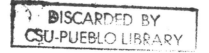

Contemporary Authors®

ISSN 0010-7468

Contemporary Authors®

A Bio-Bibliographical Guide to
Current Writers in Fiction, General Nonfiction,
Poetry, Journalism, Drama, Motion Pictures,
Television, and Other Fields

volume 262

GALE
CENGAGE Learning™

Detroit • New York • San Francisco • New Haven, Conn • Waterville, Maine • London

Contemporary Authors, Vol. 262

Project Editor: Amy Elisabeth Fuller

Editorial: Michelle Kazensky, Lisa Kumar, Mary Ruby, Rob Russell, Amanda Sams

Permissions: Margaret Gaston-Chamberlain, Lisa Kinkade, Tracie Richardson

Imaging and Multimedia: Lezlie Light

Composition and Electronic Capture: Gary Oudersluys

Manufacturing: Drew Kalasky

For product information and technology assistance, contact us at
Gale Customer Support, 1-800-877-4253.
For permission to use material from this text or product, submit all requests online at **www.cengage.com/permissions.**
Further permissions questions can be emailed to
permissionrequest@cengage.com

Gale
27500 Drake Rd.
Farmington Hills, MI, 48331-3535

LIBRARY OF CONGRESS CATALOG CARD NUMBER 62-52046

ISBN-13: 978-0-7876-9520-0
ISBN-10: 0-7876-9520-3

ISSN 0010-7468

This title is also available as an e-book.
ISBN-13: 978-1-4144-3762-0
ISBN-10: 1-4144-3762-5
Contact your Gale sales representative for ordering information.

Printed in the United States of America
1 2 3 4 5 6 7 12 11 10 09 08

380328

Contents

Indexing note: All *Contemporary Authors* entries are indexed in the *Contemporary Authors* cumulative index, which is published separately and distributed twice a year.

As always, the most recent Contemporary Authors cumulative index continues to be the user's guide to the location of an individual author's listing.

Preface

Contemporary Authors (*CA*) provides information on approximately 130,000 writers in a wide range of media, including:

- Current writers of fiction, nonfiction, poetry, and drama whose works have been issued by commercial publishers, risk publishers, or university presses (authors whose books have been published only by known vanity or author-subsidized firms are ordinarily not included)

- Prominent print and broadcast journalists, editors, syndicated cartoonists, graphic novelists, screenwriters, television scriptwriters, and other media people

- Notable international authors

- Literary greats of the early twentieth century whose works are popular in today's high school and college curriculums and continue to elicit critical attention

A *CA* listing entails no charge or obligation. Authors are included on the basis of the above criteria and their interest to *CA* users. Sources of potential listees include trade periodicals, publishers' catalogs, librarians, and other users of the series.

How to Get the Most out of *CA*: Use the Index

The key to locating an author's most recent entry is the *CA* cumulative index, which is published separately and distributed twice a year. It provides access to *all* entries in *CA* and *Contemporary Authors New Revision Series* (*CANR*). Always consult the latest index to find an author's most recent entry.

For the convenience of users, the *CA* cumulative index also includes references to all entries in these Gale Cengage Learning literary series: *Authors and Artists for Young Adults, Authors in the News, Bestsellers, Black Literature Criticism, Black Literature Criticism Supplement, Black Writers, Children's Literature Review, Concise Dictionary of American Literary Biography, Concise Dictionary of British Literary Biography, Contemporary Authors Autobiography Series, Contemporary Authors Bibliographical Series, Contemporary Dramatists, Contemporary Literary Criticism, Contemporary Novelists, Contemporary Poets, Contemporary Popular Writers, Contemporary Southern Writers, Contemporary Women Poets, Dictionary of Literary Biography, Dictionary of Literary Biography Documentary Series, Dictionary of Literary Biography Yearbook, DISCovering Authors, DISCovering Authors: British, DISCovering Authors: Canadian, DISCovering Authors: Modules* (including modules for Dramatists, Most-Studied Authors, Multicultural Authors, Novelists, Poets, and Popular/ Genre Authors), *DISCovering Authors 3.0, Drama Criticism, Drama for Students, Feminist Writers, Hispanic Literature Criticism, Hispanic Writers, Junior DISCovering Authors, Major Authors and Illustrators for Children and Young Adults, Major 20th-Century Writers, Native North American Literature, Novels for Students, Poetry Criticism, Poetry for Students, Short Stories for Students, Short Story Criticism, Something about the Author, Something about the Author Autobiography Series, St. James Guide to Children's Writers, St. James Guide to Crime & Mystery Writers, St. James Guide to Fantasy Writers, St. James Guide to Horror, Ghost & Gothic Writers, St. James Guide to Science Fiction Writers, St. James Guide to Young Adult Writers, Twentieth-Century Literary Criticism, 20th Century Romance and Historical Writers, World Literature Criticism*, and *Yesterday's Authors of Books for Children*.

A Sample Index Entry:

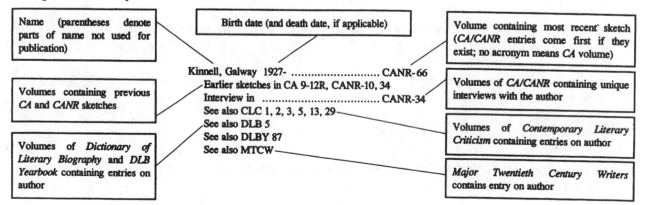

How Are Entries Compiled?

The editors make every effort to secure new information directly from the authors; listees' responses to our questionnaires and query letters provide most of the information featured in *CA*. For deceased writers, or those who fail to reply to requests for data, we consult other reliable biographical sources, such as those indexed in Gale's *Biography and Genealogy Master Index,* and bibliographical sources, including *National Union Catalog, LC MARC,* and *British National Bibliography.* Further details come from published interviews, feature stories, and book reviews, as well as information supplied by the authors' publishers and agents.

An asterisk (*) at the end of a sketch indicates that the listing has been compiled from secondary sources believed to be reliable but has not been personally verified for this edition by the author sketched.

What Kinds of Information Does An Entry Provide?

Sketches in *CA* contain the following biographical and bibliographical information:

- **Entry heading:** the most complete form of author's name, plus any pseudonyms or name variations used for writing

- **Personal information:** author's date and place of birth, family data, ethnicity, educational background, political and religious affiliations, and hobbies and leisure interests

- **Addresses:** author's home, office, or agent's addresses, plus e-mail and fax numbers, as available

- **Career summary:** name of employer, position, and dates held for each career post; resume of other vocational achievements; military service

- **Membership information:** professional, civic, and other association memberships and any official posts held

- **Awards and honors:** military and civic citations, major prizes and nominations, fellowships, grants, and honorary degrees

- **Writings:** a comprehensive, chronological list of titles, publishers, dates of original publication and revised editions, and production information for plays, television scripts, and screenplays

- **Adaptations:** a list of films, plays, and other media which have been adapted from the author's work

- **Sidelights:** a biographical portrait of the author's development; information about the critical reception of the author's works; revealing comments, often by the author, on personal interests, aspirations, motivations, and thoughts on writing

- **Interview:** a one-on-one discussion with authors conducted especially for *CA*, offering insight into authors' thoughts about their craft

- **Autobiographical essay:** an original essay written by noted authors for *CA*, a forum in which writers may present themselves, on their own terms, to their audience

- **Photographs:** portraits and personal photographs of notable authors

- **Biographical and critical sources:** a list of books and periodicals in which additional information on an author's life and/or writings appears

- **Obituary Notices** in *CA* provide date and place of birth as well as death information about authors whose full-length sketches appeared in the series before their deaths. The entries also summarize the authors' careers and writings and list other sources of biographical and death information.

Related Titles in the *CA* Series

Contemporary Authors Autobiography Series complements *CA* original and revised volumes with specially commissioned autobiographical essays by important current authors, illustrated with personal photographs they provide. Common topics include their motivations for writing, the people and experiences that shaped their careers, the rewards they derive from their work, and their impressions of the current literary scene.

Contemporary Authors Bibliographical Series surveys writings by and about important American authors since World War II. Each volume concentrates on a specific genre and features approximately ten writers; entries list works written by and about the author and contain a bibliographical essay discussing the merits and deficiencies of major critical and scholarly studies in detail.

Available in Electronic Formats

GaleNet. *CA* is available on a subscription basis through GaleNet, an online information resource that features an easy-to-use end-user interface, powerful search capabilities, and ease of access through the World-Wide Web. For more information, call 1-800-877-GALE.

Licensing. *CA* is available for licensing. The complete database is provided in a fielded format and is deliverable on such media as disk, CD-ROM, or tape. For more information, contact Gale's Business Development Group at 1-800-877-GALE.

Suggestions Are Welcome

The editors welcome comments and suggestions from users on any aspect of the *CA* series. If readers would like to recommend authors for inclusion in future volumes of the series, they are cordially invited to write the Editors at *Contemporary Authors*, Gale Cengage Learning, 27500 Drake Rd., Farmington Hills, MI 48331-3535; or call at 1-248-699-4253; or fax at 1-248-699-8054.

Contemporary Authors Product Advisory Board

The editors of *Contemporary Authors* are dedicated to maintaining a high standard of excellence by publishing comprehensive, accurate, and highly readable entries on a wide array of writers. In addition to the quality of the content, the editors take pride in the graphic design of the series, which is intended to be orderly yet inviting, allowing readers to utilize the pages of *CA* easily and with efficiency. Despite the longevity of the *CA* print series, and the success of its format, we are mindful that the vitality of a literary reference product is dependent on its ability to serve its users over time. As literature, and attitudes about literature, constantly evolve, so do the reference needs of students, teachers, scholars, journalists, researchers, and book club members. To be certain that we continue to keep pace with the expectations of our customers, the editors of *CA* listen carefully to their comments regarding the value, utility, and quality of the series. Librarians, who have firsthand knowledge of the needs of library users, are a valuable resource for us. The *Contemporary Authors* Product Advisory Board, made up of school, public, and academic librarians, is a forum to promote focused feedback about *CA* on a regular basis. The six-member advisory board includes the following individuals, whom the editors wish to thank for sharing their expertise:

International Advisory Board

Well-represented among the 130,000 author entries published in *Contemporary Authors* are sketches on notable writers from many non-English-speaking countries. The primary criteria for inclusion of such authors has traditionally been the publication of at least one title in English, either as an original work or as a translation. However, the editors of *Contemporary Authors* came to observe that many important international writers were being overlooked due to a strict adherence to our inclusion criteria. In addition, writers who were publishing in languages other than English were not being covered in the traditional sources we used for identifying new listees. Intent on increasing our coverage of international authors, including those who write only in their native language and have not been translated into English, the editors enlisted the aid of a board of advisors, each of whom is an expert on the literature of a particular country or region. Among the countries we focused attention on are Mexico, Puerto Rico, Germany, Luxembourg, Belgium, the Netherlands, Norway, Sweden, Denmark, Finland, Taiwan, Singapore, Spain, Italy, South Africa, Israel, and Japan, as well as England, Scotland, Wales, Ireland, Australia, and New Zealand. The sixteen-member advisory board includes the following individuals, whom the editors wish to thank for sharing their expertise:

- **Lowell A. Bangerter,** Professor of German, University of Wyoming, Laramie, Wyoming.

- **Nancy E. Berg,** Associate Professor of Hebrew and Comparative Literature, Washington University, St. Louis, Missouri.

- **Frances Devlin-Glass,** Associate Professor, School of Literary and Communication Studies, Deakin University, Burwood, Victoria, Australia.

- **David William Foster,** Regent's Professor of Spanish, Interdisciplinary Humanities, and Women's Studies, Arizona State University, Tempe, Arizona.

- **Hosea Hirata,** Director of the Japanese Program, Associate Professor of Japanese, Tufts University, Medford, Massachusetts.

- **Jack Kolbert,** Professor Emeritus of French Literature, Susquehanna University, Selinsgrove, Pennsylvania.

- **Mark Libin,** Professor, University of Manitoba, Winnipeg, Manitoba, Canada.

- **C. S. Lim,** Professor, University of Malaya, Kuala Lumpur, Malaysia.

- **Eloy E. Merino,** Assistant Professor of Spanish, Northern Illinois University, DeKalb, Illinois.

- **Linda M. Rodríguez Guglielmoni,** Associate Professor, University of Puerto Rico—Mayagüez, Puerto Rico.

- **Sven Hakon Rossel,** Professor and Chair of Scandinavian Studies, University of Vienna, Vienna, Austria.

- **Steven R. Serafin,** Director, Writing Center, Hunter College of the City University of New York, New York City.

- **David Smyth,** Lecturer in Thai, School of Oriental and African Studies, University of London, England.

- **Ismail S. Talib,** Senior Lecturer, Department of English Language and Literature, National University of Singapore, Singapore.

- **Dionisio Viscarri,** Assistant Professor, Ohio State University, Columbus, Ohio.

- **Mark Williams,** Associate Professor, English Department, University of Canterbury, Christchurch, New Zealand.

CA Numbering System and Volume Update Chart

Occasionally questions arise about the *CA* numbering system and which volumes, if any, can be discarded. Despite numbers like "29-32R," "97-100" and "262," the entire *CA* print series consists of only 357 physical volumes with the publication of *CA* Volume 262. The following charts note changes in the numbering system and cover design, and indicate which volumes are essential for the most complete, up-to-date coverage.

CA First Revision
- 1-4R through 41-44R (11 books)
  Cover: Brown with black and gold trim.
  There will be no further First Revision volumes because revised entries are now being handled exclusively through the more efficient *New Revision Series* mentioned below.

CA Original Volumes
- 45-48 through 97-100 (14 books)
  Cover: Brown with black and gold trim.
  101 through 262 (162 books)
  Cover: Blue and black with orange bands.
  The same as previous *CA* original volumes but with a new, simplified numbering system and new cover design.

CA Permanent Series
- *CAP*-1 and *CAP*-2 (2 books)
  Cover: Brown with red and gold trim.
  There will be no further Permanent Series volumes because revised entries are now being handled exclusively through the more efficient *New Revision Series* mentioned below.

CA New Revision Series
- CANR-1 through CANR-168 (168 books)
  Cover: Blue and black with green bands.
  Includes only sketches requiring significant changes; **sketches are taken from any previously published CA, CAP, or CANR volume.**

If You Have:	You May Discard:
CA First Revision Volumes 1-4R through 41-44R and *CA Permanent Series* Volumes 1 and 2	*CA* Original Volumes 1, 2, 3, 4 Volumes 5-6 through 41-44
CA Original Volumes 45-48 through 97-100 and 101 through 262	**NONE:** These volumes will not be superseded by corresponding revised volumes. Individual entries from these and all other volumes appearing in the left column of this chart may be revised and included in the various volumes of the *New Revision Series*.
CA New Revision Series Volumes *CANR*-1 through *CANR*-168	**NONE:** The *New Revision Series* does not replace any single volume of *CA*. Instead, volumes of *CANR* include entries from many previous *CA* series volumes. All *New Revision Series* volumes must be retained for full coverage.

A Sampling of Authors and Media People Featured in This Volume

Ishmael Beah

Beah's memoir, *A Long Way Gone: Memoirs of a Boy Soldier,* tells about war from the point of view of a young boy trained to kill without remorse. Beah served as a child soldier in the Sierra Leone Army in the mid-1990s until he was rescued by the United Nations and sent to a camp for rehabilitation. He later served as a member of the Human Rights Watch Children's Rights Division Advisory Committee and ultimately immigrated to the United States, where he was adopted by an American woman. His wrenching story joins an elite class of writing by Africans about African wars.

Charles, Prince of Wales

Prince Charles is the heir apparent to the throne of England. He is also an author, having published books primarily on art and his favorite hobby, gardening. An outspoken environmentalist, his books *Highgrove: Portrait of an Estate, The Garden at Highgrove,* and *The Elements of Organic Gardening,* describe his personal experiments with organic gardening methods. In *A Vision of Britain: A Personal View of Architecture,* he delves into issues of urban development, while *Watercolors* is a collection of his own paintings. He serves on the Prince of Wales's Foundation for Architecture and Urban Development and is the founder of an organic food company.

Rachel Hadas

Hadas grew up on the Upper West Side of Manhattan, near Columbia University, surrounded by the generation of New York intellectuals that largely dominated the American literary and political scene from the 1930s through the 1960s. She emerged in the 1980s as perhaps the most prolific poet among the New Formalists with five published books of poetry. Her residence in Greece forms the background and subject matter for most of the poems in two apprentice volumes: *Starting from Troy* and *Slow Transparency.* Her later work is influenced by her role as a mother and her work with people with AIDS. An autobiographical essay by Hadas is included in this volume of *CA.*

Eric R. Kandel

A Nobel Prize-winning scientist, Kandel has also written several award-winning books in the areas of neuroscience, psychiatry, and psychology. Kandel was born in Austria and lived through the Nazi invasion of that country in the 1930s. A personal witness to the horrors of Kristallnacht, the destruction of thousands of Jewish homes, businesses, and synagogues on November 9 and 10, 1938, Kandel escaped Austria before World War II began. His autobiography, *In Search of Memory: The Emergence of a New Science of the Mind,* shares details of his childhood in Nazi-occupied Austria, his Brooklyn schooling, his education as a scientist, and his illustrious career as a researcher.

Jill Paton Walsh

As a prolific British author of young adult fiction, Paton Walsh explores a variety of topics and eras, including life, death, and honor in Anglo-Saxon England; Victorian child labor in England; and growing up in World War II England. She has also written several novels set in England's Cornish coast, where she spent part of her childhood. An autobiographical essay by Paton Walsh is included in this volume of *CA.*

Molly Peacock

Peacock is an American poet who uses strong rhyme schemes, skillful alliteration, and biting humor to explore such themes as fate, family, sexuality, pain, and the many facets of love. Her memoir, *Paradise, Piece by Piece,* details her difficult childhood and her father's alcoholism. *Cornucopia: New and Selected Poems, 1975-2002* brings together many of Peacock's best poems from earlier collections. An autobiographical essay by Peacock is included in this volume of *CA.*

Sapphire

Born Ramona Lofton, Sapphire is an African American poet and novelist whose traumatic upbringing and work with children in Harlem inform her work. A controversial writer, she frequently addresses themes of incest, rape, child abuse, sexuality, and racism. Her first novel, *Push,* received the Stephen Crane award for outstanding first work of fiction. Sapphire has published multiple collections of poetry, including *Meditations on the Rainbow* and *Black Wings & Blind Angels.*

Roberto Mangabeira Unger

As a young man, Unger left Brazil for Harvard University to study law. In 1970, when there was a military crackdown in Brazil, Unger decided not to return home and instead became one of Harvard's youngest-ever law professors. By the 1980s he was considered the leader of the Critical Legal Studies movement at Harvard. Unger's books draw from a broad spectrum of disciplines, including politics, religion, and philosophy, and promote legal and political reform.

Acknowledgments

Grateful acknowledgment is made to those publishers, photographers, and artists whose work appear with these authors's essays. Following is a list of the copyright holders who have granted us permission to reproduce material in this volume of *CA*. Every effort has been made to trace copyright, but if omissions have been made, please let us know.

Photographs/Art

Hadas, Rachel: All photographs reproduced by permission.

Peacock, Molly: All photographs reproduced by permission.

Walsh, Jill Paton: All photographs reproduced by permission.

A

Indicates that a listing has been compiled from secondary sources believed to be reliable, but has not been personally verified for this edition by the author sketched.

ALDERMAN, B.J. 1948-

PERSONAL: Born 1948. *Education:* Pittsburg State University, B.S., 1970.

ADDRESSES: Home—Kansas City, MO.

CAREER: Journalist and writer.

AWARDS, HONORS: Edward H. Tihen Historical Research Grant, Kansas State Historical Society, 2003, 2007.

WRITINGS:

The Secret Life of the Lawman's Wife, Praeger (Westport, CT), 2007.

Contributor to periodicals, including *Chronicle of the Old West, Missouri Life,* and *American Western* magazine.

SIDELIGHTS: In her book *The Secret Life of the Lawman's Wife,* author B.J. Alderman provides an historical account of the important role a sheriff's wife played in managing jails throughout the United States from about 1800 until the 1960s. Using letters, diaries, interviews, and local historical accounts, Alderman reveals how these women, who were not paid for their work, helped feed prisoners, took statements and conducted interviews, sewed and repaired jail linens and other items, and served as their husbands' backups. As a result, they often risked their lives and fought with escapees. A *Reference & Research Book News* contributor noted that these women "sustained the law enforcement system of the US for generations." In fact, the women performed all of their jailhouse duties while raising children and keeping a home, which typically included extensive gardening. Reviewers commended the author for revealing the difficult life and heroism of these women. Frances Sandiford, writing in *Library Journal,* called the tales in *The Secret Life of the Lawman's Wife* "captivating, and sometimes incredible," adding that "history buffs, women's studies, and people who simply want a good read" will appreciate the book.

BIOGRAPHICAL AND CRITICAL SOURCES:

PERIODICALS

Choice: Current Reviews for Academic Libraries, Ocobter, 2007, review of *The Secret Life of the Lawman's Wife.*
Library Journal, March 1, 2007, Frances Sandiford, review of *The Secret Life of the Lawman's Wife,* p. 96.
Reference & Research Book News, February, 2007, review of *The Secret Life of the Lawman's Wife.*

*   *   *

ALTON, Nikki
See DAVIS, Genie

AMIRREZVANI, Anita 1961-

PERSONAL: Born November 13, 1961, in Tehran, Iran; immigrated to the United States with family, 1962; daughter of Ahmad Amirrezvani and Katherine Smith. *Education:* Attended Vassar College; University of California, Berkeley, A.B., 1983.

ADDRESSES: E-mail—aa@bloodofflowers.com.

CAREER: Journalist, writer, and editor. Telelerning, Inc., San Francisco, CA, editor, 1983-84; *PC World* magazine, San Francisco, senior associate editor, 1989-96; *Contra Costa Times,* Walnut Creek, CA, assistant entertainment editor, 1994-95, staff writer, beginning 1995; *San Jose Mercury News,* San Jose, CA, dance critic, 2000-05. Also worked as a freelance writer and was writer-in-residence at the Hedgebrook Foundation for Women Writers (twice), Langley, WA.

MEMBER: Phi Beta Kappa.

AWARDS, HONORS: National Arts Journalism Program fellow, 1997.

WRITINGS:

The Blood of Flowers: A Novel, Little, Brown (New York, NY), 2007.

Also author of monthly "Consumer Watch" column, 1987-89; contributor to professional journals.

SIDELIGHTS: Anita Amirrezvani's debut work, *The Blood of Flowers: A Novel,* was called a "sumptuous tale of female fortitude and ingenuity" by Margaret Flanagan in *Booklist.* The story revolves around a nameless teenager living in seventeenth-century Iran. Following her father's death, the teenaged girl and her mother become servants to relatives. Eventually because of her poverty, the girl is forced into a temporary marriage called a "sigheh." The young girl eventually makes a better life for herself as she learns the trade of carpet weaving from her uncle, who is a master weaver. *Library Journal* reviewer Evelyn Beck commented that "the plucky narrator's rocky road

toward independence is stirring and surprisingly erotic." The author also interweaves with the young girl's story the numerous folktales told by her mother.

"Before I started to develop the plot, one of my main concerns was to provide a more nuanced view of Iran than we normally see in news headlines," the author said in an interview on *Bookreporter.com.* She went on to note: "I wanted to show what life might look like from the perspective of a young woman who lived long ago, and to draw readers so completely into old Iran that they would be able to smell the rosewater and picture the deep indigos and crimsons of handmade carpets." Most reviewers believed that the author accomplished her goals. "*The Blood of Flowers* is a wonderfully rich tapestry of characters and events," wrote Douglas R. Cobb on the *Curled Up with a Good Book* Web site. A *Publishers Weekly* contributor noted: "Sumptuous imagery and a modern sensibility . . . make this a winning debut."

BIOGRAPHICAL AND CRITICAL SOURCES:

PERIODICALS

Booklist, April 15, 2007, Margaret Flanagan, review of *The Blood of Flowers: A Novel,* p. 29.
Bookseller, April 14, 2006, Nicholas Clee, "Headline Wins Hot Iran Novel," p. 13; March 9, 2007, Benedicte Page, "Rugs to Riches: Benedicte Page Talks to Anita Amirrezvani about Her Debut Novel, Which Explores the Hardships of 17th-Century Iran and the Art of Carpet Making," p. 22.
Entertainment Weekly, June 15, 2007, Allyssa Lee, review of *The Blood of Flowers,* p. 83.
Library Journal, March 1, 2007, Evelyn Beck, review of *The Blood of Flowers,* p. 66.
Publishers Weekly, January 22, 2007, Suzanne Mantell, "Blood of Flowers," p. 63; February 12, 2007, review of *The Blood of Flowers,* p. 59.
School Library Journal, April, 2007, Ellen Bell, review of *The Blood of Flowers: A Novel,* p. 168.

ONLINE

Bloodofflowers.com, http://www.bloodofflowers.com (October 14, 2007), includes biography of author.

BookLoons, http://www.bookloons.com/ (October 14, 2007), Hilary Williamson, review of *The Blood of Flowers.*

BookReporter.com, http://www.bookreporter.com/ (June 29, 2007), interview with author.

Brown BookLoft, http://www.brownbookloft.com/ (August 20, 2007), review of *The Blood of Flowers.*

Compulsive Reader, http://www.compulsivereader. com/ (October 14, 2007), Liz Hall-Downs, review of *The Blood of Flowers.*

Curled Up with a Good Book, http://www.curledup. com/ (October 14, 2007), Douglas R. Cobb, review of *The Blood of Flowers.*

Payvand's Iran News, http://www.payvand.com/news/ (May 8, 2007), "An Interview with Anita Amirrez-vani, Author of *The Blood of Flowers.*"

PopMatters, http://www.popmatters.com/ (July 23, 2007), Lara Killian, review of *The Blood of Flowers.*

Reading Matters, http://kimbofo.typepad.com/reading matters/ (April 9, 2007), review of *The Blood of Flowers.*

*   *   *

ANSTRUTHER, Ian 1922-2007

(Sir Ian Anstruther of That Ilk, Ian Fife Campbell Anstruther)

OBITUARY NOTICE— See index for *CA* sketch: Born May 11, 1922, in Buckinghamshire, England; died July 29, 2007. Farmer, philanthropist, and author. Anstruther did not have to work for a living, so he spent much of his adult life engaged in activities that gave him pleasure and added meaning to his daily routine. He once modestly described himself to *CA* as a farmer, but the property he acquired through a bequest from his aunt and de facto foster mother Joan Campbell was in fact the valuable Thurloe Estate, a large residential parcel located in the South Kensington section of London. Anstruther took his stewardship of the estate quite seriously, managing the property from 1950 until changes in British law allowed certain leaseholders to purchase their holdings outright. Despite his acquired wealth, Anstruther was born into relatively modest surroundings. His parents were technically members of the nobility but were not in any line of succession, even within their own family. Their tumultuous marriage eventually nudged the boy out of the family and into the household of his aunt, where he prospered and ultimately became the owner of her estate. His titles as baronet of Balcaskie of Scotland and baronet of Anstruther of Scotland and England came to him via an equally circuitous route from a childless cousin. He lived a quiet life as manager of Thurloe and as a farmer at Barlavington in rural Sussex. Anstruther developed an appreciation for libraries, where he spent substantial amounts of time among dusty tomes and literary antiquities. In 1992 he endowed the Anstruther Wing created by the London Library to house and preserve up to 25,000 rare volumes. Anstruther wrote a few nonfiction books himself, including *"I Presume": A Study of H.M. Stanley, The Knight and the Umbrella* (an account of the colorful reenactment of a medieval tournament by Lord Archibald Eglinton in 1839), *The Scandal of the Andover Workhouse, Oscar Browning: A Biography,* and *Coventry Patmore's Angel.*

OBITUARIES AND OTHER SOURCES:

PERIODICALS

Times (London, England), August 8, 2007, p. 49.

*   *   *

ANSTRUTHER, Ian Fife Campbell
See ANSTRUTHER, Ian

*   *   *

ANSTRUTHER OF THAT ILK, Sir Ian
See ANSTRUTHER, Ian

*   *   *

ANTHONY, Lawrence 1950-

PERSONAL: Born 1950, in Johannesburg, South Africa.

ADDRESSES: Home—Province of Kwa-Zulu, South Africa. *E-mail*—la@thulathula.com.

CAREER: Environmentalist, conservationist, and writer. Thula Thula game reserve, Province of Kwa-Zulu, South Africa, head of conservation; The Earth Organization, founder, 2003. Also coformed first Society for the Prevention of Cruelty to Animals (SPCA) in Iraq.

WRITINGS:

(With Graham Spence) *Babylon's Ark: The Incredible Wartime Rescue of the Baghdad Zoo,* Thomas Dunne Books (New York, NY), 2007.

SIDELIGHTS: Longtime head conservationist on the Thula Thula game reserve in South Africa, Lawrence Anthony directed the amazing rescue of the Baghdad Zoo following the invasion of Iraq by the United States, Great Britain, and their coalition in 2003. The story of the zoo's rescue is told in *Babylon's Ark: The Incredible Wartime Rescue of the Baghdad Zoo,* which Anthony wrote with Graham Spence. In the book, Anthony recounts how he made his decision to save the zoo as he watched the invasion on television from South Africa and recalled how other zoos had fared during wartime. The memoir follows Anthony as he arrives in Iraq, begins repairing cages and other facilities in a badly damaged zoo, and then fights for the zoo's survival, at no small risk to himself. "The story of the zoo is in many ways a microcosm of what happened in Baghdad in those first chaotic, hopeful and ultimately disheartening months," wrote Joshua Kucera in the *San Francisco Chronicle. Babylon's Ark* has received favorable reviews from the critics. "Heartfelt, but never treacly . . . animal lovers will shed tears . . . [while others] will find their souls stirred with the injustice doled out to defenseless creatures," wrote a contributor to the *Kaite's Book Shelf* Web site. Nancy Bent, writing in *Booklist,* commented that the author's "obvious love of animals and his anger at what they suffer . . . [lends] poignancy and immediacy to the story."

Anthony told *CA:* "I wanted to record my real life experiences with wildlife. The opportunity came during the war in Iraq when I found my way into Bagh-

dad during the coalition invasion to help the abandoned animals of the Baghdad Zoo. My work is influenced by my experiences with the natural world.

"When writing, I recall actual life experiences, which I place on tape and structure these experiences into a story. I have a coauthor who will draft a rough chapter and then we work together to complete it. The most surprising thing I have learned as a writer is how involved readers get in the story. I hope that my work communicates to readers."

BIOGRAPHICAL AND CRITICAL SOURCES:

BOOKS

Anthony, Lawrence, and Graham Spence, *Babylon's Ark: The Incredible Wartime Rescue of the Baghdad Zoo,* Thomas Dunne Books (New York, NY), 2007.

PERIODICALS

Booklist, February 1, 2007, Nancy Bent, review of *Babylon's Ark,* p. 10.
Entertainment Weekly, March 9, 2007, Josh Rottenberg, review of *Babylon's Ark,* p. 113.
Kirkus Reviews, December 15, 2006, review of *Babylon's Ark,* p. 1250.
Publishers Weekly, December 11, 2006, review of *Babylon's Ark,* p. 54.
San Francisco Chronicle, March 16, 2007, Joshua Kucera, "One Man's Quest to Save Iraq Zoo after US Invasion."
SciTech Book News, June, 2007, review of *Babylon's Ark.*

ONLINE

Kaite's Book Shelf, http://kaitesbookshelf.blogspot.com/ (June 10, 2007), "Welcome to the Condemned Monkey House," review of *Babylon's Ark.*
Lawrence Anthony Home Page, www.lawrence anthony.co.za (October 14, 2007).

Paraview, http://www.paraview.com/ (October 14, 2007), biography of author.

*　　*　　*

ANTON, Shari

PERSONAL: Married; children: two.

ADDRESSES: Home—WI. *E-mail*—sharianton@wi.rr. com.

CAREER: Writer. Formerly held various jobs, including personnel clerk and executive secretary.

MEMBER: Romance Writers of America, Wisconsin Romance Writers of America (WisRWA), Hearts through History Romance Writers, Novelists Inc., Authors Guild.

WRITINGS:

Emily's Captain, Harlequin Historicals (Don Mills, Ontario, Canada), 1997.
The Conqueror, Harlequin Historicals (Don Mills, Ontario, Canada), 2000.
Midnight Magic (first book in "The Magic Trilogy"), Warner Forever (New York, NY), 2005.
At Her Service, Warner Forever (New York, NY), 2005.
Twilight Magic (second book in "The Magic Trilogy"), Warner Forever (New York, NY), 2006.

"THE WILMONT STORIES" SERIES

By King's Decree, Harlequin Historicals (Don Mills, Ontario, Canada), 1998.
Lord of the Manor, Harlequin Historicals (Don Mills, Ontario, Canada), 1998.
Queen's Grace, Harlequin Historicals (Don Mills, Ontario, Canada), 1999.
Knave of Hearts, Harlequin Historicals (Don Mills, Ontario, Canada), 2001.

"THE HAMELIN STORIES" SERIES

The Ideal Husband, Warner Books (New York, NY), 2003.
Once a Bride, Warner Books (New York, NY), 2004.

Contributor to anthologies, including *Christmas at Wayfarer Inn,* Harlequin Historical Christmas Anthology, 2001. Also author of Web blog.

SIDELIGHTS: Shari Anton writes historical romance novels. Her first book, *Emily's Captain,* takes place during the Civil War and features Union spy Jared Hunter sent to rescue his commanding officer's daughter, Emily, and bring her north from Georgia. However, Emily sympathizes with the Southern cause, and Jared soon finds himself posing as a Confederate officer to get Emily to accompany him as they travel through dangerous lands. "Shari Anton's portrait of the Civil War conveys the tragedy and the horror" of the period, wrote Kathe Robin on the *Romantic Times Online.*

Anton is also author of "The Wilmont Stories," a series of medieval romance novels that begins with *By King's Decree,* which tells the love story of Baron Gerard of Wilmont and Ardith of Lenvil, who is resigned to a solitary life because she is barren. *Romantic Times* Web site contributor Maria C. Ferrer called the novel "a delicious romance full of treachery, greed, revenge and heated passion." In the fourth entry in the series, *Knave of Hearts,* Stephan of Wilmont, a knight, finds himself caught between two cousins, one an old love he abandoned and the other looking for a younger husband after two older ones have died. Gabrielle Panter wrote on the *Romantic Times Online* that *Knave of Hearts* is "an entertaining tale of romance with love lost, found, and rekindled."

Anton begins "The Hamelin Stories" series with *The Ideal Husband.* The novel features the disgraced Leah of Pechem, who finds herself stranded in France. On a voyage home to England, the ship goes down, and Leah begins caring for Geoffrey Hamelin, a gentleman who washed up on shore. She pretends that the unconscious Geoffrey is her husband and then, as Geoffrey has lost his memory, maintains the ruse after they are rescued. Kathe Robin, writing on the *Romantic Times Online,* noted that the author "weaves history into her highly romantic tale with aplomb, crafting a beautiful love story." *Once a Bride,* the second book in "The Hamelin Stories" series, features Eloise, daughter of the disgraced Lord Hamelin. Eloise is forced to relent to Roland St. Marten, who has come to oversee the estate on behalf of its new owner, Lord Kenworth. To her surprise, Eloise and Roland begin to fall in love but can only make their love acceptable if they can prove Lord Hamelin's innocence. Robin, once again writing on the *Romantic Times Online,* commented that the author "weaves a spellbinding romance, rich in historical backdrop, fiery characters and sexual tension."

Midnight Magic is the first book in "The Magic Trilogy," which revolves around three sisters. The story begins in 1145 with the marriage of Gwendolyn to Alberic, who has been granted an estate and his choice of one of three sisters as a reward for slaying William de Leon on behalf of King Stephen. Gwendolyn's other two sisters are sent off to a nunnery after not being chosen, and Gwendolyn enters a marriage where she is surprised to find herself falling in love. "This is a well-written historical romance, filled with legends of the days of Merlin and King Arthur," wrote Marie Hashima Lofton on the *BookLoons* Web site. "It has a quality of the ethereal." The next book in the series, *Twilight Magic,* features Gwendolyn's sister Emma, who has the gift of seeing the future in a pool of water. When she meets the man she loves, the Flemish mercenary Darian of Bruges, Emma must prove him innocent of murdering an English nobleman. Writing in *Booklist,* John Charles called *Twilight Magic* an "expertly crafted, utterly beguiling medieval romance." A *Publishers Weekly* contributor noted the romance novel's "appealing characters and playful repartee."

BIOGRAPHICAL AND CRITICAL SOURCES:

PERIODICALS

Booklist, January 1, 2005, John Charles, review of *At Her Service,* p. 829; December 1, 2005, John Charles, review of *Midnight Magic,* p. 29; November 15, 2006, John Charles, review of *Twilight Magic,* p. 36.

MBR Bookwatch, January, 2005, Harriet Klausner, review of *At Her Service.*

Publishers Weekly, October 30, 2006, review of *Twilight Magic,* p. 43.

Voice of Youth Advocates, June, 2002, review of *The Conqueror,* p. 89.

ONLINE

BookLoons, http://www.bookloons.com/ (October 14, 2007), Marie Hashima Lofton, review of *Midnight Magic.*

Hachette Book Group, http://www.hachettebook groupusa.com/ (October 14, 2007), brief profile of author.

My Space, http://www.myspace.com/sharianton (October 14, 2007).

Romantic Times Online, http://www.romantictimes. com/ (October 14, 2007), Kathe Robin, reviews of *At Her Service, Emily's Captain, Midnight Magic, Once a Bride, The Conqueror, The Ideal Husband,* and *By Queen's Grace*; Maria C. Ferrer, review of *By King's Decree*; Gabrielle Pantera, review of *Knave of Hearts*; Michell Phifer, review of *Lord of the Manor.*

Shari Anton Home Page, http://www.sharianton.com (October 14, 2007).

Shari Anton's Blog, http://www.blogger.com/profile/ 04624755109245094179 (October 14, 2007).

*   *   *

ANTONIONI, Michelangelo 1912-2007

OBITUARY NOTICE— See index for *CA* sketch: Born September 29, 1912, in Ferrara, Italy; died July 31, 2007, in Rome, Italy. Film director and screenwriter. As a filmmaker, Antonioni has been called the greatest artistic stylist of all time. It was not always so. When *L'Avventura* premiered at the Cannes Film Festival in 1960, people booed, hissed, and walked out of the theater. The movie incorporated many elements that would come to be recognized as Antonioni's trademarks: a story line that meanders at its own pace and without apparent objective; periods of silence and agonizing pauses; cinematography that sometimes seems to supersede plot and character. A frequent subject of his earlier films, in particular, is the aimlessness, boredom, spiritual emptiness, and despair that he witnessed among the Italian privileged classes after World War II, and every element of his films embodies that lack of personal direction. *L'Avventura* is the story of a young woman who disappears on a yachting trip, or the story of her lover and best friend and their search for her, or simply the story of the lover and the friend. There is no distinct beginning or end, no resolution to the mystery. A similar description could be applied to Antonioni's most popular movie, *Blow-Up* (1966), in which a young fashion photographer becomes obsessed with investigating a murder that may or may not have happened. One of Antonioni's American successes was *The Passenger,* a 1975 thriller starring Jack Nicholson as a broadcast journalist who ends up in Africa, assuming the identity of a dead gun-runner for reasons that are never explained, and whose choice ultimately spells his doom. Antonioni has been called a perfectionist, whose pensive pre-shoot meditations and occasional outbursts of temper kept his actors on edge as much as his directorial techniques kept audiences and critics off balance. He acquired much of his training in the early 1940s at the prestigious Centro Sperimentale di Cinematografia in Rome, where he worked with Roberto Rossellini and other major figures in the Italian film industry. By the time that *L'Avventura* appeared at Cannes, he had made several documentaries and written screenplays for other directors such as Federico Fellini. Antonioni directed at least a dozen feature films in his career, though not all of them were widely distributed throughout the United States. In 1985 he suffered a stroke that left him speechless and hampered his career, but he was never able to abandon his muse altogether. Antonioni filmed *Beyond the Clouds* in 1995 with hand gestures, line drawings, and the assistance of others who could interpret his wishes. In the same year he received an honorary Academy Award for career achievement.

OBITUARIES AND OTHER SOURCES:

BOOKS

Antonioni, Michelangelo, *That Bowling Alley on the Tiber: Tales of a Director,* translated by William Arrowsmith, Oxford University Press (New York, NY), 1986.

Antonioni, Michelangelo, *The Architecture of Vision: Writings and Interviews on Cinema,* edited by Marga Cottino-Jones, Marsilio Publishers (St. Paul, MN), 1996.

Contemporary Literary Criticism, Volume 144, Thomson Gale (Detroit, MI), 2001.

International Dictionary of Films and Filmmakers, Volume 2: *Directors,* St. James Press (Detroit, MI), 2000.

PERIODICALS

Chicago Tribune, August 1, 2007, sec. 2, p. 9.
Los Angeles Times, August 1, 2007, p. B6.
New York Times, August 1, 2007, pp. A1, A16.
Times (London, England), August 1, 2007, p. 53.

*   *   *

ANTRIM, Taylor 1974-

PERSONAL: Born 1974. *Education:* Graduate of Stanford University and Oxford University; University of Virginia, M.F.A.

ADDRESSES: E-mail—ltantrim@hotmail.com.

CAREER: Writer and editor. *ForbesLife,* editor.

AWARDS, HONORS: Poe-Faulkner fellow, University of Virginia.

WRITINGS:

The Headmaster Ritual (novel), Houghton Mifflin (Boston, MA), 2007.

Contributor to periodicals, including the *New York Times, Vogue, Esquire, San Francisco Chronicle,* and *Village Voice.*

SIDELIGHTS: Taylor Antrim's first novel, *The Headmaster Ritual,* was called "impressive for a first-year effort" by *Washington Post* contributor Ron

Charles. The author sets the scene in an elite, private boarding school in Massachusetts. The school's headmaster is a radical who may support North Korean terrorists. As the author explores the headmaster's fanaticism, he also develops the stories of two people who will profoundly influence each other: Dyer Martin, a new history teacher running from a failed relationship and a disastrous job, and James, son of the school's headmaster. A contributor to the *New Yorker* noted that the author examines "the rituals of boarding-school life—the rigid hierarchies, the code of silence." Some reviewers felt that Antrim was overly ambitious, but they still had praise for the novel. For example, although *New York Times Book Review* contributor Darin Strauss found *The Headmaster Ritual* "ambitious and confounding," the reviewer went on to note: "In its best moments . . . *The Headmaster Ritual* is a good old-fashioned campus novel." Writing in *Library Journal*, Kevin Greczek commented: "The book's real accomplishment . . . is the parallel personal development of Dyer and James."

BIOGRAPHICAL AND CRITICAL SOURCES:

PERIODICALS

Books, June 2, 2007, Kristin Kloberdanz, review of *The Headmaster Ritual*, p. 7.

Book World, July 15, 2007, Ron Charles, "Class Struggles," review of *The Headmaster Ritual*, p. 6.

Library Journal, March 1, 2007, Kevin Greczek, review of *The Headmaster Ritual*, p. 66.

New Yorker, August 6, 2007, review of *The Headmaster Ritual*, p. 71.

New York Times Book Review, August 12, 2007, Darin Strauss, review of *The Headmaster Ritual*.

Washington Post, July 15, 2007, Ron Charles, "Class Struggles," review of *The Headmaster Ritual*, p. BW06.

ONLINE

Houghton Mifflin, http://www.houghtonmifflinbooks. com/ (October 14, 2007), brief profile of author.

Taylor Antrim Home Page, http://www.taylorantrim. com (October 14, 2007).*

ARRUDA, Suzanne M. 1954-
(Suzanne Middendorf Arruda)

PERSONAL: Born 1954, in Greensburg, IN; married; children: two. *Education:* Purdue University, B.S.; Kansas State University, M.S.; Washburn University, M.Ed.

ADDRESSES: Home—Pittsburg, KS. *E-mail*—sarruda@cox.net.

CAREER: Writer, instructor. Kansas State University, Manhattan, lab technician, research assistant, biology instructor; Kansas Department of Wildlife and Parks, museum worker; Pittsburg State University, Pittsburg, KS, biology instructor. Has also taught high school science and worked part time at a zoo.

MEMBER: Mystery Writer's of America, Joplin Writer's Guild (past president and secretary), Missouri Writer's Guild, Sisters in Crime, Kansas Center for the Book, Women in the Outdoors (charter member of the Southeast Kansas chapter).

AWARDS, HONORS: Best fiction award, Missouri Writer's Guild, 2007, for *The Mark of the Lion: A Jade Del Cameron Mystery*.

WRITINGS:

(As Suzanne Middendorf Arruda) *From Kansas to Cannibals: The Story of Osa Johnson*, Avisson Press (Greensboro, N.C.), 2001.

(As Suzanne Middendorf Arruda) *Freedom's Martyr: The Story of Jose Rizal, National Hero of the Philippines*, Avisson Press (Greensboro, NC), 2003.

(As Suzanne Middendorf Arruda) *The Girl He Left Behind: The Life and Times of Libbie Custer*, Avisson Press (Greensboro, NC), 2004.

A Stocking for Jesus, Pauline Press (Boston, MA), 2005.

"JADE DEL CAMERON" MYSTERIES

Mark of the Lion: A Jade Del Cameron Mystery, New American Library (New York, NY), 2006.

Stalking Ivory: A Jade Del Cameron Mystery, New
    American Library (New York, NY), 2007.
*The Serpent's Daughter: A Jade Del Cameron
    Mystery,* Obsidian (New York, NY), 2007.

Also the author of a Web log; contributor of science
articles for adults and young readers to magazines and
newspapers.

SIDELIGHTS: A part-time zookeeper and a teacher,
Suzanne M. Arruda has published both biographies for
young adult readers as well as a popular historical
mystery series for adults that is set in East Africa following World War I. Arruda, as she noted on her Web
site, has been "an armchair explorer ever since I first
picked up a book of missionary tales." Growing up on
stories of the adventures of such historical figures as
African bush pilot Beryl Markham and museum collector Roy Chapman Andrews, who was used as an
inspiration for the Indiana Jones character in popular
films, Arruda was well equipped to give her mystery
series a ring of veracity. Her fictional protagonist,
American Jade Del Cameron, drives an ambulance in
France during World War I. In the debut title, *Mark of
the Lion: A Jade Del Cameron Mystery,* Jade travels to
British East Africa where she hopes to find the brother
of her fallen betrothed, David. It was his dying wish
that she do so, and the trail leads to Africa, for it is
there that David's father died. Securing a position as a
travel writer to finance her expedition, Jade is soon
over her head in an investigation that turns up mystery
upon mystery in this novel that provides the reader an
"exciting early 20th century safari," according to
Crescent Blues Book Reviews writer Augusta
Scattergood. Further praise came from *Booklist*
contributor Stephanie Zvirin, who wrote, "Arruda
manufactures an intriguing backdrop for the debut of
her new series," and from a *Kirkus Reviews* critic who
concluded that this first installment offered "an enjoyable romp through a colorful place and period in
which the heroine has a Douglas-Fairbanks-in-a-split-
skirt-charm." Similarly, a *Publishers Weekly* reviewer
found *Mark of the Lion* a "charming book."

In *Stalking Ivory: A Jade Del Cameron Mystery,* Jade
is on assignment at an elephant sanctuary only to be
shocked by the slaughter of several of these protected
pachyderms by poachers. She vows to find the
perpetrators, whether they are Abyssinian raiders or
the mysterious safari leader, Harry Hascombe. A *Pub-*

lishers Weekly reviewer noted, "The resilient Jade will
charm readers as she asserts her independence." A
Kirkus Reviews critic, on the other hand, was less
impressed with the heroine, but commented that the
"poaching/elephant lore . . . is unimpeachable."

BIOGRAPHICAL AND CRITICAL SOURCES:

PERIODICALS

Booklist, December 15, 2005, Stephanie Zvirin,
    review of *Mark of the Lion: A Jade Del Cameron
    Mystery,* p. 25.
Kirkus Reviews, November 15, 2005, review of *Mark
    of the Lion,* p. 1211; November 15, 2006, review
    of *Stalking Ivory: A Jade Del Cameron Mystery,*
    p. 1153.
Publishers Weekly, October 24, 2005, review of *Mark
    of the Lion,* p. 42; October 23, 2006, review of
    Stalking Ivory, p. 35.
School Library Journal, November, 2001, Michele
    Capozzella, review of *From Kansas to Cannibals:
    The Story of Osa Johnson,* p. 167; May, 2004,
    Karen Sutherland, review of *Freedom's Martyr:
    The Story of Jose Rizal, National Hero of the
    Philippines,* p. 160; October, 2004, Lynn Evarts,
    review of *The Girl He Left Behind: The Life and
    Times of Libbie Custer,* p. 184.
Voice of Youth Advocates, December 1, 2006, John
    Charles, review of *Mark of the Lion,* p. 390.

ONLINE

Armchair Interviews, http://www.armchairinterviews.
    com/ (August 25, 2007), Kathy Perschmann,
    review of *Stalking Ivory.*
Berkley Prime Crime, http://www.berkleysignet
    mysteries.com/ (August 25, 2007), "Suzanne
    Arruda."
Catholicmom.com, http://www.catholicmom.com/
    (August 25, 2007), Lisa M. Hendey, review of *A
    Stocking for Jesus.*
Crescent Blues Book Reviews, http://www.crescent
    blues.com/ (August 25, 2007), Augusta Scatter-
    good, review of *Mark of the Lion.*
Missouri Writers Guild Web site, http://www.
    missouriwritersguild.org/ (August 25, 2007), "Su-
    zanne M. Arruda."

Suzanne Arruda Home Page, http://www.suzanne
arruda.com (August 25, 2007).

* * *

ARRUDA, Suzanne Middendorf
See ARRUDA, Suzanne M.

* * *

ASIM, Jabari 1962-

PERSONAL: Born 1962; married; wife's name Liana;
children: five.

ADDRESSES: Office—Washington Post, P.O. Box
17370, Arlington, VA 22216.

CAREER: Writer, journalist, columnist, editor, poet,
and playwright. *St. Louis Post-Dispatch,* St. Louis,
MO, served as book editor, copy editor of the daily
editorial and commentary pages, and arts editor of the
weekend section; *Washington Post Book World,*
Washington, DC, senior editor.

WRITINGS:

(Editor, with Shirley LeFlore) *Wordwalkers,* Creative
Arts & Expression Laboratory (St. Louis, MO),
1988.
The Road to Freedom (novel for young adults),
Jamestown Publishers (Lincolnwood, IL), 2000.
(Ed itor) *Not Guilty: Twelve Black Men Speak Out on
Law, Justice, and Life,* Amistad Press (New York,
NY), 2001.
*The N Word: Who Can Say It, Who Shouldn't, and
Why,* Houghton Mifflin (Boston, MA), 2007.

Also author of the plays *Caribbean Beat,* produced by
Muny Student Theatre Project; *Peace, Dog,* produced
by The New Theatre; *Believe I'll Testify,* produced by
Gettys Productions; and *New Blood Symphony* and
Didn't It Rain, both staged by Pamoja Theatre
Workshop. Contributor of essays to anthologies,
including *The Furious Flowering of African-American
Poetry,* University Press of Virginia, and *Step into A*

*World: A Global Anthology of the New Black Litera-
ture,* Wiley. Contributor of fiction and poetry to
anthologies, including *In The Tradition: An Anthology
of Young Black Writers,* Harlem River Press; *Brother-
man: The Odyssey of Black Men in America,* Ballan-
tine; *Soulfires: Young Black Men on Love and Violence,*
Viking Penguin; *Beyond the Frontier: African-
American Poetry for the 21st Century,* Black Classic
Press; and *Role Call: A Generational Anthology of
Social & Political Black Literature & Art,* Third World
Press. Contributor to periodicals, including the *Interna-
tional Herald Tribune, Los Angeles Times Book
Review, Salon.com, Detroit News, Village Voice,
Hungry Mind Review, XXL, Code, Emerge, Phoenix
Gazette,* and *BlackElectorate.com.* Assistant editor of
Drumvoices Revue and founding editor of *EyeBall.*

CHILDREN'S BOOKS

Whose Knees Are These?, illustrated by LeUyen
Pham, Little, Brown (New York, NY), 2006.
Daddy Goes to Work, illustrated by Aaron Boyd,
Little, Brown (New York, NY), 2006.
Whose Toes Are Those?, illustrated by LeUyen Pham,
Little, Brown (New York, NY), 2006.

SIDELIGHTS: Jabari Asim is a longtime journalist
and newspaper editor who, in addition to being a
syndicated columnist, has written fiction, plays,
poetry, social criticism, and children's books. In his
book *The N Word: Who Can Say It, Who Shouldn't,
and Why,* Asim explores the history of racism and
bigotry in the United States by examining the use of
the word "nigger" as a derogatory appellation for
African Americans. "I had my preconceived notions
about the word, but I tried for them to not be a guid-
ing influence," the author told Mark Anthony Neal in
an interview on the *Salon.com.* "I wanted to be as
open-minded as I could honestly be. I wanted to look
into it and see where it led me."

"*The N Word* is the first comprehensive look at this
most incendiary word in our divided culture," commented a contributor to the *Frost Illustrated* Web site.
"Unlike any previous book . . . *The N Word* is a
cultural history that traces the origins, growth, and current state of the slur." In addition to examining the
roots and uses of the "N" word, from minstrel shows
to movies to modern rap culture, Asim also examines
the evolution of racial views in America. In the book's
final chapters, he discusses the black community's use
of the word.

In a review of *The N Word* for the *Library Journal,* Emily-Jane Dawson noted that the author "is most eloquent when relating how African Americans have been characterized in our culture." Other reviewers had even higher praise for the book. "*The N Word* should be considered among the gold standard of serious attempts to historically ground discussions of American popular culture," wrote Todd Steven Burroughs in the *Black Issues Book Review.* A *Publishers Weekly* contributor noted that the author "sweeps over . . . sensitive and contradictory terrain . . . with practicality, while dispensing gentle provocations."

Asim is also editor of *Not Guilty: Twelve Black Men Speak Out on Law, Justice, and Life,* which was inspired by the shooting of an innocent black man by New York City police officers. The book includes twelve black writers, including E. Lynn Harris and Mark Anthony Neal, commenting on what it means to be black in America. "The twelve essays are well-written pieces that speak not only to race and racism but class, street culture, fatherhood, education and perceptions that African Americans have about themselves," wrote Tracy Grant in the *Black Issues Book Review.* A *Publishers Weekly* contributor noted that "these essays work as an instrument for taking apart the myths of 'monolithic black experience and the singular black perspective' on civil society."

In addition to his adult-oriented works, the author has written several illustrated children's books, including *Whose Knees Are These?,* illustrated by LeUyen Pham. The rhymed story focuses on various knees, from the knees of toddlers themselves to grown up knees. In the process the story asks readers to identify the owners of the various knees. Kornelia Longoria, writing on the *Armchair Interviews* Web site, noted that she has read the story often to her own daughter and wrote: "Every time you read it, it is as much fun as the first time." Asim and illustrator Pham also teamed up for the similar book *Whose Toes Are Those?* Commenting on both books in the *School Library Journal,* Amelia Jenkins wrote: "The stories are sweet and simple."

Daddy Goes to Work, illustrated by Aaron Boyd, features a young African American girl describing a day when she accompanies her dad to the office. Told in rhyming couplets, the story begins with the little girl having breakfast with her father, riding with him to work, and then her helping out during the day. Writing in *Booklist,* Gillian Engberg noted that the author's "words emphasize the warmth between father and daughter."

BIOGRAPHICAL AND CRITICAL SOURCES:

PERIODICALS

Black Issues Book Review, January-February, 2002, Tracy Grant, review of *Not Guilty: Twelve Black Men Speak Out on Law, Justice, and Life,* p. 65; March-April, 2007, Todd Steven Burroughs, review of *The N Word: Who Can Say It, Who Shouldn't, and Why,* p. 28.

Booklist, October 1, 2001, Vernon Ford, review of *Not Guilty,* p. 273; February 1, 2006, Gillian Engberg, review of *Daddy Goes to Work,* p. 66; February 1, 2007, Vernon Ford, review of *The N Word,* p. 21.

Books, May 13, 2007, Rebecca L. Ford, "Attempting to Put a Racial Slur in Its Place," review of *The N Word,* p. 8.

Kirkus Reviews, April 15, 2006, review of *Daddy Goes to Work,* p. 401.

Library Journal, November 1, 2001, review of *Not Guilty,* p. 119; March 1, 2007, Emily-Jane Dawson, review of *The N Word,* p. 92.

New York Law Journal, December 31, 2002, Thomas Adcock, review of *Not Guilty,* p. 2.

Publishers Weekly, October 15, 2001, review of *Not Guilty,* p. 59; January 22, 2007, review of *The N Word,* p. 179.

Reference & Research Book News, May, 2002, review of *Not Guilty,* p. 134.

School Library Journal, June, 2006, Amy Lilien-Harper, review of *Daddy Goes to Work,* p. 104; June, 2006, Amelia Jenkins, review of *Whose Knees Are These?* and *Whose Toes Are Those?,* p. 104.

Washington Post, November 5, 2001, Jeffrey Rosen, "Twelve Thoughtful Men," review of *Not Guilty,* p. 4.

ONLINE

Armchair Interviews, http://reviews.armchair interviews.com/ (August 14, 2007), Kornelia Longoria, review of *Whose Knees Are These?*

California Newsreel, http://www.newsreel.org/ (August 14, 2007), biography of author.

Frost Illustrated, http://www.frostillustrated.com/ (August 14, 2007), review of *The N Word.*

Racialicious.com, http://www.racialicious.com/ (June 13, 2007), review of *The N Word.*

Salon.com, http://www.salon.com/ (April 15, 2007), Mark Anthony Neal, "Who Gets to Use the N Word?,"interview with author.

Truthdig.com, http://www.truthdig.com/ (November 5, 2006), Jabari Asim, "Stir over Slurs"; (August 14, 2007), biography of author.*

*   *   *

ASSEFI, Nassim

PERSONAL: Ethnicity: "Iranian-American." *Education:* Wellesley College, B.A. (magna cum laude), 1991; University of Washington School of Medicine, M.D. (with high honors), 1997; postgraduate training at Harvard Medical School, 1997-2000.

ADDRESSES: Home—Istanbul, Turkey. *E-mail*—nassim@nassimassefi.com.

CAREER: Physician, activist, and writer. Physician specializing in women's health and immigrant/refugee medicine. University of Washington, School of Medicine, Seattle, junior faculty member, 2000-03; Management Sciences for Health, Kabul, Afghanistan, senior program associate, 2004-05; Family Health Alliance, Los Angeles, CA, women's health adviser, 2006—; freelance writer, 2006—. Has also worked as an academic in Seattle, a humanitarian aid worker and underground salsa dance teacher in Kabul, and an aspiring musician in Havana, Cuba.

MEMBER: Phi Beta Kappa, Sigma Xi Scientific Honor Society, Alpha Omega Alpha.

AWARDS, HONORS: University of Washington high merit full-tuition scholarship, 1988; Leadership America Scholar, 1990; M.A. Cartland Shackford Medical Fellowship Prize, 1991; Franklin Smith, M.D., Ph.D. Teaching Prize, 1993; Whiteley Center Scholar, 2001-04; Rainshadow Award for community service, 2004.

WRITINGS:

Aria, Harcourt (Orlando, FL), 2007.

Aria has been translated into Dutch, Portuguese, Taiwanese, Slovene, and Persian.

Contributor to the anthology *This Side of Doctoring,* edited by Eliza Lo Chin, Sage Press, 2003; contributor to periodicals, including *Wellesley* magazine and *Hedgebrook Journal*; contributor to numerous scientific journals, including the *Journal of Adolescent Health, British Medical Journal, Journal of Sexual and Reproductive Health,* and the *Clinical Journal of Women's Health.*

SIDELIGHTS: Nassim Assefi's first novel, *Aria,* was called "a small gem of a debut" by John Marshall in the *Seattle Post-Intelligencer.* In the novel, Assefi tells the story of Yasaman (Jasmine) Talahi, an Iranian-American physician who seeks spiritual truth after her five-year-old daughter, Aria, accidentally dies. Aria's father also died before she was born, leaving Jasmine alone to travel the world, from Guatemala to Tibet. A *Publishers Weekly* contributor commented that the author's "themes—loss as physical distance and the spiritual harm that can result from solitary grieving—come through." Jasmine ultimately ends up in Iran, where her parents still live but reject Aria for her modern, Western lifestyle. Marshall noted: "Writer Assefi faces her greatest challenge in Talahi's return to Iran and proves equal to the daunting difficulty of depicting an estranged family's reunion in all its intensity and complexity." Other reviewers also praised the novel. "There is much of talent in this remarkable book," wrote Bob Williams on the *Compulsive Reader* Web site. "It is a serious meditation on the greatest misfortune in life and an interesting display of the growth of the persons involved." Williams went on to write that the novel "stands out as notable achievement and should appeal to many discriminating readers."

Assefi told *CA:* "My first novel, *Aria,* was the result of a ten-year gestation and an accident. Here is the story: In 1996, I was trapped alone in a monsoon in Yogyakarta, Indonesia. My best friend and travel companion had departed the day before. I had run out of books to read and had already written my postcards. I was a twenty-three-year-old medical student on holiday, a privileged Iranian-American with a lucky life unacquainted with suffering. As I waited for the rains to end, I had little else to do but sit with myself. The spiritually perplexing issues posed to me by my patients with unimaginably difficult lives percolated through my mind. I realized I was woefully unprepared for making sense of the maelstrom of sickness and dying that I was witnessing in the clinical setting, and I had no spiritual framework for understanding the experience of war on people's lives. I began to write. A novel was born, the story of how great loss might manifest in the context of a comfortable U.S. life. I had seen grief take a variety of forms in different parts of the world. This seemed worthy of further exploration. I kept writing after my return from Indonesia, stealing quiet moments in the interstices of medical work. Finally, in January of 2006, I was blessed to find a wonderful agent who sold the book almost immediately.

"I write best in the mornings, for a maximum of four hours. My most effective writing has been done at writing residencies. Writing is a long, slow process for me—sometimes years of gestation and percolation before I commit words to the computer screen, then rewriting, revising, and editing."

When asked the most surprising thing she has learned as a writer, Assefi answered: "Patience, perseverance, and following my instincts."

Her favorite of her books is "the one I'm currently composing because by the time I publish a book, it has taken so many years in production that I may have tired of the subject and feel critical about its writing quality."

"I hope to humanize misunderstood parts of the world, particularly the Middle East and Persian-speaking Asia (Iran, Afghanistan, Tajikistan). I hope my readers connect with my characters, change their preconceived notions about life in the Muslim world, and feel less willing to support U.S. invasions in the region. I believe that good stories can change the world."

BIOGRAPHICAL AND CRITICAL SOURCES:

PERIODICALS

Library Journal, February 15, 2007, Shalini Miskelly, review of *Aria,* p. 109.

Publishers Weekly, January 1, 2007, review of *Aria,* p. 28.

Seattle Post-Intelligencer, May 3, 2007, John Marshall, review of *Aria.*

ONLINE

Annie Appleseed Project Web site, http://www.annieappleseedproject.org/ (October 14, 2007), "Reiki for Fibromyalgia Studied in Seattle," information on author in physician role.

Bookslut, http://www.bookslut.com/ (October 14, 2007), Jill Meyers, review of *Aria.*

Compulsive Reader, http://www.compulsivereader.com/ (October 14, 2007), Bob Williams, review of *Aria.*

Curled Up with a Good Book, http://www.curledup.com/ (October 14, 2007), Luan Gaines, review of *Aria.*

Howard Hughes Medical Institute, http://www.hhmi.org/ (April 27, 2006), "A Scientist-Novelist Helps Heal a People."

Nassim Assefi Home Page, http://nassimassefi.com (October 14, 2007).

Whit Press, http://www.whitpress.org/ (October 14, 2007), profile of author.

*   *   *

AUERBACH, Ann Hagedorn
See HAGEDORN, Ann

B

BAKKER, Tamara Faye
See MESSNER, Tammy Faye

*   *   *

BAKKER, Tammy
See MESSNER, Tammy Faye

*   *   *

BAKKER, Tammy Faye
See MESSNER, Tammy Faye

*   *   *

BALCHIN, W. George Victor
See BALCHIN, W.G.V.

*   *   *

BALCHIN, W.G.V. 1916-2007
(W. George Victor Balchin, William Balchin, William George Victor Balchin)

OBITUARY NOTICE— See index for *CA* sketch: Born June 20, 1916, in Aldershot, Hampshire, England; died July 30, 2007. Geographer, explorer, educator, and author. Early in his career, Balchin sailed into the Arctic, where he explored and mapped the northern reaches of Norway, including the glaciated peak named in his honor, now known as Balchinfjellet. He spent most of the rest of his career in academia. Balchin lectured at King's College, London, for nearly ten years following the end of World War II, developing a subcategory of geography that he called "local climate" research. It was one of several contributions that would eventually elevate the status of British geographical research from a subfield of geology into a respectable academic discipline that could stand on its own. Balchin's primary contribution came in the mid-1950s, when he was invited to create a geography department at the University of Wales, University College of Swansea. He not only established the department, but also added several laboratories, including a facility for studying the effects of waves and running water. That facility became a model for other institutions around the world. Balchin was also active as an officer of the Glamorgan County Naturalists Trust and other similar bodies. He remained at Swansea until 1978. Balchin spent his retirement in Ilkley, Yorkshire, but remained active in the Royal Geographical Society and the Geographical Association. He also continued to write books of national and regional interest, including *Cornwall: The Making of Its Landscape* (1954), *Cornwall: The Landscape through Maps* (1967), *Living History of Britain* (1981), and *The Cornish Landscape* (1983).

OBITUARIES AND OTHER SOURCES:

PERIODICALS

Times (London, England), September 6, 2007, p. 74.

ONLINE

Times Online, http://www.timesonline.co.uk/ (September 6, 2007).

BALCHIN, William
    See BALCHIN, W.G.V.

*   *   *

BALCHIN, William George Victor
    See BALCHIN, W.G.V.

*   *   *

BARONOVA, Irina 1919-

PERSONAL: Born March 13, 1919, in Petrograd, Russia; married German Sevastianov, 1936 (divorced); married Cecil G. Tennant, 1946 (died, 1967); remarried German Sevastianov; children: three.

ADDRESSES: Home—Byron Bay, Australia.

CAREER: Dancer and writer. Paris Opéra, Paris, France, made debut at the age of eleven, soloist, 1930; Théâtre Mogador, Paris, soloist, 1931; engaged by George Balanchine (at age thirteen) as ballerina, Ballets Russes de Monte Carlo, 1932, remaining with company (various Ballets Russes companies under the direction of de Basil), until 1939; ballerina, Original Ballet Russe, 1940-41, and Ballet Theatre (later American Ballet Theatre), New York, NY, 1941-42; also performed with Roxy Theater, New York, NY, 1943, and Massine's Ballet Russe Highlights, 1945; guest artist, Original Ballet Russe, touring Cuba and Rio de Janeiro, Brazil, 1946; also appeared in several films, including *Florian,* 1940, and *Yolanda,* 1943, *Train of Events,* 1949, and *Toast of Love,* 1951; appeared in plays and musicals, including as Anna Viskinova in the musical *Follow the Girls,* London, 1945; as ballerina in *Bullet in the Ballet* British tour, 1946; and as Tania Karpova in *Dark Eyes,* U.S., 1947, and London, England, 1948; Royal Academy of Dancing, London, England, member of Technical Committee and occasional teacher.

WRITINGS:

Irina: Ballet, Life and Love, University Press of Florida (Gainesville, FL), 2005.

SIDELIGHTS: In her memoir, *Irina: Ballet, Life and Love,* Irina Baronova tells her story of being a young Russian immigrant and ballet prodigy who made her debut at the Paris Opéra when she was apprxoimately eleven years old. After being spotted by George Balanchine, a world-renowned choreographer, she became one of his three famous "baby ballerinas." During her time at the Ballet Russe de Monte Carlo, she worked with ballet greats such as Léonide Massine and Bronislawa Nijinska and with artists such as Pablo Picasso and Salvador Dali. In the memoir, the author also recounts her work in Hollywood films and the American Ballet Theatre, as well as her personal life, including divorces and family problems. "She has concentrated on the first forty-eight years of her life, preferring to deal with the era of her development, her career as a ballet artist, and her halcyon years in Great Britain as the wife of Cecil Tennant and mother of three brilliant children," noted Leland Windreich on the *Ballet-Dance Magazine* Web site. Although some reviewers thought that Baranova provided too much detail in her memoir, most had high praise for *Irina.* David Jays, writing in the *Moscow Times,* noted: "It isn't retrospection but recall that makes this autobiography a delight. The detail is fabulous." A *Publishers Weekly* contributor noted that the author's "prose is a testament to the woman she is: passionate, vivacious and overwhelmingly optimistic."

BIOGRAPHICAL AND CRITICAL SOURCES:

BOOKS

Baronova, Irina, *Irina: Ballet, Life and Love,* University Press of Florida (Gainesville, FL), 2005.

International Dictionary of Ballet, St. James Press (Detroit, MI), 1993.

PERIODICALS

Moscow Times, September 29, 2006, David Jays, "Footloose," review of *Irina.*

New York Times Book Review, September 10, 2006, Jennifer Homans, "Baby Ballerina," review of *Irina.*

Publishers Weekly, June 12, 2006, review of *Irina,* p. 39.

Sydney Morning Herald, October 29, 2005, Valerie Lawson, "A Rich Life Fully Lived," review of *Irina.*

ONLINE

ABC.net.au, http://www.abc.net.au/ (October 27, 2005), "Ballerina Irina Baronova," profile of author.
Ballet-Dance Magazine, http://www.ballet-dance.com/ (January, 2006), Leland Windreich, review of *Irina.*
International Movie Database, http://www.imdb.com/ (October 14, 2007), information on author's film work.*

*   *   *

BEAH, Ishmael 1980-

PERSONAL: Born 1980, in Sierra Leone; immigrated to the United States, 1998. *Education:* Oberlin College, B.A, 2004.

ADDRESSES: Home—New York, NY.

CAREER: Author. Member, Human Rights Watch Children's Rights Division Advisory Committee. *Military service:* Served in the Sierra Leone Army, 1994-96.

WRITINGS:

A Long Way Gone: Memoirs of a Boy Soldier, Farrar, Straus & Giroux (New York, NY), 2007.

SIDELIGHTS: Ishmael Beah's *A Long Way Gone: Memoirs of a Boy Soldier* tells about war from the point of view of a young boy trained to kill without remorse. Beah's first dozen years or so in Sierra Leone were happy ones, but when civil war broke out, his village was raided by both sides of the conflict. He and his brother lost their family, and the siblings soon were separated from each other as well. Struggling to survive, Beah ran into the Sierra Leone Army, which gave him shelter. However, their motives were not selfless, and they offered the boy the choice of either joining the army or being abandoned. Terrified, Beah became a soldier and was trained to use a weapon. The army gave their young soldiers drugs and made them watch violent movies, all the while telling them that the rebels were responsible for killing their loved ones. This kind of indoctrination was effective, and Beah was turned into a murdering machine. Beah describes the two years he was in the army frankly, relating how he killed many people himself.

In 1996, Beah had the good fortune of being rescued by the United Nations and sent to a camp where he was rehabilitated. While there were problems with this process—government and rebel soldiers were thrown together and treated the same, as if they had not been bitter enemies—U.N. counselors did help Beah. He was adopted by an uncle. When his uncle, too, died, he was adopted by another woman, who helped him immigrate to the United States. Once there, Beah attended and graduated from Oberlin College. Beah remains astounded and chagrined over how he had been turned into a barbaric soldier. "The thing that causes me to wince most is when I remember all the really bad stuff we did that I laughed at," he is quoted as saying in a *Time* article by Belinda Luscombe. "You wonder how anyone with a soul could do that."

While some critics of *A Long Way Gone* pointed out narrative flaws in Beah's writing style, many reviewers were impressed by the work. If Beah's descriptions of the atrocities he personally committed "are to be given credence, his personal body count must total many dozens," remarked William Boyd in the *New York Times Book Review.* "Such knowledge is shocking, but it's the reader's imagination that delivers the cold sanguinary shudder, not the author's boilerplate prose. It is a vision of hell that Beah gives us, one worthy of Hieronymus Bosch, but as though depicted in primary colors by a naive artist." Nevertheless, Boyd asserted that "Beah's memoir joins an elite class of writing: Africans witnessing African wars." In a *Miami Herald* review, Connie Ogle attested that "Beah's story is a wrenching survivor's tale, but there's no self-pity or political digression to be found. Raw and honest, *A Long Way Gone* is an important account of the ravages of war, and it's most disturbing as a reminder of how easy it would be for any of us to break, to become unrecognizable in such extreme circumstances." "Told in a conversational, accessible style, this powerful record of war ends as a beacon to all teens experiencing violence around them," Matthew L. Moffett further observed in the *School Library Journal.*

BIOGRAPHICAL AND CRITICAL SOURCES:

BOOKS

Beah, Ishmael, *A Long Way Gone: Memoirs of a Boy Soldier,* Farrar, Straus & Giroux (New York, NY), 2007.

PERIODICALS

Biography, spring, 2007, Lynne Jones, review of *A Long Way Gone.*

Black Issues Book Review, March 1, 2007, Angela P. Dodson, "Starbucks Offers a Jolt of Serious Reading," p. 6.

Booklist, November 15, 2006, Hazel Rochman, review of *A Long Way Gone,* p. 19.

Books, February 11, 2007, Jeff Rice, "Memoir Paints Portrait of a Child as a Soldier," p. 4; June 23, 2007, Kristin Kloberdanz, review of *A Long Way Gone,* p. 7.

Bulletin of the Center for Children's Books, May, 2007, Elizabeth Bush, review of *A Long Way Gone,* p. 359.

Entertainment Weekly, February 16, 2007, Gilbert Cruz, "Tug of War," p. 82.

Kirkus Reviews, January 15, 2007, review of *A Long Way Gone,* p. 58; March 1, 2007, review of *A Long Way Gone,* p. 3.

Library Journal, March 1, 2007, James Thorsen, review of *A Long Way Gone,* p. 91.

Miami Herald, March 7, 2007, Connie Ogle, "Ishmael Beah Leads a Harrowing Journey into the Heart of Sierra Leone's Bloody Civil War."

Nation, May 28, 2007, Fatin Abbas, review of *A Long Way Gone,* p. 34.

National Post, March 24, 2007, Stewart Bell, review of *A Long Way Gone,* p. 13.

New York Times, March 10, 2007, Julie Bosman, "Disturbing Memoir Outsells Literary Comfort Food at Starbucks," p. 7.

New York Times Book Review, February 25, 2007, William Boyd, "Babes in Arms," p. 12.

New York Times Magazine, January 14, 2007, Ishmael Beah, "The Making, and Unmaking, of a Child Soldier," p. 36.

Publishers Weekly, December 18, 2006, review of *A Long Way Gone,* p. 55.

School Library Journal, April, 2007, Matthew L. Moffett, review of *A Long Way Gone,* p. 171.

Spectator, June 9, 2007, Caroline Moorehead, "Lost and Found."

Time, February 12, 2007, Belinda Luscombe, "Pop Culture Finds Lost Boys," p. 62.

USA Today, January 11, 2007, Carol Memmott, "'Gone' to Starbucks," p. 01.

ONLINE

Gather.com, http://www.gather.com/ (March 20, 2007), Lucy B., review of *A Long Way Gone.*

Ishmael Beah Home Page, http://www.alongwaygone.com/ishmael_beah.html (September 25, 2007).*

*   *   *

BEALMEAR, Robert Fate
See FATE, Robert

*   *   *

BENGELSDORF, Irving S. 1922-2007
(Irving Swem Bengelsdorf)

OBITUARY NOTICE— See index for *CA* sketch: Born October 23, 1922, in Chicago, IL; died of kidney failure, June 22, 2007, in Oceanside, CA. Science columnist, editor, journalist, chemist, and educator. Bengelsdorf was best known as a science writer, but he spent nearly ten years as a research chemist in the early days of his career, including posts at the General Electric Research Laboratory, the Texaco-U.S. Rubber Research Center, and the U.S. Borax Research Corporation. Later he worked at the Jet Propulsion Laboratory in La Cañada, California, as a grant writer and director of science communication. Bengelsdorf devoted much of his time to explaining science to the general reader. His column "Of Atoms and Men" appeared in the *Los Angeles Times,* where he worked as the science editor from 1963 to 1970. Afterward he taught science communication at the California Institute of Technology in Pasadena and appeared occasionally at other institutions, including the University of Southern California and the University of California at Los Angeles. Bengelsdorf received several awards for science journalism in the 1960s, including the James T. Grady Award of the American Chemical Society, Westinghouse Awards from the American Association for the Advancement of Science, and a Claude Bernard Science Journalism Award from the National Society for Medical Research. Though most of his writing appeared in newspapers, such as the *Times* and later the *Los Angeles Herald Examiner,* Bengelsdorf also wrote the book *Space Ship Earth: People and Pollution* (1969).

OBITUARIES AND OTHER SOURCES:

PERIODICALS

Los Angeles Times, July 20, 2007, p. B6.

*   *   *

BENGELSDORF, Irving Swem
    See BENGELSDORF, Irving S.

*   *   *

BENSON, Ophelia

PERSONAL: Female.

ADDRESSES: Home and office—Seattle, WA. *E-mail*—opheliabenson@msn.com.

CAREER: Writer and editor. Cofounder, *Butterflies and Wheels.com.*

WRITINGS:

(With Jeremy Stangroom) *The Dictionary of Fashionable Nonsense: A Guide for Edgy People,* Souvenir (London, England), 2004.

(With Jeremy Stangroom) *Why Truth Matters,* Continuum (New York, NY), 2006.

Deputy editor, and author of monthly column "Interrogations," for *Philosophers'.*

SIDELIGHTS: Ophelia Benson is the cofounder and editor of *Butterflies and Wheels,* a Web site designed to inform readers of the truth behind pseudoscience. In addition, with Jeremy Stangroom she has written *The Dictionary of Fashionable Nonsense: A Guide for Edgy People* and *Why Truth Matters.* The purpose of the first volume is to debunk the plethora of myths and beliefs that are assumed to be true simply because they have gained attention or common acceptance in society. Benson and Stangroom argue that certain phrases and words in particular, such as "anything goes" and "ideology," are used in order to talk around a subject and distract listeners or readers from the truth. Phil Mole, in a review for the *Skeptical Inquirer,* called the book "an excellent contribution to the small but important genre of satirical dictionaries," adding that he "recommended [the book] to anyone wishing a deeper understanding of the follies of our time."

Why Truth Matters addresses what Benson and Stangroom state to be an ever-dwindling interest in getting to the truth in any given situation in favor of a more postmodern, accepting method of dealing with a problem. They provide readers with numerous examples across a spectrum of subjects, from science to politics to literature, illustrating how this new tendency is weakening the progress of humanity. Johann Hari, in a review for the London *Independent on Sunday* quoted on his *Johann Hari Archives* Web site, remarked that the book is "a defense of Enlightenment values and the pursuit of uncomfortable truths from the feminist left." *Library Journal* contributor Jason Moore observed: "The book's strong point is its reasonable and concise overview of the major arguments and viewpoints."

Benson told *CA:* "Writing is my way of arguing with the world, as well as my way of thinking about it, talking to it, considering it from new angles. I like the essay as a form, and essayists are among my favorite writers—Montaigne and William Hazlitt especially. I like essays, articles, and books to be no longer than they need to be; I don't like padding or diffuseness, although I do like complex syntax and thought. I don't like simple writing or language, but I do like concision."

BIOGRAPHICAL AND CRITICAL SOURCES:

PERIODICALS

Choice: Current Reviews for Academic Libraries, October 1, 2006, C.S. Seymour, review of *Why Truth Matters,* p. 309.

Library Journal, May 1, 2006, Jason Moore, review of *Why Truth Matters,* p. 89.

Reference & Research Book News, February 1, 2007, review of *Why Truth Matters.*

Skeptical Inquirer, May 1, 2005, Phil Mole, "Nonsense in Vogue," review of *The Dictionary of Fashionable Nonsense: A Guide for Edgy People,* p. 56.

Times Higher Education Supplement, December 24, 2004, "The Hip and the Dead," p. 28.

Times Literary Supplement, January 28, 2005, Toby Lichtig, review of *The Dictionary of Fashionable Nonsense,* p. 33; October 20, 2006, Jack Darach, review of *Why Truth Matters,* p. 32.

ONLINE

Butterflies and Wheels, http://www.butterfliesand wheels.com/ (August 22, 2007), biography of Ophelia Benson.

Johann Hari Archives, http://www.johannhari.com/ (March 13, 2006), Johann Hari, review of *Why Truth Matters,* from the *Independent on Sunday.*

Third Camp, http://www.thirdcamp.com/ (August 21, 2007), Arash Sorx, interview with Ophelia Benson.

3:AM Magazine Online, http://www.3ammagazine. com/ (January 31, 2007), David Thompson, interview with Ophelia Benson.

Virtual Philosopher Blog, http://nigelwarburton. typepad.com/virtualphilosopher/ (January 3, 2007), Nigel Warburton, interview with Ophelia Benson.

Why Truth Matters Web site, http://www.whytruth matters.com (August 21, 2007), biography of Ophelia Benson.

*   *   *

BERG, Scott W.

PERSONAL: Education: University of Minnesota, B.A.; Miami University of Ohio, M.A.; George Mason University, M.F.A.

ADDRESSES: Home—Washington, DC. *Office*—English Department, George Mason University, 4400 University Dr., MSN 3E4, Fairfax, VA 22030. *E-mail*—scottwberg@grandavenues.com; sberg@gmu. edu.

CAREER: George Mason University, Fairfax, VA, creative writing faculty member.

WRITINGS:

Grand Avenues: The Story of the French Visionary Who Designed Washington, D.C., Pantheon Books (New York, NY), 2007.

Contributor to periodicals, including the *Washington Post.*

SIDELIGHTS: Scott W. Berg trained as an architect before becoming a writing teacher. Berg's first book, *Grand Avenues: The Story of the French Visionary Who Designed Washington, D.C.,* reflects his ongoing interest in architecture and civil engineering. It tells the story of Pierre L'Enfant, the French planner who designed the layout of Washington, DC, as it is known today. L'Enfant gained attention as the architect for the Federal Hall in New York, and went on to raise eyebrows with some of his more daring suggestions for the layout of the capitol, including the placement of Congress adjacent to the Potomac River, which was an untouched area at the time, and placing much of the proposed city on swamp land. Writing for the *Metroactive* Web site, Richard Busack commented: "With admittedly little documentation to go on, Berg silhouettes L'Enfant against the leading lights of his time." Brad Hooper, in a review for *Booklist,* remarked that "all the wrinkles about both the plan and the man himself are ironed out in this approachable biography." A reviewer for *Publishers Weekly* declared that "Berg performs sterling service in excavating this little-known story from the archives."

BIOGRAPHICAL AND CRITICAL SOURCES:

PERIODICALS

Booklist, January 1, 2007, Brad Hooper, review of *Grand Avenues: The Story of the French Visionary Who Designed Washington, D.C.,* p. 36.

Publishers Weekly, December 11, 2006, review of *Grand Avenues,* p. 61.

Reference & Research Book News, May 1, 2007, review of *Grand Avenues.*

Washington Post Book World, April 1, 2007, Benjamin Forgey, review of *Grand Avenues,* p. 3.

ONLINE

Metroactive, http://www.metroactive.com/ (March 27, 2007), Richard von Busack, review of *Grand Avenues.*

Scott W. Berg Home Page, http://www.scottwberg.com (August 21, 2007).*

* * *

BERGMAN, Ernst Ingmar
See BERGMAN, Ingmar

* * *

BERGMAN, Ingmar 1918-2007
(Ernst Ingmar Bergman, Buntel Eriksson, Ernest Riffle)

OBITUARY NOTICE— See index for *CA* sketch: Born July 14, 1918, in Uppsala, Sweden; died July 30, 2007, on the island of Fårö, Sweden. Film director, screenwriter, stage director, playwright, and author. Bergman is regarded as one of the world's greatest filmmakers, having directed and scripted dozens of award-winning movies. His admirers tend to describe him as "respected," rather than "beloved," however, and report "appreciating" his films, rather than "enjoying" them. Bergman's work was not considered light fare. He tackled the monumental themes of man's relationship with God, the relationships of men and women, the torment of mental illness, and the innate character of the artist. Several of his early films fall into the first category and are generally described as dark, gloomy, and pessimistic—rejections of the existence of a loving, caring God and an outgrowth of his childhood as the son of a strict, even abusive minister. Among such films was one of his most popular, *The Seventh Seal* (1956), in which a medieval knight plays chess with the Devil against a background of the Black Death. Other films, such as *Scenes from a Marriage* (1973), deal with male-female relationships, and Bergman was often praised for his strong and independent female characters. One of his later and most popular films was originally produced for television: *Fanny and Alexander* (1981) is a long film about two children growing up in Sweden in the early 1900s. Some critics have claimed that it blends all of Bergman's themes into a single work of art and treats them with a gentler hand than his earlier anguished efforts. His last film was *Saraband,* broadcast on Swedish television in 2003. Bergman was affiliated with the Svensk Filmindustri for nearly thirty years; he established his own film companies, Cinematograph in Sweden, in 1968, and Personafilm in West Germany, in 1977. Less well known, especially to English-speaking audiences, is Bergman's work as a stage director and playwright, and occasional novelist and nonfiction author, sometimes under pseudonyms. He was, according to some reports, even more actively involved in the theater than the film industry, directing several stage plays each year and writing some of them. He directed the Civic Theater in Malmö, Sweden, in the 1950s, and operated the Royal Dramatic Theater in Stockholm in the 1960s. Bergman won most of the awards available to a film director and screenwriter, including the Irving G. Thalberg Memorial Award and four Academy Awards from the U.S. Academy of Motion Picture Arts and Sciences (one Academy Award was for *Fanny and Alexander*). In 2003, he received the Film Preservation Award of the International Federation of Film Archives. Bergman spent his last days on the isolated island of Fårö, off the southeastern coast of Sweden, where he said that he felt most comfortable and secure.

OBITUARIES AND OTHER SOURCES:

BOOKS

Bergman, Ingmar, *The Magic Lantern: An Autobiography,* Viking (New York, NY), 1988.

Bergman, Ingmar, *Images: My Life in Film,* Arcade (New York, NY), 1994.

Dictionary of Literary Biography, Volume 257: *Twentieth-Century Swedish Writers after World War II,* Thomson Gale (Detroit, MI), 2002.

International Dictionary of Films and Filmmakers, Volume 2: *Directors,* 4th edition, St. James Press (Detroit, MI), 2000.

PERIODICALS

Chicago Tribune, July 31, 2007, sec. 3, p. 5.
Los Angeles Times, July 31, 2007, pp. A1, A6-A7.
New York Times, July 31, 2007, pp. A1, A20.
Times (London, England), July 31, 2007, p. 55.

*   *   *

BERNSTEIN, Harry 1910-

PERSONAL: Born April 17, 1910, in Stockport, England; brought to the United States, 1922; married, c. 1935; wife's name Ruby (died, 2002); children: Adraenne, Charles.

ADDRESSES: Home—Brick, NJ.

CAREER: Writer. Has worked as a book and script reader for movie studio Columbia Pictures, a freelance writer for periodicals, and as an editor for a trade magazine, until 1972.

WRITINGS:

The Invisible Wall: A Love Story That Broke Barriers (memoir), Ballantine Books (New York, NY), 2007.

Also author of about two dozen unpublished novels, including *The Smile, The Peekskill Episode,* and *Hard Times and White Collars.* Contributor to periodicals, including *Popular Mechanics, Family Circle,* and *New York Daily News.*

SIDELIGHTS: Widely praised for his first published book, the memoir *The Invisible Wall: A Love Story That Broke Barriers,* Harry Bernstein has particularly drawn attention for breaking into publishing at age ninety-six. Actually, he has been writing for many years, including contributions to magazines and nearly thirty unpublished novels. It was not until his wife died in 2002, though, that his disappointment over earlier failures was overcome by a need to reflect on his life. "I was too much alone. My wife was dead. My friends were mostly gone . . . ," he said in a

Seattle Times interview with Mark DiIonno. "I had no future to think about, no present. And so I found myself thinking about my past, and the people I knew and the place I grew up. I was looking for a home." He found writing about his childhood to be a satisfying creative release.

Several critics of the memoir compared it to *Angela's Ashes,* the book by Frank McCourt about his desperately poor childhood in Ireland. Bernstein's memoir is about his early years in the Jewish section of Lancashire before World War I. The title, *The Invisible Wall,* refers to the fact that Christian families lived on one side of town and Jews on the other. Though they often got along, the city remained divided by religion. Bernstein, one of five children in an impoverished home, recalls his alcoholic, abusive father and kind, loving mother. But the story centers around his sister Lily, who falls in love with a Christian boy and how their relationship first tears apart, then joins together the community. Because the events happen some eighty years ago, the dialogue and events are subject to some artistic license. A *Kirkus Reviews* critic commented that readers would therefore be advised to consider it "less a memoir, more an autobiographical novel." The author readily admitted to Motoko Rich in the *New York Times* that his book "is not necessarily an accurate day-to-day detailing of your life, . . . [but] certain scenes are projected in your mind as if they are on a screen and you are looking at it."

Many reviewers praised the results, with *Library Journal* contributor Ingrid Levin describing it as a "gripping coming-of-age memoir." In *Booklist,* Hazel Rochman stated: "Far from rambling oral history, the chapters are tense with danger and with tenderness," while a *Publishers Weekly* writer concluded that "the conversational account takes on the heft of a historical novel with stirring success."

BIOGRAPHICAL AND CRITICAL SOURCES:

BOOKS

Bernstein, Harry, *The Invisible Wall: A Love Story That Broke Barriers,* Ballantine Books (New York, NY), 2007.

PERIODICALS

America's Intelligence Wire, March 30, 2007, "96-Year-Old Author Proves It's Never Too Late to Write That Book."

Booklist, November 1, 2006, Hazel Rochman, review of *The Invisible Wall,* p. 17.

Bookseller, March 10, 2006, "Debut Writer, Aged 95," p. 10.

Entertainment Weekly, March 23, 2007, Tanner Stransky, review of *The Invisible Wall,* p. 65.

Kirkus Reviews, December 15, 2006, review of *The Invisible Wall,* p. 1250.

Library Journal, March 15, 2007, Ingrid Levin, review of *The Invisible Wall,* p. 78.

New York Times, April 7, 2007, Motoko Rich, "Successful at 96, Writer Has More to Say," p. 7.

New York Times Book Review, April 4, 2007, William Grimes, "Recalling a Time When a Street Divided Two Worlds," p. 9.

Publishers Weekly, December 11, 2006, review of *The Invisible Wall,* p. 54; January 29, 2007, "PW Talks with Harry Bernstein: A Writer Takes Off at 90: In His Memoir *The Invisible Wall,* Harry Bernstein Tells of Growing Up Jewish in a World War I-Era Northern English Town," p. 53.

School Library Journal, June 2007, Ellen Bell, review of *The Invisible Wall,* p. 181.

USA Today, March 20, 2007, Bob Minzesheimer, "Writing on the 'Wall,'" p. 01.

ONLINE

Guardian Online, http://www.guardian.co.uk/ (February 12, 2007), Ed Pilkington, "Divided Loyalties."

Happy News, http://www.happynews.com/ (April 1, 2007), Rebecca Santana, "Author, 96, Proves It's Never Too Late."

International Herald Tribune Online, http://www.iht.com/ (April 10, 2007), Motoko Rich, "At 96, Harry Bernstein Finds Literary Success with His Memoir."

Nextbook, http://www.nextbook.org/ (March 20, 2007), Joey Rubin, "Late Bloomer."

Seattle Times Online, http://seattletimes.nwsource.com/ (April 16, 2007), Mark DiIonno, "93-Year-Old Writer Discovers Success—at Last."*

*   *   *

BHAGAT, Chetan 1974-

PERSONAL: Born April 22, 1974, in Delhi, India; son of Rekha Bhagat; married Anusha Suryanarayan; children: twin sons. *Education:* Indian Institute of Technology, Delhi, India, B.S., 1995; India Institute of Management, M.B.A, 1997. *Hobbies and other interests:* Yoga.

ADDRESSES: Home—India. *Agent*—Bhavna Sharma, Corporate Voice/Weber Shandwick Pvt. Ltd, 212, 2nd Fl, Okhla Industrial Estate, Phase-III, New Delhi, India 110 020.

CAREER: Goldman Sachs (investment bank), Hong Kong, China, associate, beginning 1998; Deutsche Bank, Hong Kong, investment banker.

MEMBER: Mensa Society.

AWARDS, HONORS: Society Young Achiever's Award, 2004, for *Five Point Someone;* Rupa & Co. recognition award, 2005, for *Five Point Someone.*

WRITINGS:

Five Point Someone: What Not to Do at IIT (novel), Rupa (New Delhi, India), 2004.

One Night @ the Call Center (novel), Rupa (New Delhi, India), 2005, published as *One Night at the Call Center: A Novel,* Ballantine Books (New York, NY), 2007.

Contributor to professional journals.

ADAPTATIONS: Film rights for *Five Point Someone* and *One Night @ the Call Center* have been optioned.

SIDELIGHTS: An engineering graduate who has pursued a career in banking, Chetan Bhagat has created a sensation in his native India for his comical novels featuring young Indian professionals coping with a country that is rapidly changing. His debut book, *Five Point Someone: What Not to Do at IIT,* is about a group of students at the India Institute for Technology, where Bhagat himself graduated. Feeling that they might become soulless working drones should they strive to get responsible jobs after college, the seven friends instead indulge in drugs, American rock music, and drinking. "Parental pressure, familial obligations, gender roles, dating, sex, drugs, suicide— just about every teen issue is addressed, and the book has struck a chord in India," reported Jeff Plunkett in a *Time International* article. The critic noted, though, that Bhagat does not go so far as to have his characters fail at school. They all graduate, despite cheating on exams and pursuing their hedonistic ways. "It's not all funny," observed a writer for the blog *Krishna-Talkies.* "Chetan has put some insights into the high level of pressure in professional colleges and how it affects the students."

Five Point Someone became a best seller in India and was optioned for film. The same has proven true with Bhagat's follow-up work, *One Night @ the Call Center* (also published as *One Night @ the Call Center: A Novel*). Here the setting is one of India's many call center companies, where the characters answer questions from Americans about various products. While the money is good, the young workers hate the company and its managers, who have no qualms about firing perfectly good employees for the sake of downsizing. They are also instilled with the belief that the average adult American has the intelligence of a typical ten-year-old Indian child. To prevent themselves from being fired for no good reason, the protagonists hatch a plan to encourage incoming calls about a Microsoft software package. The ploy goes horribly awry, however, to the point where lives are at stake and only a phone call from God Himself rescues the workers.

"Bhagat has issues with what he calls the high pedestal on which America has been placed," explained Jonathan Boorstein in a *Direct* review of *Five Point Someone.* "He maintains he is just telling the youth of India the reality of the United States and then they can make up their own minds." Some critics, as Shashi Tharoor pointed out in *Foreign Policy,* have observed that it "isn't great literature. Serious critics will no doubt quibble with the two-dimensional characterization, the pedestrian prose, the plot's contrived deus ex machina, and the author's hokey spiritualism. But none of that matters. Bhagat's tone is pitch-perfect, his observer's eye keenly focused on nuance and detail."

BIOGRAPHICAL AND CRITICAL SOURCES:

PERIODICALS

Books, April 22, 2007, review of *One Night @ the Call Center: A Novel,* p. 12.
Call Center, October 1, 2006, "India Explores Call Center Culture in Film," p. 45.

Direct, February 1, 2006, Jonathan Boorstein, "Hello, Delhi."
Far Eastern Economic Review, March, 2006, Sadanand Dhume, "Untouchables: My Family's Triumphant Journey out of the Caste System in Modern India," p. 58.
Foreign Policy, March 1, 2006, Shashi Tharoor, "India Finds Its Calling," p. 78.
Publishers Weekly, March 19, 2007, review of *One Night @ the Call Center,* p. 41.
Time International, August 9, 2004, Jeff Plunkett, "Teenage Wasteland: Can Slackers Succeed at India's Elite Universities?," p. 51.

ONLINE

Chetan Bhagat Home Page, http://www.chetanbhagat.com/ontcc/index.php (September 24, 2007).
Krishna-Talkies, http://krishnatalkies.blogspot.com/ (September 14, 2005), review of *Five Point Someone: What Not to Do at IIT.*
Rediff.com, http://in.rediff.com/ (February 8, 2006), Lindsay Pereira, "I Could Be Working in a Call Centre," interview with Chetan Bhagat.*

*   *   *

BLATANIS, Konstantinos 1966-

PERSONAL: Born December 4, 1966, in Athens, Greece; son of Fotios and Panayo Blatanis. *Ethnicity:* "Greek." *Education:* State University of New York at Buffalo, M.A.; Aristotle University, Thessaloniki, Greece, Ph.D.

ADDRESSES: Home—Athens, Greece. *E-mail*—kblatanis@yahoo.gr.

CAREER: National and Kapodistrias University of Athens, Athens, Greece, lecturer in American literature and modern drama.

AWARDS, HONORS: Fulbright fellow in the United States.

WRITINGS:

Popular Culture Icons in Contemporary American Drama, Fairleigh Dickinson University Press (Madison, NJ), 2003.

SIDELIGHTS: Konstantinos Blatanis told *CA:* "Writing can be a number of different and contradictory things all at the same time. It is often difficult but rewarding, intimidating yet inviting, tedious while invigorating. More than anything else, it is true that writing always entails a promise. I undertook my project on popular culture icons in American popular culture with the promise that I would find out more about a long series of modern American plays that I considered attractive, intriguing, and challenging. At the same time, I worked with the hope that my research would lead me to a greater and deeper understanding of issues pertaining directly to the current culture enveloping both the playwrights and me. Needless to say, the very plays I dealt with and the playwrights themselves were my primary sources of inspiration."

BIOGRAPHICAL AND CRITICAL SOURCES:

PERIODICALS

Modern Drama, spring, 2005, Robert Baker-White, review of *Popular Culture Icons in Contemporary American Drama,* pp. 215-217.

* * *

BOCZKOWSKI, Pablo J. 1965-

PERSONAL: Born September 24, 1965, in Buenos Aires, Argentina. *Education:* Universidad de Buenos Aires, license in psychology, 1989; Cornell University, M.A., 1997, Ph.D., 2001.

ADDRESSES: Home—Evanston, IL. *Office*—Northwestern University, 2240 Campus Dr., Evanston, IL 60208. *E-mail*—pjb9@northwestern.edu.

CAREER: Massachusetts Institute of Technology, Cambridge, assistant professor, 2001-05; Northwestern University, Evanston, IL, associate professor, 2005—.

AWARDS, HONORS: Outstanding book awards, National Communication Association, 2004, 2005, and International Communication Association, 2005, all for *Digitizing the News: Innovation in Online Newspapers.*

WRITINGS:

Digitizing the News: Innovation in Online Newspapers, MIT Press (Cambridge, MA), 2004.

* * *

BOHANNAN, Paul 1920-2007
(Paul James Bohannan)

OBITUARY NOTICE— See index for *CA* sketch: Born March 5, 1920, in Lincoln, NE; died of complications from Alzheimer's disease, July 13, 2007, in Visalia, CA. Anthropologist, sociologist, educator, and author. Bohannan began his career as an explorer of culture in Nigeria and ended it as a scholarly interpreter of culture in America. In the early 1950s he and his wife lived among the Tiv of Nigeria. For nearly five years they recorded, in both writings and more than a thousand photographs, a vanishing way of life among a tribe that had rarely been studied before. The anthropologist then spent another year among the Wanga of Kenya before leaving Africa. Bohannan taught anthropology at Oxford University, where he had earlier studied as a Rhodes scholar, then at Princeton University. In the 1960s and early seventies he taught at Northwestern University, He moved to California in 1976, teaching first at the University of California in Santa Barbara and later at the University of Southern California, where he retired in 1987. Whereas Bohannan had studied a wide range of living habits and social customs in Africa, in America he focused mainly on the phenomenon of divorce among the middle class, which he likened to an "industry" that supported such a huge number of lawyers, judges, investigators, family counselors, and others that it virtually rivaled the automotive industry in scope. During a career that spanned nearly forty years and a twenty-year retirement, Bohannan wrote or edited more than thirty books, often in collaboration with his wife, Laura Bohannan, prior to their own divorce in 1975. His writings include *The Tiv of Nigeria* (1953) and *The Tiv: An African People from 1949 to 1953* (2000), which features restored photographs from his original field research, *Love, Sex, and Being Human: A Book about the Human Condition for Young People* (1969), *All the Happy Families: Exploring the Varieties of Family Life* (1985), and *We, the Alien: An Introduction to Cultural Anthropology* (1992).

OBITUARIES AND OTHER SOURCES:

PERIODICALS

Los Angeles Times, August 2, 2007, p. B6.

* * *

BOHANNAN, Paul James
    See BOHANNAN, Paul

* * *

BONNER, Robert E. 1967-

PERSONAL: Born 1967.

ADDRESSES: Office—Michigan State University, East Lansing, MI. *E-mail*—bonnerro@msu.edu; robert. bonner@dartmouth.edu.

CAREER: Michigan State University, East Lansing, MI, assistant professor of history.

WRITINGS:

Colors and Blood: Flag Passions of the Confederate South, Princeton University Press (Princeton, NJ), 2002.
The Soldier's Pen: Firsthand Impressions of the Civil War, Hill & Wang (New York, NY), 2006.

SIDELIGHTS: Historian Robert E. Bonner has started off his publishing credits by writing about the American Civil War. In *Colors and Blood: Flag Passions of the Confederate South,* he focuses on the importance of symbolism in inspiring nationalism among the citizens and soldiers of the young Confederacy. "The author argues that members of the Confederate war generation were distinctly aware of a flag's potential importance in expressing political commitments and eliciting military courage," remarked Aaron Palmer in *History: Review of Books.* Palmer further observed that Bonner does not explore the "minutiae" of the history behind flag colors and their meanings, adding that he "gives martial flags ample consideration, but the book's chief contribution is to the study of Confederate nationalism." "*Colors and Blood* meticulously catalogs the ways in which Confederate symbols evoked multiple and complex meanings during the American Civil War," observed Lisa Tendrich Frank in the *Journal of Southern History.* She added: "Those interested in the debate about southern identity and symbols, whether in the past or the present, will be well served to start with this work."

Reviewing *The Soldier's Pen: Firsthand Impressions of the Civil War* for the *Civil War News,* critic Michael Russert noted that there have already been numerous previously published collections of Civil War soldiers' writings. This one, however, is different because it draws heavily on unpublished writings from the Gilder Lehrman Collection in New York City, and because Bonner stresses the perspective of war letters, diaries, and related writings as legitimate forms of literature. Thus, Bonner "has successfully accomplished a distinctive and significant approach to the writings of Civil War soldiers," according to Russert, while also providing "the reader with a riveting and perceptive survey of Civil War soldiers' expressions."

BIOGRAPHICAL AND CRITICAL SOURCES:

PERIODICALS

American Heritage, November, 2002, review of *Colors and Blood: Flag Passions of the Confederate South,* p. 14.
American Historical Review, October, 2003, James C. Cobb, review of *Colors and Blood,* p. 1152.
American Studies, summer, 2005, William L. Barney, review of *Colors and Blood.*
Booklist, November 15, 2006, Jay Freeman, review of *The Soldier's Pen: Firsthand Impressions of the Civil War,* p. 19.
Choice: Current Reviews for Academic Libraries, May, 2003, P. Harvey, review of *Colors and Blood,* p. 1607; June 2007, S.E. Woodworth, review of *The Soldier's Pen,* p. 1812.
Civil War Times, December, 2004, Justin Hardy, review of *Colors and Blood,* p. 68.
Comparative Studies in Society and History, April, 2004, Douglas J. Smith, review of *Colors and Blood,* p. 419.

History: Review of New Books, winter, 2005, Aaron Palmer, review of *Colors and Blood,* p. 63.

Journal of American History, December, 2003, George C. Rable, review of *Colors and Blood,* p. 1030.

Journal of Southern History, May, 2004, Lisa Tendrich Frank, review of *Colors and Blood,* p. 437.

Reviews in American History, June, 2003, Eileen Ka-May Cheng, "Flag Culture and the Confederacy: Bloodshed and National Identity," p. 268.

Virginia Magazine of History and Biography, spring, 2003, Anne Sarah Rubin, review of *Colors and Blood.*

ONLINE

Civil War News Online, http://www.civilwarnews.com/ (April 1, 2007), Michael Russert, review of *The Soldier's Pen.**

*   *   *

BOOTH, Philip 1925-2007
(Philip Edmund Booth)

OBITUARY NOTICE— See index for *CA* sketch: Born October 8, 1925, in Hanover, NH; died of complications from Alzheimer's disease, July 2, 2007, in Hanover, NH. Poet, educator, and author. Booth's award-winning poetry is firmly grounded in the weathered landscape of New England, where he spent much of his life. He was a student of Robert Frost at Dartmouth College and taught at Dartmouth in New Hampshire, Bowdoin College in Maine, and Wellesley College in Massachusetts. Though he spent more than twenty years as a poet in residence and professor at Syracuse University in New York, he never strayed far from his native ground. He returned often to the family home in Castine, Maine, eventually moving there in the 1980s. According to his critics, Booth's poetry evokes the spare language and tidal rhythms of the rugged Maine coastline, and his themes resonate with the spirit of New England life in the distinctive voice of its native souls. Booth's poetry earned him several awards in his lifetime, including Guggenheim and National Endowment for the Arts fellowships and poetry awards from *Poetry Northwest, Saturday Review,* and *Virginia Quarterly Review,* but he never sought public recognition. Instead he spent much of his time in solitude, delving ever more deeply into his own thoughts. Booth's poetry collections, nearly a dozen in number, include *The Islanders* (1961) and *Weathers and Edges* (1966). He continued writing into his seventies, including the work in *Pairs: New Poems* (1994) and *Lifelines: Selected Poems, 1950-1999.* Booth also wrote a book of essays titled *Trying to Say It: Outlooks and Insights on How Poems Happen* (1996). Though he rarely made public appearances. a few of his readings were recorded by the Library of Congress in 1958 and 1965.

OBITUARIES AND OTHER SOURCES:

PERIODICALS

Los Angeles Times, July 12, 2007, p. B6.
New York Times, July 9, 2007, p. A17.

*   *   *

BOOTH, Philip Edmund
See BOOTH, Philip

*   *   *

BORCHARDT, Alice 1939-2007
(Alice O'Brien Borchardt)

OBITUARY NOTICE— See index for *CA* sketch: Born October 6, 1939, in New Orleans, LA; died of cancer, July 24, 2007, in Houston, TX. Nurse and novelist. Borchardt spent nearly thirty years as a licensed nurse before rumors of impending layoffs at the hospital where she worked prompted her to explore other career options. Ultimately she followed her younger sister, novelist Anne Rice, into the field of fantasy and supernatural fiction. Borchardt's first novels, published when she was in her middle to late fifties, were traditional, steamy historical romances, set, like her other books would be, in colorful times past. *Devoted* (1995) and *Beguiled* (1997) relate the saga of Elin the Viking and her lover Bishop Owen as they fight their way through the trials and tribulations of life in medieval France. Borchardt then turned her attention to the vampire genre that made her sibling popular. In the trilogy that begins with *The Silver Wolf* (1999) and ends with *The Wolf King* (2001), Borchardt plunges into the milieu of eighth-century Rome. There, in the waning days of the Roman Empire, the werewolf Regeane must fight the corrupt and greedy forces of family members who would bend her to their will in the search for wealth and political power. Aided by her soul mate, gladiator-werewolf Maeniel, Regeane fights her enemies in both the natural and supernatural worlds. Borchardt's other writings include fantasy novels set in mists of Camelot, such as *The Dragon Queen: The Tales of Guinevere* (2001).

OBITUARIES AND OTHER SOURCES:

PERIODICALS

Los Angeles Times, August 3, 2007, p. B8.
Washington Post, August 4, 2007, p. B6.

*   *   *

BORCHARDT, Alice O'Brien
　　See BORCHARDT, Alice

*   *   *

BORINSKY, Alicia

PERSONAL: Born in Buenos Aires, Argentina; married Jeffrey Mehlman, a writer; children: two. *Education:* University of Pittsburgh, M.A., Ph.D., 1971.

ADDRESSES: Home—Boston, MA. *Office*—Modern Foreign Languages and Literatures, Boston University, 718 Commonwealth Ave., Boston, MA 02215.

CAREER: Scholar, educator, writer, and poet. Boston University, Boston, MA, professor of Spanish, director of the Writing in the Americas Program, and member of the Boston University-Chelsea Management Team. Visiting professorships at Harvard University and Washington University, St. Louis, MO.

AWARDS, HONORS: Boston University Metcalf Award for Excellence in Teaching, 1985; Latino Literature Prize for Fiction, 1996, for *Dreams of the Abandoned Seducer*; John Simon Guggenheim fellowship, 2002.

WRITINGS:

La ventrilocua y otras canciones, [Buenos Aires, Argentina], 1975.
Ver/ser visto: Notas para una analítica poética, Antoni Bosch (Barcelona, Spain), 1978.
Mujeres tímidas y la Venus de China, Corregidor (Buenos Aires, Argentina), 1987.
Mina cruel, (novel), Corregidor (Buenos Aires, Argentina), 1989, translation by Cola Franzen published as *Mean Woman,* University of Nebraska Press (Lincoln, NE), 1993.
Theoretical Fables: The Pedagogical Dream in Contemporary Latin American Fiction (literary criticism), University of Pennsylvania Press (Philadelphia, PA), 1993.
La pareja desmontable, Corregidor (Buenos Aires, Arentina), 1994.
Sueños del seductor abandonado: Novela vodevil (novel), Corregidor (Buenos Aires, Argentina), 1995, translation by Cola Franzen in collaboration with the author published as *Dreams of the Abandoned Seducer,* University of Nebraska Press (Lincoln, NE), 1998.
Madres alquiladas, Corregidor (Buenos Aires, Argentina), 1996.
Cine continuado (novel), Corregidor (Buenos Aires, Argentina), 1997, published as *All Night Movie,* Northwestern University Press (Evanston, IL), 2002.
Golpes bajos: Instantáneas, Corregidor (Buenos Aires, Argentina), 1999, also published as *Golpes bajos/Low Blows: Instantáneas/Snapshots,* University of Wisconsin Press (Madison, WI), 2007.
La mujer de mi marido, Corregidor (Buenos Aires, Argentina), 2000.
Las ciudades perdidas van al paraíso, Corregidor (Buenos Aires, Argentina), 2003.

Author's work has been translated, anthologized, and published in the *Massachusetts Review, Confluencia, American Voice, Under the Pomegranate Tree, New American Writing, Tameme,* and *Beacons.*

SIDELIGHTS: Alicia Borinsky's first novel, *Mina cruel,* published as *Mean Woman* in the United States, tells a story of sexual intrigue and power. The general of an unidentified country and his mistress, Rosario, are the book's focus as the author "explores the idea that the will to absolute political power, as a psychological construct, is closely tied to the sexual," as noted by *Nation* contributor Barbara Jamison. The reviewer also wrote: "*Mean Woman*'s driving conceptual force seems closer analogically to a current of kinetic energy than anything that sits easily within the formal constraints the late-twentieth-century reader still tends to impose on the novel." For example, the two characters reappear in different guises throughout the book; Rosario is also known as Carmela, Cristina, the Friend, and Self-Made Woman. "Darkly humorous lines . . . about women abound," wrote a *Publishers Weekly* contributor in a review of *Mean Woman*. "With keen irony, Borinsky's disjointed narrative skewers . . . hypocrisies," wrote Yvonne Fraticelli in the *Review of Contemporary Fiction*. Fraticelli also noted: "In the midst of oppression, Borinsky finds cause for celebration in the courage and resourcefulness of women."

In Borinsky's 1995 novel, *Sueños del seductor abandonado: Novela vodevil*, published as *Dreams of the Abandoned Seducer* in the United States in 1998, the author reflects on diverse characters in what a *Publishers Weekly* contributor called "a riddle-plagued novel." The novel is a series of short vignettes that focus on various women, such as the barely teenage Clara, who strips for two gay lovers. Alan Tinkler, writing in the *Review of Contemporary Fiction*, called the novel "a postmodern exploration of society and love." Commenting on a story about ugly women being incarcerated unless they are rich, Tinkler noted: "Borinsky's novel is not crass; she finds value in the ridiculous."

In *All Night Movie*, published in Argentina as *Cine continuado*, the author writes about modern-day Argentina as a culture in chaos. "Here characters appear for a quirky narrative turn or two and then tumble back within the enfolding narrative's furious rush toward . . . nonclosure," wrote Joseph Dewey in the *Review of Contemporary Fiction*. *Rain Taxi* Web site contributor Amy Havel noted: "Driven by stunning prose and whirlwind of frenzied action, the novel presents an oddball cast of characters, most of whom have a very skewed sense of tender loving care." The wide cast of characters includes a group of renegade nuns looking for the "Scarred Girl" and members of an Eva Perón cult. Havel praised the book, noting that "the many voices that Borinsky has created eventually begin to chime together, and the pleasure of entering this other world really takes off."

Golpes bajos: Instantáneas, published in the United States as *Golpes bajos/Low Blows: Instantáneas/*

Snapshots, is a collection of eighty-eight short stories. In one tale, "Voyage of the Millennium," the author tells the story of a woman who wins a contest only to commit suicide when she learns that her cat is not allowed to come along. In another tale, a man who will not conform to a culture of consumerism may face torture. "For readers who persevere, rewards lurk beneath the metafictional façade," wrote a *Kirkus Reviews* contributor. Naomi Lindstrom, writing in *World Literature Today*, noted that in these stories "ostentation, snobbery, consumerism, and fashion correctness are often the targets of satire."

Borinski is also author of *Theoretical Fables: The Pedagogical Dream in Contemporary Latin American Fiction*. This book of literary criticism focuses on South American writers from the 1920s through the 1980s, including Macedonio Fernandez, Gabriel García Márquez, José Donoso, and Manuel Puig. "While the selection of authors cannot be called broadly representative, it is successful for this book in that it presents writers with whom Borinsky has a special empathy and whose work she can discuss knowingly and imaginatively," wrote Naomi Lindstrom in *World Literature Today*. Lindstrom also noted in the same essay that *Theoretical Fables* "is a true pleasure to read."

BIOGRAPHICAL AND CRITICAL SOURCES:

BOOKS

Notable Hispanic American Women, Book 2, Thomson Gale (Detroit, MI), 1998.

PERIODICALS

Belles Lettres: A Review of Books by Women, summer, 1994, review of *Mean Woman*.
Choice: Current Reviews for Academic Libraries, February, 1994, M.S. Arrington, Jr., review of *Theoretical Fables: The Pedagogical Dream in Contemporary Latin American Fiction*, p. 939.
Kirkus Reviews, November 1, 2002, review of *All Night Movie*, p. 1547; December 15, 2006, review of *Golpes bajos/Low Blows: Instantáneas/Snapshots*, p. 1231.
Library Journal, September 1, 1993, Mary Margaret Benson, review of *Mean Woman*, p. 220.

Nation, December 20, 1993, Barbara Jamison, review of *Mean Woman,* p. 775.

Publishers Weekly, July 12, 1993, review of *Mean Woman,* p. 73; May 4, 1998, review of *Dreams of the Abandoned Seducer,* p. 204.

Reference & Research Book News, March 1994, review of *Theoretical Fables,* p. 45.

Review of Contemporary Fiction, summer, 1994, Yvonne Fraticelli, review of *Mean Woman,* p. 210; spring, 1999, Alan Tinkler, review of *Dreams of the Abandoned Seducer,* p. 198; summer, 2003, Joseph Dewey, review of *All Night Movie,* p. 128; summer, 2007, Alan Tinkler, review of *Dreams of the Abandoned Seducer.*

Times Literary Supplement, March 21, 2003, Tim Glencross, "Tango Time," review of *All Night Movie,* p. 21.

Women's Review of Books, July, 2003, Martha Gies, "A Postmodern Challenge," review of *All Night Movie,* p. 34.

World Literature Today, autumn, 1994, Naomi Lindstrom, review of *Theoretical Fables,* p. 797; winter, 2000, Naomi Lindstrom, review of *Golpes bajos: Instantáneas,* p. 119.

ONLINE

Boston University Modern Foreign Languages and Literatures Department Web site, http://www.bu.edu/mfll/ (October 14, 2007), faculty profile of author.

Rain Taxi, http://www.raintaxi.com/ (summer, 2003), Amy Havel, review of *All Night Movie.**

*   *   *

BOWIE, Phil

PERSONAL: Father a woodworker; mother a journalist. *Education:* Attended University of Massachusetts and Clemson University. *Hobbies and other interests:* Playing the violin, travel, walking, reading, riding his motorcycle.

ADDRESSES: Home—New Bern, NC. *E-mail*—philbowie@always-online.com.

CAREER: Has worked as a draftsman, photographer, copywriter, graphic artist, community college creative writing teacher, editor of a city magazine, and water quality researcher for the Neuse River Foundation; cofounder of a graphics company; freelance writer; licensed pilot.

AWARDS, HONORS: Won a national contest for story "The Cat from Hell."

WRITINGS:

Guns (novel; "John Hardin" series), Medallion Press, 2006.

Diamondback (novel; "John Hardin" series), Medallion Press, 2007.

Contributor of short stories and articles to periodicals, including *Reader's Digest, Saturday Evening Post, Yankee, Grit, Amicus Journal, Southern Boating, Troika, Hatteras World, Grit, Overdrive, AOPA Pilot, Southern Aviator,* and *Heartland USA.*

SIDELIGHTS: Phil Bowie is a kind of jack-of-all-trades. He has worked as a photographer, graphic artist, businessman, editor, and even as a water quality researcher. A writer, too, who once earned an award for writing the short story "The Cat from Hell" with Stephen King, he has written hundreds of articles and short fiction works for various magazines. It was not until he published *Guns,* though, that he added "novelist" to his list of credits. *Guns* is the first in a series of stories featuring John Hardin, a former criminal turned pilot. In his earlier life, Hardin became mixed up with arms dealers, but he then served as a witness against his former boss and was put under federal protection in the witness protection program. Moving to a small town out west, he started his life over until his name gets in the newspaper for rescuing a couple from a boat during a storm. The news item comes to the attention of his former boss, who sends out a hitman to murder Hardin. But Hardin's girlfriend is accidently killed instead. The rest of the story involves Hardin's plans for revenge.

Critics of *Guns* found the book to be a somewhat flawed but still skillful work for a first-time novelist. A *Publishers Weekly* critic felt that the author "leans on . . . details too often, slowing down what could be an absorbing, fast-paced tale," but appreciated that Bowie "did the homework" in researching the story.

"Bowie is a skilled writer," asserted Clayton Bye for the *Gotta Write Network*. "I wouldn't have guessed this was his first novel. Take away the lengthy monologues he blatantly uses to provide backstory and you've got a terrific book."

BIOGRAPHICAL AND CRITICAL SOURCES:

PERIODICALS

Publishers Weekly, June 12, 2006, review of *Guns,* p. 36.

Sun Journal (New Bern, NC), August 20, 2006, Tom Mayer, "'Guns': Setting Sights on What You Know," interview with Phil Bowie.

ONLINE

Gotta Write Network, http://www.gottawritenetwork. com/ (October 30, 2006), Clayton Bye, review of *Guns.*

Phil Bowie Home Page, http://www.philbowie.com (September 24, 2007).*

*   *   *

BRACEWELL, Ronald N. 1921-2007
(Ronald Newbold Bracewell)

*OBITUARY NOTICE—*See index for *CA* sketch: Born July 22, 1921, in Sydney, New South Wales, Australia; died of a heart attack, July 12, 2007, in Stanford, CA. Mathematician, physicist, electrical engineer, radio-astronomer, educator, and author. Bracewell's research and inventions in the field of radio astronomy have had wide-ranging repercussions throughout the scientific world. His primary contribution was the "Fournier transform" process that enabled scientists to convert radio signals into visual images that could be printed and transmitted around the world. The process had varied applications, beginning with Bracewell's eleven-year project to monitor and map daily sunspot activity for an entire solar year. His research enabled scientists at the National Aeronautics and Space Administration to predict sunspot events that could have had a negative impact on the first U.S. moon landing in 1969. Bracewell was also able to monitor

the path of the Soviet satellite Sputnik I and offer data that might have improved the design of the American Explorer I satellite, had his advice been heeded. Bracewell's research on radio signals led to the development of medical diagnostic procedures such as computed tomography (commonly known as CT or CAT scanning) and magnetic resonance imaging (MRI). Bracewell was born in Australia, educated in Australia and England as a mathematician and physicist, and eventually spent most of his career in the electrical engineering department at Stanford University. He was also a director of the Sidney Sussex Foundation. Toward the end of his career, Bracewell became interested in the use of radio signals to explore the potential existence of extraterrestrial intelligence, and he was an active proponent of government support for the Search for Extra-Terrestrial Intelligence project, informally known as SETI. The phrase "Bracewell probe" was coined to describe the robotic devices he believed alien civilizations might use to communicate with the people of Earth. In 1974 Bracewell published the book *The Galactic Club: Intelligent Life in Outer Space.* His more conventional scientific writings include *Radio Astronomy* (1955) and *The Fournier Transform and Its Applications* (1965).

OBITUARIES AND OTHER SOURCES:

PERIODICALS

Los Angeles Times, August 17, 2007, p. B9.

*   *   *

BRACEWELL, Ronald Newbold
See BRACEWELL, Ronald N.

*   *   *

BRADBURY, J.C. 1973-
(John Charles Bradbury)

PERSONAL: Born September 28, 1973, in Charlotte, NC; married; children: one daughter. *Education:* Wofford College, B.A., 1996; George Mason University, M.A., 1998, Ph.D., 2000. *Hobbies and other interests:* "Sabermetrics, fishing (especially fly fishing).

ADDRESSES: Office—Department of Health, Physical Education, and Sports Science, Kennesaw State University, 1000 Chastain Rd., Kennesaw, GA 30144-5591. *E-mail*—jcbradbury@gmail.com; jbradbu2@kennesaw.edu.

CAREER: George Mason University, Fairfax, VA, research associate at the Mercatus Center's Regulatory Studies Program, 1999-2000, instructor in economics, 1999-2000; North Georgia College and State University, Dahlonega, assistant professor of business administration, 2000-01; University of the South, Sewanee, TN, visiting professor of economics, 2001-03, assistant professor of economics, 2003-06; Kennesaw State University, Kennesaw, GA, associate professor in department of health, physical education, and sport science, 2006—.

AWARDS, HONORS: C.G. Koch and J.M. Buchanan research fellowship, J.M. Buchanan Center of George Mason University, 1997-2000; graduate research fellowship, Political Economy Research Center, 1998.

WRITINGS:

The Baseball Economist: The Real Game Exposed, Dutton (New York, NY), 2007.

Contributor to books, including *Encyclopedia of Public Choice,* Kluwer Academic Press, 2003; and *Democratic Constitutional Design and Public Policy: Analysis and Evidence,* MIT Press (Cambridge, MA), 2006. Contributor to periodicals, including the *Journal of Sports Economics, Journal of Regulatory Economics,* and *Economic Inquiry.* Author of blog *Sabernomics.*

SIDELIGHTS: J.C. Bradbury is an educator and economist who uses the laws of economic trade to address issues regarding the sport of baseball. He began chronicling his fascination with the applicability of economics to game dynamics on his blog, *Sabernomics,* and has gathered a number of his thoughts in his first book, *The Baseball Economist: The Real Game Exposed.* Bradbury's purpose is to illuminate baseball from a wide range of angles, applying economic principles as he goes. He compares batsmen between the American and National Leagues, looks at the concept of having a batter on deck, and goes on to analyze scouts, statistics, salaries, the use of drugs, and team expansion. An interviewer for the *Southpaw Blog* remarked: "Although Bradbury is an academic, his writing style is fluid and accessible. He doesn't use many technical terms, but when he does, he explains them clearly and briefly, in a fashion that makes the material more easily understood. This is a book that's worth your buck." In a review in *Booklist,* David Pitt similarly praised Bradbury's effort as having "a smooth, accessible style," adding that he "makes the tricky game of numbers seem both straightforward and exciting." A reviewer for *Publishers Weekly* commented on the handling of the concept that Major League Baseball functions like a monopoly, stating that "Bradbury, while not forging new ground, shines in the closing chapters" where he refutes the idea. Bob Timmmermann, reviewing the book in *Baseball Toaster,* concluded: "I can't say I agree with everything Bradbury says, but I still wish there were more books like this, which suggest new ways of approaching some of the most interesting baseball questions."

BIOGRAPHICAL AND CRITICAL SOURCES:

PERIODICALS

Booklist, January 1, 2007, David Pitt, review of *The Baseball Economist: The Real Game Exposed,* p. 40.
Publishers Weekly, January 22, 2007, review of *The Baseball Economist,* p. 182.

ONLINE

Baseball Toaster, http://griddle.baseballtoaster.com/ (April 18, 2007), Bob Timmermann, review of *The Baseball Economist.*
J.C. Bradbury Home Page, http://bradbury.sewanee.edu (August 22, 2007).
Kenneshaw University Web site, http://www.kenneshaw.edu/ (August 21, 2007), faculty biography of J.C. Bradbury.
Region Web site, http://woodrow.mpls.frb.fed.us/pubs/region/ (August 21, 2007), review of *The Baseball Economist.*
Sabernomics, http://www.sabernomics.com (August 21, 2007), author's blog.

Southpaw Blog, http://108mag.typepad.com/the_southpaw/ (March 10, 2007), interview with J.C. Bradbury.*

* * *

BRADBURY, John Charles
See BRADBURY, J.C.

* * *

BRIBIESCAS, Richard G.

PERSONAL: Education: Harvard University, Ph.D., 1997.

ADDRESSES: Office—Department of Anthropology, Yale University, P.O. Box 208277, New Haven, CT 06520-8277. *E-mail*—richard.bribiescas@yale.edu.

CAREER: Yale University, New Haven, CT, associate professor of anthropology, director of the reproductive ecology laboratory.

AWARDS, HONORS: Postdoctoral Research Fellow in Medicine, Massachusetts General Hospital; Woodrow Wilson Faculty Research Fellowship.

WRITINGS:

Men: Evolutionary and Life History, Harvard University Press (Cambridge, MA), 2006.

SIDELIGHTS: Richard G. Bribiescas is an anthropologist whose research interests include endocrinology, human evolutionary physiology, and life history theory. He has traveled extensively in Paraguay, Venezuela, and Japan to study the evolution of hunter/gatherers in preparation for his first book, *Men: Evolutionary and Life History.* His purpose in this book is to throw light on the question of why humans have evolved the way they have, men in particular. Some facets of human behavior, such as the appeal of sexual intercourse, can be explained strictly in evolutionary terms. Others, however, such as why a

man's brain appears to be physically different from a woman's, allow for speculation concerning life history, such as gene interactions based on reproductive choices. Most of Bribiescas's research involved men, and he compared both their biology and certain behaviors to other human men, as well as to the males of other species. *Booklist* reviewer Ray Olson felt that "Bribiescas presents . . . a text that demands to be closely read, with great fascination." Gloria Maxwell, writing in *Library Journal,* found the book intriguing, particularly Bribiescas's theories "as to why men tend to engage in warfare and genocide and exert control over economics and politics throughout the world." In a review for the *New Statesman,* James Plumb concluded that "Bribiescas writes in an intelligent and thoughtful manner."

BIOGRAPHICAL AND CRITICAL SOURCES:

PERIODICALS

Booklist, November 1, 2006, Ray Olson, review of *Men: Evolutionary and Life History,* p. 7.
Library Journal, November 15, 2006, Gloria Maxwell, review of *Men,* p. 93.
New Statesman, January 8, 2007, James Plumb, "What Makes Men Tick?," review of *Men,* p. 53.

ONLINE

Yale University Department of Anthropology Web site, http://www.yale.edu/anthro/ (August 21, 2007), faculty biography of Richard G. Bribiescas.*

* * *

BROCHEUX, Pierre

PERSONAL: Education: Ph.D.

ADDRESSES: Home—France.

CAREER: University of Paris VII, Denis Diderot, Paris, France, faculty and head of the department of history.

WRITINGS:

(Editor) Robert Aarsse, and others, *Histoire de l'Asie du Sud-Est: révoltes, réformes, révolutions,* Presses Universitaires de Lille (Lille, France), 1981.

(With Daniel Hémery) *Indochine, la colonisation ambiguë: 1858-1954,* Découverte (Paris, France), 1994, revised edition, 2001.

The Mekong Delta: Ecology, Economy, and Revolution, 1860-1960, Center for Southeast Asian Studies (Madison, WI), 1995.

(With others, and managing editor) *Du conflit d'Indochine aux conflits indochinois,* Complexe (Brussels, Belgium), 2000.

Ho Chi Minh, Presses de Sciences (Paris, France), 2000, translation by Claire Duiker published as *Ho Chi Minh: A Biography,* Cambridge University Press (New York, NY), 2007.

(Editor, with Gisele Bousquet) *Viêt Nam Exposé: French Scholarship on Twentieth-Century Vietnamese Society,* University of Michigan Press (Ann Arbor, MI), 2002.

Hô Chi Minh: du révolutionnaire à l'icône, Payot (Paris, France), 2003, translation published as *Ho Chi Minh: From Revolutionary to Icon,* Cambridge University Press (New York, NY), 2006.

Contributor to *L'Indochine Française, 1940-1945,* edited by Paul Isoart, Presses Universitaires de France (Paris, France), 1982. Managing editor, with G. Boudarel and D. Hémery, *Guide de recherches sur le Vietnam: Bibliographies, archives et bibliothèques de France,* Editions L'Harmattan (Paris, France), 1983.

SIDELIGHTS: Pierre Brocheux is an historian who has specialized in southeastern Asia, especially Vietnam and the area formerly known as French Indochina. He has published several histories of the region that cover topics ranging from economics and agriculture to demographic changes, politics, and the Vietnam War. Collaborating with Daniel Hémery in *Indochine, la colonisation ambiguë: 1858-1954,* Brocheux tackles the complex subject of French colonialism in Indochina. With the main emphasis being the period before 1945, Brocheux and Hémery spend more time on Vietnam than other parts of the former French-controlled region, while noting that the region's political evolution was influenced by many diverse peoples and not just the result of France imposing its rule on the area. "It looks at French colonization not only as a process imposed and improvised from the outside but also the result of internal dynamics within Indochinese societies, the convergence between global trends and local changes, and the interaction then cohabitation between colonisers and colonized," reported Nguyen Manh Hung in *Pacific Affairs.* "It further points out that French colonization, however exploitative and oppressive, did make a positive contribution to the modernization of the colonized societies." The result is a "sympathetic look at French colonization without losing sight of the heavy burden that the peoples of Indochina had to bear." Van Nguyen-Marshall similarly commented in another *Pacific Affairs* article: "This approach, which shatters the older binary depiction of a monolithic and oppressive colonizing power versus a united indigenous nationalist movement, has become in the last two decades the accepted norm in colonial studies." While Nguyen-Marshall admitted that, told from the view of the native population, the French rule "may not have been at all ambiguous," he concluded: "Despite these reservations, this is a solid work of research that will be valuable for both experts and students."

In *The Mekong Delta: Ecology, Economy, and Revolution, 1860-1960,* Brocheux, who spent part of his childhood in Vietnam, discusses the importance of the fertile region and the Mekong River, which is an important tributary for Vietnam, Cambodia, Laos, and Thailand. The delta lands are fragile, too, however, and subject to environmental and agricultural disasters. It is "likely to be an area that we need to understand more fully," Joakim Öjendal observed in a review for *MekongRiver.org.* "Pierre Brocheux has given us an instrument for doing just that, and from this point of view, his study is extremely timely." But the critic regretted that the work "lacks interpretation, analysis and perhaps a hypothesis on which Brocheux could test his material. Tellingly, the introduction and the conclusion are but a few pages each, in spite of the fact that there is an overwhelmingly rich information base to dig from. This becomes somewhat frustrating as there is no reason to believe that Brocheux lacks this capacity." Öjendal still insisted: "Having said that, this work must be considered as a major contribution to the factual knowledge of life in the Mekong Delta in this particular period, and although it may be lacking a more thorough analysis, the reader is free to make his or her own conclusions." Benoit de Treglode more enthusiastically asserted in the *Journal of Southeast Asian Studies* that "Brocheux skillfully analyzes the manner in which the fusion of the region's ecological, ethnical and historical elements create a social space distinct from those which existed in the north and the center of the country."

More recently, Brocheux's biography of the founder of modern Vietnam was translated as *Ho Chi Minh: From Revolutionary to Icon*. Researching the life of Ho is a task full of roadblocks. The Vietnamese government has censored or otherwise altered many of the records about their esteemed late leader's life, while many records of Ho's days in Europe as a young man have been lost as well. Even the details of Ho's life that are available are often contradictory, such as his birth date, which ranges from 1890 to 1903, depending on the source. In Brocheux's book, Ho is depicted as a charismatic and idealistic leader who becomes caught up in the communist rule he helped establish, ultimately making him "a tragic figure," as a *Publishers Weekly* writer reported. The reviewer felt that "Brocheux's account is too brief and haphazard" to be very revealing, but other critics were more impressed. Patti C. McCall called the biography a "fascinating account" in *Library Journal*, while on the *Asia by the Book* Web site Janet Brown concluded that "this biography is dense with historical and political background. Yet the man shines through the thicket of facts, with his wit and his poetry making Ho alive on the page. . . . Pierre Brocheux brings out a concise but skillful portrait from history's obscuring layers of sainthood and demonization."

BIOGRAPHICAL AND CRITICAL SOURCES:

PERIODICALS

American Historical Review, December, 1996, Mark W. McLeod, review of *The Mekong Delta: Ecology, Economy, and Revolution, 1860-1960,* p. 1599.

Journal of Asian Studies, November, 1995, John K. Whitmore, review of *Indochine, la colonisation ambiguë: 1858-1954,* p. 1147; August, 1996, David Hunt, review of *The Mekong Delta,* p. 779.

Journal of Southeast Asian Studies, September, 1996, Philippe Papin, review of *Indochine, la colonisation ambiguë,* p. 405; September, 1997, Benoit de Treglode, review of *The Mekong Delta,* p. 463;

February, 2003, Anne Raffin, review of *Indochine, la colonisation ambiguë: 1858-1954,* p. 192; October, 2004, review of *Viêt Nam Exposé: French Scholarship on Twentieth-Century Vietnamese Society,* p. 573.

Journal of Third World Studies, fall, 1995, Robert Lawless, review of *The Mekong Delta.*

Library Journal, February 15, 2007, Patti C. McCall, review of *Ho Chi Minh: A Biography,* p. 127.

Pacific Affairs, spring, 1996, Nguyen Manh Hung, review of *Indochine, la colonisation ambiguë: 1858-1954;* summer, 1996, Hy V. Luong, review of *The Mekong Delta;* fall, 2001, Alexander Woodside, review of *Ho Chi Minh;* fall, 2002, Van Nguyen-Marshall, review of *Indochine, la colonisation ambiguë: 1858-1954.*

Publishers Weekly, December 18, 2006, review of *Ho Chi Minh: From Revolutionary to Icon,* p. 53.

ONLINE

Asia by the Book, http://weblogs.thingsasian.com/tablogs/page/asiabook/ (July 8, 2007), review of *Ho Chi Minh: A Biography.*

MekongRiver.org, http://www.mekongriver.org/ (September 25, 2007), Joakim Öjendal, review of *The Mekong Delta.*

New York Sun Online, http://www.nysun.com/ (April 25, 2007), Carl Rollyson, "The Many Lives of Ho Chi Minh."*

    * * *

BROOKE, Edward
 See BROOKE, Edward W.

    * * *

BROOKE, Edward W. 1919-
 (Edward Brooke, Edward William Brooke)

PERSONAL: Born October 26, 1919, in Washington, DC; son of Edward W. (an attorney) and Helen Brooke; married Remigia Ferrari-Scacco, 1947 (divorced, 1978); married Anne Fleming, 1979; children: (first marriage) Remi Cynthia, Edwina Helene; (second marriage) Edward. *Education:* Howard University, B.S., 1940; Boston University, LL.B., 1948, LL.M., 1949.

ADDRESSES: Home—Miami, FL.

CAREER: Attorney, legislator, consultant, and writer. Attorney in private practice, c. 1948-60; Boston Finance Commission, chairman, c. 1960-62; private law practice, Roxbury, MA, 1948-60; Boston Finance Commission, chairman, 1961-62; Commonwealth of Massachusetts, Attorney General, 1963-67; U.S. Senate, Washington, DC, senator, 1967-79; Csaplar & Bok, Boston, MA, counsel, beginning 1979; O'Connor & Hannan, Washington, DC, partner, beginning 1979; Bcar & Stearns, New York, NY, limited partner, beginning 1979. Chairperson of the National Low-Income Housing Coalition, 1979; chairperson of the board of The Opera Co. of Boston Inc.; chairperson of the board of directors of the Boston Bank Company; member of the board of directors of the Washington Performing Arts Society; chairman of the World Policy Council; member of board of directors of Meditrust Inc., Boston; member of national council, Boy Scouts of America; member of national board, Boys Clubs of America. *Military service:* U.S. Army, 1942-45; served in World War II in European theater of operations; attained rank of captain; awarded Bronze Star.

MEMBER: American Bar Association (fellow), American Academy of Arts and Sciences (fellow), Massachusetts Bar Association, Boston Bar Association, American Veterans of World War II, Korea, and Vietnam, Administrative Conference of the U.S.

AWARDS, HONORS: Distinguished Service Award, AMVETS, 1952; Grand Cross of Italy; Spingarn Medal, National Association for the Advancement of Colored People (NAACP), 1967; Charles Evans Hughes Award, National Conference of Christians & Jews, 1967; Mary Hudson Onley Achievement Award, 2001; Presidential Medal of Freedom, 2004; more than thirty honorary degrees.

WRITINGS:

(With Gieshard Paris) *Gieshard Paris and Edward Brooke Address the 53rd Annual Meeting of the National Urban League,* Library of Congress (Washington, DC), 1963.
The Challenge of Change, Little, Brown (Boston, MA), 1966.

United States Foreign Assistance for Haiti: Report of Senator Edward W. Brooke, Library of Congress (Washington, DC), 1974.
Report of Developments in United States Relations with the Soviet Union, Poland, and Italy, U.S. Government Printing Office (Washington, DC), 1976.
(With Sam Nunn) *An All-Volunteer Force for the United States?,* American Enterprise Institute for Public Policy Research (Washington, DC), 1977.
A Report on West European Communist Parties, Superintendent of Documents (Washington, DC), 1977.
Bridging the Divide: My Life, Rutgers University Press (New Brunswick, NJ), 2007.

SOUND RECORDINGS

Keynote Meeting and Address at the 1963 National Urban League Conference (sound recording), Library of Congress (Washington, DC), 1963.
Busing (sound recording), Library of Congress (Washington, DC), c. 1970s.
Conversation between Senators Claiborne Pell, Edward Brooke and Vice President Nelson Rockefeller (sound recording), Library of Congress (Washington, DC), c. 1970s.
Statement by Edward W. Brooke (sound recording), Library of Congress (Washington, DC), c. 1970s.
Speech by Edward W. Brooke at Brigham Young University (sound recording), Brigham Young University (Provo, UT), 1978.
Broadcasts of Senator Edward Brooke's News Conference (sound recording), Library of Congress (Washington, DC), 1978.
Statements by Carroll Sheehan and Edward W. Brooke (sound recording), Library of Congress (Washington, DC), 1978.

The Edward W. Brooke Collection of Film and Video Materials relating to his Political Career, 1963-1978 is held by the Library of Congress, Washington, DC.

SIDELIGHTS: The first black man popularly elected to the U.S. Senate since Reconstruction and then to be reelected, Edward W. Brooke began his career as a lawyer before he entered politics. He is also the author of *The Challenge of Change,* published in 1966 during the Civil Rights movement, and *Bridging the Divide: My Life,* a memoir published in 2007. The first book focuses on the life of African Americans in the United States and on politics. A member of the Republican Party, Brooke nevertheless criticizes the party in his book. Brooke rebuked the Republican leadership for the strategic error of not targeting the votes of young, urban, and minority citizens, and for fielding out-of-touch, arch conservative candidates like Barry Goldwater, whose failed 1964 presidential bid, in Brooke's view, devastated any promising relationship between the party and the electorate. In his book, the author also writes of his experience as a black soldier during World War II. As Brooke notes, blacks were treated as second-class citizens despite having established themselves as brave and effective soldiers.

In *Bridging the Divide,* Brooke writes not only of his own life but also of his generation of black men and the challenges that they faced. Among the numerous aspects of his life that the author discusses are his marriages, his political career, his battle with a rare form of male breast cancer, and his vision for America. Of special note is Brooke's discussion of former President Richard M. Nixon, with whom Brooke had many differences. Brooke, who had endorsed Nixon in the 1968 and 1972 campaigns, clashed with the president on a number of issues, including Brooke's failure to vote for three Nixon nominees to the Supreme Court. Brooke became the first senator to publicly call for Nixon's resignation for his involvement in the Watergate scandal.

In his memoir, the author also writes of how he would like to be remembered, which is not as a black man who had a noted political career in a government dominated by whites but as an individual who helped further a multiracial society. "I've embarked on this book hoping there will be lessons in it, that it will provide insight on American politics," Brooke noted on *Washingtonpost.com.* "Believing with Plato that the unexamined life is not worth living, I have attempted here to offer an honest and frank accounting of my personal and political life. As the readers of my book *Bridging the Divide* will learn, the two became all too entwined." Referring to the memoir as "engaging," Vanessa Bush noted in *Booklist:* "Brooke looks back on his time in the Senate as a 'golden age.'"

BIOGRAPHICAL AND CRITICAL SOURCES:

BOOKS

Brooke, Edward W., *Bridging the Divide: My Life,* Rutgers University Press (New Brunswick, NJ), 2007.

Contemporary Black Biography, Thomson Gale (Detroit, MI), 1994.

Cutler, John Henry, editor, *Ed Brooke: Biography of a Senator,* Bobbs-Merrill (Indianapolis, IN), 1972.

Notable Black American Men, Thomson Gale (Detroit, MI), 1998.

PERIODICALS

America's Intelligence Wire, February 18, 2004, "U.S. Census Bureau Black History Month Daily Feature for Feb. 19: Edward Brooke"; February 14, 2007, "Rutgers: Former U.S. Senator Calls for Political Cooperation in Speech at Rutgers."

Booklist, February 1, 2007, Vanessa Bush, review of *Bridging the Divide,* p. 21.

Christian Science Monitor, May 6, 1996, "Affordable Housing," p. 20.

Crisis, January-February, 2007, Kenneth J. Cooper, "First Black U.S. Senator Elected by Popular Vote Tells His Story," p. 46.

Ebony, October, 1984, Llynn Norment, "The New Life of Former Senator Edward Brooke," p. 58; August, 2003, Marsha Gilbert, "Edward W. Brooke: Former Senator Battles Breast Cancer," p. 78; February, 2007, "Bridging the Divide," p. 31.

Jet, March 19, 1981, "Ex-Senator Brooke Helps Deliver His First Son," p. 17; April 18, 1983, "NAACP Wins Court Battle over Use of Its Initials," p. 5; December 10, 1984, "Edward W. Brooke Named Boston Bank's Chairman," p. 13; August 24, 1992, "Mother of Ex-Sen. Brooke Dies at 100," p. 18; July 12, 2004, "Brooke Gets Medal of Freedom," p. 4.

Los Angeles Times, August 3, 1989, William J. Eaton, "HUD Aides Said to Make Millions from $61,000," p. 19.

Miami Herald, March 19, 2007, Donna Gehrke-White, "A Vote for Miami: Former Sen. Edward Brooke Promotes His New Memoir from His New Home."

New York Times, July 23, 1989, Philip Shenon, "Documents Show Active Pierce Role on Fund Requests; File of Ex-Aide Disclosed; Former Secretary of Housing Intervened on Behalf of at Least Two Republicans," p. 1; November 22, 1992, "Aide Implicates Ex-Senator in Federal Housing Inquiry," p. 34; June 10, 2003, Lynette Clemetson, "Surprise Role for Ex-Senator: Male Breast Cancer Patient," p. 1.

Political Science & Politics, September, 1999, Judson L. Jeffries, "U.S. Senator Edward W. Brooke and Governor L. Douglas Wilder Tell Political Scientists How Blacks Can Win High-Profile Statewide Office," p. 583.

Political Science Quarterly, summer, 1990, Raphael J. Sonenshein, "Can Blacks Win Statewide Elections?"

U.S. News & World Report, February 19, 2007, Diane Cole, "History on the Hill," p. 36.

ONLINE

Bioguide.congress.gov, http://bioguide.congress.gov/ (August 14, 2007), biography of author.

Washingtonpost.com, http://www.washingtonpost.com/ (February 8, 2007) "Ex-Sen. Brooke Discusses Memoir, Race in Politics."

OTHER

Excerpts from Senate Committee Hearing Regarding President Carter's Budget Proposal (sound recording), Library of Congress, 1978.

Human Rights in Haiti: Hearing before the Subcommittee on International Organizations of the Committee on International Relations, House of Representatives, Ninety-fourth Congress, First Session, November 18, 1975 (sound recording), U.S. Government Printing Office, (Washington, DC), 1975.

Interview with Edward W. Brooke (sound recording), Library of Congress, c. 1977.

Meet the Press, [1973-04-22] (sound recording), Library of Congress, 1973.

* * *

BROOKE, Edward William
    See BROOKE, Edward W.

* * *

BROPHY, Sarah

PERSONAL: Education: Earned Ph.D.

ADDRESSES: Office—English Department, McMaster University, 1280 Main St. W., Hamilton, Ontario L8S 4L8, Canada. *E-mail*—brophys@mcmaster.ca.

CAREER: McMaster University, Hamilton, Ontario, Canada, faculty member in department of English.

AWARDS, HONORS: Social Sciences and Humanaities Research Council postdoctoral fellowship, 2001-02; McMaster Students Union Teaching Award for the Faculty of Humanities, 2004.

WRITINGS:

(Editor) *Witnessing AIDS: Writing, Testimony, and the Work of Mourning,* University of Toronto Press (Buffalo, NY), 2004.

Contributor to periodicals, including *Teaching Life-Writing Texts: MLA Options for Teaching, Topia, Canadian Children's Literature, Essays on Canadian Writing, The Eighteenth-Century: Theory and Interpretation,* and *Literature and Medicine.*

SIDELIGHTS: Canadian writer Sarah Brophy is a researcher interested in life-writing, with a particular focus on the social meaning of certain life-altering situations, such as illness and reproduction. Her research delves into personal narratives, including biography and autobiography, taking into consideration gender, sexuality, race, and cultural concerns. Her first book, *Witnessing AIDS: Writing, Testimony, and the Work of Mourning,* looks at the grief engendered by this illness, both from the perspective of the person who is dying and the people in their lives who are forced to watch them suffer. Brophy notes that, as a society, we tend to avoid the pain of true grieving. As a result, we miss out on the growth in our capacity for love that the experience would otherwise encourage. Her research includes the works of many AIDS patients, primarily diaries of homosexual men with the disease and books by friends, family, and caregivers. Many reviewers noted her focus on homosexual men, as well as the lack of cultural differences between them. G. Thomas Couser commented in *Biography:* "The book's contribution to the ongoing critical reckoning with AIDS life writing is found not in crosscultural comparisons, then, but in her dominant, and unifying, concern with mourning as a broadly cultural, rather than merely personal, phenomenon." Daniel Burr, in a review for the *Lambda Book Report,* remarked that Brophy's effort is "difficult because it forces the reader to confront, without any comfortable consolations or pious certainties, the deeper dimensions of a world crisis."

BIOGRAPHICAL AND CRITICAL SOURCES:

PERIODICALS

Biography, spring, 2005, G. Thomas Couser, review of *Witnessing AIDS: Writing, Testimony, and the Work of Mourning,* p. 295.

Canadian Book Review Annual, January 1, 2005, Ian C. Nelson, review of *Witnessing AIDS,* p. 244.

Lambda Book Report, January 1, 2005, Daniel Burr, "The Ends of Grief," review of *Witnessing AIDS,* p. 37.

Reference & Research Book News, August 1, 2004, review of *Witnessing AIDS,* p. 258.

ONLINE

McMaster University English Department Web site, http://www.humanities.mcmaster.ca/ (August 21, 2007), faculty biography of Sarah Brophy.

*   *   *

BROWN, Scott G. 1966-
(Scott Gregory Brown)

PERSONAL: Born November 1, 1966, in Mississauga, Ontario, Canada; son of Eric (a high school physics teacher) and Judy (an elementary schoolteacher) Brown. *Education:* University of Toronto, B.A., 1990, M.A., 1992, Ph.D., 1999. *Hobbies and other interests:* Writing music, playing piano, playing baseball.

ADDRESSES: Home—Barrie, Ontario, Canada. *Office*—University of Toronto, Toronto, Ontario, Canada. *E-mail*—scottg.brown@utoronto.ca.

CAREER: University of Toronto, Toronto, Ontario, Canada, sessional lecturer, 1989—.

WRITINGS:

Mark's Other Gospel: Rethinking Morton Smith's Controversial Discovery, Wilfrid Laurier University Press (Waterloo, Ontario, Canada), 2005.

Contributor to periodicals, including *Journal of Biblical Literature, Expository Times, Biblical Archaeology Review, Revue Biblique, Catholic Biblical Quarterly,* and *Harvard Theological Review.*

*   *   *

BROWN, Scott Gregory
See BROWN, Scott G.

*   *   *

BUCKLEY, Kristen 1968-

PERSONAL: Born 1968, in Upper Saddle River, NJ; partner of Brian Regan; children: Peyton (daughter) and Liam. *Education:* Attended Manhattan School of Music and Hunter College. *Hobbies and other interests:* Writing, music, sports, art.

ADDRESSES: Home—Los Angeles, CA.

CAREER: Author, screenwriter, guitarist. Worked in Hollywood as a production assistant and as a book scout.

WRITINGS:

(With Brian Regan, Bob Tzudiker, and Noni White) *102 Dalmatians* (screenplay; based on the novel by Dodie Smith), Buena Vista Pictures, 2000.

(With Brian Regan and Burr Steers) *How to Lose a Guy in 10 Days* (screenplay), Paramount Pictures, 2003.

The Parker Grey Show (novel), Berkley Books (New York, NY), 2003.

Tramps Like Us: A Suburban Confession (memoir), Cyan Communications (London, England), 2007.

Also author of film adaptation of *The Parker Grey Show;* script doctor for *The Accidental Husband, Dramarama,* and *The Champions.*

SIDELIGHTS: Kristen Buckley paid her dues in Hollywood as a production assistant, performing such tasks as holding the cigarette of Leonardo DeCaprio and reminding Sam Waterson to change his clothes between takes, before becoming a successful screenwriter with films that include *How to Lose a Guy in 10 Days,* starring Kate Hudson and Matthew McConaughey, and *102 Dalmatians,* starring Glenn Close.

Buckley wanted to write books in order to have more control over her work and spent five years writing her first novel at night. The protagonist of *The Parker Grey Show* is a guitarist (as is her creator) who works as a waitress in a New York City bar and who is recovering from a failed four-year romance with a man addicted to prescription drugs. She is befriended by Lil, who lives in a huge loft owned by her father and who is the mistress of a billionaire she refers to as Mr. Smith. During the day Parker watches soap operas in the loft and fantasizes about an actor named M.

Lil is mistaken for Mr. Smith's daughter and is kidnapped, and Smith, afraid his wife will learn of the affair, asks Parker to act on his behalf in negotiating with the kidnappers. Parker meets M., both at the bar where she works and the loft, which is chosen as the setting for a film in which he appears.

Buckley grew up in Upper Saddle River, New Jersey. The title of her memoir *Tramps Like Us: A Suburban Confession* is taken from the lyrics of "Born to Run" by Jersey native Bruce Springsteen. Buckley is the oldest of four children, and she and her siblings were all adopted, they from Korea. She notes that contrary to the stereotype, they were mathematically challenged. She writes of her life from childhood to her teen years and recalls the divorce of her parents when she was six and the characters who populated her life, including mobsters. Included is an index of the period that ends with Elvis Presley's death.

Reviewing the book for the *Blogcritics* Web site, Glen Boyd wrote that this memoir "would be a keeper for its title alone, but Kristen Buckley actually lives up to it with a great read."

BIOGRAPHICAL AND CRITICAL SOURCES:

BOOKS

Buckley, Kristen, *Tramps Like Us: A Suburban Confession,* Cyan Communications (London, England), 2007.

PERIODICALS

Booklist, March 1, 2007, Michael Cart, review of *Tramps Like Us,* p. 45.
Library Journal, March 15, 2007, Maria Kochis, review of *Tramps Like Us,* p. 78.
Publishers Weekly, July 7, 2003, review of *The Parker Grey Show,* p. 54.

ONLINE

Bildungsroman, http://slayground.livejournal.com/ (April 20, 2007), Little Willow, author interview.
Blogcritics, http://www.blogcritics.org/ (May 27, 2007), Glen Boyd, review of *Tramps Like Us.*
Bookburger, http://bookburger.typepad.com/ (April 16, 2007), "Kristen Buckley—Between the Buns," author interview.
Kristen Buckley Home Page, http://www.theparker greyshow.com (September 20, 2007).
Kristin Buckley MySpace Page, http://www.myspace. com/ (September 20, 2007).
PopGurls.com, http://www.popgurls.com/ (December 22, 2003), Michelle, Vanessa, "20 Questions with Author Kristen Buckley," interview; (April 19, 2007), Michelle, "20 Questions with Author Kristen Buckley (Again)," interview.
Smith, http://smithmag.net/ (June 11, 2007), "Interview: Kristen Buckley, Author of *Tramps Like Us.*"*

*   *   *

BUCKMAN, Daniel 1967-

PERSONAL: Born 1967.

ADDRESSES: Home—Chicago, IL.

CAREER: Writer. *Military service:* U.S. Army, served as a paratrooper.

WRITINGS:

NOVELS

Water in Darkness, Akashic Books (New York, NY), 2001.

The Names of Rivers, Akashic Books (New York, NY), 2002.

Morning Dark, St. Martin's Press (New York, NY), 2003.

Because the Rain, St. Martin's Press (New York, NY), 2007.

SIDELIGHTS: Daniel Buckman, who served as a paratrooper with the U.S. Army, has created a protagonist in his debut novel, *Water in Darkness,* who has just finished a tour. Jack Tyne's father died twenty years earlier while serving in Vietnam, and Jack has grown up without his influence and guidance, something he has dearly missed. He finds a substitute father in Vietnam veteran, now drug user, Danny Morrison, and although they make a connection, the relationship is not a smooth one. Danny tries to teach Jack to distrust everyone, an attitude Jack finds difficult to adopt. The lives of both men deteriorate, and Jack's disillusionment grows, based both on his own experiences and on the stories told to him by Danny.

John Kenyon reviewed the novel for the *PopMatters* Web site, writing: "The slim volume is a gritty tale rendered with tough, spare prose that fits the story like a flak jacket. On the surface it reads like your typical coming-of-age story. But the subject matter—the generation sent adrift because their fathers were scarred by the Vietnam War—gives this story a richness and depth that allow it to transcend the trite trappings of the genre."

Buckman's second novel, *The Names of Rivers,* is the story of a multigenerational family headed by Bruno Konick, who served during World War II and who participated in the liberation of Dachau. His sons Bruce and Len fought in Vietnam, and Luke, Bruce's son, is caught up with the memories of the former soldiers in his family.

Three generations of Illinois men populate *Morning Dark.* Big Walt is a World War II hero who built the family's wealth as a successful plumbing contractor. His son, Walt Junior, is a Vietnam veteran who has tried to live up to his father's expectations but who has failed at several marriages and in managing his father's business. His nephew has been dishonorably discharged and is attempting to reconstruct his life. Walt Junior retreats to a log cabin and is approached by teen drug dealer Shirley, who convinces him to let her process methamphetamine in the cabin, a scheme that leads to disastrous results.

Library Journal reviewer Thomas L. Kirkpatrick wrote: "Buckman is a master of character development and interpersonal analysis, and his slice-of-life tale of family dysfunction is right on target." "This is a book that won't be easily forgotten," concluded Betty Dickey in *Booklist.*

Mike Spence, the protagonist in *Because the Rain,* is a former paratrooper, now writer turned policeman, who is obsessed with Vietnamese prostitute Annie, as is one of her clients, Donald Goetzler, a tortured Vietnam vet. All become involved in the aftermath of a violent act that mingles the present with memories of times past.

Reviewing the novel in *Booklist,* Ian Chipman wrote that Buckman's writing ranges from "brusque, Hemingwayesque jabs to lilts of startling beauty detailing the tiniest gestures of longing." "It's a bleak but redeeming read," concluded a *Publishers Weekly* contributor.

BIOGRAPHICAL AND CRITICAL SOURCES:

PERIODICALS

Booklist, June 1, 2002, Thomas Gaughan, review of *The Names of Rivers,* p. 1677; September 1, 2003, Betty Dickie, review of *Morning Dark,* p. 52; March 1, 2007, Ian Chipman, review of *Because the Rain,* p. 59.

Kirkus Reviews, August 15, 2003, review of *Morning Dark,* p. 1030.

Library Journal, July 2002, Thomas L. Kilpatrick, review of *The Names of Rivers,* p. 115; September 1, 2003, Thomas L. Kilpatrick, review of *Morning Dark,* p. 204; March 1, 2007, Thomas L. Kilpatrick, review of *Because the Rain,* p. 68.

Publishers Weekly, April 29, 2002, review of *The Names of Rivers*, p. 39; September 1, 2003, review of *Morning Dark*, p. 62; December 18, 2006, review of *Because the Rain*, p. 38.

ONLINE

PopMatters, http://www.popmatters.com/ (September 20, 2007), John Kenyon, review of *Water in Darkness.**

*   *   *

BURKE, Gerald 1914-2007

OBITUARY NOTICE— See index for *CA* sketch: Born August 3, 1914; died July 15, 2007. Town planner, educator, and author. Burke became a chartered surveyor and chartered town planner after discovering the career field while working as a clerk at the College of Estate Management in Reading, England. Following service in the British Army during World War II he returned to the college, earned his certification, and began teaching classes for land surveyors. After brief study in the Netherlands and a few years working and teaching in Kenya in the 1950s, Burke found his way back to the College of Estate Management again. He was the head of the town planning department in 1972 when he and the college were absorbed into the University of Reading. It was in the city of Reading, during a period of redevelopment in which charming Victorian structures demolished to make room for utilitarian modern buildings, that Burke reportedly developed his interest in urban conservation. In 1976 Burke moved to Oxford Polytechnic (now Oxford Brookes University) to establish a department of estate management. He finished his formal career there in 1981 but continued his work as an educator into the 1990s, with a videotaped series of lectures on town planning intended for home study and distance learning. Burke's writings include *Greenheart Metropolis* (1966), *Towns in the Making* (1971), *Townscapes* (1976), and *Town Planning and the Surveyor* (1980).

OBITUARIES AND OTHER SOURCES:

PERIODICALS

Times (London, England), August 14, 2007, p. 47.

ONLINE

Times Online, http://www.timesonline.co.uk/ (August 9, 2007).

*   *   *

BURNEY, Claudia Mair 1964-

PERSONAL: Mair rhymes with "fire"; born 1964; married; children: seven.

ADDRESSES: Home—Inkster, MI. *Agent*—MacGregor Literary, 2373 N.W. 185th Ave., Ste. 165, Hillsboro, OR 97124-7076. *E-mail*—claudia.mair.burney@gmail.com.

CAREER: Writer.

WRITINGS:

Murder, Mayhem, and a Fine Man (mystery novel; "Amanda Brown Bell" series), NavPress (Colorado Springs, CO), 2006.
Death, Deceit, and Some Smooth Jazz (mystery novel; "Amanda Brown Bell" series), NavPress (Colorado Springs, CO), 2006.
Zora and Nicky: A Novel in Black and White (romance novel), David C. Cook (Colorado Springs, CO), 2008.

Also author of the blog *Ragamuffin Diva*. Contributor to *Justice in the Burbs: Being the Hands of Jesus Wherever You Live,* by Will and Lisa Samson, Baker Books (Grand Rapids, MI), 2007. Contributor to periodicals, including *Discipleship Journal* and the *Handmaiden.*

SIDELIGHTS: Claudia Mair Burney first garnered notice with her blog *Ragamuffin Diva,* where she writes about life, faith, books, and anything else that comes to mind. The popularity of the blog led Burney to her first publishing contract, and the start of her "Amanda Brown Bell" series of mystery novels. *Murder, Mayhem, and a Fine Man* is the debut book in the series. It introduces Amanda Brown Bell, a nearly-forty forensic psychologist and amateur detective who finds herself solving mysteries instead of sitting home and watching her favorite crime show on television. This volume also introduces Amanda to Lieutenant Jazz Brown, her love interest, but Burney keeps the primary focus on the murder mystery. The story involves a victim killed by way of poisoned communion wine and the cult that might be responsible. Harriet Klausner, in a review for her own Web site, called the book "a good murder mystery wrapped like a moebius string in and out of a quirky relationship drama."

Death, Deceit, and Some Smooth Jazz, the next title in Burney's series, finds Jazz attempting to reconcile with Amanda. When Jazz is accused of murdering his ex-wife, however, the resulting investigation becomes the focus of the story. Michelle Sutton, in a review on the *Novel Reviews Blog,* called the book "masterful writing and highly entertaining," adding that "the storyline was complex and well-thought-out."

Burney told *CA:* "I started [writing] when I found a page of a play on the floor at school when I was in the sixth grade. It occurred to me that I could write a play. And I did, and kept going from there."

When asked what influences her work, she said: "Everything. Beauty. Terror. All of life that I can grasp or even see gets into the gumbo that is my writing, but the rue, so to speak, is my Christian worldview. But it's not narrow or preachy. It's a big, holy cosmology. Bigger than that, really. So big it gets me in trouble sometimes."

When asked to describe her writing process, she said: "I start. Keep asking myself what happens next until I'm done. In between there is a lot of eating, procrastinating, bemoaning my fate, and doubting my skill. And then I eat again.

"You never arrive, and publishing is not what you think it will be. It will both bless and profoundly disappoint you."

When asked which of her books is her favorite, she responded, "Impossible to say. They all taught me something. They all heal and wound me. It's quite a paradoxical life for me.

"I want people to close my books and feel like God loves them no matter what and hasn't given up on them. We really aren't alone. None of us."

BIOGRAPHICAL AND CRITICAL SOURCES:

ONLINE

Harriet Klausner Review Archive, http://harriet klausner.wwwi.com/ (August 21, 2007), Harriet Klausner, review of *Murder, Mayhem, and a Fine Man.*

MacGregor Literary Agency Web site, http:// macgregorliterary.com/ (August 21, 2007), author biography.

Novel Reviews Blog, http://novelreviews.blogspot.com/ (July 11, 2006), Gina Holmes, review of *Murder, Mayhem, and a Fine Man;* (December 28, 2006), Michelle Sutton, review of *Death, Deceit, and Some Smooth Jazz.*

Soul Scents, http://www.soulscents.com/ (August 21, 2007), review of *Murder, Mayhem, and a Fine Man.*

*   *   *

BURTON, Rebecca 1970-

PERSONAL: Born 1970, in Australia; partner's name Wayne.

ADDRESSES: Home—South Australia.

CAREER: Novelist.

AWARDS, HONORS: Varuna Award, for *Leaving Jetty Road.*

WRITINGS:

Leaving Jetty Road, Angus & Robertson (Pymble, New South Wales, Australia), 2004, Knopf (New York, NY), 2006.

SIDELIGHTS: Australian novelist Rebecca Burton brings to life the world of a group of South Australian teens in her young-adult novel *Leaving Jetty Road.* In the novel, Natalie, Lise, and Sofia have been best friends throughout their years at their private high school. As they start their senior year, the girls decide to make a joint vow to become vegetarians. This choice ultimately causes changes that will allow each girl to come into her own as an individual. For example, when a job at a local vegetarian restaurant sparks romance in Nat's life, her role as official peacemaker takes a back seat to her tenuous relationship with Josh. Shy and somewhat of a loner, Lise finds that vegetarianism helps her deal with the eating disorder that has kept her hiding in the background, while popular Sofia is distracted from her academics when she develops a crush on a young man who is mature enough to be ambivalent about her charms.

Praising Burton's novel as "well-written" and "never-didactic," Frances Bradburn added in *Booklist* that *Leaving Jetty Road* is an "absorbing story about the tug and pull of old friendships as a teen's world expands." The author's themes—conveyed to readers through the intertwining narrations of Nat and Lise—will "have wide appeal, as will this story," predicted *Kliatt* contributor Claire Rosser, and *School Library Journal* reviewer Rhona Campbell cited Lise's narrative in particular for presenting teen readers with "a painfully honest confessional of the insecurities and self-loathing leading her into serious anorexia nervosa." Calling *Leaving Jetty Road* "psychologically intense," a *Publishers Weekly* reviewer nonetheless deemed Burton's story "optimistic" because as the story concludes the three teens "overcome their obstacles even as they choose different paths."

BIOGRAPHICAL AND CRITICAL SOURCES:

PERIODICALS

Booklist, June 1, 2006, Frances Bradburn, review of *Leaving Jetty Road,* p. 58.
Bulletin of the Center for Children's Books, June, 2006, Cindy Welch, review of *Leaving Jetty Road,* p. 445.
Kirkus Reviews, June 1, 2006, review of *Leaving Jetty Road,* p. 569.
Kliatt, May, 2006, Claire Rosser, review of *Leaving Jetty Road,* p. 6.

Publishers Weekly, July 24, 2006, review of *Leaving Jetty Road,* p. 59.
School Library Journal, August, 2006, Rhona Campbell, review of *Leaving Jetty Road,* p. 116.

ONLINE

HarperCollins Australia Web site, http://www.harpercollins.com/au/ (September 15, 2007), "Rebecca Burton."*

* * *

BYRNES, Michael
(Michael J. Byrnes)

PERSONAL: Married; children: two daughters. *Education:* Montclair State University, B.S.; Rutgers University, M.B.A.

ADDRESSES: Home—NJ. *Agent*—Mulcahy & Viney Ltd., 15 Canning Passage, Kensington, London W8 5AA, England.

CAREER: Founder and chief executive officer of an insurance brokerage firm in NJ.

WRITINGS:

The Sacred Bones (novel), HarperCollins (New York, NY), 2007.

SIDELIGHTS: Michael Byrnes is the founder of a highly successful insurance brokerage business in New Jersey, but his free time is devoted to writing. Byrnes's debut novel, *The Sacred Bones,* is an archeological thriller/mystery set in Jerusalem at the Temple Mount. When an artifact is stolen from beneath the mount and those responsible leave a bloody trail in their wake, tensions between Palestinians and Israelis are ratcheted up yet another notch. The Vatican steps in, hiring an American forensic scientist named Charlotte Hennesey to work with Italian anthropologist Giovanni Bersei to investigate the scene. Byrnes takes the tension to still a higher level when Hennesey and Bersei discover evidence suggesting that the skeleton buried beneath the mount might be the remains of Jesus. Several critics compared Byrnes's debut to Dan Brown's *The Da Vinci Code.* Jeff Ayers, writing for *Library Journal,* remarked that "back stories and discussion are clunky at times, halting the narrative pace," and called the story "improbable." A *Kirkus Reviews* contributor found the book "unimpressive." Terry South, however, asserted on the *Quality Book Reviews Blog* that "Byrnes has penned a superbly crafted debut novel that tantalizes with a sense of drama and of suspense as the story races forward. It is evident that he has done a great deal of research."

BIOGRAPHICAL AND CRITICAL SOURCES:

PERIODICALS

Bookseller, July 7, 2006, "Byrnes' Debut Sells," p. 13.
Kirkus Reviews, December 15, 2006, review of *The Sacred Bones,* p. 1232.

Library Journal, February 1, 2007, Jeff Ayers, review of *The Sacred Bones,* p. 62.

ONLINE

Mary Martin, http://www.marymartin.com.au/ (June 1, 2007), Denise Pickles, review of *The Sacred Bones.*
Mulcahy & Viney Ltd. Web site, http://www.mvagency. com/ (August 22, 2007), profile of Michael Byrnes.
Quality Book Reviews Blog, http://terrysouth. livejournal.com/ (August 22, 2007), Terry South, review of *The Sacred Bones.**

*   *   *

BYRNES, Michael J.
   See BYRNES, Michael

C

CARTER, Maureen

PERSONAL: Female.

ADDRESSES: E-mail—maureencarter@gmail.com.

CAREER: Worked as a newspaper reporter; BRMB radio, Birmingham, England, news reader; twenty years with the British Broadcasting Corporation (BBC), Birmingham, began as broadcast journalist, became assistant editor; worked in London, England, as a presenter on *Newsnight.*

WRITINGS:

"BEV MORRISS" CRIME SERIES

Working Girls, Creme de la Crime (Abingdon, England), 2004.
Dead Old, Creme de la Crime (Chesterfield, England), 2005.
Baby Love, Creme de la Crime (Chesterfield, England), 2006.
Hard Time, Creme de la Crime (Chesterfield, England), 2007.

SIDELIGHTS: Maureen Carter enjoyed a successful career in broadcast journalism before becoming the author of a series featuring Detective Sergeant Bev Morriss. In reviewing *Working Girls,* the first book in the series, for her blog *Rullsenberg Rules,* Lisa Rullsenberg noted that Carter exhibits "a real sense of character and a sharp ear for both spoken and internal dialogue." Rullsenberg also commented that "she brings the demands of journalism for spare if still engagingly fluid prose to conveying such a compelling tale without losing sight of what dramatic genre fiction needs. Good plots, convincing settings, internally consistent characterisation." Other characters in the series set in Birmingham, England, include the cocky Detective Inspector Mike Powell.

The third book in the series, *Baby Love,* finds Bev moving into a new home. She hasn't fully unpacked and her romance with Oz Khan, also a detective, is on shaky ground. She has been taken off of a high-profile rape case and assigned to a baby kidnapping, largely because of her bluntness and uninhibited nature, which is now threatening her career. The single mother of baby Zoe is Natalie Beck, a teen who lives with her mother, Maxine, with whom Bev has a history.

ReviewingTheEvidence.com contributor Sharon Wheeler commented that Carter "writes clean, spare prose which nails both the bleakness of the city and the pressures of Bev's job. The book's conclusion is dark and frightening." "Carter writes like a longtime veteran, with snappy patter and stark narrative," commented David Pitt in *Booklist.*

Carter told *CA:* "My years in journalism inform and influence both how I write and what I decide to write about. As both a print and broadcast reporter, I covered hundreds if not thousands of stories, many of them serious crimes. I worked alongside police officers and observed how they operate, and interviewed many detectives, crime victims, grieving relatives, and, less often, criminals. As an author, crime fiction is the perfect genre for me. It allows me to write in depth about issues I formerly covered in, say, a one-and-a-half minute film for TV news. As a reporter I was accustomed to creating arresting openings, structuring stories, writing tightly, editing as I worked and always delivering on deadline. This is how I write now. I set a minimum daily target and don't stop until I've hit it. I adore writing but don't do it for me. I write because I want my books to entertain and give pleasure to readers. I hope my work and the characters I create make readers laugh, cry, and think."

BIOGRAPHICAL AND CRITICAL SOURCES:

PERIODICALS

Booklist, February 1, 2007, David Pitt, review of *Baby Love,* p. 34.

ONLINE

Maureen Carter Home Page, http://www.maureen carter.co.uk (September 4, 2007).

ReviewingTheEvidence.com, http://www.reviewingthe evidence.com/ (August 8, 2007), Sharon Wheeler, review of *Baby Love.*

Rullsenberg Rules, http://rullsenbergrules.blogspot. com/ (July 4, 2007), Lisa Rullsenberg, review of *Working Girls.*

*   *   *

CATHERWOOD, Christopher

PERSONAL: Son of Frederick Catherwood (former vice president of the European parliament); married Paulette Moore. *Education:* Balliol College, University of Oxford, B.A., M.A.; Sidney Sussex College, University of Cambridge, M.Litt.; University of East Anglia, Ph.D.

ADDRESSES: Home—Cambridge, England. *Office*—INSTEP Cambridge, Warkworth House, Warkworth Ter., Cambridge CB1 1EE, England.

CAREER: Institute of Economic and Political Studies, University of Cambridge, Cambridge, England, tutor; School of Continuing Studies, University of Richmond, Richmond, VA, instructor, writer in residence; INSTEP, Cambridge, England, instructor. Consultant to the Strategic Futures Team of Prime Minister Tony Blair, 2002; visiting scholar at various institutions.

AWARDS, HONORS: Rockefeller fellow, 2001; Royal Geographical Society fellow; Royal Asiatic Society fellow; Royal Historical Society fellow.

WRITINGS:

Joy Unspeakable: Power & Renewal in the Holy Spirit, H. Shaw (Wheaton, IL), 1985.

Prove All Things: The Sovereign Work of the Holy Spirit, Kingsway Publications (Eastbourne, England), 1985.

The Sovereign Spirit: Discerning His Gifts, H. Shaw (Wheaton, IL), 1985.

Five Evangelical Leaders, H. Shaw (Wheaton, IL), 1985.

(Editor) David Martin Lloyd-Jones, *I Am Not Ashamed: Advice to Timothy,* Hodder & Stoughton (London, England), 1986.

Saved in Eternity: The Assurance of Our Salvation, Crossway Books (Westchester, IL), 1988.

Safe in the World: The Assurance of Our Salvation, Crossway Books (Westchester, IL), 1988.

Growing in the Spirit: The Assurance of Our Salvation, Crossway Books (Westchester, IL), 1989.

Sanctified through the Truth: The Assurance of Our Salvation, Crossway Books (Westchester, IL), 1989.

(Editor) David Martyn Lloyd-Jones, *The Heart of the Gospel,* Crossway Books (Westchester, IL), 1991.

The Kingdom of God, Crossway Books (Westchester, IL), 1992.

Enjoying the Presence of God, Vine Books (Ann Arbor, MI), 1992.

(Compiler) *The Best of Martyn Lloyd-Jones,* Kingsway Publications (Eastbourne, England), 1992.

Martyn Lloyd-Jones: A Family Portrait, Kingsway Publications (Eastbourne, England), 1995.

Why the Nations Rage, Hodder & Stoughton (London, England), 1997, revised and updated version published as *Why the Nations Rage: Killing in the Name of God,* Rowman & Littlefield (Lanham, MD), 1997.

Crash Course on Church History, Hodder & Stoughton (London, England), 1998, revised edition published as *Church History: A Crash Course for the Curious,* Crossway Books (Wheaton, IL), 2007.

From Wales to Westminster: The Story of Dr. Martyn Lloyd-Jones, Christian Focus (Fearn, England), 1999.

Whose Side Is God On? Nationalism and Christianity, Church Publishing (New York, NY), 2003.

Christians, Muslims, and Islamic Rage: What Is Going on and Why It Happened, Zondervan (Grand Rapids, MI), 2003.

The Balkans in World War Two: Britain's Balkan Dilemma, Palgrave Macmillan (New York, NY), 2003.

Churchill's Folly: How Winston Churchill Created Modern Iraq, Carroll & Graf (New York, NY), 2004, published as *Winston's Folly: Imperialism and the Creation of Modern Iraq,* Constable (London, England), 2004.

Seeking the Face of God: Nine Reflections on the Psalms, Crossway Books (Wheaton, IL), 2005.

(With Leslie Alan Horvitz) *Encyclopedia of War Crimes and Genocide,* Facts on File (New York, NY), 2006.

A Brief History of the Middle East, Carroll & Graf (New York, NY), 2006.

A God Divided: Understanding the Differences between Islam, Christianity, and Judaism, Victor (Colorado Springs, CO), 2007.

Provided editorial assistance for *Britain & the World 1815-1986: A Dictionary of International Relations,* by David Weigall, Batsford (London, England), 1987.

SIDELIGHTS: Historian and writer Christopher Catherwood is the author of books that include histories such as *Churchill's Folly: How Winston Churchill Created Modern Iraq,* published in England as *Winston's Folly: Imperialism and the Creation of Modern Iraq,* a study of Churchill's part in the creation of modern Iraq while he served as colonial secretary in the 1920s. As a consultant to British Prime Minister Tony Blair in 2002, Catherwood studied foreign relations during the period when Blair was the primary supporter of President George W. Bush's Iraq policy. Looking back to British involvement in the Middle East, he notes that Churchill was responsible for carving up the Ottoman Empire after World War I, with the intention of balancing French power and creating smaller competitive nations that would be too busy disagreeing with each other to be troublesome to Britain.

Churchill had urged the Arabs to fight the Turks, promising Syria to the Hashimites as a reward, but when Syria came under the rule of the French, the transfer was of Iraq instead. This fragmenting resulted in an Iraq with three major ethnic and religious groups—Shia and Sunni Muslims and Kurds, as well as minority factions, all of which were ruled by Saudi king Feisal, who was appointed by Churchill. Churchill chose Feisal because he thought him to be easily manipulated, so that Mesopotamia's oil riches could be British controlled, but the king soon exerted his independence, and when British occupation ended, instability became the rule, eventually resulting in the leadership of Saddam Hussein. "Catherwood demonstrates yet again that one generation's pragmatism can be a later generation's tragedy," concluded a *Publishers Weekly* contributor.

Encyclopedia of War Crimes and Genocide, written with Leslie Alan Horvitz, includes more than four hundred entries that describe human rights violations, crimes against humanity, and acts of genocide, responsible individuals, countries where they occurred, terms of various treaties, and organizations that have dealt with these crimes, such as Amnesty International. The appendix of this volume written for an adult and young adult readership includes the text of the Geneva Conventions.

Catherwood is the grandson of preacher David Martyn Lloyd-Jones, about whom he has written several volumes. He has also edited and published many of his grandfather's sermons. *Crash Course on Church History,* revised and published as *Church History: A Crash Course for the Curious,* is a history of the Christian faith from the time of Christ to the present. Catherwood notes that countries that were once the center of the Christian world are now Muslim as an aftermath of the Islamic wars of the seventh century. Catherwood also writes of the joining of church and politics, including Constantine's legalization of Christianity in the Roman Empire, and makes comparisons to the influence of religion on politics in contemporary times. He points out the dangers of Roman Catholic doctrine that embraces the idea that Mary was the mother of God, an official position only since 1950, and he notes that Mother Theresa was a universalist.

A reviewer for the *Shepherd's Scrapbook* Web site wrote: "Catherwood is downright engaging. You will not agree at every turn, but he will make you think as he broadens your perspective of the global church and how God has shaped the church by key events and people over the past 2,000 years."

BIOGRAPHICAL AND CRITICAL SOURCES:

PERIODICALS

Booklist, November 15, 2006, Brendan Driscoll, review of *A Brief History of the Middle East,* p. 20; January 1, 2007, Arthur Meyers, review of *Encyclopedia of War Crimes and Genocide,* p. 136.

Choice, November, 1998, J.W. Frost, review of *Why the Nations Rage: Killing in the Name of God,* p. 537; May, 2005, R.A. Callahan, review of *Churchill's Folly: How Winston Churchill Created Modern Iraq,* p. 1659; December, 2006, D. Altschiller, review of *Encyclopedia of War Crimes and Genocide,* p. 626.

Contemporary Review, January, 2005, review of *Winston's Folly: Imperialism and the Creation of Modern Iraq,* p. 59.

European History Quarterly, October, 2005, Ann Lane, review of *The Balkans in World War Two: Britain's Balkan Dilemma,* p. 585.

Guardian (London, England), November 27, 2004, John Charmley, review of *Winston's Folly.*

Kirkus Reviews, June 15, 2004, review of *Churchill's Folly,* p. 564.

Library Journal, April 1, 1998, Leroy Hommerding, review of *Why the Nations Rage,* p. 94.

Middle East Journal, autumn, 2004, review of *Churchill's Folly,* p. 705.

New Statesman, July 26, 2004, Anton La Guardia, review of *Winston's Folly,* p. 51.

Publishers Weekly, November 15, 1985, William Griffin, review of *Five Evangelical Leaders,* p. 32; June 14, 2004, review of *Churchill's Folly,* p. 53.

Reference & Research Book News, August, 2006, review of *Encyclopedia of War Crimes and Genocide.*

ONLINE

Shepherd's Scrapbook, http://spurgeon.wordpress.com/ (April 24, 2007), review of *Church History: A Crash Course for the Curious.*

CAUSEY, Toni McGee

PERSONAL: Born in LA; married; husband's name Carl; children: two. *Education:* Attended Louisiana State University.

ADDRESSES: Home—Baton Rouge, LA. *E-mail*—website@tonimcgeecausey.com.

CAREER: Co-owner of a civil construction company in Baton Rouge, LA.

WRITINGS:

Bobbie Faye's Very (Very, Very, Very) Bad Day (novel), St. Martin's Griffin (New York, NY), 2007.

SIDELIGHTS: Toni McGee Causey is a Louisiana native who, with her husband, owns a civil engineering firm. Her career as a writer began with a three-book deal with St. Martin's Press. In the first book in the series, *Bobbie Faye's Very (Very, Very, Very) Bad Day,* Bobbie Faye Sumrall lives a life of chaos, beginning in this story with a flooded trailer, the result of a faulty washing machine. Her no-account brother Roy has been kidnapped, and the ransom is to be a tiara she inherited from her mother. She had planned on wearing the tiara when she reigns as queen of the Lake Charles, Louisiana, Contraband Festival Days, a pirate-themed celebration, but the tiara is stolen when she goes to the bank to collect it. Playing the part of a modern-day pirate, Bobbie Faye takes command of a truck and its hunky driver, Trevor, and they embark on a wild ride through bayou country to avoid the police, FBI, and assorted villains who are on her trail.

In reviewing the novel on *Bookreporter.com,* Joe Hartlaub wrote: "There are many things to love about this book—the plot, the pacing, the dialogue—but my own favorite element is the characterization. . . . But if you want a short description of this great novel, think *Die Hard* in the swamp." "Causey doesn't miss a beat in this wonderful, wacky celebration of Southern eccentricity," wrote a *Publishers Weekly* contributor.

BIOGRAPHICAL AND CRITICAL SOURCES:

PERIODICALS

Publishers Weekly, March 26, 2007, review of *Bobbie Faye's Very (Very, Very, Very) Bad Day,* p. 66.

ONLINE

Bookreporter.com, http://www.bookreporter.com/ (September 23, 2007), Joe Hartlaub, review of *Bobbie Faye's Very (Very, Very, Very) Bad Day,.*

Toni McGee Causey Home Page, http://tonimcgee causey.com (September 23, 2007).*

*   *   *

CENDREY, Jean-Yves 1957-

PERSONAL: Born 1957, in Nevers, France; married Marie N'Diaye (a writer); children: three.

ADDRESSES: Home—Berlin, Germany.

CAREER: Writer.

WRITINGS:

Principes du cochon (novel; title means "Principles of the Pig"), P.O.L. (Paris, France), 1988.

Atlas menteur (novel; title means "Lying Atlas"), P.O.L. (Paris, France), 1989.

Les Morts vont vite (novel; title means "Deaths Go Quickly"), P.O.L (Paris, France), 1991.

Oublier Berlin: Carnets (title means "To Forget Berlin: Notebooks"), P.O.L. (Paris, France), 1994.

Trou-Madame; suivi de, *Une Journée de ma vie d'athlète,* P.O.L (Paris, France), 1997.

Les Petites Sœurs de sang (title means "Little Sisters of Blood"), Olivier (Paris, France), 1999.

Une Simple Créature (title means "One Simple Creature), Olivier (Paris, France), 2001.

Les Jouets vivants (title means "Living Toys"), Olivier (Paris, France), 2005.

Les Jouissances du remords: Un Moment de ma vie par un ennemi intime (title means "Pleasures of Remorse: One Moment of My Life by an Intimate Enemy"), Olivier (Paris, France), 2007.

(With wife, Marie N'Diaye) *Puzzle: Trois Pièces: Théâtre* (title means "Three Plays: Theatre"), Gallimard (Paris, France), 2007.

Corps Ensaignant, Gallimard (Paris, France), 2007.

SIDELIGHTS: French writer Jean-Yves Cendrey is the author of a number of novels, including *Principes du cochon* (title means "Principles of the Pig"). One of his later books, *Les Jouets vivants* (title means "Living Toys"), was a great critical success. The story is based on the actual crimes of pedophile Marcel Lechien, a teacher in Cormeilles, Normandy, who was brought to trial in 2002 and convicted of violating dozens of six-year-old students. The abuse was never acknowledged by other adults in the community who claimed not to believe the accounts of the victim children.

After moving to the village, Cendrey and his wife discovered that the teacher of one of their children had been sexually abusing his students for more than three decades. Cendrey, who was himself a victim of childhood abuse, opens the book with a recollection of the death of his father and his own resistance to attending his funeral. He then proceeds to describe how he interviewed former pupils of the teacher, and when he was certain of the evidence, physically took the teacher to the police. Cendrey and his family later left the village after denouncing the crimes and the villagers who had delayed justice and allowed the abuse to continue with their silence. The teacher received a sentence of fifteen years imprisonment.

BIOGRAPHICAL AND CRITICAL SOURCES:

PERIODICALS

French Review, February, 2000, Tom Conner, review of *Trou-Madame,* p. 586; February, 2001, Alain-Philippe Durand, review of *Les Petites Sœurs de sang,* p. 591.

ONLINE

Publishing Trends, http://www.publishingtrends.com/ (September 24, 2007), Virginie Petracco, review of *Les Jouets vivants.*

*   *   *

CENTER, Katherine
(Katherine Pannill Center, Katherine Pannill)

PERSONAL: Born in Houston, TX; married Gordon Center (a teacher); children: one boy, one girl. *Education:* Vassar College, B.A.; University of Houston, M.A.

ADDRESSES: Home—Houston, TX. *E-mail*— Katherine@katherinecenter.com.

CAREER: Writer. Worked in a bookstore and as a teacher of creative writing for Writers in the Schools.

AWARDS, HONORS: Vassar College fiction prize; University of Houston fellowship.

WRITINGS:

The Bright Side of Disaster (novel), Ballantine (New York, NY), 2007.

SIDELIGHTS: Houston native Katherine Center's novel *The Bright Side of Disaster* is her debut featuring Jenny Harris, who lives in an historic Houston neighborhood. When her very attractive friend Nadia rejects the advances of garage-band musician Dean, he moves on to Jenny and eventually into her apartment. Jenny is soon pregnant, but her mother rules out a quick wedding and plans a big event after the baby is born. The wedding never occurs, however, as Dean disappears just as she is about to give birth, and when she does, baby Maxie becomes the sole object of her affection.

Jenny is supported by new and old friends and her mother, and tries to bring her parents, who have been divorced for fifteen years, together again. Neighbor John Gardner becomes an important part of Jenny's life, but then Dean reappears, which presents a dilemma.

Guidelive.com reviewer Joy Tipping called Center's characterization and dialogue "sharply honed and spot on. You may want to conk some of these people over the head with a logic-inducing thump, but you'll know them. They're your neighbors, your best friends, your impossible exes . . . and yes, your mommy groups." Reviewing the book for the *MidWeek News* Web site, Erica Semenchuk wrote: "Katherine Center's debut novel has a lot of what a truly enjoyable novel has—an engaging plot, loveable characters, a little humor, some romance and even a dose of drama and suspense, which makes it very difficult to put down."

BIOGRAPHICAL AND CRITICAL SOURCES:

PERIODICALS

Books, June 2, 2007, Kristin Kloberdanz, review of *The Bright Side of Disaster,* p. 8.

Library Journal, June 1, 2007, Amanda Glasbrenner, review of *The Bright Side of Disaster,* p. 107.

Publishers Weekly, March 5, 2007, review of *The Bright Side of Disaster,* p. 33.

ONLINE

Guidelive.com, http://www.guidelive.com/ (September 2, 2007), Joy Tipping, review of *The Bright Side of Disaster.*

Katherine Center Home Page, http://katherinecenter. com (September 23, 2007).

MidWeek News, http://midweeknews.com/ (August 30, 2007), Erica Semenchuk, review of *The Bright Side of Disaster.*

Readers Read, http://www.readersread.com/ (September 23, 2007), "Interview with Katherine Center."*

* * *

CENTER, Katherine Pannill
See CENTER, Katherine

* * *

CHARLES, PRINCE of WALES 1948-
(Charles Philip Arthur George Windsor)

PERSONAL: Born November 14, 1948, in London, England; son of Queen Elizabeth II and Prince Philip, Duke of Edinburgh; married Diana Frances Spencer, July 29, 1981 (divorced August 28, 1996; died August 31, 1997); married Camilla Parker Bowles, April 9, 2005; children: (first marriage) William Arthur Philip Louis (Prince William of Wales), Henry Charles Albert David (Prince Henry of Wales). *Education:* Attended University College of Wales at Aberystwyth, 1969, University of Wales, 1975, and Royal Naval College, Dartmouth; Trinity College, Cambridge, B.A, 1970, M.A, 1975; Royal Air Force College, graduated, 1971. *Religion:* Church of England. *Hobbies and other interests:* Gardening, painting, active in eighteen nonprofit charities as president of The Prince's Charities.

ADDRESSES: Home—London, England.

CAREER: Became Duke of Cornwall, Duke of Rothesay, Earl of Carrick, Baron of Renfrew, Lord of the Isles and Great Steward of Scotland, 1952; created knight of the Order of the Garter, 1958, invested, 1959; created Prince of Wales and Earl of Chester, 1958; high steward, Royal Borough Windsor and Maidenhead, 1974. Barrister, Gray's Inn, 1974; chancellor, University of Wales, 1976; president, Prince's Trust, 1977, United World Colleges, 1978-92, Prince of Wales Business Leaders Forum, 1990, Prince of Wales's Foundation for Architecture and Urban Environment, 1992, Royal College of Music, 1993, and Prince's Trust-Bro, 1996; vice president, National Trust, 1996. Duchy Originals (organic food company), founder, 1990—. Member, Queen's Trust, 1977, the National Gallery, 1993, the Oxford Center for Islamic Studies, 1993, and the National Trust Centenary Appeal, 1995. Honorary member, Institute of Mechanical Engineers; royal fellow, Australian Academy of Science. *Military service:* Served in the British Royal Navy; colonel, Welsh Guards, 1974; commander of the HMS *Barrington,* 1975; colonel-in-chief, 22nd Cheshire Regiment, 1977; Air Reserves, Canada, 1977; Lord Strathcona's Horse Regiment (Royal Canadians), 1977; air commodore in chief, Royal New Zealand Air Force, 1977; Parachute Regiment, 1977; Royal Australian Armoured Corps, 1977; Royal Regiment Canada, 1977; Royal Winnepeg Rifles, 1977; Royal Pacific Islands Regiment, 1984; Royal Canadian Dragoons, 1985; Army Air Corps, 1992; Royal Dragoon Guards, 1992; Royal Gurkha Rifles, 1994; air vice marshall, Royal Air Force, 1998; royal honorary colonel, Queen's Own Yeomanry, 2000; lieutenant general, British Army, 2002; 1st Queen's Dragoon Guards, 2003; Black Watch (Royal Highland Regiment), Canada, 2004; Toronto Scottish Regiment (Queen Elizabeth The Queen Mother's Own), 2005; air chief marshall, 2006; commodore-in-chief, Royal Naval Command, Plymouth, 2006; royal colonel, 51st Highland, 7th battalion Royal Regiment of Scotland (Territorial Army), 2006; Royal Navy, vice admiral 2002, admiral, 2006; Black Watch, 3rd battalion Royal Regiment of Scotland; honorary air commodore, Royal Air Force Valley.

MEMBER: Royal Aeronautical Society (honorary member), Royal College of Surgeons (honorary fellow), Society of St. George's and Descendents of Knights of Garters (president, 1975), Royal Forestry Society, Royal Thames Yacht Club (admiral, 1974), Incorporation of Gardeners of Glasgow (honorary life member).

AWARDS, HONORS: Coronation medal, 1953; Freedom of City of Cardiff, 1969; Royal Borough of New Windsor, 1970, of City of London, 1971, of Chester, 1973, of City of Canterbury, 1978, of City of Portsmouth, 1979, of City of Lancaster, 1993, and of City of Swansea, 1994; Queen's Silver Jubilee medal, 1977; Liveryman, Fishmongers Co, 1971, Freeman, Drapers' Co, 1971, Freeman, Shipwrights' Co, 1978, Hon. Freeman, Goldsmith's Co, Liveryman, Farmers' Co, 1980, Liveryman, Pewterers' Co, 1982, and Liveryman, Fruiterers' Co, 1989; Master Mariners of Merchants, City of Edinburgh, 1979; honorary fellow, Trinity College, Cambridge, 1988; named Author of Year, 1989; Spoleto prize, 1989; Premio Fregene, 1990; Order of Merit, 2002; Global Environment Citizen award, Center for Health and Global Environment, Harvard Medical School, 2007; decorated grand cross of the Southern Cross, Brazil; White Rose, Finland; House of Orange, The Netherlands; Order of Oak Crown, Luxembourg; Order of Ojasvi Rajanya, Nepal; Legion of Honor, France; knight of the Order of the Elephant, Denmark; grand cordon of the Supreme of Chrysanthemum, Japan; Order of the Republic of Egypt; great master, Order of Bath.

WRITINGS:

The Old Man of Lochnagar (fairy tale), Hamilton (London, England), 1980.

Charles in His Own Words, compiled by Rosemary York, W.H. Allen (London, England), 1981.

A Vision of Britain: A Personal View of Architecture, Doubleday (London, England), 1989.

Watercolours, Little, Brown (London, England), 1991.

The People's Prince: A Collection of Major Addresses, Veritas (Cranbrook, Western Australia, Australia), 1992.

Islam and the West, Oxford Centre for Islamic Studies (Oxford, England), 1993.

(With Charles Clover) *Highgrove: Portrait of an Estate,* Chapmans (London, England), 1993, published as *Highgrove: An Experiment in Organic Gardening and Farming,* Simon & Schuster (New York, NY), 1994.

(Selector) *Travels with the Prince: Paintings and Drawings: In Aid of the Prince of Wales's Charitable Foundation,* Sheeran Lock (London, England), 1998.

The Garden at Highgrove, photographs by Andrew Lawson and Christopher Simon Sykes, Weidenfeld & Nicolson (London, England), 2000.

The Elements of Organic Gardening, Kales Press, 2007.

Contributor to *The Real Common Worship,* edited by Peter Mullen, Edgeways (Harleston, England), 2000, and *The Prince of Wales and the Duchess of Cornwall Annual Review.* Author of introduction, *Cornwall County Guide,* Cornwall County Council, c. 1996.

SIDELIGHTS: Charles, Prince of Wales, is the heir apparent to the throne of England. The son of Queen Elizabeth II and Prince Philip, he was born just after World War II, and his arrival signaled a hopeful new chapter in Britain after years of war. Born to a life of privilege, as a boy Charles was a quiet and dutiful son who was well liked by the people of England. Upon the death of his grandfather King George VI in 1952, he was named Duke of Cornwall, and four years later the Queen declared him the Prince of Wales, as well as bestowing upon him various other royal titles. The prince has not lived a life of idle prosperity, however. He attended military schools, and when he graduated from Trinity College, Cambridge, he became the first member of his family to receive a university degree. Charles entered the Royal Navy in the 1970s, commanding his own ship, the HMS *Barrington.* He served in Canada, Australia, and New Zealand, as well, but by 1977 he returned to his duties as a member of the royal family. Prince Charles was a good-will ambassador to various nations abroad during this time. Conscious of his position as a role model for his country, he also became involved in charity work. When the prince announced his engagement to the beautiful Diana Spencer in 1981, England, and indeed much of the world, was abuzz at the prospect. Their wedding that summer seemed the epitome of a fairy-tale. The world would not know for a number of years, though, that the marriage was largely a sham and that the prince actually had yearned for another woman.

At first, however, the marriage seemed to go well. Diana, now Princess Diana, gave birth to two sons, and she, like her husband, was a favorite of the English people. She was publicly visible for her charitable work, particularly her concern over land mines that had been left behind after wars but which routinely exploded, killing children, adults, and wildlife. By the mid-1990s, it was becoming apparent to everyone that Diana and Charles's marriage was falling apart. The two separated, and tabloids discovered that Charles was having an affair with Camilla Bowles; Diana was not an innocent in this, though; she, too, had affairs. The fairy tale ended with divorce in 1996, and Diana was sometimes criticized for her close relationship with Dodi al Fayed, the son of the owner of the famous London department store Harrod's. Relentlessly pursued by the paparazzi, Princess Diana and Fayed were killed in 1997 when their limousine crashed inside a Paris tunnel while speeding away from reporters. The tragedy marked a low point for the entire House of Windsor, but the prince and his sons were able to go on with their lives. Prince Charles eventually married Camilla Bowles in a civil ceremony in 2005. Some have felt that his reputation has been tarnished by this long chapter in his life, while others have admired his ability to maintain decorum in the face of a harassing press.

Prince Charles has continued to focus on his role as a diplomat and as a model for the British people. He remains thoroughly involved in many charities, and he established Prince Charles's Charities, an umbrella group for which he is president and which administers the work of eighteen different nonprofit organizations. He is also an author, having published books primarily on art and his favorite hobby, gardening. His first book, *The Old Man of Lochnagar,* was actually a fairy tale story based on a bedtime story he used to tell his younger brothers when they were children. In 1989 he published *A Vision of Britain: A Personal View of Architecture,* a work that stoutly criticizes many modern trends in architecture. Here, he complains that modern buildings are ugly, do not integrate well with their surrounding landscapes, and are not built on a human-friendly scale. Roberta Brandes Gratz remarked in a *Nation* review: "He truly understands what is wrong with architecture planning and urban design today, not only in Britain but also in the United States. The Prince has written a highly readable, beautifully illustrated and exceedingly wise book." She added: "Prince Charles seems to understand intuitively some of the larger issues of urban development—how traditional downtown retail and commercial codes are threatened by the rise of the shopping mall, for example."

Painting and gardening are the subjects of several other of the prince's books. His *Watercolours* reproduces seventy-three of his own paintings, mostly of scenic views, which are accompanied by his "chatty, unpretentious facing-page commentaries," according to a *Publishers Weekly* reviewer. With *Highgrove: Portrait of an Estate, The Garden at Highgrove,* and *The Elements of Organic Gardening,* the prince combines his interest in gardening and environmentalism. Highgrove is a property in the English Cotswolds. Here, the prince, working with other gardeners and horticulturists, has created an experiment where organic gardening methods are the rule. Rare and exotic varieties of fruits and vegetables are grown, environment-saving sewage systems are used, and crops are rotated to maintain healthy soils. Bonnie L. Poquette, writing a review of *The Elements of Organic Gardening* in the *Library Journal,* observed that the prince had been "an outspoken environmentalist" long before "it was fashionable." The reviewer praised the book for its "practical slant and personal, inspirational tone."

BIOGRAPHICAL AND CRITICAL SOURCES:

BOOKS

Newsmakers 1995, Thomson Gale (Detroit, MI), 1995.

PERIODICALS

Cosmopolitan, February, 1997, George Plimpton, "Whither Now, Princess Di?," p. 332.

Ecologist, September 1, 1998, "Seeds of Disaster," p. 252.

Economist, September 16, 1989, review of *A Vision of Britain: A Personal View of Architecture,* p. 95; November 25, 1995, "The Undermining of Charles," p. 54; November 23, 1996, "Princely Performance," p. 64.

Entertainment Weekly, July 10, 1992, Lisa Schwarzbaum, "To Di For," p. 24.

Environment, September, 2000, Timothy O'Riordan, "Science and Intuition," p. 1.

Food Chemical News, January 29, 2001, "Britain's Prince Charles Re-ignited the Food Biotechnology Debate This Month," p. 17; January 21, 2002, "Britain's Prince Charles Has Given His Support to a Scientist Who Believes that the Human Equivalent of Mad Cow Disease May Be Caused by Pollution Rather Than by Eating Beef Infected with Bovine Spongiform Encephalopathy," p. 14; June 24, 2002, "Britain's Prince Charles This Month Said Companies That Fund Agricultural

Biotechnology Research Should Be Made Liable for Any Damage That Occurs," p. 25; February 17, 2003, "The Prince of Wales Will Be Notably Absent," p. 19; June 5, 2006, "Royal Endorsement," p. 4.

Horticulture, the Magazine of American Gardening, January, 1994, Christopher Reed, review of *Highgrove: An Experiment in Organic Gardening and Farming,* p. 77.

Insight on the News, August 6, 2001, Suzanne Fields, "A New Image for Victorian England," p. 48.

Japan Economic Newswire, January 8, 1989, "Prince Charles May Represent Queen at Emperor's Funeral," p. 890108014.

Library Journal, August 1, 2007, Bonnie L. Poquette, review of *The Elements of Organic Gardening,* p. 108.

Life, August, 1992, Robert Lacy, "Alone Together," p. 26.

Maclean's, June 25, 2007, Kenneth Whyte, "Tina Brown Talks with Kenneth Whyte about Married Women and the Prince of Wales, Diana's Big Lie, and Dodi's Fatal Error," p. 14.

Nation, March 5, 1990, Roberta Brandes Gratz, review of *A Vision of Britain,* p. 314

New Leader, October 6, 1986, Ray Alan, "Buckingham Dallas," p. 5; January 12, 1987, "The Long March of the Prince of Wales," p. 10.

Newsweek, March 11, 1996, Jonathan Dimbeleby, "The Private Prince," p. 32; October 13, 1997, "Diana in Her Own Words: In Transcripts of Talks with the Princess, Her Sad, Candid Voice Details the Horrors of Her Marriage," p. 64; July 20, 1998, "The Prince and the Paramour," p. 63; September 26, 2005, "Newsmakers," p. 71.

New York Times, June 21, 2000, Warren Hoge, "A Coming of Age, Regal but Guarded," p. 4; March 14, 2003, "Prince Charles's Top Aide Quits after Inquiry," p. 6; July 1, 2003, "Royal Account's Bottom Line: Charles Makes a Princely Sum," p. 6; November 8, 2003, "Prince Charles Denies a Rumor, but Won't Say What It's About," p. 5; November 23, 2004, "Charles Joins Fray over Himself," p. 5; February 11, 2005, "Charles Calls End to the Affair: He'll Happily Wed His Camilla," p. 1; February 23, 2005, "Queen to Skip Wedding. She'll Attend Blessing Later. Stay Tuned," p. 5; February 24, 2005, "Charles Gets Some Good News: The Wedding, at Least, Is Legal," p. 4; March 9, 2005, "World Briefing Europe: Britain: Prince Cleared for Civil Ceremony," p. 6; April 10, 2005, "Charles and

Camilla, Married at Last, and with Hardly a Hitch," p. 1; November 5, 2005, "Organic Farming's American Heartland Awaits Royals," p. 11; March 18, 2006, "World Briefing Europe: Britain: Charles Wins Judgment on Travelog," p. 7; January 29, 2007, "The Prince, in the City, Dribbles and Scores," p. 1; May 24, 2007, "World Briefing Europe: Britain: Charles's Waxwork Goes Green," p. 10.

New York Times Magazine, March 6, 2005, Daphne Merkin, "A Fairy Tale for Grown-Ups," p. 13.

Nursing Standard, May 16, 2007, "The Prince of Wales Has Commended a Hospital Food Programme in Cornwall That Has Won the Approval of 92 Per Cent of Patients," p. 10.

People, October 31, 1988, Brad Darrach, "Prince Charles; a Dangerous Age," p. 96; July 15, 1991, "Ah! There's the Rub," p. 53; February 14, 1994, "Age of Chivalry: Pals Say Charles Dumped His Lover for the Throne," p. 56; March 7, 1994, "Royal Romance Comics," p. 193; December 4, 1995, "True Confessions: Defying the Palace, a Calculating Princess Diana Takes the Offensive in the Battle for Britain's Sympathies—and Admits to an Affair of Her Own," p. 92; February 12, 1996, "Prince Charles & Camilla Parker Bowles," p. 171; November 17, 1997, "Healing Holiday: Prince Harry's African Tour with Dad Adds Some Spice to His Life," p. 62.

Philadelphia Inquirer, January 30, 2007, Michael Klein, "The Philadelphia Inquirer Inqlings Column: Like a Little Scotch with That, YRH?"

Planning, November 2, 2001, Miffa Salter, "Salter on . . . Our Latest Obsession with Tsars," p. 9; January 26, 2007, "Royal Flight Plan Stuns Campaigners," p. 48.

PR Week, October 31, 2003, "Opinion: How Do You Make Prince Charles Seem Normal?," p. 8; May 26, 2006, "Media Relations: What the Papers Say—Princes Pull Off a Right Royal Coup," p. 13.

Publishers Weekly, August 2, 1991, review of *Watercolours,* p. 58; October 4, 1993, review of *Highgrove,* p. 75.

Reviewer's Bookwatch, July, 2007, Able Greenspan, review of *The Elements of Organic Gardening.*

Sex Roles: A Journal of Research, March, 2006, David Linton, "Camillagate: Prince Charles and the Tampon Scandal," p. 347.

Spectator, August 18, 2001, Peter Oborne, "The Next Royal Wedding," p. 10; September 28, 2002, "Someone Has It in for the Prince of Wales,"

p. 12; October 5, 2002, "The Prince Is Right; Simon Heffer Says the Prince of Wales Is Performing a Public Service by Making His Views Known to the Government," p. 16; April 16, 2005, "Let Them Reign in Peace," p. 58; February 25, 2006, "Publish the Prince's Diaries: They Would Become an Instant Classic," p. 12; October 28, 2006, "Will Charles Be the First Multicultural Monarch?"

Time, November 11, 1985, Richard Stengel, "A Prince and His Princess Arrive; Charles and Di Mix Style and a Dash of Fun," p. 56; December 4, 1995, "Now on TV: Diana, Goddess of the Haunt," p. 91; November 7, 2005, "People," p. 133.

Town & Country, May, 2001, John Cantrell, "A Princely Paradise," p. 57.

USA Today, February 11, 2005, Cesar G. Soriano, "Prince Charles and Camilla to Wed," p. 1; February 11, 2005, "With Time, Palace and Church Change Their Tune on Divorce," p. 5; April 7, 2005, "Charles and Diana and Charles and Camilla," p. 6; April 8, 2005, "FINALLY Their Happily Ever After," p. 1; April 11, 2005, "Reserved for Royalty," p. 3; October 31, 2005, "Visit Is a Royal Bore for Most in the USA," p. 1; November 2, 2005, "'Our Hearts Go Out to You,'" p. 3; November 7, 2005, "Charles, Camilla Getting Around," p. 3; August 10, 2006, "Big-Time Divorce, British Style," p. 3; August 30, 2007, "Diana Still Creating a Royal Stir," p. 2.

Victoria, August, 2001, "A Gardener at Heart," p. 10.

ONLINE

Prince of Wales Web site, http://www.princeofwales.gov.uk (September 26, 2007).*

* * *

CHOURAQUI, Andre 1917-2007
(Andre Nathanael Chouraqui)

OBITUARY NOTICE— See index for *CA* sketch: Born August 11, 1917, in Ain Temouchent, Algeria; died July 9, 2007, in Jerusalem, Israel. Linguist, translator, poet, and writer. Chouraqui was raised in Algeria in the 1920s, when Algerian Jews like himself lived in close proximity and relative harmony with Muslims and Christians. He spent most of his adult life trying to revive and spread that harmony wherever he went. In the 1970s he produced a twenty-six-volume translation of the Old and New Testaments of the Bible into modern French, using his skills as a linguist to inject into the French translation as much of the meter and rhythm of the original biblical languages as possible. Ten years later Chouraqui produced a similar French translation of the Koran. This work did not escape controversy in the Muslim world. In his introduction to the translation, Chouraqui wrote about the connections that he believed existed between the teachings of Islam and those of Judaism and Christianity. Muslim religious purists countered, on the other hand, that the God of Mohamed must be regarded and treated quite separately from the God of Abraham or the God of Christ. Chouraqui saw his mission as one of uniting people of faith in the veneration of one God, though he did not consider himself a theologian or religious scholar per se. Chouraqui lived in Israel after World War II, working briefly as a government advisor and even serving as a deputy mayor of Jerusalem. He traveled in the West, including three trips to the Vatican to meet with three different popes, and eventually achieved his goal of securing official Vatican recognition of the State of Israel in 1993. Chouraqui wrote several books, including the poetry collection *Cantique pour Nathanael* (1960), a biography of Zionist statesman Theodor Herzl, and various books about Jerusalem as a city and spiritual center of Israel. His essay collections *Lettre à un ami arabe* (1969) and *Lettres à un ami chretien* (1971) represent his contributions to the Jewish-Arab-Christian dialogue.

OBITUARIES AND OTHER SOURCES:

BOOKS

Choraquie, Andre, *A Man in Three Worlds,* translated by Kenton Kilmer, University Press of America (Lanham, MD), 1984.
Chouraqui, Andre, *L'Amour fort comme la mort: Une Autobiographie,* Editions R. Laffont (Paris, France), 1990.

PERIODICALS

Los Angeles Times, July 12, 2007, p. B6.
Times (London, England), August 8, 2007, p. 48.

CHOURAQUI, Andre Nathanael
   See CHOURAQUI, Andre

*   *   *

CLARK, Clare 1967-

PERSONAL: Born 1967, in London, England; married; children: two. *Education:* Trinity College, Cambridge, received degree in history; attended New York University.

ADDRESSES: Home—London, England.

CAREER: Writer. Also worked for Saatchi and Saatchi, London, England; worked for Bartle Bogle Hegarty, London, England, and New York, NY, beginning 1994; became board member.

AWARDS, HONORS: New York Times Editors' Choice award, *Washington Post* Best Book of the Year citation, Orange Prize long list citation, and Quality Paperback Book Club New Voices Award, all for *The Great Stink.*

WRITINGS:

The Great Stink (novel), Harcourt (Orlando, FL), 2005.
The Nature of Monsters (novel), Harcourt (Orlando, FL), 2007.

SIDELIGHTS: Historian and author Clare Clark's first novel, *The Great Stink,* is set against the background of nineteenth-century London. The book, according to a *Publishers Weekly* reviewer, is "a gripping and richly atmospheric glimpse into the literal underworld of Victorian England: the labyrinthine London sewer system." Clark explained in an article appearing in the *Independent Online:* "I found an account of the event that the newspaper famously dubbed the Great Stink. In the early 19th century, the new fashion for water closets meant that instead of household waste being stored in cesspits, as was customary, it was being flushed into the rudimentary drainage system and from there into the Thames. By the 1840s the river was a vast open sewer." "For over a decade Parliament ducked the problem," Clark recounted, "but during the scorching summer of 1858 the stench grew so overpowering that curtains soaked in chloride of lime were hung in the windows of the House."

The Great Stink takes place in 1858, when the intense heat wave has finally forced officials to take steps to address the malodorous sewers of London. Their chosen representative is William May, a veteran of the Crimean War suffering from undiagnosed post-traumatic stress disorder. May's job is to discover how the great stink is escaping from the sewers and to fix the problem. "If William succeeds," Susann Cokal declared in her *New York Times Book Review* critique of the novel, "he will ruin the livelihood of a scavenger called Long Arm Tom, whose life's work has lain not in disposing of sewage but in making the most of it." Long Arm Tom, according to several critics, invited comparisons with characters from the works of Charles Dickens. He "might have enjoyed quaffing ale and swapping horror stories with Dickens's immortal Bill Sykes," concluded a *Kirkus Reviews* contributor. However, Tom's closest Dickensian parallels are probably Gaffer Hexam and Boffin from *Our Mutual Friend*, Cokal explained. "His favorite source is the Thames, ultimate destination of all these effluvia and just as foul as the Stygian tunnels—bobbing with excrement and the occasional corpse, bearing its reek to the nostrils of rich and poor alike."

In *The Nature of Monsters*, Clark steps back another century, to the early 1700s, and examines the conflict between the Age of Reason and the Age of Faith. The key figure in the novel is Eliza Tally, a teenager from the countryside who travels to London partly to take a job as a housemaid and partly to avoid the shame of a pregnancy outside of marriage. Eliza's employer, the apothecary Grayson Black, however, is planning to use her and her unborn child as subjects in an experiment: to determine the extent to which an unborn child can be shaped by its mother's experience. In particular, Black wants to see if he can manipulate Tally's unborn child by exposing her to a variety of phenomena. In a desperate attempt to preserve her life and her freedom, Eliza befriends Black's mute servant girl Mary—also a victim of Black's immoral experiments—and the two of them seek refuge in an uncaring city. "Clark's empathetic portrait of the powerless and the victimized," a *Publisher Weekly* contributor said, "will [again] remind many readers of Dickens." "As she did so successfully in *The Great Stink*," Barbara Love stated in

the *Library Journal*, "Clark again transports readers to another time and place in this mesmerizing tale." "It is bracing to come across a writer who is mistress of such unrelenting Swiftian nastiness," wrote Hilary Mantel in the *Guardian*. "She meets the 18th century on its own terms: knocks its wig off, twists its private parts and spits in its eye."

BIOGRAPHICAL AND CRITICAL SOURCES:

PERIODICALS

Booklist, September 1, 2005, Margaret Flanagan, review of *The Great Stink,* p. 58; March 15, 2007, Margaret Flanagan, review of *The Nature of Monsters,* p. 23.

Books, January 15, 2006, Michael Upchurch, "Novel Carries Readers into the Past and Underground," p. 7.

Bookseller, February 16, 2007, review of *The Nature of Monsters,* p. 12.

Book World, October 16, 2005, Ron Charles, "Going with the Flow: The Suspense—among Other Things—Gets Deep in This Redolent Story about London's Sewers," p. 6.

Kirkus Reviews, July 1, 2005, review of *The Great Stink,* p. 699.

Library Journal, July 1, 2005, Barbara Love, review of *The Great Stink,* p. 65; March 1, 2007, Barbara Love, review of *The Nature of Monsters,* p. 69.

New Statesman, March 12, 2007, Jasmine Gartner, "Hold On to Your Bodice," p. 59.

New York Times Book Review, September 25, 2005, Susann Cokal, "The Waste Land," p. 31; June 17, 2007, "Prenatal Scare," p. 12.

Publishers Weekly, June 20, 2005, review of *The Great Stink,* p. 54; August 8, 2005, Michelle Wildgen, review of *The Great Stink,* p. 105; March 5, 2007, review of *The Nature of Monsters,* p. 39.

Times Literary Supplement, February 18, 2005, Lucasta Miller, "Lower Depths," p. 22.

ONLINE

Curled Up with a Good Book, http://www.curledup.com/ (October 1, 2007), Luan Gaines, "An interview with Clare Clark, author of *The Nature of Monsters.*"

Guardian Online, February 17, 2007, http://books.
guardian.co.uk/ (October 1, 2007), Hilary Mantel,
"How to Beget a Monkey."
Harcourt Books, http://www.harcourtbooks.com/
(October 1, 2007), "Interview with Clare Clark,
author of *The Nature of Monsters.*"
Independent Online, February 11, 2007, http://www.
independent.co.uk/ (October 1, 2007), Clare Clark,
"Clare Clark: Nocturnal Services."

*   *   *

CLEARY, Christopher 1974-

PERSONAL: Born October 28, 1974, in New Brigh-
ton, PA; son of John (a teacher) and Marianne (a
teacher) Cleary; married June 16, 1998; wife's name
Brigette (a teacher). *Ethnicity:* "American." *Educa-
tion:* Kent State University, B.F.A., 1997; DeVry
University, M.P.M., 2003. *Hobbies and other interests:*
Reading, basketball, movies, the music group Pearl
Jam, the Pittsburgh Steelers football team.

ADDRESSES: E-mail—chriscleary@immortalitypress.
com.

CAREER: Writer. Formerly worked as an administrator at a law firm in Atlanta, GA.

WRITINGS:

Writing on the Wall (young adult novel), Immortality
Press, 2007.

PLAYS

Merge with the Infinite, produced at B005 Theater,
1995.
As Yet Untitled, produced at B005 Theater, 1996.
Gettin' It On, produced at Wright-Curtis Theater,
1997.

Contributor to periodicals.

BIOGRAPHICAL AND CRITICAL SOURCES:

ONLINE

Immortality Press Web site, http://www.immortality
press.com (August 13, 2007).

COCHRAN, Heather

PERSONAL: Born in VA; married; children: Wren.
Education: Wellesley College, B.A.; University of
Pennsylvania, M.B.A.

ADDRESSES: Home—Los Angeles, CA. *Agent*—
Katherine Fausset, Curtis Brown, Ltd., 10 Astor Pl.,
New York, NY 10003. *E-mail*—Hkcochran@yahoo.
com.

CAREER: Writer. Has also worked as a bicycle
courier, a construction worker in West Africa, and a
rock-climbing instructor; Academy of Motion Picture
Arts and Sciences, currently a film archivist.

WRITINGS:

Mean Season (novel), Harlequin/Red Dress Ink (Don
Mills, Ontario, Canada), 2004.
The Return of Jonah Gray (novel), Mira (Don Mills,
Ontario, Canada), 2007.

SIDELIGHTS: Heather Cochran debuted as a novelist
with her 2004 title, *Mean Season,* a "a warm, engaging, often funny" work, according to *Booklist* reviewer
Kristine Huntley. The novel features Leanne Gitlin, a
woman in the crux of change. A native of Pinecob,
West Virginia, she has never left home and begins to
wonder if her homespun ways are doing her any good.
Part of the inspiration for these thoughts is the arrival
of movie star Joshua Reed, who is filming a movie in
Pinecob. Leanne happens to be the head of his fan
club, and when he is sentenced to house arrest after a
drunk-driving incident, it is Leanne's house where he
is forced to stay. Reed is a noxious house guest,
however, completely disabusing Leanne of any of the
glamour of actors. She begins to think it is time for a
real relationship with the local man she has been
interested in for years. Further praise for this first
novel came from a *Publishers Weekly* reviewer, who
termed *Mean Season* a "poignant, gently comic story
about growing up and moving on." Similarly, in
People, Andrea L. Sachs commented on the "considerable emotional heft that works seamlessly with the
comic relief" in this novel.

Cochran's second novel, *The Return of Jonah Gray,*
explores love amid the ruins of an IRS audit. Sasha
Gardner, a thirty-something auditor, becomes romanti-

cally involved with the man she is charged with auditing, a gardening journalist named Jonah Gray. The more she examines his financial history, the more she feels drawn to him. She discovers, in fact, that he left his prestigious job at a national newspaper and returned to his hometown newspaper in order to be able to care for his aging father. A reviewer for *Publishers Weekly* commended this second book, remarking that "Cochran's novel is better written than most in the genre, and her take on the divergent lives of arborists and accountants is both poignant and humorous." Huntley, again writing in *Booklist,* also had a positive assessment, calling it "both quirky and highly original."

BIOGRAPHICAL AND CRITICAL SOURCES:

PERIODICALS

Booklist, September 15, 2004, Kristine Huntley, review of *Mean Season,* p. 218; March 15, 2007, Kristine Huntley, review of *The Return of Jonah Gray,* p. 32.
People, September 27, 2004, Andrea L. Sachs, review of *Mean Season,* p. 56.
Publishers Weekly, July 19, 2004, review of *Mean Season,* p. 142; January 8, 2007, review of *The Return of Jonah Gray,* p. 35.

ONLINE

Heather Cochran Home Page, http://www.heather cochran.com (September 14, 2007).*

*   *   *

COCKEY, Tim
    See HAWKE, Richard

*   *   *

COHN, Jonathan

PERSONAL: Married; children: two. *Education:* Attended Harvard University.

ADDRESSES: Home—Ann Arbor, MI. *Office*—New Republic, 1331 H St. N.W., Ste. 700, Washington, DC 20005.

CAREER: Writer for *American Prospect,* 1991-97; *New Republic,* Washington, DC, executive editor for two years, senior editor, 1997—. Henry J. Kaiser Family Foundation, media fellow, 2002-04; Demos (think tank), senior fellow.

WRITINGS:

Sick: The Untold Story of America's Health Care Crisis—and the People Who Pay the Price, HarperCollins Publishers (New York, NY), 2007.

Has contributed to periodicals, including *Boston Globe, Mother Jones, New York Times, Slate,* and *Washington Monthly.*

SIDELIGHTS: As a journalist Jonathan Cohn has covered domestic and social policies, with a special focus on social welfare and health-care issues. His 2007 book, *Sick: The Untold Story of America's Health Care Crisis—and the People Who Pay the Price,* takes a more in-depth view of America's health-care crisis by humanizing the problem. Cohn presents numerous striking personal stories of people who have lost their insurance due to job loss; they subsequently watch as family members suffer and die. Speaking with Mary Carmichael in *Newsweek,* Cohn noted: "Our health-care problems have definitely gotten worse since the 1990s. People are really struggling to afford medical care. But does that mean the public is ready to embrace universal health care? I'm not so sure." Yet that is in part the prescription that Cohn delivers, for, as he recounts, the United States is the only industrialized nation that does not guarantee its citizens health care. Totally privatized, capitalist-system medicine does not seem to be meeting the challenge of the increasing numbers of uninsured.

Sick received widespread critical attention. Writing in the *New York Times Book Review,* Sally Satel faulted Cohn for failing to provide enough alternatives to the current health-care delivery system, but nonetheless praised the work as "important" in furthering the debate. *Library Journal* contributor Dick Maxwell declared the same work "a convincing collection of stories about people dealing with the inequities and problems in the present system," while a *Kirkus Reviews* critic called *Sick* a "compelling portrait of a deeply troubled system." Similar praise came from a *Publishers Weekly* reviewer: "Cohn is eloquent, and he's good at using case studies to dramatize and explain complex issues." *Columbia Journalism Review* critic Kevin Drum observed that "Cohn is a terrific storyteller, as well as one who doesn't insist on twisting his tales into polemics."

BIOGRAPHICAL AND CRITICAL SOURCES:

PERIODICALS

Booklist, March 1, 2007, Vanessa Bush, review of *Sick: The Untold Story of America's Health Care Crisis—and the People Who Pay the Price,* p. 45.

Chicago Tribune Books, May 26, 2007, Robert D. Johnston, "An Ailing System: A Look at America's Health-Care Crisis and a Possible Cure," p. 9.

Columbia Journalism Review, July 1, 2007, Kevin Drum, "A Spoonful of Sugar: How to Explain the Health Care Crisis," p. 60.

Commentary, July 1, 2007, Yuval Levin, "Diagnosis & Cure," p. 80.

Kirkus Reviews, February 1, 2007, review of *Sick,* p. 108.

Library Journal, March 1, 2007, Dick Maxwell, review of *Sick,* p. 99.

Newsweek, April 16, 2007, Mary Carmichael, "It's a Chronic Condition; Our Current Health-Care Debate Is Rooted in the 1930s," p. 43.

New York Times Book Review, April 8, 2007, Sally Satel, review of *Sick.*

Publishers Weekly, January 22, 2007, review of *Sick,* p. 175.

Washington Monthly, May 2007, Phillip Longman, "Misdiagnosed: Why All the Money in the World Won't Fix What's Wrong with America's Health Care System," p. 59.

Washington Post Book World, April 1, 2007, review of *Sick,* p. 9; May 20, 2007, "What Ails Us," p. 7.

ONLINE

New Republic Web site, http://www.tnr.com/ (September 14, 2007), brief biography of Jonathan Cohn.

Newsweek Online, http://www.msnbc.msn.com/ (April 10, 2007), Mary Carmichael, "Healthy Reading: 'Sick' Examines U.S. Health Care."

Sick the Book, http://www.sickthebook.com (September 14, 2007).*

*   *   *

COHN, Norman 1915-2007
  (Norman Rufus Cohn)

OBITUARY NOTICE— See index for *CA* sketch: Born January 12, 1915, in London, England; died of generative heart disease, July 31, 2007, in Cambridge, England. Historian, linguist, educator, and author. Cohn's wide-ranging, award-winning research explored what he himself described as a single theme: a recurring human compulsion to save the world and open the door to paradise by eradicating a group of people, often a marginalized and relatively helpless group of outsiders, suspected of causing the ills of their day. This compulsion, he believed, consumed the downtrodden masses from ancient times to the present day, whether the trigger was religious, political, or economic, and it wreaked the most damage under the direction of a charismatic leader convinced of his own infallibility. Cohn saw distinct parallels between medieval apocalyptic movements that tended to gain strength at the approach of a millennium and the totalitarian political regimes of the twentieth century. His historical research was grounded in rigorous training in ancient and modern languages, his background as the child of a religiously mixed marriage, and his post-World War II encounters with Jewish and Soviet refugees of war and genocide. Cohn taught French and history at various British universities, serving most notably as the Astor-Wolfson professor of History at the University of Sussex, where he also directed the university's Columbus Centre for research on genocide and persecution. He was best known, however, for his influential studies of sects and messianic movements. Cohn was awarded the Cleveland Foundation's Anisfield-Wolf Book Award in race relations for *Warrant for Genocide: The Myth of the Jewish World-Conspiracy and the Protocols of the Elders of Zion* (1966), a surprise best seller given its scholarly tone. Cohn's other writings include *The Pursuit of the Millennium: Revolutionary Millenarians and Mystical Anarchists of the Middle Ages* (1957), *Europe's Inner Demons: An Enquiry Inspired by the*

Great Witch-Hunt (1975), *Cosmos, Chaos, and the World to Come: The Ancient Roots of Apocalyptic Faith* (1993), and *Noah's Flood: The Genesis Story in Western Thought* (1996).

OBITUARIES AND OTHER SOURCES:

PERIODICALS

Chicago Tribune, August 28, 2007, p. 6.
Los Angeles Times, September 2, 2007, p. B15.
New York Times, August 27, 2007, p. A19.
Times (London, England), August 23, 2007, p. 69.

* * *

COHN, Norman Rufus
See COHN, Norman

* * *

COLANTUONI, Joe 1948-

PERSONAL: Born April 28, 1948, in Brooklyn, NY; son of Vincent Colantuoni.

ADDRESSES: E-mail—bch4joe@comcast.net.

CAREER: Writer.

WRITINGS:

The Surfmaster: A Tale of Love and Hope (nonfiction), Outskirts Press (Parker, CO), 2006.
The Melody of the Soul (nonfiction), Outskirts Press (Parker, CO), 2007.

SIDELIGHTS: Joe Colantuoni told *CA:* "I always wanted to be writer. As a youth, I worked on short stories in the manner of Edgar Allan Poe and Rod Serling. Two years ago, I started documenting dreams and 'visions.' I wanted to leave a legacy for my fam- ily of what I really believed in and how I felt one's life should be lead. Both books are loosely based on real events which happened to me or people I have met.

"I want my books to touch people and make them examine how they are living their lives. The feedback that I am receiving seems to indicate that the books are affecting the readers positively. Readers are seeing themselves in my work. I believe that I have written books that have a universal appeal because they both speak to the human nature. I look forward to additional writing and meeting more people who have read my books."

* * *

COTE, Nancy

PERSONAL: Born in Fall River, MA; daughter of Edward (a milk deliverer) and Lorraine (a homemaker) Marek; married Michael Cote (a high school teacher); children: Melissa, Katherine, John. *Ethnicity:* "Austrian descent." *Education:* Attended University of Massachusetts and Dartmouth College; earned B.F.A.

ADDRESSES: Home—Somerset, MA. *E-mail*—nancycote@comcast.net.

CAREER: Writer and illustrator. Rhode Island School of Design, instructor.

MEMBER: Society of Children's Book Writers and Illustrators, Freelance Artists Network, Rhode Island School of Design Freelance Group.

AWARDS, HONORS: Oppenheim Toy Portfolio Gold Seal Award for *When I Feel Angry* and *Mrs. Greenberg's Messy Hanukkah;* Sidney Taylor Notable Book Award for *Mrs. Greenberg's Messy Hanukkah.*

WRITINGS:

AUTHOR AND ILLUSTRATOR; CHILDREN'S BOOKS

Palm Trees, Four Winds Press (New York, NY), 1993.

Flip-Flops, Albert Whitman (Morton Grove, IL), 1998.

It Feels Like Snow, Boyds Mills Press (Honesdale, PA), 2003.

It's All about Me, Putnam (New York, NY), 2005.

ILLUSTRATOR:

(With Denise Harris) Clement Moore, *The Night before Christmas: A Pop-Up Book,* Bell Books (Honesdale, PA), 1993.

Sharon Phillips Denslow, *Woollybear Good-Bye,* Four Winds Press (New York, NY), 1994.

Amy Hest, *Ruby's Storm,* Four Winds Press (New York, NY), 1994.

Virginia Kroll, *Fireflies, Peach Pies, and Lullabies,* Simon & Schuster Books for Young Readers (New York, NY), 1995.

Linda Glaser, *The Borrowed Hanukkah Latkes,* Albert Whitman (Morton Grove, IL), 1997.

Marion Hess Pomeranc, *The Can-Do Thanksgiving,* Albert Whitman (Morton Grove, IL), 1998.

Abby Levine, *Gretchen Groundhog, It's Your Day!,* Albert Whitman (Morton Grove, IL), 1998.

Sarah Marwil Lamstein, *I Like Your Buttons!,* Albert Whitman (Morton Grove, IL), 1999.

Cornelia Maude Spelman, *When I Feel Angry,* Albert Whitman (Morton Grove, IL), 2000.

Leslie Kimmelman, *Round the Turkey: A Grateful Thanksgiving,* Albert Whitman (Morton Grove, IL), 2002.

Leslie Kimmelman, *Happy 4th of July, Jenny Sweeney!,* Albert Whitman (Morton Grove, IL), 2003.

Linda Glaser, *Mrs. Greenberg's Messy Hanukkah,* Albert Whitman (Morton Grove, IL), 2004.

Virginia Kroll, *Jason Takes Responsibility,* Albert Whitman (Morton Grove, IL), 2005.

Pat Brisson, *Tap-Dance Fever,* Boyds Mills Press (Honesdale, PA), 2005.

Teresa Bateman, *Hamster Camp: How Harry Got Fit,* Albert Whitman (Morton Grove, IL), 2005.

Virginia Kroll, *Good Neighbor Nicholas,* Albert Whitman (Morton Grove, IL), 2006.

Virginia Kroll, *Honest Ashley,* Albert Whitman (Morton Grove, IL), 2006.

Lori Anne Ries, *Mrs. Fickle's Pickles,* Boyds Mills Press (Honesdale, PA), 2006.

Virginia Kroll, *Good Citizen Sarah,* Albert Whitman (Morton Grove, IL), 2007.

Virginia Kroll, *Makayla Cares about Others,* Albert Whitman (Morton Grove, IL), 2007.

Lacy Finn Borgo, *Big Mama's Baby,* Boyds Mills Press (Honesdale, PA), 2007.

Also illustrator of textbooks. Contributor of art work to magazines, including *Highlights* and *High Five.*

SIDELIGHTS: Nancy Cote told *CA:* "My first book, *Palm Trees,* was inspired by my daughter's curly hair. I had never thought of myself as a writer, but the story just unfolded in my mind and I desperately wanted to illustrate it. I initially wrote the story in rhyme and submitted it to one of the major publishers in New York City. I was soon contacted by an editor who loved the story idea and asked me to rewrite it in prose. It took me close to a year, and when I felt as though I could not change another word, I re-illustrated the story and resubmitted it to another major publisher. Within a few weeks, I was notified that it had been accepted for publication.

"Several books later, I still have a hard time referring to myself as an author, I am an illustrator with a creative mind. I've developed a love for writing over the years, but personally I find writing to be a much more difficult process than illustrating. Drawing and painting have always been like breathing for me. I've done it all my life without thinking about it. It's always been what I have loved to do most.

"Lately I've become more and more excited about writing as well. It is the most incredible feeling to create characters that children can relate to and be inspired by. I feel so strongly in touch with my feelings and memories of childhood and see the world every day as though I am seeing it for the first time. For this I am very grateful and know that my senses are my riches in life.

"To have the opportunity to be able to translate my thoughts into words and pictures is a dream come true. I feel indescribably fortunate to have a full-time career in the field of children's publishing. I have so many ideas for stories in my head that it has become difficult to narrow down which ideas I would like to focus on first.

"My life as an illustrator alone keeps me quite busy, but I now make time to continue my writing as well. I have discovered that, if I allow my imagination to be free, there are stories to be developed all around me. I have no pattern as to how I begin developing an idea. It may start with an illustration, a certain word, a piece of music, or through memory or even a dream. There is no formula in my thought process. I am very spontaneous and do not live by any routine. So in essence, one might say I live from moment to moment. But that is what keeps me happy—this sense of freedom."

Cote later told *CA:* "I am often asked how I got interested in the field of Children's Books. The summer that I graduated from college, we adopted our first daughter, Melissa. My husband, Mike, and I loved being parents and soon had two additional children, Kate and John. I read that reading to children was one of the most important things that you could do for child development and began a daily routine of reading dozens of books each day that we borrowed from our local libraries. We all loved reading so much that all three children became avid readers before they entered kindergarten. I developed a passion for the stories and illustrations found in Children's Books and became inspired to write and illustrate my own.

"My first story was inspired by my daughter Melissa's curly hair and many of the characters in my work are comprised of traits found in my friends and family. I have always used our family pets as characters in my work as well. Our family has always been very uninhibited and we talk, laugh and express ourselves fully. My approach to writing and illustrating is fairly simple. I am very much in touch with my inner child and enjoy each and every moment of life. Everything inspires me and I find that I have infinite resources in just waking up each morning. My family and I love the outdoors and go hiking whenever we can. I love bike riding and running, meeting new people and spending time with family and friends. I look for adventures everyday and find them wherever I go. I truly appreciate all animals and love being able to depict the relationships that people have with pets and nature. Music is an important tool for me as I work. I feel that it frees my approach and it helps me to become more expressive. I work in a studio that is heated with only the use of a wood stove. It keeps me cozy and warm as I work each day. My two dogs Maggie (basset hound) and Frankie (mini dachshund) join me in my studio and keep me company. I like to volunteer wherever I am needed and I teach a class in Children's Book Illustration at Rhode Island School of Design in the Continuing Ed. Certificate Program."

COUCH, Dick 1943-

PERSONAL: Born 1943, in MS; married; wife's name Julia. *Education:* United States Naval Academy, graduated, 1967. *Hobbies and other interests:* Skiing, hiking, fly fishing.

ADDRESSES: Home—Ketchum, ID. *E-mail*—dick@dickcouch.com.

CAREER: Central Intelligence Agency, former Maritime Operations Officer, beginning 1972; lecturer at the Naval Academy, the Air Force Academy, the Naval Special Warfare Center, the JFK Special Forces Center and School, the FBI Academy, the Naval Postgraduate School, the Joint Special Operations University, and the Academy Leadership Forum. *Military service:* Navy SEALS, 1967-72; Naval Reserve until 1997; served in Vietnam; attained rank of captain.

WRITINGS:

NONFICTION

The Warrior Elite: The Forging of SEAL Class 228, photographs by Cliff Hollenbeck, Crown Publishers (New York, NY), 2001.
To Be a U.S. Navy SEAL, photographs by Cliff Hollenbeck, MBI (St. Paul, MN), 2003.
The Finishing School: Earning the Navy SEAL Trident, foreword by Bob Kerrey, Crown Publishers (New York, NY), 2004.
Down Range: Navy SEALs in the War on Terrorism, foreword by Richard Danzig, Crown (New York, NY), 2005.
Chosen Soldier: The Making of a Special Forces Warrior, foreword by Robert D. Kaplan, Crown Publishers (New York, NY), 2007.

FICTION

Seal Team One, Avon (New York, NY), 1991.
Pressure Point, Putnam (New York, NY), 1992.
Silent Descent, Putnam (New York, NY), 1993.
Rising Wind, Naval Institute Press (Annapolis, MD), 1996.

The Mercenary Option, Pocket Books (New York, NY), 2003.

Covert Action, Pocket Books (New York, NY), 2005.

SIDELIGHTS: Dick Couch is the author of several nonfiction works and novels, many of which concern the elite U.S. Navy SEALs. Couch writes from personal experience, for he was a platoon leader of a SEAL squad during the Vietnam War and led one of the few successful operations to free American POWs. His first work, the novel *Seal Team One,* appeared in 1991. This debut novel follows the fortunes of James McConnell, a skeet shooter with dreams of entering the Navy and training as a frogman. Accomplishing this, he is sent to Vietnam as a SEAL unit leader. A reviewer for *Publishers Weekly* was less than complimentary about this work, calling it "violence-glorifying," as well as "rife with racist and misogynist comments." Couch's second novel, *Pressure Point,* a thriller set in the Pacific Northwest, was better received. A *Publishers Weekly* contributor praised this tale of a Palestinian terrorist intent on stealing a Trident missile: "Taut writing and crisp dialogue further enhance the appeal of one of the year's better adventure novels." In *Rising Wind,* the Navy SEALs are again called in, this time to foil the plans of a Japanese terrorist who threatens to unleash America's horde of chemical weapons on the American mainland. Writing in *Booklist,* Gilbert Taylor reported that "within the bounds of this all-action-no-message genre, Couch commands comfortably right through the climactic firefight."

Couch turns to nonfiction in other works. With *The Warrior Elite: The Forging of SEAL Class 228,* he was allowed close access to the training of SEALs; he also was able to use his own personal experience as a SEAL to present an "energetic read for sailors, SEALs, and the greater population of armchair SEALs," according to a *Kirkus Reviews* critic. He documents the six-month training such volunteers undergo in the Basic Underwater Demolition/SEAL program, or BUD/S. Himself a graduate of Class 45, Couch examines the three-part training program, beginning with arduous physical training, a period that ends in what is called Hell Week, with the use of sleep deprivation and long bouts in the water to weed out less likely candidates. Those who survive this first part of training progress to the next phases, where they learn special skills, including demolition and night swimming. The *Kirkus Reviews* critic noted that the "superior element here is the empathy and texture within [Couch's] character depictions." Similar praise came from *Booklist* reviewer Roland Green, who felt that Couch's books is "unique" among many other books about the SEALs.

Couch focuses on another branch of elite fighting forces in his 2007 work, *Chosen Soldier: The Making of a Special Forces Warrior.* Here he follows the training of an Army Special Forces Class, better known as the Green Berets. Couch tracked a batch of recruits for ten months to construct his narrative, noting that only one in five makes it through the training. As with *The Warrior Elite,* Couch focuses on many individual recruits as well as their trainers in this "book worthy of the quality of the soldiers it profiles," according to *Booklist* contributor Green. A *Kirkus Reviews* critic was less impressed with *Chosen Soldier,* however, describing it as "macho prose full of praise for would-be warriors and the men who train them, seemingly designed to enthrall young men, boost recruitment and please the army." A higher assessment came from a *Publishers Weekly* reviewer who concluded that "Couch loves the Green Berets too much to look beneath the surface; still, he tells an entertaining story."

BIOGRAPHICAL AND CRITICAL SOURCES:

PERIODICALS

Booklist, May 15, 1996, Gilbert Taylor, review of *Rising Wind,* p. 1568; October 15, 2001, Roland Green, review of *The Warrior Elite: The Forging of SEAL Class 228,* p. 360; March 15, 2007, Roland Green, review of *Chosen Soldier: The Making of a Special Forces Warrior,* p. 7.

California Bookwatch, June 2007, review of *Chosen Soldier.*

Christian Science Monitor, November 8, 2001, review of *The Warrior Elite,* p. 20.

Kirkus Reviews, September 1, 2001, review of *The Warrior Elite,* p. 1259; December 15, 2006, review of *Chosen Soldier,* p. 1252.

Library Journal, June 1, 1992, Elsa Pendleton, review of *Pressure Point,* p. 172.

Military History, June, 2002, Doug Pricer, review of *The Warrior Elite,* p. 70; June 2007, review of *Chosen Soldier,* p. 69.

New York Times Book Review, July 26, 1992, Newgate Callendar, review of *Pressure Point,* p. 13.

Publishers Weekly, May 10, 1991, review of *Seal Team One,* p. 277; May 11, 1992, review of *Pressure Point,* p. 53; April 1, 1996, review of *Rising Wind,* p. 56; January 8, 2007, review of *Chosen Soldier,* p. 45.

Tribune Books (Chicago, IL), March 16, 2003, review of *The Warrior Elite,* p. 2.

Vietnam, October 2005, Carl O. Schuster, "First Tested in Combat in Vietnam, Navy SEALs Today Undergo Training Based Heavily on the Lessons of Experience," p. 50.

Wall Street Journal, December 21, 2001, David M. Shribman, review of *The Warrior Elite,* p. 10.

Washington Post Book World, October 16, 2005, Chris Bray, review of *Down Range: Navy SEALs in the War on Terrorism,* p. 9.

ONLINE

Random House Web site, http://www.randomhouse. com/ (September 14, 2007), brief biography of Dick Couch.

United States Naval Academy Web site, http://www. usna.edu/ (September 14, 2007), "Captain Dick Couch, USN Retired."*

* * *

COULSON, Joseph 1957-

PERSONAL: Born 1957, in Detroit, MI. *Education:* State University of New York at Buffalo, Ph.D.

ADDRESSES: Home—Cambridge, MA.

CAREER: Author. Former teacher; former editorial director, Great Books Foundation, Chicago, IL.

AWARDS, HONORS: Gray Writing Fellowship; Book of the Year Award, Gold Medal in Literary Fiction, *ForeWord* magazine, for *The Vanishing Moon.*

WRITINGS:

POETRY

The Letting Go, Hundred Pound Press (Detroit, MI), 1984.

A Measured Silence, Hundred Pound Press (Detroit, MI), 1986.

Graph, Bombshelter Press (Los Angeles, CA), 1990.

NOVELS

The Vanishing Moon, Archipelago Books (New York, NY), 2004.

Of Song and Water, Archipelago Books (Brooklyn, NY), 2007.

PLAYS

(With William Relling, Jr.) *A Saloon at the Edge of the World,* produced as *Edge of the World,* 1996.

(With William Relling, Jr.) *Junkyard of the Gods,* 1999.

EDITOR

(Editor, with Peter Temes, Jim Baldwin) *Modern American Poetry,* Great Books Foundation (Chicago, IL), 2002.

(Editor, with Nancy Carr and Steve Hettleman) *Reader's Guide to "The Scarlet Letter,"* Great Books Foundation (Chicago, IL), 2003.

(Editor, with Donald Whitfield and Ashley Preston) *Keeping Things Whole: Readings in Environmental Science,* Great Books Foundation (Chicago, IL), 2003.

(Editor, with Mike Levine and Steve Hettleman) *Reader's Guide to "Narrative of the Life of Frederick Douglass, an American Slave,"* Great Books Foundation (Chicago, IL), 2004.

SIDELIGHTS: Joseph Coulson is an American poet and novelist. His 2004 novel, *The Vanishing Moon,* is "a somberly beautiful family saga," according to *Booklist* reviewer Donna Seaman. The book opens in the worst years of the Great Depression and follows the fortunes and misfortunes of the Tollman family: children Phil, Stephen, Maggie, and Myron, and their blind mother and less-than-competent father. At one point the family is so poor that they live in a tent near Cleveland. Set there and in Detroit, where Coulson was raised, the novel is told through the eyes of many characters. It follows the Tollman children through the Second World War, into the era of the Civil Rights

Movement, and on to the 1960s and the Vietnam War. Coulson particularly focuses on the difficult relationship of the brothers Phil and Stephen over several generations. Seaman went on to observe: "Assured and purposeful, first-time novelist Coulson infuses each surprising and evocative moment with great feeling and mythic resonance as he leapfrogs forward in time." Reba Leiding, writing in *Library Journal*, had further praise for this first novel: "Coulson movingly evokes the feel of Rust Belt cities in hard times." *Curled Up with a Good Book* critic Luan Gaines also had high praise for the book, writing that "Coulson balances the heartbreak of reality with scenes of unearthly beauty, the tenderness and passion of first love and the impulsive yearning of young men for a world that has a place for them." Gaines further commended the "fully-fleshed characters" in this debut novel.

Coulson's second novel, *Of Song and Water*, features an itinerant jazz guitarist Jason "Coleman" Moore in a tale that once again spans the decades. This time the author covers the 1930s through to more contemporary times, with the plot again partly set in Detroit. Michael Lindgren, writing for *KGB Bar*, described this novel as an "overtly poetic Midwestern Gothic," as well as a "convincing if static portrait of loss and regret." Told in flashbacks that leap through time, *Of Song and Water* delves into the lives not only of Coleman, but also his grandfather and father, who were both sailors on the Great Lakes, just like Coleman once was. Down on his luck and drinking too much, Coleman can no longer play guitar because of injuries to his hand. The book details his difficult relations with the women in his life, from his ex-wife to his lover to his teenage daughter. Also complicated are the relationships between the white Coleman and other jazz musicians, many of whom are black. Seaman, writing again in *Booklist*. pronounced *Of Song and Water* a "complexly elegiac tale [that] is, in part, a tribute to [Coulson's] mentor, poet and Great Lakes mariner Stephen Tudor." *Library Journal* contributor Christine DeZelar-Tiedman felt that despite some confusion caused by Coulson's nonlinear story line, "the book has a certain flow and rhythm that seems appropriate to its themes, and all loose ends are tied up satisfactorily." Higher praise came from a *Publishers Weekly* reviewer who commented that "Coulson moves fluidly between the past and the present, and the novel is ultimately quiet, affecting and redemptive." Likewise, Lindgren concluded: "The novel's evocative power stems largely from its deftly-managed narrative structure."

BIOGRAPHICAL AND CRITICAL SOURCES:

PERIODICALS

Booklist, January 1, 2004, Donna Seaman, review of *The Vanishing Moon,* p. 820; March 1, 2007, Donna Seaman, review of *Of Song and Water,* p. 59.
Boston Magazine, April, 2007, Sara Corrigan, review of *Of Song and Water,* p. 30.
Library Journal, December, 2003, Reba Leiding, review of *The Vanishing Moon,* p. 164; January 1, 2007, Christine DeZelar-Tiedman, review of *Of Song and Water,* p. 88.
Publishers Weekly, January 15, 2007, review of *Of Song and Water,* p. 31.

ONLINE

Archipelago Books Web site, http://www.archipelago books.com/ (September 14, 2007), brief biography of Joseph Coulson.
Curled Up with a Good Book, http://www.curledup. com/ (September 14, 2007), Luan Gaines, review of *The Vanishing Moon.*
Five Branch Tree, http://www.fivebranchtree.blogspot. com/ (August 13, 2007), review of *Of Song and Water.*
Joseph Coulson Home Page, http://www.joseph coulson.com (September 14, 2007).
KGB Bar, http://www.kgbbar.com/ (September 14, 2007), Michael Lindgren, review of *Of Song and Water.**

*   *   *

CRANDALL, Susan

PERSONAL: Born in Noblesville, IN; married; children: one son, one daughter. *Hobbies and other interests:* Writing, reading, movies, music, outdoor activities.

ADDRESSES: Home—Noblesville, IN. *E-mail*—susan@susancrandall.net.

CAREER: Worked as a dental hygienist. *More* magazine, editor.

AWARDS, HONORS: Two National Readers Choice Awards; Golden Quill; RITA Award, Romance Writers of America.

WRITINGS:

NOVELS

Back Roads, Warner Books (New York, NY), 2003.

The Road Home, Warner Books (New York, NY), 2004.

Magnolia Sky, Warner Books (New York, NY), 2004.

Promises to Keep (sequel to *The Road Home*), Warner Forever (New York, NY), 2005.

On Blue Falls Pond, Warner Forever (New York, NY), 2006.

A Kiss in Winter, Warner Forever (New York, NY), 2007.

SIDELIGHTS: Author Susan Crandall is fond of outdoor adventure, and her most frequent partner in such pursuits has been her daughter, Brook Wilkinson. Together they have been involved in racing cars, bungee jumping, long-distance bicycling, and, in 2003, climbing Mt. Kilimanjaro in East Africa. Crandall's adventurous spirit carries over into her novels, which feature women who lead challenging and interesting lives.

Crandall's debut, *Back Roads,* features Leigh Mitchell, the thirty-year-old sheriff of Glens Crossing, Indiana. Leigh's response to newcomer Will Scott's invitation to ride the carnival's Ferris wheel with him is uncharacteristic. She agrees, and then accepts his offer of a beer. When they dance, the romance is set in motion, although Will, who has a past that he must keep hidden, knows that he is making a mistake in beginning this new relationship. Will once spent time with an aunt in Glens Crossing, however, and he finds it impossible to leave the place he came to love and the woman with whom he is now falling in love. He takes a job as a mechanic, but soon after, when a local teen is missing, he becomes a suspect. He is unwilling to share his past with Leigh, who must investigate, and she is torn between her faith in Will and his reluctance to tell her more. *BookLoons* Web site reviewer Martina Bexte wrote: "*Back Roads* is an accomplished and very satisfying first novel."

Crandall takes a character from her second book, *The Road Home,* and makes him the protagonist in *Magnolia Sky.* Luke Boudreau's reversal of an order was partly responsible for the death of his fellow Army Ranger and friend, Calvin Abbott, as they carried out a rescue mission. Now he is in Grover, Mississippi, visiting Calvin's mother, Olivia, younger brother, Cole, and the wife he did not know Calvin had. Olivia welcomes him warmly and insists that Luke stay awhile, particularly to help ease Cole's loss of his older brother. Luke helps with the family's landscaping business, all the while falling in love with Analise, Calvin's widow.

Promises to Keep is the sequel to *The Road Home,* and is the story of Molly Boudreau, a Boston pediatrician who abandons her practice to shelter a baby orphaned as the result of a gangland-style shooting. Molly returns to her hometown of Glens Crossing, but is tracked down by Dean Coletta, the brother of the victim, a war correspondent who believes Molly knows more than she is admitting about his sister's killing.

The protagonist of *On Blue Falls Pond* is Glory Harrison, who returns to the Tennessee town where her husband and unborn child died as the result of a fire. She discovers that Scott, the small son of Eric Wilson, the fire chief who saved her life, has developmental or mental problems that are going untreated because Eric's former wife refuses to acknowledge them. Although she no longer wants Eric, she also doesn't want anyone else to have him, including Glory.

Caroline Rogers is torn between her dream and a new love who settles in the place she had planned to leave in *A Kiss in Winter.* Caroline has raised her stepsiblings since the deaths of their parents, and she will soon be able to pursue a career as a photographer and leave her small hometown in Kentucky. Psychiatrist Mick Larson leaves his practice and buys her family farm, creating the obstacle which Caroline may or may not want to overcome. *Library Journal* contributor Kristin Ramsdell wrote that in this story Crandall explores various issues "with consummate skill and perceptiveness."

BIOGRAPHICAL AND CRITICAL SOURCES:

PERIODICALS

Booklist, August 1, 2004, Lynne Welch, review of *Magnolia Sky,* p. 1908; February 15, 2005, Lynne

Welch, review of *Promises to Keep,* p. 1067; December 15, 2005, Diana Tixier Herald, review of *On Blue Falls Pond,* p. 30; January 1, 2007, Diana Tixier Herald, review of *A Kiss in Winter,* p. 67.

Library Journal, December 1, 2006, Kristin Ramsdell, review of *A Kiss in Winter,* p. 103.

Mediaweek, October 6, 2003, Anne Torpey-Kemph, "It's All Uphill This Week for *More* Editor Susan Crandall and Her 24-year-old Daughter Brook Wilkinson, an Assistant Editor at *Conde Nast Traveler,*" p. 17.

ONLINE

BookLoons, http://www.bookloons.com/ (August 9, 2007), Martina Bexte, reviews of *Back Roads* and *Magnolia Sky.*

OnceWritten.com, http://www.oncewritten.com/ (September 15, 2003), Monica Poling, review of *Back Roads.*

Susan Crandall Home Page, http://www.susancrandall.net (September 4, 2007).*

* * *

CRESPI, Camilla T. 1942-
(Trella Crespi, Camilla Trinchieri)

PERSONAL: Born 1942, in Prague, Czechoslovakia; dual American and Italian citizenship, became U.S. citizen, 1997. *Education:* Graduate of Barnard College; Columbia University, M.F.A.

ADDRESSES: E-mail—camcrespi@aol.com.

CAREER: Worked in the Italian film industry; sold pasta, worked as a translator and at an advertising firm, all in New York, NY.

WRITINGS:

(As Camilla Trinchieri) *The Price of Silence* (crime novel), Soho Press (New York, NY), 2007.

"SIMONA GRIFFO" MYSTERY SERIES

(As Trella Crespi) *The Trouble with a Small Raise,* Zebra (New York, NY), 1991.

(As Trella Crespi) *The Trouble with Moonlighting,* Zebra (New York, NY), 1991.

(As Trella Crespi) *The Trouble with Too Much Sun,* Zebra (New York, NY), 1992.

The Trouble with Thin Ice, HarperCollins (New York, NY), 1993.

The Trouble with Going Home, HarperCollins (New York, NY), 1995.

The Trouble with a Bad Fit: A Novel of Food, Fashion, and Mystery, HarperCollins (New York, NY), 1996.

The Trouble with a Hot Summer, HarperCollins (New York, NY), 1997.

SIDELIGHTS: Camilla T. Crespi has written under several versions of her name, including, most recently, her birth name, Camilla Trinchieri. She penned the first three books of her "Simona Griffo" mystery series as Trella Crespi, then changed to the name by which she is most recognized. Crespi is the daughter of an Italian father and American mother. She worked in the Italian film industry as a dubber with many well-known Italian actors and producers. She came to New York in 1980 and wrote her first book as fictional revenge on the boss who wouldn't give her a raise. *The Trouble with a Small Raise* was the first in her series and marked the beginning of her career as an author.

The Trouble with Thin Ice is the fourth book in the series. Simona Griffo, an Italian expatriate, lives in Greenwich Village, works in advertising, and is in a relationship with New York homicide detective Stan Greenhouse, who is the father of fourteen-year-old Willy. She is also a pasta lover, perhaps drawn from her creator's own experiences selling pasta in the Village when she first came to New York. In this story the couple attends the wedding of friends, but the happy occasion is soon overshadowed by the murder of a widow who had announced that she was selling her Frank Lloyd Wright-designed home to the interracial couple.

The Trouble with Going Home finds Simona back in Rome with her mother who becomes involved when Tamar, the American student of art teacher Mirella Monti, is stabbed. Simona steps in to help and soon discovers that Tamar had discovered something in the archives of the prince she was dating that may be a clue to her death. In *The Trouble with a Bad Fit: A*

Novel of Food, Fashion, and Mystery, Simona and Stan investigate the murder of an aging fashion model. In reviewing the novel for the *New York Times Book Review,* Suzy Menkes noted that "Ms. Crespi has an eye for fashion detail that gives the novel a cutting edge."

Simona and her Russian partner, Dimitri, vacation in the Hamptons and investigate murder in *The Trouble with a Hot Summer,* described by a *Publishers Weekly* contributor as being "a story as lazy and easy to take as a summer afternoon."

BIOGRAPHICAL AND CRITICAL SOURCES:

PERIODICALS

Booklist, January 1, 1994, Mary Carroll, review of *The Trouble with Thin Ice,* p. 809; July 1, 1997, GraceAnne A. DeCandido, review of *The Trouble with a Hot Summer,* p. 1801.

Library Journal, April 1, 1996, Rex E. Klett, review of *The Trouble with a Bad Fit: A Novel of Food, Fashion, and Mystery,* p. 121.

New York Times Book Review, April 21, 1996, Suzy Menkes, review of *The Trouble with a Bad Fit.*

Publishers Weekly, December 6, 1993, review of *The Trouble with Thin Ice,* p. 59; November 28, 1994, review of *The Trouble with Going Home,* p. 45; March 18, 1996, review of *The Trouble with a Bad Fit,* p. 61; June 2, 1997, review of *The Trouble with a Hot Summer,* p. 56.

School Library Journal, September, 1997, Pam Johnson, review of *The Trouble with a Hot Summer,* p. 239.

ONLINE

Camilla T. Crespi Home Page, http://members.aol.com/camcrespi (August 10, 2007).*

*   *   *

CRESPI, Trella
See CRESPI, Camilla T.

*   *   *

CROSS, Janine

PERSONAL: Born in England; Canadian citizen; children: two.

ADDRESSES: Home—North Vancouver, British Columbia, Canada. *E-mail*—janinecross@shaw.ca.

CAREER: Writer. Has worked in a chocolate factory and a veterinary hospital; cofounded a private school.

WRITINGS:

Touched by Venom: Book One of the Dragon Temple Saga, Roc (New York, NY), 2005.
Shadowed by Wings: Book Two of the Dragon Temple Saga, Roc (New York, NY), 2006.
Forged by Fire: Book Three of the Dragon Temple Saga, Roc (New York, NY), 2007.

Also author of a comedy book.

SIDELIGHTS: Janine Cross is the author of the "Dragon Temple Saga," a "dystopian feminist fantasy trilogy," as a *Publishers Weekly* contributor described the three novels. Writing about the second novel in the series, *Shadowed by Wings: Book Two of the Dragon Temple Saga,* another reviewer for *Publishers Weekly* felt compelled to deliver the following warning: "These are not [fantasy novelist Ann] McCaffrey dragons. Think X-rated Tolkien set in the Middle East." Indeed, Cross caused a stir in the fantasy community with her edgy depiction of a society worshipping and at the same time enslaving dragons, and with her graphic descriptions of both violence and sex— including rape and bestiality. Cross explained, in part, her inspiration for writing the fantasy trilogy, as quoted by Lynn Viehl on *Paperback Writer:* "One thing in particular inspires/drives me: how human beings, women and children being my main interest, can survive tragedy and persecution, torture and deprivation—not only survive but continue with life. These things are happening every day, and have happened in our little corner of the world in the not-so-distant past, too. Really, my books are the stories of these people." Marcus Richards, writing on *Blogcritics.org,* noted that Cross was using dragons to a new and more complex purpose in her saga: "Cross has created a world where the dragons are both the focal point for human existence, and the tool for a religious elite to exert control over a conquered people."

The first novel in the series, *Touched by Venom: Book One of the Dragon Temple Saga,* lays the groundwork for the series, introducing the young female protagonist

Zarq. As a contributor for *Mad Times* related in a review of *Shadowed by Wings:* "The protagonist is a woman in a male-dominated society who's become addicted to dragon venom which when ingested is a stimulant and hallucinogen." Zarq's situation goes from bad to worse as her serf family and other inhabitants of Malacar are ruled by the tenets of the Temple of the Dragons. Only the noble born are allowed to keep dragons, and women are most definitely second-class citizens. Sent into exile into the Dead Zone, Zarq learns the cruel truths of life, but ultimately is set to tending male dragons after a "unsexing" ritual. Marcus felt that Cross's opening installment is "a brilliant depiction of a despotic theocracy whose sole purpose is to insure that a very few people have power over the majority," and went on to observe that her "writing has a gritty reality to it that is not often been seen in fantasy until recently, but is becoming more prevalent." Others took exception to the grittiness of the writing. A *Kirkus Reviews* critic, for example, found *Touched by Venom* to be "a truly ridiculous and at times revolting fantasy," as well as "wretched drivel." Liz Henry, however, writing in *Strange Horizons*, had a far different assessment of *Touched by Venom*, describing it as a "thoughtful, enjoyable work of feminist speculative fiction. . . . a woman's hero-tale, the story of a survivor; a true dystopian fantasy, and one written with an awareness of non-Western cultures." Similarly, *Library Journal* contributor Jackie Cassada thought it is "a fascinating story of love and vengeance," and found that Cross "combines skillful storytelling with sensually evocative details."

Cross carries the story forward in *Shadowed by Wings*, in which the now teenaged Zarq continues to fight for her own station in the male-dominated society. She hopes that she, in fact, will become a dragon master, while at the same time she must battle her addiction to the venom of the dragons. Cross brings her trilogy to a conclusion with *Forged by Fire: Book Three of the Dragon Temple Saga*, in which Zarq has established her own dragon colony, but seeks to unravel the ancient secret of the dragons to rid the society of the oppression of the Dragon Temple and the autocratic stranglehold it holds on the populace. Cassada, reviewing this final installment in *Library Journal*, commented that Cross "combines an unusual approach to dragons and dragon lore with strong characters and an exotic, tribal culture." Further praise for this concluding volume came from a *Publishers Weekly* reviewer who felt that Cross "handles challenging themes of addiction, graphic sexuality, racism, slavery and the oppression of children and women."

BIOGRAPHICAL AND CRITICAL SOURCES:

PERIODICALS

Kirkus Reviews, October 1, 2005, review of *Touched by Venom: Book One of the Dragon Temple Saga,* p. 1056.

Library Journal, November 15, 2005, Jackie Cassada, review of *Touched by Venom,* p. 64; April 15, 2007, Jackie Cassada, review of *Forged by Fire: Book Three of the Dragon Temple Saga,* p. 78.

Publishers Weekly, September 12, 2005, review of *Touched by Venom,* p. 47; June 12, 2006, review of *Shadowed by Wings: Book Two of the Dragon Temple Saga,* p. 35; February 12, 2007, review of *Forged by Fire,* p. 67.

ONLINE

Bewildering Stories, http://www.bewilderingstories.com/ (September 15, 2007), Danielle L. Parker, review of *Touched by Venom.*

Blogcritics.org, http://www.blogcritics.org/ (May 3, 2006), Richard Marcus, review of *Touched by Venom.*

Janine Cross Home Page, http://janinecross.ca (September 15, 2007).

Mad Times, http://www.tomcat.com/madtimes/ (December 30, 2006), review of *Shadowed by Wings.*

Paperback Writer, http://www.pbackwriter.blogspot.com/ (November 16, 2005), Lynn Viehl, review of *Touched by Venom.*

SF Canada, http://www.sfcanada.ca/ (September 15, 2007), Celu Amberstone, "An Author's Cinderella Story: Interview with Janine Cross."

SF Site, http://www.sfsite.com/ (September 15, 2007), Donna McMahon, review of *Touched by Venom.*

Strange Horizons, http://www.strangehorizons.com/ (February 6, 2006), Liz Henry, review of *Touched by Venom.*

*   *   *

CROSSLEY, James G.

PERSONAL: Education: University of Nottingham, Ph.D.

ADDRESSES: Office—Department of Biblical Studies, University of Sheffield, Arts Tower, Western Bank, Sheffield S10 2TN, England. *E-mail*—jgcrossley10@yahoo.co.uk; james.crossley@sheffield.ac.uk.

CAREER: University of Sheffield, Sheffield, England, lecturer in New Testament studies.

WRITINGS:

The Date of Mark's Gospel: Insight from the Law in Earliest Christianity, T & T Clark International (New York, NY), 2004.

(Editor, with C. Karner) *Writing History, Constructing Religion,* Ashgate Publishing (Burlington, VT), 2005.

Why Christianity Happened: A Sociohistorical Account of Christian Origins (26-50 CE), Westminster John Knox Press (Louisville, KY), 2006.

Judaism, Jewish Identities, and the Gospel Tradition: Essays in Honour of Maurice Casey, Equinox (Oakville, CT), 2008.

Coeditor of the Equinox "Biblical World" series; maintains a blog, *Earliest Christian History.*

SIDELIGHTS: James G. Crossley is a new Testament scholar whose studies include the origins of Christianity. Crossley maintains a blog where he posts published and soon-to-be published writings. In an interview with Jim West of *Biblioblogs.com,* Crossley said of his blog *Earliest Christian History,* "Yet testing my work was never the reason for starting the blog. One key reason was political, and in different senses of the phrase. It now seems naive to me at least, but I once thought there were more politically radical people in scholarship, though I don't think that anymore. This disappointed me when it hit home and it disappointed me in terms of blogging because there, I thought, more than anywhere in biblical scholarship, would such views be found. The situation is quite the opposite, I think."

In *Why Christianity Happened: A Sociohistorical Account of Christian Origins (26-50 CE),* Crossley notes that Jesus observed Jewish law and followed dietary rules but that within two decades following his death, the Christian movement was discarding these laws. He argues that this swing was instrumental in the spread of the Christian religion. Converts included those who practiced Judaism lite, engaging with their more observant friends and neighbors but disregarding the rules regarding abstinence from eating pork or practicing circumcision, for example.

Crossley told *Chronicle of Higher Education* interviewer David Glenn: "And it's in this context that Paul can come along and give his great teachings on justification by faith. I think that you can see that context as a social, or almost an economic, phenomenon."

Crossley told *CA:* "At present, Noam Chomsky, Edward Said, Maurice Casey, Derek Gregory, and Gilbert Achcar are particularly influential on my work."

When asked which of his books is his favorite, Crossley said: "The forthcoming one: because I have just written it, it is at least relevant for once, it involves my major interest in politics and foreign policy, and I tend to put my other books to the back of my mind and forget about them."

When asked what kind of effect he hopes his books will have, he said: "Of the previous books, I hope that some New Testament scholars would at least attempt to look at early Jewish sources in more detail rather than pay lip service to 'Second Temple Judaism.' I would also hope that some New Testament scholars may pay closer attention to the social historical causes underlying Christian origins."

BIOGRAPHICAL AND CRITICAL SOURCES:

PERIODICALS

Chronicle of Higher Education, February 9, 2007, David Glenn, "Why Early Christians Stopped Observing Jewish Codes," interview.

Journal of Religion, October, 2005, Daniel J. Harrington, review of *The Date of Mark's Gospel: Insight from the Law in Earliest Christianity,* p. 649.

Journal of Theological Studies, October, 2006, David Instone-Brewer, review of *The Date of Mark's Gospel,* p. 647.

ONLINE

Biblioblogs.com, http://www.biblioblogs.com/ (August 10, 2007), Jim West, "Jim West Interviews James Crossley."

Earliest Christian History, http://www.earliestchristian history.blogspot.com (August 10, 2007), author's blog.

University of Sheffield Web site, http://www.shef.ac.uk/ (August 10, 2007), author biography.

*   *   *

CUMMINS, Ann

PERSONAL: Born in Durango, CO; daughter of Cyril P. and Barbara R. Cummins; married Steven Evans Willis (a musician), April 14, 2001. *Education:* Johns Hopkins University, M.F.A., 1987; University of Arizona, Tucson, M.F.A., 1989.

ADDRESSES: Home—Oakland, CA; Flagstaff, AZ. *Office*—Department of English, Northern Arizona University, Flagstaff, AZ 86011-6032. *E-mail*—ann. cummins@nau.edu.

CAREER: Northern Arizona University, Flagstaff, professor of English.

AWARDS, HONORS: Arizona Commission on the Arts, fellow, 1990, 1994; Lannan Foundation fellow, 2002-03.

WRITINGS:

Red Ant House: Stories, Houghton Mifflin (Boston, MA), 2003.
Yellowcake (novel), Houghton Mifflin (Boston, MA), 2007.

Author's work represented in anthologies, including *The Best American Short Stories 2002,* Houghton Mifflin (Boston, MA). Contributor to periodicals, including *McSweeney's* and the *New Yorker.*

SIDELIGHTS: Ann Cummins is the daughter of Irish immigrants who settled in Colorado. Her father, a uranium mill worker, moved the family to Shiprock, New Mexico, when she was nine, and Cummins graduated from high school on the Navajo Indian reservation.

The English professor's first book is a collection titled *Red Ant House: Stories.* The stories are set in small Southwestern towns, and protagonists tend to be young people lacking parents or guidance, but even in the tales about adults, there is frequently the overriding emotion of loss and the need to escape. Two of the stories, "Trapeze" and "Bitterwater," are about white families living on the reservation. Cummins lost her own father to lung disease while she was writing "Headhunter," which she told *Homestead Review Online* interviewer Kathryn Petrucelli was her favorite. She said: "I think my characters tend to be lonely souls. And I do think they are looking for moments of connection with the different people who fascinate them. They also are attracted to fascinating people. They're pulled into dramas by people who would not normally be good friends to them. Frequently I'll find my plot in those kinds of tensions: characters who are very different and the attractions are centered on the differences."

In reviewing the collection for the *Literary Potpourri* Web site, Laura M. Schneider wrote: "Cummins drills to the center of what makes these characters tick, what they long for, fear and what they dream—and how this works into life on the desolate landscape where her characters reside. Many of the characters are the types who imagine they're invisible to the rest of the world. She reminds us that there's always something to see on the surface, but just imagine what you'll find if you dig a little deeper. This collection, mutually charming and disturbing, is a wonderful beginning for this promising writer."

Cummins draws on her knowledge of the uranium mining industry in her debut novel, *Yellowcake.* The title refers to the uranium concentrate used in making nuclear fuel. Ryland Mahoney, a foreman at a uranium mine until it closed in 1991, now depends on an oxygen tank to stay alive. Dying of cancer is Woody Atcitty, a Navajo man whose bank-officer daughter joins with Ryland's wife to seek compensation from the mining company. Ryland wants nothing to do with the action however, refusing to believe that his job caused his illness. The story is a saga of two families with very different values that, nevertheless, become intertwined because of the relationships of its members and the impact of mining on both people and the natural environment. "Cummins brilliantly conflates the insidious damage wrought by radiation sickness with the maladies of the soul," concluded *Booklist* contributor Donna Seaman.

BIOGRAPHICAL AND CRITICAL SOURCES:

PERIODICALS

Booklist, April 1, 2003, Brendan Dowling, review of *Red Ant House: Stories,* p. 1375; February 1, 2007, Donna Seaman, review of *Yellowcake,* p. 29.
Entertainment Weekly, March 16, 2007, Ben Spier, review of *Yellowcake,* p. 72.
Kirkus Reviews, February 1, 2003, review of *Red Ant House,* p. 159; November 15, 2006, review of *Yellowcake,* p. 1143.
Library Journal, January 1, 2007, Jenn B. Stidham, review of *Yellowcake,* p. 88.
Publishers Weekly, April 7, 2003, review of *Red Ant House,* p. 46.
Washington Post Book World, March 25, 2007, review of *Yellowcake,* p. 6.

ONLINE

Bookreporter.com, http://www.bookreporter.com/ (August 11, 2007), Stephen M. Deusner, review of *Red Ant House.*
Homestead Review Online (literary magazine of Hartnell College), http://hartnell.edu/ (August 11, 2007), Kathryn Petrucelli, interview (transcript of interview recorded July 14, 2003).
Literary Potpourri, http://www.literarypotpourri.com/ (August 11, 2007), Laura M. Schneider, review of *Red Ant House.*
Northern Arizona University Department of English Web site, http://jan.ucc.nau.edu/ (August 11, 2007), faculty biography.*

*   *   *

CURRIER, Chester S.
See CURRIER, Chet

CURRIER, Chet 1945-2007
 (Chester S. Currier)

OBITUARY NOTICE— See index for *CA* sketch: Born March 26, 1945, in NY; died of prostate cancer, July 29, 2007, in Santa Monica, CA. Financial journalist, columnist, and publisher of crossword puzzles. Currier began his career with the Associated Press news syndicate as a general news reporter for the Kansas City bureau in 1970. He moved to the New York, New York, office in 1973, where his interests soon turned to business news and Wall Street. He reported on the stock market, investments, mutual funds, and personal finance for many years. He was the author of several popular columns, including "Ticker Talk," "Weekly Wall Street," and "On the Money." In 1999 Currier became a columnist for the *Bloomberg News;* his last column was published one month before his death. His financial writings were published in books such as *Investor's Encyclopedia* (1985), *15 Minute Investor: Prosperity and Peace of Mind for the Price of a Newspaper* (1986), and *No Cost/Low Cost Investing* (1987). Currier was also an aficionado of crossword puzzles; he created hundreds of "Sunday-Size" puzzles for the Associated Press, beginning in 1979. Some of these were collected in the books *Associated Press Sunday Crossword Book* (1983) and *Scads of Crosswords: 300 Challenging Sunday-Size Puzzles from the Associated Press* (2005).

OBITUARIES AND OTHER SOURCES:

PERIODICALS

New York Times, August 3, 2007, p. C9.

D

DABASHI, Hamid 1951-

PERSONAL: Born June 15, 1951, in Ahvaz, Khuzestan, Iran; married Golbarg Bashi (a professor). *Education:* University of Pennsylvania, Ph.D., 1984.

ADDRESSES: Office—Department for Middle East and Asian Languages and Cultures, Columbia University, New York, NY 10027 *E-mail* hd14@columbia.edu.

CAREER: Columbia University, New York, NY, currently Hagop Kevorkian Professor of Iranian Studies and Comparative Literature. Founder of Dreams of a Nation, a Palestinian Film Project. Advisor to various film companies; jury member for international film awards; media consultant on Middle East issues.

AWARDS, HONORS: Postdoctoral fellowship, Harvard University.

WRITINGS:

(Editor, annotator, and author of introduction, with Seyyed Hossein Nasr and Seyyed Vali Reza Nasr) *Shiism: Doctrines, Thought, and Spirituality,* State University of New York Press (Albany, NY), 1988.

(Editor, annotator, and author of introduction, with Seyyed Hossein Nasr and Seyyed Vali Reza Nasr) *Expectation of the Millennium: Shiism in History,* State University of New York Press (Albany, NY), 1989.

Authority in Islam: From the Rise of Muhammad to the Establishment of the Umayyads, Transaction Publishers (New Brunswick, NJ), 1989.

(Editor) Parviz Sayyad, *Parviz Sayyad's Theater of Diaspora: Two Plays, "The Ass" and "The Rex Cinema Trial,"* foreword by Peter Chelkowlski, Mazda Publishers (Costa Mesa, CA), 1993.

Theology of Discontent: The Ideological Foundations of the Islamic Revolution in Iran, New York University Press (New York, NY), 1993, 2nd edition, Transaction Publishers (New Brunswick, NJ), 2006.

(With Peter Chelkowski) *Staging a Revolution: The Art of Persuasion in the Islamic Republic of Iran,* New York University Press (New York, NY), 1999.

Truth and Narrative: The Untimely Thoughts of Ayn al-Qudat al-Hamadhani, Curzon (Richmond, Surrey, England), 1999.

Onomadopean: Visite à Amir Parsa, Editions Caracterers (Paris, France), 2000.

Close Up: Iranian Cinema, Past, Present, and Future, Verso (New York, NY), 2001.

Shirin Neshat: La última palabra = The Last Word, MUSAC (León, Spain), 2005.

(Editor and author of introduction) *Dreams of a Nation: On Palestinian Cinema,* preface by Edward Said, Verso (New York, NY), 2006.

Iran: A People Interrupted, New Press (New York, NY), 2007.

Masters and Masterpieces of Iranian Cinema, Mage Publishers (Washington, DC), 2007.

Also contributor of numerous articles to professional journals. Dabashi's works have been translated into

Japanese, German, French, Spanish, Italian, Russian, Hebrew, Danish, Arabic, Korean, Persian, Portuguese, Polish, Turkish, Urdu, and Catalan.

SIDELIGHTS: Hamid Dabashi is an internationally recognized culture critic whose areas of expertise include Iranian studies, medieval and modern Islam, comparative literature, world cinema, and the philosophy of art. He has written widely on all these subjects, publishing numerous books and articles both in the United States and around the world. With his *Authority in Islam: From the Rise of Muhammad to the Establishment of the Umayyads,* Dabashi looks to the historic role of Islam in a work at once "original, creative and insightful," according to John L. Esposito in the *Journal of the American Oriental Society.* Esposito further commented: "In this sociological study, Dabashi utilizes [pioneering sociologist Max] Weber's concept of charismatic authority to analyze the threefold (Sunni, Shii, and Khariji) socio-cultural responses to and transformation of Muhammad's authority and prophetic movement." Dabashi's study ranges from pre-Islamic Arab culture through the influence of Muhammad and to the consolidation of the first Muslim caliphate, the Umayyad dynasty of the seventh century. Esposito found this book a "significant addition to scholarship on the history and sociology of Islam,"

Dabashi's *Theology of Discontent: The Ideological Foundations of the Islamic Revolution in Iran,* which he began in the early 1970s before the Iranian Revolution of 1979, focuses on many of the major Iranian personalities whose thoughts ultimately led to the revolution. Dabashi attempts to show that the revolution in Iran was the final outgrowth of and reaction to nineteenth-century colonialism. *Staging a Revolution: The Art of Persuasion in the Islamic Republic of Iran,* written with Peter Chelkowski, examines how those behind the Iranian Revolution used various media to establish their message both during the revolution and the war with Iraq in the 1980s. According to Daniel Pipes in the *Middle East Quarterly,* these media included "political speeches, print and electronic media, school books, movies, songs, poems, slogans, graffiti, murals, posters, banners, stamps, banknotes, coins, calendars, and even chewing-gum wrappers." The authors gather all these various propaganda measures within the covers of their book. "What a catalogue the authors have assembled of esthetic depravity and political falsification," noted Pipes.

Daniel Brumberg, writing in the *Political Science Quarterly,* had further praise for the same title, declaring it an "extraordinary study."

Dabashi takes a more general look at his birthplace in the more recent *Iran: A People Interrupted,* in which he argues that Iran and its people are much more complex than the West, particularly the United States, believes. For Dabashi, Iran has been existing in the past and may continue to be a victim of colonialism. Despite its leadership that "flirts with fascism and seeks smoke screens of its own," as a *Kirkus Reviews* critic observed, it is a "democracy all the same, even if a flawed one." The same critic called the book "an eye-opening, if partial, consideration of a nation in need of understanding." A *Publishers Weekly* reviewer provided a mixed assessment of *Iran,* commenting that it is "peppered alternately with delightful vignettes from [Dabashi's] Iranian youth and dense academic-speak." For this same contributor the work is "unlikely to win over the uninitiated."

Dabashi is also the author of several works on Iranian cinema. His *Close Up: Iranian Cinema Past, Present, and Future* "places Iranian films into the broader context of the political and intellectual struggles that have characterized twentieth-century Iranian history," according to *Cineaste* reviewer Rahul Hamid. For Hamid, *Close Up* "provides much-needed historical, political, and artistic context as well as critical insight into Iranian cinema." Similarly, Dabashi's *Masters and Masterpieces of Iranian Cinema* "explores the development of Iranian cinema objectively and subjectively via the people who created it, without the need for restrictive answers," concluded Benjamin D. Malczewski in *Library Journal.*

BIOGRAPHICAL AND CRITICAL SOURCES:

PERIODICALS

Annals of the American Academy of Political and Social Science, July, 1994, Mehran Kamrava, review of *Theology of Discontent: The Ideological Foundations of the Islamic Revolution in Iran,* p. 185.
Choice, April, 1993, M. Swartz, review of *Theology of Discontent,* p. 1330; March, 2002, R.D. Sears, review of *Close Up: Iranian Cinema, Past, Present, and Future,* p. 1247.

Chronicle of Higher Education, October 13, 2006, Richard Byrne, "A Collision of Prose and Politics."

Cineaste, spring, 2002, Rahul Hamid, review of *Close Up*.

Contemporary Sociology, September, 1991, Serif Mardin, review of *Authority in Islam: From the Rise of Muhammad to the Establishment of the Umayyads*, p. 733; September, 1994, Said Amir Arjomand, review of *Theology of Discontent*, p. 671.

Film Quarterly, summer, 2003, Azadeh Farahmand, review of *Close Up*.

Fuse Magazine, February, 2001, review of *Close Up*, p. 43.

International Journal of Middle East Studies, May, 1996, Ervand Abrahamian, review of *Theology of Discontent*, p. 299; May, 2002, Ali Asghar Seyed-Gohrab, review of *Truth and Narrative: The Untimely Thoughts of Ayn al-Qudat al-Hamadhani*, p. 375.

Journal of Asian History, spring, 1991, Victor Danner, review of *Expectation of the Millennium: Shiism in History*.

Journal of Religion, April, 1991, Michael Sells, review of *Expectation of the Millennium*, p. 298.

Journal of the American Oriental Society, January 1, 1993, John L. Esposito, review of *Authority in Islam*, p. 122.

Kirkus Reviews, December 15, 2006, review of *Iran: A People Interrupted*, p. 1253.

Library Journal, April 1, 2007, Benjamin D. Malczewski, review of *Masters and Masterpieces of Iranian Cinema*, p. 93.

Medium Aevum, fall, 2000, Alan Jones, review of *Truth and Narrative*.

Middle East Journal, winter, 1992, review of *Authority in Islam*.

Middle East Quarterly, June, 2000, Daniel Pipes, review of *Staging a Revolution: The Art of Persuasion in the Islamic Republic of Iran*, p. 86.

Muslim World, July 1, 1989, Ismail K. Poonawala, review of *Shiism: Doctrines, Thought, and Spirituality*, p. 262; July 1, 1990, Jane I. Smith, review of *Expectation of the Millennium*, p. 282; April, 1991, Steven P. Blackburn, review of *Authority in Islam*, p. 168; January 1, 1995, Mahmood Monshipouri, review of *Theology of Discontent*, p. 156; July 2006, Joseph Lumbard, review of *Truth and Narrative*, p. 532.

Political Science Quarterly, spring, 2001, Daniel Brumberg, review of *Staging a Revolution*.

Publishers Weekly, January 8, 2007, review of *Iran*, p. 45.

Reference & Research Book News, May, 2006, review of *Theology of Discontent*.

Sight and Sound, December, 2006, Ali Jaafar, review of *Dreams of a Nation: On Palestinian Cinema*, p. 94; May, 2007, Sheila Whitaker, review of *Masters and Masterpieces of Iranian Cinema*, p. 100.

Sociological Analysis, spring, 1991, Robert Bianchi, review of *Authority in Islam*.

Times Higher Education Supplement, January 21, 1994, Dermot Clinch, review of *Theology of Discontent*, p. 18; July 5, 2002, "Iran Holds Up Its Mirror of Truths," p. 26.

World Politics, July, 1995, review of *Theology of Discontent*, p. 555.

ONLINE

Campus Watch, http://www.campus-watch.org/ (June 12, 2003), "Interview with Hamid Dabashi."

Columbia University Web site, http://www.columbia.edu/ (September 15, 2007), faculty profile of Hamid Dabashi.

Discoverthenetworks.org, http://www.discoverthenetworks.org/ (September 15, 2007), brief profile of Hamid Dabashi.

Hamid Dabashi Home Page, http://www.hamiddabashi.com (September 15, 2007).

Iranian.com, http://www.iranian.com/ (August 22, 2006), Peyvand Khorsandi, "Dabashi on Picnics."

ZNet, http://www.zmagazine.org/ (August 4, 2006), Foaad Khosmood, "Lolita and Beyond."*

* * *

DALEY-CLARKE, Donna

PERSONAL: Education: University of East Anglia, M.A.

CAREER: Writer.

AWARDS, HONORS: Commonwealth First Novel Prize, 2006, for *Lazy Eye;* also Hawthornden fellowship and writer's awards from the Society of Authors, the Jerwood foundation, and the Arts Council England.

WRITINGS:

Lazy Eye, Scribner (London, England), 2005, MacAdam Cage (San Francisco, CA), 2007.

Short fiction has been read on Radio 4 in Great Britain, has appeared in magazines, and has been anthologized.

SIDELIGHTS: In her first novel, *Lazy Eye,* Donna Daley-Clarke tells the story of Geoffhurst Johnson, a young black man in Great Britain who witnesses the murder of his mother by his father after a heated argument in the kitchen. The story is told in flashbacks by various characters in the book, including Geoffhurst and Geoffhurst's father, Sonny. The title of the book refers to Geoffhurst's lazy eyes, which make him see things in more than one way. "I haven't read many better descriptions of a killer losing control," wrote a *Telegraph.co.uk* contributor about Sonny's version of the murder. The novel also details Sonny's life as a one of the first black footballers in Great Britain who, partly because of the prejudice he faces on and off the field, ultimately self-destructs. *Lazy Eye* received widespread praise from the critics. Caroline M. Hallsworth, writing in the *Library Journal,* noted that Daley-Clarke's "prose is lyrical and original." In a review on the *Black Britain* Web site, Julie Ann Ryan referred to *Lazy Eye* as "imaginative and funny" and also noted: "Whenever the story seemed to be dragging down a little the author would inject something into the story line just at the right time to get the readers attention again and draw you back into its world."

BIOGRAPHICAL AND CRITICAL SOURCES:

PERIODICALS

Booklist, March 1, 2007, Hazel Rochman, review of *Lazy Eye,* p. 61.
Bookseller, February 10, 2006, "British Wins at Commonwealth," p. 11.
Library Journal, March 1, 2007, Caroline M. Hallsworth, review of *Lazy Eye,* p. 69.
Publishers Weekly, January 29, 2007, review of *Lazy Eye,* p. 43.

ONLINE

Black Britain, http://www.blackbritain.co.uk/ (July 10, 2006), Julie Ann Ryan, "Donna Daley Clarke rekindles memories in *Lazy Eye.*"

British Council, http://www.britishcouncil.org/ (October 6, 2007), Donna Daley-Clarke, "Writers Talk Books."
Telegraph.co.uk, http://www.telegraph.co.uk/ (July 27, 2005), "Witness to a Murder," review of *Lazy Eye.**

*   *   *

DANDO-COLLINS, Stephen

PERSONAL: Male.

ADDRESSES: Home—Noosa Heads, Queensland, Australia.

CAREER: Writer. Also worked as a graphic designer, copywriter, creative director, senior advertising agency executive, and independent marketing consultant.

WRITINGS:

Finklestein's Miracle, Dandy Books (Leura, New South Wales, Australia), 1989.
Cobbers: The Complete Lives and Loves of the Bloke and Ginger Mick, Angus & Robertson (Sydney, New South Wales, Australia), 1997.
Caesar's Legion: The Epic Saga of Julius Caesar's Elite Tenth Legion and the Armies of Rome, John Wiley (New York, NY), 2002.
Standing Bear Is a Person: The True Story of a Native American's Quest for Justice, Da Capo Press (Cambridge, MA), 2004.
Nero's Killing Machine: The True Story of Rome's Remarkable Fourteenth Legion, John Wiley (Hoboken, NJ), 2005.
Cleopatra's Kidnappers: How Caesar's Sixth Legion Gave Egypt to Rome and Rome to Caesar, John Wiley (Hoboken, NJ), 2006.
Mark Antony's Heroes: How the Third Gallica Legion Saved an Apostle and Created an Emperor, John Wiley (Hoboken, NJ), 2006.

SIDELIGHTS: Stephen Dando-Collins began his career writing novels and eventually turned his attention to history. Commenting on the author's book, *Standing Bear Is a Person: The True Story of a Native*

American's Quest for Justice, Whispering Wind contributor Dawn Karima Pettigrew noted: "Stirring events, memorable characters, formidable obstacles and an impressive conflict combine with uncluttered writing to create a worthwhile work." In the book, the author focuses on an incident in which Standing Bear led twenty-seven other Ponca Indians off a reservation that they were sent to by the U.S. government, land that was unsuitable for farming. Many Ponca Indians died as a result, including Standing Bear's own son, which spurred Standing Bear to leave the reservation so he could take his son to his tribe's traditional burying grounds. Standing Bear's rebellion eventually came to the notice of the Omaha Soldier Lodge and made headlines in the *Omaha Daily Herald,* leading to a courtroom drama. In addition to Pettigrew, several other critics had high praise for Dando-Collins's account. Writing in *Booklist,* Rebecca Maksel commented that the author "captures the full drama of Standing Bear's struggle." *Kliatt* contributor Patricia Moore referred to *Standing Bear Is a Person* as a "smoothly written and gripping narrative," also commenting that it is presented with "clear and fast-paced prose."

The author has also written several books focusing on military legions in the Roman army. In *Cleopatra's Kidnappers: How Caesar's Sixth Legion Gave Egypt to Rome and Rome to Caesar,* Dando-Collins focuses on the Sixth Legion's successful defense of Julius Caesar's empire when attacked by the Egyptian Army in Alexandria. The author also writes of the politics of the time and of Caesar's famous interlude with Cleopatra, Queen of Egypt. "The author entertains and, through chatty digressions on 'Roman civilization,' military practices, myths, and historical and geographical curiosities, also instructs the general reader," wrote Adrian Tronson in the *Historian.* Several reviewers noted, however, that some of the author's "history" is highly conjectural, including David S. Michaels, writing on *RomanaArmy.com.* Nevertheless, Michaels also commented that the author "is a competent writer who can spin a fairly lively narrative. His style weaves together straightforward exposition with novelistic details and snatches of dialog." In addition, Michaels wrote of the book: "At root it is a sometimes compelling tale of brave men enduring a bitter trial of strength to emerge victorious."

Mark Antony's Heroes: How the Third Gallica Legion Saved an Apostle and Created an Emperor recounts how this legion, which was formed in Gaul, played a key role in the Roman army as Rome established its imperial power in the century prior to Christ's birth. "This is an interesting and well-written work that should appeal to general readers," wrote Jay Freeman in *Booklist.* Referring to the author as "a good storyteller," *Library Journal* contributor Clay Williams also wrote: "The period he covers is fascinating for the historiography it has inspired."

BIOGRAPHICAL AND CRITICAL SOURCES:

PERIODICALS

Booklist, December 15, 2004, Rebecca Maksel, review of *Standing Bear Is a Person: The True Story of a Native American's Quest for Justice,* p. 701; November 15, 2006, Jay Freeman, review of *Mark Antony's Heroes: How the Third Gallica Legion Saved an Apostle and Created an Emperor,* p. 20.

Choice: Current Reviews for Academic Libraries, October, 2002, R.T. Ingoglia, review of *Caesar's Legion: The Epic Saga of Julius Caesar's Elite Tenth Legion and the Armies of Rome,* p. 335.

Historian, winter, 2006, Adrian Tronson, review of *Cleopatra's Kidnappers: How Caesar's Sixth Legion Gave Egypt to Rome and Rome to Caesar.*

Journal of Military History, July, 2005, review of *Nero's Killing Machine: The True Story of Rome's Remarkable Fourteenth Legion,* p. 899.

Kirkus Reviews, October 1, 2004, review of *Standing Bear Is a Person,* p. 946.

Kliatt, January, 2006, Patricia Moore, review of *Standing Bear Is a Person,* p. 33.

Library Journal, December 1, 2004, Elizabeth Morris, review of *Standing Bear Is a Person,* p. 134; October 1, 2005, Sean Michael Fleming, review of *Cleopatra's Kidnappers,* p. 92; January 1, 2007, Clay Williams, review of *Mark Antony's Heroes,* p. 122.

Reference & Research Book News, February, 2005, review of *Caesar's Legion,* p. 280; February, 2005, review of *Standing Bear Is a Person,* p. 60.

Whispering Wind, November-December, 2004, Dawn Karima Pettigrew, review of *Standing Bear Is a Person,* p. 37.

ONLINE

RomanArmy.com, http://www.romanarmy.com/cms/ (October 7, 2007), David S. Michaels, review of *Cleopatra's Kidnappers.**

DARTY, Peggy

PERSONAL: Married.

ADDRESSES: Home—CO; FL. *E-mail*—peggydarty@
aol.com.

CAREER: Writer. Has worked in film, researched for
the Columbia Broadcasting System, Inc. (CBS), and
taught in writing workshops around the country.

MEMBER: Red Hat Society.

WRITINGS:

FICTION

Mountain to Stand Strong, Zondervan (Grand Rapids,
MI), 1984.
Kincaid of Cripple Creek, Zondervan (Grand Rapids,
MI), 1985.
Cimarron Sunset, Zondervan (Grand Rapids, MI),
1986.
The Wailing Winds of Juneau Abbey, Zebra (New
Westminster, British Columbia, Canada), 1990.
The Crimson Roses of Fountain Court, Zebra (New
Westminster, British Columbia, Canada), 1991.
The Captured Bride of Aspenwood, Zebra (New West-
minster, British Columbia, Canada), 1992.
The Widowed Bride of Raven Oaks, Zebra (New West-
minster, British Columbia, Canada), 1992.
The Precious Pearls of Cabot Hall, Zebra (New West-
minster, British Columbia, Canada), 1992.
Angel Valley, Palisades (Sisters, OR), 1995.
Morning Mountain, Barbour Publishing (Uhrichsville,
OH), 1995.
Sundance, Palisades (Sisters, OR), 1996.
Seascape, Palisades (Sisters, OR), 1996.
Song of the Dove, Barbour Publishing (Uhrichsville,
OH), 1997.
Moonglow, Palisades (Sisters, OR), 1997.
Promises, Palisades (Sisters, OR), 1997.
Memories, Palisades (Sisters, OR), 1998.
Spirits, Palisades (Sisters, Or), 1998.
Summer Place, Barbour Publishing (Uhrichsville,
OH), 1998.
Look Homeward, Angel, Heartsong Presents (Uhrichs-
ville, OH), 2000.

My Beloved Waits, Heartsong Presents (Uhrichsville,
OH), 2001.
Lilly's Dream, Heartsong Presents (Uhrichsville, OH),
2004.

"COZY MYSTERY" SERIES

When the Sandpiper Calls, WaterBrook Press
(Colorado Springs, CO), 2005.
When Bobbie Sang the Blues, WaterBrook Press
(Colorado Springs, CO), 2007.
When Zeffie Got a Clue, WaterBrook Press (Colorado
Springs, CO), 2008.

Contributor to books, including *A Christmas Joy,* 1995;
*Resolutions: Four Inspiring Novellas Show a Loving
Way to Make a Fresh Start,* 1999; *A Christmas Joy
Resolutions: Four Inspiring Novellas Show a Loving
Way to Make a Fresh Start, Historical Collection,*
2000; *Getaways: Four Inspirational Love Stories to
Sweep You Away on Romantic Excursions,* Barbour
Publishing (Uhrichsville, OH), 2000; *Florida: Four
Inspirational Romances in One Complete Volume,* Bar-
bour Publishing (Uhrichsville, OH), 2001; *Silent
Stranger,* Barbour Publishing (Uhrichsville, OH),
2005.

SIDELIGHTS: Peggy Darty has written numerous
novels, novellas, and articles. Among her books is a
series of cozy mysteries that take place in a seaside
community in Florida. *When Bobbie Sang the Blues* is
the second book in the series and was called "a warm,
fun-filled read perfect for an afternoon in the ham-
mock with a glass of lemonade," by *Novel Reviews*
Web site contributor Ane Mulligan. The story revolves
around mystery writer Christy Castleman's Aunt
Bobbie. When Bobbie arrives in Summer Breeze,
Florida, she quickly becomes a noted town character
as she drives around in her old red truck looking for
items to find and restore for her store. However, when
Bobbie's ex-husband is found dead in her pickle bar-
rel, Aunt Bobbie becomes the prime suspect in his
murder. Used to dealing with fictional mysteries,
Christy deals with a real-life mystery as she sets out to
prove her aunt's innocence. "The imagery and
dialogue used in this novel is fresh and fun," wrote
Lacy Williams on the *Armchair Interviews* Web site.
Williams went on to note: "Although the suspense in
this book will keep you on your toes, Darty's masterful use of words and plot creates a light touch that

doesn't scare." *TitleTrakk.com* contributor Darcie Gudger wrote: "Darty weaves in interesting sub-plots and even a bit of romance to satisfy a broad range of readers."

BIOGRAPHICAL AND CRITICAL SOURCES:

PERIODICALS

Kirkus Reviews, December 15, 2006, review of *When Bobbie Sang the Blues,* p. 1244.
MBR Bookwatch, February, 2007, Harriet Klausner, review of *When Bobbie Sang the Blues.*
Publishers Weekly, December 11, 2006, review of *When Bobbie Sang the Blues,* p. 49.

ONLINE

Armchair Interviews, http://armchairinterviews.com/ (October 7, 2007), Lacy Williams, review of *When Bobbie Sang the Blues.*
Barbour Books Web site, http://www.barbourbooks. com/ (October 7, 2007), brief profile of author.
Novel Reviews, http://novelreviews.blogspot.com/ (April 12, 2007), Ane Mulligan, review of *When Bobbie Sang the Blues.*
Peggy Darty Home Page, http://www.peggydarty.com (October 7, 2007).
TitleTrakk.com, http://www.titletrakk.com/ (October 7, 2007), Darcie Gudger, review of *When Bobbie Sang the Blues.**

*　　*　　*

DASA, Satyaraja
　　See ROSEN, Steven

*　　*　　*

DAVIES, David Stuart 1946-

PERSONAL: Born 1946; married; wife's name Kathryn.

CAREER: Writer. English teacher for twenty years.

WRITINGS:

Holmes of the Movies: The Screen Career of Sherlock Holmes, New English Library (London, England), 1976, C.N. Potter (New York, NY), 1977.
Bending the Willow, Ash Tree Press (Ashcroft, British Columbia, Canada), 1996.
Fixed Point—The Life and Death of Sherlock Holmes: An Audio Dramatization, adapted for audio by Meredith Granger, Classic Specialties Audio (Cincinnati, OH), 1996.
Sherlock Holmes—The Last Act (play; produced at Salisbury Playhouse, 1999), Calabash Press (Ashcroft, British Columbia, Canada), 1996.
(Editor) *Selected Short Stories from the 19th Century,* Wordsworth Classics (Ware, England), 2000.
Starring Sherlock Holmes, Titan Books (London, England), 2001.
Clued Up on Sherlock, Atlas Publishing Limited (New Milton, Hampshire, England), 2004.
Forests of the Night (novel), Robert Hale (London, England), 2005, published as *Forests of the Night: A Johnny Hawke Novel,* Thomas Dunne Books (New York, NY), 2007.
(Editor) *Return from the Dead: Classic Mummy Stories,* Wordsworth Classics (Ware, England), 2006.
(Editor and author of introduction) *Vintage Mystery and Detective Stories,* Wordsworth Editions (Ware, England), 2006.
Comes the Dark, Hale Crime (London, England), 2006.

SHERLOCK HOLMES NOVELS

Sherlock Holmes and the Hentzau Affair, Ian Henry Publications (London, England), 1991.
The Tangled Skein, foreword by Peter Cushing, Calabash Press (Ashcroft, British Columbia, Canada), 1998.
The Scroll of the Dead, Calabash Press (Ashcroft, British Columbia, Canada), 1998.
The Shadow of a Rat, Calabash Press (Ashcroft, British Columbia, Canada), 1999.
The Veiled Detective, Robert Hale (London, England), 2004.

Also author of comic book series featuring "Skelington Bones," Sherlock Holmes's comic-book alter-ego; editor of anthologies, including *Tales of Unease.* Editor of the crime fiction magazine, *Sherlock,* and *Red Herrings,* the monthly publication for members of the Crime Writers Association.

SIDELIGHTS: David Stuart Davies is a former high school English teacher turned writer who has written Sherlock Holmes novels, books about films featuring Sherlock Holmes, and a novel featuring his own fictional detective. As for his interest in Sherlock Holmes, Davies noted in an interview on the *Sherlock Holmes Shoppe* Web site: "I first encountered Sherlock Holmes in the school library. As fate would have it, the Basil Rathbone series of films was being televised at the same time. The potent combination of Conan Doyle's prose and Rathbone's performance as The Great Detective ensured my life-long love of Mr. Holmes and his world." Among the books by Davies about films featuring Sherlock Holmes is *Starring Sherlock Holmes,* which includes numerous photographs, plot summaries, and interviews. "Lavish pictures, knowledgeable writing, what more could you want?" wrote Eve Sanders on *Sherlockiana.net.*

Although the author of several novels featuring Sherlock Holmes, Davies turns to an original character for his novel *Forests of the Night: A Johnny Hawke Novel.* Readers are introduced to Hawke, a policeman in 1939 London who loses his eye in an shooting accident and then leaves the force to become a private detective. His first case is to find the spinsterish Pamela Palfrey, a young woman who has been missing for months. However, when Hawke investigates, he finds that Palfrey, contrary to her family's belief, was no wallflower but rather a beautiful woman who had escapades with many men. Eventually, Hawke discovers Pamela's body, leading to an encounter with a fading film star. "This book is compelling," wrote Andrea Sisco on the *Armchair Interviews* Web site. "His dialogue is filled with dry humor and just sparse enough to evoke strong emotions from the reader." A *Kirkus Reviews* contributor wrote that the author "effectively captures the London of a later era in this taut page-turner."

BIOGRAPHICAL AND CRITICAL SOURCES:

PERIODICALS

Booklist, December 15, 2006, Bill Ott, review of *Forests of the Night: A Johnny Hawke Novel,* p. 25.

Kirkus Reviews, November 15, 2006, review of *Forests of the Night,* p. 1154.
Publishers Weekly, November 13, 2006, review of *Forests of the Night,* p. 37.

ONLINE

Armchair Interviews, http://armchairinterviews.com/ (October 8, 2007), Andrea Sisco, review of *Forests of the Night.*
David Stuart Davies Home Page, http://www.david stuartdavies.com (October 7, 2007).
Nashville Scholars, http://www.nashvillescholars.net/ (October 7, 2007), Jim Hawkins, "David Stuart Davies: Sherlockian Editor," interview with author.
Scifipedia, http://scifipedia.scifi.com/ (October 7, 2007), brief profile of author.
Sherlock Holmes Shoppe, http://www.sherlock-holmes. com/ (October 7, 2007), "Meet David Stuart Davies."
Sherlockiana.net, http://www.sherlockiana.net/ (October 7, 2007), Eve Sanders, review of *Starring Sherlock Holmes;* Charles Prepolec, review of *Starring Sherlock Holmes.**

*   *   *

DAVIES, Freda 1930-
(Amy Pirnie)

PERSONAL: Born 1930, in London, England. *Education:* Graduated from Bristol University, England.

CAREER: Writer. Formerly a teacher.

WRITINGS:

"DETECTIVE INSPECTOR KEITH TYRELL AND HIS TEAM" SERIES

A Fine and Private Place, Constable (London, England), 2001.
Bound in Shallows, Carroll & Graf Publishers (New York, NY), 2003.
Flawed Scales, Constable (London, England), 2005.

"PEMBROKE STORIES" SERIES

The Tanner's Wife: A Pembroke Story, Caeriw Publishing (Pembroke, Wales), 2005.

Ninian's Daughter: A Pembroke Story, Caeriw Publishing (Pembroke, Wales), 2006.

A Portion for Foxes: A Pembroke Story, Caeriw Publishing (Pembroke, Wales), 2007.

"SUE BENNETT MURDER MYSTERY" SERIES; AS AMY PIRNIE

Let Heaven Fall (British edition published under name Freda Davies), Allison & Busby (London, England), 1995, Carroll & Graf (New York, NY), 2006.

Lesser Creatures, Carroll & Graf (New York, NY), 2007.

SIDELIGHTS: Freda Davies has written under her own name and the pseudonym Amy Pirnie. Published under her own name are the volumes of the "Pembroke Stories" and "Detective Inspector Keith Tyrell and His Team" series. The former series describes life in a growing town in the early twelfth century and involves events in the life and times of Nest. Known as the Helen of Wales, Nest was the daughter of a king, mistress of Henry I of England, and mother of the first Fitzgeralds of Ireland.

In *A Fine and Private Place,* the first book in the "Detective Inspector Keith Tyrell and His Team" series, Freda introduces Detective Inspector Tyrell, who is called in to identify the skeletal remains uncovered on the property of Sir Edward Driffield in the small English village of Tolland. Dog tags identify the remains as an American soldier gone AWOL during World War II. Tyrell determines that the missing soldier was murdered and sets out to discover the murderer as well as the killer of Mehmet Orhan, a child pornographer whose body turns up in somebody else's grave. Barry Forshaw, writing on the *Crime Time* Web site, commented: "The unassuming manner of Davies' writing cleverly wrongfoots the reader, and ensures total attention." A *Kirkus Reviews* contributor noted that the author "kicks off her series with a splendid evocation of village life, offbeat family portraits, a pair of complex puzzles, and a believable, low-key hero."

Bound in Shallows finds Tyrell investigating the murder of an unidentified young woman in the Forest of Dean, a mysterious place known for its pagan background, which still lives on with its inhabitants. Two more murders occur, and Tyrell goes against the popular theory that it is a serial killer on the loose. Instead, he surmises that more than one killer is involved in the deaths. Also featured in the story is Tyrell's ongoing personal battle with Detective Chief Inspector Richard Whittaker, who tries to thwart Tyrell every chance he gets. Referring to the police procedural as "absorbing," a *Publishers Weekly* contributor later wrote in the same review: "There's a lot going on here, but Davies pulls it all together in a realistic page-turner." Rex E. Klett wrote in the *Library Journal* that the story "is strengthened by authentic surrounds, departmental idiosyncrasies, and clever plotting."

As Amy Pirnie she is author of the "Sue Bennett Murder Mystery" series. The first book in the series, *Let Heaven Fall,* was first published in England in 1995 under the author's birth name and introduces readers to Sue Bennett, a London science reporter who gets involved in mysteries. The second book in the series, *Lesser Creatures,* finds Sue trying to track down the culprit or culprits who bombed the newspaper building where she works, killing several of her colleagues while police believe the bomb was meant for her. A *Publishers Weekly* contributor commented that the author "moves the story along with clean, brisk prose." Writing in *Kirkus Reviews,* a contributor noted that the author "tosses romance and adventure into the mix and comes up with a winner."

Davies told *CA:* "I have always enjoyed writing and find committing murders and solving them great fun. I was influenced by Professor Keith Simpson, an expert pathologist and charismatic lecturer. The most surprising thing I have learned as a writer is just how enjoyable the process is when it is going well. [My] writing process occurs as early in the day as possible. I start at page one and am always surprised by the way plots develop from the kernel of an idea. As to my favorite book, I have not stopped writing long enough to look back and decide—yet."

BIOGRAPHICAL AND CRITICAL SOURCES:

PERIODICALS

Booklist, October 15, 2001, David Pitt, review of *A Fine and Private Place,* p. 385.

Kirkus Reviews, September 1, 2001, review of *A Fine and Private Place,* p. 1247; September 15, 2003, review of *Bound in Shallows,* p. 1155; November 15, 2006, review of *Lesser Creatures,* p. 1157.

Library Journal, November 1, 2001, Rex E. Klett, review of *A Fine and Private Place,* p. 135; November 1, 2003, Rex E. Klett, review of *Bound in Shallows,* p. 127.

Publishers Weekly, October 1, 2001, review of *A Fine and Private Place,* p. 40; September 29, 2003, review of *Bound in Shallows,* p. 46; November 20, 2006, review of *Lesser Creatures,* p. 42.

ONLINE

BookLoons, http://www.bookloons.com/ (August 26, 2007), Tim Davis, review of *Lesser Creatures.*

Crime Time, http://www.crimetime.co.uk/ (August 26, 2007), Barry Forshaw, review of *Bound in Shallows.*

Romantic Times, http://www.romantictimes.com/ (August 26, 2007), Toby Bromberg, review of *A Fine and Private Place;* Kim Colley, review of *Bound in Shallows.*

Shots, http://www.shotsmag.co.uk/ (August 26, 2007), Maureen Carlyle, review of *Bound in Shallows.*

*   *   *

DAVIS, Dee 1959-

PERSONAL: Born 1959; married; children: one daughter. *Education:* Holds a B.A. and an M.P.A.

ADDRESSES: Home—New York, NY. *Agent*—Kimberly Whalen, Trident Media Group, 41 Madison Ave., 36th Fl., New York, NY 10010. *E-mail*—dee@deedavis.com.

CAREER: Writer. Worked for ten years in public relations and six years at Association Management.

MEMBER: Romance Writers of America.

AWARDS, HONORS: Best Paranormal Romance for 2000, Booksellers' Best, for *Everything in Its Time;* has also won the Golden Leaf, Texas Gold, and Prism awards.

WRITINGS:

A Match Made on Madison (novel), St. Martin's Griffin (New York, NY), 2007.

ROMANCE FICTION

Everything in Its Time, Jove Books (New York, NY), 2000.

After Twilight, Ivy Books (New York, NY), 2001.

Just Breathe, Ivy Books (New York, NY), 2001.

Dark of the Night, Ivy Books (New York, NY), 2002.

Midnight Rain, Ivy Books (New York, NY), 2002.

The Promise, Love Spell (New York, NY), 2002.

Dancing in the Dark, Ivy Books (New York, NY), 2003.

Wild Highland Rose, Dorchester Publishing (New York, NY), 2003.

(With Claudia Dain and Evelyn Rogers) *Silent Night* (novellas), Leisure Books (New York, NY), 2004.

Endgame, Harlequin (Don Mills, Ontario, Canada), 2005.

Enigma, Harlequin (Don Mills, Ontario, Canada), 2005.

Exposure, Harlequin (Don Mills, Ontario, Canada), 2005.

(With Julie Kenner and Kathleen O'Reilly) *Hell with the Ladies* (novellas), Berkley Sensation (New York, NY), 2006.

Eye of the Storm, Harlequin (Don Mills, Ontario, Canada), 2006.

(With Julie Kenner and Kathleen O'Reilly) *Hell on Heels* (novellas), Berkley Sensation (New York, NY), 2007.

SIDELIGHTS: Dee Davis dreamed of becoming a writer from a young age, drifting off into her own imaginary worlds at the worst times—from sitting at her desk at school to driving past her exit on the freeway. However, she took a more practical approach to life, studying political science, history, and public administration, and taking a job working in public relations that enabled her to write as well as work the public-speaking circuit. In addition, Davis married and lived in Vienna for several years, all of which provided grist for the mill. When she finally determined to do something about her dreams, she began writing romance novels. Her first published book, *Everything in Its Time,* was released in July,

2000, and was well received. It won the Booksellers' Best Paranormal Romance of the Year award, and was also honored as a Holt Medallion finalist, a Texas Bronze winner for best historical, and a Dorothy Parker Award honorable mention for best debut novel. Other books by Davis have been nominated for or won additional awards, and garnered favorable reviews.

Eye of the Storm tells the story of Simone Sheridan, a former CIA ops agent who finds her past coming to haunt her just as she thinks she is getting her life back under control. *Booklist* reviewer Mary K. Chelton praised the book, remarking that the "ending is as inevitable as surprising in this one-sitting read." In *A Match Made on Madison* Davis looks at the high-powered business of modern-day matchmaking. Heroine Vanessa Carlton looks at matchmaking as more of an arrangement, where love is just a bonus, and so she accepts her former mentor's challenge to see which of them will be first to match up rich and powerful playboy Mark Grayson. Grayson, of course, turns his attentions on Vanessa, though not for her ability to find him a wife. A *Publishers Weekly* reviewer objected to the "obligatory designer name-dropping, but it's her heroine's exalted venue-hopping that's the source of much fun." Maria Hatton commented in *Booklist* that Davis's effort "takes readers on an enjoyable adventure as we root for Vanessa."

BIOGRAPHICAL AND CRITICAL SOURCES:

PERIODICALS

Booklist, November 1, 2002, Megan Kalan, review of *Midnight Rain,* p. 478; May 15, 2006, Mary K. Chelton, review of *Eye of the Storm,* p. 29; December 1, 2006, Maria Hatton, review of *A Match Made on Madison,* p. 31.

Kirkus Reviews, November 15, 2006, review of *A Match Made on Madison,* p. 1143.

MBR Bookwatch, March 1, 2005, Harriet Klausner, review of *Endgame.*

Publishers Weekly, May 28, 2001, review of *Just Breathe,* p. 57; November 20, 2006, review of *A Match Made on Madison,* p. 31.

ONLINE

Dee Davis Home Page, http://www.deedavis.com (August 22, 2007).

Writers Write, http://www.writerswrite.com/ (August 22, 2007), Claire E. White, interview with Dee Davis.

* * *

DAVIS, Genie
(Nikki Alton)

PERSONAL: Born in MD; married; children: two. *Hobbies and other interests:* Road trips, microwaveable meals, and feeding her cats.

ADDRESSES: Home—CA.

CAREER: Writer, producer, director of television documentaries, commercials, and corporate videos.

AWARDS, HONORS: Road to Romance Reviewers' Choice award.

WRITINGS:

Dreamtown, Fiction Works (Lake Tahoe, NE), 2001.
The Model Man, Kensington Publishing (New York, NY), 2006.
Five o'Clock Shadow, Kensington Publishing (New York, NY), 2007.

Work represented in anthologies, including (as Nikki Alton) *The Cowboy* (erotica), Kensington Aphrodesia, 2006.

SIDELIGHTS: Genie Davis writes romance novels and television documentaries and scripts for corporate films. She is also the author of erotica, under the pseudonym Nikki Alton. Her debut novel, *The Model Man,* finds the protagonist, Christie, posing as a psychic when homicide detective Joe Richter enters her life. Together they drive to the home of a deceased male model; during the drive, Christie is able to extract information from him about stolen champagne, about which she is supposed to provide some clues. Christie is then attacked in her apartment and the attacker is found with his hands severed. When she talks to the police, they say that there is no Joe Richter on the force. *Booklist* reviewer Diana Tixier Herald wrote that the romantic mystery "is truly a find. The protagonists are interesting; their love affair is convincing."

The main character in *Five o'Clock Shadow* is Jessie Adams, a California disk jockey whose best friend, Lisa, is threatened with the loss of her music club because of rezoning. Jessie runs for the vacant position on the town council, hoping to win and then have to power to sway the decision in Lisa's favor. Jessie is in a relationship with detective Frank Jackson, and when her opponents begin dying and Jessie receives death threats telling her to drop out of the race, Frank is there to protect her. The novel was reviewed for *BookLoons* by Martina Bexte, who wrote: "Genie Davis has written a fun and breezy story. Jessie is a delight. . . . Frank is a great love interest." Bexte concluded by calling *Five o'Clock Shadow* "an entertaining romance with just the right touch of mystery."

BIOGRAPHICAL AND CRITICAL SOURCES:

PERIODICALS

Booklist, December 1, 2005, Diana Tixier Herald, review of *The Model Man,* p. 30; January 1, 2007, Maria Hatton, review of *Five o'Clock Shadow,* p. 67.

ONLINE

BookLoons, http://www.bookloons.com/ (August 12, 2007), Martina Bexte, review of *Five o'Clock Shadow.*

Genie Davis Home Page, http://www.geniedavis.com (August 12, 2007).*

*   *   *

DEANS, Bob

PERSONAL: Born in VA; married; wife's name Karen; children: three.

ADDRESSES: Home—Bethesda, MD. *Office*—Cox Newspapers, Washington Bureau, 400 N. Capitol St., N.W., Ste. 750, Washington, DC 20001-1536.

CAREER: Journalist and writer. Fairchild Publications, Atlanta-based reporter, 1980, then editor, New York, NY, 1981-1983; *Post and Courier,* Charleston, SC, reporter, 1983; *Atlanta Journal-Constitution,* Atlanta, GA, business reporter, beginning 1984; Cox Newspapers, Washington, DC, chief Asia correspondent in Tokyo, Japan, 1987-91, then national correspondent and then White House correspondent, 1992—.

MEMBER: White House Correspondents Association (president, 2002-2003).

WRITINGS:

Behind the Headlines, Japan Society (New York, NY), 1996.
The River Where America Began: A Journey along the James, Rowman & Littlefield (Lanham, MD), 2007.

SIDELIGHTS: Longtime journalist Bob Deans is the author of *The River Where America Began: A Journey along the James.* In this historical account, the author writes of the James River and the establishment of Jamestown, the first English colony in America. Deans begins by tracing the origins of the river and those who lived along it from the beginning of civilization in America dating back 15,000 years. He then delves into the establishment of Jamestown and the history of the new British colonies. The history continues through the Revolutionary and Civil Wars. Among the historical events the author discusses are the meeting of Captain John Smith and Pocahontas, an Indian attack on the Jamestown settlement in 1622, the Bacon rebellion of 1676, the American Revolution, and Abraham Lincoln's journey up the James River in 1865 to tour the defeated town of Richmond, Virginia. In the process, Deans also provides a history of the many contributions Virginians made to the developing colonies and subsequently the United States. "His succession of stories brims with drama," wrote Thomas J. Davis in the *Library Journal.* Writing in *Booklist,* Gilbert Taylor noted that the author's "fast-moving presentation successfully engages interest in an overview of Jamestown and its aftermath."

BIOGRAPHICAL AND CRITICAL SOURCES:

PERIODICALS

Booklist, March 1, 2007, Gilbert Taylor, review of *The River Where America Began: A Journey along the James,* p. 56.

Christian Science Monitor, May 10, 2007, "Jamestown: Where the American Story Began," p. 9.

Library Journal, February 15, 2007, Thomas J. Davis, review of *The River Where America Began,* p. 130.

ONLINE

Coxwashington.com, http://www.coxwashington.com/ (October 7, 2007), profile of author.

PFD New York, http://www.pfdny.com/ (October 7, 2007), brief profile of author.

River Where America Began Web site, http://theriverwhereamericabegan.com (October 7, 2007).*

*   *   *

DEEN, Hanifa

PERSONAL: Born in Kalgoorlie, Western Australia, Australia. *Education:* Attended the University of Western Australia.

ADDRESSES: Home—Melbourne, Victoria, Australia. *Agent*—Jenny Darling & Associates Pty Ltd., P.O. Box 413, Toorak, Victoria 3142, Australia. *E-mail*—Hanifa.Deen@arts.monash.edu.au.

CAREER: Multicultural and Ethnic Affairs Commission of Western Australia, deputy commissioner, Human Rights and Equal Opportunity Commission of Western Australia, hearing commissioner. Monash University, Victoria, Australia, senior research fellow with the Centre for Muslim Minorities and Islamic Policy. Served on the board of directors of Special Broadcasting Services.

AWARDS, HONORS: New South Wales Premier's Literary Award, 1996, for *Caravanserai: Journey among Australian Muslims.*

WRITINGS:

Caravanserai: Journey among Australian Muslims, Allen & Unwin (St. Leonards, New South Wales, Australia), 1995, revised edition, Fremantle Arts Centre Press (Fremantle, Western Australia, Australia), 2003.

Broken Bangles, Doubleday/Anchor Books (New York, NY), 1998.

The Crescent and the Pen: The Strange Journey of Taslima Nasreen, Praeger (Westport, CT), 2006.

The Jihad Seminar, Scribe (Melbourne, Victoria, Australia), 2007.

SIDELIGHTS: Hanifa Deen is a third-generation Australian who is of Pakistani descent. A human rights activist and social commentator, she wrote *Caravanserai: Journey among Australian Muslims* after the start of the Gulf War and revised it to reflect sentiment following the tragedy of September 11, 2001. She saw the changes that occurred in the Australian Muslim community. While they were earlier embraced as Australians first, 9/11 cast suspicion on its Muslim citizens. The word "caravanserai" means the central court of an inn where the covered wagons of a caravan stop for the night. It indicates shelter, but Muslims experienced only increasing hostility as the undefined "war on terror" expanded and opinions turned even more negative. *New Internationalist* reviewer Julie Young wrote: "Much has gone wrong and Hanifa Deen's vignettes give us many powerful examples from those who bear the brunt of such ostracism and marginalization."

Broken Bangles is the result of Deen's travels studying the lives of Muslim women in Bangladesh and Pakistan. She reveals that in many Islamic communities, Muslim society has political subsets much the same as exist in other countries. Although their left, middle-of-the-road, and right may reflect differing degrees of liberalism or conservatism, they do exist. She also notes that the burqa, the head covering worn by Muslim women in Bangladesh and other countries, which is so frowned upon by the West, is typically worn by the middle class, because the fabric could interfere with work. She writes that the fundamentalist treatment of women comes largely from a need to control them financially and not because of their sex or any behavior that might be blamed.

The title of the book refers to the bangles a woman collects throughout her life, beginning with those given to her by her in-laws on her wedding day. When her husband dies, the wife breaks her bangles and becomes socially deprived without the protection of her husband, which is why Muslim women often hoard what they can to prepare for such a time. Deen presents the lives of Muslim women through a myriad of voices, including well-known writers, rural women, social workers, expatriates, and others. Dana de Zoysa reviewed the volume for the *Curled Up with a Good Book* Web site, writing: "Ms. Deen's ability to elevate the particular to the level of the general without directly saying so raises *Broken Bangles* to the quality of a good novel."

"The idea of bangles provides a vivid metaphor for the unbroken cycle of patriarchal control that draws together this diverse range of stories," wrote Maria Degabriele for *Intersections*. "Indeed, the metaphor of brokenness suggests sites of women's resistance and increasing visibility. Nevertheless, the author never imposes the metaphor on the life of the stories themselves."

Taslima Nasreen is a Bangladeshi writer, physician, and activist who in 1993 was accused by the government of damaging religious sentiment. She had spoken out against male oppression, repression of free speech, and fanaticism. A fatwa was issued against her by a fundamentalist group after publication of her book *Lajja,* which translates as "Shame," the same title given by Salman Rushdie to his fictionalized history of the partition of the subcontinent. Nasreen fled Bangladesh and went into hiding. Deen heard the story but could not understand why the women of Bangladesh had not taken a stand on Nasreen's behalf. Deen wrote *The Crescent and the Pen: The Strange Journey of Taslima Nasreen* after five years of research and interviews conducted in Bangladesh and other locations to discover the truth behind the story. *Booklist* reviewer David Pitt concluded that *The Crescent and the Pen* is "timely and extremely relevant in the post-9/11 climate."

BIOGRAPHICAL AND CRITICAL SOURCES:

PERIODICALS

Booklist, January 1, 2007, David Pitt, review of *The Crescent and the Pen: The Strange Journey of Taslima Nasreen,* p. 41.

Choice, May 1, 2007, J.C. Richards, review of *The Crescent and the Pen,* p. 1531.

New Internationalist, December 1, 2003, Julie Young, review of *Caravanserai: Journey among Australian Muslims,* p. 31.

Overland, September 22, 2004, "Muslim Appearances, Western Gaze," p. 133.

Reference & Research Book News, February 1, 2004, review of *Caravanserai,* revised edition, p. 46; February 1, 2007, review of *The Crescent and the Pen.*

ONLINE

Australian Broadcasting Corporation Web site, http://www.abc.net.au/ (September 24, 2003), Rachel Kohn, "Travels among Australian Muslims," interview ("The Ark on Radio National" transcript).

Center for Muslim States and Societies, University of Western Australia Web site, http://www.cmss.uwa.edu.au/ (August 14, 2007), brief author biography.

Curled Up with a Good Book, http://www.curledup.com/ (August 14, 2007), Dana de Zoysa, review of *Broken Bangles.*

Curtin University of Technology Web site, http://lsn.curtin.edu.au/ (August 14, 2007), brief author biography.

Intersections (online journal of Murdoch University), http://wwwsshe.murdoch.edu/au/intersections/ (August 14, 2007), Maria Degabriele, review of *Broken Bangles.*

Monash University Web site, http://arts.monash.edu.au/ (August 14, 2007), brief author biography.*

* * *

DESNOËTTES, Caroline

PERSONAL: Born in France.

ADDRESSES: Home—France.

CAREER: Painter, designer, and author.

WRITINGS:

Le musée des couleurs, Réunion des musées nationaux (Paris, France), 1996.

Le musée des animaux, Réunion des musées nationaux (Paris, France), 1997.

Le musée des potagers, Réunion des musées nationaux (Paris, France), 1998.

Le musée des enfants, Réunion des musées nationaux (Paris, France), 1998.

Le musée des nombres, Réunion des musées nationaux (Paris, France), 1999.

Le musée de la musique, Réunion des musées nationaux (Paris, France), 2000.

Le musée des contraires, Réunion des musées nationaux (Paris, France), 2000.

La peinture au fil du temps, Réunion des musées nationaux (Paris, France), 2000.

Le musée de la nature, Réunion des musées nationaux (Paris, France), 2001.

Renoir, Réunion des musées nationaux (Paris, France), 2001.

Degas, Réunion des musées nationaux (Paris, France), 2001.

Les 5 sens au musée, Réunion des musées nationaux (Paris, France), 2003.

Colors of the Museum of Fine Arts, Houston, Museum of Fine Arts (Houston, TX), 2003.

Lire les sons qui sifflent, illustrated by Isabelle Huy de Pananster, Hatier (Paris, France), 2004.

Lire les sons qui chantent, illustrated by Isabelle Huy de Pananster, Hatier (Paris, France), 2004.

Au royaume du Nil, illustrated by Isabelle Huy de Pananster, Réunion des musées nationaux (Paris, France), 2004.

Trésors du Moyen-age, illustrated by Isabelle Huy de Pananster, Réunion des musées nationaux (Paris, France), 2005.

Lire les sons qui résonnent, illustrated by Isabelle Huy de Pananster, Hatier (Paris, France), 2005.

Lire les sons qui claquent, illustrated by Isabelle Huy de Pananster, Hatier (Paris, France), 2005.

L'art autour du monde, Réunion des musées nationaux (Paris, France), 2005.

Le musée du corps, Réunion des musées nationaux (Paris, France), 2006.

Regarde la peinture à travers les siècles, Albin Michel Jeunesse (Paris, France), 2006, translated as *Look Closer: Art Masterpieces through the Ages,* Walker (New York, NY), 2006.

Où es-tu Mona?, Réunion des musées nationaux (Paris, France), 2006.

Découvre les secrets del'Art, Albin Michel Jeunesse (Paris, France), 2007.

Tam tam couleurs, Réunion des musées nationaux (Paris, France), 2007.

BIOGRAPHICAL AND CRITICAL SOURCES:

PERIODICALS

Kirkus Reviews, October 1, 2006, review of *Look Closer: Art Masterpieces through the Ages,* p. 1013.

School Library Journal, December, 2006, Wendy Lukehart, review of *Look Closer,* p. 161.*

*   *   *

DeTERRE, Veronica
See HOLLAND, JoJean

*   *   *

DIRCK, Brian R. 1965-

PERSONAL: Born 1965. *Education:* University of Central Arkansas, B.A.; Rice University, M.A.; University of Kansas, Ph.D., 1998.

ADDRESSES: Home—Fishers, IN. *Office*—History Department, Anderson University, 100 E. 5th St., Anderson, IN 46012. *E-mail*—brdirck@anderson.edu.

CAREER: Historian, educator, and writer. Anderson University, Anderson, IN, began as assistant professor, became professor.

WRITINGS:

Lincoln and Davis: Imagining America, 1809-1865, University Press of Kansas (Lawrence, KS), 2001.

Waging War on Trial: A Handbook with Cases, Laws, and Documents, ABC-Clio (Santa Barbara, CA), 2003, published as *Waging War on Trial: A Sourcebook with Cases, Laws, and Documents,* Hackett Publishing (Indianapolis, IN), 2003.

The Executive Branch of Federal Government: People, Process, and Politics, ABC-Clio (Santa Barbara, CA), 2007.

(Editor and contributor) Lincoln Emancipated: The President and the Politics of Race, foreword by Allen C. Guelzo, Northern Illinois University Press (DeKalb, IL), 2007.

Lincoln the Lawyer, University of Illinois Press (Urbana, IL), 2007.

Also author of blog A Lincoln Blog.

SIDELIGHTS: Brian R. Dirck is an historian who has written extensively about Abraham Lincoln. In his 2001 book, Lincoln and Davis: Imagining America, 1809-1865, the author presents dual and contrasting biographies of the leaders of the North and South during the Civil War. "Dirck does not offer complete biographies, but his well-written work places Lincoln and Davis side by side to examine their world views," wrote Russell H. Allen in History: Review of New Books. Allen went on to note that the book "is psychohistory, as it studies forces that developed personal characteristics that determined human ideas and actions." Among the factors that the author explores concerning the opposing presidents are political stances, religious believes, and philosophies about war. In the process the author reveals what he sees as very different world views held by the two men, with Lincoln being more rational and legally oriented in his thinking while Davis revealed himself to be a much more emotional man who relied heavily on his personal beliefs. "Lincoln and Davis is thoughtful, provocative, well written, and extensively documented (it contains over fifty pages of notes)," wrote John S. Robey in Perspectives on Political Science. Robey also wrote in the same review: "Dirck presents us with a compelling revision of Davis, demonstrating that many of Davis's ideals were eventually incorporated into the American mosaic." A Publishers Weekly contributor remarked that the author "does present a provocative and potentially fruitful new interpretation of U.S. culture and intellectual history."

Dirck is also editor of and contributor to Lincoln Emancipated: The President and the Politics of Race, which presents essays by academics who specialize in Lincoln. In essays focusing on Lincoln's views of slavery and race, some essayists found that Lincoln's desire to free the slaves was not all-encompassing. They write that Lincoln stated that his primary intention during the Civil War was to keep the Union united, whether that meant freeing the slaves or not. Overall, the essays take a wide-ranging view of Lincoln, from Lincoln as a racist within the confines of his times to a man who showed an evolution in thinking about racism and slavery. The author's essay, "Abraham Lincoln, Emancipation, and the Supreme Court," focuses on various proposals concerning emancipation made by Lincoln in 1862, including the Emancipation Proclamation and Lincoln's efforts to pressure both border states and the U.S. Congress to gradually enact laws that would lead to the end of slavery. "The volume [Dirck] has edited in no way amounts to hagiography," wrote Peter Bridges on the California Literary Review Web site. "It is a useful addition to Lincolniana." Craig Buettinger, writing on the HNN: History News Network Web site, commented that "this volume takes the side that Lincoln was a progressive thinker who necessarily trimmed his policies to get by the societal racism, the Chief Justice, and the proslavery, border-state Unionists."

BIOGRAPHICAL AND CRITICAL SOURCES:

PERIODICALS

Choice: Current Reviews for Academic Libraries, June, 2002, R.A. Fischer, review of Lincoln and Davis: Imagining America, 1809-1865, p. 1863.

Chronicle of Higher Education, November 16, 2001, review of Lincoln and Davis.

Civil War History, March, 2003, Daniel Walker Howe, review of Lincoln and Davis, p. 94.

History: Review of New Books, winter, 2002, Russell H. Allen, review of Lincoln and Davis, p. 52.

Internet Bookwatch, July, 2007, review of Lincoln Emancipated: The President and the Politics of Race.

Journal of American History, September, 2002, David Herbert Donald, review of Lincoln and Davis, p. 638.

Journal of Southern History, August, 2003, Michael Fellman, review of Lincoln and Davis, p. 695.

Library Journal, October 15, 2001, John Carver Edwards, review of Lincoln and Davis, p. 90.

Perspectives on Political Science, summer, 2002, John S. Robey, review of Lincoln and Davis.

Publishers Weekly, October 8, 2001, review of Lincoln and Davis, p. 58.

Reference & Research Book News, November, 2003, review of *Waging War on Trial: A Handbook with Cases, Laws, and Documents,* p. 182.

ONLINE

Anderson University Web site, http://www.anderson. edu/ (October 7, 2007), faculty profile of author.
California Literary Review, http://calitreview.com/ (June 10, 2007), Peter Bridges, review of *Lincoln Emancipated.*
HNN: History News Network, http://hnn.us/ (August 28, 2007), Craig Buettinger, review of *Lincoln Emancipated.**

* * *

DISHWASHER PETE
See JORDAN, Pete

* * *

DIXON, Keith 1971-

PERSONAL: Born 1971, in Durham, NC; married Jessica Lee Behrer (a teacher), November 5, 2004. *Education:* Hobart College, Geneva, NY, graduated 1993.

ADDRESSES: Home—New York, NY. *E-mail*—kdwriter@gmail.com.

CAREER: Writer and editor. *New York Times,* became editor for News Technology department, 1993—.

WRITINGS:

NOVELS

Ghostfires, St. Martin's Press (New York, NY), 2004.
The Art of Losing, St. Martin's Press (New York, NY), 2007.

SIDELIGHTS: Referring to Keith Dixon's first novel, *Ghostfires, Bookreporter.com* Web site contributor Joe Hartlaub called it "an impressive debut from a writer who unquestionably will have more to say in the future." The novel focuses on William, Warren, and Ben Bascomb, three generations of Bascombs who face disturbing problems. The sour relationship between Warren and his son, Ben, is predated by William Bascomb's own negative feelings about Warren, whom William blamed for the death of his wife during Warren's birth. As for Warren and Ben, their mutual hostility is fueled by the fact that Warren has kept his son financially solvent through bad business dealings while Ben provides Dialudid and other drugs that his father has become addicted to after a burn accident, an addiction that cost him his medical license for five years. Furthermore, Ben helped his mother commit suicide as an act of mercy as she suffered from terminal cancer. The two men's problems come to a head when Ben ends up in a psychiatric award after a failed robbery, leaving Warren looking for drugs and willing to commit desperate acts to get them. "Insightful and impressively crafted, this is a novel from which no one emerges unscathed," wrote Michele Leber in *Booklist. Library Journal* contributor Judith Kicinski noted that the author "examines exquisitely how misfortune and weakness defeat a single family."

Dixon's next novel also received favorable reviews from the critics. "*The Art of Losing* is a dark, captivating novel in which Dixon relentlessly pursues the twin themes of greed and loss, stripping his characters clean as he does so," wrote *New York Times Book Review* contributor Natalie Moore of Dixon's sophomore effort. In *The Art of Losing,* Mike Jacobs is a broke filmmaker in New York City who joins a friend's plan to fix a horse race. Mike's job is to place the bets with bookmakers who already have barred Mike's friend, Sebby Laslo, from betting with them. When the horses they bet on don't win due to an accident involving the jockeys, who were in on the plan, Mike and Sebby find themselves deep in debt with people who will not hesitate to hurt and even kill them if they don't come through with the money. As a result, Mike finds himself descending into evil as he resorts to violence and murder in an effort to pay off the bookies and save his life. "Dixon has written a cautionary tale that is not easy to enjoy but even harder to forget," wrote Dennis Dodge in *Booklist.* A *Kirkus Reviews* contributor commented: "So well and darkly done that readers may find themselves opting for a noir moratorium in the interest of mental health."

BIOGRAPHICAL AND CRITICAL SOURCES:

PERIODICALS

Booklist, December 15, 2003, Michele Leber, review of *Ghostfires,* p. 726; December 15, 2006, Dennis Dodge, review of *The Art of Losing,* p. 27.

Entertainment Weekly, February 23, 2007, Jeff Labrecque, review of *The Art of Losing,* p. 104.

Kirkus Reviews, November 15, 2003, review of *Ghostfires,* p. 1326; November 15, 2006, review of *The Art of Losing,* p. 1144.

Library Journal, January, 2004, Judith Kicinski, review of *Ghostfires,* p. 154.

New York Times, November 7, 2004, "Jessica Behrer, Keith Dixon," wedding announcement, p. 16.

New York Times Book Review, February 8, 2004, Daniel Woodrell, "Other People's Drug Money," review of *Ghostfires,* p. 14; April 1, 2007, Natalie Moore, "Going Down Gambling," review of *The Art of Losing,* p. 18.

Philadelphia Inquirer, February 21, 2007, Frank Wilson, review of *The Art of Losing.*

Publishers Weekly, December 15, 2003, review of *Ghostfires,* p. 54; September 25, 2006, review of *The Art of Losing,* p. 41.

ONLINE

Bookreporter.com, http://www.bookreporter.com/ (October 7, 2007), Joe Hartlaub, review of *Ghostfires.*

Keith Dixon Home Page, http://www.readkeithdixon. com (October 7, 2007).

Noir Writer, http://noirwriter.blogspot.com/ (March 11, 2007), Steve Allan, "Sunday Interview: Keith Dixon."

PopMatters, http://www.popmatters.com/ (February 23, 2007), Frank Wilson, review of *The Art of Losing.*

*   *   *

DMILITANT
See LITTLETON, Darryl

*   *   *

DOHERTY, Brian 1968-

PERSONAL: Born 1968. *Education:* University of Florida, bachelor's degree.

ADDRESSES: Office—Reason, 3415 S. Sepulveda Blvd., Ste. 400, Los Angeles, CA 90034. *E-mail*—bdoherty@reason.com; brian@thisisburningman.com.

CAREER: Writer, journalist, and editor. *Regulation* magazine, managing editor, 1993-94; *Reason,* Los Angeles, CA, associate editor, 1994-2003, senior editor, 2004—. Also worked at the Cato Institute, Washington, DC, and played base in punk rock bands; founder of Cherry Smash Records, 1993.

AWARDS, HONORS: Warren Brookes Fellow in Environmental Journalism, Competitive Enterprise Institute, 1999.

WRITINGS:

This Is Burning Man: The Rise of a New American Underground, Little, Brown (New York, NY), 2004.

Radicals for Capitalism: A Freewheeling History of the Modern American Libertarian Movement, PublicAffairs (New York, NY), 2007.

Contributor to periodicals, including the *Washington Post, Los Angeles Times, Mother Jones, Spin, National Review, Weekly Standard, San Francisco Chronicle,* and *Suck.*

SIDELIGHTS: In his first book, *This Is Burning Man: The Rise of a New American Underground,* journalist and magazine editor Brian Doherty writes about the annual Burning Man get-together, a weeklong event held in the Nevada dessert near Reno each August that is capped off with the burning of a giant stick figure of a man. An annual attendee of the "new-age" event since 1995, Doherty outlines the event's history and growth into a multimillion dollar occurrence that offers an alternative lifestyle for a week, including new ways of doing commerce and practicing art. In addition to reminiscing about his own time at the festival, the author includes more than one hundred interviews with other attendees. Michelle Chihara, writing in *Mother Jones,* called *This Is Burning Man* "an intelligent and exhaustive effort to chronicle the explosion of one of America's most implausible subcultures." A *Publishers Weekly* reviewer noted: "This insider's look at a cornerstone of American subculture is informative, though nearly as chaotic as Burning Man itself."

According to a contributor to *Campaigns & Elections,* Doherty's second book, *Radicals for Capitalism: A Freewheeling History of the Modern American*

Libertarian Movement, is a "well-researched history [that] avoids polemics in outlining a vital political orientation that cuts across the political spectrum." Once again, the author writes about a movement that he has belonged to for many years. In an interview with Jamie Glazov for *FrontPageMagazine.com,* the author noted his reasons for writing the book, commenting: "I believe that libertarian ideas and the people who advocated them in the twentieth century deserve attention and credit; they really are pushing the political ideas at the heart of the American founding, and did so in the twentieth century against great odds and great hostility, especially after FDR and the New Deal." In his comprehensive history of the Libertarian movement, the author profiles many of the founding members, including Ayn Rand, Milton Friedman, Ludwig von Mises, Murray Rothbard, and F.A. Hayek. He also details Libertarian beliefs, which focus on fostering a small government with the primary purpose of protecting its citizens, a philosophy that differs from the Republican political party in that Libertarians do not favor the legislating of morality. The author also presents his case that Libertarianism may be an answer for many of the problems facing the United States.

Referring to *Radicals for Capitalism* as "delightful," *Fortune* contributor Daniel Okrent also called the book a "smart, lively narrative [that] digs deep into libertarianism." Writing in the *National Review,* Jonah Goldberg commented that "*Radicals for Capitalism* is, quite simply, the best book of its kind ever written." Goldberg continued: "This should not be interpreted as faint praise merely because it is the only book of its kind ever written (at least that I am aware of). It is an extraordinary accomplishment."

BIOGRAPHICAL AND CRITICAL SOURCES:

PERIODICALS

Booklist, August, 2004, Mike Tribby, review of *This Is Burning Man: The Rise of a New American Underground,* p. 1879.

Campaigns & Elections, April, 2007, review of *Radicals for Capitalism: A Freewheeling History of the Modern American Libertarian Movement,* p. 62.

Fortune, March 19, 2007, Daniel Okrent, "Geniuses, Idealists and Nuts," p. 212.

Kirkus Reviews, July 1, 2004, review of *This Is Burning Man,* p. 615.

Library Journal, March 1, 2007, Michael O. Eshleman, review of *Radicals for Capitalism,* p. 96.

Mother Jones, September-October, 2004, Michelle Chihara, review of *This Is Burning Man,* p. 88.

National Review, May 14, 2007, Jonah Goldberg, "Live Free or Else!," review of *Radicals for Capitalism,* p. 41.

New York Times Book Review, September 19, 2004, Dave Itzkoff, review of *This Is Burning Man;* April 1, 2007, David Leonhardt, "Free for All," review of *Radicals for Capitalism.*

PR Week, November 20, 2006, "Media: Journalist Q&A— Brian Doherty, Reason," p. 10.

Publishers Weekly, July 5, 2004, review of *This Is Burning Man,* p. 49; December 11, 2006, review of *Radicals for Capitalism,* p. 58; December 18, 2006, review of *Radicals for Capitalism,* p. 60.

Reason, October, 2004, "Reason News," p. 10.

ONLINE

FrontPageMagazine.com, http://www.frontpagemag. com/ (April 3, 2007), Jamie Glazov, review of *Radicals for Capitalism.*

Radicals for Capitalism Web site, http://radicalsfor capitalism.com (October 7, 2007).

Reason, http://www.reason.com/ (October 7, 2007), brief profile of author.

This Is Burning Man Web site, http://www.thisis burningman.com (October 7, 2007).*

*   *   *

DOIDGE, Norman

PERSONAL: Education: Attended the University of Toronto; holds a degree in medicine; Columbia University Department of Psychiatry, degrees in psychiatry and psychoanalysis.

ADDRESSES: Home—Toronto, Ontario, Canada; New York, NY. *Office*—Columbia University Psychoanalytic Center, 1051 Riverside Dr., New York, NY 10032. *Agent*—Chris Calhoun, Sterling Lord Literistic, Inc., 65 Bleecker St., New York, NY, 10012.

CAREER: Psychiatrist, researcher, and writer. *Books in Canada—The Canadian Review of Books,* Toronto, Ontario, Canada, editor-in-chief, 1995-98; *National*

Post, Toronto, Canada, author of column "On Human Nature," 1998-2001; University of Toronto, Clarke Institute of Psychiatry, Toronto, head of the psychotherapy centre and the assessment clinic, and instructor in philosophy, political science, law, and psychiatry; Columbia University Center for Psychoanalytic Training and Research, New York, NY, member of research faculty.

MEMBER: American College of Psychoanalysts.

AWARDS, HONORS: E.J. Pratt Prize for poetry; Canadian Broadcasting Corporation/*Saturday Night* Literary Award, for an unpublished work, 1994; four Canadian National Magazine gold awards, including the National Magazine Award President's Medal for the best article published in Canada, 2000; research fellow, Columbia-National Institute of Mental Health; clinical fellow, department of psychiatry, Columbia University; U.S. National Psychiatric Endowment Award in psychiatry; CORST Prize in Psychoanalysis and Culture, American Psychoanalytic Association; M. Prados Prize, Canadian Psychoanalytic Association.

WRITINGS:

The Brain That Changes Itself: Stories of Personal Triumph from the Frontiers of Brain Science, Viking (New York, NY), 2007.

Contributor to periodicals, including *Saturday Night, Reader's Digest, Time, Maclean's, Gravitas, Books in Canada, Medical Post, Melbourne Age, Weekly Standard,* and the *Chicago Sun-Times.*

SIDELIGHTS: Norman Doidge started writing poetry at a young age and won accolades early in his career, including the E.J. Pratt Prize for poetry when he was just nineteen years old. He went on to study classics and philosophy at the University of Toronto, and then earned his medical degree to eventually become a psychiatrist. He splits his time between New York City, where he serves as part of the research faculty at the Columbia University Center for Psychoanalytic Training and Research, and Toronto, where he heads up the Psychotherapy Centre and the Assessment Clinic for the Clarke Institute of Psychiatry and also serves on the teaching faculty at the University of Toronto. He is the author of *The Brain That Changes Itself: Stories of Personal Triumph from the Frontiers of Brain Science,* which looks at modern improvements and theories in the field of neuroscience, focus-

ing in particular on the ways in which the brain alters in response to illness or injury in an effort to adapt itself and continue functioning on the highest possible level. In addition, Doidge takes his study deeper, considering ways in which people might alter their brains consciously through the choices they make. The book covers a variety of circumstances, including the effects of stroke and ongoing pain, and the effects of such mental stimuli as pornography. Ronald Pies, in a review for the *Psychiatric Times,* praised Doidge's effort, remarking: "Doidge is a fine writer, and his book has a lucid and engaging style. The text is thoroughly referenced, and most of the scientific claims are well substantiated." A contributor to *Kirkus Reviews* found that the book was "somewhat scattershot, but Doidge's personal stories, enthusiasm for his subject and admiration for its researchers keep the reader engaged."

BIOGRAPHICAL AND CRITICAL SOURCES:

PERIODICALS

Book World, March 4, 2007, Elizabeth Williamson, review of *The Brain That Changes Itself: Stories of Personal Triumph from the Frontiers of Brain Science,* p. 11.

California Bookwatch, June, 2007, review of *The Brain That Changes Itself.*

Humanist, July 1, 2007, Kenneth W. Krause, review of *The Brain That Changes Itself,* p. 45.

Kirkus Reviews, December 15, 2006, review of *The Brain That Changes Itself,* p. 1254.

Library Journal, February 15, 2007, Mary Ann Hughes, review of *The Brain That Changes Itself,* p. 135.

O, the Oprah Magazine, May, 2007, Kathryn Matthews, "Romance Rehab: Can a Woman Learn to Kick the Bad-Man Habit? Can a Playboy Ever Be Trusted to Settle Down? Yes! and New Brain Research Shows How," p. 205.

Psychiatric Times, August 1, 2007, review of *The Brain That Changes Itself,* p. 57.

Publishers Weekly, December 4, 2006, review of *The Brain That Changes Itself,* p. 45.

ONLINE

International Herald Tribune Online, http://www.iht.com/ (May 30, 2007), Abigail Zuger, review of *The Brain That Changes Itself.*

Union-Tribune Online (San Diego, CA), http://www. signonsandiego.com/ (May 27, 2007), Julia Keller, "Physicians with Pens."*

*   *   *

DOLNICK, Ben 1982-

PERSONAL: Born 1982, in Chevy Chase, MD. *Education:* Graduated from Columbia University.

ADDRESSES: Home—Brooklyn, NY. *E-mail*—zoologynovel@gmail.com.

CAREER: Writer. Previously worked as a zookeeper at New York City's Central Park Zoo, a bookseller, a research assistant in an immunology lab, and a tutor.

WRITINGS:

Zoology: A Novel, Vintage Books (New York, NY), 2007.

SIDELIGHTS: Ben Dolnick studied English and writing at Columbia University in New York prior to working an assortment of odd jobs, including as a tutor, a research assistant at an immunology lab, and as a zookeeper at the Central Park Zoo. He went on to mine his zookeeping experience in his debut work of fiction, *Zoology: A Novel.* The book focuses on the coming-of-age traumas of Henry Elinsky, whose first year of college is harder than he expected. Henry soon finds himself helping out back at his old elementary school where his father teaches music, and wondering what the adult world has in store for him. When his brother offers to let him visit him in New York for the summer, it seems to be the adventure he is looking for, and Henry sets off. Once in New York, he applies for a job at the Central Park Zoo, where he is hired to work in the children's area. The job is less than glamorous, but Henry toughs it out, meeting new people both in his apartment building and at work, dealing with family emergencies, and seeking out his destiny. *Library Journal* reviewer Jan Blodgett found Dolnick's effort to be "written with humor and insight." Nola Theiss, writing for *Kliatt,* commented that "the New York City settings, especially the zoo and the apartment building, give the story some original and funny situations." A critic for the *New Yorker* stated that Dolnick "demonstrates an engaging lightness of touch."

Dolnick told *CA:* "I discovered pretty early on—and occasionally to my parents' dismay—that I enjoyed imitating people, seeing if I could 'get' their voices right. This started out as just mimicking a waiter or a teacher, but pretty soon I discovered fiction writing as a means of getting people in a more significant and satisfying way. And of course I don't think I'd be a writer if I didn't love to read. Every time I read something I love, I find myself wanting to rush to my keyboard.

"I have a huge and ever-changing list of writers I love, all of whom I hope influence me one way or another. There's Alice Munro, whom I just can't say enough about. And Philip Roth, Nicholson Baker, George Saunders, William Maxwell, Penelope Fitzgerald, William Trevor. . . . "

When asked to describe his writing process, Dolnick said: "I'm afraid it isn't particularly systematic. I get an idea in my head and then spend a long time worrying at it, typing paragraphs and deleting them, feeling guilty for not writing more, wondering if this could possibly work, and after a year or two of that I realize that I'm actually, to my amazement, pretty close to having a book, and then a kind of pleasant rush kicks in.

"I'm sure there are lots of surprises I'm not thinking of, but one thing is how similar the task of writing remains, even once you've been published. I think a part of me expected that after publication, all doubts and difficulties would vanish, to be replaced by a steady stream of confident production. Not so, or at least not for me. It's just the same self-doubting, disorganized process as ever.

"I wouldn't mind it if [my books] made someone, or multiple someones, feel the way that I feel when I read a particularly beloved piece of writing. Which is to say, the reader would feel less alone, more alert to the busy-ness of his or her mind—and, even if the story isn't particularly cheery, happier."

BIOGRAPHICAL AND CRITICAL SOURCES:

PERIODICALS

Kliatt, May, 2007, Nola Theiss, review of *Zoology: A Novel,* p. 24.

Library Journal, May 1, 2007, Jan Blodgett, review of *Zoology,* p. 72.

New Yorker, June 11, 2007, review of *Zoology,* p. 130.

Publishers Weekly, March 5, 2007, review of *Zoology,* p. 39.

School Library Journal, July, 2007, Mary Ann Harlan, review of *Zoology,* p. 129.

ONLINE

Armchair Interviews Web site, http://reviews.armchairinterviews.com/ (October 2, 2007), Diane A. Brown, review of *Zoology.*

Ben Dolnick Home Page, http://www.bendolnick.com (October 2, 2007).

BookLoons.com, http://www.bookloons.com/ (October 2, 2007), Lyn Seippel, review of *Zoology.*

Random House Web site, http://www.randomhouse.com/ (October 2, 2007), author profile.

*   *   *

DOUGLAS, Charles
See McAULAY, Alex

*   *   *

DOUGLAS, Richard
See WHITING, Charles

*   *   *

DRABBLE, Phil 1914-2007

OBITUARY NOTICE— See index for *CA* sketch: Born May 14, 1914, in Bloxwich, England; died July 29, 2007. Television personality, naturalist, and author. Drabble is remembered as the host of the popular, long-running television program *One Man and His Dog,* but the series was only one facet of a long and varied life. Drabble spent his childhood roaming the British countryside in the company of his father. When his schooling was complete, he became a factory worker and remained one until he was nearly fifty years old. About halfway through this career, however, he began to write about the countryside of his youth and his fondness for pets, especially dogs. Finally Drabble resigned from factory work and returned to the country. He invested his entire savings into a country lodge and farm in Staffordshire, where he established a wildlife sanctuary and Christmas tree farm. He continued to support himself through his writing, which by this time had expanded into the genres of radio and television. It was about 1975 when the British Broadcasting Corporation asked him to present a program pitting teams of shepherds and their sheepdogs against one another in a televised competition. Drabble himself was quite certain that such an apparently boring enterprise would end in failure, but somehow it became a Saturday afternoon success, and Drabble stayed with the program for nearly twenty years. His background as a rustic landowner, pet lover, and informed commentator added authenticity to the pastoral setting and attracted viewers from city, suburb, and countryside alike. In 1993 Drabble retired to his sanctuary near Goat Lodge, where he spent the rest of his life in the company of his beloved wildlife. Over a period of fifty years, Drabble wrote more than twenty books, including *The Penguin Book of Pets* (1964), *Badgers at My Window* (1969), *Country Seasons* (1976), *It's a Dog's Life* (1983), and *My Wilderness in Bloom* (1986).

OBITUARIES AND OTHER SOURCES:

BOOKS

Drabble, Phil, *A Voice in the Wilderness,* Pelham Books (London, England), 1991.

PERIODICALS

Times (London, England), August 1, 2007, p. 55.

*   *   *

DUVE, Karen 1961-

PERSONAL: Born 1961, in Hamburg, Germany.

ADDRESSES: Home—Brunsbüttel, Germany.

CAREER: Freelance writer, 1990—. Has worked as a proofreader and a taxi driver.

AWARDS, HONORS: Award for new prose, city of Arnsberg, Germany, 1991; Open Mike- Pankow Workshop Literary Prize, Berlin, Germany, 1994; Bettina von Arnim Award, third place, 1995; Gratwander Award, 1996; Heinrich Heine scholarship, 1997; guest of the Goethe Institute, Vietnam, 2000; Literature Award, city of Hamburg, Germany, 2001; Hebbel Award, 2004; International IMPAC Dublin Literary Award, 2004, for Rain.

WRITINGS:

Im tiefen Schnee ein stilles Heim (short stories), Achilla Presse (Hamburg, Germany), 1995.

(With Judith Zaugg) *Bruno Orso fliegt ins Weltall* (comic), Maro Verlag (Augsburg, Germany), 1997.

(With Thies Völker) *Lexikon berühmter Tiere,* Eichborn (Frankfurt on Main, Germany), 1997.

Keine Ahnung: Erzahlungen, Suhrkamp (Frankfurt on Main, Germany), 1999.

Regenroman, Eichborn (Berlin, Germany), 1999, translation by Anthea Bell published as *Rain,* Bloomsbury (London, England), 2003.

(With Thies Völker) *Lexikon berühmter Pflanzen,* Eichborn (Frankfurt on Main, Germany), 1999.

Dies Ist Kein Liebeslied: Roman, Eichborn (Frankfurt on Main, Germany), 2002, translation published as *This Is Not a Love Song,* Bloomsbury (London, England), 2005.

Weihnachten mit Thomas Müller, Eichborn (Frankfurt on Main, Germany), 2003.

Die Entfuhrte Prinzessin: Von Drachen, Liebe Und Anderen Ungeheuern: Roman, Eichborn (Berlin, Germany), 2005.

Ne apie meil e daina, Algimantas (Vilnius, Lithuania), 2005.

Thomas Müller und der Zirkusbär, Eichborn (Frankfurt on Main, Germany), 2006.

SIDELIGHTS: German-born writer Karen Duve worked as a proofreader and a taxi driver in her native Hamburg following high school until 1990, when she became a full-time freelance writer. Since then, she has authored numerous novels and short stories, and has won several awards for her writing. Her novel, *Regenroman,* was her first to be translated into English, appearing as *Rain.* The book follows the adventures of Leon Ulbricht, a writer who has been hired to compile a gangster's memoirs. Leon must go to East Germany, where the gangster lives, in order to conduct the necessary research and interviews, and

what he first imagines will be a wonderful, vacation-like trip, soon turns into a dreary, uncomfortable task. The gangster and his wife are at odds, and the town seems destined to float away beneath the unending rain. Barbara Baker, in a review for the Goethe Institute Web site, remarked that "among the strong points of the novel must be Karen Duve's sharp eye for detail, which builds out every scene vividly." Baker went on to note, however, that "the balance between realism and fantasy, between 'comedy' and violence is shaky, leaving the reader to conjecture that Duve's chief purpose is to be original." However, a critic for *Kirkus Reviews* found the book to be "an amiable and good-humored take on an old story, with an interesting West vs. East slant that enlivens what could have been some very stale city-slicker clichés."

Die Entfuhrte Prinzessin: Von Drachen, Liebe Und Anderen Ungeheuern: Roman is a fairy tale of sorts, telling the story of the Princess Lisvana, her two suitors, and a humorous dwarf. Harald Leusmann, in a review of the German edition for *World Literature Today,* dubbed Duve's effort "a wonderful read," and went on to note that "one gets easily and pleasantly lost in her narrative labyrinth."

BIOGRAPHICAL AND CRITICAL SOURCES:

PERIODICALS

Kirkus Reviews, December 15, 2002, review of *Rain,* p. 1786.

Publishers Weekly, March 17, 2003, review of *Rain,* p. 55.

Times Literary Supplement, September 19, 2003, Elizabeth Winter, "Rain and Fire," review of *Rain,* p. 29.

World Literature Today, July 1, 2006, Harald Leusmann, review of *Die Entfuhrte Prinzessin: Von Drachen, Liebe Und Anderen Ungeheuern: Roman,* p. 66.

ONLINE

Bloomsbury USA Web site, http://www.bloomsburyusa.com/ (October 3, 2007), author profile.

Eichborn Berlin Web site, http://www.eichborn-berlin.de/ (October 3, 2007), author profile.

Goethe Institute Web site, http://www.goethe.de/ (October 3, 2007), Barbara Baker, review of *Rain.**

E

ELLIS, Albert 1913-2007
(Albert Isaac Ellis)

OBITUARY NOTICE— See index for *CA* sketch: Born September 27, 1913, in Pittsburgh, PA; died of kidney and heart failure, July 24, 2007, in New York, NY. Psychologist, counselor, educator, administrator, and author. Ellis revolutionized the field of psychotherapy and supplanted Sigmund Freud in a 1982 survey of clinical psychologists as the most influential contributor to his field. Ellis, in fact, rejected Freud's emphasis on sex and childhood trauma as primary causes of mental problems and also his conviction that effective treatment required years and years of psychoanalysis. He criticized such long-term therapy as a treatment that made patients *feel* better without helping them to *become* better. Ellis's own solution, which he called rational emotive behavioral therapy (or cognitive behavioral therapy), was much faster and more direct, as well as confrontational and blunt, even to the point of obscenity. He considered neurosis a form of "whining," to use his own word, and exhorted patients to quit complaining and take action. Ellis had a similarly direct, action-oriented, and uninhibited approach to the topic of sex, and his encouragement, combined with the profanities he used for effect, made his teaching and writings spectacularly popular and heavily publicized. He was, not surprisingly, censured by many of his colleagues in the 1950s, even called a crackpot. Over the years, however, most of his teachings came to be accepted, many were adopted by leading professionals, and he was regarded with the highest respect. Ellis began his career not with a medical degree, but with a doctorate in psychology. He worked as a personnel manager and a state government psychologist. In 1959 he created the Institute for Rational Living (now the Albert Ellis Institute), where he worked until 2005 and lived until his death. He taught classes at Rutgers University, New York University, and other institutions and held weekly public seminars at his New York, New York, facility into his nineties. Ellis earned many awards in his long career. He was named "humanist of the year" by the American Humanist Association and "distinguished sex researcher" by the Society for the Scientific Study of Sex. He won a distinguished psychologist award from the Academy of Psychologists in Marital and Family Therapy and an American Psychological Association award for distinguished professional contributions to knowledge. Throughout his long career, Ellis also managed to write more than one hundred books, many of which became best sellers. One of his most popular titles was *Sex without Guilt* (1958). Other popular books were less suggestive, including *How to Prevent Your Child from Becoming a Neurotic Adult* (1966), *How to Stubbornly Refuse to Make Yourself Miserable about Anything—Yes, Anything!* (1988), *Optimal Aging: Get Over Getting Older* (1998), and *The Road to Tolerance* (2004).

OBITUARIES AND OTHER SOURCES:

BOOKS

Gale Encyclopedia of Psychology, 2nd edition, Thomson Gale (Detroit, MI), 2001.

PERIODICALS

Chicago Tribune, July 25, 2007, p. 12.
Los Angeles Times, July 25, 2007, p. B8.

New York Times, July 25, 2007, pp. A1, A16; August 2, 2007, p. A2.
Washington Post, July 25, 2007, p. B7.

*   *   *

ELLIS, Albert Isaac
    See ELLIS, Albert

*   *   *

EMCKE, Carolin 1967-

PERSONAL: Born 1967. *Education:* Attended Harvard University and the London School of Economics; J.W. Goethe University, Frankfurt, Germany, M.A., Ph.D.

ADDRESSES: Home—Berlin, Germany.

CAREER: Writer, editor, and philosopher. Has worked as a freelance writer for German television; *Der Spiegel,* Berlin, Germany, editor and foreign correspondent, 1998—; Yale University, New Haven, CT, visiting lecturer, 2003-04.

AWARDS, HONORS: Political book award, Friedrich Ebert Stiftung, and Lettre Ulysses Award short list, both for *Von Den Kriegen: Briefe an Freunde,* both 2005; Ernst Blöch Förderpreis, for scholars and philosophers showing great promise, 2006.

WRITINGS:

Kollektive Identitäten, Sozialphilosophische Grundlagen (Leer, Germany), 2000.
Von Den Kriegen: Briefe an Freunde, S. Fischer (Frankfurt am Main), 2004, translation published as *Echoes of Violence: Letters from a War Reporter,* Princeton University Press (Princeton, NJ), 2007.

SIDELIGHTS: Carolin Emcke is a writer, philosopher, and educator, who studied both in the United States, at Harvard University, and in Europe, at the J.W. Goethe University in Frankfurt and the London School of Economics. She began working at *Der Spiegel,* a German news magazine, in 1998, first as a staff writer and then as an editor and foreign correspondent reporting from combat areas. She is the author of *Kollektive Identitäten* and *Von Den Kriegen: Briefe an Freunde,* the latter of which was released in English translation as *Echoes of Violence: Letters from a War Reporter. Echoes of Violence* compiles a series of letters that Emcke wrote to friends over the course of her work as a correspondent, and chronicles her experiences and thoughts about the political and social situations in places such as Kosovo, Romania, Nicaragua, Iraq, Pakistan, and Lebanon, as well as on the events of 9/11, during which she was in New York City. The book was critically well received both in Europe and the United States. Chris Nash, in a contribution for the *Australian Review of Public Affairs Online,* faulted Emcke for her sense of detachment from the events she witnessed, but acknowledged that this was partly a result of her role as journalist. Nash remarked: "Emcke is to be applauded for the power of her writing, her commitment to the importance of ordinary people's suffering, and her honesty in laying out her thoughts and reactions for all to see." Kathy English, writing in *Biography,* opined that Emcke's effort "combines gripping narrative with philosophic reflection."

BIOGRAPHICAL AND CRITICAL SOURCES:

BOOKS

Emcke, Carolin, *Echoes of Violence: Letters from a War Reporter,* Princeton University Press (Princeton, NJ), 2007.

PERIODICALS

Biography, spring, 2007, Kathy English, review of *Echoes of Violence.*
Booklist, March 1, 2007, Vanessa Bush, review of *Echoes of Violence,* p. 56.

ONLINE

Australian Review of Public Affairs Online, http://www.australianreview.net/ (October 2, 2007), Chris Nash, review of *Echoes of Violence.*

EVANS, Justin 1971(?)-

PERSONAL: Born c. 1971; married; children: son. *Education:* Columbia University, B.A.; New York University, M.B.A.

ADDRESSES: Home—New York, NY. *Agent*—Diane Bartoli, Artists Literary Group, 27 W. 20th St., 10th Fl., New York, NY 10011. *E-mail*—justin@ justinevans.com.

CAREER: Writer. Paramount Pictures, New York, NY, former talent scout; *New York Times,* New York, NY, former member of advertising group and business strategist; The Nielsen Company, New York, NY, former business strategist; The Pluck Corporation, New York, NY, strategy executive.

WRITINGS:

A Good and Happy Child: A Novel, Shaye Areheart Books (New York, NY), 2007.

SIDELIGHTS: Justin Evans earned his degree in English from Columbia University and went on to earn an M.B.A. in finance from New York University. He has worked in business development and strategy for a number of organizations, including The Pluck Corporation, a social media technology company where he now serves as a strategy executive, in addition to pursuing his interest in writing. Evans's debut, *A Good and Happy Child: A Novel,* was published in 2007 to favorable reviews. The book tells the story of George Davies, from the time he was a child struggling with the death of his father until he is himself an adult and father. Problems develop when an invisible visitor appears to George and torments him regarding the circumstances of his father's death. Even as George eventually goes into therapy to deal with his hallucinations, there are individuals in his life suggest-

ing he is actually being haunted by a real demon. A reviewer for *Publishers Weekly* opined that "this stunning novel marks the debut of a serious talent," and went on to praise Evans's effort for its "psychological depth and riveting suspense." Ian Chipman, in a review for *Booklist,* dubbed the book "an edgy, compelling read more unnerving than scary—that will slide its hooks deep inside and throttle you." In a critique for *Kirkus Reviews,* one writer found *A Good and Happy Child* to be "a psychological thriller that keeps the reader on edge until the last page."

BIOGRAPHICAL AND CRITICAL SOURCES:

PERIODICALS

Booklist, March 1, 2007, Ian Chipman, review of *A Good and Happy Child: A Novel,* p. 62.
Books, June 2, 2007, Kristin Kloberdanz, review of *A Good and Happy Child,* p. 9.
Entertainment Weekly, May 25, 2007, Thom Geier, review of *A Good and Happy Child,* p. 89.
Kirkus Reviews, January 15, 2007, review of *A Good and Happy Child,* p. 40.
Library Journal, March 1, 2007, Marianne Fitzgerald, review of *A Good and Happy Child,* p. 72.
Publishers Weekly, March 12, 2007, review of *A Good and Happy Child,* p. 34; March 26, 2007, "PW Talks with Justin Evans: Everyone Where I Grew up Believed in Ghosts," p. 62.

ONLINE

Bookreporter.com, http://www.bookreporter.com/ (October 3, 2007), Joe Hartlaub, review of *A Good and Happy Child.*
Justin Evans Home Page, http://www.justinevans.com (October 3, 2007).
USA Today Online, http://www.usatoday.com/ (May 16, 2007), Carol Memmott, review of *A Good and Happy Child.**

F

FATE, Robert 1935-
(Robert Fate Bealmear)

PERSONAL: Born 1935, in Oklahoma City, OK; married; wife's name Fern (a ceramics artist); children: Jenny. *Education:* Studied at universities in California, Oklahoma, Greece, and France, including the Sorbonne.

ADDRESSES: Home—Los Angeles, CA. *E-mail*—robert-fate@sbcglobal.net.

CAREER: Writer. Worked variously as an oilfield roughneck, a TV cameraman in Oklahoma, a fashion model in New York, NY, a chef at restaurant in Los Angeles, CA, and an FX technician in Hollywood, CA. *Military service:* Served in the U.S. Marines following high school.

MEMBER: Writers Guild of America—West, Mystery Writers of America, Sisters in Crime (Los Angeles and national chapters), International Association of Crime Writers (North American Branch).

AWARDS, HONORS: Academy Award for Technical Achievement.

WRITINGS:

Baby Shark, Capital Crime Press (Fort Collins, CO), 2006.

Baby Shark's Beaumont Blues, Capital Crime Press (Fort Collins, CO), 2007.

SIDELIGHTS: Robert Fate was born and raised in Oklahoma City, Oklahoma. After graduating from high school, he joined the U.S. Marines. Upon completing his military service, Fate decided to make use of the G.I. Bill, and attended universities in various locations both in the United States and Europe, including travel as part of his education. Over the course of his studies and travels, he wrote steadily, compiling short fiction, poetry, magazine articles, plays, scripts, and eventually a novel. Fate also worked at an assortment of colorful jobs in different locations, including as a chef for an upscale Los Angeles restaurant, a roughneck in an Oklahoma oil field, and a model in New York. Working in Los Angeles as an FX technician, he won an Academy Award for technical achievement. However, writing remained his true love, and he finally found success with his novel, *Baby Shark,* which was published to critical praise and became the first in a series. The book tells the story of Kristin "Baby" VanDijk, the teenage daughter of a pool hustler, whose life changes at the hands of a motorcycle gang whose members rape and beat her and murder her father. Bent on revenge and knowing the police are unlikely to get her justice, Kristin sets out in her father's footsteps as a junior hustler to find the men responsible for his death. In a review for the *Hollywood Comics* Web site, Kevin R. Tupple remarked that Fate's first effort is "a powerful, often violent novel that does actually live up to the media hype."

Fate's follow-up novel, *Baby Shark's Beaumont Blues,* finds Kristin working as a private investigator while keeping up her pool-hustling skills. Along with her partner, Otis, she has been hired to find a missing oil heiress who has been kidnapped in anticipation of her very lucrative eighteenth birthday. *Library Journal* reviewer Teresa Jacobsen wrote that "witty dialog, colorful characters, and nonstop action make this pulp-style piece sparkle."

BIOGRAPHICAL AND CRITICAL SOURCES:

PERIODICALS

Library Journal, February 15, 2007, Teresa Jacobsen, review of *Baby Shark's Beaumont Blues,* p. 118.
Publishers Weekly, March 5, 2007, review of *Baby Shark's Beaumont Blues,* p. 43.

ONLINE

Armchair Interviews, http://reviews.armchairinterviews.com/ (October 3, 2007), Kim Reis, review of *Baby Shark.*
Associated Content, http://www.associatedcontent.com/ (January 30, 2007), J.B. Thompson, review of *Baby Shark.*
BookPleasures.com, http://www.bookpleasures.com/ (October 3, 2007), Norm Goldman, interview with Robert Fate.
Hollywood Comics, http://www.hollywoodcomics.com/ (May 30, 2007), Kevin R. Tupple, "Kevin's Corner," review of *Baby Shark.*
Robert Fate Home Page, http://www.robertfate.com (October 3, 2007).
Who Dunnit, http://www.who-dunnit.com/ (October 3, 2007), review of *Baby Shark.**

*　　*　　*

FERNER, Mike

PERSONAL: Male.

ADDRESSES: Home—Toledo, OH. *E-mail*—info@mikeferner.org; mike.ferner@sbcglobal.net.

CAREER: Journalist, writer, and peace activist. Has served as organizer for American Federation of State, County and Municipal Employees (an employees'

union) and communications director for the Farm Labor Organizing Committee and the Program on Corporations, Law & Democracy. *Military service:* U.S. Navy, Navy Hospital Corpsman during Vietnam War.

MEMBER: Veterans for Peace.

WRITINGS:

Inside the Red Zone: A Veteran for Peace Reports from Iraq, foreword by Cindy Sheehan, Praeger (Westport, CN), 2006.

SIDELIGHTS: A Vietnam War veteran who eventually left the U.S. Navy as a conscientious objector, Mike Ferner has continued as a peace activist demonstrating against the Iraq War that began in 2003. His protests have sometimes put him at odds with the law, and in 2006 he was convicted of vandalism for spray painting "Troops Out Now" on a highway bridge. His first book, *Inside the Red Zone: A Veteran for Peace Reports from Iraq,* was called "essential for . . . understanding . . . the psyche and structure" of Iraq by an *Internet Bookwatch* contributor. In his book, Ferner reports on his visits to Iraq prior to the U.S. invasion in March, 2003, and then again a year later. The author focuses much of the book on the ordinary Iraqi citizens and their daily lives in the city and in the country, both before and after the war. The author writes in his introduction to the book: "Reading this modest volume will not provide you with the definitive political analysis of Iraq." He goes on to explain: "This book tells the story of a month I spent in Iraq just before the U.S. invasion as a member of a delegation of peace activists, and the two months I spent there a year later, as an independent journalist to write stories about ordinary people and how the war changed their lives . . . and mine." *Inside the Red Zone* has received favorable reviews, especially for revealing the lives of ordinary Iraqis. "Along with photographs and letters, Ferner offers a compellingly human perspective on the war," wrote Vanessa Bush in *Booklist.*

BIOGRAPHICAL AND CRITICAL SOURCES:

BOOKS

Ferner, Mike, *Inside the Red Zone: A Veteran for Peace Reports from Iraq,* foreword by Cindy Sheehan, Praeger (Westport, CN), 2006.

PERIODICALS

Blade, January 2, 2006, "Former City Councilman Is Accused of Vandalism: Police Say Ferner, Brother Sprayed Anti-war Graffiti"; January 6, 2006, "Editorial: Defacing a Reputation"; July 19, 2006, "Ferner Jury Selection Set to Begin Final Phase Today"; July 20, 2006, "Ferner Is Guilty of Vandalism on Sylvania Township Bridge"; August 5, 2006, "Ferner Gets House Arrest, Probation for Vandalism"; August 9, 2006, "Editorial: Fair Sentence for Ferner."

Booklist, December 1, 2006, Vanessa Bush, review of *Inside the Red Zone,* p. 11; June 1, 2007, Brad Hooper, review of *Inside the Red Zone,* p. 16.

Internet Bookwatch, May, 2007, review of *Inside the Red Zone.*

Reference & Research Book News, February, 2007, review of *Inside the Red Zone.*

ONLINE

Dr. Laniac's Laboratory, http://www.drlaniac.com/ (January 19, 2006), Mike Ferner, "The War on Dissent Gets Creepy."

Infoshop News, http://www.infoshop.org/ (July 10, 2006), "Anti-War Graffiti—Mike Ferner Found Guilty of Vandalism."

Mike Ferner Home Page, http://www.mikeferner.org (October 4, 2007).

Online Journal, http://www.onlinejournal.com/ (July 5, 2006), Mike Ferner, "Busted for Wearing a Peace T-Shirt; Has This Country Gone Completely Insane?"

Press Action, http://www.pressaction.com/ (April 1, 2006), Mike Ferner, "Four Words That Speak Volumes."

Selves and Others, http://www.selvesandothers.org/ (October 4, 2007), brief profile of author.

Truthout, http://www.truthout.org/ (March 14, 2006), Mike Ferner, "Hungering for Justice at My First Congressional Testimony."*

*   *   *

FERRIS, Joshua 1974-

PERSONAL: Born 1974, in Danville, IL; married. *Education:* University of Iowa, B.A., 1996; University of California at Irvine, M.F.A., 2003.

ADDRESSES: Home—Brooklyn, NY. *Agent*—Julie Barer, Barer Literary, LLC, 156 5th Ave., Ste. 1134, New York, NY 10010. *E-mail*—ferris.joshua@gmail.com.

CAREER: Writer. Davis Harrison Dion, Chicago, IL, advertising staff member, 1998; Draft Worldwide, Chicago, former staff member.

AWARDS, HONORS: Glenn Schaeffer Prize, for an emerging writer.

WRITINGS:

Then We Came to the End: A Novel, Little, Brown (New York, NY), 2007.

Contributor to anthologies, including *Best New American Stories* and *New Stories from the South: Best of 2007.* Contributor of short fiction to periodicals, including the *Iowa Review, Prairie Schooner,* and *Phoebe.*

SIDELIGHTS: Joshua Ferris is a graduate of the University of Iowa, where he studied English and philosophy, and of the M.F.A. program at the University of California at Irvine. His short stories have appeared in various publications, including the *Iowa Review, Best New American Stories, Prairie Schooner, Phoebe,* and *New Stories from the South: Best of 2007.* While working on his writing in his spare time, Ferris was employed as a copywriter for an advertising agency in Chicago, a job that served as the inspiration for his debut, *Then We Came to the End: A Novel.* Published to both critical and popular praise, the book began as a form of catharsis, into which he poured his frustrations regarding his day job. However, the eventual result was instead a book about the average worker and his feelings regarding corporate America in a time of economic downturns and layoffs. The book is also noted for its stylistic achievement, in that its viewpoint is first person plural. Alden Mudge, in a review for *BookPage,* noted: "This choral voice is technically difficult. But the effect here is both exhilarating and thought-provoking." James Poniewozik, writing in the *New York Times Book Review Online,* called Ferris's effort "expansive, great-hearted, and acidly funny." Stephen

Morrow, writing in the *Library Journal*, remarked that "with so many books on office life, it's nice to see someone add fresh spark and originality to the subject." A critic for *Kirkus Reviews* praised the book, stating that it "succeeds as both a wickedly incisive satire of office groupthink and a surprisingly moving meditation on mortality and the ties that band."

BIOGRAPHICAL AND CRITICAL SOURCES:

PERIODICALS

Advertising Age, March 5, 2007, Simon Dumenco, "Overthink This: Your World Just Came Out in Hardcover," p. 30.

Books, March 11, 2007, Art Winslow, "Down and Out at a Chicago Ad Agency: Office Culture, Layoffs Provide Backdrop for Energetic Debut Novel," p. 3.

Campaign, October 13, 2006, "Diary: Draft Man Swaps Focus Groups for Feature Films," p. 23.

Entertainment Weekly, March 2, 2007, Tina Jordan, review of *Then We Came to the End: A Novel,* p. 72.

Kirkus Reviews, December 15, 2006, review of *Then We Came to the End,* p. 1234.

Library Journal, January 1, 2007, Stephen Morrow, review of *Then We Came to the End,* p. 91.

London Review of Books, July 19, 2007, Christopher Tayler, "Walk Spanish," p. 19.

New Yorker, March 26, 2007, review of *Then We Came to the End,* p. 91.

O, the Oprah Magazine, March, 2007, Vince Passaro, "The Office: A Funny, Fanged Novel about Showing Up for Work at an Ax-wielding Ad Agency," p. 196.

Publishers Weekly, January 8, 2007, review of *Then We Came to the End,* p. 32.

Spectator, March 31, 2007, Eric Weinberger, "We Also Do Some Work."

Times Literary Supplement, April 6, 2007, Nicholas Clee, "Routine Regrets," p. 23.

ONLINE

BookPage, http://www.bookpage.com/ (October 3, 2007), Alden Mudge, "All in a Day's Work," interview with Joshua Ferris.

Hachette Book Group USA, http://www.hachettebook groupusa.com/ (October 3, 2007), author profile.

Mostly Fiction Book Reviews, http://www.mostly fiction.com/ (March 28, 2007), Poornima Apte, review of *Then We Came to the End.*

New York Times Book Review Online, http://www. nytimes.com/ (March 18, 2007), James Poniewozik, "Pink Slip Blues," review of *Then We Came to the End.*

PopEntertainment.com, http://www.popentertainment. com/ (May 17, 2007), Ronald Sklar, "Joshua Ferris Is Not Close to the End."

PopMatters, http://www.popmatters.com/ (April 4, 2007), Michael Upchurch, review of *Then We Came to the End.**

*   *   *

FINKELSTEIN, Adrian

PERSONAL: Education: Hadassah Medical School, Hebrew University, Jerusalem, Israel, M.D., 1968.

ADDRESSES: Home—Malibu, CA. *Office*—Malibu Holistic Health Center, Hypnotic Past Life Regression & Yoga, 22837 Pacific Coast Hwy., Ste. B, Malibu, CA 90265. *E-mail*—sardro@gte.net.

CAREER: Psychiatrist. Chicago Medical School, University of Health Sciences, Chicago, IL, assistant professor of psychiatry, 1972-75; Mount Sinai Medical Center, Chicago, chief of outpatient psychiatry, 1972-75; Rush Medical School and University, Chicago, assistant professor of psychiatry, 1975-90; University of California at Los Angeles, clinical assistant professor of psychiatry, 1990—; Malibu Holistic Health Center, Malibu, CA, psychiatrist.

MEMBER: American Medical Association, Alumni Menninger Association, American Holistic Medical Association, International Association of Regression Research and Therapies.

AWARDS, HONORS: First Distinguished Research Graduate Award Recipient, Menninger School of Psychiatry, and first Distinguished A.E. Bennett Award, national forum, Central Neuropsychiatric Association, both in 1972.

WRITINGS:

A Psychiatrist's Search for G-d: Back to G-d: Finding Joy in Divine Union, 50 Gates Publishing (Malibu, CA), 1996.

Your Past Lives and the Healing Process: A Psychiatrist Looks at Reincarnation and Spiritual Healing, 50 Gates Publishing (Malibu, CA), 1996.

Marilyn Monroe Returns: The Healing of a Soul, Hampton Roads (Charlottesville, VA), 2006.

Also author of the unproduced screenplay, *Search for Love,* and a time travel video, 2002. Maintains a blog.

SIDELIGHTS: Adrian Finkelstein is a noted psychiatrist working at the Malibu Holistic Health Center in Malibu, California, and also as an assistant professor of psychiatry at the University of California at Los Angeles. A staunch believer in the concept of reincarnation, Finkelstein is perhaps best known for his writings on the subject, including *Your Past Lives and the Healing Process: A Psychiatrist Looks at Reincarnation and Spiritual Healing* and *Marilyn Monroe Returns: The Healing of a Soul.* In the latter work, Finkelstein states his belief that Marilyn Monroe was reincarnated, and that she has returned in the form of Sherrie Lea Laird, a professional singer from Canada. Laird, who was born within a year of Monroe's death, suffered from flashbacks that seemed to come from a previous life. The book goes on to present evidence in support of Finkelstein's claim that Laird is a reincarnated Monroe, including information garnered from Laird under hypnosis, during which time Finkelstein performed past-life regressions on the singer and videotaped the results. He goes on to look at the concept of reincarnation from a scientific point of view. A reviewer for *PR Newswire* remarked that "you don't have to be a believer to be fascinated by this detective story of a doctor and patient team in search of Marilyn, and even outright skeptics will be intrigued by the eerie similarities between Marilyn and Sherrie Lea."

BIOGRAPHICAL AND CRITICAL SOURCES:

PERIODICALS

Library Journal, June 15, 2006, Mary E. Jones, review of *Marilyn Monroe Returns: The Healing of a Soul,* p. 86.

PR Newswire, August 8, 2005, "The Reincarnation of Marilyn Monroe"; July 24, 2007, review of *Marilyn Monroe Returns.*

Science Books & Films, September 1, 2006, Eric R. Kandel, review of *Marilyn Monroe Returns,* p. 206.

UPI NewsTrack, August 6, 2006, "Toronto Woman Says She Is Marilyn Monroe."

World Entertainment News Network, August 11, 2006, "Psychiatrist Believes Client Is Monroe Reincarnated."

ONLINE

Adrian Finkelstein Home Page, http://www.pastlives. com (October 3, 2007).

Past Lives and Self-Healing with Adrian Finkelstein, M.D., http://www.marilynmonroereincarnated.net/ blog (October 3, 2007).*

*   *   *

FINNEGAN, Lisa

PERSONAL: Education: Fordham University, M.A.

ADDRESSES: E-mail—lisafinnegan@hotmail.com.

CAREER: Freelance journalist. Former reporter for *Port Jefferson Record,* Long Island, NY, *Saratogian,* Saratoga Springs, NY, *Press Enterprise,* Bloomsburg, PA, and States News Service, Washington, DC; *Occupational Hazards,* Washington, DC, former editor and staff writer; Fordham University, Bronx, NY, former associate director of public affairs for media relations.

MEMBER: American Psychological Association.

AWARDS, HONORS: Deadline reporting award, Long Island Press Club, 1990, for story "Woman Killed in Stony Brook Home"; depth reporting award from New York State Associated Press Association, and local reporting award from New York Newspaper Publishers Association, both 1992, both for story "What's Wrong with Welfare?"; depth reporting award from New York

State Associated Press Association, and local reporting award from New York Newspaper Publishers Association, both 1993, both for "Workers at Risk."

WRITINGS:

No Questions Asked: News Coverage since 9/11, foreword by Norman Soloman, Praeger Publishers (Westport, CT), 2006.

Contributor to periodicals, including the *Boston Globe, Denver Post, Colorado Springs Gazette, Anchorage Daily News, Washington Lawyer, Asia Times, Manager, Flatirons, Fordham Urban Law Journal,* and *Newsday.*

SIDELIGHTS: Journalist and freelance writer Lisa Finnegan began her career as a reporter for the *Port Jefferson Record* in Long Island, New York, covering primarily local government issues. From there she went on to work at several newspapers, eventually ending up at the States News Service in Washington, DC. She has written about government, the environment, and health and safety issues. Following the September 11, 2001, terrorist attacks, Finnegan earned a master's degree in educational psychology at Fordham University, where she met Professor Harold Takooshian, with whom she went on to research current attitudes toward terrorism. Finnegan went on to write *No Questions Asked: News Coverage since 9/11,* which addresses the manner in which the American press treated the Bush administration's post-9/11 policies and questions what the role of the press should have been during this time. She also looks at the current situation on the global political arena and how it has been affected by these failures on the part of the press. Vanessa Bush remarked in *Booklist:* "This is a penetrating look at American news coverage at a critical time in U.S. history." Carl Sessions Stepp, writing in the *American Journalism Review,* further commented: "Finnegan's most provocative proposition is that press docility stemmed from a calculation of self-interest. . . . Unfortunately, Finnegan doesn't back this with evidence." However, a contributor for *Reference & Research Book Review* felt that Finnegan "documents the many ways that the American media has come to serve essentially as a propaganda organ for government."

BIOGRAPHICAL AND CRITICAL SOURCES:

PERIODICALS

American Journalism Review, April 1, 2007, Carl Sessions Stepp, "Bungling the WMD Story," p. 65.

Booklist, February 1, 2007, Vanessa Bush, review of *No Questions Asked: News Coverage since 9/11,* p. 7.
California Bookwatch, March 1, 2007, Diane C. Donovan, review of *No Questions Asked.*
Reference & Research Book News, February 1, 2007, review of *No Questions Asked.*

ONLINE

Greenwood Publishing Group, http://www.greenwood. com/ (August 22, 2007), profile of Lisa Finnegan.
No Questions Asked, http://www.noquestionsasked. com (August 22, 2007), brief biography of Lisa Finnegan.*

* * *

FLORINE, Hans 1964-
   (Hans E. Florine)

PERSONAL: Born June 18, 1964, in Fort Lee, VA; son of Thomas (a veterinarian) and Maryann (a teacher, business administrator, real estate speculator, and homemaker) Florine; married Jacqueline Adams (a model and homemaker), October 7, 2000; children: Marianna, Pierce. *Ethnicity:* "White." *Education:* California Polytechnic State University, San Luis Obispo, B.S., 1988.

ADDRESSES: Home—Lafayette, CA. *E-mail*—hand@ hansflorine.com.

CAREER: Parker Seals, Culver City, CA, production manager, 1988-90; self-employed rock climber, and public speaker, 1990-2000. Touchstone Climbing, in marketing, 2000—; affiliate of National Competition Climbing Federation. TranSystems, Oakland, CA, administrator, 2007—.

MEMBER: American Alpine Club, National Speakers Association.

WRITINGS:

(With Bill Wright) *Climb On! Skills for More Efficient Climbing,* Falcon Press (Guilford, CT), 2002, 2nd edition published as *Speed Climbing! How to Climb Faster and Better,* 2004.

Also creator of the audio program *Speed Is Power,* produced by Topics Entertainment in 2005. Contributor to periodicals, including *Adventure Sports, Climbing, Podcast Climber, Summit Journal,* and *Rock and Ice.*

SIDELIGHTS: Hans Florine told *CA:* "I write to share knowledge, so I can see others accomplish more and be inspired in turn to do more myself."

BIOGRAPHICAL AND CRITICAL SOURCES:

ONLINE

Hans Florine Home Page, http://www.hansflorine.com (August 13, 2007).

* * *

FLORINE, Hans E.
    See FLORINE, Hans

* * *

FONTES, Ron 1952-

PERSONAL: Born July 19, 1952, in Los Angeles, CA; son of Ruben Paul (a master sergeant, then mail carrier) and Pauline (a department store clerk) Fontes; married Marie Elena Taft, August 6, 1981 (marriage ended); married Justine Korman (a writer), November 21, 1998. *Education:* Austin Peay State University, B.S., 1978. *Hobbies and other interests:* Photography, filmmaking.

ADDRESSES: Home and office—Readfield, ME. *E-mail*—critter@gwi.net.

CAREER: Illustrator and designer. Creative Corp., Clarksville, TN, designer, 1971-73; Art Factory, Nashville, TN, 1977-78; McDonald and Associates Advertising, Nashville, designer, 1978-80; Western Publishing, designer and staff artist for Whitman Comics line, 1980-81; Marvel Comics, New York, NY, production supervisor of special projects, 1981-85; freelance illustrator and pasteup artist. Sonive Publish-

ing, Readfield, ME, cofounder with wife, Justine Korman Fontes, 2004. Speaker at conventions, including DragonCon, 2008.

WRITINGS:

FICTION

(With Justine Korman) *My Friend Fang,* illustrated by Kathy Wilburn, Bantam Books (New York, NY), 1992.

(Adaptor, with Justine Korman) *Poky Puppy's First Christmas,* Golden Books (New York, NY), 1993.

(Adaptor, with Justine Korman) *The Teapot's Tale,* Golden Books (New York, NY), 1993.

(With Justine Korman) *The Ghost Who Couldn't Boo,* illustrated by Ellen Blonder, Random House (New York, NY), 1994.

(With Justine Korman) *The Grumpy Easter Bunny,* Troll Communications, 1995.

(With wife, Justine Korman Fontes) *How the Leopard Got Its Spots: Three Tales from around the World,* illustrated by Keiko Motoyama, Golden Books (New York, NY), 1999.

(With Justine Fontes) *How the Turtle Got Its Shell,* illustrated by Keiko Motoyama, Golden Books (New York, NY), 2000.

(With Justine Fontes) *How the Camel Got It's Hump,* illustrated by Keiko Motoyama, Golden Books (New York, NY), 2001.

(Adaptor, with Justine Fontes) *The Great Pumpkin Strikes Again!* (based on the cartoon by Charles M. Schulz), Little Simon (New York, NY), 2004.

(Adaptor, with Justine Fontes) *Lucy Must Be Traded* (based on the television special), Little Simon (New York, NY), 2004.

"DISNEY'S AMERICAN FRONTIER" SERIES; WITH JUSTINE KORMAN; FICTION

Davy Crockett at the Alamo, illustrated by Charlie Shaw, Disney Press (New York, NY), 1991.

Davy Crockett and the Creek Indians, illustrated by Charlie Shaw, Disney Press (New York, NY), 1991.

Davy Crockett and the Highwaymen, illustrated by Charlie Shaw, Disney Press (New York, NY), 1992.

Calamity Jane at Fort Sanders, illustrated by Charlie Shaw, Disney Press (New York, NY), 1992.

Annie Oakley in the Wild West Extravaganza!, illustrated by Charlie Shaw, Disney Press (New York, NY), 1993.

Wild Bill Hickok versus the Rebel Raiders, illustrated by Charlie Shaw, Disney Press (New York, NY), 1993.

Davy Crockett Meets Death Hug, illustrated by Charlie Shaw, Disney Press (New York, NY), 1993.

"BIKER MICE FROM MARS" SERIES; WITH JUSTINE KORMAN; FICTION

Hands off My Bike!, Random House (New York, NY), 1994.

The Masked Motorcyclist, illustrated by Bob Ostrom, Random House (Ne York, NY), 1994.

ADAPTOR, WITH JUSTINE KORMAN; "BABE, PIG IN THE CITY" SERIES; FICTION; BASED ON THE NOVEL BY DICK KING-SMITH

Babe, Pig in the City, Random House (New York, NY), 1998.

Friends to the Rescue, Random House (New York, NY), 1998.

Beware of Dog!, Random House (New York, NY), 1998.

ADAPTOR, WITH JUSTINE KORMAN; "THE FUNNIE MYSTERIES" SERIES; FICTION; BASED ON CHARACTERS BY JIM MINKINS

Quailman Battles the Giant Space Slug, Golden Books (New York, NY), 1999.

The Case of the Baffling Beast, illustrated by William Preston, Disney Press (New York, NY), 2000.

NONFICTION; WITH JUSTINE FONTES

Abraham Lincoln: Lawyer, Leader, Legend, Dorling Kindersley (New York, NY), 2001.

George Washington: Soldier, Hero, President, Dorling Kindersley (New York, NY), 2001.

Brazil, Children's Press (New York, NY), 2003.

China, Children's Press (New York, NY), 2003.

France, Children's Press (New York, NY), 2003.

India, Children's Press (New York, NY), 2003.

Ireland, Children's Press (New York, NY), 2003.

Israel, Children's Press (New York, NY), 2003.

Italy, Children's Press (New York, NY), 2003.

Kenya, Children's Press (New York, NY), 2003.

Mexico, Children's Press (New York, NY), 2003.

Russia, Children's Press (New York, NY), 2003.

Delaware, the First State, World Almanac Library (Milwaukee, WI), 2003.

North Dakota, the Peace Garden State, World Almanac Library (Milwaukee, WI), 2003.

West Virginia, the Mountain State, World Almanac Library (Milwaukee, WI), 2003.

Wyoming, the Equality State, World Almanac Library (Milwaukee, WI), 2003.

Proteins, Children's Press (New York, NY), 2005.

Rachel Carson, Children's Press (New York, NY), 2005.

GRAPHIC NOVELS

Captain Fortune, RipOff Comics, 1994.

(Editor, with Justine Fontes) *Tale of the Terminal Diner,* Sonic Publishing (Readfield, ME), 2004.

(And illustrator) *Captain Fortune,* Sonic Publishing (Readfield, ME), 2005.

(With Justine Fontes; and illustrator, with David Barneda) *The Batsons,* Sonic Publishing (Readfield, ME), 2005.

(With Justine Fontes; and illustrator) *Itchy Mitch,* Mondo (New York, NY), 2006.

(And illustrator) *Bloodlust,* Sonic Publishing (Readfield, ME), 2006.

(With Justine Fontes; and illustrator, with Paul Plumer) *Wooden Sword/Rudis Princeps: Vesuvius; Via Appia; Arena* (English and Latin text), three volumes, Sonic Publishing (Readfield, ME), 2006.

(With Justine Fontes) *Atalanta: The Race against Destiny,* Graphic Universe (Minneapolis, MN), 2007.

(With Justine Fontes) *Demeter and Persephone: Spring Held Hostage,* Graphic Universe (Minneapolis, MN), 2007.

(With Justine Fontes) *Captured by Pirates,* illustrated by David Witt, Graphic Universe (Minneapolis, MN), 2007.

(With Justine Fontes) *The Trojan Horse: The Fall of Troy,* Graphic Universe (Minneapolis, MN), 2007.

FILM AND TELEVISION ADAPTATIONS; WITH JUSTINE KORMAN FONTES, EXCEPT AS NOTED

101 Dalmations (based on the motion picture), Golden Books (New York, NY), 1988.

Hook: The Storybook (based on the motion picture), Random House (New York, NY), 1991.

Teenage Mutant Ninja Turtles: Secret of the Ooze (based on the television series), Random House (New York, NY), 1991.

(Solo adaptor) *The Rocketeer,* Disney Press (New York, NY), 1991.

Batman Returns Movie Storybook, Western Publishing (Racine, WI), 1992.

Lion King: Zazu's View (based on the motion picture), Golden Books (New York, NY), 1994.

Lion King: Friends in Need (based on the motion picture), Golden Books (New York, NY), 1994.

Squanto: A Warrior's Tale, illustrated by Darlene Craviotto and Bob Dolman, 1994.

X-Men: Masquerade, illustrated by Aristides Ruiz, Random House (New York, NY), 1994.

Ace Ventura: When Nature Calls, Random House (New York, NY), 1995.

Babe: A Little Pig Goes a Long Way (based on the novel by Dick King-Smith), Random House (New York, NY), 1995.

Congo: The Movie, Random House (New York, NY), 1995.

Pocahontas (based on the animated film), Golden Books (New York, NY), 1995.

Pocahontas: Voice of Wind (based on the animated film), Golden Books (New York, NY), 1995.

Lion King: No Worries (based on the motion picture), Golden Books (New York, NY), 1995.

Lion King: The Cave Monster (based on the motion picture), Golden Books (New York, NY), 1996.

Mars Attacks! (based on the motion picture), Troll Communications, 1996.

The Hunchback of Notre Dame (based on the animated film), Golden Books (New York, NY), 1996.

Disney's Flubber, Golden Books (New York, NY), 1997.

Tower of Terror (based on the television program), Disney Press (New York, NY), 1997.

Mushu's Story, Disney Press (New York, NY), 1998.

A Bug's Life, Disney Press (New York, NY), 1998.

Stuart Little: George and Stuart, HarperFestival (New York, NY), 1999.

Stuart Little: My Family Album, HarperFestival (New York, NY), 1999.

Stuart Little: Search and Find, HarperFestival (New York, NY), 1999.

Toy Story II: Rex to the Rescue!, Disney Press (New York, NY), 1999.

Disney's Pepper Ann: Too Cool to Be Twelve, Golden Books (New York, NY), 1999.

Disney's Toy Story: A Read-Aloud Story Book, Mouse Works (New York, NY), 1999.

Star Wars Episode I: Anakin's Pit Droid (based on the film series), Random House (New York, NY), 2000.

To Fly with Dragons (based on characters created by Ron Rodecker), Random House (New York, NY), 2000.

It's the Great Pumpkin, Charlie Brown (based on the characters by Charles M. Schulz), Little Simon (New York, NY), 2001.

Jurassic Park III: Rescue Mission, Random House (New York, NY), 2001.

A Charlie Brown Christmas (based on the television special), Little Simon (New York, NY), 2001.

It's the Easter Beagle, Charlie Brown! (based on the television special), illustrated by Paige Braddock, Little Simon (New York, NY), 2001.

A Charlie Brown Valentine (based on the television special), illustrated by Paige Braddock, Little Simon (New York, NY), 2001.

Star Wars: Attack of the Clones: Battle in the Arena, Random House (New York, NY), 2002.

A Charlie Brown Thanksgiving (based on the television special), Little Simon (New York, NY), 2002.

Dr. Seuss' The Cat in the Hat Storybook (based on the motion picture), Random House (New York, NY), 2003.

Lucy Must Be Traded (based on the television special), Little Simon (New York, NY), 2004.

Adaptor, with Justine Fontes, of numerous other readers, junior novelizations, storybooks, and novelty books based on television and film screenplays.

OTHER

(With Justine Fontes and Serge Rion) *Walt Disney Pictures Presents: Dinosaur Joke Book,* Disney Press (New York, NY), 2000.

Also author of screenplays, including *Bloodlust.* Author, with Justine Fontes, of numerous novelty books, readers, and book-club editions.

SIDELIGHTS: Ron Fontes told *CA:* "I have told stories in pictures and words all my life. At age three I drew a grasshopper, right down to the hairs on its legs. My mother taught me to read using flashcards. By age six I was chuckling over jokes in my cousin's comic books.

"My serious pursuit of art started with a bad case of swimmer's ear that kept me in bed for nearly a year. Dizzy if I sat up or rolled over, I learned to keep very still—and to draw. I also had plenty of time to read and I taught myself all about ancient civilizations. I could only listen to television.

"At age sixteen I stayed up late every night to draw and co-script a science-fiction comic-strip series with my friend, John Browne. John's father was a professional writer who helped us place "Stellar Ops" in our local newspaper. But adventure strips were dying, and when John moved to Orlando, Florida, I focused on other projects, including one about a gladiator.

"I worked my way through the local college, Austin Peay State University. When the art department rejected my classical drawing style and my interest in comics, I switched to theatre. Costuming, acting, directing, and doing make-up for seventy-two shows over the next six years taught me many aspects of visual storytelling.

"After college, the need to earn a living pulled me away from acting into advertising, where I quickly rose to art director of a top Nashville agency. A painful divorce freed me to fulfill my lifelong dream of moving to New York City, and I wound up working in the comic-book department of Western Publishing/Little Golden Books."

"While waiting for the subway one morning, I met my future wife, Justine Korman, an editorial assistant at little Golden Books who lived nearby in Greenwich Village. When Western closed its comic-book department, I fulfilled another lifelong dream: Through a mixture of amazing coincidence and preparation, I became the production supervisor in Marvel Comics' Special Projects Department. At Marvel I worked with comic legends like Spider-Man artist John Romita, Sr., Sol Brodsky, and Stan Lee.

"When working in comics proved less fun than reading them, and Justine needed help with her growing children's book career, I became a children's book writer. Together, we have written everything from board books to junior novels, fiction and nonfiction, and original and adaptations of movies and cartoon shows like *Batman Returns* and 'Peanuts.'

"Aspiring to tell 1,001 tales, Justine and I are near the halfway mark, including mega-bestsellers like the Little Golden Books retelling of *The Lion King*. Since moving to Maine in 1988, we have kept in touch with publishers, family, and friends with *critter news,* a strictly-for-fun newsletter now published quarterly in color. The newsletter has been a place to develop personal projects like our spooky-kooky family *The Batsons* and *Tales of the Terminal Diner,* the story of an aspiring cartoonist who finds a magic ring that grants wishes. In 2004 we launched Sonic Publishing."

BIOGRAPHICAL AND CRITICAL SOURCES:

PERIODICALS

Booklist, October 1, 2007, Jesse Karp, review of *Captured by Pirates,* p. 52.

Publishers Weekly, September 7, 1992, Elizabeth Devereaux, review of *My Friend Fang,* p. 59; January 14, 2002, review of *It's the Easter Beagle, Charlie Brown,* p. 62.

School Library Journal, April, 1993, Jean H. Zimmerman, review of *Calamity Jane at Fort Sanders,* p. 118; August, 2001, Barbara Buckley, review of *Abraham Lincoln: Lawyer, Leader, Legend,* p. 168: March, 2004, Sandra Welzenbach, review of *Brazil,* p. 192; May, 2007, Alana Abbott, review of *Demeter and Persephone: Spring Held Hostage,* p. 165; September, 2007, Alana Abbott, review of *Captured by Pirates,* p. 222.

Voice of Youth Advocates, February, 2007, Amy Luedke, review of *The Trojan Horse: The Fall of Troy,* p. 558.

ONLINE

Sonic Comics Web site, http://www.sonicpublishing. com (October 17, 2007), "Ron Fontes."*

*   *   *

FORMAN, James 1928-2005

PERSONAL: Born October 4, 1928, in Chicago, IL; died January 10, 2005, in Washington, DC, from colon cancer; son of Jackson Forman (a jitney driver) and Octavia Rufus; married Mary Forman (divorced); married Mildred Thompson (divorced); married Constancia Ramilly (divorced); children: Chaka (son), James. *Ethnicity:* African American. *Education:* Attended Wilson Junior College and the University of Southern California; Roosevelt University, B.A., 1957; attended African Research and Studies Program, Boston University, 1958, and Chicago Teachers College, 1959-60; Cornell University, M.A., 1980; Union of Experimental Colleges and Universities with the Institute for Policy Studies, Ph.D., 1985.

CAREER: Writer, educator, and civil rights activist. *Chicago Defender,* Chicago, IL, reporter, 1958-59, 1960; Chicago public schools, teacher, 1960; Student Nonviolent Coordinating Committee (SNCC), executive secretary, 1961-66, SNCC, administrator of the national office, Atlanta, GA, 1967; SNCC, director of International Affairs Commission, New York, NY, 1967; Black Panther Party, minister of foreign affairs, 1968; Unemployment and Poverty Action Committee, Washington, DC, president, mid-1970s-1980s; *Washington Times,* founder, 1981; Black American News Service, founder, early 1980s. *Military service:* U.S. Air Force, 1947-51; served in the Korean War.

MEMBER: Student Nonviolent Coordinating Committee (executive secretary, 1961-66; director of Internal Affairs Commission, 1967), Black Panther Party.

AWARDS, HONORS: Fannie Lou Hamer Freedom Award, the National Conference of Black Mayors, 1990.

WRITINGS:

La Libération viendra d'une chose noire, F. Maspero (Paris, France), 1968.

Law and Disorder, T. Nelson (New York, NY), 1972.

Self-Determination and the African-American People, Open Hand Publishing (Seattle, WA), 1981, published as *Self-Determination: An Examination of the Question and Its Application to the African-American People,* 1984.

The Making of Black Revolutionaries, Macmillan (New York, NY), 1985, reprinted, University of Washington Press (Seattle, WA), 1997.

Sammy Younge, Jr.: The First Black College Student to Die in the Black Liberation Movement, Open Hand Publishing (Washington, DC), 1986.

High Tide of Black Resistance and Other Political and Literary Writings, Open Hand Publishing (Seattle, WA), 1994.

SIDELIGHTS: James Forman was a writer, educator, and civil rights activist. As a reporter for the *Chicago Defender,* the prominent black newspaper of the time, he traveled to Little Rock, Arkansas, in 1958 to cover the desegregation of Central High School. He later wrote articles for the newspaper about black tenant farmers being thrown off the land in Fayetteville, Tennessee, because they dared to participate in a local voter registration, and he represented the farmers to the chairman of the National Association for the Advancement of Colored People. He also served as a teacher in the Chicago school system. However, Forman is best known for his participation in the Student Nonviolent Coordinating Committee (SNCC), and his association with the Black Panther Party. In 1969, he offered African Americans a "Black Manifesto," which called upon the government and the public to offer reparations to African Americans for years of oppression and discrimination. He worked as SNCC executive secretary from 1961 to 1966, and was a key participant in the organization of the major civil rights rallies of the decade. He went on to write several books on civil rights, including *Sammy Younge, Jr.: The First Black College Student to Die in the Black Liberation Movement* and *High Tide of Black Resistance and Other Political & Literary Writings,* and remained an active voice in the fight for civil rights until his death. Forman passed away in 2005, from colon cancer. In an obituary for *Jet,* one writer noted: "Throughout his civil rights career, Forman stayed in the highest leadership ranks of the Civil Rights Movement where his ideas quickly were formulated into policy."

BIOGRAPHICAL AND CRITICAL SOURCES:

PERIODICALS

African American Review, summer, 1996, review of *High Tide of Black Resistance and Other Political and Literary Writings.*

Biography Today, April, 2005, "James Forman, 1928-2005: American Civil Rights Activist," p. 41.

Emerge, April, 1996, Victoria Valentine, "In the Fore of the Movement.," p. 24.

Library Journal, December, 1997, review of *The Making of Black Revolutionaries,* p. 160.

Morning Edition, January 12, 2005, "Profile: Career of Civil Rights Activist James Forman, Who Died This Week at Age 76."

New York Times Book Review, July 14, 1985, review of *The Making of Black Revolutionaries,* p. 40.

NPR Special Coverage, January 12, 2005, "Interview: Barbara Ransby Looks Back on the Life of James Forman."

Publishers Weekly, August 9, 1985, review of *The Making of Black Revolutionaries,* p. 73.

ONLINE

Stanford University Web site, http://www.stanford.edu/ (October 3, 2007), Clayborne Carson and Penny A. Russell, profile of James Forman.

OBITUARIES

PERIODICALS

Black Scholar, March 22, 2005, "James Forman."

Jet, January 31, 2005, "James Forman, 76, Key Activist among Youth during Civil Rights Movement in '60s Dies."

New York Times, January 12, 2005, Martin Douglas, "James Forman Dies at 76; Was Pioneer in Civil Rights," p. A18.

Sojourners Magazine, April 1, 2005, "Honoring the Elders."

UPI NewsTrack, January 12, 2005, "Rights Activist James Forman Dead at 76."

ONLINE

Washington Post Online, http://www.washingtonpost. com/ (January 11, 2005), Joe Holley, "Civil Rights Leader James Foreman Dies."*

* * *

FRIMANSSON, Inger 1944-

PERSONAL: Born 1944, in Stockholm, Sweden.

ADDRESSES: Home—Södertälje, Sweden. *Agent*—Salomonsson Agency, Stora Nygatan 20, 111 27 Stockholm, Sweden. *E-mail*—inger@frimansson.se.

CAREER: Journalist, writer.

AWARDS, HONORS: Little Nobel Prize, 1963; two Swedish Academy Writers' Awards for best Swedish crime novel.

WRITINGS:

Trots Allt: Samtal Med Föräldrar till Utvecklingsstörda, Rabén & Sjögren (Stockholm, Sweden), 1976.

16 kvinnor berättar, Stegelands (Stockholm, Sweden), 1977.

Dubbelsängen (title means *The Double Bed*), Prisma (Stockholm, Sweden), 1984.

Den Förtrollade Prinsen, Prisma (Stockholm, Sweden), 1986.

Den Nya Omsorgslagen, Handikappbyrån på Socialstyrelsen (Stockholm, Sweden), 1986.

Djuret under tummarna, Prisma (Stockholm, Sweden), 1989.

Mannen med barnvagnen, Hammarström & Åberg (Stockholm, Sweden), 1990.

Jag kan också gå på vattnet, Prisma (Stockholm, Sweden), 1991.

Handdockan, Prisma (Stockholm, Sweden), 1992.

Mannen som flö över bergen, Prisma (Stockholm, Sweden), 1993.

Skräpsommaren, Rabén & Sjögren (Stockholm, Sweden), 1993.

Soldaternas dotter, Rabén Prisma (Stockholm, Sweden), 1995.

Kärlek, trohet, vänskap, hat, Bonnier Carlsen (Stockholm, Sweden), 1995.

Stilla under regnbågsytan, Prisma/Vår Bostad (Stockholm, Sweden), 1995.

Där Inne Vilar Ögat: Noveller, Rabén Prisma (Stockholm, Sweden), 1996.

Fruktar jag intetont, Rabén Prisma (Stockholm, Sweden), 1997.

God Natt Min Älskade, Prisma (Stockholm, Sweden), 1998.

Mannen Med Oxhjärtat, Norstedt (Stockholm, Sweden), 1999.

Elden, Bonnier Carlsen (Stockholm, Sweden), 1999.

Katten Som Inte Dog, Norstedt (Stockholm, Sweden), 2000.

Mord i Midsommartid, Semic (Stockholm, Sweden), 2000.

Ett Mycket Bättre Liv (title means *A Much Better Life*), Norstedt (Stockholm, Sweden), 2001.

Midvintermord, Semic (Stockholm, Sweden), 2001.

De Nakna Kvinnornas Ö, Norstedts (Stockholm, Sweden), 2002, published in English as *Good Night, My Darling,* Pleasure Boat Studio: A Literary Press (New York, NY), 2007.

Svept i rosa papper, Bonnier Carlsen (Stockholm, Sweden), 2002.

Bebådelsedag, Stormdals (Stockholm, Sweden), 2003.

Mörkerspår, Norstedts (Stockholm, Sweden), 2003.

Ge mig en drink, jag är rädd!, Systembolaget (Stockholm, Sweden), 2003.

Inga livstecken, Bonnier Carlsen (Stockholm, Sweden), 2004.

Svarta diamanter, AlfabetaAnamma (Stockholm, Sweden), 2004.

Noveller för Värdens, Barn Informationsförlaget (Stockholm, Sweden), 2004.

Skuggan I vattnet, Norstedts (Stockholm, Sweden), 2005.

Mord i juletid, Semic (Stockholm, Sweden), 2005.

Ligga som ett O, Norstedts (Stockholm, Sweden), 2007.

SIDELIGHTS: Swedish writer Inger Frimansson was born in 1944, in Stockholm. She began writing at a young age and was the winner of a number of literary prizes as a child and young adult, including the Little Nobel Prize in 1963. She worked as a journalist for many years before delving into fiction professionally in 1984 with her first novel, *Dubbelsängen* ("The Double Bed."). Eventually, she began writing psychological thrillers and crime fiction. Frimansson is the author of more than two dozen books, and her work has been translated into several languages and published in Norway, Latvia, Holland, Finland, Denmark, Spain, Bulgaria, and Germany, as well as in Sweden and the United States. *Ett Mycket Bättre Liv,* or "A Much Better Life," is the story of a missing child. Four-year-old Angelica is feeling poorly at her nursery school, and so is put down to sleep during the school's tenth-year-anniversary party festivities. When one of the staff is called away for a moment, the little girl disappears. Frimansson avoids the cliché of the manhunt or the discovery of a body, instead focusing on the little girl's experiences after she is taken, and

the emotions of the teacher who feels guilty for the child's abduction while in her care. Charlotte Whittingham, writing for the *Swedish Book Review Online,* remarked: "The character portraits are skillfully drawn and the individuals whose thoughts we follow are credible."

Good Night, My Darling is a tale in the tradition of Snow White, in which three-year-old Justine's mother dies, leaving her with her father, the owner of a candy empire, and a wicked stepmother named Flora. The twist to Frimansson's fairy tale is that a more-adult Justine seduces her hunter rather than fleeing from him or succumbing to his axe. Later in life, Justine takes her psychological issues in hand and begins exacting her own sort of revenge, making for a disturbing story. David Pitt, in a review for *Booklist,* opined that the book "settles into a dark corner of your mind and just sits there, hanging around long after you have moved on."

BIOGRAPHICAL AND CRITICAL SOURCES:

PERIODICALS

Booklist, March 1, 2007, David Pitt, review of *Good Night, My Darling,* p. 66.

Library Journal, March 15, 2007, Mary Todd Chesnut, review of *Good Night, My Darling,* p. 57.

ONLINE

Euro Crime Web site, http://www.eurocrime.co.uk/ (October 3, 2007), Diane Bane, review of *Good Night, My Darling.*

Inger Frimansson Home Page, http://www.frimansson.se (October 3, 2007).

International Noir Fiction Blog, http://international noir.blogspot.com/ (March 11, 2007), Glen Harper, review of *Good Night, My Darling.*

Swedish Book Review Online, http://www.swedish bookreview.com/ (October 3, 2007), Charlotte Whittingham, review of *Ett Mycket Bättre Liv.*

*　　*　　*

FROST, Karolyn Smardz

PERSONAL: Education: Earned B.A. and M.A.; University of Waterloo, Ph.D.

ADDRESSES: Home—Collingwood, Ontario, Canada, and Nova Scotia, Canada. *Agent*—Bukowski Agency, 14 Prince Arthur Ave., Ste. 202, Toronto, Ontario M5R 1A9, Canada.

CAREER: Postdoctoral fellow, York University, 2004-05.

AWARDS, HONORS: Received research fellowships from Multiculturalism Canada, the Ontario Heritage Foundation, the Virginia Historical Society, the Anderson Center at Red Wing, Minnesota, the Bentley Historical Library of the University of Michigan, the Kentucky African American Heritage Commission, and the Filson Historical Society of Louisville, KY.

WRITINGS:

The Archaeology Education Handbook: Sharing the Past with Kids, AltaMira Press (Walnut Creek, CA), 2000.

The Underground Railroad: Next Stop, Toronto!, Natural Heritage Books (Toronto, Ontario, Canada), 2002.

I've Got a Home in Glory Land: A Lost Tale of the Underground Railroad, Farrar, Straus & Giroux (New York, NY), 2007.

SIDELIGHTS: Historian and archaeologist Karolyn Smardz Frost specializes in the history of African Canadians, and her book *I've Got a Home in Glory Land: A Lost Tale of the Underground Railroad* relates the story of two of them. Thornton and Lucie Blackburn were fugitives from slavery in Kentucky who made their escape to freedom in Michigan in 1831. Within a couple of years, however, they were arrested and threatened with deportation to Kentucky. They were secretly freed, though, and spirited across the Detroit River into Canada, where they became the subjects of a notable court case in which Canadian justices ruled that American slaves who had escaped into Canada could not be extradited to the United States.

The Blackburns first came to Frost's attention, wrote *New York Times* contributor David S. Reynolds, when she was leading an excavation, "an archaeological dig beneath a Toronto schoolyard that uncovered the remains of the Blackburns' home—some broken household items, horseshoe nails, a dog collar, bricks heaped in a pit. The find was significant enough to attract worldwide attention and establish the place as a historic site on the Canadian Underground Railroad. Frost then spent two decades piecing together the Blackburns' tale from scattered sources like court records, census reports and artifacts almost two centuries old." The author's attention to "her subject and love of . . . documentation are evident," Vanessa Bush stated in her *Booklist* review, "in this engrossing look at a couple who defied slavery."

BIOGRAPHICAL AND CRITICAL SOURCES:

PERIODICALS

American Anthropologist, September 1, 2001, review of *The Archaeology Education Handbook: Sharing the Past with Kids,* p. 844.

American Antiquity, October, 2002, Robert Brooks, review of *The Archaeology Education Handbook,* p. 782.

Biography, spring, 2007, Robin Breon, review of *I've Got a Home in Glory Land: A Lost Tale of the Underground Railroad,* p. 249.

Booklist, February 1, 2007, Vanessa Bush, review of *I've Got a Home in Glory Land,* p. 27.

New York Times, June 17, 2007, David S. Reynolds, "North toward Home."

ONLINE

Natural Heritage Books, http://www.naturalheritage books.com/ (September 1, 2007), author bio.

Ontario Historical Society, http://www.ontario historicalsociety.ca/ (September 1, 2007), author biography.

Vanguard, http://www.novanewsnow.com/ (September 1, 2007), Eric Bourque, review of *I've Got a Home in Glory Land.**

*   *   *

FUREY, Leo

PERSONAL: Education: St. Francis Xavier University, B.A. (with honors); Memorial University, degree in education and a graduate degree; University of Ottowa, graduate degree.

ADDRESSES: Home—Canada. *Agent*—Anne McDermid & Associates Ltd., 83 Willcocks St., Toronto, Ontario M5S 1C9, Canada.

CAREER: Writer. Newfoundland and Labrador Film Development Corporation, Canada, executive director.

WRITINGS:

The Long Run: A Novel, Key Porter Books (Toronto, Ontario, Canada), 2004, Trumpeter (Boston, MA), 2006.

SIDELIGHTS: Canadian writer Leo Furey serves as the executive director of the Newfoundland and Labrador Film Development Corporation. He is also the author of a variety of short fiction and poetry, and his debut book, *The Long Run: A Novel,* was released in 2004. The novel tells the story of Aiden Carmicheal, a young boy at the Mount Kildare Orphanage and a member of a secret club with several of his friends there, led by an American boy called Blackie, who was abandoned at the orphanage by his mother and is the only black child there. Rules at the orphanage are strict, and punishments for the slightest infraction are harsh. The boys distract themselves by training in secret for a marathon held each summer, going out to run even in the coldest weather. Furey mines his own childhood raised in an orphanage, accurately reproducing the emotions of his youth, as well as the smart dialogue. Alide Kohlhaas, in a review for the *Lancette Journal of the Arts,* remarked: "Furey writes like a seasoned author, who knows how to shape scenes, cre- ate vivid images, and tell an absorbing tale cleanly and truthfully." Kohlhaas concluded that Furey's effort "will put the reader through quite an emotional grinder." *Booklist* reviewer Joanne Wilkinson commented that the book "encapsulates the life-affirming resilience of youth." A reviewer for *Publishers Weekly* found the book to be "a moving and uplifting story."

BIOGRAPHICAL AND CRITICAL SOURCES:

PERIODICALS

Booklist, September 1, 2006, Joanne Wilkinson, review of *The Long Run: A Novel,* p. 54.
Canadian Literature, spring, 2006, Timothy Callin, "Escape Routes."
Publishers Weekly, August 21, 2006, review of *The Long Run,* p. 47.

ONLINE

Lancette Journal of the Arts, http://www.lancetteer. com/ (October 3, 2007), Alide Kohlhaas, review of *The Long Run.*
Anne McDermid & Associates, http://www.mcdermid agency.com/ (October 3, 2007), author profile.*

*   *   *

FUTEHALI, Zahida
   See WHITAKER, Zai

G

GARBERA, Katherine

PERSONAL: Married; children: two.

ADDRESSES: Home—FL. *Agent*—The Knight Agency, 570 East Ave., Madison, GA 30650. *E-mail*—kathy@katherinegarbera.com.

CAREER: Writer.

AWARDS, HONORS: Romantic Times Book Club Career Achievement Award nomination for both series fantasy and series adventure.

WRITINGS:

Some Kind of Incredible, Silhouette Books (New York, NY), 2001.
Cinderella's Convenient Husband, Silhouette Books (New York, NY), 2002.
Tycoon for Auction, Silhouette Books (New York, NY), 2003.
Cinderella's Christmas Affair, Silhouette Books (New York, NY), 2003.
Cinderella's Millionaire, Silhouette Books (New York, NY), 2003.
In Bed with Beauty, Silhouette Books (New York, NY), 2003.
Sin City Wedding, Silhouette Books (New York, NY), 2004.
One Hot Weekend, Harlequin (New York, NY), 2004.
Night Life, Silhouette Books (New York, NY), 2004.

Let It Ride, Silhouette Books (New York, NY), 2004.
Exposed: Athena Force, Silhouette Books (New York, NY), 2004.
Mistress Minded, Silhouette Books (New York, NY), 2004.
Her Baby's Father, Silhouette Books (New York, NY), 2004.
Rock Me All Night, Silhouette Books (New York, NY), 2005.
(With Nalini Singh) *Desert Warrior,* Silhouette Books (New York, NY), 2005.
The Amazon Strain, Silhouette Books (New York, NY), 2005.
(With Emilie Rose) *A Passionate Proposal,* Silhouette Books (New York, NY), 2005.
Their Million-Dollar Night, Silhouette Books (New York, NY), 2006.
His Wedding-Night Wager, Silhouette Books (New York, NY), 2006.
Her High-Stakes Affair, Silhouette Books (New York, NY), 2006.
The Once-a-Mistress Wife, Silhouette (New York, NY), 2006.
Exclusive, Silhouette Books (New York, NY), 2006.
Body Heat, Brava/Kensington (New York, NY), 2006.
The Ultimate Romantic Challenge, Brava (New York, NY), 2006.
Make-Believe Mistress, Silhouette Books (New York, NY), 2007.
Six-Month Mistress, Harlequin (New York, NY), 2007.
High-Society Mistress, Silhouette Books (New York, NY), 2007.
Legends and Lies, Silhouette Books (New York, NY), 2007.
(With others) *The Night before Christmas* (novella), Kensington (New York, NY), 2007.

Sex with a Stranger, Silhouette Books (New York, NY), 2007.

SIDELIGHTS: Katherine Garbera is the author of numerous romantic novels, and over the course of her successful writing career has received many accolades, including a nomination for the *Romantic Times* Book Club Career Achievement Award for both series fantasy and series adventure. In addition, her books have appeared on the Waldenbooks and Borders best-seller lists for series romance, and the extended best-seller list for *USA Today.* In an interview on her home page, Garbera explained her choice of writing subject by stating simply: "I write romance because I love that feeling that comes when you first fall in love." Garbera's books are known for their sensual descriptions, along with fun plots and intriguing characters.

Although Garbera's novels do stand on their own, many fall within loose series, with crossover characters or settings that are shared between books. One example of this is the "Cinderella" books, which include *Cinderella's Convenient Husband, Cinderella's Christmas Affair,* and *Cinderella's Millionaire.* The last title tells the story of CFO Joe Barone, who works for the family gelato business. Having lost his wife to cancer, Joe is no longer interested in love, instead throwing himself into his work. This backfires, however, when a contest run by the family in an effort to develop a new flavor gelato results in the winner coming to visit their corporate offices, and that winner turns out to be Holly Fitzgerald, a hard-working girl who has never had time to play with emotions or relationships. Joe's and Holly's individual emotional distance serves as the spark that ignites the chemistry between them, and so begins an awkward, sometimes-painful courtship. Shirley Lyons, in a review for *Romance Reader Reviews,* remarked on the speed with which these two overcome their personal issues in order to fall in love, but noted that in category romance, the quick turnaround is often built into the structure of the story. Lyons concluded: "Category romance is often meant to be a fairy tale and in this case, *Cinderella's Millionaire* hits the mark."

High-Society Mistress falls within Garbera's "Mistress" series. The book focuses on Tempest Lambert, a spoiled but emotionally deprived young woman who was sent to boarding school following her mother's death. As a result, she resents her wealthy father for having shipped her off and ignored her. As an adult, Tempest engages in a series of meaningless affairs, swiftly earning herself the reputation of "high-society mistress," as her only apparent discriminating factor is the man's wealth. She eventually ends up falling for Gavin, who has his own grudge against her father. Shirley Lyons, again reviewing for *Romance Reader Reviews,* found this couple less convincing, remarking that the book "was too much revenge and too little love."

The Ultimate Romantic Challenge revolves around widow Alexandra Haughton, whose husband died only a year into their marriage, and who then loses both of her parents relatively soon after. Devastated, she goes to work for her in-laws and leads something of a reclusive life, engaging in only meaningless affairs and refusing to invest her heart again. But when Sterling Powell arrives to purchase the Charleston hotel owned by the Haughtons, Alexandra is forced to deal with him. Maria Hatton, reviewing for *Booklist,* praised the book overall, and in particular noted that "Sterling is quite the romantic hero in Garbera's very sensual, satisfying story."

BIOGRAPHICAL AND CRITICAL SOURCES:

PERIODICALS

Booklist, November 15, 2006, Maria Hatton, review of *The Ultimate Romantic Challenge,* p. 37.
MBR Bookwatch, January, 2005, Harriet Klausner, review of *Night Life.*

ONLINE

Karmela Johnson Book Reviews, http://www.karmelajohnson.com/ (October 3, 2007), review of *Exposed: Athena Force.*
Katherine Garbera Home Page, http://www.katherinegarbera.com (October 3, 2007).
Romance Reader Reviews, http://www.theromancereader.com/ (October 3, 2007), Laura Scott, review of *The Ultimate Romantic Challenge;* Cathy Sova, review of *Some Kind of Incredible;* Irene Williams, review of *Her Baby's Father;* Shirley Lyons, reviews of *Cinderella's Millionaire* and *High-Society Mistress.*

Romantic Times Online, http://www.romantictimes. com/ (October 3, 2007), Pat Cooper, review, of *Make-Believe Mistress* and *The Once-a-Mistress Wife.**

*   *   *

GEE, Darien Hsu
    See KING, Mia

*   *   *

GERSON, Mark David 1954-

PERSONAL: Born October 3, 1954, in Montreal, Quebec, Canada; son of Sydney and Edith Gerson; children: Guinevere. *Education:* Concordia University, Montreal, Quebec, Canada, B.Comm., 1975.

ADDRESSES: Home—Albuquerque, NM.

CAREER: Concordia University, Montreal, Quebec, Canada, assistant director of public relations, 1976-81; writer and creative writing teacher, 1981—.

AWARDS, HONORS: Discovery Award, Southwest Literary Center, 2006, for *The MoonQuest.*

WRITINGS:

The MoonQuest (fantasy novel), LightLines Media (Santa Fe, NM), 2007.

Also author of the blog *Mark David Gerson's New Earth Chronicles.*

SIDELIGHTS: Mark David Gerson told *CA:* "It was March, 1994, and I was teaching a creative writing workshop in Toronto. As participants settled into writing, an odd-looking man in an even odder-looking coach pulled by two odd-colored horses rode onto my blank page—a blank page I hadn't even planned on filling, as I rarely write during these workshops. These characters would become the mysterious O'ric and his two mystical mares, Rykka and Ta'ar. And their tale would become the opening scene of the first draft of a novel that would reveal neither its story nor its title to me for many months.

"When I write, I write what I teach, which is that the story has a life and imperative of its own. My job as a writer is to listen, make myself available, and surrender to that story as fully as I can. That's how I wrote *The MoonQuest,* which is why the story emerged only as I wrote it. Outlining and plotting have never worked for me. Even though it's sometimes more stressful, I prefer to strap myself into the vehicle of my creative project and allow myself to be taken on a ride of surprise, wonder, and discovery.

"Most of *The MoonQuest*'s first two drafts were written in rural Nova Scotia on Canada's Atlantic seaboard and, as it turned out, I penned each of the subsequent revisions in the ensuing eleven years in a different part of Canada or the United States. As I prepare to return to work on *The StarQuest,* the first of two planned sequels, I can't help but wonder if each of its drafts will also find its way onto the page in a different part of the world.

"My philosophy in all I teach and write is to empower individuals to break through all that blocks them, creatively and spiritually, and to live more authentic lives as a result. Although it was not part of any conscious plan, *The MoonQuest,* with its tale of the freeing of once-banned storytelling, fits perfectly into that mold as will, I imagine, its sequels."

*   *   *

GERVAY, Susanne

PERSONAL: Born in Australia; daughter of Hungarian parents. *Education:* University of Sydney, B.A.; Advanced College of Education—Victoria, Dip.Ed.; University of New South Wales, M.Ed.; University of Technology—Sydney, M.A.

ADDRESSES: Home and office—Sydney, New South Wales, Australia. *Agent*—Rick Raftos, Raftos Management, Level 4/116-122 Kippax St., Surry Hills, New South Wales 2010, Australia. *E-mail*—info@sgervay. com.

CAREER: Educator, author, and child development specialist. Lecturer in English and communication at colleges in Sydney, New South Wales, Australia. Sydney's Literary and Arts Hotel, The Hughenden, Sydney, co-owner with sister, Elizabeth Gervay, beginning 1992. Sydney Children's Writers and Illustrators Network at the Hughenden, chair.

MEMBER: Society of Children's Book Writers and Illustrators Australia/New Zealand (co-head), New South Wales Writers Centre (member of board).

AWARDS, HONORS: Australian National University Short Story Award, 1996; Children's Literature Prize for Peace shortlist, 1996, for *Next Stop the Moon;* National Society of Women Writers Short Story Award, 1999; Family Therapy Award shortlist, Children's Book Council Notable Award, and WAYBRA award shorlist, all for *I Am Jack;* International Board on Books for Young People Outstanding Youth Literature on Disability honor, for *Butterflies;* Society of Women Writers Biennial Book Award, 2003, for *The Cave,* and 2005, for *Super Jack;* Lady Culter Award for services to children, 2007.

WRITINGS:

Jamie's a Hero, illustrated by Cathy Wilcox, Angus & Robertson (Pymble, New South Wales, Australia), 1994.

Next Stop the Moon, Angus & Robertson (Pymble, New South Wales, Australia), 1995.

Shadows of Olive Trees, Hodder Headline (Sydney, New South Wales, Australia), 1996.

Victoria's a Star, illustrated by Cathy Wilcox, Angus & Robertson (Pymble, New South Wales, Australia), 1996.

I Am Jack, illustrated by Cathy Wilcox, HarperCollins (Sydney, New South Wales, Australia), 2001.

Butterflies, HarperCollins (Sydney, New South Wales, Australia), 2001.

The Cave, HarperCollins (Sydney, New South Wales, Australia), 2002.

SuperJack (sequel to *I Am Jack*), illustrated by Cathy Wilcox, HarperCollins (Sydney, New South Wales, Australia), 2003.

That's Why I Wrote This Song, lyrics and music by daughter, Tory Gervay, HarperCollins (Sydney, New South Wales, Australia), 2007.

Contributor to anthology *H20: Stories of Water,* ABC Books, 2005. Contributor of short fiction to periodicals, including *Southerly, Quadrant, Westerly, Mattoid,* and *Ling.*

Author's work has been translated into several languages, including Korean and Bahasa.

ADAPTATIONS: Several books have been adapted for audiobook, including *I Am Jack* and *SuperJack,* Vocaleyes. *I Am Jack* was adapted as a play produced by MonkeyBaa Theatre, 2008.

SIDELIGHTS: "Writing is my voice and central to discovering meaning," Susanne Gervay told *CA.* "My collaborative work, *That's Why I Wrote This Song,* with my daughter Tory, was especially emotional. Tory wrote the music and lyrics, and sings her songs 'I Wanna Be Found' and 'Psycho Dad,' which underpin my novel. The integration of music, film, and text in story was a difficult but amazing journey."

BIOGRAPHICAL AND CRITICAL SOURCES:

PERIODICALS

Magpies, September, 1996, review of *Victoria's a Star,* p. 33; March, 2001, review of *Butterflies,* p. 38; July, 2002, review of *The Cave,* p. 43; November, 2003, review of *Super Jack,* p. 34, and *That's Why I Wrote This Song,* p. 41.

ONLINE

Australian Broadcasting Corporation, http://www.abc.net.au/rn/ (July 30, 2007), interview with Gervay.

Susanne Gervay Home Page, http://www.sgervay.com (September 15, 2007).

*　　*　　*

GHELFI, Brent

PERSONAL: Married; children: two sons.

ADDRESSES: Home—Phoenix, AZ.

CAREER: Lawyer, entrepreneur, and writer. Owns and operates businesses; previously served as a clerk on the U.S. Court of Appeals and as a partner in law firm in Phoenix, AZ.

WRITINGS:

NOVELS

Volk's Game, Henry Holt (New York, NY), 2007.
Volk's Shadow, Henry Holt (New York, NY), 2008.

SIDELIGHTS: Commenting on Brent Ghelfi's first novel, *Volk's Game, Armchair Interviews* Web site contributor Debra Kiefat called the novel "a powerful, visual read that captures the attention of anyone interested in espionage and intrigue." In a review on *Bookreporter.com,* Ghelfi received further praise from Joe Hartlaub, who noted: "Ghelfi's prose is like a dark drug that pulls you further under its spell with each taste, so that by the end of the book, the reader is exhausted and, though satiated, ready and frantic for more." The novel introduces readers to Russian double agent Alexei Volkovoy, called "Volk." On the one hand, Volk is a maimed veteran of the war against Chechnya and a powerful gangster. He also works as a covert military operative. The plot revolves around Volk's plan to steal a painting by Leonardo Da Vinci that is hidden underneath another painting exhibited at the St. Petersburg museum. Barbara Conaty, writing in the *Library Journal,* noted that the author's "deft and controlled writing [that] viscerally describes the snarling Russian underworld." A contributor to the *Literary Illusions* Web site wrote that the author's debut "is just too damn entertaining and its protagonist Alexei Volkovoy . . . is just too captivatingly violent to ignore."

BIOGRAPHICAL AND CRITICAL SOURCES:

PERIODICALS

Library Journal, March 1, 2007, Barbara Conaty, review of *Volk's Game,* p. 73.
Publishers Weekly, April 2, 2007, review of *Volk's Game,* p. 38.

ONLINE

Armchair Interviews, http://armchairinterviews.com/ (October 7, 2007), Debra Kiefat, review of *Volk's Game.*
BellaOnline, http://www.bellaonline.com/ (October 7, 2007), Karm Holladay, review of *Volk's Game.*
Bookreporter.com, http://www.bookreporter.com/ (October 7, 2007), Joe Hartlaub, review of *Volk's Game.*
Eclectic Closet, http://antheras.blogspot.com/ (June 11, 2007), Janelle Martin, review of *Volk's Game.*
Literary Illusions, http://www.literaryillusions.com/ (February 24, 2007), review of *Volk's Game.*
Mostly Fiction Book Reviews, http://www.mostly fiction.com/ (June 14, 2007), Tony Ross, review of *Volk's Game.*
Volk's Game Web site, http://www.volksgame.com (October 7, 2007).*

*   *   *

GIFFORD, Bill

PERSONAL: Born in Washington, DC. *Education:* Attended Dartmouth College.

ADDRESSES: Home—Mount Gretna, PA.

CAREER: Writer. *Outside* magazine, correspondent, 1990—.

WRITINGS:

Ledyard: In Search of the First American Explorer, Harcourt (Orlando, FL), 2007.

Contributor to periodicals, including *Rolling Stone, Bicycling, Men's Health, Washington Post, Men's Journal,* and *Slate.*

SIDELIGHTS: Outdoors writer Bill Gifford has been a longtime correspondent for *Outside* magazine. In his first book, *Ledyard: In Search of the First American Explorer,* Gifford writes about an explorer, John Ledyard, who is little known today but was greatly admired in his time by such men as U.S. President Thomas Jefferson. A contributor to *Kirkus Reviews* called *Ledyard* "an enthusiastic account," adding that "Gifford clearly relishes the chance to retrace his idol's steps." The author recounts Ledyard's wide range of adventures, from sailing with Captain Cook on his last voyage of exploration to getting arrested by Catherine the Great's men and expelled from Russia and its seas. By the 1820s, Ledyard was a renowned explorer considered among the pantheon of American personalities of the day. Among his most famous expeditions described in the book are treks across North America and into the unexplored regions of Africa. Along with Ledyard's story, the author also recounts through journal excerpts his own adventures while researching the book. Candice Millard, writing in the *New York Times Book Review,* noted that the biography "makes an important contribution to the existing literature through its personal approach to Ledyard's life." *Booklist* contributor George Cohen wrote that "this rich and immensely detailed biography brings this obscure explorer to life."

BIOGRAPHICAL AND CRITICAL SOURCES:

PERIODICALS

Booklist, November 15, 2006, George Cohen, review of *Ledyard: In Search of the First American Explorer,* p. 18.
Internet Bookwatch, March, 2007, review of *Ledyard.*
Kirkus Reviews, November 15, 2006, review of *Ledyard,* p. 1160.
Library Journal, January 1, 2007, Ingrid Levin, review of *Ledyard,* p. 118.
New York Tiimes Book Review, February 18, 2007, Candice Millard, "Hard Traveler," review of *Ledyard.*
Publishers Weekly, October 16, 2006, review of *Ledyard,* p. 42.
Reference & Research Book News, May, 2007, review of *Ledyard.*

ONLINE

Armchair Interviews, http://reviews.armchair interviews.com/ (October 9, 2007), Sharron Stockhausen, review of *Ledyard.*

Bill Gifford Home Page, http://www.billgifford.com (October 7, 2007).
Outside, http://outside.away.com/ (October 7, 2007), brief profile of author.*

*   *   *

GILLER, Marc D. 1968-
(Marc Daniel Giller)

PERSONAL: Born 1968; married; children: two. *Education:* Texas A & M University, B.S.

ADDRESSES: Home—FL. *Agent*—Kimberley Cameron, Reece Halsey North, 98 Main St., #704, Tiburon, CA 94920.

CAREER: Writer. Information systems manager for a Florida law firm. Previously worked as a photographer, producer, and computer trainer.

WRITINGS:

Hammerjack: A Novel, Bantam Books (New York, NY), 2005.
Prodigal: A Novel, Bantam Books (New York, NY), 2006.

SIDELIGHTS: Marc D. Giller's first science fiction work, *Hammerjack: A Novel,* features Cray Alden, a former "superhacker" of computers. Such hackers are nicknamed "hammerjacks." Cray has gone straight and now works as an investigator for Corporate Special Services tracking down hackers. He comes upon a scheme to take over the Earth via a dominating biological supercomputer. Carl Hays, writing in *Booklist,* referred to *Hammerjack* as "a winning blend of crime novel motifs and computer technology." Writing on *SFFWorld.com,* Rob H. Bedford noted that the author "has crafted an impressive novel, one that should appeal to the same people enjoying Richard K. Morgan's novels as well as readers looking for something fast paced with a healthy injection of technological evolution."

Prodigal: A Novel is a sequel to *Hammerjack* and features another former hammerjack, or computer hacker. Lea Prism, who appears in *Hammerjack,* finds herself battling the same cult she previously encountered. The cult's goal is to use human flesh as a computer substrate as part of its efforts to overthrow a multinational corporation and world power known as the Collective. In the course of her investigation, Lea has the opportunity to wreak revenge on the people who put her lover, Cray Alden, in frozen hibernation in cyberspace. In a review in *Booklist,* Carl Hays noted that the author "proves exceptional at keeping the reader entertained with heady technological extrapolation and full-throttle action." Writing on the *Yet Another Book Review* Web site, Shaun Green commented that the author's "take on classic cyberpunk concepts have a delicious edge of authenticity."

BIOGRAPHICAL AND CRITICAL SOURCES:

PERIODICALS

Booklist, May 1, 2005, Carl Hays, review of *Hammerjack: A Novel,* p. 1576; October 1, 2006, Carl Hays, review of *Prodigal: A Novel,* p. 44.

Kirkus Reviews, April 1, 2005, review of *Hammerjack,* p. 392.

Library Journal, October 15, 2006, Jackie Cassada, review of *Prodigal,* p. 54.

ONLINE

Armchair Interviews, http://reviews.armchair interviews.com/ (August 16, 2007), Bob Pike, review of *Hammerjack.*

BellaOnline, http://www.bellaonline.com/ (August 16, 2007), Laura Lehman, review of *Hammerjack.*

BookLoons, http://www.bookloons.com/ (August 16, 2007), Hilary Williamson, review of *Hammerjack.*

Gothic Revue, http://www.gothicrevue.com/ (August 16, 2007), Azrael Racek, review of *Hammerjack* and "Interview with Marc Giller."

Hammerjack.net, http://www.hammerjack.net/ (August 16, 2007), biography of author.

HubPages, http://hubpages.com/ (August 16, 2007), Daniel Greenfield, review of *Hammerjack.*

Random House Web site, http://www.randomhouse. com/ (August 16, 2007), brief biography of author.

SciFi.com, http://www.scifi.com/ (August 16, 2007), D. Douglas Fratz, review of *Hammerjack.*

SFFWorld.com, http://www.sffworld.com/(May 29, 2005), Rob H. Bedford, review of *Hammerjack.*

SF Site, http://www.sfsite.com/ (August 16, 2007), Victoria Strauss, review of *Hammerjack.*

TamaraSilerJones.com, http://www.tamarasilerjones. com/ (August 16, 2007), "Interview with Marc Giller and Tamara Siler Jones."

Yet Another Book Review, http://www.yetanotherbook review.com/ (August 16, 2007), Shaun Green, review of *Prodigal.**

*   *   *

GILLER, Marc Daniel
   See GILLER, Marc D.

*   *   *

GLAZEBROOK, Philip 1937-2007
(Philip Kirkland Glazebrook)

OBITUARY NOTICE— See index for *CA* sketch: Born April 3, 1937, in London, England; died July 2, 2007. Travel writer, novelist, and critic. Glazebrook traveled widely, but his interests focused on Central and South Asia. His travel writings covered ground that was new to many English-speaking readers, despite the opinion of some critics that his topics evoked the flavors and scents of times gone by. He described his own writing as a quest for the sources of travelers' fascination with the Orient, concluding that the East seemed to inspire a nostalgia for gallantry and romance that was fast disappearing in the commercialized world of Western Europe. Glazebrook had begun his career as a novelist and continued to dabble in fiction throughout his life. His travel writing resonated with the voice of the novelist, it is said, enhancing the accounts of his journeys. His travel books include *Byzantine Honeymoon: A Tale of the Bosphorus* (1979), *Journey to Kars: A Modern Traveler to Ottoman Lands* (1984), *Journey to Khiva: A Writer's Search for Central Asia* (1994), and *The Electric Rock Garden* (2001), set near the India-Pakistan border in the 1970s. Glazebrook also wrote reviews for British and American newspapers and at least one screenplay. His novels include the mystery *The Eye of the Beholder* (1977) and two novels about a fictional nineteenth-century travel writer, Captain Vinegar.

OBITUARIES AND OTHER SOURCES:

PERIODICALS

Times (London, England), August 2, 2007, p. 55.

*   *   *

GLAZEBROOK, Philip Kirkland
   See GLAZEBROOK, Philip

*   *   *

GOLD, Ben-Zion 1923-

PERSONAL: Born 1923, in Radom, Poland; immigrated to United States, 1947. *Religion:* Judaism.

CAREER: Rabbi, educator, and writer. Harvard University, Cambridge, MA, Harvard Hillel director, 1958-1990.

WRITINGS:

Tradition and Contemporary Reality (sermons and speeches), Puritan Press (Cambridge, MA), 1990.
The Life of Jews in Poland before the Holocaust: A Memoir, University of Nebraska Press (Lincoln, NE), 2007.

SIDELIGHTS: For more than three decades, Ben-Zion Gold served as director of Harvard Hillel, a Harvard University Jewish organization that sponsors lectureships, forums, and study groups focusing on the Jewish culture and religion. In a history of Hillel on the Harvard Hillel Web site, a contributor noted: "[Gold] had visions of a community that would serve the broad spectrum of Jews at Harvard and hopes that the University would in time be more accepting of Jewish difference."

In his book *The Life of Jews in Poland before the Holocaust: A Memoir,* Gold recounts his family's traditional Jewish life in Radom, Poland, before the German invasion in 1940 and reveals the legacy of the Jewish culture prior to World War II. The author then proceeds to describe his life in segregated ghettos after the German invasion, how he avoided being sent to a concentration camp, and his efforts to build a new life. "There is an imbalance in the way we remember the Jews of Europe," the author writes in his introduction to *The Life of Jews in Poland before the Holocaust.* "Thousands of books have been written about the Holocaust, but only a few have been written about the life of Polish Jews before they were murdered." The author goes on to comment: "The Holocaust was undoubtedly the greatest tragedy in Jewish history, but it would be a mistake to treat it as a heritage. Our heritage is the way the Jews of Europe lived and what they created before the Holocaust." George Cohen, writing in *Booklist,* noted that the author also "writes about . . . the relations between Poles and religious Jews as 'burdened by prejudices on both sides.'"

BIOGRAPHICAL AND CRITICAL SOURCES:

BOOKS

Gold, Ben-Zion, *The Life of Jews in Poland before the Holocaust: A Memoir,* University of Nebraska Press (Lincoln, NE), 2007.

PERIODICALS

Booklist, February 15, 2007, George Cohen, review of *The Life of Jews in Poland before the Holocaust,* p. 19.

ONLINE

Harvard Hillel, http://64.78.11.207/ (August 28, 2007), "History of Harvard Hillel."
University of Nebraska Press, http://www.nebraska press.unl.edu/ (October 4, 2007), brief profile of author.*

*   *   *

GOODMAN, David 1959-

PERSONAL: Born 1959; married; children: two.

ADDRESSES: Home—VT.

CAREER: Writer and journalist. *Mother Jones* magazine, contributing writer. Has appeared on national radio and television shows, including *PBS NewsHour with Jim Lehrer, Pacifica Radio, Democracy Now!, NPR's Fresh Air, Morning Edition, Talk of the Nation,* and *CNN.*

WRITINGS:

Classic Backcountry Skiing: A Guide to the Best Ski Tours in New England, Appalachian Mountain Club Books (Boston, MA), 1989.

Backcountry Skiing Adventures: Classic Ski and Snowboard Tours in Maine and New Hampshire, Appalachian Mountain Club Books (Boston, MA), 1999.

Fault Lines: Journeys into the New South Africa, photographs by Paul Weinberg, University of California Press (Berkeley, CA), 1999.

Backcountry Skiing Adventures: Classic Skiing and Snowboarding Tours in Vermont and New York, Appalachian Mountain Club Books (Boston, MA), 2000.

(With sister, Amy Goodman) *The Exception to the Rulers: Exposing Oily Politicians, War Profiteers, and the Media That Love Them,* Hyperion (New York, NY), 2004.

(With Amy Goodman) *Static: Government Liars, Media Cheerleaders, and the People Who Fight Back,* Hyperion (New York, NY), 2006.

Contributor to books, including *In the Name of Democracy,* Metropolitan, 2005. Contributor to periodicals, including the *Washington Post, Outside, Christian Science Monitor, Boston Globe,* and the *Nation.*

SIDELIGHTS: Journalist David Goodman has written backcountry skiing and travel books and is also the author of two books with his sister, Amy Goodman, a journalist and host of the National Public Radio program *Democracy Now!* In their first book together, *The Exception to the Rulers: Exposing Oily Politicians, War Profiteers, and the Media That Love Them,* David and Amy Goodman provide no-holds-barred reporting about politics and government as they address an array of topics, including media responsibility, human rights, and government accountability issues. The authors also discuss such current events as

massacres in East Timor, the Iraq War, and the state of journalism today in covering human rights abuses. *Kliatt* contributor Nola Theiss noted that the authors provide "many firsthand accounts of situations where journalists were forbidden to report what they have actually seen."

In their next book together, *Static: Government Liars, Media Cheerleaders, and the People Who Fight Back,* the Goodmans focus on the government administration of George W. Bush and what they see as the administration's Orwellian approach to providing and controlling information. In addition, they profile antiwar activist Cindy Sheehan and a British ambassador who released information on human rights abuses. "They also remind us of the unseemly ties between Republican Party supporters and Pentagon contracts in Iraq," wrote a contributor to *Publishers Weekly. PopMatters* Web site contributor Joe Silva commented: "Reading like an Administration rap sheet and a stern indictment of the media that let them down, *Static* is a look at the details beneath the headline horrors that most disinterested Americans never get to."

BIOGRAPHICAL AND CRITICAL SOURCES:

PERIODICALS

California Bookwatch, November, 2006, review of *Static: Government Liars, Media Cheerleaders, and the People Who Fight Back.*

Guild Practitioner, spring, 2005, David Gespass, review of *The Exception to the Rulers: Exposing Oily Politicians, War Profiteers and the Media That Love Them.*

Kliatt, September, 2005, Nola Theiss, review of *The Exception to the Rulers,* p. 37.

Parks & Recreation, January, 1990, review of *Classic Backcountry Skiing: A Guide to the Best Ski Tours in New England,* p. 87.

Publishers Weekly, June 12, 2006, review of *Static,* p. 41.

ONLINE

Democracy Now, http://tour.democracynow.org/ (October 9, 2007), brief profile of author.

Hyperion, http://www.hyperionbooks.com/ (October 9, 2007), brief profile of author.

Next Left, http://www.thenextleft.com/ (October 9, 2007), review of *Static.*

PopMatters, http://www.popmatters.com/ (November 21, 2006), Joe Silva, review of *Static.**

* * *

GOODMAN, Henrietta 1970-

PERSONAL: Born 1970; married twice (divorced twice); children: two. *Education:* Holds an M.A.; University of Montana, M.F.A.

CAREER: Poet, writer, and educator. University of Montana, Missoula, adjunct assistant professor, 2001—, writing center tutor and coordinator, 2003—. Marjorie Davis Boyden Wilderness Writing Residency, 2002.

AWARDS, HONORS: Individual Artist Fellowship, Montana Arts Council, 2001; Beatrice Hawley Award, Alice James Books, 2007, for *Take What You Want.*

WRITINGS:

Take What You Want (poetry), Alice James Books (Farmington, ME), 2007.

Contributor of poetry to periodicals, including *Mid-American Review, Willow Springs, Runes: A Review of Poetry,* and *Northwest Review.*

SIDELIGHTS: In her first book of poetry, titled *Take What You Want,* Henrietta Goodman covers a wide range of issues from familial and sexual love to motherhood. Many of the poems incorporate aspects of fairy tales, dreams, and animal life. For example, the narrator of several poems is Gretel, the young female protagonist in the Germanic fairy tale "Hansel and Gretel." Goodman's Gretel, however, is now an older, wiser woman. In one poem, Gretel recalls the mistake she and Hansel made when they mistook the smoke from the witch's chimney as smoke from their own home. Some of the poems are reflections on love lost, such as "Farewell Note in Czech." Overall, the collection of poems represents twelve years of work by the author. In an interview on the *Every Other Day* Web site, Goodman discussed the how feedback from one of her students impacted the manuscript for *Take What You Want:* "I was able to begin revising in a way I'd never done before. I gained perspective on the manuscript, saw it as a whole, with themes that needed more exploration, and weak spots that needed to be cut." Referring to the debut book of poetry as "impressive," *Library Journal* contributor Sue Russell felt that "readers will look forward to witnessing the transformations to come in Goodman's future work."

BIOGRAPHICAL AND CRITICAL SOURCES:

PERIODICALS

Library Journal, February 1, 2007, Sue Russell, review of *Take What You Want,* p. 75.

ONLINE

Alice James Books, http://www.alicejamesbooks.org/ (August 29, 2007), biography of Henrietta Goodman.

Every Other Day, http://www.kickingwind.com/ (August 1, 2007), interview with author and poems from *Take What You Want.**

* * *

GOOD TIME GEORGE
See MELLY, George

* * *

GOOLRICK, Robert 1948-

PERSONAL: Born 1948.

CAREER: Writer. Previously worked in advertising.

WRITINGS:

The End of the World as We Know It: Scenes from a Life (memoir), Algonquin Books of Chapel Hill (Chapel Hill, NC), 2007.

SIDELIGHTS: Commenting on Robert Goolrick's memoir *The End of the World as We Know It: Scenes from a Life, Newsweek* contributor Malcom Jones wrote: "The beauty of the story is in its language and its keen appreciation for the details that turn a childhood into an understated Chekhovian nightmare." *The End of the World as We Know It* recounts the author's loveless childhood with alcoholic parents who never expressed affection and eventually lived in squalor. The book, which *Entertainment Weekly* contributor Jennifer Reese called an "unnerving, elegantly crafted memoir," leads to an unexpected climax when the author reveals a family "secret" of abuse. Goolrick also includes the details of his suicide attempt when he was thirty-five, his subsequent self-maiming, and his eventual commitment to an institution. "In the end, Goolrick has written a moving, unflinchingly rendered story of how the past can haunt a life," wrote a *Publishers Weekly* contributor. Other critics also praised the book. "*The End of the World as We Know It* is barbed and canny, with a sharp eye for the infliction of pain," commented Janet Maslin in the *New York Times Book Review*. A *Kirkus Reviews* contributor made special note of the author's style, calling it "lush and poetic while never becoming purple."

BIOGRAPHICAL AND CRITICAL SOURCES:

BOOKS

Goolrick, Robert, *The End of the World as We Know It: Scenes from a Life,* Algonquin Books of Chapel Hill (Chapel Hill, NC), 2007.

PERIODICALS

Booklist, December 15, 2006, Deborah Donovan, review of *The End of the World as We Know It,* p. 14.

Entertainment Weekly, March 23, 2007, Jennifer Reese, review of *The End of the World as We Know It,* p. 66.
Kirkus Reviews, December 15, 2006, review of *The End of the World as We Know It,* p. 1255.
Newsweek, April 20, 2007, "Mystery and Manners," review of *The End of the World as We Know It.*
New York Times Book Review, March 26, 2007, Janet Maslin, "Beautiful People, Wretched Childhood," review of *The End of the World as We Know It.*
Publishers Weekly, November 27, 2006, review of *The End of the World as We Know It,* p. 40.

ONLINE

Bookslut, http://www.bookslut.com/ (October 9, 2007), Erin Walter, review of *The End of the World as We Know It.*

*   *   *

GRAHAM, John 1926-2007

OBITUARY NOTICE— See index for *CA* sketch: Born September 1, 1926, in Washington, DC; died of extensive blood loss, July 16, 2007, in Charlottesville, VA. Educator and author. For more than thirty years Graham taught students at the University of Virginia about the world of literature. He specialized in the eighteenth century but taught a wide variety of classes, ranging from rhetoric to romanticism, speech to satire, and communications to children's literature. Before arriving at the university in 1958, he had taught at private schools in Maryland and New Hampshire and at Marquette University and Georgetown University, his alma mater. Generally reflecting his scholarly interests, Graham's writings included studies of iconic authors such as Ernest Hemingway and John Hawkes and works on the craft of writing. His hobbies, however, included children's literature, and he wrote two modestly successful children's books: *A Crowd of Cows* (1968) and *I Love You, Mouse* (1976).

OBITUARIES AND OTHER SOURCES:

PERIODICALS

Washington Post, August 7, 2007, p. B6.

GRANDES, Almudena 1960-

PERSONAL: Born 1960, in Madrid, Spain; married Luis García Montero (a poet). *Education:* Attended Complutensian University, Madrid, Spain.

CAREER: Writer and novelist.

AWARDS, HONORS: La Sonrisa Vertical Prize, 1989, for *Las edades de Lulú;* Crisol Readers Prize.

WRITINGS:

Las edades de Lulú (novel), Tusquets (Barcelona, Spain), 1989, translation by Sonia Soto published as *The Ages of Lulu,* Grove Press (New York, NY), 1994.

Te llamaré Viernes (novel), Tusquets (Barcelona, Spain), 1991.

Malena es un nombre de tango (novel), Tusquets (Barcelona, Spain), 1994.

Modelos de mujer (short stories; title means "Models of Woman"), Tusquets Editores (Barcelona, Spain), 1996.

Atlas de geografía humana (novel), Tusquets (Barcelona, Spain), 1998.

Los Aires difíciles (novel), Tusquets Editores (Barcelona, Spain), 2002, translation by Sonia Soto published as *The Wind from the East,* Seven Stories Press (New York, NY), 2007.

Mercado de Barceló (short stories), illustrated by Ana Juan, Tusquets Editores (Barcelona, Spain), 2003.

Castillos de cartón (novel), Tusquets Editores (Barcelona, Spain), 2004.

Estaciones de paso (short stories), Tusquets Editores (Barcelona, Spain), 2005.

El Corazón helado (novel), Tusquets Editores (Barcelona, Spain), 2007.

Contributor to books. Author's books have been translated into twenty-one languages.

ADAPTATIONS: The Ages of Lulu and *Malena es un nombre de tango* were adapted for film, 1996.

SIDELIGHTS: Almudena Grandes is an acclaimed, best-selling novelist in Spain and has also achieved an international reputation. She garnered wide acclaim with her first novel, *Las edades de Lulú.* Published in English as *The Ages of Lulu,* the novel reached the million-plus mark in sales worldwide and tells the erotic story of Maria Luisa Ruiz-Poveday y Garcia de la Casa, commonly referred to as Lulu. Seduced by a friend of her older brother, Lulu goes on to study under him at university, where he introduces her to unusual sexual practices. A *Publishers Weekly* contributor referred to *The Ages of Lulu* as a "luridly inventive first novel." John Shreffler, writing in *Booklist,* called the novel "powerfully written and imparting a disturbing, immediate impact." The reviewer went on to note that the author had written a "powerful essay into the darker side of female sexuality."

Malena es un nombre de tango, the author's third novel, is narrated by Malena, which is also the name of a tango. A tomboy at the beginning of the novel, Malena goes through a sexual awakening as she encounters her first love and then marries. At the same time, Malena begins to delve into her family history and ultimately uncovers family secrets. "This novel is a 'Buddenbrooks' narrated by a bright, naughty woman at odds with her world, liberating her animal self," wrote a contributor to the *Economist.*

In her 1996 short-story collection titled *Modelos de mujer* ("Models of Woman"), Grandes presents stories about love which are all told by a diverse cast of women in often unusual situations. For example, the author includes a ghost story set in an asylum as well as a story about being brought up by a maid in Madrid. Another tale features an alcoholic mother who brings her daughter under control through the use of drugs. "All the stories are funny," wrote a contributor to the *Economist.*

Grandes's 2002 novel, *Los Aires difíciles,* was published in English as *The Wind from the East.* The story features Sara Gomez and Juan Olmedo, who both retire to a small coastal town to find that they are neighbors. The couple becomes close, first through their sharing of a maid, who tells each respective employer about the other. Eventually, they meet and form a companionship that they believe will help them forget the tragedies from their past. Leda Schiavo, writing in the *School Library Journal,* noted that the author's "appealing story and entertaining descriptions will hold readers' attention." A *Kirkus Reviews* contributor commented on the book's length, noting: "Grandes's serenely composed, ponderous work celebrates the healing power of friendship. It's long-running, but ultimately satisfying."

BIOGRAPHICAL AND CRITICAL SOURCES:

PERIODICALS

Booklist, June 1, 1994, John Shreffler, review of *The Ages of Lulu,* p. 1770.

Economist, July 20, 1996, reviews of *Malena es un nombre de tango* and *Modelos de mujer,* p. 14; November 13, 1999, review of *Atlas de geografía humana,* p. 14.

Internet Bookwatch, August, 2007, review of *The Wind from the East.*

Kirkus Reviews, November 15, 2006, review of *The Wind from the East,* p. 1146.

Library Journal, June 1, 1994, David A. Berona, review of *The Ages of Lulu,* p. 158.

Publishers Weekly, May 2, 1994, review of *The Ages of Lulu,* p. 280; October 23, 2006, review of *The Wind from the East,* p. 30.

School Library Journal, December, 2002, Leda Schiavo, review of *Los Aires difíciles,* p. 36.

Variety, April 17, 2006, Jonathan Holland, "Rough Winds," review of film *Los Aires difíciles,* p. 31.

World Literature Today, spring, 1995, review of *Malena es un nombre de tango.*

ONLINE

Almudena Grandes Home Page, http://www.almudena grandes.com (October 9, 2007).

EPDLP.com, http://www.epdlp.com/ (October 9, 2007), brief profile of author.

Escritoras.com, http://www.escritoras.com/ (October 9, 2007), brief profile of author.

Orion Books, http://www.orionbooks.co.uk/ (October 9, 2007), brief profile of author.

Seven Stories Press, http://www.sevenstories.com/ (October 9, 2007), brief profile of author.*

GRANGER, Farley 1925-
   (Farley Earle Granger, II)

PERSONAL: Born July 1, 1925, in San Jose, CA; son of Farley Earle and Eva H. Granger; longtime companion of Robert Calhoun.

ADDRESSES: Agent—Jay Julien, 1501 Broadway, New York, NY 10036.

CAREER: Actor. Appeared in over forty films between 1943 and 1995, including *North Star,* Samuel Goldwyn, 1945; *Rope,* Warner Brothers, 1948; *They Live by Night,* RKO Radio Pictures, 1948; *Side Street,* Metro-Goldwyn-Mayer, 1950; and *Strangers on a Train,* Warner Brothers, 1951. Appeared on episodes of the TV programs *United States Steel Hour,* 1953; *Playhouse 90,* 1956; *Get Smart,* 1965; *Ellery Queen,* 1975; *Love Boat,* 1977; and *Murder, She Wrote,* 1984. Appeared on TV series *As the World Turns* and *One Life to Live,* 1976-77. *Military service:* U.S. Armed Forces, 1944-46.

MEMBER: National Repertory Theatre, Circle Repertory Theatre.

AWARDS, HONORS: Daytime Emmy Award for Outstanding Supporting Actor in a Daytime Drama, 1977, for *One Life to Live;* Obie Award, 1986, for *Talley and Son;* Artistic Achievement Award, Philadelphia International Gay and Lesbian Film Festival, 2007.

WRITINGS:

(With Robert Calhoun) *Include Me Out: My Life from Goldwyn to Broadway,* St. Martin's Press (New York, NY), 2007.

SIDELIGHTS: Farley Granger is best known as a leading film actor and Broadway star with a career spanning over fifty years, from the 1940s to the 1990s. In 2007 he published his memoirs, written with his longtime partner, Robert Calhoun, titled *Include Me Out: My Life from Goldwyn to Broadway.* Granger's career began at the age of seventeen, when the great producer Samuel Goldwyn happened to watch Granger in a local theatre production of *The Wookie.* Granger was signed to a seven-year contact with Goldwyn, and went on to star in a number of films alongside leading ladies such as Ann Blyth, Shelley Winters, and Marilyn Monroe. Granger's relationship with Goldwyn eventually soured and he opted to settle out of his contract. Granger continued his acting career in films, such as the Italian masterpiece *Senso;* in television, with recurring roles in several daytime soap operas; and in theatre, in productions such as *The Crucible* and *The Glass Menagerie.*

In addition to recounting Granger's professional career, *Include Me Out* shares details from Granger's personal life, including what he describes as fluid sexuality, with relationships with both men and women. In an interview with *Philadelphia Inquirer* contributor Carrie Rickey, Granger stated his lifelong philosophy: "I've always been open to things." A critic for *Kirkus Reviews* described *Include Me Out* as "an engaging, colorful memoir," further adding: "Granger, who knows the dramatic when he sees it, fills his story with vivid moments from his career." Writing for *Gay and Lesbian Review Worldwide,* Michael Ehrhardt commented: "This is a memoir that will prove compulsive reading to old movie buffs as well as those who are fascinated by the inner workings of Hollywood." A *Publishers Weekly* reviewer noted that "Granger and Calhoun write with a stylish and iridescent flair."

BIOGRAPHICAL AND CRITICAL SOURCES:

PERIODICALS

Gay and Lesbian Review Worldwide, July 1, 2007, Michael Ehrhardt, "What Happened in Hollywood," review of *Include Me Out: My Life from Goldwyn to Broadway,* p. 36.
Kirkus Reviews, December 15, 2006, review of *Include Me Out,* p. 1255.
Philadelphia Inquirer, July 12, 2007, Carrie Rickey, "Stunner and Shunner," review of *Include Me Out.*
Publishers Weekly, January 1, 2007, review of *Include Me Out,* p. 47.

ONLINE

Farley Granger Home Page, http://www.farleygranger. net (September 30, 2007).*

GRANGER, Farley Earle, II
   See GRANGER, Farley

*   *   *

GRAY, Dianne E.

PERSONAL: Born in York, NE; married; husband's name Lee (a professor); children: two daughters. *Education:* Earned two bachelor's degrees (computer science and psychology); Hamline University, M.A. *Hobbies and other interests:* Reading, playing tennis.

ADDRESSES: Home and office—Winona, MN. *E-mail*—dgray@prairievoices.com.

CAREER: Writer. Worked as a computer programmer, systems analyst, and information system manager for twenty years; GrayGoose Software, Winona, MN, cofounder and software developer. Has also taught at University of Wisconsin-La Crosse.

AWARDS, HONORS: Willa Literary Award, Women Writing the West, and Best Books for Young Adults selection, American Library Association (ALA), both 2001, both for *Holding Up the Earth;* Pen USA Award finalist, Willa Literary Award finalist, ALA Best Books for Young Adults nomination, and Nebraska Book Award, Nebraska Center for the Book, 2003, all for *Together Apart;* Minnesota Book Award, Friends of the Saint Paul Public Library, and Nebraska Book Award, both 2007, both for *Tomorrow, the River.*

WRITINGS:

HISTORICAL FICTION

Holding Up the Earth, Houghton Mifflin (Boston, MA), 2000.
Together Apart, Houghton Mifflin (Boston, MA), 2002.
Tomorrow, the River, Houghton Mifflin (Boston, MA), 2006.

SIDELIGHTS: Nebraska native Dianne E. Gray is the author of a number of critically acclaimed young-adult novels, including *Holding Up the Earth,* the recipient of a Willa Literary Award from Women Writing the West. Gray, who enjoyed a long career in computer information systems before trying her hand at creative writing, is also the developer of the interactive story-writing software Hodgepodge, which is marketed through GrayGoose Software, a company she founded with her husband.

Gray's debut novel, *Holding Up the Earth,* concerns five generations of young women and their relationship to a small Nebraska farm. The tale centers on fourteen-year-old Hope, an orphan who has been shuttled from one foster home to another since her mother died in an automobile accident eight years earlier. Sarah, a college professor and Hope's newest foster mother, invites the teen to spend the summer on the farm where she grew up and where Sarah's mother, Anna, still resides. There Hope is introduced to the letters of Abigail Chapman, a girl whose father established the homestead and whose letters describe the hardships of pioneer life in 1869. Hope also reads from a diary belonging to Rebecca, a servant girl who lived on the farm at the turn of the twentieth century. She also learns that Anna saved the farm during the Great Depression, and discovers that Sarah fought against government intrusion on the nearby prairie. "What Hope understands is that many young women before her suffered great hardship and survived, in some ways healed by the land, working on the farm," observed *Kliatt* reviewer Claire Rosser. "While all the narratives are not equally compelling, many themes and symbols create a rich quilt of memories," noted *School Library Journal* critic Elizabeth A. Kaminetz, and a *Horn Book* contributor called *Holding Up the Earth* "a carefully structured work full of recurring connections and patterns, peopled with strong female characters."

Set in Nebraska in 1888, *Together Apart* focuses on teenagers Hannah and Isaac, friends who survived a deadly storm known as the "School Children's Blizzard" by huddling beneath a haystack. Months later, Isaac flees his abusive stepfather. When a grief-stricken Hannah, who lost her two brothers in the storm, also leaves her family farm, both teens ultimately find themselves at the home of Eliza Moore. A widowed suffragist, Moore puts the pair to work on the *Women's Gazette,* a feminist newsletter that she publishes. Hannah and Isaac also help Eliza open a "resting room" for visiting farm women and their children, and

through their efforts the teens begin to overcome their painful histories. Writing in *Horn Book,* Christine M. Heppermann stated that the author's "measured prose gracefully brings Hannah and Isaac to the conclusion that, if they could sustain each other through one storm, they would do well to face the future together." According to a reviewer in *Publishers Weekly,* "the blossoming love story will keep readers involved, and Gray's memorable characters reveal the late 19th-century society's attitudes toward women's rights and class consciousness."

Hannah and Isaac return in *Tomorrow, the River,* Gray's third work of historical fiction. Now married and the owners of a Mississippi riverboat, the duo is joined one summer by Hannah's fourteen-year-old sister, Megan. After a brief but exciting train trip during which she encounters a host of colorful characters, Megan boards the *Oh My* at Burlington, Iowa. When Isaac suffers a horrible injury, Megan must take on a greater share of the responsibilities, and she learns to fish, swim, and pilot the boat. "History and river life are skillfully woven into the fast-moving plot," noted Kathryn Kosiorek in *School Library Journal.* Heppermann commented that "it's rewarding to follow Megan's transformation from a girl unsure of her strengths and future to a confident young woman," and *Booklist* contributor Hazel Rochman described *Tomorrow, the River* as "a survival adventure and a realistic coming-of-age story."

On her home page, Gray remarked: "My advice to anyone who ever thought they might like to write—go for it, no matter if you are ten or ten times ten. You're never too young or too old to begin." She added that aspiring authors should "tune in to the world around you. There's magic there, in the simplest, everyday things, if only you open your eyes and ears and heart."

BIOGRAPHICAL AND CRITICAL SOURCES:

PERIODICALS

Booklist, January 1, 2001, Gillian Engberg, review of *Holding Up the Earth,* p. 959; September 15, 2002, Hazel Rochman, review of *Together Apart,* p. 226; December 1, 2006, Hazel Rochman, review of *Tomorrow, the River,* p. 38.

Book Report, May, 2001, Linden Dennis, review of *Holding Up the Earth,* p. 58.

Bulletin of the Center for Children's Books, November, 2000, review of *Holding Up the Earth,* p. 105; November, 2002, review of *Together Apart,* p. 108.

Horn Book, September, 2000, review of *Holding Up the Earth,* p. 568; November-December, 2002, Christine M. Heppermann, review of *Together Apart,* p. 757; January-February, 2007, Christine M. Heppermann, review of *Tomorrow, the River,* p. 67.

Kirkus Reviews, October 1, 2006, review of *Tomorrow, the River,* p. 1014.

Kliatt, November, 2000, Claire Rosser, review of *Holding Up the Earth,* p. 18; September, 2002, Claire Rosser, review of *Together Apart,* p. 9; November, 2006, Janis Flint-Ferguson, review of *Tomorrow, the River,* p. 11.

Publishers Weekly, October 23, 2000, review of *Holding Up the Earth,* p. 76; September 23, 2002, review of *Together Apart,* p. 73.

School Library Journal, October, 2000, Elizabeth A. Kaminetz, review of *Holding Up the Earth,* p. 160; December, 2002, Catherine Ensley, review of *Together Apart,* p. 138; December, 2006, Kathryn Kosiorek, review of *Tomorrow, the River,* p. 140.

Voice of Youth Advocates, October, 2000, review of *Holding Up the Earth,* p. 264; February, 2003, review of *Together Apart,* p. 475.

ONLINE

Dianne E. Gray Home Page, http://www.prairievoices.com (October 17, 2007).

Gray Goose Software, http://www.graygoosesoftware.com (October 17, 2007).

*   *   *

GREENOUGH, Beverly Sills
See SILLS, Beverly

*   *   *

GROUNDWATER, Beth

PERSONAL: Married; children: two. *Education:* College of William and Mary, B.S., 1978; Virginia Polytechnic Institute and State University, M.A.

ADDRESSES: E-mail—website07@bethgroundwater.com; bgroundwater@earthlink.net.

CAREER: Author. Former software engineer and project manager.

MEMBER: Mystery Writers of America, Sisters in Crime (secretary of Rocky Mountain chapter), Short Mystery Fiction Society, Pikes Peak Writers (vice president), Rocky Mountain Fiction Writers.

AWARDS, HONORS: First-place short story, PPW Paul Gillette Memorial Writing Contest, 2003, for "New Zealand"; first place, Rocky Mountain Fiction Writers Short Story Anthology Contest, 2004, for "New Zealand"; first place, Great Manhattan Mysteries Conclave Short Story Anthology Contest, 2005, for "Flamingo Fatality"; first place, *Storyteller* Magazine Flash Fiction Contest, 2005, for "Lucky Bear"; first place, *Mom Writer's Literary Magazine* Short Story Contest, 2006.

WRITINGS:

A Real Basket Case (novel), Five Star (Waterville, ME), 2007.

Contributor to anthologies, including *Manhattan Mysteries* and *Dry Spell: Tales of Thirst and Longing.* Author of the blog *Beth Groundwater.* Short stories have been published in anthologies and magazines, including *Wild Blue Yonder, Mom Writer's Literary Magazine,* and *The Map of Murder.*

SIDELIGHTS: A former software engineer with a knack for puzzles, Beth Groundwater turned to fiction writing as a second career and has become an award-winning short-story writer and mystery novelist. Her first story, "New Zealand," was published in 2004, and she has since seen her work published in numerous magazines and anthologies. *A Real Basket Case,* Groundwater's debut novel, introduces the character Claire Hanover, owner of a Colorado gift basket company, mother to grown children, and wife of a workaholic husband. A friend convinces a lonely Claire to get a massage from a handsome athletics instructor. The results are devastating: the masseur is killed mid-treatment and Claire's husband is found with the murder weapon. In an interview with Lonnie Cruse in *Poe's Deadly Daughters*, Groundwater shared how she decided on the novel's plot: "I had a 'What If?' inspiration: What if a man is killed in a married woman's bedroom and her husband is found holding the gun that shot him, BUT he didn't do it and the woman wasn't having an affair with the victim? That led to all kinds of questions that had to be answered."

Reviewing the novel for *Spinetingler Magazine*, J.B. Thompson remarked: "Groundwater's well-crafted characters comprise a nicely balanced cast, and she does a good job incorporating a blend of humor and relationship drama into a deftly twisted plot." Kevin Tipple commented on his blog, *Kevin's Corner:* "Full of twists and turns along with plenty of suspects, the book . . . is sure to keep readers entertained all the way to the end. Clearly the start of a series and a good one at that, this is a book that is sure to please a lot of readers." *Booklist* reviewer Barbara Bibel predicted that *A Real Basket Case* would "appeal to *Desperate Housewives* fans and those who like cozies with a bit of spice."

Groundwater told *CA:* "My first forays into fiction writing were my Freddie stories written when I was in fifth and sixth grade. Freddie had all sorts of wild adventures, including visiting an underground mole city after burrowing down in a giant screw-mobile. Once I retired from my career as a rare commodity, a software engineer who could write, I began writing fiction again for fun. On my long road to publication, I collected over one hundred rejections on my short stories to get seven published. I also was rejected by eighty-nine literary agents before the ninetieth decided I might have some talent and took me on. My first book contract was signed within a few months. Persistence is indeed important for writers! I am an avid and eclectic reader, devouring about a book a week. I love mysteries, of course, but also read literary, women's fiction, romance, and even some science fiction."

BIOGRAPHICAL AND CRITICAL SOURCES:

PERIODICALS

Booklist, February 1, 2007, Barbara Bibel, review of *A Real Basket Case*, p. 34.

Crime Spree, March-April, 2007, Judy Clemens, review of *A Real Basket Case*.

Kirkus Reviews, January 1, 2007, review of *A Real Basket Case*.

ONLINE

Beth Groundwater Home Page, http://www.beth groundwater.com (August 22, 2007).

Kevin's Corner, http://www.hollywoodcomics.com/kevin/ (January 15, 2007), Kevin Tipple, review of *A Real Basket Case*.

Poe's Deadly Daughters, http://poesdeadlydaughters. blogspot.com/ (March 9, 2007), Lonnie Cruse, review of *A Real Basket Case*.

Romance Reviews Today, http://romrevtoday.com/ (October 12, 2007), Courtney Michelle, review of *A Real Basket Case*.

Spinetingler Magazine, http://www.spinetinglermag. com/ (August 22, 2007), J.B. Thompson, review of *A Real Basket Case*.

* * *

GUHRKE, Laura Lee

PERSONAL: Education: Graduated from college.

ADDRESSES: Home—ID. *E-mail*—laura@lauralee guhrke.com.

CAREER: Romance novelist. Worked previously as a caterer and as an advertising agent in Los Angeles, CA.

AWARDS, HONORS: RITA Award, Romance Writers of America; *Romantic Times* Award for Best European Historical Romance, 2004.

WRITINGS:

"GUILTY" SERIES

Guilty Pleasures, Avon Books (New York, NY), 2004.
His Every Kiss, Avon Books (New York, NY), 2004.

The Marriage Bed, Avon Books (New York, NY), 2005.

She's No Princess, Avon Books (New York, NY), 2006.

"GIRL-BACHELOR" SERIES

And Then He Kissed Her, Avon Books (New York, NY), 2007.

The Wicked Ways of a Duke, Avon Books (New York, NY), 2008.

OTHER

Prelude to Heaven, HarperCollins (New York, NY), 1994.

To Dream Again, HarperCollins (New York, NY), 1995.

Conor's Way, HarperCollins (New York, NY), 1996.

The Seduction, HarperCollins (New York, NY), 1997.

Breathless, Sonnet Books (New York, NY), 1999.

The Charade, Sonnet Books (New York, NY), 2000.

Not So Innocent, Sonnet Books (New York, NY), 2002.

Contributor to various periodicals, including *Romance Writers Report, British Weekly,* and *Irish-American Press.*

SIDELIGHTS: Laura Lee Guhrke is a historical romance novelist whose books are regularly featured on the *USA Today* best-seller list. After earning a business degree in college, the Idaho native spent time in Los Angeles, where she tried her hand at selling advertising and catering meals for Hollywood events. Guhrke ultimately moved back to Idaho and set her sights on a career as a writer, drawn to the independence of working for herself and to the romance genre as a source of personal pleasure. Her first novel, *Prelude to Heaven,* was published in 1994, and she has written at least one novel nearly every year since.

Among Guhrke's early novels, *Breathless* is representative of her strength at creating memorable characters and attention-grabbing plots. The book's protagonist, Lily Morgan, is a librarian in a turn-of-the-century Georgian town, making a quiet life for herself after a scandal surrounding her divorce five years prior. A boisterous men's club in town becomes the focus of Lily's ire, and the same lawyer who was at the center of her divorce debacle becomes an obstruction in Lily's personal crusade to close the club. The two become sudden allies, however, when one of the club's female "entertainers" is murdered. Writing for the *Romance Reader* Web site, Lesley Dunlap remarked: "I had scarcely begun reading *Breathless* (a most non-descriptive title) when I felt that it was going to be a terrific book. My instincts were right. It's funny. It's touching. It's great." *Romantic Times* online reviewer Kathe Robin exclaimed that Guhrke "weaves a lively story where Southern respectability joins with simmering passion to heat up the pages giving readers a memorable romance."

The Charade, Guhrke's follow-up to *Breathless,* is set in Boston in the years prior to the Revolutionary War. Trying to escape a destiny as an indentured servant in Virginia, former pickpocket Katie is blackmailed into spying for the British in an attempt to uncover the root of the growing rebellion. As it happens, the object of Katie's investigation becomes the object of her desires, and her own survival is threatened as she is drawn into the role of double agent. Lesley Dunlap appreciated the novel's "well-developed characters, cohesive plot and relatively uncommon setting" in a review for the *Romance Reader* Web site. A *Publishers Weekly* critic found the book had "well-researched historical background and a fast-paced plot."

In *Not So Innocent,* Guhrke introduces the character of Sophie Haversham, a psychic who is compelled to report to the police a crime that has not yet happened. The Scotland Yard inspector who receives the report is skeptical until he becomes the intended victim of a murder. As part of the subsequent investigation, the inspector delves into the details of Sophie's personal life, only to succumb to a growing attraction. Describing the novel as "a delightful yet intensely satisfying mystery of late 1800s London," Denise M. Clark remarked in a review for the *Curled Up with a Good Book* Web site: "Tolerance and acceptance is subtly woven throughout the plot, which twists and turns until the reader is giddy with anticipation to identify the person behind the attempted murder."

Emmaline Dove, the central character in *And Then He Kissed Her,* has been dealing with the less-than-acceptable behavior of her boss for some time, believing that her dedicated work as the publisher's secretary would be taken into account when she asks him to consider her newly written book for publication. Instead, her employer, Harry, doesn't even read it, prompting Emmaline to quit and take her book with her. The unintended result is that Harry sees her in a different light for the first time, leaving open the possibility for both professional and physical connections down the road. *Booklist* reviewer John Charles called the novel "a sparkling and deliciously fun romantic battle of wits." "Fresh, smart, and romantic" was how a contributor to the *Dear Author* Web site described the book, noting that the story "never lagged, not once."

BIOGRAPHICAL AND CRITICAL SOURCES:

PERIODICALS

Booklist, March 1, 2007, John Charles, review of *And Then He Kissed Her,* p. 70.
Publishers Weekly, February 14, 2000, review of *The Charade,* p. 179.

ONLINE

Curled Up with a Good Book, http://www.curledup.com/ (October 26, 2007), Denise M. Clark, review of *Not So Innocent.*
Dear Author, http://dearauthor.com/ (March 19, 2007), review of *And Then He Kissed Her.*
Laura Lee Guhrke Home Page, http://www.lauraleeguhrke.com (October 1, 2007).
Romance Reader, http://www.theromancereader.com/ (October 1, 2007), Lesley Dunlap, reviews of *The Charade* and *Breathless.*
Romantic Times, http://www.romantictimes.com/ (October 1, 2007), Kathe Robin, review of *Breathless.**

*   *   *

GUTHRIE, Allan

PERSONAL: Born in Orkney, Scotland; married; wife's name Donna (an adult literacy tutor).

ADDRESSES: *Home*—Edinburgh, Scotland. *E-mail*—allan@allanguthrie.co.uk.

CAREER: Crime novelist, editor, and literary agent. Point Blank Press, Rockland, MD, and Jenny Brown Associates, Edinburgh, Scotland, commissioning editor. Worked for a bookstore as a bookseller, information technologies trainer, and stockroom manager.

AWARDS, HONORS: Theakston's Old Peculier Crime Novel of the Year, 2007, for *Two-Way Split;* nominated for Edgar Allan Poe Award for best paperback original, 2006, for *Kiss Her Goodbye.*

WRITINGS:

FICTION

Two-Way Split, Point Blank (Rockland, MD), 2004.
Kiss Her Goodbye, Dorchester (New York, NY), 2005.
Hard Man, Harcourt (New York, NY), 2007.
Kill Clock (novella), Barrington Stoke (Edinburgh, Scotland), 2007.

Author of the blog *Hard Man* (now discontinued). Author's works have been translated into Italian.

SIDELIGHTS: Allan Guthrie is a crime writer whose hard-hitting works are often inspired by his native city of Edinburgh, Scotland. Guthrie attributes his success as an author in part to luck: Best-selling writer Ian Rankin encouraged audience members at an international book festival to read a novel by the previously unknown Guthrie. Within a year, Guthrie had secured a three-book deal with the Scottish publishing company Polygon, earning the company's largest advance to date. Several of his books have since been nominated for major awards, including a nomination to the Edgar Allan Poe Award shortlist.

The novel that started it all, *Two-Way Split,* features a group of characters connected by a crime. A botched robbery leaves an elderly woman dead, and her son Pearce—who happens to be an ex-con who served time for bringing his sister's killer to personal justice—is set on revenge. Pearce is featured in another of Guthrie's novels, *Hard Man,* when he is enlisted by a dysfunctional dad-son combo to help retrieve the baby of the family—a married sixteen-year-old pregnant girl with another man's baby—from her abusive husband. Pearce is still grieving his mother, and not interested in the job—until someone decides it would be a good idea to get his attention by killing his beloved dog. In a review for the *Crime Scene Scotland* Web site, Russel D. McLean wrote that the novel "comes out roaring, with a black, almost surreal, vision of Edinburgh. His [Guthrie's] violent, stripped-down novels are enough to send traditional mystery fans scampering behind the sofa." McLean continued: "*Hard Man* delivers on a potential that has so far only been hinted at. There's a sense of velocity from the word go, and as the novel progresses, events move entirely out of control until the final third delivers a denouement that is as inspired as it is insane." A *Kirkus Reviews* contributor described the novel as "by turns hilarious and horrifying," noting: "Guthrie's original voice grabs the reader and doesn't let go."

Guthrie's other books include *Kiss Her Goodbye,* which earned him nominations for the Edgar, Gum-shoe, and Anthony awards, and *Kill Clock,* a novella targeting adults who struggle as readers, such as those with dyslexia.

BIOGRAPHICAL AND CRITICAL SOURCES:

PERIODICALS

Kirkus Reviews, March 1, 2007, review of *Hard Man,* p. 196.

ONLINE

Allan Guthrie Home Page, http://www.allanguthrie. co.uk (October 1, 2007).

Crime Scene Scotland, http://crimescenescotland reviews.blogspot.com/ (October 26, 2007), Russel D. McLean, review of *Hard Man.*

H

HAARSMA, P.J.

PERSONAL: Born in Canada; married Marissa Grieco; children: Skylar (daughter). *Education:* Mc-Master University, B.S.; attended University of California—Los Angeles Film School.

ADDRESSES: Home—Los Angeles, CA.

CAREER: Writer and professional photographer and filmmaker. Owner and producer for film production company for over fifteen years. Creator and developer of "Rings of Orbis" online role-playing game; director of film *Devious Beings.* Presenter at schools. Volunteer for Kids Need to Read project.

AWARDS, HONORS: New York Public Library Books for the Teen Age designation, 2007, for *Virus on Orbis 1.*

WRITINGS:

"SOFTWIRE" SCIENCE-FICTION NOVEL SERIES

Virus on Orbis 1, Candlewick Press (Cambridge, MA), 2006.
Betrayal on Orbis 2, Candlewick Press (Cambridge, MA), 2008.

Also author of film scripts, including *Devious Beings.*

SIDELIGHTS: P.J. Haarsma turned from a career in film production to science fiction with his "Softwire" series of novels, which include *Virus on Orbis 1* and *Betrayal on Orbis 2.* Set in an imaginative world and inspired by Haarsma's own love of science, the "Softwire" novels are also the basis for the online role-playing game "Rings of Orbis," which Haarsma created and developed and which serves as a companion to the fiction series.

Haarsma's fiction debut, *Virus on Orbis 1,* is the first novel in the "Softwire" series and focuses on a group of orphaned children who are enslaved to an alien people on a remote interspace hub called the rings of Orbis. As readers meet twelve-year-old Johnny Turn-bull, he is living on a spaceship, together with his sister and dozens of other parentless children. The ship was designed to carry a group of adults to a planet far from Earth, where they hoped for a better life. When the adults dies, the fertilized embryos also carried on the ship are all born simultaneously after being incubated and brought to term by the ship's computer. Landing on Orbis 1, the children discover that they are destined to fulfill their parents' obligations: they are indentured to the planet's native creatures until they can repay the cost of their space voyage. On Orbis 1, Johnny discovers that he has the ability to communicate with the planet's computers, and because of this talent he is labeled a Softwire. When the ageing computers on Orbis 1 begin to malfunction, Johnny is blamed and must discover the true cause of the malfunction in order to protect himself and his friends.

In her *Booklist* review of *Virus on Orbis 1,* Diana Tixier Herald wrote that the novel will capture readers' interest due to its mix of "exotic aliens, dangerous situations, and fast-paced adventure." In *Kliatt,* Lesley Farmer noted that Haarsma's young hero is "very likeable," and that the novel's subplot "provides a supernatural spin." Noting the story's fast-moving plot, Melissa Christy Burton added in her *School Library Journal* review that in this debut novel Haarsma "deftly introduces the futuristic setting without getting bogged down in long and detailed descriptive passages."

BIOGRAPHICAL AND CRITICAL SOURCES:

PERIODICALS

Booklist, November 15, 2006, Diana Tixier Herald, review of *Virus on Orbis 1,* p. 59.
Bulletin of the Center for Children's Books, November, 2006, April Spisak, review of *Virus on Orbis 1,* p. 125.
Kirkus Reviews, September 1, 2006, review of *Virus on Orbis 1,* p. 904.
Kliatt, September, 2006, Lesley Farmer, review of *Virus on Orbis 1,* p. 12.
School Library Journal, December, 2006, Melissa Christy Burton, review of *Virus on Orbis 1,* p. 142.

ONLINE

IGN.com, http://comics.ign.com/ (October 4, 2006), Stephen Horn, interview with Haarsma.
P.J. Haarsma Home Page, http://www.pjhaarsma.com (October 27, 2007).
Rings of Orbis Web site, http://www.ringsoforbis.com (October 27, 2007).*

*   *   *

HADAS, Rachel 1948-

PERSONAL: Born November 8, 1948, in New York, NY; daughter of Moses (a classical scholar) and Elizabeth Hadas; married Stavros Kondylis, 1970 (divorced, 1978); married George Edwards (a composer and teacher), July 22, 1978; children: Jonathan. *Education:* Harvard University, B.A. (magna

Rachel Hadas

cum laude), 1969; Johns Hopkins University, M.A., 1977; Princeton University, Ph.D. (with special distinction), 1982.

ADDRESSES: Office—Department of English, Newark College of Arts and Sciences, Rutgers University, Hill Hall, 360 Dr. M.L. King, Jr. Boulevard, Newark, NJ 07102; fax 201-648-1450. *E-mail*—rhadas@rutgers. edu.

CAREER: Rutgers University, Newark, NJ, instructor, 1980-81, assistant professor, 1982-87, associate professor, 1987-92, professor of English, beginning 1992, currently Board of Governors Professor of English. Has also taught in the English department at Columbia University, 1992 and 1993, the Hellenic Studies Program at Princeton University, 1995, the Creative Writing Program at Princeton University, 1996, the Sewanee Writers' Conference and the West Chester Poetry Conference.

MEMBER: Poetry Society of America (member of governing board, 1983-84), Modern Language Association of America, Modern Greek Studies Association (member of governing board, 1996-98), National Council of Teachers of English, National Book Critics Circle (member of governing board, 1994-97), American Academy of Arts and Sciences, Phi Beta Kappa.

AWARDS, HONORS: Isobel M. Briggs traveling fellowship, 1969-70; writers grant, Vermont Council on the Arts, 1975-76, for poetry; fellow of MacDowell Colony and scholar at Bread Loaf Writers' Conference, both 1976; Ingram-Merrill Foundation Award, 1977, 1994, for poetry; Sidonie M. Clauss Prize, Princeton University, 1982-83, for best dissertation in comparative literature; Guggenheim fellow in poetry, 1988-89; American Academy and Institute of Arts and Letters Literature Award, 1990; McGinnis Award, *Southwest Review,* 1990, for best essay to appear in magazine in previous year; Elizabeth Matchett Stover Poetry Award, *Southwest Review,* 1991; Hellas Award, *Hellas Magazine,* 1993, for best poem to appear in magazine in previous year; elected to American Academy of Arts and Sciences, 1995; Sharp Family Foundation Award, *Yale Review,* 1995; and O.B. Hardison Award of the Folger Shakespeare Library.

WRITINGS:

Starting from Troy (poems), D.R. Godine (Boston, MA), 1975.

(Editor, with Charlotte Mandel and Maxine Silverman) *Saturday's Women: Eileen W. Barnes Award Anthology,* introduction by Mandel, Saturday Press (Upper Montclair, NJ), 1982.

Slow Transparency (poems), Wesleyan University Press (Middletown, CT), 1983.

Form, Cycle, Infinity: Landscape Imagery in the Poetry of Robert Frost and George Seferis, Bucknell University Press (Lewisburg, PA), 1985.

A Son from Sleep (poems), Wesleyan University Press (Middletown, CT), 1987.

Pass It On (poems), Princeton University Press (Princeton, NJ), 1989.

Living in Time (essays and poems), Rutgers University Press (New Brunswick, NJ), 1990.

Unending Dialogue: Voices from an AIDS Poetry Workshop, Faber & Faber (Boston, MA), 1991, expanded edition, 1993.

Mirrors of Astonishment, Rutgers University Press (New Brunswick, NJ), 1992.

Others Worlds Than This: Translations (from Latin, French, and Modern Greek Poetry), Rutgers University Press (New Brunswick, NJ), 1994.

The Empty Bed, Wesleyan University Press (Middletown, CT), 1995.

The Double Legacy, Faber & Faber (Boston, MA), 1995.

Halfway down the Hall: New and Selected Poems, Wesleyan University Press (Middletown, CT), 1998.

Merrill, Cavafy, Poems, and Dreams (poems), University of Michigan Press (Ann Arbor, MI), 2000.

Indelible (poems), Wesleyan University Press (Middletown, CT), 2001.

Laws (poems), Zoo Press (Lincoln, NE), 2004.

The River of Forgetfulness (poems), David Roberts (Cincinnati, OH), 2006.

(With Dick Davis and Timoth Steele) *Three Poets in Conversation,* Between the Lines (London, England), 2006.

TRANSLATIONS

Stephanos Xenos, *Trelles* (poems; title means "Follies"), [Athens, Greece], 1978.

Seneca, *Oedipus* ("Roman Drama Series"), Johns Hopkins University Press (Baltimore, MD), 1994.

Euripides, *Helen* ("Greek Drama Series"), University of Pennsylvania Press (Philadelphia, PA), 1997.

Work represented in anthologies, including *Ardis Anthology of American Poetry.* Contributor of poems, articles, translations, and reviews to many magazines, including *Atlantic Monthly, National Forum, Harper's, New Yorker, New Republic, Partisan Review, Ploughshares,* and *Writing.*

SIDELIGHTS: Rachel Hadas, a poet, translator, essayist, critic, and professor of literature, grew up on the Upper West Side of Manhattan near Columbia University and surrounded by the generation of New York intellectuals that largely dominated the American literary and political scene from the 1930s through the 1960s. Yet Hadas experienced an unusual journey from Radcliffe and Harvard in the 1960s to her emergence in the 1980s, with five published books of poetry (some mixed with prose), as perhaps the most prolific poet among the New Formalists. Instead of proceeding directly to graduate school to study classics or creative writing, Hadas spent much of her twenties married to a Greek, living with him on the island of Samos, running an olive-oil press, and being tried for and acquitted of arson in connection with the press's mysterious destruction.

Hadas majored in classics at Radcliffe College and was elected to Phi Beta Kappa during her junior year. At Harvard she took her only poetry-writing course as an undergraduate with Robert Fitzgerald, the poet and classicist who taught such other poets as Robert B. Shaw, Katha Pollitt, Brad Leithauser, Mary Jo Salter, and Dana Gioia. Hadas was the poetry editor of the *Harvard Advocate* during her senior year (1968-1969). Her residence in Greece forms the background and subject matter for most of the poems in two apprentice volumes: her chapbook *Starting from Troy* and the book-length *Slow Transparency*. While critics noted the rich emotional background and vividly beautiful landscape that ground these poems, as well as Hadas's obvious intelligence and her technical proficiency with a variety of meters and verse forms, some reviewers found that neither volume is fully successful in exploiting these resources. *Slow Transparency* moves in time from childhood into adulthood and in location from a Greek island to rural New England. While *Times Literary Supplement* contributor Anne Stevenson believed that Hadas's "poems suffer from being worked on for too long under the shadow of Wallace Stevens," she added that "there is intelligence here, and imagination which augurs well for the future." Jorie Graham in the *New York Times Book Review* pointed out the poet's tendency to over-editorialize, but also stated that "in those poems where thinking is not inflated to fit shapeliness, Miss Hadas confronts the details of her life with some genuine power."

Hadas's third poetry collection, *A Son from Sleep,* is dedicated to her son, Jonathan, the subject of many of the poems. Several critics have noted that as motherhood and domesticity have become more central to Hadas's work, her poetry has become more accessible linguistically and emotionally direct. One theme that emerges in *A Son from Sleep* is the connection between the intellectual nourishment Hadas still receives from memories of her late father and the physical nourishment she provides for her son through her body. This theme continues in Hadas's fourth volume of poems, *Pass It On.* This collection is, according to *Dictionary*

of Literary Biography contributor Robert McPhillips, her strongest to date and "fully consolidates the potential only sporadically on view in her earlier books. Not only is it a completely unified volume focused on the various ways life and knowledge are passed down from generation to generation—from parents to children, from teachers to students, from books in general, and through the writing of poems—it also makes clear that Hadas's greatest strengths as a poet are less apparent in individual lyrics than they are in the larger units of poetic sequences and in full-length books."

As both a poet and an essayist, Hadas uses both prose and poetry to muse on time in *Living in Time.* Her long poem, "The Dream Machine," which a *Publishers Weekly* reviewer considered "a profound meditation on reality," is surrounded by two sections of essays that discuss what time means, how poets have viewed it in the past, and how men with AIDS taking a workshop run by Hadas react to having only a little time left to live. Her experience working with AIDS victims also colors her poetry collection, *The Empty Bed,* a series of poems about death, memory, and friendship in the face of losing a loved one. "With the softest, sweetest touch, Hadas skillfully articulates the initial sorrow and eventual acceptance of final good-byes," wrote a *Booklist* contributor of the title. Her poems are elegies, both for her AIDS students and for her mother, who died of cancer. In her prose collection, *The Double Legacy,* Hadas reflects on the loss of her mother and one of her close friends, a victim of AIDS. "A loosely organized collection of essays whose subjects range from a trip to a mailbox to the role of mourning in literature, [the book] is as deeply subjective . . . as Ms. Hadas herself promises it will be," wrote Daniel Mendelsohn in the *New York Times Book Review.*

In *Halfway down the Hall,* poems previously published in Hadas's early books, including *Starting from Troy* and *A Son from Sleep,* reappear in the company of thirty-three new pieces. "The rhymes she chooses are gentle and scholarly but always fresh, deft, natural," said Judy Clarence in a *Library Journal* review of the title. Joel Brouwer, writing in *Progressive,* noted that many of the poems in the collection revolve around art, from museums to ballet. "Art may not be able to overthrow mortality's dominion, but it can help us understand and endure. . . . It can delight us, too—as these witty, elegant poems demonstrate," he concluded.

Indelible, a collection of new poetry, revisited many of the themes of her earlier works contained in *Halfway down the Hall.* Divided into three sections, the book contains lamentations for the dead, musings on mythology, and personal pieces. "The book's instants of emotional vulnerability will please Hadas's readers, and are often what compel the most," wrote a *Publishers Weekly* contributor.

Of Hadas's work on the whole, poet Grace Schulman wrote on *Poets.org,* "The poems are urgent, contemplative, and finely wrought. In them, antiquity illuminates the present as Rachel Hadas finds in ordinary human acts 'what never was and what is eternal.'" Gloria Brame, who interviewed Hadas on Brame's home page, said of her poetry, "Rachel brings vivid immediacy to the life of the mind as well as to the ordinary realities of everyday life." A *Publishers Weekly* critic, in a review of *The Empty Bed,* called Hadas "one of our most elegiac poets." Discussing how "no one reads poetry anymore" in her review of *Laws,* Amanda Kolson Hurley in the *Washington Times* recommended, "Readers who have been disappointed by their encounters with modern poetry—and readers who haven't—should discover the work of Rachel Hadas." Kolson further noted that Hadas's poetry in *Laws* "displays the fluid gracefulness, the generosity of intellect and emotion, that have come to distinguish her best writing." Hadas "has a gift for finding the profound in the ordinary, instilling the ordinary with importance," wrote Bob Braun in the Newark, New Jersey, *Star-Ledger.*

Hadas once explained to *CA:* "Why do I write? To make things clear or at least clearer, whether to myself or to others; to hold on in some fashion to what has been and is continually being lost—these may be the most consistent threads in a thirty-year career, but there are others. One strand is the lyric impulse to address a loved one, living or dead; another is the challenge of translating; another is the work I have done with people with AIDS as well as other students—helping them to write and myself being helped in the process.

"My work is influenced by all the books I have loved, starting with children's books from *The Color Kittens* to *The Princess and the Goblin,* moving on through poetry, belle-lettres, philosophers I have read and enjoyed—I might mention Proust, Thoreau, Nabokov, Seneca, Catullus, Cavafy, and in our own day James Merrill.

"My writing process is hardly carved in stone. I don't have a daily routine; when time permits, I try to work fast, and later on, typing up my scribbles, begin to shape them, to see what forms inhere and discard the rest. Whether I'm writing poetry or prose, there is a strong sense of discovery, of—in words I am borrowing from Robert Frost, another writer I turn back to often—discovering what I hadn't known I knew."

AUTOBIOGRAPHICAL ESSAY: Rachel Hadas contributed the following autobiographical essay to *CA*

AUTHOR'S NOTE: My initial problem with the assignment of writing even a brief autobiography was this: a chronological account of my own life seemed doomed to be intolerably boring, lifeless, plodding, and inaccurate—not to mention being something of a duplication of what already exists in the form of a curriculum vitae and an annotated bibliography. How much simpler, I thought, to urge any curious reader simply to read what I've written. Wasn't it because I was a writer in the first place that anyone would look me up? I think it was Apollinaire who said that each of his poems commemorated an event in his life. Motherhood, a friend's death, a winter walk—read what I've written, I want to snap, if you're curious how it felt to me. I've even been tempted to excerpt some of my own essays—after all, they're personal—in lieu of an autobiography.

Alas, both these expedients are unfair to the reader who, whether or not she has read any of my work, is simply in search of facts about me. So in lieu of an autobiography I offer here an alphabetized list of items. Alphabetical order seems to me a more neutral principle than chronological order. Other ordering principles, like the periodic table of the elements in Primo Levi's wonderful book of that title, were beyond my reach—but let me pay tribute here to the compelling and inventive ways to order their own stories found by Iris Origo in *Images and Shadows* and Sharon Olds in *Satan Says.*

Unlike section D ("Dramatis Personae") of James Merrill's "The Book of Ephraim," another important source, the following list isn't restricted to characters; it includes categories such as Education and Friendship, one of which normally finds a slot in a c.v. while the other doesn't. The resulting index to my life is undoubtedly incomplete, idiosyncratic, and confusing—but so is any account of a life, not to mention the life itself.

A final note: in order to halfway satisfy my lust to encourage potential researchers to read my work, I not only list my books here but refer to passages in the books that are relevant to particular items on the list.

ANSEN, 1922–

My dear friend, whom, thanks to John Hollander, I met in Athens in 1969: an expatriate, a poet, a wonderfully hospitable and generous, eccentric polymath, who read Dante with me in his apartment in Kolonaki, in a tall old house, now demolished, on Alpekis Street. I've written about Alan in my afterword to *Contact Highs,* (his *Selected Poems*) and elsewhere. At a time in my life when I was drifting and frightened, Alan always made me feel completely safe and welcome. He had much more to teach me about literature than just about any of the professors I'd had at Harvard, though some of what I learned from him (love for Auden's work, or for that matter for Alan's own rumbustious poems) ripened only later. Giving me a book about Auden's poetry, Alan inscribed it, "A cart before a heavenly horse." Just so: now, teaching myself, chained to the academic routine, I sometimes feel like a nonheavenly horse, but I was shown the heavenly cart before my real work began.

Disorderly Houses, Alan's 1959 volume from Wesleyan, is dedicated in part to Pindar, "whose [houses] never were." Alan's life might be chaotic—the dying flowers in their vases, the boys coming and going. There is surface scuzz and mess, and there is also devotion to the world of art.

ARSON

In the spring of 1973, in the olive oil press my then husband Stavros and I were running on the island of Samos, there were a couple of unexplained fires. We went to America for the summer, and when we came back he and I were separately indicted for arson, the idea apparently being that we had "burned down the factory" (it was still standing) for the insurance money. Eventually we were tried and acquitted, a process both slowed down and probably mellowed by the fact that in the meantime (summer 1974) the Greek junta had fallen and democracy had been restored.

My memories of these nightmarish events are intermittent, comical, and scary. It's much easier to recall what I was wearing for the trial (one long day in March 1975), or that I had my period, or that during lunch on the Vathy waterfront I talked about New York schools with the lawyers, than to grasp the whole episode in all its long drawn-out absurdity and danger. What's clear now is that the trial, and the long, long months leading up to it, gave me a gift. For henceforth what might have seemed challenging situations (defending a Ph.D. thesis, for example) were comparatively benign: I knew people were on my side. And having been under house arrest, that is, forbidden to leave the country until the trial, has given me a greater appreciation of freedom.

ARTISTS' COLONIES

At the MacDowell Colony in Peterborough, New Hampshire, my first night at dinner—it was July 1, 1976—I made the acquaintance of a tall, gaunt composer who could tell by looking at me, he said, that I wasn't a composer and was probably a poet. I'd never met a composer before, though I've met many since, and composing twenty seconds of music a day seemed a very slow pace to me.

The tall thin composer was George Edwards; two years later we got married. We've gone off at intervals to artists' colonies ever since, George always to MacDowell (he's there as I write this), I to Virginia, Ragdale, and Yaddo. After ten or twelve days at a colony, I find I want to get back to my home routine, and after about two weeks I'm too restless to work well. But in the first spread of space and time colonies afford, a tremendous amount of work of different kinds gets accomplished. Turning forty at Ragdale, writing prose about the past, I felt as if I were on an island in the middle of my life; I could see with new clarity where I had been, if not where I was going. And at Virginia, the fall after my mother's death, I filled a roomy studio with my grief: papers piled on the floor, grandfather's letters on a side table, me at the desk, writing, weeping, writing.

With her son, Jonathan, 1985

People who have children especially need the time offered by artists' colonies, but the pull of a child also means, perhaps for women in particular, that one's stay may be short. For those two or three weeks, a colony represents the only form of house arrest (see "Arson") that I can now imagine without shuddering.

CHARLES BARBER, 1956–1992

In his short life an actor, director, dancer, critic, essayist, and poet, Charles was my student in a poetry workshop at Gay Men's Health Crisis from late 1989 until shortly before his death in the summer of 1992. He was also my beloved friend; he had a rare gift for friendship, and I am still basking in the affection we shared even as I continue to mourn his loss. Many, many of my poems in the past six years are in one way or another addressed to Charles; his death, together with that of my mother, is the subject of *The Double Legacy*.

BREAD LOAF

I was a s at the Writers' Conference in 1976, but my cherished and formative memories of Bread Loaf date from 1958, 1960, and 1961 (I think these dates are right), when I was a faculty brat, since my father taught at the School of English. I remember croquet, Ping Pong, milkshakes in the Barn, the peculiar smell of the bathrooms in Maple, the faculty wives shopping for cocktail hors d'oeuvres, plays at the Little Theater. Wylie Sypher, tall, genial, and bald, wearing a seersucker jacket and binoculars around his neck, was a dedicated birdwatcher; Lucy, his wife, a foot shorter, trotted after him with hard-boiled eggs (his midmorning snack) in a basket. Lucy corresponded with me for years, sent me cookies when I was in college, met me for lunch at the Wurst Haus in Cambridge, and—most important of all, I now think—had the imagination and generosity to send me many of those little books about great artists that the Boston Museum of Fine Arts used to publish. "An unbirthday present," she'd write on the flyleaf. The cookies are gone, and lunches, and Wylie, and Lucy. Even the purple finches that flocked in a certain larch tree one summer are gone. But the little books about Degas and Gauguin, Botticelli and Van Gogh, and Goya are still on my shelves. This coming Saturday morning my son will start art classes.

CHILDREN

Our son, Jonathan Hadas Edwards, was born on February 4, 1984, and promptly began allowing me, at the age of thirty-five, to relive my childhood—nursery rhymes, a dependence on my mother, the joys of children's books. I've written about some of these matters in *A Son from Sleep* and "The Cradle and the Bookcase" and in my long poem "The Dream Machine." Jonathan as he grows up walks through other poems, notably—on his way to school—"The Red Hat." But he is not a model, a subject, a muse; he's a separate, complicated, sometimes opaque, and quickly changing person, who so far, I hope, defies Proust's gloomy prediction that children inherit the worst qualities of both parents.

THE DOUBLE LEGACY

This little book of prose consists of various essays around the central theme of mourning. "Double" refers to two deaths that happened six weeks apart in 1992: first my mother, then Charles Barber.

DREAMS

Dreams and poems are engaged in some of the same tasks and use some of the same tools. Both, in my experience, somehow know and can convey unappealing truths to which the waking person, the person living her daily life in prose, seems to lack access—or is it rather that she lacks courage? I was writing poems foreshadowing the end of my first marriage long before I had admitted to myself that it was ending. A dream informed me of my mother's fatal cancer a week or two before her diagnosis.

Both poetry and dreams make lavish use of images; both often move laterally, erratically, by means of what I think of as lyric leaps. Both can be screamingly clear or hermetically difficult to construe. Both are mysterious in their provenance, seeming to come from deep within the self yet also reaching us as if from outside. Both can be zanily solipsistic yet can also command an impersonal kind of authority.

Unlike poems, of course, dreams often melt away, leaving, as Prospero puts it, not a wrack behind. The medium I use for simultaneously fixing dreams in my memory and trying to make sense of them is poetry. It's hardly surprising, then, that many of the dreams I succeed in remembering touch upon the same themes many of my poems do—people I have loved and lost and continue to love.

A recent dream about the poet James Merrill tugged at me all the next day, though each time I tried to reconstruct it, fewer details were available. I'd seemed to be standing with Jimmy and a few other people at twilight just outside a building, an apartment house, under a canopy. Inside had been a kind of boudoir with a travertine dressing table and a tall, four-paneled mirror. There was the sense of going out on the town for the evening and also of looking out on the passing world, critically but not unkindly, with laughter. There was much more I couldn't recall—the substance of what was said. . . . What made the dream especially poignant was that I was aware in it that Jimmy didn't have long to live. It was such a strong and pleasurable dream that I hated to wake up.

Not until late afternoon did it dawn on me (hardly the *mot juste* in this connection) that the day's date, August 6, was precisely half a year after the date of Jimmy's death. I felt at once abashed to have been so slow to realize this; grateful for the continued loving intimacy the dream had abundantly conveyed; and mystified at how I had subliminally recalled this six-month mark. "There are subconscious connections, Mom," said my son wisely. Indeed there are. The significance of the date finally became clear to me at the moment when, trudging barefoot along a Vermont dirt road that humid, sleepy Sunday afternoon, I was thinking about a passage in Merrill's *Mirabell* I'd recently reread, in which Merrill's companion has a dream about his parents precisely a year after their deaths. February sixth to August sixth. It finally clicked.

I haven't, or haven't yet, captured the details of my August 6 dream in a poem. Perhaps I never will. But so much buried love, memory, and meaning clustered even in the few vignettes I was able to retrieve that it was as if I'd tapped into a rich vein of subterranean significance. Remembering the dream, I felt desolate but also consoled; bereaved but also lucky. Dreams are a triumphant loophole in the wall of silence that separates the living from the dead.

During the twenty-six years of my friendship with James Merrill, I dreamed about him many times. Death, while it has changed the tone of these dreams, hasn't broken the continuity of the messages.

It would be pleasant to dream of great poets of the past, as Elizabeth Bishop dreamed of George Herbert. Robert Frost did appear to me once in a dream some years ago, but never Dickinson or Keats, Shakespeare or Sappho. I can hardly complain, though, as long as Merrill continues to be a living presence in my dreams.

EDUCATION

Nursery school: Tompkins Hall, at 21 Claremont Avenue, across the street from Barnard College. Cooperative; the mothers—faculty wives—used to help out. I remember playing on the roof, and having my temperature taken, and eating—or throwing up—a baked apple. I remember quiet-voiced, gray-haired, buck-toothed, besmocked Miss Edith Morton. But 21 Claremont came alive for me again in the fall of 1976, when George, whom I'd met earlier that summer, and who was about to start teaching in the Columbia Music

Rachel and Jonathan, Maine, 1988

Department, moved into his Columbia Housing-provided apartment on the ground floor of 21 Claremont, right across the hall from where I'd gone to nursery school. Sometimes we'd see lines of small children moving through the lobby, undeterred by obstacles like (one day) George's upright piano being maneuvered around a corner. "Make way for ducklings," George murmured.

Elementary school was much farther away from home (home being 460 Riverside Drive); too far, I now think. I went, as my older sister had, to Hunter College Elementary School, then on Park Avenue and Sixty-eighth Street. In the mornings, if we were early, all the children would have to walk around and around the block until we could go into the lobby. The elevators were big and smelly.

But my imagination out-Orwelled the reality. I remember worrying that kindergarten would be a big dark room with hapless children bent over their desks. (Had I been reading Dickens at age five? Where else did such a stern Victorian fantasy come from?) In fact Hunter was benign enough. Reading was easy for me, though the penmanship teacher admonished me to "Write, Rachel, don't draw!" By third or fourth grade I was helping some of the other kids with reading. French started in fourth grade, with Mme. Hopstein pointing down her throat and gargling "La gorrrrge."

The art teacher, Marie Boylan, looked like a 1950s (well, this was the fifties) poodle: rhinestones, swirling felt skirts, lots of pink and turquoise. Pug-faced, pear-shaped, ancient-seeming Dr. Anna Chandler presided over a Hunter Elementary special called Audio-Visual Enrichment, AVE for short. We sat in the dark and looked at slides; I'm sure many people often fell asleep, as I did, but we also learned about Winslow Homer and Pollaiuolo, Albert Ryder and Raphael.

For some unexplained reason, I was one of six children "accelerated"—skipped, or rather shot from cannons, from fourth to sixth grade—none of whom succeeded in passing the newly established test to get into Hunter High. So instead of following my sister to Hunter, I was sent to Riverdale for seventh through twelfth grades. A pattern of lopsidedness had already been set: I was good at English and French and Latin, passable at history—forget math and science. I was only ten at the start of seventh grade, "flat as a pancake," as my best friend Barbara Foley put it, but I made up for my youthfulness by the time I was sixteen or so with determined frivolity . . . or was I just in search of boys to write love poems about? My best memories of Riverdale are of the sun on the fields in the morning—I was a terrible hockey player, but it was nice to feel almost in the country—and of the relief, as I experienced it at ages maybe ten to fourteen, of not having boys in the class (Riverdale wasn't coed at that time). Every afternoon the school bus would take us up the hill (a hill so steep it allowed for many precious snow days) from the Girls' School down by the river to the Boys' School, where the boys would join us for the bus ride home to Manhattan. Every afternoon on that bus most of the girls would get out their compacts and apply eyeliner and foundation and lipstick.

At Radcliffe I majored in classics, for several reasons. First, sibling rivalry—my sister was an English major already, and I didn't want to follow in her footsteps any more than I already had. Secondly, majoring in English seemed silly when I could and did read Dickens and Shakespeare, Keats and Jane Austen, and the poems of my father's student, the emerging poet John Hollander, on my own. Finally, I was in some ways a very cautious and conservative young person. Taking courses that involved more of what I knew how to do already—looking up words in lexicons—felt comfortable and safe. Was there parental pressure to study classics? Not any more than there had been to do well in school and go on to college; it was in the air my sister and I breathed. No one made an issue of reminding me that my mother's father had been a classicist, or that my mother had been studying Latin prose composition at Columbia the summer she and my father met. My father did, toward the end of my freshman year, send me a brief letter complimenting me on my grades and adding that I didn't have to major in classics and didn't have to get all A's. I think he meant it, or that he thought he did, but there was little time to discuss my future; he died the August following my freshman year.

The teaching in the Harvard Classics Department wasn't, for the most part, inspiring. I do remember with most fondness two early-morning classes on the third floor of the Fogg Museum: David Mitten's Greek sculpture and Sterling Dow's Greek history. Homer with Gregory Nagy and Aristophanes with Harold Gotoff offered more memorable moments than a dry-as-dust Oedipus with Wendell Clausen, who preferred Alexandrian poets to classical tragedians. My Latin training was stronger than my Greek, and I probably learned the most about poetry (genre, meter, imagery, temperament, tradition) from G.P. Goold on Roman elegy and, above all, J.P. Elder on Lucretius.

However dubious my motives may have been, and however large a percentage of what I learned I have forgotten, I've never regretted majoring in classics. Recently, translating some Seneca and Tibullus—and my next project is a play of Euripides—has taken me back to the days hunched over a lexicon in Whitman Hall, with trimeter and hexameter ringing in my ears. To reenter, however gingerly, the world of classical scholarship is a removal, a renewal, a return to the source. Nor have I ever regretted that the only poetry-writing class I took was with Robert Fitzgerald, a piercingly, almost alarmingly low-key, gentle, and charming man. Robert Lowell's gigantic reputation made me nervous, not that I knew much about his work or indeed about the man himself, but a palpable aura of charismatic damage surrounded him—damage his students, it seemed to me, eagerly imitated and shared.

I was in love a lot at college, sometimes with spectacularly unsuitable people (a heroin addict who dropped out of Harvard soon after I met him and is probably dead by now stands out in my memory),

sometimes with young men who are so kind and ardent and interesting in my faded memories that I only wish I could recall them better. There was also a married poet; there was a health food store-running hippie up in Vermont. After my father's death I was off course for years to come, easily attaching and detaching myself, panicky, dependent. My first husband, the man who said, "I grew you up and then you left me," was not someone I met at Harvard, and neither was George.

I finished college in 1969 and was away from educational institutions and out of the country for the next few years, but in 1976-77 I went to the writing seminars at Johns Hopkins. One could study either poetry or prose, and about half the students were teaching fellows in a freshman course called "Contemporary American Letters," a subject about which I knew very little. The syllabus featured work by writers like Pynchon, Barthelme, and Barth; I learned as much as my students. The poetry workshop was useful chiefly because of some of my fellow poets. Tom Sleigh, Molly Peacock, Lisa Zeidner, and, above all, Phillis Levin had a lot to teach me about poetry and about critiquing others' work sharply but not cruelly. Different styles flew around the room like germs; there was no prevailing aesthetic that I remember. The year at Hopkins, I was mostly in New York on weekends, visiting George (we had met at MacDowell that summer). On the train rides to and from Baltimore, it was a pleasure to be alone and write! Back at Hopkins, I audited graduate courses in the Romantics with Jerome McGann and the pre-Socratics with Diskin Clay. Library books piled up on the floor: "Beppo," "Julian and Maddalo," Solon's "Hymn to the Muses." I stopped using my married name—I was separated from my first husband—and reverted to Hadas.

It was clear by the middle of my year at Hopkins that an M.A. in poetry (it wasn't called an M.F.A. for some reason) and a token would get me a ride on the subway. I wanted to be back in New York, where George was teaching at Columbia. After dipping a toe into the waters of graduate school at Hopkins, the prospect of going deeper was less frightening. I wanted a program that would make use of my newly acquired modern Greek without letting me turn my back on the classics. The doctoral program in comparative literature at Princeton was, as graduate studies go, painless, even pleasurable. I remember Robert Fagles's seminars on epic and tragedy, Edmund Keeley's tutorials in modern Greek poetry, Theodore Weiss's repair work on my ignorance of American poetry, Clarence Brown's uncanny seminar on Stevens, Ralph Freedman on Rilke and Valery, William Meredith (who had waltzed with my mother at Bread Loaf in 1960 or thereabouts) giving a guest seminar on Auden—all this was a wonderful corrective to poetry workshops on the one hand and readings of Sophocles that emphasized the aorist tense on the other.

Last spring I had the pleasure of teaching a course at Princeton in the Hellenic Studies Program; I'd gotten older, but everything else had pretty much stayed the same.

So many years spent in classrooms! And this September marks my fifteenth fall at Rutgers. My father once wrote, "I am a teacher. Except for wars and holidays I have never been out of the sound of a school bell." I've been spared the wars.

THE EMPTY BED

This collection was going to be called *Red House,* the title of a poem in turn named after a Malevich painting. The present title is probably too gloomy; even though much of the book is elegiac. I now see *The Empty Bed* as the middle of a trilogy whose first and last volumes are *Unending Dialogue* and *The Double Legacy.*

FATHER, MOSES HADAS, 1900–1966

My father was forty-eight when, the younger of two daughters from his second marriage, I was born; he already had a teenage daughter and son from his first. When he died I was seventeen. Not only did I not have very many years in which to get to know him, but the years we overlapped were the busiest in his busy life. Furthermore, his was not at all a transparent personality. There's an alarming amount about his life that probably no one now living knows (my half-brother David knows more than most people); I'd have to hire an investigative journalist to do the sleuthing if I wanted to find out in any detail about my father's family connections, childhood, education in Atlanta and New York, life as a rabbi, first marriage. . . . But in a way, what I already know is enough for me. It's not as if even that small stock of memory doesn't

The author's father, Dr. Moses Hadas

constantly change, abetted by a letter unearthed here, an anecdote shared there, and the fact that I am fast approaching the age my father was when I was born.

To put it another way, love is enough for me—living and dead, absent and present, the love we shared. Rightly or wrongly, I've always thought I probably resemble him in temperament (not looks) more than any of his other three children. I used to feel what I thought of as a pointing finger, admonishing me not to be lazy, not to waste time. Your father, my shrink would say. But in time I came to be able to localize the insistent prodding and found it originated inside me. My father, then, was in a way myself.

Tired at the end of his long days of teaching (he taught classics at Columbia for forty years), tired with a tiredness I understand better every semester, my father would lie down when he got home from work, do the *Times* crossword puzzle, relax. I'd lie down next to him for companionable help with my Latin homework;

we read a good deal of Cicero's *De Senectute* together. One afternoon I asked him to transliterate the word "fuck," spelled in Greek OYK, in a poem of e.e. cummings. I thought I knew what the letters sounded out but wasn't sure. He looked at the word a long time. "I can't read it," he said.

The temperamental match: no matter how many honorary degrees he got, no matter how many accolades from grateful students, my father always needed more praise than seemed forthcoming—from inside as well as outside. (Inside the family? inside himself? where was the pointing finger?) Alas, it was, of course, easier to wow students than the quiet wife and the two recalcitrant teenagers who faced him across the dinner table. Once I remember telling my father to shut up; of course I had to leave the table. But beyond or beneath all this, I understood increasingly as I got to be sixteen or so the need he felt for unconditional praise and love. (Did I share this vulnerability already?) Besides, though he boasted some at dinner, my father was anything but long-winded about his own concerns and doings. He wasn't one of those men who feel the need to tell their families what they've been telling other people at work all day. If anything, often by dinnertime words would have all but deserted him; he'd point to the butter or horseradish in silence. I understand it so well now, the queasy-making roughness in any teacher's life of the alternation of speech and silence.

This is not the place to rehearse my father's long and complicated career as a rabbi, in the Office of Strategic Services, or at Columbia. Virtually no personal papers have been left behind; my half-brother and sister know more than I do, as do various distant cousins who surface from time to time. Of course I can and do read and reread various of my father's books; I welcome hearing anecdotes about him. What matters most to me at this stage is that, dead for almost thirty years, my father has come closer to me than when I was a seventeen-year-old shell-shocked by his death. Lovable, charismatic, mysterious, vulnerable, talkative, silent, contradictory, versatile, exhausted—human.

Love is a leap, an arc, an improvisation, a surprise. An overcommitted forty-eight when I was born, a grandfather by the time I was six or so, my father had no empty place for me in his heart. Love turns out not to work that way; it creates its own resting place, which death is then powerless to abolish.

FATHER-IN-LAW

Was it no more than a remarkable coincidence that both the men I married had, unknown to me, lost their fathers at eighteen or so, the same age I had? Maybe I was drawn to some signal of that shared loss, some enzyme or odor of adolescent bereavement, some gap in the story. The practical result suited me fine: I never had to deal with a father-in-law, only memories. Living or dead, one father was enough for me.

FORM, CYCLE, INFINITY: LANDSCAPE IMAGERY IN THE POETRY OF ROBERT FROST AND GEORGE SEFERIS

My doctoral dissertation at Princeton; also my way of marrying the landscapes of Greece and Vermont, two places where I'd spent a lot of time, under the twin auspices of two fearsome old men.

FRIENDS

One of the great blessings of my life. Friends surface and vanish; if one lives in New York, someone is always passing through town on their way someplace else or for some brief, hectic event. And then it turns out life is like that: we're passing through. Friends are associated with times and places in a life: the benches surrounding a sandbox in Riverside Park, a seminar room, a certain stretch of Broadway, or summers in Vermont or Maine or wherever. Friends can be pried loose from their context and find a new niche: Missy Roberts, my best friend when we were growing up on Riverside Drive (our mothers were best friends too) more or less disappeared from my life about 1960 for the next thirty years, but luckily for me, now she's back. Reeve Lindbergh was on a lofty pedestal, concealed in her white hilltop farmhouse in Peacham, for fifteen years or more, but she's down on my human level now, and I know and love her much better than before.

When I was auditing his course in pastoral at Princeton, Paul Alpers said something to the effect that the impulse to pull away from a group, go sit under a tree, and discuss things with one other person was a pastoral impulse. If so, I'm one of nature's shepherds. I want to buttonhole my beloved interlocutor and get him or her away from the crowd, face to face—or even not face to face so long as, the way one can on walks in the country, we're looking in the same direction.

Because in my experience many poets are letter writers, the line between friend and colleague or acquaintance can be blurry. Of course, there are hierarchies, pecking orders, disappointments. I've unintentionally gotten close to one or two people whom somewhere along the way I wounded unforgivably. These contretemps made me feel cautious or guilty or angry, as the case may be. And the passage of time always tempts one to draw the line: no more time and space for friends. Luckily, the world doesn't work that way.

If I had the slightest talent for writing fiction, friendship might well be a subject I'd want to explore. Certainly it's among the themes of much great fiction from Jane Austen to Tolstoy and beyond. And yet lyric poetry, with its plethora of pronouns, its incurably personal and immediate point of view, its penchant for apostrophe, is just as much the genre of friendship as it is of love. From Sappho's message of longing to Keats's chatty sonnets to Montale's wry meditations, lyric is usually addressed to someone. Maybe I'm so drawn to friendship in theory and practice because I'm an addict of the apostrophic mode. Mark Rudman, Eleanor Cory, Reeve Lindbergh, Lisa Hull, Charlie Barber—among many others, let me lovingly name you here.

GMHC

Gay Men's Health Crisis, one of the first organized responses to AIDS in New York City in the early eighties, is now a formidably large and complex bureaucracy. From early 1988 into 1994, I ran a poetry workshop for clients, most often in a windowless basement room I grew very fond of. I want to name the people who worked with me and some of whose poems can be found in *Unending Dialogue:* Charles Barber, Glenn Besco, Dan Conner, Tony Giordano, Kevin Imbusch, Glenn Philip Kramer, Raul Martinez-Avila, Gustavo Motta, Michael Pelonero, and James Turcotte. Between 1990 and 1995, all of them died.

GRANDPARENTS

My father's father, David Hadas, emigrated from somewhere in the Pale to Atlanta around 1900 and died many years before I was born. My father's mother, Gertrude Draizen Hadas, was, I think, alive for at least some of my childhood, but although she lived in Manhattan, she wasn't interested in meeting this second and incompletely Jewish crop of grandchildren. My father was not in the habit of talking about his early years, and these grandparents are almost completely mysterious to me, though I know (how?) that she was blond, and that he ran a dry goods store, had a horse and cart, was a scholar, and wrote a book. But was it essays or Talmudic studies? And was it in Hebrew or Yiddish?

My mother's father, Lewis Parke Chamberlayne (1879–1917), died when she was only two, perhaps of influenza. A classicist who had gone from the University of Virginia to study for his doctorate at the University of Halle in Germany, he was a gifted poet and translator. A very incomplete but still precious set of his papers came to me when my mother died, including an essay about his boyhood in Petersburg, Virginia, near the site of the Battle of the Crater. His father, who died when my grandfather was small, had been a captain under General Lee; the children playing in the yard found bits of bone.

My mother's mother, Elizabeth Claiborne Mann Chamberlayne, who was born in the 1880s and died around 1956, is the only one of my grandparents I ever saw. She visited us in New York more than once and was staying with us when her arteriosclerosis suddenly worsened and she died. I remember her tall, big-boned, deep-voiced presence; I remember her reading to us; I remember that she was scandalized when the family cat Butterscotch climbed onto the dining-room table and licked butter off the butter plate (no one else seemed to care). I remember walking on Riverside Drive holding her hand and calling her "Grandma" just to hear how the word sounded. I remember peering into the little room halfway down the hall and seeing her lying on the bed, dead.

DAVID HADAS, 1931–

Summers in Vermont during my childhood, this gentle, funny man was halfway between a brother and a father to me and my sister. He had two, small children of his own, but he read my sister and me Dickens, taught Beth to drive, was endlessly available and affectionate. A great reader, often lying down to read (it clearly runs in the family), David was legendary for getting through Calvin's *Institutes* one summer. He doesn't publish, but he can and does teach anything from the Book of Job to Stanley Elkin's novels. He currently teaches and has taught for many years at Washington University in St. Louis.

ELIZABETH HADAS, 1946–

My sister Beth, two and a half years older than I, in relation to whom I defined myself when we were growing up. I used to beg her to play with me, and often enough she complied; we used to have elaborate games of paper dolls on Sunday mornings when our parents slept late. She went to Hunter, I went to Riverdale; I followed her to Radcliffe but not into an English major. Since 1970 she has lived in Albuquerque, where she is now head of the University of New Mexico Press. Despite temperamental clashes, I have great respect for her judgment and integrity. We don't always like the same books, but we continue to listen to each other's opinions on books. The same things make us laugh, and our laughs sound alike.

LIVING IN TIME

A collection of essays with a long poem sandwiched in the middle. I'll always be grateful to Kenneth Arnold, former director of Rutgers University Press, for his leap of faith in publishing this and two subsequent books by me.

MARRIAGE

In November 1970, I was married at City Hall in Manhattan to Stavros Kondilis. We weren't divorced until 1978, but I saw him for the last time (so far) in September 1976, when he put me on the train to Johns Hopkins. I've written about this youthful marriage in "Mornings in Ormos" and other essays, as well as more obliquely in poems. Twenty-five years on, this marriage seems remote and unlikely rather than unpleasant. Stavros kept me company and in his own way took care of me as I mourned for my father and decided, by not deciding, what to do next. When I finally did take several steps, including leaving him, he was sad rather than bitter.

My second husband, George Edwards, and I celebrated our seventeenth anniversary last summer. George grew up in Wellesley, studied at Oberlin, did graduate work

George and Jonathan, 1988

in composition at Princeton, and taught music theory at New England Conservatory before coming to Columbia in 1976 and moving into the building where I had gone to nursery school. Inconceivably naive after my years abroad, I asked George in the early days why, if he was a composer, he taught music theory and didn't simply compose. "To support my habit," he replied. We've both been supporting our respective habits ever since.

JAMES MERRILL, 1926–1995

This catalog-in-lieu-of-a-memoir is being written toward the end of a year colored by the death of this incomparably rare genius—a matchless writer and an equally matchless friend. Soon after his death on February 6, 1995, I wrote the following tribute (originally published in *PN Review,* July-August 1995. Copyright © 1995 by Rachel Hadas).

The last poem I wanted to show Jimmy Merrill was a ballad written by Saint-Exupéry at the age of eighteen or so, which had leaped out at me from a less memorable though usually interesting source, Stacy Schiff's recent biography of the aviator/writer. The slightly aggrieved, wistful tone of Saint-Exupéry's lines is perfectly captured in Mary McCarthy's 1986 description of Merrill's voice, both, one gathers, in life and in his work—as "a very light voice . . . no organ tones; rather a boy's voice that has only just changed and keeps a slight hoarseness." (From *For James Merrill: A Birthday Tribute,* New York: Jordan Davies, 1986.) The speaker is a schoolboy's desk which has been cruelly exiled, and there is something inexpressibly Merrillian about its tone of urbane aggrievement.

I prefer not to allegorize the desk and its master. But I know Jimmy would have enjoyed the rhyme of "rococo" and "status quo," and I would have enjoyed hearing him laugh. Besides, as far as I could remember, *Le Petit Prince* was one book we'd never talked about.

Last November, I flew to St. Louis to participate in a cluster of events I then thought and still think of as James Merrill Weekend. There were to be readings, lectures, a panel discussion—all to celebrate the fact that Merrill's papers were lodged (is that the word?) in the library of Washington University. For some reason, as the plane climbed into the cold morning sky, I felt unusually conscious of connections, of chronology, of the present moment as one in a series. I tried to make order in my mind, to isolate various past events like dots that I would later be able to connect into an intelligible shape—events of which, since I had met Jimmy in 1969, this weekend would be the latest in a long series. I didn't think at that time it would be the last.

Nor, in a way, was it. In December there were chatty phone conversations, though final exams and houseguests prevented me from getting across town to see Jimmy's tree. On January 12 there was a delicious long phone call from Tucson; among the things we talked about were a mutual friend's childhood and Jimmy and Peter's project of finding a few suitable lines from Auden's *Thanksgiving for a Habitat* to be translated into German and hung on the wall of the *Kirchstetten bierstube* under what Jimmy said was a wonderful photo of Auden by Rollie McKenna.

Even after the numbing news of Jimmy's death, there were other social events in which he was a presence: the vigil in his apartment the day before the funeral, and then the funeral itself. In all this, the living person had hardly receded at all. It may well be that very bad news is slow to sink in; I'm not sure that by the day of the funeral any of Jimmy's innumerable friends had really understood that he was gone. On the other hand, his living presence is part of me. To quote from a card he sent me in 1976 giving news of some back problem, it "will pass & recur, pass & recur, and finally go away, with me, for good." Not until every last person who knew Jimmy is gone will he really go away for good—and even to say so is monstrously untrue, for it is to ignore the poems.

As I looked out the plane window that November morning, images would open out into events, or at least scenes. December (isn't it?) 1969: the first time I'm at David and Jimmy's house in Athens. Jimmy, standing at the top of the stairs to greet guests, is wearing a belt with a beautiful silver buckle. As if I were waist high, the buckle seems to be what I first focus on.

Sometime in 1973 or '74, sitting at my kitchen table in Samos, I type a letter to my mother on my rusty but trusty Olympia portable, quoting for her lines from "Days of 1935" that make me splutter with laughter each time I read them. The wealthy child, kidnapped by his fantasy couple Floyd and Jean, overhears his captors making love, and they know he overhears them and perform all the more passionately in that knowledge. It's a wonderful variation on the primal scene, with borrowed parents all the sexier for their sleaze.

January 1975: Jimmy and I, sitting in the living room, are among the people gathered in Chester Kallman's Athens apartment. Earlier that morning, Chester has been found dead in bed. There are other people around, making phone calls, making coffee in the kitchen. Next to me on the sofa or even in one of Chester's huge, enveloping black leather armchairs, Jimmy puts his hand comfortingly on mine. I liked Chester, but I am not devastated by his loss; probably I'm too young and callous to be in need of consoling. But I love the feeling of Jimmy's hand on mine, and we sit like that for a few moments. After Chester is buried the next day in the Jewish section of an Athenian cemetery, everyone in the car back to Kolanaki is out of sorts. Has Alan Ansen taken exception to Bernie Weinbaum's tears, or are people worried by the fact that Chester died intestate, or is it something else? In the *zacharoplasteion* where we testily repair for drinks and cake, there are problems about who should sit next to whom. "How characteristic of Chester," murmurs Jimmy, "that his funeral should leave everyone in a blind rage."

Whereas Jimmy's funeral only left everyone blind with tears.

*

I was barely twenty-one when Jimmy and I met; I'm older now than he was then. In the years of our friendship, the age gap of twenty-years shrank, by the end, to almost nothing. Now, fast becoming a *vieux meuble rococo* in my turn, I often find myself irritated by the rawness, the shyness, the inarticulate strengths, troubles, and weaknesses of students in their early twenties. The impulse to retreat, to kvetch, to withdraw—I see it daily, in my contemporaries and colleagues as well as myself. And then I remember Jimmy's generosity and patience, his unfailing appetite for the human comedy, his kindness to—among countless other people—a self-absorbed, confused, and fearful young woman still shaken by her father's death a couple of years before.

Not that Jimmy took my father's place exactly. For one thing, I got to know him when I was already (if barely) an adult. For another, we were in constant touch for the next quarter-century. Unlike my father, Jimmy knew both my husbands well. He knew and loved my son; he knew and encouraged me with all my books. I cannot imagine the past years without his friendship.

MIRRORS OF ASTONISHMENT

This collection of poems began as a group of sequences, but some shorter pieces made their way into the central section, which is probably now my favorite.

MOTHER, ELIZABETH CHAMBERLAYNE HADAS, 1915–1992

Quiet and shy in life, at once articulate and withheld, loving and understated, my mother has, according to what's becoming a familiar pattern, become more present to me in the years since her death. That death and its aftermath, in tandem with the parallel last days of my friend Charles Barber, are the subject matter of *The Double Legacy*. But just as in life my mother often faded into the background of even a small gathering, so in death she was in some ways eclipsed by him. He was so young and beautiful, and I'd known him so short a time, I was so greedy for more, that I couldn't

bear the fact of Charlie's slipping away—whereas my mother, having been part of me for my whole life, couldn't slip away. Or could she?

I'd rather explore my mother's life than her death. Alas, very few papers survive, though she scrupulously kept the transcripts from her studies in classics at Columbia, where she studied in the summer of 1942 and met my father. My mother was born in Columbia, South Carolina, where her father was teaching classics at the university. After his sudden death, his widow took her two small daughters back to Richmond, Virginia, where my mother grew up (she also spent a good deal of time with her grandparents in Petersburg). She went north to college, Bryn Mawr, taught at St. Timothy's School, and was studying for her M.A. in Latin at Columbia when she met my father. They married in 1945, in Washington, D.C., where he was working for the OSS (he had been overseas earlier) and she worked for the Library of Congress until my sister was born. When they moved to New York in 1947 or 1948, she worked for a while at the New York Public Library; after I was born, she stayed home with us girls until we were in seventh and ninth grade, respectively, and then went to work part-time teaching Latin at the Spence School, where she remained for twenty-five years. When she retired in 1984, it was partly to help me with my son, for whom she was a blessedly present grandparent for the first eight years of his life. I wish it could have been longer. But loving relationships and cherished memories aren't the worst of all possible worlds.

Until the last couple of years of her life, my mother was almost never ill. More than sturdy, she seemed indefatigable, walking, gardening, baby-sitting. Her unemphatic presence, like her intelligence and judgment, was so dependable and undramatic that I was apt to take them all for granted—a mistake I no longer have the luxury of making.

ORMOS

Port town on the Marathokampos, a village on the southwest coast of Samos, in the eastern Aegean. Marathokampos was my husband Stavros's village; we lived in Ormos for almost four years in the early seventies. I visited there briefly ten years later, but another dozen years have passed since I've seen the place.

In the port of Ormos, Greece, 1972

Ormos was on the edge of the world. I loved the nearness of our tiny house to the ocean; the clarity of its north/south orientation (one looked out the kitchen window south to the sea) reminded me of the grid of Manhattan, where as a child I'd looked out the window west to the Hudson River and the setting sun. Elementally bare yet also lush bright colors—the green of fig leaves, the sapphire of the Aegean—Ormos was, from my egotistical perspective, a background for the dramas of my belated adolescence or young wifehood (both phrases seem all wrong), as well as whatever larger domestic or civic or historical dramas played themselves out against what I called in an early poem the blue proscenium of sea.

OTHER WORLDS THAN THIS

Collection of my favorite translations from Latin (Seneca's *Oedipus,* some poems of Tibull), French (favorite poems of Hugo, Baudelaire, Rimbaud, Valery, and La Forgue) and modern Greek (Karyotakis).

PASS IT ON

The first collection of my work I organized on my own, without help or advice from anyone—which solo practice I've adhered to ever since. The thematic strands seemed to braid themselves without much help even from me: the book had something to tell me.

THE PRINCESS AND THE GOBLIN

George MacDonald's children's story—the first book of any difficulty I ever read to myself—turns up in more than one of my essays. The powerful, magical great-grandmother and the beloved, bearded father no doubt attracted me, but the most crucial thing I took away from the book was the idea of giving someone a present that one can also keep at the same time. Like a name. Like a book. Like teaching. Like writing.

PUMPKIN HILL

Around 1955, my parents bought a tumbledown farmhouse and thirty acres of land in an area called

Pumpkin Hill between St. Johnsbury and Danville in northern Vermont. For the last forty years, I've spent most of my summers there as well as an occasional fall and even, once, winter until March. The house isn't winterized; isn't glamorous; is barely comfortable. Most of the people who've spent time there have had things they wanted to do more urgently than to fix the place up—work in the garden, write a poem, translate, compose. As long as the house is standing (and we've fixed the foundation so that it will, we've been told, last our time), and there are still cows across the road; the place is a priceless blessing.

RIVERSIDE DRIVE

One of the points of my inner compass. I grew up in a ground-floor apartment (thunderous sneezes from doormen in the lobby; doorknob trembling while on the other side of the door brass is being polished) at 460 Riverside Drive, toward the northern end of the long block between 116th and 119th Streets. My parents moved in, in 1947 or 1948, and the apartment was vacated only with my mother's death in 1992. When I walk in the park now I like to look at the lighted window and know another family is living there.

It was a dark apartment, and my father never had his own study, and the fact that we were on the ground floor meant there was less floor space and less privacy and less of a view than if we had been higher up. Still, it was wonderful to look across the street at Riverside Drive and beyond that the park and the river. I felt almost as if I were near the ocean.

RUTGERS

Like many people, I didn't even know that Rutgers had a campus in Newark until, in the spring of 1981, consulting MLA job lists, I compiled a long list of colleges within commuting distance of New York where I hoped I might find a probably part-time teaching job. One thing led to another, and I've been at Rutgers Newark since the fall of 1981. I can be irritated or exhausted or distracted or bored or full of stagefright or unprepared or many of those things at once, but essentially I love teaching and am very fortunate in my Rutgers colleagues and students.

SLOW TRANSPARENCY

My first full-length book of poems. Like many such, it was compiled over the course of years and is hence very full and probably somewhat disjunct. It avoids

narrative but nevertheless more than touches upon both some of the events of my years in Greece and my marriage to George Edwards.

A SON FROM SLEEP

Many of the poems in this book were written when Jonathan was an infant. No doubt, the resulting work is more generic than I intended or thought at the time. After a reading, a man came up to me and said enthusiastically: "When our baby was little, my wife was writing those poems too."

STARTING FROM TROY

My first book, a chapbook in the Godine series. The earliest poems in it were written when I was a senior in high school; others date from college and my early years in and immediately after Greece. James Merrill, who very kindly read the galley proofs in Athens in 1974 and early 1975, said the book was about growing up, losing a father, and transferring my affections to a husband.

TRANSLATIONS

The task of translating combines two kinds of challenges: that of an assignment and that of a puzzle. To translate a poem is a workout; it's also serendipitous and mysterious. Where is the author going, and how to follow him or her down the track? But also, why has this particular text turned up to be translated at this stage of my life? Recently, I was offered the choice of translating either the *Hecuba*, the *Iphigenia among the Taurians*, or the *Helen* of Euripides; I couldn't avoid pondering the emblematic aspect of this choice.

UNENDING DIALOGUE: VOICES FROM AN AIDS POETRY WORKSHOP

This hybrid book grew out of the poetry workshop that I ran at the Gay Men's Health Crisis. Its heart is forty-five poems by my students there, preceded by an essay of mine and followed by some of my own poems, with commentary.

Rachel Hadas contributed the following update to *CA* in 2007:

It would be easy to mark the years that have elapsed since 1995, when the original version of my autobiography was published in the *Contemporary Authors* series, by an incredulous gasp: "Wow, they went fast!" As Horace reminds us, *labuntur anni*—the years glide or slide by. My son, born in 1984, was eleven in 1995. Now he's almost twenty-three. The changes these same years have wrought in me are, I like to think, less obvious: from forty-seven to fifty-eight? No big deal.

Another way of measuring the passage of time would be to tick off the books I've published since then. In 1995 a prose collection, *The Double Legacy,* appeared; so did a volume of poems, *The Empty Bed,* and my translation of Seneca's tragedy *Oedipus.* These have been followed by *Halfway down the Hall: New and Selected Poems,* 1998. Also in 1998, my translation of Euripides' *Helen* was published. Since then, three more collections have followed: *Indelible* (2001), *Laws* (2004), and *The River of Forgetfulness* (2006). *Helen* was one of three Greek plays in translation in the volume in which it appeared; and, as it happens, an interview with me conducted by Isaac Cates likewise takes up a third of the volume *Poets in Conversation* published, in the fall of 2006, by the British Waywiser Press in their "Between the Lines" series of interviews with poets. I am presently starting to put together a new book of poems entitled *The Ache of Appetite,* and I also hope to publish my recent translation of Racine's tragedy *Iphigenie.* (More about translations later.)

Book publications, like my son's graduation from college in 2006, are, I'm well aware, rather private events. The years since 1995 have been marked by immense public convulsions, from 9/11 to Hurricane Katrina. History will be much more interested in terrorism or geopolitics or global warming than in a private life. Still, that life is my subject, so I'll go on ruminating about the past twelve years as they have affected me. But I hope I won't be doing so in utter, blithe ignorance of what Hannah Arendt called "the public realm." This realm has sidled into some of the poems in my last couple of books.

But the small realm of my life since 1995 is striking for how much *hasn't* changed. Indeed, given current trends in American life, the continuities have been exceptional. I live in the same apartment as I did then, teach at the same university, am married to the same man. (It's true that our cats died in 1998 at the ripe old ages of twenty each and have been replaced by another pair who may outlive us.) I still teach and write, and write and teach. Changes in my work, like changes in my face and body, have certainly occurred, but stealthily—more stealthily even than a child's growth, which is hard to see day by day but obvious if measured annually. Still, in the years since a dark change, but a change whose beginning was so inconspicuous as to be unknowable, has been taking place near me.

I've recently been thinking about Howard Nemerov's poem "The Dependencies," which is about the subtle transitions that occur in nature. Nemerov was writing, primarily at least, about the sly changing of the seasons. Yet like other poems I've recently read or reread, the signal or announcement his poem makes me think of is the insidious progress of diseases that cause neurological damage and dementia.

And this is why: my husband George Edwards, a composer who taught at Columbia University for many years, is, at the ripe old age of sixty-three, suffering from a dementia of the Alzheimer's type. He was diagnosed early in 2005, but with the phenomenon I've come to think of as 20/20 hindsight, it is now perfectly clear that as early as 1999 George had begun to cease to be his energetic and witty self. I had been making all kinds of semiconscious excuses for his progressive withdrawal and passivity. In the murky world of dementia, nothing is simple or clear; more than likely my various justifications had some truth to them. The decline is still astoundingly subtle. And yet, as of this writing, George no longer teaches, composes, writes, plays the piano, or reads beyond a glance at the headlines. Since he avoids conversations and keeps moving further toward silence, how subtle, really, can it be?

There is much more to be said about this illness, and I've said a little of it in two recent prose pieces—an essay entitled "Notes from the Kingdom of Illness," published in *Literary Imagination* in the spring of 2006, and the much shorter "Into the Murky World," published in a periodical entitled *Families, Systems, and Health* (Vol. 25, No. 1, pp. 127-129). I mention the titles of these two vastly different quarterlies because they are so eloquent of the sea-change in what I write about—if not how—and the venues I am finding. And the titles of my essays, I now see, both indicate my feeling that I am living in a new place.

Whatever the venue, whatever the raw material, writing has never stopped being a good friend: a truth-teller, a companion, a life raft. This has been true for me all along. In the mid seventies, my poems seemed to know, though I did not, that my first marriage was ending. Later, around 1990, my dreams (and hence, by a short path, my poems) informed me of my mother's fatal cancer before my harried workaday self could stand to see it. And late in 2004, in the sleepless nights during those weeks and months when George's illness could no longer be ignored or explained away, I looped back in my memory for months, years—and then, when I found the courage, I consulted my journals and poems from those years. Sure enough: I had been pushing the subtle and then less subtle signs that something was wrong to the periphery. But my poems and journal entries, like my dreams, captured, even if they didn't wholly understand, the growing ache of absence, the spooky loneliness of going on living alongside someone who was no longer fully there.

I don't expect to stop writing poetry—far from it. But the prose I write has been moving away from essays about or reviews of poetry and toward what I have called, in those two prose pieces I've mentioned, either "the kingdom of illness" or "the murky world." And no doubt this preoccupation with illness is predictable and logical, given that my husband has a chronic and progressive condition which will keep on slowly transforming the rest of our lives together.

Yet it's not that simple. I was already interested in the world of illness as early as 1998, starting with my work with AIDS and poetry. This interest has seemed to follow its own track. In May 2006, I was invited to serve as scholar-facilitator in the Literature and Medicine program coordinated by the New Jersey Council on the Humanities, run at various hospitals throughout the state; I'll be running the seminars at the University of Medicine and Dentistry of New Jersey in Newark through mid-2007. The young woman from the state Humanities Council who phoned me from Trenton last May knew nothing of either my work with AIDS or my husband's illness. But for whatever reason, one strand in my work connects to a strand in the larger cultural fabric.

That, at least, is what I think is happening in my career, whose new swerve (to change metaphors) reflects a convergence of several developments. My husband's recently diagnosed illness and my own prior curiosity about how illness and poetry might interact— these surely played a role. The shift in my writing wouldn't have happened without a certain restlessness on my part, and it was facilitated by cultural changes much bigger than my own work.

My own restlessness: I'd been feeling increasingly ready to put poetry, and literature in general, to work somehow in what used to be called "the real world." Teaching is, of course, one wonderful way to do this. My most popular courses at Rutgers in the past five or six years, courses like Mythology in Literature or Children's Literature, have addressed not so much poetry as the role of the imagination. I wanted, though I've only recently come to think of it this way, to find a way of making my love and knowledge of literature useful, of putting them to work.

Dr. Rita Charon's authoritative new study, *Narrative Medicine,* points out that the fields of literature and medicine each have something to offer the other. Charon writes: ". . . what medicine *lacks* today—in singularity, humility, accountability, empathy—can in part be provided by intensive narrative training." But what I really found myself pouncing on when I recently read this book was the other half of Charon's equation: "Literary studies . . . on the other hand, seek practical ways to transduce their conceptual knowledge into powerful influence in the world . . . " Stir "poetry" into the mix of "literary studies," and you get a sense of what I am discovering I'm in the process of trying to do.

My life has forced me to see if literature can help with my own lonely plight as a well spouse. It has also recently brought me face to face with a variety of physicians, some much more humane than others. My career, in many ways, has always been about literature; but lately the connection has started to feel like a lifeline. I know my needs; I also, increasingly, know I have something that others need. Furthermore, it has struck me with more and more force over the past year or two that, whereas publishing poems often means wrangling with distracted or languid editors (though there are honorable exceptions), the kind of practical literary work I've been trying to describe is something there's no need to try to sell or place. I am eagerly asked to do it and paid for doing it. Like teaching, such work often has institutional support; like teaching, it involves going into a room and talking to people and hearing what they have to say in return. Indeed, this work clearly is a form of teaching—but the syllabus has opened out in ways I could never have predicted.

Maybe my poetry is simply going stale; maybe if I freshened up or retooled my poetic style, which I sometimes think is incorrigibly bookish, there would be more of a demand for my poems. But I don't really believe this. I think the swerve in my career says as much if not more about the culture at large as it does about my own path. I also think, though this may be wishful thinking, that everything I've done up to now, from my AIDS work, writings, translations, mothering, and many years of teaching, to my experience as a well spouse—that all of this life has been some kind of preparation for and hence useful to the way I see my work evolving in however many productive years remain to me. I hope they'll be many, but who knows?

But back to my point about the culture at large and its own swerve away from poetry: here's a little scrap of dialogue that illustrates what I mean. In February of 2004 I was one of several writers invited to participate in an international conference in Delphi about the influence of Greece, or Greekness, in our work. From the hotel in Athens, the day I arrived, I phoned my half-brother David, who was then terminally ill, though alert and cheerful, in St. Louis, where he had taught English at Washington University for almost four decades. I don't remember our exact words, but the conversation went something like this. "Remind me what you'll be doing in Delphi," said David. "Did they invite you there to read your poems?"

I explained that the conference involved writers discussing their work.

"Yes, that's the way it usually is," he said. "People don't want to actually listen to poetry, but they wouldn't have invited you unless you'd written it, and they do want to hear you talk about it."

Like much else that David said near the end of his life, this matter-of-fact gem of wisdom has proven to be a gift that keeps on giving. "Talking about it" is another form of applying or using literature.

Finally, two other developments in my career in the past decade have also involved practical applications: translating and editing. I've enjoyed translating since high school, when I rendered Verlaine's *L'Art Poetique* into rhymed quatrains I wish I could dig up now. At the beginning of this update I made mention of my translations, from Latin and Ancient Greek respectively, of Seneca's tragedy *Oedipus* and Euripides' romance *Helen.* The latter was published in 1998; yet only last year did I use my version of this remarkable play in the Mythology in Literature course which I often teach. I'm evidently getting more impatient, however. Last summer I translated Racine's tragedy *Iphigenie,* and this translation, which has yet to find a publisher, will be on the syllabus of this spring's mythology course.

The other practical application I have in mind is editing; but again, translation is involved. For the past few years (I'm a bit vague about precisely how many), I have been engaged in coediting a massive anthology, to be published by Norton, of Greek poetry in translation from Homer to the present. This was and still is a daunting mission: collaboration, deadlines, even editing were new territory to me. But the deadline has proven mercifully flexible; my coeditors, Edmund Keeley, Peter Constantine, and Karen Van Dyck, have been wonderful to work with; and as for editing—isn't it one more way to transform the word on the page (or rather, in this case, a venerable, vital, and magnificent canon) into a book which will have a palpable influence in the world?

Two years ago, the tsunami hit. At just this time, my husband's terrifying illness felt like a tsunami in our lives. Now, two years later, his slow decline continues, but it remains slow. I am often tired, frustrated, angry, and sometimes lonely. How could it be otherwise? But I also feel intensely alive, productive, and in some ways fortunate. Poetry, teaching, and the entire world of literature as it touches our lives keeps nourishing me. So long as I in turn feel able to contribute something to the larger dialogue, so long as there is conversation, I can keep going.

BIOGRAPHICAL AND CRITICAL SOURCES:

BOOKS

Contemporary Poets, 6th edition, St. James Press (Detroit, MI), 1996.

Rachel and George, 1988

Dictionary of Literary Biography, Volume 120: *American Poets since World War II,* Thomson Gale (Detroit, MI), 1992.

PERIODICALS

Belles Lettres, January, 1996, Lois Marie Harrod, review of *The Empty Bed,* p. 36.

Booklist, May 15, 1995, Elizabeth Gunderson, review of *The Empty Bed,* p. 1627.

Library Journal, September 15, 1998, Judy Clarence, review of *Halfway down the Hall: New and Selected Poems,* p. 83; April 1, 1999, Barbara Hoffert, review of *Halfway down the Hall,* p. 96; September 1, 2000, Ellen Sullivan, review of *Merrill, Cavafy, Poems, and Dreams,* p. 208.

Nation, May 3, 1986, Grace Schulman, "Prizewinning Poets," p. 620.

New York Times Book Review, March 4, 1984, Jorie Graham, review of *Slow Transparency;* May 6, 1990; January 21, 1996, Daniel Mendelsohn, "Keep Your Mind in Hell"; December 23, 2001, Eric McHenry, review of *Indelible,* p. 17.

Poetry, November, 1984; June, 1990; December, 1991; May, 1994; February, 1997.

Progressive, February, 1999, Joel Brouwer, review of *Halfway down the Hall,* p. 43.

Publishers Weekly, August 31, 1990, Penny Kaganoff, review of *Living in Time,* p. 59; September 28, 1992, review of *Mirrors of Astonishment,* p. 71; March 27, 1995, review of *The Empty Bed,* p. 80; October 30, 1995, review of *The Double Legacy,* p. 51; July 27, 1998, review of *Halfway down the Hall,* p. 72; October 22, 2001, review of *Indelible,* p. 72.

Record (Bergen County, NJ), April 12, 1996, Antoinette Rainone, "Celebrating a Poet's Life," p. 10.

Star Ledger (Newark, NJ), February 24, 2005, Bob Braun, "A Poet's Simple Words Open the Door to Live's Complexities," p. 15.

Times Literary Supplement, July 20, 1984, Anne Stevenson, review of *Slow Transparency.*

Washington Times, May 23, 2004, Amanda Kolson Hurley, "Poems of Old Truths Relearned," p. B06.

ONLINE

Gloria G. Brame's Home Page, http://gloria-brame.com/glory/rachel.htm (June 11, 2007), interview with Hadas.

Poets.org, http://www.poets.org/poet.php/prmPID/195 (June 11, 2007), profile of Hadas.

Rachel Hadas's Home Page, http://www.rachelhadas.com (June 11, 2007).

Rutgers University Web site, http://mfa.newark.rutgers.edu/ (June 11, 2007), profile of Hadas.*

*   *   *

HAGEDORN, Ann
(Ann Hagedorn Auerbach)

PERSONAL: Born in Dayton, OH. *Education:* Denison University, B.A.; University of Michigan, M.L.S. (with highest honors); Columbia University, M.A. (with highest honors); Goethe Institute, German language proficiency degree; also attended Yale University. *Hobbies and other interests:* Playing the violin and concertina, bicycling, sailing, reading, and writing.

ADDRESSES: Home—Ripley, OH; New York, NY.

CAREER: Writer. *San Jose Mercury News,* San Jose, CA, staff writer, 1985-86; *Wall Street Journal,* New York, NY, staff writer, 1986-1993; *New York Daily News,* New York, NY, special projects editor and investigative reporter, 1993-95. Also worked as a research librarian, University of Kansas, and a member of library faculty, New York University. Guest lecturer and professor at Columbia University and Northwestern University; guest lecturer at Vassar College, Berea College, Denison University, Wilmington College, Ohio State University, Xavier University, and Antioch Writer's Workshop.

AWARDS, HONORS: Associated Press award for business writing, for article in *New York Daily News* on George Steinbrenner; Ohioana Book Award citation winner in nonfiction category, and Most Notable Books in America citation, American Library Association, both 2004, both for *Beyond the River: The Untold Story of the Heroes of the Underground Railroad.*

WRITINGS:

AS ANN HAGEDORN AUERBACH

Wild Ride: The Rise and Tragic Fall of Calumet Farm, Inc., America's Premier Racing Dynasty, Henry Holt (New York, NY), 1994.
Ransom: The Untold Story of International Kidnapping, Henry Holt (New York, NY), 1998.

OTHER

Beyond the River: The Untold Story of the Heroes of the Underground Railroad, Simon & Schuster (New York, NY), 2002.
Savage Peace: Hope and Fear in America, 1919, Simon & Schuster (New York, NY), 2007.

SIDELIGHTS: Former journalist Ann Hagedorn is both an author of nonfiction books and a guest lecturer in writing and journalism at universities across the United States. Her first book, *Wild Ride: The Rise and Tragic Fall of Calumet Farm, Inc., America's Premier Racing Dynasty,* traces the multigenerational story of one of horseracing's most successful companies, which eventually went bankrupt in the early 1990s amid charges of fraud and corruption. Hagedorn's sophomore title, *Ransom: The Untold Story of International Kidnapping,* is centered around the story of the 1995 kidnapping of several men—one of them American—in the Indian region of Kashmir. The book also includes numerous accounts from kidnapping victims, as well as commentary on kidnappers' motives and what might be done to stop them.

Beyond the River: The Untold Story of the Heroes of the Underground Railroad is a factual account of the role that the town of Ripley, Ohio, played in helping both escaped and freed slaves continue their journey into Canada. One character in particular—the abolitionist Reverend John Rankin—receives particular attention for the sacrifices made and risks taken in protecting the lives of American slaves. Hagedorn places the town's efforts in context by sharing details about the greater abolitionist movement in the United States. Writing in the *Journal of Southern History,* Leonne M. Hudson wrote: "This superbly written volume is thoroughly documented with primary sources and contains several photographs." Hudson continued: "With a sense of freshness and passion, Hagedorn succeeds splendidly in recreating the historical legacy of the Underground Railroad." A *Publishers Weekly* reviewer pointed out that "Hagedorn's decision to relocate to Ripley during the book's completion no doubt inspired her immediate and vivid prose, bringing these historical figures to a wider audience." "Hagedorn's book could have offered more background on the slave empire and the workings of the Underground Rail-road beyond Ripley," remarked *Time* reviewer Richard Lacayo, "but the ground-level focus gives Hagedorn's story the flavor and fire of an era when even the newspapers had names like the *Agitator* and the *Castigator.*"

In *Savage Peace: Hope and Fear in America, 1919,* Hagedorn focuses on the year after the close of World War I, a time of great optimism in the United States. In reality, racism was rampant and prompted violence, paranoia was widespread, and women were still fighting for the right to vote. The book, wrote *History News Network* Web site reviewer Murray Polner, is "a dramatic and valuable reminder of a period that resembles our more recent time of troubles after WWII, during the Vietnam era, and in the proxy war in Central America when political and governmental demagogues hounded and persecuted critics and dissenters." A contributor to *Kirkus Reviews* found the *Savage Peace* "fluently written, constantly surprising—and timely, in a between-the-lines sort of way." Describing the book as a "vivid account of a nation in tumult and transition," a critic for *Publishers Weekly* noted: "The nexus of global and national upheaval is chillingly relevent."

BIOGRAPHICAL AND CRITICAL SOURCES:

PERIODICALS

Journal of Southern History, May, 2004, Leonne M. Hudson, review of *Beyond the River: The Untold Story of the Heroes of the Underground Railroad,* p. 431.

Kirkus Reviews, February 1, 2007, review of *Savage Peace: Hope and Fear in America, 1919,* p. 111.

Publishers Weekly, January 6, 2003, review of *Beyond the River,* p. 50; January 15, 2007, review of *Savage Peace,* p. 40.

Time, February 17, 2003, Richard Lacayo, "Making Tracks to Freedom: A Chronicle of One Defiant Family Who Formed a Vital Link in the Pre-Civil War Underground Railroad," p. 70.

ONLINE

Ann Hagedorn Home Page, http://www.annhagedorn.com (October 2, 2007).

History News Network, http://hnn.us/ (May 21, 2007), Murray Polner, review of *Savage Peace.*

*   *   *

HALL, Joseph Tillman
See HALL, J. Tillman

*   *   *

HALL, J. Tillman 1916-2007
(Joseph Tillman Hall)

OBITUARY NOTICE— See index for *CA* sketch: Born January 16, 1916, in Big Sandy, TN; died following a stroke, June 6, 2007, in Inglewood, CA. Educator, administrator, folk dancer, and author. Hall was best known for the youth dance group that he founded, more or less as a hobby, in 1950. The Westchester Lariats began as an after-school square dance group that Hall created in his western Los Angeles neighborhood. He later revealed his initial doubts that a country dance group would succeed on the West Coast, but his young dancers became nationally recognized. They performed on the television program *The Lawrence Welk Show* and even toured U.S. and European cities on a regular basis. The Lariats, who were still performing at the time of their founder's death, added international folk dances to their roster and made thousands of appearances in the twenty-five years that Hall and his wife were in charge. Professionally, Hall was an academic who taught physical education at the University of Southern California for more than twenty years. Officially retired in 1989, he assumed the leadership of the university's Emeriti Center, where he recruited dozens of other university retirees to go out into the community and continue teaching informally what they had once taught for a living. Some of their favorite venues were local senior centers and retirement homes. Hall also established the University of Southern California Living History Project to videotape oral interviews with aging educators and administrators. He continued that work until 1996. Hall wrote or coauthored books on physical fitness, education, and dance, including *Dance! A Complete Guide to Social Folk & Square Dancing* (1963), *Folk Dance* (1969), the two-volume work *Until the Whistle Blows: A Collection of Games, Dances, and Activities . . .* (1976-77), *Total Fitness for Men* (1980), and *Physical Education in the Elementary School* (1980).

OBITUARIES AND OTHER SOURCES:

PERIODICALS

Los Angeles Times, June 24, 2007, p. B13.

*   *   *

HALL, Meredith 1949-

PERSONAL: Born 1949; divorced; children: three. *Education:* Graduated from Bowdoin College, c. 1993; University of New Hampshire, M.A.

ADDRESSES: Home—Pownal, ME. *Office*—University of New Hampshire, 310 Hamilton Smith Hall, Durham, NH 03824.

CAREER: Writer and educator. University of New Hampshire, Durham, writing teacher.

MEMBER: Phi Beta Kappa.

AWARDS, HONORS: Gift of Freedom Award, A Room of Her Own Foundation, 2004; Pushcart Prize, 2004, for "Shunned"; fellowships with Maine Arts Commission, MacDowell Colony, Jental Arts, Helene Wurlitzer Foundation, and Djerassi, all 2005; University of New Hampshire President's Citation for Excellence in Teaching; Thomas Williams Prize in Fiction; Forbes Rickard Poetry Prize; Bertram Louis Smith Prize in English; Elbridge Sibley Award in Anthropology.

WRITINGS:

Without a Map: A Memoir, Beacon Press (Boston, MA), 2007.

Contributor to *New York Times, Creative Nonfiction, Southern Review, Five Points, Prairie Schooner,* and several anthologies.

SIDELIGHTS: In 1965, Maine native Meredith Hall was a sixteen-year-old high school student who became pregnant and was inevitably forced by her parents to give her child up for adoption. After several years wandering around Europe and the Middle East, she returned to Maine, got married, and started a family. Hall was ultimately reconnected with her grown son, and felt compelled to share her story in the book *Without a Map: A Memoir.* In an interview with contributor Ray Routhier on the *Portland Press Herald/Maine Sunday Telegram* Web site, Hall commented: "I thought that I was writing about the griefs that come from the loss of people we love deeply—my child, my mother and my father. As I wrote, I was flooded with love and great tenderness for my parents. And I was surprised to feel great love and tenderness for the young girl who had experienced those losses. . . . I also came to see that I live my life with a certain calm and fullness, a deep sense of gratitude and awe."

In the opinion of *Library Journal* contributor Elizabeth Brinkley, "The message of redemptive compassion makes this a worthwhile and moving read." A reviewer for *Publishers Weekly* found that the "painful memoir builds to a quiet resolution." *Entertainment Weekly* writer Alanna Nash described Hall as a "brave writer of tumultuous beauty." "Stunning" was how Emily Book described the book in a review for *Booklist.* Cook went on to note Hall's "spare, unsentimental prose."

BIOGRAPHICAL AND CRITICAL SOURCES:

BOOKS

Hall, Meredith, *Without a Map: A Memoir,* Beacon Press (Boston, MA), 2007.

PERIODICALS

Booklist, December 15, 2006, Emily Cook, review of *Without a Map,* p. 12.
Entertainment Weekly, April 20, 2007, Alanna Nash, review of *Without a Map,* p. 65.
Library Journal, February 1, 2007, Elizabeth Brinkley, review of *Without a Map,* p. 88.
Publishers Weekly, January 22, 2007, review of *Without a Map,* p. 178.

ONLINE

Meredith Hall Home Page, http://meredithhall.org (October 3, 2007).
Portland Press Herald/Maine Sunday Telegram Online, http://pressherald.mainetoday.com/ (April 15, 2007), Ray Routhier, review of *Without a Map.**

*   *   *

HALM, Heinz 1942-

PERSONAL: Born February 21, 1942, in Andernach, Rhein, Germany; married Christa Guédé. *Education:* University of Bonn, Germany, Ph.D., 1967; University of Tübingen, Germany, habilitation, 1975.

CAREER: Writer, educator, university administrator, Islamist, and historian. University of Tübingen, Tübingen, Germany, professor, 1980, dean of faculty of cultural sciences, 1994-95, studiendakan faculty, cultural sciences, 1996-2000, currently professor of Islamic studies; University of Paris IV Sorbonne, associate professor, 1987-89. Guest professor, Leiden University, 1993.

MEMBER: European Union of Arabists and Islamists.

WRITINGS:

Die Traditionen Uber Den Aufstand Ali Ibn Muhammads, Des "Herrn Der Zang"; Eine Quellenkritische Untersuchung, (Bonn, Germany), 1967.

Soldaten in Bruckeburg, Grimme (Buckeburg, Germany), 1971.

Die Ausbreitung Der Safi'itischen Rechtsschule Von Den Anfangen Bis Zum 8./14. Jahrhundert, Reichert (Wiesbaden, Germany), 1974.

Kosmologie Und Heilslehre Der Fruhen Ismailiya: Eine Studie Zur Islamischen Gnosis, Franz Steiner (Weisbaden, Germany), 1978.

Aegypten Nach Den Mamlukischen Lehensregistern, Reichert (Wiesbaden, Germany), 1979.

Die Islamische Gnosis: Die Extreme Schia Und Die Alawiten, Artemis Verlag (Zurich, Switzerland), 1982.

Die Schia, Wissenschaftliche Buchgesellschaft (Darmstadt, Germany), 1988.

Das Reich Des Mahdi: Der Aufstieg Der Fatimiden (875-973), C.H. Beck (Munich, Germany), 1991, published as *The Empire of the Mahdi: The Rise of the Fatimids,* translated by Michael Bonner, E.J. Brill (Leiden, Germany), 1996.

Shiism, translated by Janet Watson, Edinburgh University Press (Edinburgh, Scotland), 1991, 2nd edition, published as *Shi'ism,* with new material translated by Marian Hill, Columbia University Press (New York, NY), 2004.

Der Schiitische Islam: Von Der Religion Zur Revolution, C.H. Beck (Munich, Germany), 1994.

The Fatimids and Their Traditions of Learning, I.B. Tauris/Institute of Ismaili Studies (New York, NY), 1997.

Shi'a Islam: From Religion to Revolution, Markus Wiener Publishers (Princeton, NJ), 1997.

Der Islam: Geschichte Und Gegenwart, C.H. Beck (Munich, Germany), 2000.

Geschichte Der Arabischen Welt, C.H. Beck (Munich, Germany), 2001.

Die Kalifen Von Kairo: Die Fatimiden in Aegypten, 973-1074, C.H. Beck (Munich, Germany), 2003.

The Arabs: A Short History, translated by Allison Brown and Thomas Lampert, Markus Wiener Publishers (Princeton, NJ), 2007.

The Shiites: A Short History, 2nd updated and enlarged edition, translated by Allison Brown, Markus Wiener Publishers (Princeton, NJ), 2007.

Contributor to books, including the *Encyclopaedia of Islam* and the *Encyclopaedia Iranica.* Contributor to scholarly journals and periodicals.

SIDELIGHTS: Heinz Halm is a professor at the University of Tübingen in Germany, where he is a prolific Islamicist and a specialist in Ismaili studies. His numerous books cover topics related to Islam, Arabic history, the Shiites, and the Shi'a religion, and other areas of Islamic culture, religion, and history.

Halm explores the many facets of learning and education among the Fatimids, the early Ismaili Shi'a group that conquered Egypt in 969 and founded the Egyptian city of Cairo, in *The Fatimids and Their Traditions of Learning.* The book is a "comprehensive account of the traditions of learning among the Fatimids, written by a distinguished scholar and an authority in Fatimid/Ismaili studies," commented Ismail K. Poonawala in the *Journal of the American Oriental Society.* The Fatimids, who claimed to be descended from Fatima, daughter of Muhammad, were well organized, closely connected, and educated, and were aided from within by scholar-missionaries called Dais. Within the book, Halm looks at the Dai and their leader, and in particular examines the group's "training, education, and accomplishments," Poonawala stated. "Halm has succeeded in his task of illuminating the many-sided personality of the dai," Poonawala concluded.

Similarly, with *The Empire of the Mahdi: The Rise of the Fatimids,* Halm provides an "integrated, comprehensive, and persuasive narrative of early Isma'ili activities," culminating in the Fatimid conquest of Egypt, noted Richard W. Bulliet in the *Historian.* He recounts the battles over the inheritance of religious authority, the development of Fatimid power through propaganda, revolts that arose and failed, tribal armies of the Berbers who helped extend the Imam's power, the rise of militant movements throughout the Middle East, and more. "Against this background, Halm's achievement looms large. Specialists will disagree with him on details, but they will applaud the flow and liveliness of his narrative," Bulliet concluded. Reviewer Farhad Daftary, writing in the *Journal of the American Oriental Society,* stated that Halm's "treatment of the complex issues of early Ismailism fully reflects the state of modern scholarship in the field, to which he himself has made valuable contributions over the last two decades." Daftary also concluded his review with high praise for Halm's work: "All in all, Halm's *The Empire of the Mahdi* is a masterly treatment of a crucial and complex early phase in the long history of the Ismailis and as such it represents a major contribution to modern Ismaili studies in general and Fatimid studies in particular."

In *Shi'a Islam: From Religion to Revolution,* Halm seeks to "lessen the reader's confusion about the bewildering events in the Middle East," noted James F. DeRoche in the *Library Journal.* Halm recounts the history and doctrine of Shi'a and its belief that it represents the true imams and the only legitimate heirs and successors to the Islamic prophet Muhammad. Halm carefully describes numerous rituals of the Shi'a that demonstrate grief and penitence over the martyrdom of successive imams. Thirdly, the author covers in depth the history and development of the Shi'ite religious hierarchy of mullahs and ayatollahs. Relevant to modern issues in the Middle East, Halm describes how the mullahs and ayatollahs came to represent Shi'a and how they gained their religious and political power, and the religious doctrine that they use to justify and retain their strict rule. DeRoche called the book an "excellent source," while *Booklist* reviewer Gilbert Taylor observed that Halm gives "fair treatment" to the "origins and tenets of Shi'ite Islam."

BIOGRAPHICAL AND CRITICAL SOURCES:

PERIODICALS

Asian Affairs, June, 1998, Francis Robinson, review of *The Fatimids and Their Traditions of Learning,* p. 203.
Booklist, March 15, 1997, Gilbert Taylor, review of *Shi'a Islam: From Religion to Revolution,* p. 1207.
Choice, May, 1997, review of *Shi'a Islam,* p. 1516.

Historian, spring, 1999, Richard W. Bulliet, review of *The Empire of the Mahdi: The Rise of the Fatimids,* p. 651.
International Journal of Middle East Studies, May, 1999, Said Amir Arjomand, review of *Shi'a Islam,* p. 276.
Journal of the American Oriental Society, April 1, 1998, Farhad Daftary, review of *The Empire of the Mahdi,* p. 298; July 1, 1999, Ismail K. Poonawala, review of *The Fatimids and Their Traditions of Learning,* p. 542.
Library Journal, April 15, 1997, James F. DeRoche, review of *Shi'a Islam,* p. 86; October 1, 1998, review of *Shiism,* p. 62.
Muslim World, January, 1998, Abdulaziz Sachedina, review of *Shi'a Islam,* p. 102.
Reference & Research Book News, May, 1997, review of *The Empire of the Mahdi,* p. 30; November, 1997, review of *The Fatimids and Their Traditions of Learning,* p. 33.

ONLINE

Institute of Ismaili Studies Web site, http://www.iis.ac.uk/ (October 3, 2007), biography of Heinz Halm.*

*   *   *

HANDLER, Marisa 1976-

PERSONAL: Born 1976, in South Africa. *Education:* University of California, Berkeley, B.A., 1998.

ADDRESSES: Home—San Francisco, CA. *E-mail*—marisahandler@gmail.com.

CAREER: Writer, activist, singer-songwriter, and teacher.

WRITINGS:

Loyal to the Sky: Notes from an Activist, Berrett-Koehler Publishers (San Francisco, CA), 2007.

Contributor to publications including *San Francisco Chronicle, San Francisco Bay Guardian, Earth Island Journal, Salon.com, Alternet, Orion, Tikkun,* and *Bitch.*

SIDELIGHTS: Born and raised in South Africa during the height of apartheid, Marisa Handler immigrated with her family to the United States when it seemed no end to the country's political and racial inequality was in sight. She has since traveled internationally as an activist and journalist, working with justice organizations in Africa, the Middle East, Europe, South Asia, and South America. Handler's lifelong pursuit of peace and global justice been chronicled in her first book, *Loyal to the Sky: Notes from an Activist.* In addition to recounting the evolution of her career in activism, Handler also describes activism on a grander scale and how grassroots movements around the world are working to make change at the local, national, and global levels. *Booklist* reviewer Emily Cook described *Loyal to the Sky* as "a deeply intelligent, absorbing call to action." Jessica Lee, writing for the *Indypendent,* commented that the book is "the fist on the table that quiets the room full of activists quarreling over what message to put on the sign or which route to take in the march. . . . [Handler] speaks directly to those of us knocking our heads against the wall working for social and environmental change, feeling that with every step forward we end up three steps back." In a review for *Publishers Weekly,* a critic remarked that Handler describes "the histories of places many people couldn't find on a map in a lively, moving and funny voice."

BIOGRAPHICAL AND CRITICAL SOURCES:

PERIODICALS

Booklist, February 15, 2007, Emily Cook, review of *Loyal to the Sky: Notes from an Activist,* p. 30.

Publishers Weekly, January 1, 2007, review of *Loyal to the Sky,* p. 47.

ONLINE

Indypendent Online, http://www.indypendent.org/ (August 15, 2007), Jessica Lee, "The Revolution Within: A Review of *Loyal to the Sky: Notes from an Activist.*"

Marisa Handler Home Page, http://www.marisa handler.com (September 3, 2007), author biography.

*   *   *

HARDING, Duncan
      See WHITING, Charles

HARDING, Ian
      See WHITING, Charles

*   *   *

HARRISON, C.C.

PERSONAL: Female.

ADDRESSES: Home—Anthem, AZ. *E-mail*—contact@ ccharrison-author.com.

CAREER: Writer, journalist, short-story writer, and novelist.

WRITINGS:

The Charmstone, Five Star (Waterville, ME), 2007.
Running from Strangers, Five Star (Waterville, ME), 2008.

SIDELIGHTS: C.C. Harrison is a prolific author of articles and short stories. Her debut novel, *The Charmstone,* reflects her love for the desert settings of the American southwest, including Monument Valley and Navajo lands. Protagonist Amanda Bell is a socialite and museum designer who lives a comfortable life with her fiancé in Beverly Hills. When her archaeologist father is killed in a car crash, Amanda honors his last request by traveling to the Navajo reservation in Monument Valley to deliver his papers and other materials to the cultural center. Though the stark environment of the reservation is a strong contrast to the posh surroundings she enjoyed in Beverly Hills, Amanda finds herself growing more and more attracted to the beauty of the land and the culture of its inhabitants. Soon, she decides to stay on to catalogue and archive her father's papers and the cultural center's collections. While there, she encounters Durango Yazzie, a Hollywood director and Navajo who has returned to the reservation to deepen his knowledge and connection to his culture. As romantic sparks are kindled between the two, the details of Amanda's father's car crash draw both characters' interest. Amanda discovers numerous inconsistencies in the accident report, and the fact that her father's body was never found leads both her and

Durango to suspect there is more to the case than was reported. When she investigates further, Amanda receives threats and intimidating messages indicating she should leave the area and stop looking into her father's death. The case gets even more complicated with the involvement of a shady news reporter, the reappearance of Amanda's ex-fiancé, and the presence of a group of thieves who rob Indian graves and steal precious Navajo artifacts.

With this novel, "Harrison does a masterful job of painting very visible characters and challenging them with an interesting and fast moving plot," commented Dennis Collins on *MyShelf.com*. *Booklist* critic Patty Engelmann concluded that Harrison's "top-notch romantic suspense novel" illuminates both the "beauty of the land and culture of the Navajo."

BIOGRAPHICAL AND CRITICAL SOURCES:

PERIODICALS

Booklist, March 1, 2007, Patty Engelmann, review of *The Charmstone*, p. 70.

ONLINE

C.C. Harrison Home Page, http://www.ccharrison-author.com (October 3, 2007).
C.C. Harrison Web log, http://www.ccharrison.blogspot.com (October 3, 2007).
MyShelf.com, http://www.myshelf.com/ (October 3, 2007), review of *The Charmstone*.*

*   *   *

HART, Marjorie 1924-

PERSONAL: Born April 15, 1924, in Story City, IA; married William Hart (a dentist; died 1981); married Peter Cuthbert; children: three daughters and one son. *Education:* University of Iowa, B.M., San Diego State College, M.A.

ADDRESSES: Home—La Mesa, CA.

CAREER: Musician and writer. Worked previously at DePauw University and the University of San Diego as a professor of music.

WRITINGS:

Summer at Tiffany, William Morrow (New York, NY), 2007.

SIDELIGHTS: In the summer of 1945, two young coeds from the University of Iowa decided to experience the glamour and excitement of city life by getting summer jobs in New York City. During their short stay the women both experienced history—they were witness to the excitement of Victory over Japan (VJ) Day in Times Square and the devastation of an accidental plane crash into the Empire State Building—and made history as the first women to work on the sales floor at Tiffany & Co. One of the women, Marjorie Hart, shared in an interview with *San Diego Union Tribune* contributor Arthur Salm what compelled her to write of those experiences at the age of eighty-three: "I don't consider myself a writer, but I wanted a legacy for our family." Recalling love letters belonging to her mother that she found and read as a child, Hart continued: "From then on, I thought of her differently. I'd had no idea that she had those feelings. My children and grandchildren don't really know me, and I thought, maybe they'll know me like I got to know my mother when I found those letters." The resulting memoir, *Summer at Tiffany*, was described by Michelle Jones in a *BookPage* review as "charming and fun." Jones further commented: "Every once in a while a book comes along that is everything one wants it to be; such is the case with Marjorie Hart's *Summer at Tiffany*." *Booklist* reviewer Carol Haggas wrote: "Hart's infectious vivacity resonates with a madcap immediacy, delectably capturing the city's heady vibrancy." Writing for *USA Today*, Deirdre Donahue remarked: "Neither sentimental nor saccharine, this book offers insights into the women who lived through World War II."

BIOGRAPHICAL AND CRITICAL SOURCES:

PERIODICALS

Booklist, January 1, 2007, Carol Haggas, review of *Summer at Tiffany*, p. 30.

ONLINE

BookPage, http://www.bookpage.com/ (September 7, 2007), Michelle Jones, "Tiffany Charmer Is Pure Sterling."

San Diego Union Tribune, http://www.signonsandiego.com/ (July 1, 2007), Arthur Salm, "One Shining 'Summer,'" review of *Summer at Tiffany.*

USA Today, http://www.usatoday.com/ (April 18, 2007), Deirdre Donahue, "Two Women's Stories that Improve with Age," review of *Summer at Tiffany.**

*   *   *

HAWKE, Richard 1955-
(Tim Cockey)

PERSONAL: Born 1955. *Education:* Attended college.

ADDRESSES: E-mail—hawke@rhawke.com; tim cockey@mindspring.com.

CAREER: Writer.

WRITINGS:

Speak of the Devil: A Novel, Random House (New York, NY), 2005.
Cold Day in Hell: A Novel, Random House (New York, NY), 2007.

"HITCHCOCK SEWELL" SERIES; AS TIM COCKEY

The Hearse You Came In On, Hyperion (New York, NY), 2000.
Hearse of a Different Color, Hyperion (New York, NY), 2001.
Hearse Case Scenario, Hyperion (New York, NY), 2002.
Murder in the Hearse Degree, Hyperion (New York, NY), 2003.
Backstabber, Hyperion (New York, NY), 2004.

ADAPTATIONS: Author's books have been adapted for audio, including *Hearse Case Scenario,* Brilliance Audio, 2002.

SIDELIGHTS: Richard Hawke began his career by writing the "Hitchcock Sewel" humorous mystery series under the pseudonym Tim Cockey. *Library Journal* contributor Rex E. Klett called the series "delightful." The initial title in the series, *The Hearse You Came In On,* introduces readers to Hitch, an undertaker who is also an amateur detective. Hitch finds himself investigating the murder of a woman killed the day after another woman using her name came into Hitch's funeral home to arrange, so she claimed, her own funeral. In the process of the investigation, Hitch begins a romance with Baltimore cop Bonnie Nash. "Cockey possesses a terrific comic touch," wrote Bill Ott in *Booklist. Hearse of a Different Color* features Hitch and Nash on the case of a murdered waitress whose body was dumped on the steps of the Sewel & Sons funeral home. "*Hearse of a Different Color* had me laughing out loud from page one," commented Judi Clark on *The Mostly Fiction* Web site.

Hearse Case Scenario finds Hitch and his ex-wife looking for his friend Lucy, who shot her lover, Shrimp Martin, a nightclub owner. *Booklist* contributor Bill Ott wrote that the author "effectively grounds Hitch's high jinks in the real world." A *Kirkus Reviews* contributor commented: "The cast is colorful, and Hitch can be fun." In *Murder in the Hearse Degree,* Hitch investigates the death of a nanny who might have been pregnant by the husband of a one of Hitch's old flames. "Those who enjoy lighthearted mysteries with screwball characters will relish Cockey's fourth outing," noted a *Publishers Weekly* contributor. In the fifth book in the series, *Backstabber,* Hitch decides to investigate the murder of a woman's husband after he learns that the prime suspect is an old high school friend who was having an affair with her. A *Publishers Weekly* contributor wrote: "Cockey keeps the pace fast, the plot twisted and the laughs plentiful—as always, he does not disappoint."

In his first book writing as Richard Hawke, *Speak of the Devil: A Novel,* the author introduces private investigator Fritz Malone, who starts his day by stopping a mass murderer on a rampage. Before the day is over, however, Hawke, whose father was once the police commissioner, finds himself investigating a police scandal. Allison Block, writing in *Booklist,* noted: "In a genre populated with predictable PIs, Fritz Malone is a fresh, engaging blend of laconic detective and likable guy." In *Library Journal,* Jo Ann Vicarel wrote: "Read this for compelling characters and an intriguing, fast-paced plot."

Fritz returns in *Cold Day in Hell: A Novel,* this time trying to prove that a handsome, popular television host is innocent of murdering two women with whom he was having affairs. The only reason Fritz becomes involved is because one of the women came to him asking for help before she was killed. A *Publishers Weekly* contributor referred to the novel as "intriguing." Writing in *Booklist,* David Wright called it an "intelligent and well-turned mystery."

BIOGRAPHICAL AND CRITICAL SOURCES:

PERIODICALS

Booklist, January 1, 2000, Bill Ott, review of *The Hearse You Came In On,* p. 882; December 15, 2000, Bill Ott, review of *Hearse of a Different Color,* p. 790; January 1, 2002, Bill Ott, review of *The Hearse Case Scenario,* p. 816; May 1, 2004, Bill Ott, review of *Backstabber,* p. 1503; November 1, 2005, Allison Block, review of *Speak of the Devil: A Novel,* p. 28; January 1, 2007, David Wright, review of *Cold Day in Hell: A Novel,* p. 63.

Drood Review of Mystery, November, 2000, reviews of *Hearse of a Different Color* and *The Hearse You Came In On,* p. 13; May, 2001, review of *Hearse of a Different Color,* p. 10.

Entertainment Weekly, January 13, 2006, Gilbert Cruz, review of *Speak of the Devil,* p. 89.

Kirkus Reviews, December 1, 2001, review of *Hearse Case Scenario,* p. 1647; December 15, 2002, review of *Murder in the Hearse Degree,* p. 1805; June 15, 2004, review of *Backstabber,* p. 558; February 1, 2007, review of *Cold Day in Hell,* p. 102.

Library Journal, March 1, 2000, Rex E. Klett, review of *The Hearse You Came In On,* p. 127; February 1, 2001, Rex E. Klett, review of *Hearse of a Different Color,* p. 127; February 1, 2002, Rex E. Klett, review of *The Hearse Case Scenario,* p. 136; February 1, 2003, Shelley Mosley, review of *Murder in the Hearse Degree,* p. 122; December 1, 2005, Jo Ann Vicarel, review of *Speak of the Devil,* p. 112; March 1, 2007, Stacy Alesi, review of *Cold Day in Hell,* p. 74.

Publishers Weekly, February 14, 2000, review of *The Hearse You Came In On,* p. 176; December 4, 2000, review of *Hearse of a Different Color,* p. 56; January 21, 2002, review of *The Hearse Case Scenario,* p. 67; January 20, 2003, review of *Murder in the Hearse Degree,* p. 59; June 28, 2004, review of *Backstabber,* p. 34; October 3, 2005, review of *Speak of the Devil,* p. 46; December 11, 2006, review of *Cold Day in Hell,* p. 43.

ONLINE

Bookreporter.com, http://www.bookreporter.com/ (January 13, 2006), interview with author.

Mostly Fiction, http://www.mostlyfiction.com/ (February 6, 2000), Judi Clark, review of *The Hearse Case Scenario;* (February 4, 2001), Judi Clark, review of *Hearse of a Different Color;* (March 31, 2003), Judi Clark, review of *Murder in the Hearse Degree.*

Mystery Ink, http://www.mysteryinkonline.com/ (August 20, 2007), David J. Montgomery, review of *Speak of the Devil.*

Mystery Reader, http://www.themysteryreader.com/ (August 20, 2007), Lesley Dunlap, review of *Speak of the Devil.*

Richard Hawke Home Page, http://www.rhawke.com (August 20, 2007).

Tim Cockey Home Page, http://www.timcockey.com (August 20, 2007).

*   *   *

HENDERSON, Timothy J.

PERSONAL: Male.

ADDRESSES: Home—Department of History, Auburn University Montgomery, Montgomery, AL 36124. *E-mail*—thender1@aum.edu.

CAREER: Historian, educator, and writer. Auburn University Montgomery, Montgomery, AL, professor of history.

WRITINGS:

The Worm in the Wheat: Rosalie Evans and Agrarian Struggle in the Puebla-Tlaxcala Valley of Mexico, 1906-1927, Duke University Press (Durham, NC), 1998.

(Editor, with Gilbert M. Joseph) *The Mexico Reader: History, Culture, Politics,* Duke University Press (Durham, NC), 2002.

A Glorious Defeat: Mexico and Its War with the United States, Hill & Wang (New York, NY), 2007.

SIDELIGHTS: Historian Timothy J. Henderson's first book, *The Worm in the Wheat: Rosalie Evans and Agrarian Struggle in the Puebla-Tlaxcala Valley of Mexico, 1906-1927,* was called "colorfully written, carefully researched, and often highly entertaining" by *Labor History* contributor Cheryl E. Martin. The book focuses on Rosalie Caden Evans, a landowner along with her British husband, who set out to protect her 300-year-old hacienda San Pedro Coxtocan from being taken over by local peasants and others after her husband's death in 1917, seven years after the Mexican Revolution of 1910. Evans used everything within her means, including appealing to local government leaders in Mexico as well as to American and British officials, to remain owner of the valuable hacienda and the surrounding lands. As Henderson points out, Evans claimed that her mission was about more than her ownership rights but also about principles and the rights of the individual in a civilized society. Evans was eventually killed by gunfire when she was out riding one day in her buggy.

"In *The Worm in the Wheat,* Timothy J. Henderson uses the history of one foreign landowner's struggle against the postrevolutionary Mexican government to present the conflicts that resulted from Mexico's agrarian reform programme," noted Kristina A. Boyle in the *Journal of Latin American Studies.* In his review of *The Worm in the Wheat,* Martin noted in *Labor History* that the author "displays an exceptionally fine-tuned sensitivity to the complexity of Rosalie Evans's times," adding: "He skillfully leads his readers through the tangled web of agrarian politics in Puebla with all of its opportunistic and idealistic threads, while not losing sight of relevant contemporary events in Mexico City and abroad, so that even readers with little background in Mexican history can follow the narrative."

Henderson served as the editor, with Gilbert M. Joseph, of *The Mexico Reader: History, Culture, Politics.* The book presents numerous writings to provide the reader with both a general history of Mexico and a view of its culture, from the time of the Aztec Empire to the present day. Among the contributors are noted Mexican writers Carlos Fuentes and Octavio Paz. The authors also include famous texts such as Mexican revolutionary Emiliano Zapata's "Plan de Ayala." "This work is ideal for general readers," wrote Jay Freeman in *Booklist. Journal of Latin American Studies* contributor Patience A. Schell pointed out: "Through its focus on the remarkable lives and achievements of ordinary people, *The Mexico Reader* provides examples of how historical and contemporary actors have challenged their situations and continue to do so, chronicling the achievements and struggle of average Mexicans."

In *A Glorious Defeat: Mexico and Its War with the United States,* Henderson presents the Mexican-American War of of 1846-1848 from the perspective of the Mexicans. The author discusses such issues as why Mexico decided to go to war and why, after the United States was victorious, U.S. government leaders decided not to take possession of Mexico and incorporate it into the ever-growing United States. Brad Hooper, writing in *Booklist,* referred to *A Glorious Defeat* as a "unique contribution to the literature of the era." *Library Journal* contributor Stephen H. Peters commented that the book "fills a gap in the literature and will be appreciated" by both the general public and history students and scholars.

BIOGRAPHICAL AND CRITICAL SOURCES:

PERIODICALS

Agricultural History, winter, 2000, Alexander S. Dawson, review of *The Worm in the Wheat: Rosalie Evans and Agrarian Struggle in the Puebla-Tlaxcala Valley of Mexico, 1906-1927,* p. 104.

American Historical Review, April, 2000, review of *The Worm in the Wheat,* p. 586.

Americas: A Quarterly Review of Inter-American Cultural History, July, 1999, David G. LaFrance, review of *The Worm in the Wheat,* p. 130.

Booklist, January 1, 2003, Jay Freeman, review of *The Mexico Reader: History, Culture, Politics,* p. 840; January 1, 2007, Brad Hooper, review of *A Glorious Defeat: Mexico and Its War with the United States,* p. 46.

California Bookwatch, July, 2007, review of *A Glorious Defeat.*

Choice, May, 1999, D. Baldwin, review of *The Worm in the Wheat,* p. 1673; September, 2003, M.R. Lara, review of *The Mexico Reader,* p. 214.

H-Net: Humanities and Social Sciences Online, July, 2005, Timothy E. Anna, review of *The Mexico Reader.*

Hispanic American Historical Review, November, 1999, review of *The Worm in the Wheat,* p. 770; February, 2004, Eric Zolov, review of *The Mexico Reader,* p. 127.

Journal of Latin American Studies, May, 2000, Kristina A. Boylan, review of *The Worm in the Wheat,* p. 574; February, 2005, Patience A. Schell, review of *The Mexico Reader,* p. 178.

Kirkus Reviews, February 1, 2007, review of *A Glorious Defeat,* p. 111.

Labor History, November 1, 1999, Cheryl E. Martin, review of *The Worm in the Wheat,* p. 581.

Library Journal, April 1, 2007, Stephen H. Peters, review of *A Glorious Defeat,* p. 101.

Publishers Weekly, February 19, 2007, review of *A Glorious Defeat,* p. 157.

Rural Sociology, September, 2000, Pilar-Alicia Parra, review of *The Worm in the Wheat,* p. 527.

Times Literary Supplement, February 26, 1999, review of *The Worm in the Wheat,* p. 33.

ONLINE

Duke University Press, http://www.dukeupress.edu/ (August 20, 2007), brief profile of author.

*   *   *

HERNÁNDEZ, Lisa

PERSONAL: Female.

ADDRESSES: Home—Pasadena, CA. *Office*—Los Angeles City College, 855 N. Vermont Ave., Los Angeles, CA 90029. *E-mail*—hernanla@lacitycollege. edu.

CAREER: Writer, editor, educator, and short-story writer. Los Angeles City College, Los Angeles, CA, instructor in English.

AWARDS, HONORS: Chicano/Latino Literary Prize, University of California-Irvine, for *Migrations and Other Stories.*

WRITINGS:

(Editor, with Tina Benitez) *Palabras Chicanas: An Undergraduate Anthology,* Mujeres en Marcha (Berkeley, CA), 1988.

Migrations and Other Stories, Arte Publico Press (Houston, TX), 2007.

SIDELIGHTS: Author and editor Lisa Hernández is an English instructor at Los Angeles City College. She is also a coordinator of literacy programs for the Los Angeles Unified School District.

Hernández's fiction is showcased in her debut collection, *Migrations and Other Stories.* "Family secrets are at the heart of these eleven fine stories in Hernández's first collection," commented Hazel Rochman, writing in *Booklist.* In one story, protagonist Esmerelda finds that she has come to hate the weak and ineffective factory-worker husband she married in order to facilitate her immigration to America. In another, a daughter dutifully scatters her dead mother's ashes at the U.S./Mexico border, even as startling revelations about her mother's first true love loom in the background. In the title story, two California neighbors travel to Mexico, each for their own heartfelt reasons. Reynaldo returns to Mexico after several years in California, hoping to reconcile with his alienated daughter who was furious when he crossed the border into America to look for work. Reynaldo's traveling companion, a young woman, hopes to divest herself of an unwanted lover while taking in the Mexican culture and scenery and contemplating her own parents' long-ago border crossing. In "The Neighbor," seventy-nine-year-old Sarita is offended at the rough sexual relationship between two neighbors, whose sadistic affair she considers an insult to the gentle and considerate lovers she has known throughout her many years.

In assessing Hernández's fiction, a *Publishers Weekly* contributor concluded: "Short and affecting, Hernández's tales are as ardent as they are prosaic and unflinching."

BIOGRAPHICAL AND CRITICAL SOURCES:

PERIODICALS

Booklist, March 15, 2007, Hazel Rochman, review of *Migrations and Other Stories,* p. 24.

Publishers Weekly, January 22, 2007, review of *Migrations and Other Stories,* p. 160.*

*   *   *

HICKEY, Donald R. 1944-

PERSONAL: Born 1944. *Education:* University of Illinois, Urbana-Champaign, B.A., 1966, M.A., 1968, Ph.D., 1972.

ADDRESSES: Office—Department of History, Wayne State College, 1111 Main St., Wayne, NE 68787.

CAREER: Writer, historian, reviewer, lecturer, and educator. University of California, Santa Barbara, lecturer, 1976-77; Wayne State College, Wayne, NE, assistant professor, became professor of history, 1978—. U.S. Army Command and General Staff College, Ft. Leavenworth, KS, John F. Morrison Professor of Military History, 1991-92. University of Illinois, Urbana-Champaign, visiting lecturer, 1972-73, 1981; University of Colorado, Boulder, visiting assistant professor, 1973-75; Texas Tech University, Lubbock, visiting assistant professor, 1978; U.S. Naval War College, Newport, RI, visiting professor of strategy, 1995-96.

MEMBER: Phi Beta Kappa, Phi Kappa Phi.

AWARDS, HONORS: Research grant, Nebraska Committee for the Humanities, 1986; National Endowment for the Humanities Research Fellowship for College Teachers, 1988-89; Best Book Award, American Military Institute, and National Historical Society Book Prize, both 1990, both for *The War of 1812;* Burlington Northern Award for outstanding teaching, 1991; Commander's Award for Public Service, U.S. Army Command and General Staff College, 1992; Pi Gamma Mu Outstanding Faculty Member award, 1992-93; Burlington Northern Award for outstanding scholarship, 1993.

WRITINGS:

The War of 1812: A Forgotten Conflict, University of Illinois Press (Urbana, IL), 1989.

Nebraska Moments: Glimpses of Nebraska's Past, University of Nebraska Press (Lincoln, NE), 1992, new edition, 2007.

The War of 1812: A Short History, University of Illinois Press (Urbana, IL), 1995.

Don't Give Up the Ship! Myths of the War of 1812, University of Illinois Press (Urbana, IL), 2006.

(Editor, with Connie D. Clark) *Citizen Hamilton: The Wit and Wisdom of an American Founder,* Rowman & Littlefield (Lanham, MD), 2006.

Contributor to books, including the *World Book Encyclopedia; Nebraska Voices: Telling the Stories of Our State,* edited by Jim Cihlar, Nebraska Humanities Council (Lincoln, NE), 1993; *Encyclopedia of the American Presidency,* edited by Leonard Levy and Louis Visher, Simon & Schuster (New York, NY), 1994; *Encyclopedia of the United States Congress,* edited by Donald C. Bacon, 4 volumes, Simon & Schuster (New York, NY), 1994; *James Madison and the American Nation, 1751-1836,* edited by Robert A Rutland, Simon & Schuster (New York, NY), 1994; *Encyclopedia of U.S. Foreign Relations,* edited by Bruce W. Jentleson and Gaddis Smith, Oxford University Press (New York, NY), 1997; *The Conservative Press in Eighteenth- and Nineteenth-Century America,* edited by Ronald Lora and William Longton, Greenwood Press (Westport, CT), 1999; *The Oxford Companion to American Military History,* edited by John Whiteclay Chambers II et al., Oxford University Press (New York, NY), 2000; and *The American Congress: The Building of Democracy,* edited by Julian Zelizer, Houghton Mifflin (Boston, MA), 2004.

Contributor to periodicals and journals, including the *Journal of the Illinois State Historical Society, Maryland Historian, Tennessee Historical Quarterly, Soundings, Pennsylvania Magazine, New England Quarterly, Register of the Kentucky Historical Society, West Virginia History, Journal of American Studies, Indiana Magazine of History, Military Affairs, Journal of American History, Journal of the Illinois State Historical Society, Journal of the Early Republic, William and Mary Quarterly, Journal of the War of 1812, War of 1812 Magazine, Journal of the West, Business History Review,* and *History at Illinois. Midwest Review: A Journal of the History and Culture of the Missouri Valley,* editor, 1978-83; *War of 1812* series, Johns Hopkins University Press, editor, 2007—. *Military Review,* member of advisory board, 1991-92; *Journal of the Early Republic,* member of editorial board, 1993-97; *Journal of the War of 1812*, member of board of advisors, 2002—; *War of 1812 Magazine*, member of editorial board, 2006—. Author of column, *Journal of the War of 1812*, 2002—.

SIDELIGHTS: A prolific author, historian, and reviewer, Donald R. Hickey is a specialist in the history and effects of the War of 1812. His work often reveals humorous or little-known aspects of otherwise famous events and personalities. In *Don't Give Up the Ship! Myths of the War of 1812*, Hickey strives to distinguish fact from fiction about the famous conflict "by exposing the many myths and biased assumptions about the war," noted a reviewer in the *Reference & Research Book News*. Hickey first offers a prologue that summarizes the history and background of the war, and places the events that led up to it in their proper context. Throughout the rest of the book, he carefully and methodically addresses the many myths that have arisen about the War of 1812. With his analysis and efforts, Hickey "shows how myth has helped construct a history that we can understand and accept," observed a contributor to *Publishers Weekly*. He thoroughly looks at myths and misconceptions about the war's causes, its battles and campaigns, its military leadership, its political implications, and its outcomes. He considers well-told tales, such as Colonel Henry Johnson's killing of Indian chief Tecumseh in hand-to-hand combat; Captain James Lawrence's legendary utterance of "Don't give up the ship"; and notorious pirate Jean Lafitte's role in the Battle of New Orleans, and how is brother Pierre Lafitte may have had the greater influence. The *Publishers Weekly* reviewer stated that Hickey's work further galvanizes his status as a "leading scholar of the early national period." A reviewer in *Esprit de Corps* commented that "this entertaining, informative and provocative study offers a unique take on the War of 1812."

Hickey also studies influential leaders in early American history. *Citizen Hamilton: The Wit and Wisdom of an American Founder*, edited by Hickey and Connie D. Clark, provides a collection of "shining quotations and insights from one of the great figures of American history," commented an *Internet Bookwatch* reviewer. As a member of George Washington's staff during the American Revolution, and as the first treasury secretary of the United States, Hamilton was a dedicated participant in the forging of America. The quotations and remarks presented in the book attest to Hamilton's intelligence, wit, wisdom, and character.

BIOGRAPHICAL AND CRITICAL SOURCES:

PERIODICALS

American Historical Review, April, 1992, review of *The War of 1812: A Forgotten Conflict*, p. 613.

American History Illustrated, November 1, 1990, review of *The War of 1812: A Forgotten Conflict*, p. 20.

Canadian Journal of History, August, 1990, Reginald C. Stuart, review of *The War of 1812: A Forgotten Conflict*, p. 297.

Choice, July, 2007, R. Dunnavent, review of *Don't Give Up the Ship! Myths of the War of 1812*, p. 1962.

Esprit De Corps, December, 2006, review of *Don't Give Up the Ship!*, p. 46.

History: The Journal of the Historical Association, June, 1991, David Chandler, review of *The War of 1812: A Forgotten Conflict*, p. 330.

International History Review, June, 2007, Reginald C. Stuart, review of *Don't Give Up the Ship!*, p. 380.

Internet Bookwatch, June, 2007, review of *Citizen Hamilton: The Wit and Wisdom of an American Founder*.

Journal of American History, March, 1991, Douglas R. Egerton, review of *The War of 1812: A Forgotten Conflict*, p. 1351.

Journal of Military History, July, 1990, Ralph P. Dupont, review of *The War of 1812: A Forgotten Conflict*, p. 349.

Journal of Southern History, August, 1991, Frank A. Cassell, review of *The War of 1812: A Forgotten Conflict*, p. 510.

Journal of the Early Republic, summer, 1990, Harry L. Coles, review of *The War of 1812: A Forgotten Conflict;* summer, 2007, Gene Allen Smith, review of *Don't Give Up the Ship!*

Journal of the West, January, 1995, Loren N. Horton, review of *Nebraska Moments: Glimpses of Nebraska's Past*, p. 103.

Military History, March, 2007, Kenneth P. Czech, "Union 1812: The Americans Who Fought the Second War of Independence," review of *Don't Give Up the Ship!*, p. 69.

New England Quarterly, September, 1990, Albert T. Klyberg, review of *The War of 1812: A Forgotten Conflict*, p. 500.

Publishers Weekly, June 12, 2006, review of *Don't Give Up the Ship!*, p. 43.

Queen's Quarterly, summer, 1992, review of *The War of 1812: A Forgotten Conflict.*

Reference & Research Book News, February, 2007, review of *Don't Give Up the Ship!*

Reviews in American History, June, 1991, Roger H. Brown, review of *The War of 1812: A Forgotten Conflict,* p. 183.

Roundup Magazine, August, 1996, review of *Nebraska Moments,* p. 25.

Western Historical Quarterly, May, 1993, review of *Nebraska Moments,* p. 283.

William and Mary Quarterly, April, 1991, Jane Errington, review of *The War of 1812: A Forgotten Conflict,* p. 338.

ONLINE

Wayne State College Web site, http://www.wsc.edu/ (June 1, 2007), curriculum vitae of Donald R. Hickey.*

*   *   *

HICKMAN, Lisa C. 1959-

PERSONAL: Born 1959. *Education:* University of Mississippi, Ph.D.

ADDRESSES: Home—Memphis, TN.

CAREER: Writer, college professor, and independent scholar.

WRITINGS:

William Faulkner and Joan Williams: The Romance of Two Writers, foreword by Richard Bausch, McFarland (Jefferson, NC), 2006.

Contributor to periodicals, including the *Southern Quarterly, Housman Society Journal, Memphis, Memphis Flyer, Teaching Faulkner,* and the *Sunday Des Moines Register.*

SIDELIGHTS: Lisa C. Hickman is a writer and independent scholar whose works focus on Southern literature and the life and writings of acclaimed Southern writers William Faulkner and Joan Williams. In *William Faulkner and Joan Williams: The Romance of Two Writers,* Hickman explores the personal and professional relationship that developed between Faulkner and Williams from 1949 to 1953. More than three decades separated the two writers—Faulkner was fifty-one, Williams was twenty, when their association began. For Faulkner's part, he hoped that their correspondence would blossom into romance; Williams was not equally taken with that idea, but instead hoped to learn more about writing from the accomplished Faulkner. However, their relationship in all its nuances and levels was immensely important to the work and life of each author. At the time, Faulkner was involved in an unhappy marriage, his literary career was at a disheartening ebb, and he was plagued by depression, alcoholism, and substance abuse. Williams, vibrant and beautiful, was a budding writer with a deep interest in the Southern literary tradition and a single-minded focus on developing her writing abilities. Impressed by her talents and physical beauty, Faulkner offered to "serve as suitor, lover, mentor, and father figure, and she could be, in his own words, 'maid' and 'maiden,' in addition to muse and object of desire—someone to write not only to but for," noted Leonard Gill in *Memphis Magazine Online.* Although the pair never settled on the precise character of their relationship, and it did not lead to the romance that Faulkner desired, their association nonetheless deeply affected each of them. Based on the actual letters exchanged by Faulkner and Williams, and on interviews conducted with Williams before her death in 2004, Hickman creates a "fascinating book" that "treats their bond with a deft hand," observed Felicity D. Walsh in the *Library Journal.*

BIOGRAPHICAL AND CRITICAL SOURCES:

PERIODICALS

Library Journal, March 15, 2007, Felicity D. Walsh, review of *William Faulkner and Joan Williams: The Romance of Two Writers,* p. 72.

Phi Beta Kappa: The Key Reporter, summer, 2007, M. Thomas Inge, review of *William Faulkner and Joan Williams,* p. 14.

Southern Register, spring, 2007, Joan Wylie Hall, review of *William Faulkner and Joan Williams,* pp. 26-28.

ONLINE

Memphis Magazine Online, http://www.memphis magazine.com/ (October 3, 2007), Leonard Gill,

"Dearest Bill," review of *William Faulkner and Joan Williams.*

Mississippi Writers Page, http://www.olemiss.edu/mwp/ (October 3, 2007), biography of Lisa C. Hickman.

Tennessean, http://www.tennessean.com/ (October 11, 2007), Jack Brimm, breview of *William Faulkner and Joan Williams.*

* * *

HOGG, Kathleen Erin
See WOODIWISS, Kathleen E.

* * *

HOLLAND, Jo
See HOLLAND, JoJean

* * *

HOLLAND, JoJean 1936-
(Veronica DeTerre, Jo Holland, Jo Jean)

PERSONAL: Born November 26, 1936, in Pittsburgh, PA; daughter of John Baptist and Josephine Daout; married Thomas Holland, June 11, 1959 (divorced, June, 1993); children: Jeanne Victoria Holland Thoes, Jon Edward, Jennifer Jo. *Ethnicity:* "Italian-Belgian." *Education:* Geneva College, B.A., 1958; attended University of Pittsburgh, 1960-61. *Politics:* Independent. *Religion:* Christian. *Hobbies and other interests:* Gardening, rescuing cats and kittens.

ADDRESSES: Home—Mesquite, TX. *E-mail*—jdaout@sbcglobal.net.

CAREER: Dallas County Community College District, Dallas, TX, biology instructor at Cedar Valley College, 1989-2001, and editor of district newsletter, *Pulse.*

MEMBER: Texas Retired Teachers Association.

WRITINGS:

(Under name Jo Holland) *One Little Branch* (nonfiction), Brentwood Christian Press (Columbus, GA), 1988.

(Under pseudonym Veronica DeTerre) *AVAM: Avenging America* (novel), Infinity Publishing (West Conshohocken, PA), 2003.

(Under name JoJean) *Twilight in the Vineyard* (spiritual commentary), Outskirts Press (Parker, CO), 2007.

Contributor to a Christian newspaper.

SIDELIGHTS: JoJean Holland told *CA:* "Writing is a gift. I feel God has called me to use this gift. As I study or read the Bible I begin to get insights and revelations that lead to my writing. I share knowledge with others and encourage others through my writing. Islam is a major concern, and my book *AVAM: Avenging America* was written to educate people about this religion by using a fictional story."

"Since first grade, I have been an avid reader. I loved animal stories, fairy tales and mythology. Then [writer] O. Henry introduced me to the short story with a surprise ending. This started me writing my own short stories with surprise endings. I also began writing poems."

When asked who or what influence her work, she said: "In nonfiction, it is God (Yahweh, the Almighty Creator). In fiction, it often stems from my love of science.

"When writing fiction, I just sit at the computer and began to type. Then I go over what I've written, often many times. It's true that there is only good 'rewriting'! When doing nonfiction I often have scriptures come into my mind that lead me in beginning a topic."

When asked the most surprising thing she has learned as a writer, she responded: "That too often people only buy or read those books that receive lots of attention or make it to the top-sellers list or are about a well known person, event or scandal."

When asked which of her books was her favorite, Holland said: "*Twilight in the Vineyard* because it was written at the leading of Yahweh and proclaims truths that are for *now.*

"[I hope] that readers will seek the *truth* in all things, especially regarding the word of God."

HOOD, Jean 1953-

PERSONAL: Born 1953. *Education:* Graduate of University of Durham.

ADDRESSES: Home—England.

CAREER: Writer, nautical historian, and information officer. Lloyd's Register of Shipping, information officer.

WRITINGS:

Marked for Misfortune: An Epic Tale of Shipwreck, Human Endeavour, and Survival in the Age of Sail, Conway Maritime (London, England), 2003.
Trafalgar Square: A Visual History of London's Landmark through Time, B.T. Batsford (London, England), 2005.
Come Hell and High Water: Extraordinary Stories of Wreck, Terror, and Triumph on the Sea, Burford Books (Springfield, NJ), 2007.

SIDELIGHTS: Writer, nautical expert, and sea historian Jean Hood is a former information officer for Lloyd's Register of Shipping, a ship classification service that offers information on the status and condition of ships likely to be insured by marine insurance underwriters around the world.

Hood is also the author of books on maritime history and disaster. In *Come Hell and High Water: Extraordinary Stories of Wreck, Terror, and Triumph on the Sea,* she presents seventeen narratives chronicling a variety of seagoing catastrophes from the middle of the eighteenth century to the present. "A positively brilliant addition to popular maritime history is this omnibus of historic shipwrecks," commented *Booklist* critic Roland Green. Hood's reportage pinpoints causes ranging from bad weather to incompetent leadership to unsafe ships to simple bad luck. She also looks at the effect the sinkings had on their contemporaries; though many of the incidents she covers have since faded into obscurity, in their day each disaster commanded the shock and attention of the general public. Among her subjects are three eighteenth-century ships; sunken Russian submarines; and perhaps the most famous maritime disaster of all, the doomed *Titanic.* "Skill-

fully mining the archives, Hood produces a gripping narrative illuminating ship operation, nautical terms, and historical context," explaining what happened to each ship and why the disaster occurred, noted a *Publishers Weekly* reviewer.

In addition to the tragic and often dramatic stories of the vessels, their occupants, and their fates, Hood also includes detailed scholarly references for those who wish to pursue their own primary-source research. She presents a glossary of terms for those unfamiliar with nautical language, and carefully places each ship within the context of its time and the prevailing maritime law, shipbuilding standards, and available technology. Green concluded that the book is a "superior reminder" of what can happen to those who choose to go sailing on the high seas.

BIOGRAPHICAL AND CRITICAL SOURCES:

PERIODICALS

Booklist, March 1, 2007, Roland Green, review of *Come Hell and High Water: Extraordinary Stories of Wreck, Terror, and Triumph on the Sea,* p. 55.
California Bookwatch, May, 2007, review of *Come Hell and High Water.*
Publishers Weekly, January 29, 2007, review of *Come Hell and High Water,* p. 51.
Reference & Research Book News, May, 2007, review of *Come Hell and High Water.*

ONLINE

Anova Books Web site, http://www.anovabooks.com/ (October 3, 2007), biography of Jean Hood.
Burford Books Web site, http://www.burfordbooks. com/ (October 3, 2007), biography of Jean Hood.*

*   *   *

HOOPER, Dan 1976-

PERSONAL: Born 1976. *Education:* University of Wisconsin, Ph.D., 2003.

ADDRESSES: Office—Theoretical Astrophysics, Fermi National Accelerator Laboratory, Wilson Hall 6 West, P.O. Box 500, Batavia, IL 60510. *E-mail*—dhooper@fnal.gov.

CAREER: Writer, scientist, and astrophysicist. Fermi National Accelerator Laboratory, Batavia, IL, associate scientist in theoretical astrophysics. Worked as a post-doctoral researcher at Oxford University.

AWARDS, HONORS: David Schramm Fellow, Fermi National Accelerator Laboratory.

WRITINGS:

Dark Cosmos: In Search of Our Universe's Missing Mass and Energy, Smithsonian Books/Collins (New York, NY), 2006.

SIDELIGHTS: Dan Hooper is a scientist and theoretical astrophysicist whose work focuses on the "interface between particle physics and cosmology," as he noted in an autobiography on the Fermi National Accelerator Laboratory Web site. Much of his research concerns complex topics such as supersymmetry, neutrinos, extra dimensions, and cosmic rays. A major portion of his scientific work focuses on the mysterious and little-understood phenomenon of dark matter, the unseen substance that makes up the bulk of the mass of the universe. In *Dark Cosmos: In Search of Our Universe's Missing Mass and Energy,* Hooper offers a detailed exploration of cosmology that explores what is known about dark matter and dark energy, considers the far-reaching implications of the presence of such dark materials, and suggests methods of additional research that could, perhaps, locate and harness dark energy.

Hooper relates some mind-boggling facts about the world around us. He points out that only about five percent of the matter in the universe is directly observable. In other words, everything that humans can see, touch, and experience—from the most distant stars to the smallest microscopic particles and everything in between—amounts to only a fraction of the mass and material that actually exists. The remaining ninety-five percent of the mass of the universe consists of invisible dark matter and dark energy. Hooper uses theories of cosmology to carefully explain what is known about dark matter, pointing out that scientists have long known about its existence. He describes theories of dark matter, including what it is made of and how it operates. He notes that some known minigalaxies are composed entirely of dark matter. In some theories, dark matter is what appears to be making the universe expand. Hooper also brings to bear other ideas from cosmology that could account for dark matter and its possible hiding places, including the possibilities of multiple dimensions and additional universes that coexist with our own.

Hooper's book "helps us recall our sense of wonder at the universe," observed Sara Rutter, writing in *Library Journal.* A *Publishers Weekly* reviewer commented that Hooper's "clear presentation in very simple, jargon-free prose should appeal especially to young people" who are beginning to explore the wonders and mysteries of science.

BIOGRAPHICAL AND CRITICAL SOURCES:

PERIODICALS

Library Journal, October 15, 2006, Sara Rutter, review of *Dark Cosmos: In Search of Our Universe's Missing Mass and Energy,* p. 85.

Nature, March 1, 2007, "Into the Darkness: Cosmologists Face Some Tough Challenges as They Explore the Composition of the Universe," review of *Dark Cosmos,* p. 25.

New Scientist, October 4, 2003, "Has Dark Matter Been Found at Last?," p. 8.

Physics Today, July, 2007, Daniel Holz, review of *Dark Cosmos,* p. 62.

Publishers Weekly, September 11, 2006, review of *Dark Cosmos,* p. 48.

Science News, December 2, 2006, review of *Dark Cosmos,* p. 367.

SciTech Book News, March, 2007, review of *Dark Cosmos.*

ONLINE

Dan Hooper Home Page, http://home.fnal.gov/~dhooper (September 1, 2007).

Fermi National Accelerator Laboratory Web site, http://home.fnal.gov/ (September 1, 2007), autobiography of Dan Hooper.
HarperCollins Web site, http://www.harpercollins.com/ (September 1, 2007), biography of Dan Hooper.

* * *

HOWARD, Tracie

PERSONAL: Education: Georgia State University, B.A.

ADDRESSES: E-mail—tracie @traciehoward.com.

CAREER: Write r and columnist. *Savoy* magazine, travel and lifestyle editor. Previously worked in marketing in Atlanta, GA, for Xerox, Johnson & Johnson, and American Express; member of core marketing team for 1996 Atlanta Centennial Olympic Games.

WRITINGS:

NOVELS

(With Danita Carter) *Revenge Is Best Served Cold,* New American Library (New York, NY), 2001.
(Wi th Danita Carter) *Talk of the Town,* New American Library (New York, NY), 2002.
Why Sleeping Dogs Lie, New American Library (New York, NY), 2003.
Never Kiss and Tell, New American Library (New York, NY), 2004.
(With Danita Carter) *Success Is the Best Revenge,* New American Library (New York, NY), 2004.
Gold Diggers, Doubleday (New York, NY), 2007.

Author of monthly column"Tongue 'n Chic" for *Savoy* magazine.

SIDELIGHTS: Tracie Howard worked for many years in marketing before turning to writing novels that feature African American characters in story lines revolving around romance, suspense, and action. "Along with the freedom I derive from working with a blank canvas, one of the main reasons I initially felt compelled to write was my desire to depict another aspect of African American life," the author noted in an interview on her home page. "I've always felt that stories and characters depicting the lifestyles of mainstream African Americans who are doing well was underrepresented in popular fiction. Their stories provide another distinct texture that will only serve to enhance our rich cultural mosaic."

Howard's first book was cowritten with Danita Carter and titled *Revenge Is Best Served Cold.* It tells the story of the successful African-American women Morgan Nelson and Dakota Cantrell as they become involved with Blake St. James, part of the New York social elite. When Blake offers a business proposal, Morgan agrees to participate only to find that she is soon losing money. Ultimately she must confront Blake as his underhanded dealings threaten to wreck the careers of both her and Dakota. *Talk of the Town* is a sequel to *Revenge Is Best Served Cold.* In this title, the authors once again feature Morgan and Dakota. Still successfully pursuing their careers, the duo find that they are having more difficulties in handling personal matters, which include an unwanted pregnancy and a cheating husband. A third novel by Howard and Carter, *Success Is the Best Revenge,* focuses on Lyle Johnson, a successful Wall Street investment banker who also owns a bar in New York City called Street Signs. When Contessa "Tess" Aventura Dubois comes to town, she ends up buying a share of Lyle's business only to threaten everything Lyle has worked hard to achieve, both in his business and family life. Lillian Lewis, writing in *Booklist,* called *Success Is the Best Revenge* "an engrossing story with great characters."

Howard is also the sole author of several novels. Her first solo effort, *Why Sleeping Dogs Lie,* finds Mallory Baylor leaving her position as head of *Heat* magazine to forget a failed romance and begin life again. "Howard's writing is explicit and sophisticated," wrote Joycelyn A. Wilson in her review of *Why Sleeping Dogs Lie* in the *Black Issues Book Review.* "She manipulates language in such a way that places the reader right in the thick of the situation."

In *Never Kiss and Tell,* Howard features successful interior designer, Kiernan Malloy, and her husband, investment banker Taylor Hudson. Both are unhappy in their marriage when Taylor meets another women leading to a complex love triangle. Furthermore,

Taylor's love interest, psychologist Brooke Parrish, happens to have Kiernan as one of her patients. Lillian Lewis wrote in *Booklist* that the novel "is entertaining." *Gold Diggers* tells the story of four African-American women who go to New York to follow their dreams. As their stories unfold, envy and sex play a role in threatening the four women's friendship. Writing in *Booklist*, Patty Engelmann wrote that the author "explores the fleeting world of fame and bling with verve and flash."

BIOGRAPHICAL AND CRITICAL SOURCES:

PERIODICALS

Black Issues Book Review, March-April, 2004, Joyce-lyn A. Wilson, review of *Why Sleeping Dogs Lie*, p. 53.
Booklist, October 1, 2001, Lillian Lewis, review of *Revenge Is Best Served Cold*, p. 299; April 1, 2004, Lillian Lewis, review of *Success Is the Best Revenge*, p. 1346; October 15, 2004, Lillian Lewis, review of *Never Kiss and Tell*, p. 389; March 1, 2007, Patty Engelmann, review of *Gold Diggers*, p. 63.
Essence, June, 2004, Deborah Gregory, "Back to the Beach," p. 138.
Library Journal, November 1, 2001, review of *Revenge Is Best Served Cold*, p. 115; November 1, 2002, Ann Burns, review of *Talk of the Town*, p. 111; November 1, 2003, review of *Why Sleeping Dogs Lie*, p. 103.
Publishers Weekly, October 8, 2001, review of *Revenge Is Best Served Cold*, p. 44.

ONLINE

Book-remarks.com, http://www.book-remarks.com/ (October 10, 2007), "Tracie Howard," interview with author.
Tracie Howard Home Page, http://www.traciehoward. com (October 10, 2007).*

*   *   *

HUTCHINSON, George 1953-
  (George B. Hutchinson)

PERSONAL: Born 1953. *Education:* Brown University, A.B., 1975; Indiana University, Blooming-ton, M.A., 1980, Ph.D., 1983.

ADDRESSES: *Home*—IN. *Office*—Department of English, Indiana University, 442 Ballantine Hall, 1020 E. Kirkwood Ave., Bloomington, IN 47405-7103. *E-mail*—gbhutchi@indiana.edu.

CAREER: U.S. Peace Corps, Burkina Faso, well digger, 1975-77; University of Tennessee, Knoxville, chair of American Studies Program for thirteen years, Kenneth Curry Chair of English, 1982-2000; Indiana University, Bloomington, Booth Tarkington Chair of Literary Studies, 2000—. Visiting professor at University of Bonn, Germany.

MEMBER: Modern Language Association (member of advisory council and nominating committee of the American Literature Section), Phi Beta Kappa.

AWARDS, HONORS: Andrew W. Mellon Foundation summer stipend, 1986; National Endowment for the Humanities fellow, 1988, 1989-90; Darwin Turner Prize, Modern Language Association, 1995, for work in African American literature; Chancellor's Citation, University of Tennessee, 1997, for outstanding research and creative achievement; Christian Gauss Award, Phi Beta Kappa, 2007, for *In Search of Nella Larsen: A Biography of the Color Line;* named Phi Beta Kappa lecturer, University of Tennessee.

WRITINGS:

The Ecstatic Whitman: Literary Shamanism and the Crisis of the Union, Ohio State University Press (Columbus, OH), 1986.
The Harlem Renaissance in Black and White, Belknap Press (Cambridge, MA), 1995.
In Search of Nella Larsen: A Biography of the Color Line, Belknap Press (Cambridge, MA), 2006.
(Editor) *The Cambridge Companion to the Harlem Renaissance*, Cambridge University Press (New York, NY), 2007.

Contributor to periodicals, including *American Literary History, African American Review,* and *Walt Whitman Quarterly Review.*

SIDELIGHTS: George Hutchinson is a writer and academician who focuses on issues of race, the Harlem Renaissance, and the works of Walt Whitman.

Raised in Indianapolis, Hutchinson graduated from Brown University in 1975 and immediately set off for Burkina Faso, where he worked with the U.S. Peace Corps for two years. Upon his return to the United States, he completed his M.A. and Ph.D. at Indiana University, Bloomington, and began a career in academia. During his nearly twenty-year tenure at the University of Tennessee, Knoxville, Hutchinson worked his way to the position of chair of American Studies Program and the Kenneth Curry Chair of English. In 2000 he relocated to Indiana University to accept the newly created position of Booth Tarkington Chair of Literary Studies.

Hutchinson's *The Harlem Renaissance in Black and White* is divided into three parts, including the rise of intellectualism and scholarship surrounding the period, a survey of the literary institutions that aided the movement, and an in-depth study of Alain Locke's 1925 anthology, *The New Negro,* and its role in the Renaissance. Claudia Tate, writing in the *African American Review,* called the book "an impressive study in scope, detail, and analysis." Tate concluded that *The Harlem Renaissance in Black and White* "presents the rich and complex interplay between the modern cultural nationalisms of black and white America that characterized the decade of the 1920s and its aftermath." *College Literature* contributor Allison Berg stated: "Hutchinson's exhaustive analysis of the institutional and intellectual contexts of the Harlem Renaissance makes a major contribution to the field, both by establishing the interdependence of black and white intellectual formations and by debunking some of the most cherished myths about the era."

Nearly a decade later, Hutchinson published again on the subject with *In Search of Nella Larsen: A Biography of the Color Line.* This biography covers the life of Nella Larsen (1891-1964), a Harlem Renaissance writer born to a white Danish seamstress and a black laborer from the U.S. Virgin Islands (at that time, part of Denmark). This "scandalous" race mixing was made worse for Larsen when her mother married a white man and had other children, effectively making Larsen the black sheep of the family. Forced out of her home by age sixteen, she made a living for herself in New York and Alabama, and studied in Copenhagen, Denmark. Larsen's upbringing as a mixed-race child, not entirely accepted by either race, played a prominent role in her writing. Evelyn C. White in the *Washington Post Book World* called it an "exhaustive and masterfully rendered narrative." *Booklist* contributor Vanessa Bush found that the book was a "sparkling examination of a critical period in American racial and literary development." In the *Black Issues Book Review,* Sandra Rattley observed that "Hutchinson demonstrates a keen capacity for meticulous research."

Hutchinson told *CA:* "As a child, I loved writing fiction, beginning in about fourth grade. By high school I began to enjoy writing research papers for school, and a fascination for research as well as writing has remained throughout my life. It is amazing what one can discover if one looks hard enough, and the creative, self-expressive aspect of writing still enthralls me. I've been most influenced as a scholar by my maternal grandfather's reputation for scholarly boldness and integrity (he was a geologist) and by my mother's emphasis on being 'modern' and open to the new but retaining a sense of quality and what will last. My experience as a well digger in Africa completely transformed my understanding of American culture and race. I tend to write counter to intellectual fads while trying to expand our understanding of the possible in the past and present. I have also been much influenced by being the white father of black or biracial sons; it has affected my life profoundly. I was rather surprised by the generally very positive reception of *The Harlem Renaissance in Black and White* and *In Search of Nella Larsen,* because in both books I was writing against what I considered deeply entrenched prejudices in American literary scholarship. When *The Harlem Renaissance in Black and White* came out (a book I honestly didn't think anyone would publish, but was snapped up by a wonderful editor), I discovered that young scholars from all over had been waiting for such an argument about the inextricability of 'black' and 'white' in American culture. I loved working on [both] books, but perhaps *In Search of Nella Larsen* is my favorite because it took me on fascinating journeys, literally, and the writing itself demanded that I be more creative in evoking places, scenes, people, and handling narration. The research was incredibly exhilarating, full of discoveries. I hope my books will inspire people to keep questioning received wisdom, especially about race, and to attend to the truths that destabilize old habits of mind, the truths our experience (as long as we remain open to new experience) often leads us to intuit before we can articulate them."

BIOGRAPHICAL AND CRITICAL SOURCES:

PERIODICALS

African American Review, fall, 1997, Claudia Tate, review of *The Harlem Renaissance in Black and White.*

Black Issues Book Review, September 1, 2006, Sandra Rattley, review of *In Search of Nella Larsen: A Biography of the Color Line,* p. 40.

Booklist, May 15, 2006, Vanessa Bush, review of *In Search of Nella Larsen,* p. 16.

College Literature, fall, 1998, Allison Berg, review of *The Harlem Renaissance in Black and White.*

Ebony, August 1, 2006, review of *In Search of Nella Larsen,* p. 30.

New York Times Book Review, August 27, 2006, Tara McKelvey, review of *In Search of Nella Larsen,* p. 20.

Research in African Literatures, fall, 2000, Joseph McLaren, review of *The Harlem Renaissance in Black and White.*

Washington Post Book World, May 21, 2006, Evelyn C. White, review of *In Search of Nella Larsen,* p. 14.

ONLINE

Indiana University Web site, http://www.indiana.edu/ (August 18, 2007), author profile.

*   *   *

HUTCHINSON, George B.
   See HUTCHINSON, George

*   *   *

HYLTOFT, Ole 1935-

PERSONAL: Born August 16, 1935, in Copenhagen, Denmark. *Education:* Graduate of Copenhagen University, 1954; studied at Harvard University.

ADDRESSES: Home—Tisvildeleje, Denmark. *E-mail*—ole.hyltoft@wanadoo.dk.

CAREER: Writer, journalist.

WRITINGS:

Tør du være fri?, Fremad (Copenhagen, Denmark), 1968.

Hvis lille pige Er du?, Fremad (Copenhagen, Denmark), 1970.

Hjertet sidder til venstre, Fremad (Copenhagen, Denmark), 1973.

Tør du være med?, Fremad (Copenhagen, Denmark), 1974.

Revolutionens fortrop (novel), Fremad (Copenhagen, Denmark), 1975.

Hvem er angst for den stygge ulv? (novel), Fremad (Copenhagen, Denmark), 1976.

Arbejdsliv, Fremad (Copenhagen, Demmark), 1978.

De befriede (novel), Naver (Copenhagen, Denmark), 1979.

De besejrede (novel), Naver (Copenhagen, Denmark), 1979.

Byggekongen (novel), Naver (Copenhagen, Denmark), 1981.

Tante Isidora og andre fortællinger, Naver (Copenhagen, Denmark), 1982.

Hverdagen blev anderledes—fra 1920 til i dag, Aschehough (Copenhagen, Denmark), 1983.

Kulturpaven (novel), Naver (Copenhagen, Denmark), 1984.

Skabt af ild, Fremad (Copenhagen, Denmark), 1984.

Snyd fanden for en taber, Fri Børnehaver (Copenhagen, Denmark), 1986.

Mord er kun en leg, Holkenfeldt (Sprog, Denmark), 1987.

En køn en, Aschehoug, 1989.

Mordet på museet (novel; title means "Murder in the Museum"), Holkenfeldt (Sprog, Denmark), 1997.

Den poetiske politiker, Bomholtkomiteen (Copenhagen, Denmark), 2000.

Barn af partiet, Høst, 2000.

Alle disse forhåbninger, Host, 2001.

Københavnerpigen og Kongemaleren, Hovedland (Høejbjerg, Denmark), 2005.

Københavnerpigen under besættelsen, Hovedland (Høejbjerg, Denmark), 2007.

SIDELIGHTS: Danish writer Ole Hyltoft is the author of many books, including the novel *Mordet på museet* ("Murder in the Museum"), which was reviewed by Sven H. Rossel in *World Literature Today.* The museum of the title, based on a contemporary art museum south of Copenhagen, is managed by director Ann Belgrave, who, Hyltoft implies, got the job by enhancing her resume and sleeping with the mayor. Hyltoft was criticized for alluding to real characters in this novel, although he had done so before with little comment. Rossel wrote that Hyltoft "uses here a certain literary genre primarily in order to aim his satire at charlatanism in politics and art, abuse of power, and a snobbish but truly ignorant upper class. Granted, Hyltoft's satire can be quite impertinent and relentless, but mostly it hits the mark." Although this book is basically a detective novel, Rossel noted that a parallel could be drawn between the story and Hans Christian Andersen's *The Emperor's New Clothes.*

The protagonists are journalist Jes, who solves several murders and exposes corruption, and his daughter, Dina. The story includes romance and what Rossel described as a "strange yet fascinating sexual encounter between Jes and Ann, which in its erotic tension between passion and frigidity, fire and ice, can be matched by only a very few Danish writers."

BIOGRAPHICAL AND CRITICAL SOURCES:

PERIODICALS

World Literature Today, Spring, 1999, Sven H. Rossel, review of *Mordet på museet;* spring, 2001, Sven H. Rossel, review of *Barn af partiet.*

ONLINE

Ole Hyltoft Home Page, http://www.ole-hyltoft.dk (September 26, 2007).*

I-J

IFILL, Sherrilyn A.

PERSONAL: Education: Vassar College, B.A., 1984; New York University, J.D., 1987.

ADDRESSES: Office—School of Law, University of Maryland, 500 W. Baltimore St., Baltimore, MD 21201-1786. *E-mail*—sifill@law.umaryland.edu.

CAREER: Attorney, activist, consultant, educator, and author. University of Maryland, School of Law, Baltimore, professor of law, 1993—. NAACP Legal Defense and Educational Fund, Inc., assistant counsel; Reentry of Ex-Offenders Clinic, cofounder. Member of board of directors, Open Society Institute, Baltimore, and the Enoch Pratt Free Library, Baltimore.

WRITINGS:

On the Courthouse Lawn: Confronting the Legacy of Lynching in the Twenty-first Century, Beacon Press (Boston, MA), 2007.

Contributor to periodicals, including the *Baltimore Sun, Jurist, Colorlines Magazine,* and the *AFRO American.*

SIDELIGHTS: Sherrilyn A. Ifill is a prominent writer on legal issues such as diversity and impartiality in judicial proceedings. She is "nationally recognized as an advocate in the areas of civil rights, voting rights, judicial diversity and judicial decision-making," according to a biographer on the University of Maryland School of Law Web site. Ifill "also writes about the history of racial violence and contemporary reconciliation efforts." In her first book, *On the Courthouse Lawn: Confronting the Legacy of Lynching in the Twenty-first Century,* Ifill confronts the difficult history of racially motivated attacks and murder-by-lynching that once plagued the Eastern Shore region of Maryland. An area closely identified with the American South and the Confederacy, the Eastern Shore is also marked by high levels of poverty and poor educational achievement. The last lynching occurred there more than eighty years ago.

Ifill identified distinct differences in the way that blacks and whites remembered and reacted to incidents of racial hatred. A number of whites interviewed by Ifill remembered that there had indeed been lynchings in the Eastern Shore, but they knew or recalled very few details about them. In contrast, many blacks she spoke to had detailed knowledge of the lynchings and could vividly recount elements of the events, even if they had not been there. "Ifill says she found this silence by whites and their detachment from the lynchings quite extraordinary when contrasted with the rich and detailed recollections of blacks," commented Osita Iroegbu in the *Recorder.*

With her book, "Ifill depicts a region still suffering from its history of lynching and says the Eastern Shore is only one of many such communities across the nation," Iroegbu noted. Ifill explores the deep racial divisions that have split the Eastern Shore, exemplified by a controversy over erecting a monument to statesman and former slave Frederick Douglass on the Talbot County courthouse lawn. Ironically, a monument to fallen Confederate soldiers has long stood on that very same lawn. Ifill also recounts several cases of gross injustice in which blacks were convicted of crimes on the basis of flimsy evidence and testimony that would otherwise fail to stand up in court. She notes that even now, blacks and whites have tremendous difficulty discussing the history of lynching and racial violence in America. There are few who "really want to remember what for most on both sides of the divide were traumatizing events. Yet remembering is essential," observed a *Kirkus Reviews* critic. The reviewer concluded that Ifill's book is an "intriguing, immodest proposal that itself warrants discussion—and action."

BIOGRAPHICAL AND CRITICAL SOURCES:

PERIODICALS

Kirkus Reviews, November 15, 2006, review of *On the Courthouse Lawn: Confronting the Legacy of Lynching in the Twenty-first Century,* p. 1160.
Legal Times, March 26, 2007, Osita Iroegbu, review of *On the Courthouse Lawn.*
Recorder, May 11, 2007, Osita Iroegbu, "Breaking the Code of Silence," review of *On the Courthouse Lawn.*
Reference & Research Book News, May, 2007, review of *On the Courthouse Lawn.*

ONLINE

University of Maryland School of Law Web site, http://www.law.maryland.edu/ (October 10, 2007), biography of Sherrilyn A. Ifill.*

*   *   *

IYENGAR, Sujata 1970-

PERSONAL: Born 1970, in Newcastle-upon-Tyne, England; daughter of E.N. (a physician) and Mythili (a physician) Iyengar; married Richard Menke (a college professor); children: Kavya, Kartik. *Ethnicity:* "British Indian." *Education:* Girton College,

Cambridge, B.A. (hons.), 1991; University of Birmingham, M.A., 1992; Stanford University, Ph.D., 1998. *Hobbies and other interests:* Early music, vegetarian cooking.

ADDRESSES: Office—Department of English, University of Georgia, Park Hall, Athens, GA 30602-6205. *E-mail*—iyengar@uga.edu.

CAREER: University of Georgia, Athens, assistant professor, 1998-2005, associate professor of English, 2005—.

MEMBER: Modern Language Association of America, Renaissance Association of America.

AWARDS, HONORS: Special Sandy Beaver Award, University of Georgia, 2000; Schachterle Prize, Society for Literature and Science, 2003, for article "Royalist, Romancist, Racialist: Rank, Gender, and Race in the Science and Fiction of Margaret Cavendish."

WRITINGS:

Shades of Difference: Mythologies of Skin Color in the English Renaissance, University of Pennsylvania Press (Philadelphia, PA), 2004.

Contributor to books, including *Gender and Monstrous Appetite in the Middle Ages and the Renaissance,* edited by Elizabeth Herbert McAvoy and Teresa Walters, University of Wales Press (Aberystwyth, Wales), 2002; *Othello: New Critical Essays,* edited by Philip C. Kolin, Routledge (New York, NY), 2002; *Sensible Flesh: Renaissance Representations of the Tactile,* edited by Elizabeth Harvey, University of Pennsylvania Press (Philadelphia, PA), 2003; and *Color-Blind Shakespeare,* edited by Ayanna Thompson, Routledge, 2006. Contributor to periodicals, including *Postmodern Culture* and *Literature/Film Quarterly. Borrowers and Lenders: Journal of Shakespeare and Appropriation,* cofounder and coeditor, and editor of special issues, 2005, 2006.

*   *   *

JADICK, Richard 1968(?)-

PERSONAL: Born c. 1968; married; wife's name Melissa; children: one daughter.

CAREER: Urologist. *Military service:* U.S. Navy; served in the Iraq War and Operation Iraqi Freedom; achieved rank of lieutenant commander; awarded Bronze Star with Combat V for valor.

WRITINGS:

On Call in Hell: A Doctor's Iraq War Story (memoir), NAL Caliber (New York, NY), 2007.

SIDELIGHTS: Richard Jadick is a physician, urologist, surgeon, and Navy officer who served with the 1st Battalion, 8th Marine Regiment, in Iraq during Operation Iraqi Freedom. In his memoir, *On Call in Hell: A Doctor's Iraq War Story,* Jadick recounts his terrifying but ultimately heroic experiences serving as a military doctor in a combat zone. Jadick and his medical team were responsible for setting up a Forward Aid Station, or FAS, a mobile medical care unit designed to provide urgent treatment and life-saving emergency procedures for Marines injured in battle. As the fighting progressed, the FAS could be easily moved forward to follow the battle. "The FAS unquestionably saved lives by reducing considerably the amount of time" it took for seriously wounded Marines to receive critical trauma care, noted Will Holahan in the *Officer.*

Jadick's experiences were not confined to his aid station, however. Many times he went forward into hot combat zones to provide on-the-spot treatment to wounded Marines. During the second Battle of Fallujah in November, 2004, Jadick experienced firsthand the brutal effects of war. Leo Shane III, writing in *Stars and Stripes,* described how Jadick and his medical team left their aid station on November 8, 2004, to enter the Fallujah combat zone and tend to a wounded Marine. Soon, however, they were called deeper into the city and closer to the front lines. "The firefight was much more intense here: This time, bullets were striking all around their vehicle as soon as it stopped, and at least two rocket-propelled grenades bounced off the armor without detonating. And this time, it wasn't just one wounded Marine. It was seven and counting," Shane reported. Jadick plunged forward and worked to save lives. "Jadick said the corpsmen with him later told him bullets were bouncing within inches of him as he treated Marines and dragged them back to the armored ambulance. He said he didn't notice them, but knew how fierce the firefight was based on the wounds he was looking at," Shane reported.

Jadick is credited with saving more than thirty lives during that violent siege. Throughout his memoir, Jadick describes the terrible traumas endured by the Marines in combat, and his own and his team's efforts to rescue limbs, stanch bleeding, repair wounds, and save lives. "I didn't do it by myself. All I did was show up," Shane quoted Jadick as saying. "It's just stuff you do because it's your job." For his efforts, Jadick was awarded the Bronze Star with Combat V for valor. He was the only Navy physician to receive such an honor during Operation Iraqi Freedom, making him the most decorated doctor of the Iraq war. Holahan concluded that Jadick's memoir "should be a must-read for medical servicemembers and others interested in combat field medicine."

BIOGRAPHICAL AND CRITICAL SOURCES:

BOOKS

Jadick, Richard, *On Call in Hell: A Doctor's Iraq War Story,* NAL Caliber (New York, NY), 2007.

PERIODICALS

Booklist, March 1, 2007, Jay Freeman, review of *On Call in Hell,* p. 57.

Newsweek, March 20, 2006, Mark Whitaker, "The Editor's Desk," profile of Richard Jadick, p. 4; March 20, 2006, "On Call in Hell; He Left a Desk Job for the Front Lines of Fallujah—and a Horror Show Few Doctors Ever See. How Richard Jadick Earned His Bronze Star," p. 34.

Officer, June, 2007, Will Holahan, "Far-Forward Doc," review of *On Call in Hell,* p. 50.

Publishers Weekly, January 8, 2007, review of *On Call in Hell,* p. 45.

Stars and Stripes, June 14, 2006, Leo Shane III, "'I Didn't Do It by Myself,'" profile of Richard Jadick.

ONLINE

PR Newswire, http://www.prnewswire.com/ (March 12, 2007), "Most Decorated Doctor of Iraq War," profile of Richard Jadick.*

JAMES, Reina

PERSONAL: Daughter of Sid James (a comic); married.

ADDRESSES: Home—Sussex, England. *Agent*—Gillon Aitken, Aitken Alexander Associates, 18-21 Cavaye Pl., London SW10 9PT, England.

CAREER: Writer.

AWARDS, HONORS: McKitterick Award for first-time novelists over forty, Society of Authors, for *This Time of Dying.*

WRITINGS:

This Time of Dying, Portobello (London, England), 2006, St. Martin's Press (New York, NY), 2007.

SIDELIGHTS: Reina James began her career as a novelist relatively late in life, but was rewarded for her efforts with the McKitterick Award, a prize given by the Society of Authors for a debut novel by an author over forty years old. James's *This Time of Dying,* which garnered the prize, was published in England in 2006, followed by a U.S. release the following year, to critical praise. The novel is based on the historic 1918 Spanish flu pandemic in England, a timely subject given the present health concerns regarding a potential new strain of virus in the early part of the twenty-first century. Henry Speake is an undertaker of the day who finds the increase in business due to the spread of illness is too great for him to handle, and his fears are compounded by a letter he discovers, written by a doctor who believed the war was in part to blame for the flu's rapid dissemination. Speake makes friends with a schoolteacher, the widow Thompson, and together they attempt to make the best of their situation. A contributor to *Kirkus Reviews* found the book to be "a curiosity—sharp glimpses of human nature scattered over a detailed period panorama." Matthew Creasy, writing in the *Financial Times,* labeled James's effort "a muted but at times moving novel about the persistence of the ordinary during extraordinary times." *Library Journal* contributor Leann Restaino cited James's use of detail and accurate descriptions of the period, and called the result "a wonderfully engrossing read."

BIOGRAPHICAL AND CRITICAL SOURCES:

PERIODICALS

Financial Times, September 9, 2006, Matthew Creasy, review of *This Time of Dying,* p. 33.
Kirkus Reviews, January 15, 2007, review of *This Time of Dying,* p. 44.
Library Journal, February 15, 2007, Leann Restaino, review of *This Time of Dying,* p. 113.
Publishers Weekly, February 5, 2007, review of *This Time of Dying,* p. 41.

ONLINE

CommuniGate Web site, http://www.communigate.co.uk/ (October 10, 2007), "Carry On Daughter."
Guardian Online, http://books.guardian.co.uk/ (September 30, 2006), Rachel Hore, review of *This Time of Dying.**

*   *   *

JASPIN, Elliot

PERSONAL: Male.

ADDRESSES: Home—Annapolis, MD. *Office*—Cox Newspapers, Washington Bureau, 400 N. Capitol St. NW, Ste. 750, Washington, DC 20001-1536.

CAREER: Philadelphia Daily News, Philadelphia, PA, former reporter; *Providence Journal-Bulletin,* Providence, RI, former reporter; University of Missouri, former director of Missouri Institute for Computer-Assisted Reporting and associate professor of journalism; Cox Newspapers, Washington, DC, currently system editor and journalist; has also been a reporter for the *Pottsville Republican.* Fellow, Gannett Center for Media Studies, Columbia University, 1988-89.

AWARDS, HONORS: Pulitzer Prize (with Gilbert M. Gaul), 1979, for local investigative specialized reporting for the *Pottsville Republican;* Kiplinger Distinguished Contributions to Journalism Award, National Press Foundation, 1993.

WRITINGS:

(Editor) Hans G. Egli, *Jim Thorpe, Formerly, Mauch Chunk: Guide/History,* H. Egli (Jim Thorpe, PA), 1977.

Buried in the Bitter Waters: The Hidden History of Racial Cleansing in America, Basic Books (New York, NY), 2007.

ADAPTATIONS: Buried in the Bitter Waters has been adapted as an audiobook, HighBridge Audio.

SIDELIGHTS: Pulitzer Prize-winning journalist Elliot Jaspin is a specialist in computer-assisted reporting. He has been an assistant professor of journalism at the University of Missouri, where he established the first computer-assisted reporting program in the United States. The program was designed to train both students and practicing professional journalists how to better use computer-based resources to enhance their reporting and writing.

Jaspin is also a historian of racial issues in the United States. In *Buried in the Bitter Waters: The Hidden History of Racial Cleansing in America,* he examines twelve individual cases—covering 1864 through 1923 and occurring in eight different states—in which blacks were deliberately and systematically forced from their homes and out of a county. Jaspin uses the controversial term "racial cleansing" to denote the efforts of white Americans to "cleanse" their "living and working spaces to make them white-only enclaves," related Thomas J. Davis in *Library Journal.* Jaspin reports that although some of these cases involved violence, lynching, and riots, others were entirely nonviolent, the end result accomplished through fear and intimidation. Whites would simply deliver an ultimatum to blacks and their families: be out of town by a certain time, or violence may occur. Outnumbered and overwhelmed, black families had little choice but to comply. Jaspin recounts how mobs and vigilantes functioned within this context of racial cleansing, but he also makes it plain that whites in all aspects of their lives worked to exclude blacks from their towns. In some cases, entire black communities were disrupted and forced to flee. Jaspin also points out that not all the states in which racial cleansing occurred were in the South. Using historical recreations and featuring interviews with individuals who still remember the events, Jaspin identifies 260 towns in which blacks faced hostile whites determined to drive them away. Critics might dispute some of the author's conclusions about the "whites' motives, but Jaspin's facts are dauntingly indisputable," Davis observed.

"Jaspin's harrowing and exhaustively researched history of racial cleansing in the United States is painfully eye-opening," remarked a *Publishers Weekly* reviewer. *Booklist* critic Vanessa Bush called Jaspin's historical account a "chilling portrait of a shameful part of American history that has reshaped its racial geography."

BIOGRAPHICAL AND CRITICAL SOURCES:

PERIODICALS

Booklist, March 15, 2007, Vanessa Bush, review of *Buried in the Bitter Waters: The Hidden History of Racial Cleansing in America,* p. 8.

Book World, April 8, 2007, Kevin Boyle, "Ethnic Cleansing, American Style," review of *Buried in the Bitter Waters,* p. 2.

Library Journal, March 15, 2007, Thomas J. Davis, review of *Buried in the Bitter Waters,* p. 81.

Publishers Weekly, April 30, 2007, audiobook review of *Buried in the Bitter Waters,* p. 156.

Reference & Research Book News, May, 2007, review of *Buried in the Bitter Waters.*

ONLINE

Basic Books Web site, http://www.perseusbooksgroup. com/ (October 10, 2007), biography of Elliot Jaspin.

Cox Washington Web site, http://www.coxwashington. com/ (October 10, 2007), biography of Elliot Jaspin.

Creative Loafing, http://www.creativeloafing.com/ (March 7, 2007), John F. Sugg, "Whitewashed! Elliot Jaspin's Book Is the Last Thing the AJC's Editors Want You to Read," review of *Buried in the Bitter Waters.*

History News Network, April 2, 2007, Rick Shenkman, interview with Elliot Jaspin.*

JAYNE, Allen

PERSONAL: Education: Cambridge University, Ph.D.

ADDRESSES: Home—Santa Monica, CA.

CAREER: Historian, editor, and writer.

WRITINGS:

(Editor) *The Religious and Moral Wisdom of Thomas Jefferson: An Anthology,* Vantage Press (New York, NY), 1984.

Jefferson's Declaration of Independence: Origins, Philosophy, and Theology, University Press of Kentucky (Lexington, KY), 1998.

Lincoln and the American Manifesto, Prometheus Books (Amherst, NY), 2007.

SIDELIGHTS: Historian Allen Jayne writes frequently about American history, usually discussing on the country's founding fathers and other prominent figures who helped shape the early direction of the United States. In *Jefferson's Declaration of Independence: Origins, Philosophy, and Theology,* Jayne "focuses his considerable historical and analytic skills on the mind of Thomas Jefferson," according to Christopher M. Duncan in *Perspectives on Political Science.* "The result is a meticulously researched, cogently argued view of Jefferson that should force most readers to reconsider their understanding of him." Jayne carefully assembles a picture of the intellectually powerful and eclectic Jefferson through a close study of the president's reading habits in philosophy, politics, theology, and other subjects. He demonstrates Jefferson's adherence to concepts such as democracy, liberal individualism, application of reason, and even deism, all the while rejecting authority and strict adherence to Judeo-Christian orthodoxy. "Jayne renders a compelling picture of a great mind at war with tyranny in all its manifestations," Duncan remarked, and shows how these ideas shaped Jefferson's work on the U.S. Declaration of Independence. For some readers, mused reviewer David E. Maas in the *Journal of Church and State,* "it will be a shock to discover that the Declaration of Independence is a document that tries to arouse men to throw off the chains of traditional Christianity and embrace reason and the basic tenets of Deism or Unitarianism."

With *Lincoln and the American Manifesto,* Jayne describes the great president's views on the Declaration of Independence and how he considered it a document important enough to be treated as a genuine American manifesto, the "greatest embodiment of American principles," stated an *Internet Bookwatch* critic. Jayne explores the similarity between Lincoln and Jefferson's views on the rights of all people, moral truth, and the Declaration itself. Lincoln furthermore realized how the ideology espoused in the Declaration was at odds with the existence of slavery, and Jayne explores how Lincoln used the document as a "moral weapon in his fight against slavery and in defense of the Civil War," reported a reviewer in the *Reference & Research Book News.* The author firmly places Lincoln's "thought and purpose in Enlightenment concepts and deism" and his opposition to slavery in his adherence to the concepts of the Declaration of Independence, observed Randall M. Miller in a *Library Journal* review. In the end, Jayne offers readers an "illuminating look into the basic principles that kept one of the country's greatest leaders focused as he attempted to unify a deeply divided nation," concluded *Monsters and Critics* contributor Sandy Amazeen.

BIOGRAPHICAL AND CRITICAL SOURCES:

PERIODICALS

American Historical Review, June, 1999, Carl J. Richard, review of *Jefferson's Declaration of Independence: Origins, Philosophy, and Theology,* p. 899.

Choice: Current Reviews for Academic Libraries, June, 1998, P. Coby, review of *Jefferson's Declaration of Independence,* p. 1784.

Internet Bookwatch, August, 2007, review of *Lincoln and the American Manifesto.*

Journal of Church and State, winter, 1999, David E. Maas, review of *Jefferson's Declaration of Independence,* p. 148.

Journal of Law and Religion, summer, 2001, Rick Fairbanks, review of *Jefferson's Declaration of Independence,* p. 541.

Journal of Southern History, May, 1999, Norman K. Risjord, review of *Jefferson's Declaration of Independence,* p. 388.

Journal of the Early Republic, spring, 1999, Ralph Ketcham, review of *Jefferson's Declaration of Independence,* p. 118.

Library Journal, February 15, 2007, Randall M. Miller, review of *Lincoln and the American Manifesto,* p. 131.

Perspectives on Political Science, winter, 1999, Christopher M. Duncan, review of *Jefferson's Declaration of Independence,* p. 56.

Reference & Research Book News, August, 2007, review of *Lincoln and the American Manifesto.*

Virginia Magazine of History and Biography, summer, 1998, Stuart Leibiger, review of *Jefferson's Declaration of Independence,* p. 322.

ONLINE

Monsters and Critics, http://www.monstersandcritics. com/ (March 4, 2007), Sandy Amazeen, review of *Lincoln and the American Manifesto.*

Prometheus Books Web site, http://www.prometheus books.com/ (October 10, 2007), biography of Allen Jayne.*

* * *

JEAN, Jo
See HOLLAND, JoJean

* * *

JENKINSON, Bill 1962-

PERSONAL: Born 1962.

ADDRESSES: Home—Willow Grove, PA. *Agent*—James Fitzgerald Agency, 80 E. 11th St., Ste. 301, New York, NY 10003-6000.

CAREER: Sports historian. Has served as a consultant for numerous sports organizations, including the Baseball Hall of Fame, the Society for American Baseball Research, the Babe Ruth Museum, and for Major League Baseball and ESPN.

WRITINGS:

The Year Babe Ruth Hit 104 Home Runs: Recrowning Baseball's Greatest Slugger, Carroll & Graf (New York, NY), 2007.

SIDELIGHTS: Bill Jenkinson is a baseball historian, an expert on the history of long-distance home runs, and an acknowledged scholar on the life and career of famed baseball player Babe Ruth. In *The Year Babe Ruth Hit 104 Home Runs: Recrowning Baseball's Greatest Slugger,* Jenkinson seeks to reclaim Ruth's reputation from modern players who have surpassed the Bambino's accomplishments in sheer numbers, but whose records were achieved on a playing field much more favorable than that occupied by Ruth. In 2006, for example, controversial batter Barry Bonds surpassed Ruth's record of 714 home runs. Other players, such as Sammy Sosa, Hank Aaron, and Roger Maris, also make a claim to the title of baseball's greatest. To Jenkinson, however, Ruth remains the greatest baseball player of all time. In his book he offers detailed historical information and statistical data to back up his claim. Jenkinson's work "is an authoritative analysis of Ruth's hitting prowess, and it uses statistics to show that Ruth still would have been the game's greatest slugger if he had played today," commented William C. Kashatus in the *Philadelphia Inquirer.*

"In a fresh perspective on Ruth's position in the pantheon of sport and American heroes, we are spared 'gee-whiz' adulation and presented with meticulous research that stands on its own," reported J. Sebastian Sinsi in the *Denver Post.* For example, Jenkinson notes that Ruth played through much of his career with a nagging knee injury that could easily be remedied by today's medicine. He notes that Ruth powered in 198 home runs of more than 450 feet, compared to Bonds's record of 36. He carefully constructs a graphical pattern of Ruth's hits that, in terms of the book's title, would account for 104 home runs had they been hit in modern ballparks under today's rules, rather than under the more restrictive regulations of 1921. Jenkinson also factors in other elements of Ruth's life and career, taking into account such elements as equipment of the day, medical and rehabilitative treatment available to Ruth, the intense attention paid to Ruth by the press, and more. He also makes much of Ruth's well-demonstrated power as a batter and reveals statistics from a little-known exhibition series of 800 games in which Ruth participated. In modern thinking, modern sports figures are "bigger, faster, stronger, and therefore better," mused *Booklist* review Wes Lukowsky. In Jenkinson's thorough treatment of Babe Ruth's history, abilities, and accomplishments, however, "we have the carefully researched, imaginatively argued contrary position."

BIOGRAPHICAL AND CRITICAL SOURCES:

PERIODICALS

Booklist, March 15, 2007, Wes Lukowsky, review of *The Year Babe Ruth Hit 104 Home Runs: Recrowning Baseball's Greatest Slugger,* p. 13.

Boston Phoenix, August 15, 2007, "The Babe, Bill Jenkinson, and the Red Sox," review of *The Year Babe Ruth Hit 104 Home Runs.*

Denver Post, April 1, 007, J. Sebastian Sinsi, "Taking a New Look at the Babe's Best Year," review of *The Year Babe Ruth Hit 104 Home Runs.*

Philadelphia Inquirer, April 1, 2007, William C. Kashatus, "Babe Ruth: Unparalleled Power?," review of *The Year Babe Ruth Hit 104 Home Runs.*

ONLINE

James Fitzgerald Agency Web site, http://www.jfitzagency.com/ (October 10, 2007), biography of Bill Jenkinson.*

*   *   *

JOHNSON, Claudia Alta Taylor
    See JOHNSON, Lady Bird

*   *   *

JOHNSON, Claudia Taylor
    See JOHNSON, Lady Bird

*   *   *

JOHNSON, Jason 1969-

PERSONAL: Born 1969, in Enniskillen, County Fermanagh, Northern Ireland. *Education:* Attended the University of Sunderland and the University of Wisconsin—Milwaukee.

ADDRESSES: E-mail—woundlicker@gmail.com.

CAREER: During early career, worked as a bartender, car washer, supermarket employee, shoe salesman, waiter, courier, stonemason, chair-ride operator, painter, and decorator; worked for newspapers in Ireland, including the *Irish News* and *Belfast Telegraph,* and as news editor for the *Irish Sunday People,* until 2004; full-time writer, 2004—.

WRITINGS:

Wound Licker (novel), Blackstaff Press (Belfast, Northern Ireland), 2005.

Alina (novel), Blackstaff (Belfast, Northern Ireland), 2006.

SIDELIGHTS: Jason Johnson is a former journalist who left the world of reporting to become a full-time novelist in 2004. That year, he sold his debut work of fiction, *Wound Licker.* The book met with considerable critical praise. It centers on protagonist Fletcher Fee, a resident of Belfast, Northern Ireland, who has grown tired of the dismal world around him. Driven to act by unprovoked attacks on a teenage neighbor and the death of Karim, his only friend, Fee descends into retribution and violent reprisals that cannot be ignored by the police and that threaten an already shaky peace in the volatile environment of Belfast. Pursued by police and paramilitary groups alike, Fee discovers a well-concealed network of lies and corruption that jeopardizes any prospects of peace in Northern Ireland.

In *Alina,* Johnson's second novel, Harry Sender finds himself embroiled in the world of online pornography and the search for a missing Web site performer. Paid a handsome sum by the owner of the Web site, the down-on-his-luck Sender is soon liberated from his odious job as a phone company customer service representative. In return, he must search for Alina, a performer on the sexually explicit site who was quickly falling in love with her boss. Accompanied by the hedonistic and pleasure-seeking Shuff Sheridan, a volatile thug and tough guy, Sender sets out from his home in Northern Ireland for Romania to look for Alina. In this violent world, Sender soon comes to realize that the Web site he once thought was harmless is in fact doing great harm to the women who work for it, and may well corrupt him irreversibly before his search for Alina is finished. A *Bookseller* reviewer called Sender's quest a "blackly comic journey." Johnson "delivers a climax as harrowing as one might hope to find in contemporary crime fiction," noted *Booklist* reviewer Frank Sennett.

Johnson garnered additional attention when he decided to auction off the opportunity to appear as a character in a forthcoming novel. "I heard someone had sold cameo roles in an independent movie to help with the funding. I figured I could offer someone much more than that in a novel," Johnson explained in an online interview for the Canadian Broadcasting Corporation (CBC). In the end, "I have some money which allows me more time to write, and they get to live forever," Johnson commented.

BIOGRAPHICAL AND CRITICAL SOURCES:

PERIODICALS

Booklist, March 1, 2007, Frank Sennett, review of *Alina,* p. 68.

Bookseller, September 22, 2006, review of *Alina,* p. 10.

M2 Best Books, October 2, 2006, "Author Auctions Chance to Feature in Next Novel," profile of Jason Johnson.

ONLINE

CBC.ca, http://www.cbc.ca/ (November 22, 2006), interview with Jason Johnson.

Wound Licker Web site, http://www.woundlicker.com (October 10, 2007).*

*   *   *

JOHNSON, Lady Bird 1912-2007

(Claudia Alta Taylor Johnson, Claudia Taylor Johnson)

OBITUARY NOTICE— See index for *CA* sketch: Born December 22, 1912, in Karnack, TX; died July 11, 2007, in Austin, TX. Conservationist, environmentalist, businesswoman, and author. Johnson became known to the American public as the wife and widow of the controversial thirty-sixth U.S. president, Lyndon Baines Johnson, but she created an enduring legacy that may in some circles outlast his. The Johnsons came to the White House in the wake of the assassination of John F. Kennedy in 1963. It was a move they had not sought and one that Mrs. Johnson later

claimed she never wanted. Following in the footsteps of the elegant and polished Jacqueline Kennedy would have been a difficult challenge for the simple Texas-bred businesswoman with the unlikely name of Lady Bird, which she had acquired as a baby. Instead, Johnson embarked on a path of her own, one that would take her through trial and turmoil, testing her fortitude, and ultimately lead her back to the countryside she loved. As First Lady, Johnson stood behind her husband, often literally, doing his bidding and sometimes, according to eyewitnesses, enduring his verbal tirades, always without complaint. To others, however, she was no victim, but a formidable pillar of courage and support to a man who spent most of his presidency under siege. During his 1964 presidential campaign, which began after he had signed a controversial civil rights act, Mrs. Johnson bravely toured areas of the South where her husband could not safely venture, promoting his campaign with confidence and conviction. During the Vietnam War protests, she faced the most hostile and antagonistic protestors with calmness and grace. At the end of her husband's term of office, Johnson had won the respect of the American people. She was an active political campaigner, often traveling on her own. She was the first national chair of the Head Start program for early childhood education and a tireless supporter of her husband's War on Poverty. Most of all, Johnson wanted to replace ugliness with beauty. She planted flowers throughout the nation's capital with her own hands and campaigned successfully to replace highway trash and billboards with wildflowers and greenery. Johnson's beautification work, which seemed trivial to some at the time, ushered in a new era of conservation and environmental activism that persists to this day. After leaving the White House in 1969, Johnson returned to the LBJ Ranch in Texas and resumed her role as the owner of local radio and television stations, the proceeds from which had originally financed her husband's entrance into politics. She also dedicated herself to the land of Texas and the rest of the country. Johnson founded what is now the Lady Bird Johnson Wildflower Center at the University of Texas at Austin. For her contributions, Johnson was the recipient of many awards, including the U.S. Medal of Freedom and the Congressional Gold Medal. Johnson was the first presidential wife since Dolley Madison in the 1840s to record her experiences of life in the White House. Johnson's *A White House Diary* was published in 1970.

OBITUARIES AND OTHER SOURCES:

BOOKS

Johnson, Lady Bird, *A White House Diary,* Holt, Rinehart & Winston (New York, NY), 1970.

PERIODICALS

Chicago Tribune, July 12, 2007, pp. 1, 11.
Los Angeles Times, July 12, 2007, pp. A1, A20-A21.
New York Times, July 12, 2007, pp. A1, C12; July 13, 2007, p. A2.
Times (London, England), July 13, 2007, p. 60.
Washington Post, July 12, 2007, pp. A1, A12-A13.

*   *   *

JONES, Chris
(**Christopher Alexander Jones**)

PERSONAL: Male.

ADDRESSES: Home—Ottawa, Ontario, Canada.

CAREER: Journalist and author.

AWARDS, HONORS: Edward Goff Penny Award for the outstanding young journalist in Canada, 2000; National Magazine Award for feature writing, 2005, for "Home."

WRITINGS:

Falling Hard: A Rookie's Year in Boxing, Arcade Publishing (New York, NY), 2002.
Too Far from Home: A Story of Life and Death in Space, Doubleday (New York, NY), 2007, published as *Out of Orbit: The Incredible True Story of Three Astronauts Who Were Hundreds of Miles above the Earth When They Lost Their Ride Home,* Broadway Books (New York, NY), 2008.

Contributor to newspapers and periodicals, including the *National Post.*

Contributor and former sports columnist, *Esquire* magazine.

SIDELIGHTS: Chris Jones is a journalist and sports columnist. One of his articles, "Home," garnered him a National Magazine Award, and also served as the basis for a book-length work of nonfiction, *Too Far from Home: A Story of Life and Death in Space.* In the book, Jones explores an often overlooked aspect of the destruction of the space shuttle *Columbia.* When the *Columbia* tragically exploded on February 1, 2003, the remainder of the shuttle fleet was grounded indefinitely, leaving two American astronauts stranded on the International Space Station with no immediate prospects for a return home. Astronauts Kenneth Bowersox and Don Pettit, along with Russian engineer and cosmonaut Nikolai Budarin, had been in residence at the International Space Station since November, 2002, and were anticipating a ride back home on the *Columbia.* When the shuttle was destroyed, the spacefarers not only found themselves shocked and grieving over the deaths of their colleagues, but embroiled in the more immediate and practical matter of how they would survive during their unexpected extension of duty—and how, and if, they would finally leave orbit and return to solid ground.

Jones recounts in depth the ordeal of the three residents of the ISS, "who survived and even thrived during their stay in space," noted *USA Today* reviewer Don Oldenburg. Jones's narrative covers both the mundane and the cosmic, from the mechanics of eating and excreting in zero gravity, to the emotional toll of isolation in a place where rescue is difficult, to the constant danger of impact from pieces of space junk hurtling at ballistic velocities through space. Throughout, Jones also addresses the tension of their predicament, relating how the men coped with separation from their homes and families, and how their families back on earth dealt with the crisis and the very real prospect that the three astronauts might die in space. In the background, Jones touches on other issues, including the state of the U.S. space program, competition between American and Russian space agencies, and the determination and tenacity it takes to step away from the planet itself for the sake of science and knowledge. Ultimately, the astronauts returned to earth on a harrowing ride in a rickety Soyuz space capsule. "For all the professionalism and sang-froid described in *Too Far from Home,* though, there remains a real, underlying sense of what makes astronauts so far removed from the ordinary. Even when performing routine repairs, an astronaut may gaze at his or her foot and see behind it a similar-sized object that turns out to be Australia," observed Janet Maslin in the *New York Times.*

Library Journal reviewer John Carver called Jones's book a "first-rate account of the Expedition Six mission to the International Space Station." The book "combines gripping narrative and strongly defined characters," asserted a *Publishers Weekly* reviewer. "A smart read, the book proves to be an illuminating and enjoyable journey into the complexities of spaceflight's pernicious perils and tranquil beauty," Oldenburg concluded.

BIOGRAPHICAL AND CRITICAL SOURCES:

PERIODICALS

Biography, spring, 2007, Chet Raymo, "Space Station Astronauts," review of *Too Far from Home: A Story of Life and Death in Space,* p. 313.

Booklist, March 1, 2007, Gilbert Taylor, review of *Too Far from Home,* p. 48.

Entertainment Weekly, March 9, 2007, Wook Kim, review of *Too Far from Home,* p. 115.

Library Journal, February 1, 2007, John Carver, review of *Too Far from Home,* p. 85.

New York Times, March 22, 2007, Janet Maslin, "The Astronauts Columbia Left Behind," review of *Too Far from Home.*

Pittsburgh Post-Gazette, March 18, 2007, Jon Caroulis, "Two Books Probe NASA's Track Record after the Success of the Man-on-the-Moon Program," review of *Too Far from Home.*

Publishers Weekly, January 1, 2007, review of *Too Far from Home,* p. 44.

Quill & Quire, January, 2007, Dan Rowe, "Space Is the Place," review of *Too Far from Home.*

Science News, April 28, 2007, review of *Too Far from Home,* p. 271.

USA Today, March 19, 2007, Don Oldenburg, "2003 Space Odyssey *Too Far* Hits Close to Home," review of *Too Far from Home.*

JONES, Christopher Alexander
    See JONES, Chris

*   *   *

JORDAN, Pete 1967(?)-
(Dishwasher Pete)

PERSONAL: Born c. 1967; married; wife's name Amy Joy.

ADDRESSES: Home—Portland, OR, and Amsterdam, Netherlands. *E-mail*—pete@dishwasherpete.com.

CAREER: Co-owner and operator of a bicycle shop in Amsterdam, Netherlands; also worked as a dishwasher.

WRITINGS:

Dishwasher: One Man's Quest to Wash Dishes in All Fifty States, HarperCollins (New York, NY), 2007.

SIDELIGHTS: Pete Jordan is a writer, a frequent contributor to National Public Radio's *All Things Considered,* and owner and mechanic of a bicycle shop in Amsterdam, the Netherlands. For twelve years, from 1989 to 2001, Jordan occupied one of the lower employment rungs as a dishwasher in various restaurants around the United States. Adopting the nickname of Dishwasher Pete, Jordan self-published a hugely popular 'zine in which he wrote about his experiences in and out of dishrooms and kitchens in resorts, neighborhood eateries, ethnic eateries, communes, social clubs, and dinner trains. As Jordan related his adventures in suds-busting, his work became more iconic and evolved into a cultural phenomenon. In *Dishwasher: One Man's Quest to Wash Dishes in All Fifty States,* Jordan updates and revises the stories of his experiences, recounting his quest to leave his mark on dishwashing history and the cultural consciousness of America.

For Jordan, as well as for many of the fans of his 'zine and radio appearances, dishwashing was a lowly job, but it also had its share of freedom and unusual dignity. "As loathsome as the job seems to many people, among my friends it was empowering to do the crap work nobody else wants to do, and sort of remain anonymous or not take it too seriously. Just putting in your hours and leaving at the end of the day, and picking up your check," Jordan remarked to interviewer Bill O'Driscoll in the *Pittsburgh City Paper*. He describes the life of the dishwasher, the ability to walk off the job without guilt at a moment's notice, and the likelihood of being able to quickly pick up another similar job, sometimes within minutes of quitting one. He describes the relative freedom of being a dishwasher; the access to free food, whether swiped from the kitchens or plundered from the uneaten leftovers on patrons' plates. He also reports on a number of famous persons who once paid their rent with money earned from dishwashing, from former president Gerald Ford to Fifties rock 'n' roll icon Little Richard, and describes how dishwashers were important participants in the development of labor unions. Even when the responsibilities of marriage and making a living find their way into his life, Jordan retains his cheerfully low-key attitude.

Jordan's "writing is lucid and earnest," and his "passion for dishwashing and, even more so, for blowing-in-the-wind traveling, is infectious," observed a *Publishers Weekly* critic. A *Kirkus Reviews* contributor called the book an "enjoyable manifesto celebrating rootless irresponsibility, with rueful acknowledgement of the pitfalls therein." *Bookslut* reviewer Drew Nellins remarked that *Dishwasher* is not a "work of genius or a peek inside the mind of one of our greatest men. It's just an honest and fun account of a strange period in the life of a living oxymoron: a hard-working slacker."

BIOGRAPHICAL AND CRITICAL SOURCES:

BOOKS

Jordan, Pete, *Dishwasher: One Man's Quest to Wash Dishes in All Fifty States*, HarperCollins (New York, NY), 2007.

PERIODICALS

Chicago Tribune, May 23, 2007, Robert K. Elder, "The Soapy Adventures of Dishwasher Pete: Read How Our Hero Traveled the U.S. 'Busting Suds' for Twelve Years," interview with Pete Jordan.

Kirkus Reviews, March 1, 2007, review of *Dishwasher*, p. 208.
Library Journal, April 15, 2007, Janet Ingraham Dwyer, review of *Dishwasher*, p. 97.
New York Times, May 23, 2007, Charles McGrath, "Everything and the Kitchen Sink: The Memoir of a Dishwasher," review of *Dishwasher*, p. E1.
Pittsburgh City Paper, May 17, 2007, Bill O'Driscoll, "Zine Hero Dishwasher Pete Dishes on His New Book," interview with Pete Jordan.
Portland Mercury (Portland, OR), May 31, 2007, Chas Bowie, "Elbow Deep," interview with Pete Jordan.
Publishers Weekly, March 26, 2007, review of *Dishwasher*, p. 83.
Reference & Research Book News, August 2007, review of *Dishwasher*.
Seattle Post-Intelligencer, May 29, 2007, Regina Hackett, "Author Brings a Shine to Lowly Work in *Dishwasher*."

ONLINE

Bookslut, http://www.bookslut.com/ (October 10, 2007), Drew Nellins, review of *Dishwasher*.
Pete Jordan Home Page, http://www.dishwasherpete.com (October 10, 2007).
Pete Jordan MySpace Profile, http://www.myspace.com/dishwasherpete (October 10, 2007).
Powell's Books, http://www.powells.com/ (October 10, 2007), interview with Pete Jordan.*

*   *   *

JUNGERSEN, Christian 1962(?)-

PERSONAL: Born c. 1962, in Copenhagen, Denmark; son of a lawyer and a high school teacher. *Education:* Earned master's degree.

ADDRESSES: Home—New York, NY.

CAREER: Novelist. Worked previously as a screenwriter, copywriter, television script consultant, and film teacher.

AWARDS, HONORS: Danish Award for best first novel, 1999, for *Krat;* Danish Arts Foundation fellowship; Golden Laurels Prize for *Undtagelsen.*

WRITINGS:

Krat (title means "Thickets"), Centrum (Copenhagen, Denmark), 1999.

Undtagelsen, Gyldendal (Copenhagen, Denmark), 2004, translation by Anna Paterson published as *The Exception: A Novel,* Doubleday (New York, NY), 2006.

SIDELIGHTS: Danish author Christian Jungersen established a literary reputation for himself after his first published novel, *Krat,* won an award for best first novel in his native country. Jungersen's next book, *The Exception: A Novel* (published in Denmark as *Undtagelsen*), became his English debut and earned him the prestigious Golden Laurels Prize. The novel is largely set in the offices of a small business, the Danish Center for Information on Genocide, and focuses on a group of four female coworkers. When two of the coworkers begin receiving threatening e-mails, they blame it on one of their own, a woman they believe is an easy target. As the level of paranoia in the office escalates, the tension level boils over and the women's behavior reaches an extreme. *Mostly Fiction Book Reviews* contributor Eleanor Bukowsky described the novel as a "compelling and provocative work that explores a number of significant and thought-provoking issues," including genocide, the definition of evil, and the complexities of intra-office politics. Andrea Kempf found the book to be "so uncomfortably real for anyone who has worked in a small office that it is almost painful," as she wrote in a review for the *Library Journal.* "Read it and you will never look at your work colleagues in quite the same way again," proclaimed a critic for the *Economist,* who noted that *The Exception* "subtly suggests that, however deeply buried, there may, if provoked, be a killer in everyone." Writing for the *New York Times Book Review,* Marcel Theroux commented: "One comes away feeling there is a hugely empathetic imagination behind this novel, one that resists allowing us to fall into the simplifying judgments that are a necessary prelude to cruelty. Its characters seem deeply true to life in that they are not unitary, but a web of fluctuating motivations that combine good intentions, self-deception, generosity, selfishness and malice."

BIOGRAPHICAL AND CRITICAL SOURCES:

PERIODICALS

Economist, September 30, 2006, "Worked to Death in Denmark: New Fiction," review of *The Exception: A Novel,* p. 94.

Library Journal, March 1, 2007, Andrea Kempf, review of *The Exception,* p. 74.

New York Times Book Review, July 22, 2007, Marcel Theroux, "Cruel World," review of *The Exception,* p. 7.

ONLINE

Christian Jungersen Home Page, http://www.christian jungersen.com (October 8, 2007).

Mostly Fiction Book Reviews, http://www.mostly fiction.com/ (August 21, 2007), Eleanor Bukowsky, review of *The Exception.**

K

KALAS, J. Ellsworth 1923-

PERSONAL: Born 1923 in Sioux City, IA; married; wife's name Janet; children: Taddy, David. *Education:* University of Wisconsin, B.S. (with honors), 1951; Garrett-Evangelical Theological Seminary (with distinction), Northwestern University, B.D., 1954; completed post-graduate coursework at the University of Wisconsin, 1954-55, and Harvard University, 1955-56.

ADDRESSES: Office—Asbury Theological Seminary, 204 N. Lexington Ave., Wilmore, KY 40390.

CAREER: Professor and writer. Asbury Theological Seminary, Wilmore, KY, instructor in preaching, 1993-2000, professor of preaching, 2000—, president. Served as a pastor in Wisconsin and Ohio, c. 1950-88, and as an associate in evangelism with the World Methodist Council, c. 1988-93.

MEMBER: Member of Phi Eta Sigma, Phi Kappa Phi, and Iron Cross.

AWARDS, HONORS: Trustees Award for Scholarship and Kidder Preaching Prize, both Northwestern University; honorary doctorates from Lawrence University, 1965, Asbury Theological Seminary, 1986, Kentucky Wesleyan College, 2004, Asbury College, 2007.

WRITINGS:

Our First Song: Evangelism in the Hymns of Charles Wesley, Discipleship Resources (Nashville, TN), 1984.

Jesus Then and Now, Graded Press (Nashville, TN), 1987.

The Power of Believing, Word Books (Waco, TX), 1987.

Pilgrimage: Following in Jesus' Footsteps, C.S.S. Publishing (Lima, OH), 1987.

Reading the Signs: Sermons for Advent, Christmas, and Epiphany, Sundays in Ordinary Time, Cycle C Gospel Texts, C.S.S. Publishing (Lima, OH), 1988.

Parables from the Back Side: Bible Stories with a Twist, Abingdon Press (Nashville, TN), 1992.

365 Days from Genesis through Revelation, Abingdon Press (Nashville, TN), 1993.

If Experience Is Such a Good Teacher, Why Do I Keep Repeating the Course?, Dimensions for Living (Nashville, TN), 1994.

Old Testament Stories from the Back Side, Abingdon Press (Nashville, TN), 1995.

The Grand Sweep: 365 Days from Genesis through Revelation, Abingdon Press (Nashville, TN), 1996.

Parables of Jesus, Abingdon Press (Nashville, TN), 1997.

Luke's Message: Good News for the New Millennium, Abingdon Press (Nashville, TN), 1997.

The Christmas People: An Advent Story for Adults, Abingdon Press (Nashville, TN), 1998.

The Ten Commandments from the Back Side, Abingdon Press (Nashville, TN), 1998.

Christian Believer, Abingdon Press (Nashville, TN), 1999.

New Testament Stories from the Back Side, Abingdon Press (Nashville, TN), 2000.

Through Suffering to Hope: A Study of Isaiah, Abingdon Press (Nashville, TN), 2002.

The Thirteen Apostles, Abingdon Press (Nashville, TN), 2002.

Seven Words to the Cross: A Lenten Study for Adults, Abingdon Press (Nashville, TN), 2002.

(With others) *Sermons on the Gospel Readings: Series I, Cycle C,* C.S.S. Publishing (Lima, OH), 2003.

Christmas from the Back Side, Abingdon Press (Nashville, TN), 2003.

Preaching from the Soul: Insistent Observations on the Sacred Art, Abingdon Press (Nashville, TN), 2003.

The Scriptures Sing of Christmas: An Advent Study for Adults, Abingdon Press (Nashville, TN), 2004.

Preaching the Calendar: Celebrating Holidays and Holy Days, Westminster John Knox Press (Louisville, KY), 2004.

Preaching about People: The Power of Biography, Chalice Press (St. Louis, MO), 2004.

Life from the Up Side: Seeing God at Work in the World, Dimensions For Living (Nashville, TN), 2004.

Grace in a Tree Stump: Old Testament Stories of God's Love, Westminster John Knox Press (Louisville, KY), 2005.

More Parables from the Back Side, Abingdon Press (Nashville, TN), 2005.

Longing to Pray: How the Psalms Teach Us to Talk with God, Abingdon Press (Nashville, TN), 2006.

What I Learned When I Was Ten: Lessons That Shaped My Life and Faith, Abingdon Press (Nashville, TN), 2006.

A Hop, Skip, and a Jump through the Bible, Abingdon Press (Nashville, TN), 2007.

Strong Was Her Faith: Women of the New Testament, Abingdon Press (Nashville, TN), 2007.

Men Worth Knowing: Biblical Meditations for Daily Living, Westminster John Knox Press (Louisville, KY), 2007.

Contributor to *Christmas Reflections: From James W. Moore, Reginald Mallett, J. Ellsworth Kalas, James A. Harnish, Nell W. Mohney,* Dimensions for Living (Nashville, TN), 2001.

SIDELIGHTS: J. Ellsworth Kalas is president of the Asbury Theological Seminary, where he has taught preaching since 1993. He majored in literature as an undergraduate at the University of Wisconsin, going on to earn a master's degree in divinity studies from Northwestern University; he then spent several years in further studies at the University of Wisconsin and

Harvard University. In the 1950s Kalas began a career as a church pastor that spanned nearly four decades, after which he served the World Methodist Council as an associate in evangelism before beginning his tenure at Asbury.

Kalas has lent his expertise as a pastor and seminary professor to more than thirty books on Christian topics. Many of his titles provide analysis or a new perspective on specific chapters of the Bible, such as *Through Suffering to Hope: A Study of Isaiah,* or *Luke's Message: Good News for the New Millennium.* In *365 Days from Genesis through Revelation,* Kalas guides the reader through the chapter-by-chapter process of reading the complete Bible within one calendar year. His instructions include reading between three and four chapters a day, with scriptures from Psalms and Proverbs intermingled. In a review for *Publishers Weekly,* a critic found the text "highly usable, . . . well-written, well-researched and reliable."

Several of Kalas's books are extensions of his Asbury curriculum, where he has taught courses on biblical preaching, biographical sermons, and worship. In *Preaching about People: The Power of Biography,* Kalas expounds on the concept of the biographical sermon, his own contribution to the field of homiletics, or narrative preaching. He provides instruction for selecting personalities from history to emphasize a particular doctrine or enlighten the listener. *Strong Was Her Faith: Women of the New Testament* is a biographical sermon in book form, as it contains stories of eleven women who made a significant impact in the Bible's New Testament. *Library Journal* reviewer Graham Christian found the book to be "tailored for the modern nonacademic reader."

Kalas told *CA:* "I suspect I first became interested in writing soon after I began reading. The public libraries of my youth meant so much to me that I still visit the three locations during my annual visits to my home town of Sioux City, Iowa, even though one is now a vacant lot and the other two have been converted to other purposes. I found in my childhood clippings an interview for the West Junior High School newspaper where I said as an eighth grader that I 'wanted to write books someday.'

"I continue to be grateful for a summer school course at the University of Wisconsin taught by the late, great regional novelist, Mari Sandoz. My work has been influenced by the Bible (especially the King James Version, which I read in my childhood) and a variety of novelists, poets, playwrights, and essayists."

BIOGRAPHICAL AND CRITICAL SOURCES:

PERIODICALS

Library Journal, March 1, 2007, Graham Christian, review of Strong Was Her Faith: Women of the New Testament, p. 62.
Publishers Weekly, September 13, 1993, review of 365 Days from Genesis through Revelation, p. 42.

ONLINE

Asbury Theological Seminary, http://www.asbury seminary.edu/ (October 10, 2007), faculty profile of J. Ellsworth Kalas.

*　　*　　*

KALLI, Leszli 1980-

PERSONAL: Born 1980, in Colombia.

ADDRESSES: Home—Canada.

CAREER: Writer.

WRITINGS:

Secuestrada: Diario de una joven secuestrada por la guerrilla Colombiana, Espasa (Madrid, Spain), 2001, translation by Kristina Cordero published as Kidnapped: A Diary of My 373 Days in Captivity, Atria Books (New York, NY), 2007.

SIDELIGHTS: In April of 1999, eighteen-year-old Leszli Kalli set out by plane for Israel, accompanied by her father. Not long after takeoff, the plane was hijacked by members of the National Liberation Army, a Colombian guerrilla group also known as the ELN. For the next 373 days, Kalli and her father were held captive along with fourteen other passengers at an ELN camp deep in the jungle. Over a year would go by before the Colombian government would be able to negotiate with the ELN for the hostages' release. In an interview with Latina.com, Kalli commented about what the experience taught her: "I learned to value everything. Everyone has to deal with obstacles. Maybe not kidnapping, but maybe a lack of money? Now, those obstacles seem really small. I don't have any money? Who cares? I am alive, healthy and free. Now, I can face any difficulty and have the conviction that I will survive."

Kalli wrote about her experiences in the memoir Kidnapped: A Diary of My 373 Days in Captivity. Much of the book is taken directly from a diary that she kept throughout her ordeal, outlining the camp's organization, the constant threat of danger, and the boredom of captivity. A reviewer for Publishers Weekly found that the book "retains Kalli's vivid intensity, even as she's explaining the fear and tedium of daily life as a hostage." Writing in Kirkus Reviews, a critic remarked that "a prefatory essay, giving a bit more context about guerilla kidnappings in Colombia, would have been helpful."

BIOGRAPHICAL AND CRITICAL SOURCES:

BOOKS

Kalli, Leszli, Kidnapped: A Diary of My 373 Days in Captivity, Atria Books (New York, NY), 2007.

PERIODICALS

Kirkus Reviews, December 15, 2006, review of Kidnapped, p. 1257.

ONLINE

Latina.com, http://www.latina.com/ (October 11, 2007), review of Kidnapped.
Publishers Weekly Online, http://www.publishers weekly.com/ (February 5, 2007), review of Kidnapped.*

*　　*　　*

KANDEL, Eric R. 1929-

PERSONAL: Born November 7, 1929, in Vienna, Austria; son of Herman (a store owner) and Charlotte Kandel; married Denise Bystryn (a professor), 1956; children: Paul, Minouche. Education: Harvard College, B.A., 1952; New York University School of Medicine, M.D., 1956.

ADDRESSES: *Home*—New York, NY. *Office*—Department of Neuroscience, Howard Hughes Medical Institute, Columbia University, 1051 Riverside Dr., Rm. 668 Annex, New York, NY 10032; fax: 212-543-5474. *E-mail*—erk5@columbia.edu.

CAREER: Educator and writer. National Institutes of Health, Bethesda, MD, researcher, 1957-60; Massachusetts Mental Health Center, Harvard Medical School, Cambridge, MA, resident, 1960-62; laboratory of Ladislav Tauc, Paris, France, research scientist, 1962-63; Harvard Medical School, Cambridge, MA, instructor in psychiatry, 1963-65; New York University Medical School, Department of Physiology and Psychiatry, New York, NY, 1965-73; Columbia University, New York, NY, researcher, professor, and founding director of the Department of Neuroscience, 1973-84, university professor, 1984—, senior investigator, Howard Hughes Medical Research Institute, 1984—, Fred Kavli Professor and director of the Kavli Institute for Brain Science.

MEMBER: National Academy of Sciences, American Academy of Arts and Sciences, American Philosophical Society, National Institute of Medicine, Order of Merit for Arts and Sciences (Germany), Academie des Sciences (France).

AWARDS, HONORS: Lester N. Hofheimer Prize for Research, American Psychiatric Association, 1977; Karl Spencer Lashley Prize in Neurobiology, American Philosophical Society, 1981; Dickson Prize in Biology and Medicine, University of Pittsburgh, 1982; Albert Lasker Basic Medical Research Award, 1983; Rosenstiel Award, Brandeis University, 1984; Howard Crosy Warren Medal, Society of Experimental Psychologists, 1984; American Association of Medical Colleges Award for Distinguished Research in the Biomedical Sciences, 1985; Gairdner International Award of Canada for Outstanding Research in the Biomedical Sciences, 1987; National Medal of Science, 1988; J. Murray Luck Award for Scientific Reviewing, National Academy of Sciences, 1988; American College of Physicians Award in Basic Science, 1989; Robert J. and Claire Pasarow Foundation Award in Neuroscience, 1989; Bristol-Myers Squibb Award for Distinguished Achievement in Neu-

roscience Research, 1991; Warren Triennial Prize, Massachusetts General Hospital, 1992; Harvey Prize of the Technion in Haifa, 1993; Stevens Triennial Prize, Columbia University, 1995; Dana Award, 1997; Dr. A.H. Heineken Prize for Medicine from the Royal Netherlands Academy of Arts and Sciences in Amsterdam, 2000; Nobel Prize in Physiology or Medicine (with Arvid Carlsson and Paul Greengard), 2000; Centenary Medal, Royal Society of Canada, 2002; Julius Axelrod Neuroscience Award (with Arvid Carlsson and Paul Greengard), 2002; Honorary Fellow and Distinguished Service in Psychiatry Award, American College of Psychiatrists, both 2003; Salmon Award, New York Academy of Medicine, 2003; Benjamin Franklin Creativity Laureate Award, Smithsonian Associates and Creativity Foundation, 2004; David Dean Brockman Lectureship Award, American College of Psychoanalysts, 2004; Austrian Medal of Honour for Science and Art, Republic of Austria, 2005; Biotechnology Achievement Award, New York University School of Medicine, 2006; Benjamin Franklin Medal for Distinguished Achievement in the Sciences, American Philosophical Society, 2006; McKnight Foundation Recognition Award, McKnight Conference for Neuroscience, 2006; Louise T. Blouin Creativity Foundation Award, 2006; McGovern Prize, Cosmos Club, 2007; National Academies Communication Award for book of the year and *Los Angeles Times* Book Prize for *In Search of Memory: The Emergence of a New Science of Mind,* 2007. Honorary degrees from University of Vienna, University of Edinburgh, University of Turin, University of Montreal, New York University, University College of London, Rockefeller University, Jewish Theological Seminary, and Weitzmann Institute in Israel.

WRITINGS:

Cellular Basis of Behavior: An Introduction to Behavioral Neurobiology, W.H. Freeman (San Francisco, CA), 1976.

A Cell-Biological Approach to Learning, Society for Neuroscience (Bethesda, MD), 1978.

Behavioral Biology of Aplysia: A Contribution to the Comparative Study of Opisthobranch Molluscs, W.H. Freeman (San Francisco, CA), 1979.

(Editor, with James G. Schwartz) *Principles of Neural Science,* Elsevier North Holland (New York, NY), 1981, 3rd edition (with James G. Schwartz and Thomas M. Jessell), 1991.

(Editor) *Molecular Neurobiology in Neurology and Psychiatry,* Raven Press (New York, NY), 1987.

Essentials of Neural Science and Behavior, Appleton & Lange (Norwalk, CT), 1995.

(With Larry R. Squire) *Memory: From Mind to Molecules,* Scientific American Library (New York, NY), 1999.

Psychiatry, Psychoanalysis, and the New Biology of Mind, American Psychiatric Publishing (Washington, DC), 2005.

In Search of Memory: The Emergence of a New Science of Mind, W.W. Norton (New York, NY), 2006.

Contributor to *Cell, Science,* and *Current Biology.*

SIDELIGHTS: Eric R. Kandel is a Nobel Prize-winning scientist who has also written several award-winning books in the areas of neuroscience, psychiatry, and psychology. Kandel was born in Austria and lived through the Nazi invasion of that country in the 1930s. A personal witness to the horrors of Kristallnacht, the destruction of thousands of Jewish homes, businesses, and synagogues on November 9 and 10, 1938, Kandel escaped Austria with his parents and brother before World War II began, and the family settled in the United States. Kandel went on to attend Harvard College, where he earned a degree in European history and made a friendship with a young Austrian student that would forever shape his professional destiny. The parents of Anna Kris were prominent psychoanalysts and personal friends of Sigmund Freud, widely considered to be the father of psychoanalysis. Time spent with the Kris family instilled in Kandel a deep interest in the field, and he was inspired to attend medical school in order to earn a degree in psychiatry.

Kandel went on to enjoy an illustrious career as a neuroscientist, ultimately becoming the founding director of Columbia University's Center for Neurobiology and Behavior. It was at Columbia that Kandel was inspired to create a textbook to aid students in their study of neural science. He explained in a biography posted on the Nobel Prize Web site: "In college and medical school I was never a good note-taker. I always preferred sitting back, enjoying the lecture, and just scribbling down a few words here and there. When I came to Columbia to develop the neural science course, I was struck by how much energy students were devoting to writing out every single word of lectures, and I wanted to help them get over that." The result was the text book, *Principles of Neural Science,* edited with James G. Schwartz, and widely used at the undergraduate and graduate level. Kandel continued: "Our textbook was the first attempt to bridge cell and molecular biology to neural science and neural science to behavior and clinical states."

In 2006, six years after winning (with Arvid Carlsson and Paul Greengard) the Nobel Prize in Physiology or Medicine, Kandel published an autobiography sharing details of his childhood in Nazi-occupied Austria, his Brooklyn schooling, his education as a scientist, and his illustrious career as a researcher. *In Search of Memory: The Emergence of a New Science of Mind* was generally well received by critics. Many agreed that the early part of Kandel's memoir was exceptional. "By far the strongest part of the whole book are those sections where he describes events in Austria," wrote *Popular Science Online* contributor Brian Clegg, who added: "It's a tour-de-force as a popular science book by a scientist, and should be recommended reading for anyone interested in the brain." A reviewer for the *Economist* commented: "The weaving of science and memoir, in a clear and unadorned style, is especially effective in the first half of the book. In the latter half, long sections on the biotechnology industry and on Austrian anti-Semitism break up the chronology, and the book becomes harder to follow." In a review in *Publishers Weekly,* a critic described the book as a "fascinating portrait of a scientist's formation: learning to trust his instincts on what research to pursue and how to pose a researchable question and formulate an experiment." Sherwin B. Nuland took particular note of Kandel's "ability to weave seamlessly into the narrative his explications of some of the most fundamental precepts upon which contemporary biological research is based, so that a reader comes to understand their unifying themes." He added in his review for the *New York Times Book Review:* "If there is another book that does a better job of demonstrating how biological research is done, or of telling the story of a brilliant scientist's career, I don't know it."

BIOGRAPHICAL AND CRITICAL SOURCES:

PERIODICALS

Economist, March 4, 2006, "Proustian Moments; Science of the Mind," review of *In Search of Memory: The Emergence of a New Science of Mind,* p. 78.

New York Times Book Review, April 9, 2006, Sherwin B. Nuland, "The Secret Life of the Mind," review of *In Search of Memory,* p. 14.

Publishers Weekly, February 6, 2006, review of *In Search of Memory,* p. 62.

ONLINE

Nobel Prize Web site, http://www.nobelprize.org/ (October 11, 2007), profile of Eric R. Kandel.

Howard Hughes Medical Institute Web site, http://www.hhmi.org/ (December 19, 2007), profile of Eric R. Kandel.

Popular Science Online, http://www.popularscience. co.uk/ (October 11, 2007), review of *In Search of Memory.*

*   *   *

KAPLAN, Beth 1950-
(Elizabeth Kaplan)

PERSONAL: Born 1950, in New York, NY; daughter of Jacob Gordin (a biologist) and Sylvia Mary Kaplan; children: two. *Education:* London Academy of Music and Dramatic Art, undergraduate degree, c. 1972; University of British Columbia, M.F.A.

ADDRESSES: Home—Toronto, Ontario, Canada. *Agent*—Richard Curtis, Richard Curtis Associates, 171 E. 74th St., Ste. 2, New York, NY 10021. *E-mail*—Beth@bethkaplan.ca.

CAREER: Writer and educator. Ryerson University, Toronto, Ontario, Canada, instructor in memoir and personal essay writing, 1995. Worked as a professional actress during the 1970s.

AWARDS, HONORS: Canadian Jewish Playwriting Competition prize, 1994, for *Gordin in America.*

WRITINGS:

Finding the Jewish Shakespeare: The Life and Legacy of Jacob Gordin, Syracuse University Press (Syracuse, NY), 2007.

Contributor to periodicals, including *Globe and Mail.*

SIDELIGHTS: Beth Kaplan's first book, *Finding the Jewish Shakespeare: The Life and Legacy of Jacob Gordin,* began in 1982 as a thesis for her M.F.A. degree from the University of British Columbia. Gordin was Kaplan's great-grandfather and is considered to be one of the most eminent Yiddish playwrights of the modern era. Kaplan's thesis also includes Gordin's biography as well as commentary on his continuing legacy. After the project was completed, Kaplan felt compelled to further research Gordin's life, and spent the next twenty years compiling information from Yiddish texts before publishing *Finding the Jewish Shakespeare.* In a review of the book for *All about Jewish Theatre,* Carly Kaufman noted that Kaplan's "writing captures not just the events of his life, but also brings out Jacob Gordin's true persona." A reviewer for the *Midwest Book Review* found the biography to be "rich with nuanced detail." "Engaging and informative" was how *Booklist* reviewer George Cohen described the book, pointing out that Kaplan "brings the man and his creative work to life."

The daughter of a New York Jew and a British gentile, Kaplan has written numerous personal essays discussing her continuing journey to unite her disparate identities. In one article published in *Pakn Treger,* Kaplan remarked: "Though there is great charm in my mother's heritage of pastoral villages, stern Victorian grannies, and English eccentrics, I am drawn to my father's family's tales. I love the lush, dark flow of the Russian language; the stories of Elizavet grad and Odessa, Tolstoy and tsars, shtetls and pogroms, and the painful steamer trip from one century to another, from the precarious comfort of home to a rich, indifferent land. My years of research have shown me, at last, where I belong: to writing and the theater. To the Shakespeare of the Jews."

BIOGRAPHICAL AND CRITICAL SOURCES:

PERIODICALS

Booklist, March 15, 2007, George Cohen, review of *Finding the Jewish Shakespeare: The Life and Legacy of Jacob Gordin,* p. 14.

Pakn Treger, fall, 2004, Beth Kaplan, "The Family Kaplan."

ONLINE

All about Jewish Theatre, http://www.jewish-theatre. com/ (October 11, 2007), Carly Kaufman, review of *Finding the Jewish Shakespeare.*

Beth Kaplan Home Page, http://www.bethkaplan.ca (October 11, 2007).

Midwest Book Review, http://www.midwestbook review.com/ (August, 2007), review of *Finding the Jewish Shakespeare.**

* * *

KAPLAN, Elizabeth
   See KAPLAN, Beth

* * *

KEAL, Jenny 1951-

PERSONAL: Born April 23, 1951, in Southampton, England; daughter of Owen George (a steel erector) and Elizabeth Louise (a homemaker) Ward; married Michael Keal (divorced); married David Bellamy (an artist and author), September 9, 1997; children: (first marriage) Joanne Elizabeth, Caroline Jane. *Ethnicity:* "Anglo-Saxon." *Education:* Attended secretarial school for five years. *Politics:* Liberal. *Religion:* "Atheist." *Hobbies and other interests:* Gardening (vegetables), making jewelry.

ADDRESSES: Home and office—Powys, Wales. *E-mail*—jenny@davidbellamy.co.uk.

CAREER: Held clerical positions in Southampton, England, between 1967 and 1984; Paul Reeves Photography, Romsey, Hampshire, England, director, 1984-90; self-employed artist and writer in Wales, 1990—. Landscape painter.

WRITINGS:

(And illustrator) *Learn to Paint: Landscapes in Pastel,* Collins (London, England), 2003.

Contributor to *Leisure Painter.*

* * *

KEETON, Robert E. 1919-2007
   (Robert Ernest Keeton)

OBITUARY NOTICE— See index for *CA* sketch: Born December 16, 1919, in Clarksville, TX; died of complications from a pulmonary embolism, July 2, 2007, in Cambridge, MA. Lawyer, judge, educator, and author. Keeton began his career in Texas, where he practiced law and taught at Southern Methodist University before joining the faculty at Harvard University in the early 1950s. He remained at Harvard until 1979, when he was appointed a federal judge for the District of Massachusetts. He retired from the bench in 2006, when he was about eighty-five years old. Keeton's specialty was insurance law, and he is often credited with research that led to the passage of laws mandating no-fault automobile insurance in the commonwealth of Massachusetts in the 1960s, laws which served as benchmarks for insurance law throughout the United States. His other interests included the more general and wide-ranging category of tort law, which covers most crimes, intentional or otherwise, that do not involve a breach of contract. Keeton also taught future trial lawyers how to conduct themselves in the courtroom, and he was instrumental in enticing well-known lawyers into his classrooms to share their expert advice on courtroom behavior. Keeton received the Clarence Arthur Kulp Memorial Award from the American Risk and Insurance Association for his 1965 book *Basic Protection for the Traffic Victim: A Blueprint for Reforming Automobile Insurance,* the William B. Jones Award of the National Institute for Trial Advocacy, the Samuel E. Gates Litigation Award of the American College of Trial Lawyers, and other similar honors. His books, more than twenty in all, include an coedited work titled *Crisis in Car Insurance* (1968), *Venturing to Do Justice: Processes and Issues of Private Law Reform* (1969), and *Keeton on Judging in the American Legal System* (1999). He also coauthored *Insurance Law: A Guide to Fundamental Principles, Legal Doctrines, and Commercial Practices* (1988).

OBITUARIES AND OTHER SOURCES:

PERIODICALS

Los Angeles Times, August 6, 2007, p. B9.
New York Times, August 4, 2007, p. B10.

* * *

KEETON, Robert Ernest
   See KEETON, Robert E.

KELLY, Sheila M. 1931-

PERSONAL: Born February 15, 1931, in Canada; children: Mary Jill Hellman, Katherine Lynn Lum, Sara Anne Haynes. *Ethnicity:* "Manx-Scots." *Education:* University of Alberta, B.A.; University of Massachusetts, M.Sc., Ed.D. *Politics:* Independent. *Religion:* "Non-denominational."

ADDRESSES: Home—South Hadley, MA.

CAREER: Worked as schoolteacher in Saskatchewan, Canada, including a position as a demonstration teacher at University of Saskatchewan Lab School; preschool consultant and school psychologist in western Massachusetts, 1973-77; private practice as licensed clinical psychologist and consultant to two private schools, a day-care center, and Childrens' Aid Team in western Massachusetts, 1977-1995.

WRITINGS:

CHILDREN'S BOOKS; WITH SHELLEY ROTNER

Lots of Moms, Dial Books for Young Readers (New York, NY), 1996.
Lots of Dads, Dial Books for Young Readers (New York, NY), 1997.
About Twins, DK Ink (New York, NY), 1999.
Feeling Thankful, Millbrook Press (Brookfield, CT), 2000.
A.D.D. Book for Kids, Millbrook Press (Brookfield, CT), 2000.
Lots of Grandparents, Millbrook Press (Brookfield, CT), 2001.
What Can You Do? A Book about Discovering What You Do Well, Millbrook Press (Brookfield, CT), 2001.
Good-byes, Millbrook Press (Brookfield, CT), 2002.
Something's Different, Millbrook Press (Brookfield, CT), 2002.
Many Ways: How Families Practice Their Beliefs and Religions, Millbrook Press (Minneapolis, MN), 2006.

SIDELIGHTS: Sheila M. Kelly told *CA:* "My writing is a collaborative process with photographer Shelley Rotner. Our goal is few words, exactly matched to photographs. I chose subjects that related to my work, or about which I perceived a need in my therapeutic work with young children, their parents and teachers."

*   *   *

KENNEALLY, Christy

PERSONAL: Married. *Education:* National University of Ireland, B.A., B.Div.

ADDRESSES: Home—Wicklow, Ireland.

CAREER: Television presenter, scriptwriter, and author. Owner of a management training company.

WRITINGS:

The Joseph Coat and Other Patches, Dalton (Dublin, Ireland), 1977.
Out Foreign and Back, Dalton (Dublin, Ireland), 1979.
Strings and Things: Poems and Other Messages for Children, Paulist Press (New York, NY), 1984.
Miracles and Me: A Poem for Children, Paulist Press (New York, NY), 1986.
Maura's Boy: A Cork Childhood, Mercier Press (Dublin, Ireland), 1996.
Life after Loss: Helping the Bereaved, Mercier Press (Dublin, Ireland), 1999.
Second Son, Hodder Headline Ireland (Dublin, Ireland), 2005.
Small Wonders, Mercier Press (Douglas Village, Cork, Ireland), 2005.
The Remnant, Hodder Headline Ireland (Dublin, Ireland), 2006.

Writer of several television series about world religion, including *Heaven on Earth* and *Na Déithe Caillte* ("The Lost Gods").

SIDELIGHTS: Christy Kenneally is a prominent television presenter in his native Ireland, and has written and hosted a number of Irish television series. Kenneally has also written a number of books, several of which have been featured on Ireland's best-seller lists. His first novel, *Second Son,* rose to the third spot on the Irish best- seller list. Described as a "ridiculously far fetched" yet "well-written, fast paced thriller" by a *Bibliofemme* reviewer, the novel follows a New York priest named Michael Flaherty, who returns to the small Irish island where he spent his youth to search for his missing younger brother. He finds that the once simple way of life has been complicated by the establishment of an American fish factory. *The Remnant,* Kenneally's second work of fiction, also features Flaherty and a story that spans both sides of the Atlantic. A secret group called the Remnant is working from within the Vatican to commandeer the papacy in the dying pope's last days. The group is also responsible for the murders of a number of priests and nuns. Flaherty works with allies in both Italy and New York in an attempt to solve the murders and save the pope's life. A contributor to *Kirkus Reviews* commented that the novel provides "agreeable thrills and a few pleasant peeks into Italian domestic life."

BIOGRAPHICAL AND CRITICAL SOURCES:

PERIODICALS

Kirkus Reviews, December 15, 2006, review of *The Remnant,* p. 1236.

ONLINE

Bibliofemme, http://www.bibliofemme.com/ (October 11, 2007), review of *Second Son.*
Personally Speaking Web site, http://www.personally speaking.ie/ (October 11, 2007), author profile.*

*   *   *

KENNEDY, Holly

PERSONAL: Born in Alberta, Canada; married; children: two sons, a step-on, and a stepdaughter.

ADDRESSES: Home—Calgary, Alberta, Canada. *Agent*—Liza Dawson, Liza Dawson Associates, 350 7th Ave, Ste. 2003, New York, NY 10001. *E-mail*—holly@hollykennedy.com.

CAREER: Writer. Formerly worked in sales and business management.

WRITINGS:

The Tin Box, Forge Books (New York, NY), 2005.
The Penny Tree, New American Library Accent (New York, NY), 2007.

SIDELIGHTS: Holly Kennedy was one of the selected writers who traveled to Belize in 2000 to participate in the Francis Ford Coppola Writers Workshop. The short story she submitted to gain entry into the exclusive workshop was later expanded and turned into her first novel. Published in 2005, *The Tin Box* marks Kennedy's publishing debut. The novel introduces Kenly Lowen, a woman who hides a deep secret in her tin box. During her youth, she lived a nomadic life with her alcoholic father as he moved from job to job. Eventually they settle in Athabasca, a town in rural Alberta, Canada, and she befriends feisty Lexie and wiser-than-his-age Tommy, who lives with a facial disfigurement. When Kenly's father commits suicide, Tommy's mother takes her in. Kenly and Tommy grow closer and, just before he goes off to college, they lose their virginity in his tree house. Soon after, Kenly meets Ross and they also have sex. When she discovers she is pregnant, they marry. Kenly knows, however, that her child was conceived by Tommy and she must confront her husband with the truth. *BookLoons* contributor Hilary Williamson said the novel "is a beautiful story, full of surprises, that will take you through at least one full box of tissues." Writing in the *Romantic Times,* Sheri Melnick noted that "the author creatively uses flashbacks as she effortlessly plots this heartwarming novel." A contributor to *Publishers Weekly* commented that "the novel's moving conclusion is a testament to love and forgiveness."

Two years later Kennedy published her second novel, *The Penny Tree.* Annie Hillman, going through a divorce, moves back to her hometown of Eagan's Point, Washington, after losing her job in Seattle. Her younger son, Eric, has been quite ill. Meanwhile, her thirteen-year-old son, Luke, is skipping class and prefers to live with his father. Annie becomes a local celebrity when a mystery man continuously runs ads in the local paper claiming that she is the love of his life. Unable to discover the man's identity, Annie eventually confronts him on a local talk show. During all her stress, Annie finds solace by going back to a large tree to which she and her father nailed a penny once during previous hard times. Patty Engelmann, writing in *Booklist*, thought that this "heartrending story about love and family will touch readers' hearts and bring tears to their eyes." In a *Palo Alto Daily News* review, Terri Schlichenmeyer concluded that "if you want a good novel to tuck in your purse or suitcase, . . . grab this one. Reading *The Penny Tree* just makes cents."

Kennedy told *CA:* "I have wanted to be an author since I was ten years old and I never let go of that dream.

"People and the commonality of our struggles [influence my work]. We all experience grief, joy, shame, humiliation, rage, and ultimately our lives also have many 'secrets' hidden away from the rest of the world, and that's where I believe the best stories are found."

When asked to describe her writing process, Kennedy said: "It's painful. I write, rewrite, rewrite some more, and then rewrite it all over again. However, that said, before I begin a book, I always know the beginning and the end.

"[I've learned] to trust myself. The moment I second-guess my ability to tell a story, it all goes south."

When asked which of her books is her favorite, Kennedy said: "It's always 'the next one' because I feel a certain tug toward the stories I have tucked away in my mind that have yet to be told.

"I want to make people laugh and cry. I'm honored when someone e-mails to tell me my work really touched them in some way."

BIOGRAPHICAL AND CRITICAL SOURCES:

PERIODICALS

Booklist, January 1, 2007, Patty Engelmann, review of *The Penny Tree*, p. 55.

Palo Alto Daily News, June 15, 2007, Terri Schlichenmeyer, review of *The Penny Tree*.
Publishers Weekly, August 22, 2005, review of *The Tin Box*, p. 36; October 30, 2006, review of *The Penny Tree*, p. 31.

ONLINE

Best Reviews, http://thebestreviews.com/ (May 27, 2007), Harriet Klausner, review of *The Penny Tree*.
BookLoons, http://www.bookloons.com/ (August 22, 2007), Hilary Williamson, review of *The Tin Box*.
Holly Kennedy Home Page, http://www.hollykennedy. com (August 22, 2007), author biography.
Holly Kennedy Web log, http://author-in-the-trenches. blogspot.com (August 22, 2007), author profile.
January Magazine, http://www.januarymagazine.com/ (August 22, 2007), Cherie Thiessen, review of *The Tin Box*.
Romantic Times, http://www.romantictimes.com/ (August 22, 2007), Sheri Melnick, reviews of *The Tin Box* and *The Penny Tree*.

* * *

KENYON, T.K.

PERSONAL: Married; children. *Education:* University of Iowa, M.F.A., Ph.D., 2003; completed postdoctoral research at the University of Pennsylvania.

ADDRESSES: Home—Stony Point, NY.

CAREER: Research scientist and writer.

AWARDS, HONORS: Truman Capote fellow, Iowa Writers' Workshop, 1997; Alsop Review Fiction Contest, 2003.

WRITINGS:

Rabid, Kunati (Largo, FL), 2007.

Contributor to periodicals, including *New York Stories, Big Muddy*, and *American Short Fiction*. Author of the blog *Science for Non-Majors*.

SIDELIGHTS: A graduate of the Iowa Writers' Workshop, T.K. Kenyon is also a research scientist whose postdoctoral work centered on neurodegenerative disorders such as Alzheimer's and Parkinson's. Kenyon is an accomplished writer, with seven published short fiction pieces and five papers published in scholarly journals. Her first novel, *Rabid,* was published in 2007 and features a multitalented protagonist named Dante who is both priest and neuroscientist. Sent to New England to uncover a pedophilic priest, he has a crisis of faith after falling for a parishioner named Bev, who sought Dante's guidance after learning of her husband's infidelity. The novel takes a suspenseful turn when Bev's jealousy ultimately leads to murder. Writing for *Bookslut,* Barbara J. King remarked: "Kenyon pulls together all the beauty and terror found in religion and all the beauty and terror found in science to create a fictional space where every person seeks light, whether at the lab bench, or at the church altar, or both." King concluded that Kenyon "makes you think, and you have fun along the way." *Booklist* reviewer David Pitt found the novel "quite unlike most standard commercial fare, a genre-bending story—part thriller, part literary slapdown." A contributor to *Publishers Weekly* commented that "Kenyon manages to rein her characters in nicely at the conclusion of this overwritten yet impressive medical thriller."

BIOGRAPHICAL AND CRITICAL SOURCES:

PERIODICALS

Booklist, December 1, 2006, David Pitt, review of *Rabid,* p. 25.
Publishers Weekly, October 30, 2006, review of *Rabid,* p. 38.

ONLINE

Bookslut, http://www.bookslut.com/ (September, 2007), Barbara J. King, review of *Rabid.*
T.K. Kenyon Home Page, http://www.tkkenyon.com (October 9, 2007).*

* * *

KERRIGAN, John
See WHITING, Charles

KESSLER, Leo
See WHITING, Charles

* * *

KING, Mia 1968-
[A pseudonym]
(Darien Hsu Gee)

PERSONAL: Born 1968; married; has children. *Education:* Attended Wellesley College, 1987-89; Rice University, B.A., 1991.

ADDRESSES: Home—Kamuela, HI. *Agent*—Jenny Bent, Trident Media Group, 41 Madison Ave., 36th Fl., New York, NY 10010. *E-mail*—mia@miaking.com.

CAREER: Co-owner of a golf academy; has also worked as a tax manager for Price Waterhouse, in Houston, TX, Beijing, China, and Palo Alto, CA, and for Sephora.com and Venture Strategy Group, both in San Francisco, CA.

WRITINGS:

Good Things (novel), Berkley Books (New York, NY), 2007.

Author of the blog *Mia Musings* and contributor to the blog *Debutante Ball.*

SIDELIGHTS: Mia King is a pseudonym of Darien Hsu Gee, who began to tell stories when she was still a child, using her parents' manual typewriter to compose her tales and keeping a journal faithfully. Although her earliest ambition was to grow up to become a writer, she took a more practical stance, attending college and going to work in an accounting firm. She eventually quit to write her first novel, learned more about the publishing business, and even went so far as to acquire a literary agent before deciding she was not quite ready to take the plunge. Only years later, after marrying, having children, and settling in Hawaii with her family, did she finally dust off her writing dreams. The result is her first published work, *Good Things,* a book that follows a young woman as she loses everything she thinks she possesses in order to learn who she truly is. Deidre McIntosh lives in Seattle and hosts a television show on how to make your home beautiful while still keeping your life simple. When the show gets canceled and Deidre finds herself homeless and without a roommate, her own life becomes far more complicated. King maintains her home-economics theme by including recipes that Deidre mentions over the course of the story. Patty Engelmann in *Booklist* dubbed King's effort "a fresh and thoroughly enjoyable story as enticing as the delectable recipes at the end of the book." *Curled Up with a Good Book* critic Karyn Johnson called the book "a pretty smart and sassy novel."

BIOGRAPHICAL AND CRITICAL SOURCES:

PERIODICALS

Booklist, December 1, 2006, Patty Engelmann, review of *Good Things,* p. 30.
Kirkus Reviews, December 1, 2006, review of *Good Things,* p. 1191.
Publishers Weekly, November 27, 2006, review of *Good Things,* p. 30.

ONLINE

Armchair Interviews, http://reviews.armchair interviews.com/ (August 28, 2007), Jilian Vallade, review of *Good Things.*
Curled Up with a Good Book, http://www.curledup. com/ (August 28, 2007), Karyn Johnson, review of *Good Things.*
Mia King Home Page, http://www.miaking.com (August 28, 2007).
Mia King MySpace Page, http://www.myspace.com/ mia_writes (August 28, 2007).

* * *

KLEIN, Matthew 1968-

PERSONAL: Born 1968; married; wife's name Laura. *Education:* Graduated from Yale University, 1990; attended Stanford Graduate School of Business.

ADDRESSES: *Home*—Rye Brook, NY. *Agent*—Philip G. Spitzer Literary Agency, 50 Talmage Farm Lane, East Hampton, NY 11937.

CAREER: Writer and entrepreneur. Founder of Releasc Software Corporation and TechPlanet, Inc. (technology firms), during 1990s; founder of Collective 2, a trading technology company.

WRITINGS:

Switchback (novel), Orion Books (London, England), 2006.
Con Ed (novel), Warner Books (New York, NY), 2007.

SIDELIGHTS: Matthew Klein is the author of *Con Ed,* "a propulsive, noirish tale, as well as a smart allegory on the false promise of the Internet bubble," observed a critic in *Kirkus Reviews.* The owner of a trading technology firm, Klein drew on his own experiences for the novel: he presided over the demise of a computer service company during the 1990s, "a very public, spectacular failure," he told *New York Times* contributor Kate Stone Lombardi. *Con Ed* centers on Kip Largo, a middle-aged con artist who has just been released from federal prison after serving a term for securities and mail fraud. While working at a menial job, Kip is approached by Lauren Napier, the wife of a billionaire casino mogul, who proposes an elaborate scam to bilk her husband. Kip reluctantly agrees to the plan, in part to help his son, Toby, who is being hounded by Russian mobsters over a gambling debt. "As with all good capers and con games, the author is always a few moves ahead of the reader," noted Otto Penzler in the *New York Sun.* *Library Journal* critic Susan Clifford Braun stated that "there are enough twists and turns in this story to keep the reader firmly engaged and totally surprised at the end." Writing in the *New York Times,* Janet Maslin described *Con Ed* as "a bright swindling-scam comedy set in the world of the Internet nouveau-riche. It's not a groundbreaking book. It's just funny, full of tricks and very, very hard to put down."

BIOGRAPHICAL AND CRITICAL SOURCES:

PERIODICALS

Booklist, December 1, 2006, Thomas Gaughan, review of *Con Ed,* p. 26.

Cleveland Plain Dealer, April 1, 2007, Nancy Fontaine, review of *Con Ed.*

Guardian (London, England), December 9, 2006, Matthew Lewin, "The Road to War," review of *Switchback.*

Kirkus Reviews, December 1, 2006, review of *Con Ed,* p. 1191.

Library Journal, January 1, 2007, Susan Clifford Braun, review of *Con Ed,* p. 95.

New York Sun, March 14, 2007, Otto Penzler, "Con You Top This?," review of *Con Ed.*

New York Times, March 8, 2007, Janet Maslin, "Out of Jail, Out of Options, Out on a Limb," review of *Con Ed;* March 11, 2007, Kate Stone Lombardi, "If Life Imitates Art, He's in Big Trouble."

Publishers Weekly, January 8, 2007, review of *Con Ed,* p. 32.

USA Today, March 29, 2007, Carol Memmott, review of *Con Ed.*

ONLINE

BookPage, http://www.bookpage.com/ (November 1, 2007), Bruce Tierney, "Whodunit?," review of *Con Ed.*

Mostly Fiction Book Reviews, http://mostlyfiction.com/ (November 1, 2007), Guy Savage, review of *Con Ed.*

Mystery Ink Online, http://www.mysteryinkonline.com/ (November 1, 2007), David J. Montgomery, review of *Con Ed.**

* * *

KONRAD, Klaus
See WHITING, Charles

* * *

KOSLOW, Sally

PERSONAL: Born in Fargo, ND; married Robert Koslow; children: Jed, Rory. *Education:* Graduated from University of Wisconsin-Madison.

ADDRESSES: Home—New York, NY. *Agent*—Christy Fletcher, Fletcher and Parry LLC, 78 5th Ave., New York, New York 10013.

CAREER: Writer for *Mademoiselle* and *Woman's Day* magazines; *McCall's,* New York, NY, editor-in-chief, 1994-2001; *Rosie* magazine, New York, NY, corporate editor, 2001-02; *Lifetime* magazine, New York, NY, editor-in-chief, 2002-04. Also teaches writing at Sarah Lawrence College, Algonkian Novel Workshop, and New York Writer's Workshop.

WRITINGS:

Little Pink Slips (novel), Putnam (New York, NY), 2007.

Contributor to periodicals, including *New York Observer,Town & Country, O the Oprah Magazine, Glamour, Ladies' Home Journal, Hallmark,Health, Redbook,* and *Good Housekeeping.*

SIDELIGHTS: Sally Koslow, the former editor-in-chief of *McCall's,* is the author of *Little Pink Slips,* a "dishy and delightful insider's view of the elite in magazine publishing," observed *Booklist* contributor Patty Engelmann. *Little Pink Slips* centers on Magnolia Gold, a New York editor who learns that her tasteful periodical, *Lady,* will be transformed into *Bebe,* an homage to celebrity Bebe Blake. The novel was inspired by events from the author's own life: during Koslow's tenure at *McCall's,* the publishers formed a partnership with television host Rosie O'Donnell, who renamed the magazine *Rosie* and served as its editor during the periodical's ill-fated eighteen-month run. "It wasn't exactly my story," Koslow told an interviewer on *Bookreporter.com.* "I was the editor-in-chief of *McCall's* and moved from that position to another executive job at the company when the magazine became a celebrity vehicle. I never actually worked with the celebrity. On the other hand, I continued to be close to the *McCall's* staff that did work with her, so I was conversant with that experience."

Little Pink Slips received mixed reviews. *New York Times* critic Janet Maslin stated that the novel "clearly falls into the chicks-who-snitch category, populated by disgruntled, shoe-obsessed office underlings and nannies. What's different and moderately interesting about this book is that its main character is in a position of power and knows a lot about the magazine business." Maslin added, however, that Koslow "can't decide whether to demonize or enjoy Bebe, and so she remains a large, improbable presence." A critic in *Kirkus Reviews* noted that the author's "zippy prose ably captures the manic intensity and not-always-glamorous world of New York magazines—even if classy Magnolia and her so-so love life are a bit of a snooze." Kathy Weissman, writing on *Bookreporter. com,* also complimented the author's narrative style, writing, "Although Koslow can be witty . . . , her tone never gets too brittle. Underneath the smart-aleckisms is a welcome optimism and honesty."

BIOGRAPHICAL AND CRITICAL SOURCES:

PERIODICALS

Booklist, March 15, 2007, Patty Engelmann, review of *Little Pink Slips,* p. 25.
Kirkus Reviews, March 1, 2007, review of *Little Pink Slips,* p. 188.
Library Journal, March 15, 2007, Rebecca Vnuk, review of *Little Pink Slips,* p. 58.
New York Times, April 16, 2007, Janet Maslin, "At Lady Magazine, a Ruthless Chick-Eat-Chick World," p. E6.
Publishers Weekly, February 19, 2007, review of *Little Pink Slips,* p. 147.

ONLINE

Bookreporter.com, http://www.bookreporter.com/ (May 11, 2007), "Author Talk: Sally Koslow," and Kathy Weissman, review of *Little Pink Slips.*
Sally Koslow Home Page, http://www.sallykoslow.com (October 11, 2007).*

*   *   *

KOSTOV, K.N.
See WHITING, Charles

*   *   *

KOSTOV, L.
See WHITING, Charles

KRIPAL, Jeffrey J. 1962-

PERSONAL: Born 1962. *Education:* Conception Seminary College, B.A., 1985; University of Chicago, M.A., 1987, Ph.D., 1993.

ADDRESSES: Home—Houston, TX. *Office*—Department of Religious Studies, Rice University, P.O. Box 1892, Houston, TX 77005-1892; fax: (713) 348-5486. *E-mail*—jjkripal@rice.edu.

CAREER: Writer, editor, and educator. Rice University, Houston, TX, Lynette Autry associate professor of religious studies, beginning 2002, became J. Newton Rayzor professor and chair of religious studies, beginning 2004.

AWARDS, HONORS: History of Religions Prize for Best First Book of 1995, American Academy of Religion, for *Kali's Child;* Contemplative practice fellowship, American Council of Learned Societies, 2006.

WRITINGS:

Kali's Child: The Mystical and the Erotic in the Life and Teachings of Ramakrishna, University of Chicago Press (Chicago, IL), 1995, 2nd edition, 1998.
(Editor, with T.G. Vaidyanathan) *Vishnu on Freud's Desk: A Reader in Psychoanalysis and Hinduism,* Oxford University Press (New York, NY), 1999.
Roads of Excess, Palaces of Wisdom: Eroticism & Reflexivity in the Study of Mysticism, University of Chicago Press (Chicago, IL), 2001.
(Editor, with G. William Barnard) *Crossing Boundaries: Essays on the Ethical Status of Mysticism,* Seven Bridges Press (New York, NY), 2002.
(Editor, with Rachel Fell McDermott) *Encountering Kali: In the Margins, at the Center, in the West,* University of California Press (Berkeley, CA), 2003.
(Editor, with Glenn W. Shuck) *On the Edge of the Future: Esalen and the Evolution of American Culture,* Indiana University Press (Bloomington, IN), 2005.
The Serpent's Gift: Gnostic Reflections on the Study of Religion, University of Chicago Press (Chicago, IL), 2006.

Esalen: America and the Religion of No Religion, University of Chicago Press (Chicago, IL), 2007.

Contributor to books, including *Religion, Homosexuality, and Literature,* edited by Michael L. Stemmeler and José Ignacio Cabezón, Monument Press (Las Colinas, TX), 1992; *Dreams and Dreaming: A Reader in Religious Studies, Anthropology, History, and Psychology,* edited by Kelly Bulkeley, St. Martin's Press (New York, NY), 2001; and *Encyclopedia of Religion,* 2nd edition, edited by Lindsay Jones, Macmillan (New York, NY), 2004. Contributor to periodicals, including *Tikkun, History of Religions, Common Knowledge, Chronicle of Higher Education,* and *Religious Studies Review.*

SIDELIGHTS: Jeffrey J. Kripal, a professor of religious studies, is the author of the controversial, award-winning book *Kali's Child: The Mystical and the Erotic in the Life and Teachings of Ramakrishna* and the critically acclaimed work *Esalen: America and the Religion of No Religion.* "I started out in a Catholic Benedictine seminary, where I became interested in the relationship between sexuality and celibacy," Kripal told *Publishers Weekly* contributor Donna Freitas. He added, "All of my books are about sexuality and spirituality."

In *Kali's Child,* Kripal offers a portrait of Ramakrishna, a nineteenth-century Hindu saint whose teachings incorporated Tantric and homoerotic mysticism. The book "was a very public document, taking on multiple public lives as it became the focus of scholarly essays and debates and, more dramatically, became the object of two national ban movements in India," the author noted on the Rice University Web site. Writing in the *Journal of the American Oriental Society,* Malcolm McLean deemed *Kali's Child* "a major comprehensive study which must be seen as the most important yet of this fascinating and important religious figure."

In *Esalen,* Kripal examines the history of California's Esalen Institute, a spiritual retreat and alternative think tank situated on the Big Sur coast. Founded by Michael Murphy and Dick Price in 1962, Esalen is often credited as the birthplace of the "human potential movement," and the center hosted such notable figures as Aldous Huxley, Hunter S. Thompson, Joan Baez, Timothy Leary, and Allen Ginsberg. Embracing a wide range of intellectual frameworks, religious disciplines, and psychological theories, the community endorses a philosophy of a "religion of no religion." "Esalen has always been a place of gnosis where the intellectual and experiential have intersected and coexisted, giving birth to new ideas and practices," Kripal stated in an essay in the *Chronicle of Higher Education,* noting that the center "played a catalytic role in gestalt and humanistic psychology in the early 60s, educational reform in the late 60s, the embryonic alternative-medicine movement of the early 70s, and the development of citizen diplomacy with the Soviet Union in the late 70s, 80s, and 90s."

Esalen received generally strong reviews. A critic in *Publishers Weekly* called Kripal "an engaging story-teller" who writes of his subject "with reverence and playfulness," and *Library Journal* contributor L. Kriz called the work "a spellbinding journey through art, pop psychology, Tantric sex, Cold War physics, psychedelic drugs, and . . . religion." Though Diane Johnson, writing in the *New York Times Book Review,* stated, "Kripal gives in considerable, maybe even too much, detail both the gossip and the intellectual developments at Esalen," she also noted that the author "makes many sympathetic points about the present spiritual state of America, even if his argument gets somewhat lost in the more lurid details of suicides, strange deaths and amazing paths to enlightenment." As Kripal told David Ian Miller in the *San Francisco Chronicle,* "When I look at American religious history, I see a long history of puritanism, of Christian fundamentalism. It's been there from Day One. But I also see what some historians would call American metaphysical religion." The author concluded, "In some ways, the book for me was a cry of the heart over the state of our culture in our country. It's an attempted intervention. Maybe not a very effective one, but nevertheless an attempt."

BIOGRAPHICAL AND CRITICAL SOURCES:

PERIODICALS

California Literary Review, August 1, 2007, Paul Comstock, "Jeffrey J. Kripal: Author of *Esalen.*"
Chronicle of Higher Education, April 13, 2007, Jeffrey J. Kripal, "From Emerson to Esalen: America's Religion of No Religion."

Journal of the American Oriental Society, July 1, 1997, Malcolm McLean, review of *Kali's Child: The Mystical and the Erotic in the Life and Teachings of Ramakrishna,* p. 571.

Library Journal, March 1, 2007, L. Kriz, review of *Esalen: America and the Religion of No Religion,* p. 88; March 1, 2007, Steve Young, review of *The Serpent's Gift: Gnostic Reflections on the Study of Religion,* p. 88.

New York Times Book Review, May 6, 2007, Diane Johnson, "Sex, Drugs and Hot Tubs," review of *Esalen,* p. 12.

Publishers Weekly, February 12, 2007, review of *Esalen,* p. 83; March 21, 2007, Donna Freitas, "Jeffrey J. Kripal: The Wonder of Esalen."

San Francisco Chronicle, May 21, 2007, David Ian Miller, "Finding My Religion: Author Jeffrey J. Kripal talks about *Esalen: America and the Religion of No Religion.*"

ONLINE

Rice University Web site, http://www.rice.edu/ (October 11, 2007), "Jeffrey J. Kripal."

*   *   *

KUEGLER, Sabine 1972-

PERSONAL: Born December 25, 1972, in Patan, Nepal; daughter of Klaus Peter (a linguist and missionary) and Doris (a linguist and missionary) Kuegler; raised in West Papua, Indonesia; married and divorced twice; partner of Klaus Kluge; children: Sophia, Lawrence, Julian, Vanessa. *Education:* Attended boarding school in Switzerland.

ADDRESSES: Home—Munich, Germany.

CAREER: Owner of a media production company and publishing house in Munich, Germany. Has also worked for a hotel chain.

WRITINGS:

Dschungelkind, Droemer (Munich, Germany), 2005, translation published as *Jungle Child,* Virago Press (London, England), 2005, published as

Child of the Jungle: The True Story of a Girl Caught between Two Worlds, Warner Books (New York, NY), 2007.

SIDELIGHTS: Sabine Kuegler is the author of *Child of the Jungle: The True Story of a Girl Caught between Two Worlds,* "a unique, intercultural coming-of[-]age tale," observed *Booklist* contributor Deborah Donovan. In 1980, seven-year-old Kuegler, the daughter of German linguists and Christian missionaries, accompanied her family to a remote village in West Papua, Indonesia, where they lived with the primitive Fayu tribe. "Nothing could have prepared us for life in the Lost Valley," Kuegler told Katy Regan in *Marie Claire.* "We had only a simple wooden house with no running water or electricity. We had to radio in to the base every morning to let them know we were OK. The Fayu were cannibals, and even though we never witnessed this ourselves, there was always the risk that they might eat us." The Fayu proved most hospitable, however, and Kuegler quickly adjusted to life in the jungle, learning to speak the Fayu language, dining on roast bats, and hunting with a bow and arrow.

At age seventeen, Kuegler was sent to a Swiss boarding school to learn Western ways, but she experienced severe culture shock. She married young after becoming pregnant, sank into depression, and attempted suicide. According to *Library Journal* contributor Lisa Klopfer, "Kuegler ends her book in despair of ever adjusting fully to the Western world." "A lot of me refuses to adapt to life here," the author told Elizabeth Grice in the London *Telegraph.* "I have the constant feeling that I am not where I should be." She added, "I am unhappy, not with my life, but with the situation I am in—not being able to reach the point of saying I am home."

Child of the Jungle received generally strong reviews. A critic in *Publishers Weekly* stated that readers "will find this account of a most unusual childhood engrossing," and in *BookPage,* Megan Brenn-White noted that Kuegler's sense of displacement "seems a completely appropriate reaction to such a huge transition and an honest ending to a story that is incredible and very real at the same time."

BIOGRAPHICAL AND CRITICAL SOURCES:

BOOKS

Dschungelkind, Droemer (Munich, Germany), 2005, translation published as *Jungle Child,* Virago

Press (London, England), 2005, published as *Child of the Jungle: The True Story of a Girl Caught between Two Worlds,* Warner Books (New York, NY), 2007.

PERIODICALS

Booklist, December 15, 2006, Deborah Donovan, review of *Child of the Jungle,* p. 14.

Kirkus Reviews, December 15, 2006, review of *Child of the Jungle,* p. 1258.

Library Journal, January 1, 2007, Lisa Klopfer, review of *Child of the Jungle,* p. 118.

Marie Claire, July, 2006, Katy Regan, "'I Grew Up with Cannibals,'" p. 86.

Publishers Weekly, December 18, 2006, review of *Child of the Jungle,* p. 54.

Telegraph (London, England), September 20, 2005, Elizabeth Grice, "I Don't Know Where Home Is."

ONLINE

BookPage, http://www.bookpage.com/ (October 11, 2007), Megan Brenn-White, "At Home in the Jungle," review of *Child of the Jungle.*

Perceptive Travel, http://www.perceptivetravel.com/ (November 1, 2007), Anastasia M. Ashman, review of *Child of the Jungle.*

Sabine Kuegler Home Page, http://www.junglechild.co.uk (October 11, 2007).*

L

LAMB, Marion J. 1939-

PERSONAL: Born July 29, 1939, in Aldeburgh, England; daughter of Cyril (a news agent) and Charlotte (a homemaker) Lamb. *Ethnicity:* "White Anglo-Saxon." *Education:* University College, London, B.Sc. (with first-class honors), 1961, Ph.D., 1965. *Politics:* Liberal Democrat.

ADDRESSES: Home—London, England. *E-mail*—marionlamb@btinternet.com.

CAREER: Medical Research Council, Radiation Biology Unit, Didcot, England, scientist, 1964-66; University of London, Birkbeck College, London, England, began as lecturer, became senior lecturer in biology, 1966-94; researcher and writer, 1994—.

WRITINGS:

Biology of Ageing, Wiley (New York, NY), 1977.
(With Eva Jablonka) *Epigenetic Inheritance and Evolution: The Lamarckian Dimension,* Oxford University Press (New York, NY), 1995.
(With Eva Jablonka) *Evolution in Four Dimensions: Genetic, Epigenetic, Behavioral, and Symbolic Variation in the History of Life,* illustrated by Anna Zeligowski, MIT Press (Cambridge, MA), 2005.

Contributor of articles and reviews to scientific journals.

SIDELIGHTS: Marion J. Lamb told *CA:* "I decided to retire early from academic life in order to spend more time thinking and writing. With Eva Jablonka I wrote *Evolution in Four Dimensions: Genetic, Epigenetic, Behavioral, and Symbolic Variation in the History of Life,* a semi-popular book, to try to convince people, especially young biologists, that evolutionary biology cannot be reduced to 'selfish genes.'"

*   *   *

LANTIGUA, John

PERSONAL: Born in New York, NY. *Education:* Graduated from Jacksonville University.

ADDRESSES: Home—FL. *Office*—Palm Beach Post, P.O. Box 24700, West Palm Beach, FL 33416. *E-mail*—john_lantigua@pbpost.com.

CAREER: Journalist and novelist. Reporter for *Hartford Courant, Chicago Tribune,* and *Washington Post;* reporter for United Press International in Honduras and Nicaragua; *Miami Herald,* Miami, FL, reporter, 1993-98; *Palm Beach Post,* Palm Beach, FL, reporter, 2002—.

AWARDS, HONORS: Edgar Award nomination for best first novel, for *Heat Lightning;* Pulitzer Prize for investigative reporting, 1999; Overseas Press Club Award, 2002; National Magazine Award, 2002; Robert F. Kennedy Memorial Journalism Award, 2004 and 2006.

WRITINGS:

NOVELS

Heat Lightning, Putnam (New York, NY), 1987.
Burn Season, Putnam (New York, NY), 1989.
Twister, Simon & Schuster (New York, NY), 1992.
Player's Vendetta: A Little Havana Mystery, Signet (New York, NY), 1999, published as *La ficha roja/The Red Chip,* Alfaguara (Miami, FL), 2000.
The Ultimate Havana, Signet (New York, NY), 2001.
The Lady from Buenos Aires: A Willie Cuesta Mystery, Arte Público Press (Houston, TX), 2007.

Contributor to periodicals, including *Newsweek* and *Nation.*

SIDELIGHTS: John Lantigua, a Pulitzer Prize-winning journalist who has extensive reporting experience in Nicaragua and Honduras, is the author of several critically acclaimed crime novels, including *Burn Season* and *The Lady from Buenos Aires: A Willie Cuesta Mystery.* In Lantigua's debut work, *Heat Lightning,* San Francisco homicide detective David Cruz investigates the murder of Gloria Soto, a refugee from El Salvador who was shot execution-style. *Heat Lightning* "avoids the politics of the situation, relying on sharp observations of the Latino environment to flavor" the tale, observed *Publishers Weekly* critic Sybil Steinberg.

In *Burn Season,* Lantigua's second novel, Costa Rican police inspector Eddie Santos looks into a deadly car bombing outside the nightclub of former New Yorker Jack Lacey. Though Lacey is convinced the explosion was the work of a guerilla force, Santos suspects the club owner isn't entirely forthcoming. As he delves deeper into the case, Santos becomes involved with a beautiful Nicaraguan diplomat, a wealthy businessman, and a CIA agent. Steinberg praised the work's "Casablancan ambience and characters, and reporterly detail," and called *Burn Season* "another darkly gripping read." Set in Paradise, Texas, *Twister* centers on burned-out journalist Edward Thomas. While covering a story that has divided the town along religious lines, Thomas discovers a decades-old mystery involving oil, drugs, corruption, and murder. A critic in *Publishers Weekly* called Lantigua "a direct descendant of Ross Macdonald and—except for a marked lack of humor—Chandler and Hammett."

Lantigua has also written three novels featuring Miami private investigator Willie Cuesta. *Player's Vendetta: A Little Havana Mystery* concerns Roberto Player, a Miami resident whose parents were killed trying to flee from Cuba when he was just a child. After he returns from a trip to his homeland, Player tells his fiancée, Ellie Hernandez, that he knows the identity of his parents' murderer and vows to avenge their deaths. When Player promptly disappears, Ellie hires Cuesta to find him before he follows through with his plan. "There is no shortage of action in this fast-paced adventure," observed Andy Plonka in *Mystery Reader.* The critic added that "Lantigua draws a vibrant portrait of Little Havana—the physical description of the shops, homes and people inhabiting this community in Miami is real enough that reader[s] can almost believe that they have been there."

In *The Ultimate Havana,* a "fast-paced and engrossing" novel, according to *Mystery Reader* critic Jennifer Monahan Winberry, Cuesta must locate Carlos Espada, a tobacco company salesman who has mysteriously vanished. After Cuesta discovers phony Cuban cigars in Espada's ransacked office, the investigator finds himself drawn into the murky world of smuggling and counterfeiting. "*The Ultimate Havana* is written in the style of the classic, gritty P.I. novels," Winberry remarked, "taking full advantage of the steamy Miami setting and the surrounding Caribbean." An Argentine woman asks Cuesta to find her dead sister's long-lost daughter in *The Lady from Buenos Aires.* Though the novel focuses on Argentina's "dirty war" conducted by a ruthless military regime during the 1970s and 1980s, "Lantigua never forgets he's writing a mystery, not a polemic," wrote *Booklist* contributor David Pitt.

BIOGRAPHICAL AND CRITICAL SOURCES:

PERIODICALS

Booklist, March 15, 2007, David Pitt, review of *The Lady from Buenos Aires: A Willie Cuesta Mystery,* p. 29.
Internet Bookwatch, September 2007, review of *The Lady from Buenos Aires.*
Library Journal, October 1, 1987, Jo Ann Vicarel, review of *Heat Lightning,* p. 111; June 1, 2001, Barbara Hoffert, review of *La ficha roja/The Red Chip,* p. 56.

New York Times Book Review, November 26, 1989, Newgate Callendar, review of *Burn Season,* p. 33; February 2, 1992, Marilyn Stasio, review of *Twister,* p. 19.

Publishers Weekly, August 28, 1987, Sybil Steinberg, review of *Heat Lightning,* p. 68; August 25, 1989, Sybil Steinberg, review of *Burn Season,* p. 51; November 29, 1991, review of *Twister,* p. 44.

ONLINE

Mystery Reader, http://www.themysteryreader.com/ (May 21, 2001), Jennifer Monahan Winberry, review of *The Ultimate Havana;* (October 11, 2007), Andy Plonka, review of *Player's Vendetta: A Little Havana Mystery.**

*   *   *

LAVALLEY, Tamara Faye
   See MESSNER, Tammy Faye

*   *   *

LAVALLEY, Tammy Faye
   See MESSNER, Tammy Faye

*   *   *

LEE, Min Jin 1968-

PERSONAL: Born 1968, in Seoul, Korea; immigrated to the United States, 1976; married; children: Sam. *Education:* Yale University, graduated 1993; studied law at Georgetown University.

ADDRESSES: Home—New York, NY.

CAREER: Writer. Practiced law in New York, NY.

AWARDS, HONORS: NYFA fellowship; Henry Wright Prize for Nonfiction; James Ashmun Veech Prize for Fiction; *Missouri Review,* Peden Prize, for best story, and Narrative Prize, for new and emerging writer.

WRITINGS:

Free Food for Millionaires (novel), Warner Books (New York, NY), 2007.

Work represented in anthologies, including *To Be Real,* Doubleday (New York, NY), 1995, and *Breeder,* Seal Press (Emeryville, CA), 2001.

SIDELIGHTS: Min Jin Lee is a Korea-born writer who was educated at Yale and Georgetown and practiced law in New York before becoming a full-time writer. As a child, she immigrated with her family to the Elmhurst section of Queens, New York, which is also the setting of her debut novel, *Free Food for Millionaires.* Casey Han, recently graduated from Princeton University, and her sister, Tina, a M.I.T. student, are at the home of their parents, Joseph and Leah, who work in a dry cleaning store and who have dedicated their lives to providing the best they could for their daughters. Tina is the more compliant sister, but when the rebellious Casey informs her father that she is not going to attend Columbia Law School, where she has been accepted, but has chosen to instead "find herself," the enraged Joseph tells her to leave their home, and Casey is on her own.

Although she attended an Ivy League school, Casey is uncomfortable in the world of her classmates. She wants success and love and to fit in but does not want to sacrifice as her parents have. Her mentor, Sabine, was born in her mother's village, is married to a wealthy American and is part of the fashion world. Casey wants to create hats but takes a job working at a bank to support herself until she decides which path she will follow. She also immerses herself in the writings of British authors who include the Bronte sisters, Anthony Trollope, and George Eliot, and in which she sees a similarity to the Korean fairy tales told to her by her mother.

New York Times Book Review contributor Liesl Schillinger praised Lee's treatment of both generations—Casey's and that of her parents. *USA Today* reviewer Carol Memmott wrote: "As much as this is an immigrant story, it's also an American story full of class struggle, rugged individualism, social status and above all, the money haves and have-nots. Most of all it's an epic meditation on love, both familial and romantic."

BIOGRAPHICAL AND CRITICAL SOURCES:

PERIODICALS

Chicago Sun Times, August 26, 2007, Jae-Ha Kim, review of *Free Food for Millionaires.*

Library Journal, March 15, 2007, Beth E. Andersen, review of *Free Food for Millionaires,* p. 61.

New York Times Book Review, July 1, 2007, Liesl Schillinger, review of *Free Food for Millionaires,* p. 13.

Publishers Weekly, January 22, 2007, Judith Rosen, profile of author, p. 64; January 22, 2007, review of *Free Food for Millionaires,* p. 155.

USA Today, May 24, 2007, Carol Memmott, review of *Free Food for Millionaires,* p. 6.

ONLINE

Asian American Writers Workshop, http://aaww.org/ (September 27, 2007), Ginny Too, "Interview: Min Jin Lee."

BookLoons, http://www.bookloons.com/ (September 27, 2007), Rheta Van Winkle, review of *Free Food for Millionaires.*

BookPage, http://www.bookpage.com/ (September 27, 2007), Kristy Kiernan, review of *Free Food for Millionaires.*

Bookreporter.com, http://www.bookreporter.com/ (September 27, 2007), Shannon Luders-Manuel, review of *Free Food for Millionaires.*

Min Jin Lee Home Page, http://minjinlee.com (September 27, 2007).

Min Jin Lee MySpace Page, http://www.myspace.com/ (September 27, 2007).

Mostly Fiction Book Reviews, http://www.mostly fiction.com/ (June 22, 2007), Poornima Apte, review of *Free Food for Millionaires.*

Newsweek Online, http://www.msnbc.msn.com/ (July 13, 2007), Charlene Dy, "Forget the Comparisons. She's Unique: After Years of Labor, Min Jin Lee Is an Overnight Sensation."*

*   *   *

LEONARD, Angela M.
  See LEONARD, Angela Michele

LEONARD, Angela Michele 1954-
  (Angela M. Leonard)

PERSONAL: Born June 26, 1954, in Washington, DC; daughter of Walter (a college administrator and lawyer) and Betty (an executive administrative assistant) Leonard. *Ethnicity:* "African American." *Education:* Harvard University, A.B. (cum laude), 1976; Vanderbilt University, M.L.S., 1981; George Washington University, M.Phil., Ph.D., 1994. *Politics:* Independent. *Religion:* Roman Catholic.

ADDRESSES: Home—Baltimore, MD. *Office*—Loyola College in Maryland, 4501 N. Charles St., Baltimore, MD 21210. *E-mail*—aleonard@loyola.edu.

CAREER: Loyola College in Maryland, Baltimore, assistant professor, 1998—.

WRITINGS:

(Under name Angela M. Leonard; editor) *Antislavery Materials at Bowdoin College; A Finding Aid,* Bowdoin College (Brunswick, ME), 1992.

(Editor) *Daniel J. Boorstin: A Comprehensive and Selectively Annotated Bibliography,* foreword by Boorstin, Greenwood Press (Westport, CT), 2001.

*   *   *

LEONE, Angela Tehaan

PERSONAL: Married.

ADDRESSES: Home—McLean, VA.

CAREER: Writer, poet, and teacher.

MEMBER: Radius of Arab American Writers.

WRITINGS:

Swimming toward the Light (novel), Syracuse University Press (Syracuse, NY), 2007.

Contributor to periodicals, including *Washington Post, Christian Science Monitor, Washingtonian, Ladies' Home Journal,* and the *New York Times.*

SIDELIGHTS: Angela Tehaan Leone is a fiction writer, poet, and teacher of English and dramatic arts living in McLean, Virginia. While writing the novel *Swimming toward the Light,* Leone claims on her home page to have learned more about herself. Leone stated: "The memories that came back to me as I was writing, reconnected me with my ethnic heritage, which, of course, is an essential part of who I am, a part I can now fully embrace and welcome."

Despite being a work of fiction, *Swimming toward the Light* is based on Leone's own life and family. The novel features a Lebanese-American family living in Washington, DC, where young Irene attempts to develop freely despite her mother's attempts to allow any sort of chance development outside her control. A contributor to *Publishers Weekly* suggested that some readers could "be seduced by the Mideast immigrant angle," but overall, lamented that "the story and story-telling are disappointing." Emily Cook, writing in *Booklist,* concluded that "fans of Arab-American literature will especially love the details that flavor Leone's touching novel."

BIOGRAPHICAL AND CRITICAL SOURCES:

PERIODICALS

Booklist, February 1, 2007, Emily Cook, review of *Swimming toward the Light,* p. 32.
Publishers Weekly, January 8, 2007, review of *Swimming toward the Light,* p. 33.

ONLINE

Angela Tehaan Leone Home Page, http://www.angelatehaanleone.com (August 20, 2007), author biography.*

*   *   *

LEONI, Giulio 1951-

PERSONAL: Born August 12, 1951, in Rome, Italy. *Education:* Earned bachelor's degree.

ADDRESSES: *Home*—Rome, Italy. *E-mail*—giulio.leoni@istruzione.it.

CAREER: Writer and poet. Worked in human resources for the Italian government.

AWARDS, HONORS: Premio Alberto Tedeschi, 2000, for *Dante Alighieri e i delitti della Medusa.*

WRITINGS:

Dry Manhattan: Prohibition in New York City, Harvard University Press (Cambridge, MA), 2007.

NOVELS

La donna sulla luna, Mondadori (Milan, Italy), 2001.
E trentuno con la morte, Mondadori (Milan, Italy), 2003.
Il trionfo della volontà, Aliberti (Verbania, Italy), 2005.
La compagnia dei serpenti: Il deserto degli spettri, Mondadori (Milan, Italy), 2006.
La compagnia dei serpenti: Il sepolcro di Gengis Khan, Mondadori (Milan, Italy), 2007.

"DANTE ALIGHIERI" SERIES

Dante Alighieri e i delitti della Medusa, Mondadori (Milan, Italy), 2000.
I delitti del mosaico, Mondadori (Milan, Italy), 2004, translation by Anne Milano Appel published as *The Mosaic Crimes,* Harcourt (Orlando, FL), 2006, also published as *The Third Heaven Conspiracy,* Harvill Secker (London, England), 2006.
I delitti della luce, Mondadori (Milan, Italy), 2005.
La crociata delle tenebre, Mondadori (Milan, Italy), 2007.

Editor of literary quarterly *Simbola.*

SIDELIGHTS: Giulio Leoni is an Italian writer and poet whose writings are often set in his hometown of Rome and feature historic Italian figures, such as Dante Alighieri. Leoni worked in the human resources department of a large government organization after finishing his bachelor's degree in arts and literature. While doing this, he edited the quarterly poetry journal, *Simbola*. He stated on his home page: "Evidently administration wasn't in my stars, since I was much more involved with the darker sides of legends and improbabilities. And, mainly, in the pleasure of narrating." He left his job and began writing full time.

In 2006 his novel, *Delitti del Mosaico*, was translated into English by Anne Milano Appel and published as *The Mosaic Crimes*. Famed poet Dante Alighieri has been recently assigned as the prior of Florence, where he works to solve the murder of a master mosaicist of the Builders' Guild who was supervising the reconstruction of a church. A contributor to *Publishers Weekly* called it "a well-researched labyrinth of medieval Italian history and politics." A *Kirkus Reviews* critic thought that "readers will be either charmed or irritated by . . . Leoni's characterization of the poet as a cranky, sometimes obtuse genius." Laura A.B. Cifelli, writing in the *Library Journal*, concluded: "Elegantly written and beautifully translated, the language is descriptive without being flowery, smart without being pedantic."

BIOGRAPHICAL AND CRITICAL SOURCES:

PERIODICALS

Kirkus Reviews, November 15, 2006, review of *The Mosaic Crimes*, p. 1156.

Library Journal, December 1, 2006, Laura A.B. Cifelli, review of *The Mosaic Crimes*, p. 100.

Philadelphia Inquirer, April 1, 2007, Frank Wilson, review of *The Mosaic Crimes*.

Publishers Weekly, October 23, 2006, review of *The Mosaic Crimes*, p. 34.

ONLINE

Giulio Leoni Home Page, http://www.giulioleoni.it (August 21, 2007), author biography.

Green Man Review, http://www.greenmanreview.com/ (August 21, 2007), Donna Bird, review of *The Mosaic Crimes*.

OperaNarrativa.com, http://www.operanarrativa.com/ (July 25, 2006), author interview.

Thriller, http://www.thrillermagazine.it/ (August 21, 2007), Elio Marracci, author interview.

*　　*　　*

LERNER, Michael A.

PERSONAL: Male.

ADDRESSES: Office—Bard High School Early College, 525 E. Huston St., New York, NY 10002.

CAREER: Bard High School Early College, New York, NY, associate dean of studies, member of social studies faculty.

WRITINGS:

Dry Manhattan: Prohibition in New York City, Harvard University Press (Cambridge, MA), 2007.

SIDELIGHTS: Michael A. Lerner is the author of a history pinpointing the effects of prohibition on one region. In *Dry Manhattan: Prohibition in New York City*, he writes of the motives behind the passing of the eighteenth amendment to the Constitution, which took away the American freedom to drink alcohol. The people responsible had varying motives. Some wanted alcohol deemed illegal for religious reasons. Others were social reformers or businessmen who felt production would increase if their workers could not drink. A key figure was lobbyist William Anderson, who rallied upstate New York Republicans to become a greater block for prohibition than the numbers of city residents, many of whom were immigrants or children of immigrants, and most of whom were Democrats. Alcohol figured prominently in the cultures of the Irish, Italians, Jews, and Germans who enjoyed it, and for whom it was part of their celebrations. One argument for prohibition was that it would lessen the temptation for the young soldiers fighting in World War I.

Prohibition lasted from 1920 to 1933, and before it ended fine New York restaurants went out of business while speakeasies flourished. Prohibition agents, who were not official members of law enforcement but were chosen by those who supported the ban, were eventually joined by policemen because of pressure from the "dry" faction, although reluctantly, since they were then put in a position of arresting their friends and family. The working-class immigrants were targeted with greater frequency than upper-class lawbreakers, and the courts soon become clogged with cases brought for simple alcohol possession. Prohibition also provided a breeding ground for corruption, graft, and fostered a great many mob activities.

Lerner points out that although Prohibition was supported by, and was a goal of, the Women's Christian Temperance Union, not all women rallied around the cause. The largest group formed for the repeal of the law was the Women's Organization for National Prohibition Reform.

Library Journal contributor Frederick J. Augustyn wrote that Lerner's "engagingly written, fully annotated study will appeal to all social historians of the 20th century and popular culture enthusiasts."

BIOGRAPHICAL AND CRITICAL SOURCES:

PERIODICALS

Library Journal, February 15, 2007, Frederick J. Augustyn, review of *Dry Manhattan: Prohibition in New York City*, p. 132.
New Yorker, May 7, 2007, review of *Dry Manhattan*, p. 74.
New York Times Book Review, March 11, 2007, Pete Hamill, review of *Dry Manhattan*.
Publishers Weekly, December 4, 2006, review of *Dry Manhattan*, p. 43.

ONLINE

Bard High School Early College Web site, http://www.bard.edu/bhsec/ (September 28, 2007).*

*   *   *

LESY, Michael 1945-

PERSONAL: Born 1945. *Education:* Columbia University, B.A.; University of Wisconsin, M.A.; Rutgers University, Ph.D.

ADDRESSES: Office—Hampshire College, 893 West St., Amherst, MA 01002. *E-mail*—ma1HA@hampshire.edu.

CAREER: Hampshire College, Amherst, MA, professor of literary journalism, 1990—.

AWARDS, HONORS: Simon Fellow, United States Artists Foundation, 2007.

WRITINGS:

(Compiler) *Wisconsin Death Trip*, preface by Warren Susman, Pantheon Books (New York, NY), 1973.
Real Life: Louisville in the Twenties, Pantheon Books (New York, NY), 1976.
Time Frames: The Meaning of Family Pictures, Pantheon Books (New York, NY), 1980.
Bearing Witness: A Photographic Chronicle of American Life, 1860-1945, preface by Warren I. Susman, Pantheon Books (New York, NY), 1982.
Visible Light, photographs by Angelo Rizzuto and others, Times Books (New York, NY), 1985.
The Forbidden Zone, Farrar, Straus (New York, NY), 1987.
Rescues: The Lives of Heroes, Farrar, Straus (New York, NY), 1991.
Dreamland: America at the Dawn of the Twentieth Century, New Press/W.W. Norton (New York, NY), 1997.
Long Time Coming: A Photographic Portrait of America, 1935-1943, W.W. Norton (New York, NY), 2002.
Angel's World: The New York Photographs of Angelo Rizzuto, W.W. Norton (New York, NY), 2006.
Murder City: The Bloody History of Chicago in the Twenties, W.W. Norton (New York, NY), 2007.

ADAPTATIONS: Several of Lesy's books have been adapted as films, plays, dance performances, and operas; *Wisconsin Death Trip* was adapted as a film in 2000, written and directed by James Marsh, and broadcast on HBO, 2003.

SIDELIGHTS: With an educational background in social and cultural history, Michael Lesy has proceeded to explore the story of America through photographic narratives. Drawing on archival collections, his books both affirm and deny the nostalgia for the past; critics and library catalogers have often struggled to classify just what he is attempting to accomplish. Lesy himself does not really know, nor does he seem to believe that classifying his work is important. When asked by Robert Birnbaum on the *Identity Theory* Web site to label himself, Lesy replied: "I think I have a polymorphously perverse imagination and so—I will use whatever I can to try to tell some version of the truth. Whatever that is. I really believe in the truth. I think it exists. There are words for the truth in many human languages. They all have words for the truth."

Lesy's first book, *Wisconsin Death Trip,* was originally conceived as a film, but Lesy was still a graduate student at the time he conceived the project and he did not have the money to get the project off the ground. Instead, he settled on selecting photographs from the archives at the Wisconsin Historical Society, where he was aided by Paul Vanderbilt. "He had lots of pictures, and no one ever came in to see him," Lesy recalled for Birnbaum. Lesy was under the impression that Wisconsin was a dull place, but what he found in those photos was startling. A series of pictures shot in the town of Black River Falls from the 1890s to the 1910s revealed an economically depressed town whose ill fortunes were so unrelievedly grim as to be almost comical. Photos of poverty-stricken families, dead children, struggling farms and more seem "to confirm that the good old days were actually awful," commented Michael Rogers in the *Library Journal.* The book was eventually adapted as a movie by James Marsh.

Since *Wisconsin Death Trip,* Lesy has continued to offer photographic portraits of America's past accompanied by his text. As he explained to Birnbaum, he wished "to take bites out of American history in a steady way. I wanted to talk about the United States, decade by decade by decade." In some cases, such as with *Dreamland: America at the Dawn of the Twentieth Century* and *Long Time Coming: A Photographic Portrait of America, 1935-1943,* he takes a broad approach, while other books are more focused. *The Forbidden Zone,* for instance, is all about professionals—morticians, homicide detectives, prison wardens, even people working in slaughterhouses—who deal with death every day. Here, Lesy attempts to face the taboo subject of death head on. Despite the grim subject matter, "Mr. Lesy's subject is tolerable because

his prose is so clean," observed Christopher Lehmann-Haupt in a *New York Times* review. The critic, however, felt that the author's book falls short: "Instead of epiphanies [about death], we get mechanics." The more upbeat *Rescues: The Lives of Heroes* includes stories of selfless individuals, ranging from war heroes and activists for the handicapped to parents sacrificing for their children and ordinary citizens getting stabbed by assailants to protect people they did not even know. While *Publishers Weekly* critic Genevieve Stuttaford considered these tales inspiring, she added that "unfortunately, Lesy's pop-psychology efforts to analyze his heroes' actions are less successful."

Critics were more impressed by Lesy's sociological looks at America in such works as *Dreamland* and *Long Time Coming.* The works reflect both nostalgia and a sense that the past was not always as lovely as many recall. To populate the book with photos, Lesy drew on the Detroit Publishing Company collection housed at the Library of Congress. The company hired photographers to capture images around the country from around 1900 through the roaring Twenties. The pictures were designed to be lovely images of prosperous buildings, landmarks, and scenic vistas that customers would wish to buy. As Joanne Jacobson reported in a *Nation* review: "Lesy seems at once a dispassionate observer of the turn-of-the-twentieth-century American appetite for 'images of affirmation' and an impassioned advocate. . . . His book evokes the tensions between past and present that surround the entire enterprise of history-making, especially at self-conscious moments like our own, at the cusps of new centuries." Jacobson added: "These are striking images; but this is not an easy book to read. Text neither interrupts nor directs the reader's experience of the photographs. Between the introductory and concluding essays, only paired pages of brief news items, grouped year by year, break up the images. Lesy's reluctance to interfere with the material challenges the reader, conveying the sense that history is a slow, unpredictable process of accretion rather than a purposeful, linear drama." Lesy's follow up, *Long Time Coming,* uses pictures from the U.S. Farm Security Administration's photography project of the 1930s and 1940s. Critics appreciated it for reproducing and "extraordinary range of images," many of them rare, as a *Books & Culture* contributor pointed out.

Lesy's *Murder City: The Bloody History of Chicago in the Twenties* offers another collection of grim imagery, this time from gangster-era Chicago. Rather than focusing on such famous mobsters as Al Capone, Lesy primarily selects pictures that portray ordinary thugs and their hapless victims. Calling the work "fascinating, but creepy," Malcolm Jones added in a *Newsweek* review that "Lesy dissipates the romance of the roaring 20's." An *Atlantic Monthly* contributor noticed that Lesy's "deadpan" accompanying prose results in a tone that conveys "the archaic strangeness of myth."

When asked by interviewer Birnbaum what lasting impression Lesy wished to make with his photographic essays, the author and university professor responded: "It is trivial. I mean, who cares? You could say that about any literary or artistic or intellectual enterprise. For instance, your enterprise—talking to five hundred people for a magazine and over a hundred for a website. That's trivial. It's all trivial."

BIOGRAPHICAL AND CRITICAL SOURCES:

PERIODICALS

Atlantic Monthly, March, 2007, review of *Murder City: The Bloody History of Chicago in the Twenties,* p. 112.

Booklist, December 1, 1997, Gretchen Garner, review of *Dreamland: America at the Dawn of the Twentieth Century,* p. 607.

Books & Culture, July 1, 2003, "Pictures and Words," p. 7.

Forbes, July 18, 1983, review of *Bearing Witness: A Photographic Chronicle of American Life, 1860-1945,* p. 19.

Kirkus Reviews, November 15, 2006, review of *Murder City,* p. 1163.

Library Journal, April 15, 2000, Michael Rogers, review of *Wisconsin Death Trip,* p. 129; February 1, 2003, Cheryl Ann Lajos, review of *Long Time Coming: A Photographic Portrait of America, 1935-1943,* p. 84.

Nation, December 8, 1997, Joanne Jacobson, review of *Dreamland,* p. 32.

Newsweek, March 12, 2007, Malcolm Jones, "A City Where Murder Got to Be a Way of Life," p. 59.

Publishers Weekly, November 9, 1990, Genevieve Stuttaford, review of *Rescues: The Lives of Heroes,* p. 49.

Reference & Research Book News, May, 2007, review of *Murder City.*

ONLINE

Hampshire College Web site, http://www.hampshire.edu/ (September 26, 2007), faculty profile of Michael Lesy.

Identity Theory, http://www.identitytheory.com/ (September 16, 2003), Robert Birnbaum, "Author of *Wisconsin Death Trip* Talks with Robert Birnbaum."

New York Times Online, http://www.nytimes.com/ (July 23, 1987), Christopher Lehmann-Haupt, "Books of the Times," review of *The Forbidden Zone.*

United States Artists, http://www.unitedstatesartists.org/ (September 26, 2007), brief biography of Michael Lesy.

Wisconsin Death Trip Web site, http://www.wisconsin deathtrip.com (September 26, 2007).*

* * *

LETCHER, Andy 1968-

PERSONAL: Born 1968, in Devon, England. *Education:* Studied at Marlborough College, Sheffield University; Merton College, Oxford, D.Phil, 1994; King Alfred's College, University of Winchester, Ph.D., 2001.

ADDRESSES: E-mail—shroom@andyletcher.co.uk.

CAREER: Writer. Oxford Brookes University, lecturer; Telling the Bees, band member.

WRITINGS:

Shroom: A Cultural History of the Magic Mushroom, Ecco (New York, NY), 2007.

SIDELIGHTS: Andy Letcher is a nonfiction writer who has a strong interest in shamanism and contemporary paganism. Born in Devon, England, Letcher studied physics and applied ecology at Marlborough College, Sheffield University, and Merton College, Oxford. After becoming frustrated with the lack of attention to environmental issues, he toured England and France with his acid folk band, Telling the Bees, playing at a number of pagan-psychedelic festivals. He later returned an earned his Ph.D. on the topic of bardic performance in contemporary pagan movements.

In *Shroom: A Cultural History of the Magic Mushroom,* Letcher rewrites the history of hallucinogenic mushrooms, questioning the widely held assumption that mushrooms have been in use since prehistory. Using archaeological and historical evidence, he argues that, barring Mexico and Siberia, intentional mushroom use is a phenomenon of the last fifty years. In a London *Guardian* review, Daniel Butler said that *Shroom* was an "intelligent and well-researched book, which is full of surprises." Mary Grace Flaherty in a *Library Journal* review noted that the book "is thought provoking, . . . highly accessible and amusing," and also "extensively researched and engaging."

BIOGRAPHICAL AND CRITICAL SOURCES:

PERIODICALS

Booklist, January 1, 2007, Mike Tribby, review of *Shroom: A Cultural History of the Magic Mushroom,* p. 31.

Guardian (London, England), May 27, 2006, Daniel Butler, review of *Shroom.*

Kirkus Reviews, December 1, 2006, review of *Shroom,* p. 1209.

Library Journal, February 1, 2007, Mary Grace Flaherty, review of *Shroom,* p. 89.

New Statesman, June 12, 2006, Ned Denny, review of *Shroom,* p. 64.

New York Times Book Review, June 3, 2007, Dick Teresi, review of *Shroom,* p. 48.

Publishers Weekly, December 18, 2006, review of *Shroom,* p. 59.

Reason, July, 2007, Jacob Sullum, review of *Shroom,* p. 70.

Relish Now, July 8, 2007, Steve Wishnevsky, review of *Shroom,* p. 59.

ONLINE

Andy Letcher Home Page, http://www.andyletcher.co.uk (August 21, 2007), author biography.

Andy Letcher MySpace Profile, http://www.myspace.com/shroomthebook (August 21, 2007), author profile.

Brooklyn Rail, http://brooklynrail.org/ (December 12, 2007), Ben Gore, review of *Shroom.*

Dosenation.com, http://www.dosenation.com/ (August 21, 2007), James Kent, author interview and review of *Shroom.*

Erowid, http://www.erowid.org/ (December 12, 2007), Mike Jay, review of *Shroom.*

Strange Attractor, http://www.strangeattractor.com/ (August 21, 2007), review of *Shroom.*

*　　*　　*

LEVINE, Amy-Jill 1956-

PERSONAL: Born 1956. *Education:* Smith College, B.A. (magna cum laude), 1978; Duke University, M.A., 1981, Ph.D., 1984.

ADDRESSES: Office—Divinity School, Vanderbilt University, 411 21st Ave. S., Nashville, TN 37240-1121. *E-mail*—amy-jill.levine@vanderbilt.edu.

CAREER: Swarthmore College, Swarthmore, PA, department chair and Sara Lawrence Lightfoot Associate Professor of Religion; Vanderbilt University Divinity School, Nashville, TN, E. Rhodes and Leona B. Carpenter Professor of New Testament Studies and Director of the Carpenter Program in Religion, Gender, and Sexuality. Has presented three lecture series for the Teaching Company Great Lecture Series.

MEMBER: Society of Biblical Literature, Catholic Biblical Association, Association for Jewish Studies.

AWARDS, HONORS: Grants from Mellon Foundation, National Endowment for the Humanities, and American Council of Learned Societies; honorary doctorate of ministry, University of Richmond; fellow, Committee for the Scientific Examination of Religion.

WRITINGS:

The Social and Ethnic Dimensions of Matthean Salvation History, E. Mellen Press (Lewiston, NY), 1988.

(Editor) *"Women Like This": New Perspectives on Jewish Women in the Greco-Roman World,* Scholars Press (Atlanta, GA), 1991.

The Misunderstood Jew: The Church and the Scandal of the Jewish Jesus, HarperSanFrancisco (San Francisco, CA), 2006.

(Editor, with Dale C. Allison, Jr., and John Dominic Crossan) *The Historical Jesus in Context,* Princeton University Press (Princeton, NJ), 2006.

(With others) *Cambridge Companion to the Bible,* 2nd edition, edited by Bruce Chilton, Cambridge University Press (New York, NY), 2007.

Editor, with others, of the "Feminist Companion to the New Testament and Early Chrisitan Writings" series, T & T Clark International (New York, NY), 2002—. Member of editorial board, *Journal of Biblical Literature* and *Catholic Biblical Quarterly.*

SIDELIGHTS: Amy-Jill Levine is a religious scholar and the coeditor of a popular series of books on religion from a feminist perspective. Levine worked as the Sara Lawrence Lightfoot Associate Professor of Religion and chair of the department at Swarthmore College before accepting the position of E. Rhodes and Leona B. Carpenter Professor of New Testament Studies and Director of the Carpenter Program in Religion, Gender, and Sexuality at the Vanderbilt University Divinity School. With Marianne Blickenstaff and Maria Mayo Robbins, she has edited the "Feminist Companion to the New Testament and Early Chrisitan Writings" series on religion.

In 2006 Levine published *The Misunderstood Jew: The Church and the Scandal of the Jewish Jesus.* In it Levine delineates how Jesus, born and raised a Jew, taught Jewish teachings to a Jewish audience. She argues that a better understanding of Jesus' Judaic background can help lead to a fuller understanding of the Bible and Christianity. A contributor to *Publishers Weekly* concluded: "Written for the general public, this is an outstanding addition to the literature of interfaith dialogue." Wesley A. Mills, writing in the *Library Journal,* commented that "such insights are valuable and important for anyone seeking to grasp the New Testament." Reviewing the book in *America,* Daniel J. Harrington wrote that Levine's "positive proposals and sharp critiques deserve the attention of Christian biblical scholars, preachers, and theologians."

BIOGRAPHICAL AND CRITICAL SOURCES:

PERIODICALS

America, December 18, 2006, Daniel J. Harrington, review of *The Misunderstood Jew: The Church and the Scandal of the Jewish Jesus,* p. 24.

Booklist, February 15, 2007, Ilene Cooper, review of *The Misunderstood Jew,* p. 18.

Dallas Morning News, January 3, 2007, Holly Lebowitz Rossi, "Q&A with Author of 'The Misunderstood Jew'."

Library Journal, December 1, 2006, Wesley A. Mills, review of *The Misunderstood Jew,* p. 131.

Midwest Book Review, March 1, 2007, review of *A Feminist Companion to the New Testament Apocrypha.*

Other Side, July 1, 2004, Virginia Ramey Mollenkott, review of *A Feminist Companion to the New Testament and Early Christian Writings,* p. 39.

Publishers Weekly, October 30, 2006, review of *The Misunderstood Jew,* p. 54.

Reference & Research Book News, February 1, 2006, review of *A Feminist Companion to Mariology.*

ONLINE

ExploreFaith.org, http://www.explorefaith.org/ (August 20, 2007), Caren Goldman, author interview.

Great Lecture Library, http://www.thegreatlecture library.com/ (August 20, 2007), author profile.

Jesus Project, http://www.jesus-project.com/ (August 20, 2007), author profile.

Nashville Scene, http://www.nashvillescene.com/ (December 21, 2006), Maria Browning, review of *The Misunderstood Jew.*

Teaching Company Web site, http://www.teach12.com/ (August 20, 2007), author profile.

Vanderbilt University Divinity School Web site, http://www.vanderbilt.edu/gradschool/religion/ (August 20, 2007), author profile.

*   *   *

LITTLETON, Darryl (DMilitant)

PERSONAL: Male.

ADDRESSES: E-mail—darryllittleton@blackcomedy competition.com.

CAREER: Comedian. Writer for *Into the Dark with Teddy Carpenter, Cleveland City Limits,* and *Comic View.* Has appeared on a number of television comedy series, including *Townsend Television, Sweet Home Chicago, Apollo Comedy Hour, Uptown Comedy Club, Def Comedy Jam, Make Me Laugh,* and *America's Funniest People.*

AWARDS, HONORS: American Broadcasting Corporation, *America's Funniest People,* grand prize winner; Bay Area Black Comedy Competition & Festival, winner, 2006.

WRITINGS:

Black Comedians on Black Comedy: How African-Americans Taught Us to Laugh, introduction by Dick Gregory, Applause Theatre & Cinema Books (New York, NY), 2006.

SIDELIGHTS: Darryl Littleton is a comedian who got his start writing and performing sketches on the *Tom Joyner Morning Show* on CBS Radio. Littleton went on to work with Arsenio Hall, D.L. Hughley, and other leading comedians before appearing on television shows, including *The Apollo Comedy Hour, Uptown Comedy Club, Def Comedy Jam, Make Me Laugh,* and *America's Funniest People,* on which he was the grand-prize winner. Littleton also won the 2006 Bay Area Black Comedy Competition & Festival, putting him in an elite list of winners, including Jamie Foxx, Don DC Curry, and Mark Curry.

In the same year, Littleton tried his hand at writing by publishing *Black Comedians on Black Comedy: How African-Americans Taught Us to Laugh.* The book covers the rich history of African American comedians and profiles a number of leading talents. Over one hundred African American comedians were interviewed for the book, garnering responses ranging from the state of the comic industry today to personal reflections. *Library Journal* contributor Rosellen Brewer said the book was "fascinating and funny, with much little-known information." Vanessa Bush, writing in

Booklist, noted that *Black Comedians on Black Comedy* "is an interesting perspective on race and comedy." She cautioned, however, that some readers might be offended by what she called "off-color humor and language." Willard Manus, writing in a *Lively Arts* review, believed that a book on this topic was "long overdue" and found the comments from Tommy Chunn, Eddie Griffin, Deon Cole, and Ricky Harris "edifying."

BIOGRAPHICAL AND CRITICAL SOURCES:

PERIODICALS

Booklist, February 1, 2007, Vanessa Bush, review of *Black Comedians on Black Comedy: How African-Americans Taught Us to Laugh,* p. 26.
Ebony, December 1, 2006, review of *Black Comedians on Black Comedy,* p. 43.
Library Journal, November 15, 2006, Rosellen Brewer, review of *Black Comedians on Black Comedy,* p. 86.
Reference & Research Book News, February 1, 2007, review of *Black Comedians on Black Comedy.*

ONLINE

Darryl Littleton Home Page, http://www.blackcomedy competition.com (August 8, 2007), author biography.
Darryl Littleton MySpace Profile, http://www.my space.com/darryllittleton.com (August 8, 2007), author profile.
Lively Arts, http://www.lively-arts.com/ (July 3, 2007), Willard Manus, review of *Black Comedians on Black Comedy.**

* * *

LOFTON, Ramona
    See SAPPHIRE

* * *

LOWBURY, Edward 1913-2007
    (Edward Joseph Lister Lowbury)

OBITUARY NOTICE— See index for *CA* sketch: Born December 6, 1913, in London, England; died July 10, 2007, in London, England. Microbiologist, physician, educator, poet, and author. Lowbury's greatest contributions to mankind may have emerged from his medical career as a burn specialist and microbiologist, but it is his poetry that people remember. When he was awarded the Newdigate Prize for best composition in English verse by an undergraduate as a student at Oxford University, it might have seemed that he was headed for a career as a poet but, as he once told *CA,* the poetry had to be fitted into weekends and holidays so that he could focus on his medical calling. Lowbury spent thirty years as a specialist in the treatment of burns and related infections at the Birmingham Accident Hospital. He was particularly concerned about the infectious diseases that proliferated in hospital settings and founded the Control of Hospital Infection Research Laboratory in 1966. After retirement from medical practice in 1979, Lowbury spent another ten years as an honorary professor of medical microbiology at the University of Aston in Birmingham. Finally, in 1989 he was able to focus on his writing, but poetry had never been far from his mind. Over forty years as a medical professional Lowbury published more than twenty poetry collections, including *Fire: A Symphonic Ode* (1934), originally the subject of his student award. Subsequent well-received volumes include *Crossing the Line* (1947) and *Time for Sale* (1961). Another half-dozen collections emerged during his retirement, including *Collected Poems, 1934-1972* and *Mystic Bridge,* published in 1966. Lowbury's interest in the arts was not limited to poetry. He was a pianist and a founding member of the Birmingham Chamber Music Society, and one of his coauthored books was a biography of the composer Thomas Campion. Lowbury also wrote medical books, essays, and even a children's book. He edited a poetry collection by his father-in-law, Andrew Young, and coauthored a critical biography of the poet.

OBITUARIES AND OTHER SOURCES:

PERIODICALS

Times (London, England), August 6, 2007, p. 51.

*　　*　　*

LOWBURY, Edward Joseph Lister
　See LOWBURY, Edward

LOWE, Sheila

PERSONAL: Education: Earned B.S. degree.

ADDRESSES: Home—Ventura, CA. *E-mail*—Sheila@ sheilalowe.com.

CAREER: Handwriting analysis expert.

MEMBER: National Association of Document Examiners.

WRITINGS:

The Complete Idiot's Guide to Handwriting Analysis, Alpha, 1999.
Handwriting of the Famous and Infamous, Metro Books, 2000.
Poison Pen (novel), Capital Crime Press (Fort Collins, CO), 2007.

Contributor to periodicals, including *Time, Teen People,* and *Mademoiselle,* as well as several legal magazines.

SIDELIGHTS: Sheila Lowe is a court-certified handwriting expert who has written two books on the art of graphology. Lowe, who began working in the field in the 1970s and has been certified in the California court system since 1985, has a large base of clients who make use of her handwriting analysis, including corporate clients, mental health professionals, attorneys, private investigators, and staffing agencies. In a *BookPleasures.com* interview, Lowe addressed critics of the field: "If anyone expresses skepticism, I offer them an annotated bibliography that I compiled a few years ago of published research in the field. Handwriting analysis is based on common sense and has a lot of documented research behind it. Unfortunately, there's no licensing in the field, so it's easy for a charlatan to damage the profession and their clients that way."

In 2007 Lowe published her first novel, *Poison Pen,* the first in the proposed "Claudia Rose" series. Handwriting expert Claudia is hired by Ivan to analyze a suicide note left by his partner, Lindsey Alexander. Claudia, an old friend of Lindsey, believes the note was written by the murderer and assists detective Joel Jovanic in solving the case. *Booklist* contributor Sue O'Brien noted that Lowe's "well-developed heroine and the wealth of fascinating detail on handwriting analysis" would be most appealing for readers. Shirley Roe, writing in *Reviewer's Bookwatch,* found: "Sheila Lowe has a talent for suspense, intrigue, and character development. Lowe's writing style feels like a conversation with a companion, easy and flowing."

Lowe's advice to fellow writers, as told in a *Front Street Reviews* interview, would be to "learn the craft before beginning to send that manuscript out. Read the authors you enjoy with a critical eye to see what works—how they plot, their dialogue, the characterization. Get into a good critique group specific to your genre and, if possible, take a class or two."

Lowe told *CA:* "I began writing poetry when I was around nine and stories at fourteen. Maybe it had something to do with the fact that I started reading from an early age (four years old). As handwriting analysis developed as a career for me, writing about the psychology of handwriting was a natural progression. I've always loved mysteries and have wanted to write one for as long as I can remember. I finally realized that dream.

"My mystery fiction is probably influenced most by the authors I especially enjoy reading: Tami Hoag, Tess Gerritsen, John Sandford, Michael Connelly. Also, my work as a forensic handwriting analyst gives me insight into personality, and that undoubtedly has been a strong influence, both on the way I write and what I write about.

"I've learned that I work best with an outline, which I then follow rather loosely.

"Probably the most surprising thing (and not in a good way) was that the publisher relies on the author to do most of their own promotion. I'd always thought that every author automatically gets a book tour and a publicist, paid for by the publisher. Not so. At least, not unless the author already has a big name. Kind of ironic, isn't it?

"I love *The Complete Idiot's Guide to Handwriting Analysis* because it was my very first published book. I love *Handwriting of the Famous and Infamous* because the publisher approached me about it rather than the other way around. I love *Poison Pen* because it was my very first mystery published. So I guess I don't have a favorite. Maybe after I've written a few more books I will.

"I'd like the nonfiction books to teach more people about the gestalt method of analysis, which isn't very available in the United States. And I'd like the mystery fiction to make more people aware of handwriting analysis as a serious forensic tool."

BIOGRAPHICAL AND CRITICAL SOURCES:

PERIODICALS

Booklist, February 15, 2007, Sue O'Brien, review of *Poison Pen,* p. 41.
Publishers Weekly, January 29, 2007, review of *Poison Pen,* p. 45.
Reviewer's Bookwatch, February 1, 2007, Shirley Roe, review of *Poison Pen.*

ONLINE

BookPleasures.com, http://www.bookpleasures.com/ (August 8, 2007), Norm Goldman, author interview and review of *Poison Pen.*
Claudia Rose Series Web site, http://www.claudia roseseries.com (August 8, 2007), author profile.
Front Street Reviews, http://www.frontstreetreviews. com/ (August 8, 2007), author interview.
Mystery Morgue, http://www.breakthroughpromotions. com/mysterymorgue/ (August 8, 2007), author interview.
ReviewingTheEvidence.com, http://www.reviewingthe evidence.com/ (August 8, 2007), review of *Poison Pen.*
Sheila Lowe Home Page, http://www.sheilalowe.com (August 8, 2007), author biography.
Sheila Lowe Joint Web log, http://mystery-writers. blogspot.com/ (August 8, 2007), author profile.

LUTZ, Lisa 1970-

PERSONAL: Born March 13, 1970. *Education:* Attended University of California, Santa Cruz, University of California, Irvine, University of Leeds, and San Francisco State University.

ADDRESSES: E-mail—contactlisa@lisalutz.com.

CAREER: Writer.

WRITINGS:

Plan B (screenplay), Half Moon Entertainment, 2001.
The Spellman Files (novel), Simon & Schuster (New York, NY), 2007.

ADAPTATIONS: Film rights to *The Spellman Files* have been bought by Paramount.

SIDELIGHTS: Lisa Lutz studied at the University of California, Santa Cruz, University of California, Irvine, University of Leeds, and San Francisco State University but never finished her bachelor's degree. Instead, in 2000 she witnessed her first screenplay produced. *Plan B* is a mob comedy starring Diane Keaton. However, its premiere on September 11, 2001, was unfortunately timed and the film has been rarely shown in the United States. In a *BookPage* interview, Lutz explained that the producers made numerous changes to the script, adding: "I don't recommend anyone watching the version that is out right now. Nothing went well. We started to call the production 'the curse of *Plan B*.'"

Lutz began working on her novel *The Spellman Files* while holed up in a 200-year-old house in rural New York during the winter. Published three years later, the book introduces private detective Isabel "Izzy" Spellman. Izzy works for her parents' detective agency. Her brother, uncle, and even her kid sister, Rae, also work for the family business. When Rae goes missing, the family must work together to get her back safely. Donna Freydkin, writing in *USA Today*, noted that the author "manages to keep the plot dashing along and the reader hooked on her weirdly lovable snoops." In a *Mystery Reader* review, Lesley Dunlap found that "the characters do have promise." *Library Journal* contributor Shelley Mosley pondered: "It's hard to believe that this extraordinarily clever book is a debut novel."

BIOGRAPHICAL AND CRITICAL SOURCES:

PERIODICALS

Hollywood Reporter, January 31, 2006, "Par Spies Buy on Lutz's 'Spellman,'" p. 8.
Library Journal, March 15, 2007, Shelley Mosley, review of *The Spellman Files,* p. 63.
Publishers Weekly, January 1, 2007, review of *The Spellman Files,* p. 31; January 15, 2007, "PW Talks with Lisa Lutz: Really Smart Snooping," p. 29.
USA Today, April 24, 2007, Donna Freydkin, review of *The Spellman Files,* p. 6.

ONLINE

Blog Critics, http://www.blogcritics.org/ (March 2, 2007), Scott Butki, author interview.
BookPage, http://www.bookpage.com/ (August 9, 2007), Iris Blasi, author interview.
Bookreporter.com, http://www.bookreporter.com/ (August 9, 2007), Bethanne Kelly Patrick, review of *The Spellman Files.*
Internet Movie Database, http://www.imdb.com/ (August 9, 2007), author profile.
Lisa Lutz Home Page, http://www.lisalutz.com (August 9, 2007), author biography.
Mystery Reader, http://www.mysteryreader.com/ (August 9, 2007), Lesley Dunlap, review of *The Spellman Files.*
Spellman Files Web site, http://www.spellmanfiles thebook.com (August 9, 2007), author profile and interview.
Where Do You Get Your Ideas?, http://www.wheredo yougetyourideas.wordpress.com/ (June 1, 2007), author profile.

*   *   *

LYTLE, Mark H.
(Mark Hamilton Lytle)

PERSONAL: Education: Cornell University, B.A.; Yale University, M.Phil., Ph.D.

ADDRESSES: Office—Bard College, Annandale-on-Hudson, NY 12504-5000. *E-mail*—lytle@bard.edu.

CAREER: University College, Dublin, Ireland, Mary Ball Professor of American History; Bard College, Annandale-on-Hudson, NY, professor of history and environmental studies, chair of the American Studies Program, director of the Master of Arts in Teaching Program. Member of scholars panel of the Eleanor and Franklin Roosevelt Institute.

AWARDS, HONORS: Grants from the Council on International Relations, Kellogg Foundation, and National Endowment for the Humanities; Horace Kidger Distinguished Scholar Award, New England Social Studies Council, 1989; Fulbright scholar, 2001.

WRITINGS:

(With James West Davidson) *After the Fact: American Historians and Their Methods,* Knopf (New York, NY), 1981, published as *After the Fact: The Art of Historical Detection,* 1982, 5th edition, McGraw-Hill (Boston, MA), 2004.

(With James West Davidson) *The United States: A History of the Republic,* Prentice-Hall (Englewood Cliffs, NJ), 1981, 5th edition, 1990.

(With Dixon MacD. Merkt) *Shang: A Biography of Charles E. Wheeler,* Hillcrest Publications (Spanish Fork, UT), 1984.

(With James West Davidson and John E. Batchelor) *A History of the Republic,* two volumes, Prentice-Hall (Englewood Cliffs, NJ), 1986.

The Origins of the Iranian-American Alliance, 1941-1953, Holmes & Meier (New York, NY), 1987.

(With James West Davidson and Michael B. Stoff) *American Journey: The Quest for Liberty since 1865,* Prentice Hall (Englewood Cliffs, NJ), 1992.

America's Uncivil Wars: The Sixties Era: From Elvis to the Fall of Richard Nixon, Oxford University Press (New York, NY), 2006.

The Gentle Subversive: Rachel Carson, "Silent Spring," and the Rise of the Environmental Movement ("Narratives in American History" series), Oxford University Press (New York, NY), 2007.

Contributor to periodicals, including *Middle East Journal, Journal of American History, American Historical Review, Political Science Quarterly,* and *Hudson Valley Review.* Member of the editorial board of the Society for Historians of American Foreign Relations.

SIDELIGHTS: Mark H. Lytle, a professor of history and environmental studies, has written or cowritten many volumes of history and a biography of our most notable environmentalist. *The Gentle Subversive: Rachel Carson, "Silent Spring," and the Rise of the Environmental Movement* was published in celebration of the centennial of Carson's birth and is a study of the advances made by the woman who exposed the ongoing degradation of the planet through the use of chemicals, including pesticides. Lytle writes: "Carson offered a scathing critique of corporate responsibility, misguided science, and government complicity in what amounted to a pollution scandal. Ecology was subversive because it put nature rather than humans at the center of a living world in which everything is connected to everything else."

Marine biologist Carson wrote three books about the ocean, including *The Sea Around Us,* before publishing her landmark *Silent Spring* in 1962. The book is best remembered for its warning about DDT, which was banned in the United States in 1972, largely because of Carson's warnings, but which was manufactured and exported for many years after. Carson wrote of the dangers of other pesticides and of human impact on the ecosystem, but, unfortunately, these warnings have not been heeded to the same degree. Carson, who was condemned by many for suggesting that they did not have the right to do what they wished with their property, died of cancer after the publication of *Silent Sprint,* but before she would see the impact it would have for generations to come.

Lytle writes of her life as a woman scientist in a male-dominated field and notes that she supported her family and often had to reprioritize her work to care for her ill mother. "Lytle's greatest contribution is letting Carson speak for herself," wrote Valerie Weaver-Zercher in the *Christian Century.* "Her words are so germane to our ecological situation . . . that they require very little commentary. 'We haven't become mature enough to think of ourselves as only a tiny part of a vast and incredible universe,' Carson said in a television broadcast after *Silent Spring* was published.

'I think we're challenged as mankind has never been challenged before, to prove our maturity and our mastery not of nature, but of ourselves.'"

BIOGRAPHICAL AND CRITICAL SOURCES:

PERIODICALS

Audubon, September 1, 2007, Frank Graham, review of *The Gentle Subversive: Rachel Carson, "Silent Spring," and the Rise of the Environmental Movement,* p. 106.

Christian Century, May 1, 2007, Valerie Weaver-Zercher, review of *The Gentle Subversive,* p. 52.

Esprit De Corps, May, 2006, review of *America's Uncivil Wars: The Sixties Era: From Elvis to the Fall of Richard Nixon,* p. 46.

Library Journal, February 1, 2007, Patricia Ann Owens, review of *The Gentle Subversive,* p. 94.

ONLINE

Bard College Web site, http://www.bard.edu/ (September 29, 2007), brief biography.*

*   *   *

LYTLE, Mark Hamilton
See LYTLE, Mark H.

M

MacGILLIVRAY, Deborah

PERSONAL: Female.

ADDRESSES: Home—KY. *E-mail*—contact@deborah macgillivray.co.uk.

CAREER: Book reviewer for Web sites, including *Best Reviews, Paranormal Romance Reviews, Sensual Romance Reviews,* and *Rambles.* Has served as chair and assistant editor of the newsletter for Reviewers International Organization Award of Excellence and editor of Hearts through History's newsletter.

MEMBER: Romance Writers of America, History Fiction Writers Society of Britain.

AWARDS, HONORS: Romance Writers of America Award, CAPA Romance Award finalist, RIO Award of Excellence, Laurie Award, and More than Magic Award, all 2006, all for *A Restless Knight;* PEARL Award nominee and RIO Award of Excellence, both 2006, both for best short story; Jasmine Award for *The Invasion of Falgannon Isle.*

WRITINGS:

Cat o'Nine Tales, Highland Press, 2007.

"DRAGONS OF CHALLON" SERIES

A Restless Knight, Zebra (New York, NY), 2006.
In Her Bed, Zebra (New York, NY), 2007.

"SISTERS OF COLFORD HALL" SERIES

The Invasion of Falgannon Isle, Love Spell (New York, NY), 2006.
Riding the Thunder, Love Spell (New York, NY), 2007.

SIDELIGHTS: A member of the Romance Writers of America and longtime romance book critic, Deborah MacGillivray did not publish her first book until 2006. MacGillivray's debut, *A Restless Knight,* won numerous awards in 2006, including the Romance Writers of America Award, RIO Award of Excellence, and a Laurie Award. Set shortly before the conquests of William Wallace, the novel introduces three Norman knights who are ordered to establish marital connections with the nobles of Scotland as part of King Edward's campaign. Tired of fighting, Lord Julian Challon leaps at the opportunity to marry Lady Tamlyn McShane. Lady Tamlyn, although she despises Edward and should rightly reject Lord Julian, knows deep in her heart that she and Lord Julian are a good match for each other.

Kathy Boswell, writing in *Best Reviews,* noted that *A Restless Knight* "is one of those books that you want to savor just for the beauty of the words and the strong hero and heroine." Viviane Crystal, writing in *Crystal Reviews,* commented that the author "knows how to professionally develop the tension of conflict and character development in a marvelous historical fiction tale and at the same time amplify that with the sexiest scenes of great romance!" Also reviewing the debut in *Best Reviews,* Marilyn Rondeau stated: "Written with a finely tuned passionate and sensual voice this love story will simply take your breath away."

The Invasion of Falgannon Isle marks the start of the "Sisters of Colford Hall" series. The Isle of Falgannon is cursed in that no female is ever born there and none of the males will find true love until the Lady of the Isle finds love with a dark-haired Irishman. B.A. Montgomerie, the Lady of the Isle, plans to help the inhabitants by bringing women to the island. However, the men are wary of the curse. Kristi Ahlers, writing in *Best Reviews,* remarked that "this is a side of Scotland readers are rarely treated to," resulting in "a sweet, funny paranormal romance that is a breath of fresh air and a treat for romance readers." *Booklist* contributor Maria Hatton added that "what makes MacGillivray's romance so special are the eccentric characters, right down to the cat." Rondeau, again reviewing in *Best Reviews,* said that "MacGillivray has come up with a perfect recipe in this engaging tale blending in a terrific locale, quirky characters, humor, and sizzling sensuality into this very entertaining read."

BIOGRAPHICAL AND CRITICAL SOURCES:

PERIODICALS

Booklist, December 1, 2006, Maria Hatton, review of *The Invasion of Falgannon Isle,* p. 31.

ONLINE

AuthorsDen.com, http://www.authorsden.com/ (August 14, 2007), author profile.
Best Reviews, http://thebestreviews.com/ (June 29, 2006), Marilyn Rondeau, review of *A Restless Knight,* Harriet Klausner, review of *A Restless Knight;* (July 1, 2006), Kristi Ahlers, review of *A Restless Knight;* (September 23, 2006), Kathy Boswell, review of *A Restless Knight;* (August 14, 2007), Marilyn Rondeau, review of *The Invasion of Falgannon Isle;* (December 11, 2006), Kristi Ahlers, review of *The Invasion of Falgannon Isle,* and Harriet Klausner, review of *The Invasion of Falgannon Isle.*
Coffee Time Romance, http://www.coffeetimeromance. com/ (August 14, 2007), author profile.
Crystal Reviews, http://www.crystalreviews.com/ (May 4, 2006), Viviane Crystal, review of *A Restless Knight.*

Deborah MacGillivray Bebo Profile, http://www.bebo. com/scotladywriter/ (August 14, 2007), author profile.
Deborah MacGillivray Home Page, http://www. deborahmacgillivray.co.uk (August 14, 2007), author biography.
Deborah MacGillivray MySpace Profile, http://www. myspace.com/deborahmacgillivray (August 14, 2007), author profile.
Fierce Romance, http://fierceromance.blogspot.com/ (February 17, 2007), author interview.
Mystic Castle, http://www.themysticcastle.com/ (August 14, 2007), author profile and interview.
Sisters of Colford Hall Series MySpace Profile, http:// www.myspace.com/montgomerie_sisters (August 14, 2007), series profile.

*   *   *

MacGREEVY, Thomas 1893-1967

PERSONAL: Born October 26, 1893, in Tarbert, Ireland; died of heart failure, March 16, 1967, in Dublin, Ireland. *Education:* Earned a degree from Trinity College, Dublin.

CAREER: Poet, art and literary critic, and writer. British Civil Service, posts in Irish Land Commission in Dublin, Ireland, Charity Commissioners of England and Wales in London, England, and the Intelligence Division of the Admiralty, London, beginning 1910; *Connoisseur,* assistant editor, beginning c. 1925; Ecole Normale Supérieure of the University of Paris, Paris, France, lecturer in English literature, 1927-1928; *Studio,* London, chief art critic, beginning c. 1933; National Gallery, London, lecturer, beginning c. 1933; *Irish Times,* art critic, beginning c. 1941; National Gallery of Ireland, Dublin, director, 1950-1963, consultant, 1963-67. Also worked as a reviewer for *Criterion* and *Formes. Military service:* British Army, beginning 1917, served in Royal Field Artillery during World War I; became second lieutenant.

AWARDS, HONORS: Chevalier de l'Ordre de la Légion d'Honneur, 1948; Officier de la Légion d'Honneur, 1962; honorary doctorate of letters, National University of Ireland, 1962.

WRITINGS:

Richard Aldington: An Englishman, Chatto & Windus (London, England), 1931, Haskell House Publishers (New York, NY), 1974.

Thomas Stearns Eliot: A Study, Chatto & Windus (London, England), 1931, Haskell House Publishers (New York, NY), 1971.

Poems, Viking Press (New York, NY), 1934.

Jack B. Yeats: An Appreciation and an Interpretation by Thomas MacGreevy, Victor Waddington Publications (Dublin, Ireland), 1945.

Pictures in the Irish National Gallery, B.T. Batsford (London, England), 1946.

Nicolas Poussin, Dolmen Press (Dublin, Ireland), 1960.

Collected Poems, edited by Thomas Dillon Redshaw, foreword by Samuel Beckett, New Writers' Press (Dublin, Ireland), 1971.

TRANSLATOR

(With others) *Introduction to the Method of Leonardo Da Vinci, Translated from the French of Paul Valéry,* J. Rodker (London, England), 1929.

Marthe Lucie Bibesco, *Lord Thompson of Cardington: A Memoir and Some Letters,* George Routledge (London, England), 1932.

Henry de Montherlant, *Lament for the Death of An Upper Class,* John Miles (London, England), 1935, published as *Perish in Their Pride,* by, A.A. Knopf (New York, NY), 1936.

Henry de Montherlant, *Pity for Women,* George Routledge (London, England), 1937.

Ella K. Maillart, *Forbidden Journey,* Northwestern University Press (Evanston, IL), 2003.

Contributor to periodicals, including *Times Literary Supplement, Athenaeum, Father Mathew Record, Capuchin Annual,* and the *Nation.*

SIDELIGHTS: Although only one volume of Thomas MacGreevy's poetry, titled *Poems,* was published during his lifetime, many critics believe he had a profound influence on his generation of poets. For example, he is considered a groundbreaking writer in that his poetry "paved the way for younger poets such as Samuel Beckett, Brian Coffey and Denis Devlin to see a way around that proverbial shadow cast by W.B. Yeats," according to a biography by Susan Schreibman that appeared on the *Ireland Local* Web site. MacGreevy's life in Ireland and experience in World War I inspired his poetry, which was also influenced by his many literary colleagues. Among these colleagues were such acclaimed writers as James Joyce, Samuel Beckett, and T.S. Eliot. Schreibman remarked that the author "was an extraordinarily visual poet: he painted words on the page, sometimes like an impressionist, but more often like a cubist, juxtaposing the real and surreal in disturbing and unfamiliar ways." In addition to poetry, MacGreevy reviewed art and literature for publications such as the *Times Literary Supplement, Nation,* and *Athenaeum.* The author eventually became director of the National Gallery of Ireland and then resumed writing poetry later in life, as well as a memoir that has not been published.

BIOGRAPHICAL AND CRITICAL SOURCES:

ONLINE

Ireland Local, http://www.local.ie/ (July 1, 1998), Susan Schreibman, biography of Thomas MacGreevy.

Irish Writers Online, http://www.irishwriters-online.com/ (August 30, 2007), biography of Thomas MacGreevy.

Masthead Literary Arts Ezine, http://www.masthead.net.au/ (October 4, 2007), brief profile of author.

Thomas MacGreevy Archive, http://www.macgreevy.org/ (August 30, 2007), biography of Thomas MacGreevy.

University of Delaware Library, http://www.lib.udel.edu/ (August 30, 2007), biography of Thomas MacGreevy.*

*   *   *

MacKENZIE, Sally

PERSONAL: Born in Washington, DC; married; children: four sons. *Education:* University of Notre Dame, B.A. *Hobbies and other interests:* Swimming.

ADDRESSES: Home—Kensington, MD. *E-mail*—writesally@comcast.net.

CAREER: Worked for the U.S. Department of Agriculture.

WRITINGS:

"NAKED" SERIES; ROMANCE NOVELS

The Naked Duke, Zebra Books (New York, NY), 2005.
The Naked Marquis, Zebra Books (New York, NY), 2006.
The Naked Earl, Zebra Books (New York, NY), 2007.

SIDELIGHTS: Sally MacKenzie is the author of Regency romance novels, the first three about three male friends living in the early 1800s. In her first, *The Naked Duke,* Protagonist Sarah Hamilton travels from Philadelphia to the home of her uncle in England, and in doing so, she fulfills the request of her dying father who wanted his daughter properly cared for and protected. On the way she stays at an inn where a drunken Robbie Hamilton directs her to a room that was previously reserved for his friend James Runyon, Duke of Alvord. When she wakes, she finds the naked duke lying beside her. British tradition requires that she marry him, but her American independence prevents her from doing so. James, whose life is being threatened by a cousin who wishes to secure the family fortune, is in need of a wife and has been hesitating to marry the only woman who seems an option. Sarah is at first drawn to Robbie, a confirmed bachelor, but instead chooses to live with James and his sister and aunts, all of whom soon conspire to forge a union. *Booklist* reviewer Maria Hatton wrote: "MacKenzie sets a merry dance in motion in this enjoyable Regency romp."

MacKenzie follows with *The Naked Marquis,* in which Charles Draysmith has acquired the title of Marquis of Knightsdale after the death of his brother. Now charged with running the estate and caring for his two orphaned nieces, Charles is in need of a wife, a problem that could be solved if he can convince childhood friend Emma Peterson to marry him.

In *The Naked Earl,* Robbie, who is fleeing from a lady with marriage on her mind, ends up in the bed of Lady Elizabeth Tunyon, after climbing through her window. Unknown to Robbie, Elizabeth, who is the sister of his best friend, has long lusted after him. Other entanglements figure in the plot; a duchess whose husband is elderly wants an heir and pursues a young man who would seem capable of the job, which causes jealousy in the party's host. A *Publishers Weekly* contributor concluded: "MacKenzie has great fun shepherding this boisterous party toward its happy ending; readers will be glad they RSVPed."

BIOGRAPHICAL AND CRITICAL SOURCES:

PERIODICALS

Booklist, January 1, 2005, Maria Hatton, review of *The Naked Duke,* p. 831; March 15, 2007, John Charles, review of *The Naked Earl,* p. 32.
Publishers Weekly, February 5, 2007, review of *The Naked Earl,* p. 46.

ONLINE

Best Reviews, http://thebestreviews.com/ (September 30, 2007), Linda Hurst, review of *The Naked Duke.*
Bookstore, http://www.thebookstore-radcliff.com/ (September 30, 2007).
Fallen Angel Review, http://www.fallenangelreviews.com/ (September 30, 2007), Missy, review of *The Naked Duke.*
Romance Reader, http://www.theromancereader.com/ (September 30, 2007), Cathy Sova, "New Faces 166: Sally MacKenzie."
Romantic Times Online, http://www.romantictimes.com/ (September 30, 2007), Kathe Robin, reviews of *The Naked Duke, The Naked Marquis,* and *The Naked Earl.*
Sally MacKenzie Home Page, http://www.sallymackenzie.net (September 30, 2007).*

*   *   *

MACOMBER, James

PERSONAL: Born in Fall River, MA; son of Clinton and Margaret Macomber; married; wife's name Sandra. *Education:* Rhode Island College, B.A., 1970; New England School of Law, J.D., 1980.

ADDRESSES: E-mail—jim@jamesmacomber.com.

CAREER: Attorney, 1980-96; writer, 1996—. *Military service:* U.S. Air Force, 1962-66.

WRITINGS:

"JOHN CANN" SERIES

Bargained for Exchange, Scorpion Books (Bradenton, FL), 1996.
Art & Part, Scorpion Books (Bradenton, FL), 2003.
A Grave Breach, Oceanview Publishing (Ipswich, MA), 2007.

BIOGRAPHICAL AND CRITICAL SOURCES:

ONLINE

James Macomber Home Page, http://www.james macomber.com (August 14, 2007).

*   *   *

MAINIERO, Lisa A.

PERSONAL: Education: Smith College, B.A.; Yale University, M.A., M.Phil., Ph.D., 1983.

ADDRESSES: Office—School of Business, Fairfield University, 1073 N. Benson Rd., Fairfield, CT 06824. *E-mail*—Lmainiero@mail.fairfield.edu.

CAREER: Fairfield University, Fairfield, CT, professor of management.

MEMBER: American Society for Training and Development, American Management Association, Eastern Academy of Management (secretary and proceedings editor), Women in Management Division of the National Academy of Management (program chair), Phi Beta Kappa.

WRITINGS:

(With Cheryl L. Tromley) *Developing Managerial Skills in Organizational Behavior: Exercises, Cases & Readings,* Prentice Hall (Englewood Cliffs, NJ), 1989, 2nd edition, 1994.
Office Romance: Love, Power, and Sex in the Workplace, Rawson Associates (New York, NY), 1989.
(With David D. Palmer) *Managing Our Future,* Eastern Academy of Management (Fairfield, CT), 1994.
(With Margaret Brindle) *Managing Power through Lateral Networking,* Quorum (Westport, CT), 2000.
(With Sherry E. Sullivan) *The Opt-Out Revolt: Why People Are Leaving Companies to Create Kaleidoscope Careers,* Davies-Black Publishing (Mountain View, CA), 2006.

Contributor to periodicals, including *Administrative Science Quarterly, Academy of Management Review, Academy of Management Executive, Group and Organization Management, Journal of Management, Organizational Dynamics,* and *Harvard Business Review.*

SIDELIGHTS: Lisa A. Mainiero is a professor of management at the Fairfield University School of Business and the author, with Sherry E. Sullivan, of *The Opt-Out Revolt: Why People Are Leaving Companies to Create Kaleidoscope Careers.* The book examines why both men and women are choosing to go it alone rather than climb the corporate ladder. Using quantitative and qualitative research from a five-year period, the authors reason that for cultural, biological, and psychological reasons, more people are choosing to restructure their careers, with the ultimate goal of spending more time outside of the company walls. Heidi Senior in the *Library Journal* noted that "job seekers, career changers, and researchers will find this book useful." In *Armchair Interviews,* Celia Renteria Szelwach recommended the book, commenting that "human resources professionals, academics, and executive/career transition coaches will gain value from reading this book." She concluded: "It's a keeper!"

BIOGRAPHICAL AND CRITICAL SOURCES:

PERIODICALS

California Bookwatch, December 1, 2006, review of *The Opt-Out Revolt: Why People Are Leaving Companies to Create Kaleidoscope Careers.*

Library Journal, September 1, 2006, Heidi Senior, review of *The Opt-Out Revolt,* p. 158.

Publishers Weekly, June 12, 2006, review of *The Opt-Out Revolt,* p. 42.

Stamford Advocate, August 25, 2006, review of *The Opt-Out Revolt.*

ONLINE

Armchair Interviews, http://www.armchairinterviews.com/ (August 10, 2007), Celia Renteria Szelwach, review of *The Opt-Out Revolt.*

Fairfield University Web site, http://www.fairfield.edu/ (August 10, 2007), author profile.

Opt-Out Revolt Web site, http://www.optoutrevolt.com (August 10, 2007).*

*   *   *

MARKOVITS, Benjamin 1973-

PERSONAL: Born 1973, in CA; immigrated to England; married; wife's name Caroline; children: Gwen. *Education:* Attended Yale University.

ADDRESSES: Home—London, England.

CAREER: Writer. Played professional basketball in Germany.

WRITINGS:

The Syme Papers (novel), Faber & Faber (London, England), 2004.

Fathers and Daughters (novel), W.W. Norton (New York, NY), 2005, published as *Either Side of Winter,* Faber & Faber (London, England), 2005.

Imposture, W.W. Norton (New York, NY), 2007.

SIDELIGHTS: Benjamin Markovits was born in California and grew up in Texas, London, England, and Berlin, Germany. He is the son of two lawyers, including a father who collected Victoriana and who introduced his children to antiques. The family moved to England when Markovits was fourteen, but he attended college at Yale. He decided on a career in sports, however, and left academia to play professional basketball in Germany.

Markovits wrote *The Syme Papers* while working in an ice-cream parlor in Oxford. It is the story of two men, Samuel Highgate Syme, an eighteenth-century American geologist whose early findings on continental drift were never recognized, and his biographer, historian Douglas Pitt, who a century later would bring them to light within the scientific community. If Pitt is successful, he will get tenure, prevent his wife from leaving him, and perhaps gain the respect of his sons. He is hopeful that there is some truth in Syme's idea that the earth is a hollow sphere inside which concentric spheres rotate, but he mistakenly relies on the accounts of Friedrich Muller, or "Phiddy," whose opinions may have been influenced by his sexual feelings for Syme. Pitt is unable to prove his case and finally comes to terms with his failure.

Fathers and Daughters consists of four linked novellas featuring the faculty and students at an elite New York school. In each case, Markovits explores the relationships between the fathers and their daughters.

Imposture is a story based on fact. In 1816, at a villa at Lake Geneva, Byron challenged his guests to each write a frightening tale. The guests included Percy Shelley and Mary Godwin (later Shelley), a teen at the time. She won with a story that would be published as *Frankenstein,* but another idea had implications nearly as great. Byron's underachieving physician, John Polidori, created "The Vampyre," a short story that was later published and attributed to Byron and later became the inspiration for the stories featuring Count Dracula. Markovits begins the novel in 1819, with Polidori in London, having been dismissed by Byron, who has fled England following his divorce and the rumor that he and his half-sister had been sexually involved. Because he bears a strong resemblance to the man who has stolen his work, Polidori is mistaken for Byron by Eliza, who says they have previously met. The two fall in love, without Eliza learning the truth.

New Statesman reviewer Simon Baker speculated as to who the greater bloodsucker might be—Byron for stealing Polidori's work or Polidori for using Byron's identity to win a woman. Baker concluded that Markovits "leaves us mercifully free of neat conclusions about Polidori, who emerges as a complex, conflicted character. In spite of his deceit (which leads, predictably, to disaster) and his envy, he must surely, in the end, capture our sympathy because he wants the impossible: he wants, above all things, to be Byron."

BIOGRAPHICAL AND CRITICAL SOURCES:

PERIODICALS

Booklist, October 15, 2005, Joanne Wilkinson, review of *Fathers and Daughters*, p. 31; March 1, 2007, Allison Block, review of *Imposture*, p. 63.

Economist, January 13, 2007, review of *Imposture*, p. 76.

Financial Times, January 13, 2007, Jonathan Derbyshire, review of *Imposture*, p. 33.

Kirkus Reviews, August 1, 2005, review of *Fathers and Daughters*, p. 808; March 1, 2007, review of *Imposture*, p. 189.

Library Journal, October 1, 2005, David A. Berona, review of *Fathers and Daughters*, p. 68; May 15, 2007, Cynthia Johnson, review of *Imposture*, p. 81.

New Statesman, March 8, 2004, Jonathan Heawood, review of *The Syme Papers*, p. 55; January 15, 2007, Simon Baker, review of *Imposture*, p. 58.

New York Times Book Review, November 6, 2005, Bliss Broyard, review of *Fathers and Daughters*, p. 15; May 13, 2007, Jess Row, review of *Imposture*, p. 9.

Publishers Weekly, September 12, 2005, review of *Fathers and Daughters*, p. 41; February 5, 2007, review of *Imposture*, p. 36.

ONLINE

Agony Column, http://trashotron.com/agony/ (December 4, 2004), Katie Dean, review of *The Syme Papers*.

Guardian Unlimited, http://www.guardian.co.uk/ (January 13, 2007), Andrew Motion, review of *Imposture*.

Independent Online, http://www.independent.co.uk/ (January 12, 2007), Christina Patterson, "Benjamin Markovits: Leaps in the Dark," interview.

Observer, http://www.observer.guardian.co.uk/ (January 7, 2007), Kirsty Gunn, review of *Imposture*.

Reading Group Guides, http://www.readinggroupguides.com/ (September 30, 2007), "A Conversation with Benjamin Markovits."

Scotland on Sunday, http://scotlandonsunday.scotsman.com/ (January 7, 2007), Stuart Kelly, review of *Imposture*.

Sunday Times, http://www.sunday-times.co.uk (January 21, 2007), John Spurling, review of *Imposture*.

Telegraph Online, http://www.telegraph.co.uk/ (January 14, 2007), Alastair Sooke, review of *Imposture*.*

*   *   *

MARKWALD, Marilynn Morris 1928-

PERSONAL: Born November 26, 1928, in Waukegan, IL; daughter of Evan Llewellyn (a teacher) and Ethelyn LeBaron (a home decorator) Morris; married Rudolf K. Markwald (a Lutheran pastor), December 18, 1949; children: Ruth Markwald Osberg (deceased), Paul, Christine Markwald Wolf, Ruth Markwald Johnson. *Ethnicity:* "Welsh-Yankee." *Education:* Baptist Missionary Training School, B.A.; Augustana Hospital, Chicago, IL, R.N. *Religion:* Lutheran.

ADDRESSES: Home—Boerne, TX. *E-mail*—markwald@ktc.com.

CAREER: Cook County Department of Public Aid, Chicago, IL, caseworker, 1970-76; Belmont Hospital, Chicago, registered nurse, 1978-80; Hilltop Village, Kerrville, TX, registered nurse.

WRITINGS:

(With husband, Rudolf K. Markwald) *Katharine von Bora: A Reformation Life,* Concordia Publishing House (St. Louis, MO), 2002.

MARKWALD, Rudolf K. 1919-

PERSONAL: Born March 28, 1919, in Berlin, Germany; naturalized U.S. citizen; son of Bruno (an automotive engineer) and Cornelia (a homemaker) Markwald; married Marilynn Morris (a registered nurse), December 18, 1949; children: Ruth Markwald Osberg (deceased), Paul, Christine Markwald Wolf, Elizabeth Markwald Johnson. *Ethnicity:* "German." *Education:* Attended Berlin Theological Seminary and Neuendetteslau Seminary; Chicago Theological Seminary, B.D., S.T.M. *Religion:* Lutheran. *Hobbies and other interests:* History, music, lapidary.

ADDRESSES: Home—Boerne, TX. *E-mail*—markwald@ktc.com.

CAREER: Ordained Lutheran minister; pastor of Lutheran congregations in Chile and in Illinois, 1950-68; history professor and school superintendent, 1968-82; director of a Hispanic ministry in Chicago, IL. *Wartime service:* Served as a scout during World War II.

MEMBER: Rotary International (life member).

WRITINGS:

(Translator and author of commentary) *A Mystic's Passion: The Spirituality of Johannes von Staupitz in His 1520 Lenten Sermons,* Peter Lang (New York, NY), 1990.

(With wife, Marilynn Morris Markwald) *Katharine von Bora: A Reformation Life,* Concordia Publishing House (St. Louis, MO), 2002.

SIDELIGHTS: Rudolf K. Markwald told *CA:* "As an ordained Lutheran pastor and teacher my motivation for writing was to prepare sermons and lectures for more than thirty years of my ministry. But my professional commitment turned into an avocation during my retirement. I was particularly influenced in my work by the well-known professor of the University of Chicago, Dr. Joseph Gittler, one of the outstanding orators and writers in the twentieth century. My writing process is influenced by my reading and military experiences. What inspired me to write on the subjects I have chosen was my interest in sharing my insights and recollections with my family and curious readers."

MARLETTE
See MARLETTE, Doug

*　　*　　*

MARLETTE, Doug 1949-2007
(Marlette, Douglas Nigel Marlette)

OBITUARY NOTICE— See index for *CA* sketch: Born December 6, 1949, in Greensboro, NC; died after an automobile accident, July 10, 2007, in Marshall County, MS. Editorial cartoonist, comic-strip artist, novelist, and author. Marlette was best known for his cartoons that skewered hypocrisy, greed, cruelty, and self-righteousness. His targets were most often political figures and fundamentalist clergy of all denominations, and he was fiercely proud of his reputation in that regard. Marlette began his career in Charlotte, North Carolina, as a young editorial cartoonist for the *Charlotte Observer,* where he worked from 1972 to 1987. His work there earned him the distinction of becoming the first cartoonist selected to be a Nieman fellow at Harvard University. He worked briefly at the *Atlanta Constitution,* earning a Pulitzer Prize for editorial cartooning in 1988. In 1989 Marlette joined the staff at *Newsday* in New York, New York, but his uncompromising work was syndicated around the world. Marlette took pride in the equal-opportunity nature of his editorial commentary. After 2001 he was harshly criticized—even threatened—for his online drawing of a man in Arab dress driving a rental truck bearing a nuclear warhead, with the caption "What would Mohammed drive?" Yet, as he pointed out to his critics, he also lambasted Christian fundamentalists, particularly the most recognizable of the televangelists, targeted the Roman Catholic pope, and criticized the leadership of Israel. No less appealing to his sense of humor were politicians and other authority figures, whose foibles and offenses he tackled with enthusiasm. Despite his international reputation, Marlette never forgot his southern roots. He was affiliated with the *Tallahassee Democrat* and, at the time of his death, the *Tulsa World.* The gentle side of Marlette's wit emerged in his comic strip "Kudzu," which he created in 1981. "Kudzu"—named for an unusually tenacious and almost indestructible southern botanical ground cover—followed the daily activities and anxieties of the teenager Kudzu Dubose in the fictional town of Bypass, North Carolina. Though "Kudzu" was far less controversial than his editorial cartoons, Marlette could not resist tweaking southern fundamentalism through the words of local Bypass preacher, the Reverend Will B. Dunn. Marlette's editorial drawings were collected in several books, including *Drawing Blood: Political Cartoons,* published in 1980 under the sobriquet "Marlette," *Shred This Book! The Scandalous Cartoons of Doug Marlette* (1988), and *Faux Bubba: Bill & Hillary Goes to Washington* (1993). The "Kudzu" collections include *Even White Boys Get the Blues: Kudzu's First Ten Years* (1992). The cartoonist also collaborated on a musical play based on Kudzu's adventures. Marlette often commented that pictures were more powerful and expressive than mere words, but he did write novels, set in the South and reportedly semi-autobiographical in nature. His second, *Magic Times,* was published not long before his untimely death.

OBITUARIES AND OTHER SOURCES:

BOOKS

Marlette, Doug, *In Your Face: A Cartoonist at Work,* Houghton Mifflin (Boston, MA), 1991.

PERIODICALS

Chicago Tribune, July 11, 2007, p. 9.
Los Angeles Times, July 11, 2007, p. B6.
New York Times, July 11, 2007, p. C17.
Washington Post, July 11, 2007, p. B7.

* * *

MARLETTE, Douglas Nigel
See MARLETTE, Doug

* * *

MARSHALL, Alex 1959-

PERSONAL: Born 1959, in Norfolk, VA. *Education:* Earned bachelor's degree from Carnegie-Mellon University and master's degree from Columbia University.

ADDRESSES: Home—New York, NY. *Office*—Regional Plan Association, 4 Irving Place, 7th Fl., New York, NY 10003. *E-mail*—Alex@rpa.org.

CAREER: Urban planner and journalist. *Virginian-Pilot,* Norfolk, VA, staff writer, 1989-97; Regional Plan Association, New York, NY, senior fellow and editor of newsletter. Harvard University Graduate School of Design, Loeb fellow, 1999-2000.

MEMBER: Citistates Associates.

AWARDS, HONORS: German-Marshall European Community Journalism fellowship, 1994.

WRITINGS:

How Cities Work: Suburbs, Sprawl, and the Roads Not Taken, University of Texas Press (Austin, TX), 2000.
Beneath the Metropolis: The Secret Lives of Cities, edited by David Emblidge, Caroll & Graf (New York, NY), 2006.

Contributor to periodicals, including *New York Times Magazine, Metropolis, Boston Globe, Architectural Record, Washington Post, Salon.com, George, Architecture, Newsday, San Francisco Chronicle,* and *Slate.* Transportation columnist for *Governing* magazine.

SIDELIGHTS: Alex Marshall, a native of Norfolk, Virginia, began working at the local *Virginian-Pilot* as a staff writer in 1989. As a journalist Marshall wrote on a number of topics, but focused primarily on urban development and design. This eventually led to his involvement with the New York-based Regional Plan Association, a group that seeks to improve upon the transportation system and maintain economic competitiveness of the thirty-one-county New York-New Jersey-Connecticut region. His work has earned him a journalism fellowship from the German-Marshall European Community as well as a Loeb fellowship with Harvard University Graduate School of Design.

In 2000 Marshall published his first book, *How Cities Work: Suburbs, Sprawl, and the Roads Not Taken.* In it he explains the relation between cities, people, and commerce, taking primary issue with transportation systems. Marshall claims that American cities grow and are shaped by the traffic engineers and the roads they lay. This sprawl into far-reaching areas around the city's downtown area takes away commerce from the core of the city and produces a center that is usually difficult to navigate by car and is not particularly commercially affluent or people-friendly. Marshall gives four unique and differing case studies, covering Celebration, Florida, Jackson Heights, New York, Silicon Valley, California, and Portland, Oregon. Marshall faults a lack of local and regional government involvement for the decline of downtown areas.

A reviewer on the *December Communications* Web site noted that "Marshall's analysis of the role of government in building cities sheds a great deal of light on issues of sprawl." Writing in the *American Prospect*, Joanna Mareth thought that "Marshall's enthusiasm for urban places and active government is contagious." *Library Journal* contributor Drew Harrington summarized that "Marshall writes with wit, reason, and style, effectively driving home his well-researched premise that cities exist and evolve based on transportation systems, the building of wealth, and government guidance or misguidance."

Marshall's second book, *Beneath the Metropolis: The Secret Lives of Cities,* was published in 2006. Here Marshall outlines the way underground spaces are used in some of the world's largest cities. The twelve cities covered, including New York, Chicago, Los Angeles, Mexico City, Paris, Rome, and Sydney, make use of their subterranean spaces for telecommunications, water, electricity, and the movement of people. Through interviews with architects and city planners, research, and personal observations, Marshall explains the benefits and difficulties each locale has had in its underground projects. Frederick J. Augustyn, Jr., reviewing the book in the *Library Journal,* praised the "unique and colorful view" Marshall expressed in his "lavishly illustrated" volume.

BIOGRAPHICAL AND CRITICAL SOURCES:

PERIODICALS

American Prospect, June 18, 2001, Joanna Mareth, review of *How Cities Work: Suburbs, Sprawl, and the Roads Not Taken,* p. 45.

Library Journal, May 1, 2001, Drew Harrington, review of *How Cities Work,* p. 76; October 15, 2006, Frederick J. Augustyn, Jr., review of *Beneath the Metropolis: The Secret Lives of Cities,* p. 73.
Metropolis, January, 2001, James Howard Kunstler, review of *How Cities Work.*

ONLINE

Alex Marshall Home Page, http://www.alexmarshall. org (August 15, 2007), author biography.
December Communications, http://www.december. com/ (August 15, 2007), review of *How Cities Work.*
Regional Plan Association Web site, http://www.rpa. org/ (August 15, 2007), author profile.

*   *   *

MASOOD, Maliha 1972-

PERSONAL: Born 1972, in Karachi, Pakistan; immigrated to the United States, 1984; married. *Education:* Graduate of the University of Washington; Tufts University, M.A.

ADDRESSES: Home—Kirkland, WA. *E-mail*—zaatardays@gmail.com.

CAREER: Worked as an information technology research analyst; International Crisis Group, Pakistan, specialist in conflict resolution. Founder of Diwaan: Dialogue on Islam (nonprofit).

AWARDS, HONORS: Jack Straw award in creative nonfiction.

WRITINGS:

In the Middle of the East: A Muslim-American Woman's Odyssey from Cairo to Istanbul (memoir), Cune Press (Seattle, WA), 2005, published as *Zaatar Days, Henna Nights: Adventures, Dreams, and Destinations across the Middle East,* Seal Press (Emeryville, CA), 2006.

Author of the short play *Three's Company,* produced at the South Asian Theater Festival, NJ, 2007; co-writer of *Nazrah: A Muslim Woman's Perspective,* a documentary in which she also appears; work represented in anthologies, including *The Veil: Women Writers on Its History, Lore and Politics; Voices of Resistance: Muslim Women on War, Faith and Sexuality; Waking Up American;* and *Bare Your Soul: A Thinking Girls's Guide to Spirituality;* contributor to periodicals, including *Asia Times* and *Al-Ahram Weekly.*

SIDELIGHTS: Maliha Masood was born in Pakistan of Indian parents and immigrated to the United States with her family when she was a child. Seattle, Washington, became her new home. She attended the University of Washington and spent six years working as an information technology research analyst. Bored and feeling unfulfilled, she handed in her resignation and embarked on a trip to Europe and the Middle East. She bought a one-way trip to Paris, trekked through Europe for six months, then arrived in Cairo, Egypt, in September, 2000.

Zaatar Days, Henna Nights: Adventures, Dreams, and Destinations across the Middle East chronicles this period, during which Masood traveled through Egypt, Jordan, Syria, Lebanon, and Turkey, and comments on what it meant to be a female traveling alone. She began her journey at the height of Arab-Israeli tensions and returned to the United States ten days before the events of September 11, 2001.

Although her appearance helped her to blend in, her unfamiliarity with the various religious, geographic, and cultural groups into which she tried to assimilate sometimes prevented complete acceptance. Because of her lack of full understanding, she at one point gave the impression that she wanted to marry a man with one wife and was also suspected of being a spy.

In reviewing the memoir for the *Perceptive Travel* Web site, Anastasia M. Ashman wrote: "These aren't just travel hijinks. Masood's battle for self-knowledge promises to be life-long, and current affairs only compound it."

BIOGRAPHICAL AND CRITICAL SOURCES:

BOOKS

Masood, Maliha, *Zaatar Days, Henna Nights: Adventures, Dreams, and Destinations across the Middle East,* Seal Press (Emeryville, CA), 2006.

PERIODICALS

Library Journal, February 1, 2007, Elizabeth Connor, review of *Zaatar Days, Henna Nights,* p. 89.
Seattle Times, May 12, 2007, "Middle Eastern Travels Inspire a Book, a Life," interview.

ONLINE

Daily (University of Washington), http://www.thedaily.washington.edu/ (April 10, 2007), A.J. Yoon, "Memoirs of the Middle East," interview.
Jack Straw Productions, http://www.jackstraw.org/ (September 30, 2007), "2005 Writers Forum: Maliha Masood with Curator John Mifsud," interview.
Levantine Cultural Centre Web site, http://www.levantinecenter.org/ (April 26, 2007), review of *Zaatar Days, Henna Nights.*
Maliha Masood Home Page, http://www.maliha-masood.com (September 30, 2007).
Perceptive Travel, http://www.perceptivetravel.com/ (September 30, 2007), Anastasia M. Ashman, review of *Zaatar Days, Henna Nights.**

*   *   *

MATHEWS, Dan 1964-

PERSONAL: Born 1964, in CA; son of Ray (a restaurateur) and Perry (a bookkeeper) Mathews.

ADDRESSES: Home—Portsmouth, VA. *Office*—People for the Ethical Treatment of Animals, 501 Front St., Norfolk, VA 23510.

CAREER: Worked as a model; People for the Ethical Treatment of Animals, Washington, DC (now Norfolk, VA), 1985—, became senior vice president for campaigns.

WRITINGS:

Committed: A Rabble-Rouser's Memoir, Atria Books (New York, NY), 2007.

Contributor to periodicals, including the *Advocate, Out, Details, TV Guide, Genre* and the London *Guardian.*

SIDELIGHTS: Dan Mathews has been an animal activist since childhood, and as an adult he has raised awareness of animal rights and funds for People for the Ethical Treatment of Animals (PETA), often with celebrity supporters who notably include Pamela Anderson. An openly gay man, Mathews told an interviewer for the *Gay & Lesbian Review Worldwide:* "I think the connection is very clear in the way that many gays are sensitized to animal rights far more than most people. . . . People who have a cavalier attitude about cruelty to animals tend to have a similar attitude toward gay people and other minorities. So I think philosophically and emotionally gays should see the nasty attitudes towards animals and sympathize with them because they have been at the receiving end of that same attitude." Many gay celebrities, including Boy George, k.d. lang, Melissa Etheridge, and Julie Cypher have acted as spokespersons for PETA.

In *Committed: A Rabble-Rouser's Memoir,* Mathews writes of his more than two decades with PETA, where he changed the tone of campaigns, replacing posters showing the skinning and killing of animals with others that were easier to view, many of which featured celebrities. As a result of Mathews's creative activism, fashion designer Calvin Klein dropped fur from his collection, as did Ralph Lauren, Georgio Armani, and Tommy Hilfiger. Female celebrities appeared nearly nude in the "I'd Rather Go Naked Than Wear Fur" campaign posters, including Christy Turlington and Anderson, the latter wearing a bikini of lettuce leaves.

Mathews himself has dressed in a carrot costume and appeared in public in his shorts to promote vegetarianism and animal rights, and he has been arrested more than twenty times. Mathews convinced Al Sharpton to narrate a video targeting Kentucky Fried Chicken, which is a popular food item in the black community, and Sharpton agreed. Martha Stewart reversed her position on wearing fur and narrated an antifur video. Under Mathews's leadership PETA membership has grown from sixty thousand to nearly two million. In reviewing the book, *Booklist* reviewer Donna Seaman wrote: "The force of his convictions and his love of life electrify every page."

BIOGRAPHICAL AND CRITICAL SOURCES:

BOOKS

Mathews, Dan, *Committed: A Rabble-Rouser's Memoir,* Atria Books (New York, NY), 2007.

PERIODICALS

Booklist, March 1, 2007, Donna Seaman, review of *Committed,* p. 43.
Gay & Lesbian Review Worldwide, July 1, 2007, "Dan Mathews: Connecting Animal and Gay Rights," p. 34.
Houston Chronicle, September 9, 2007, Clifford Pugh, "Stop! In the Name Animal Rights: Socially Active."
Kirkus Reviews, February 1, 2007, review of *Committed,* p. 113.
Library Journal, April 15, 2007, Alicia Graybill, review of *Committed,* p. 98.
OnEarth, summer, 2007, Elizabeth Royte, review of *Committed.*
People, February 13, 1995, Peter Catro and John Hannah, "For PETA's Sake; Dan Mathews Has Turned His Antifur Fervor into a Cause Celeb," p. 157.
Publishers Weekly, January 22, 2007, review of *Committed,* p. 176; February 19, 2007, "*PW* Talks with Dan Mathews: He'd Rather Go Naked Than Wear Fur: As Someone Who's Been Jailed Wearing a Carrot Suit and While Protesting in the Nude, Dan Mathews Tells What It's Like to Crusade for People for the Ethical Treatment of Animals in *Committed: a Rabble Rouser's Memoir,*" p. 158.
USA Today, April 12, 2007, Craig Wilson, "Crusader's *Committed* Is a Monument to PETA Power," p. 8.

ONLINE

Conversations with Famous Writers, http://www.conversationsfamouswriters.blogspot.com/ (April 26, 2007), "Dan Mathews: *Committed: A Rabble Rouser's Memoir,*" interview.
Dan Mathews MySpace Page, http://www.myspace.com/ (October 1, 2007).
People for the Ethical Treatment of Animals Web site, http://www.peta.org/ (October 1, 2007), brief biography.

McAULAY, Alex 1975-
(Charles Douglas)

PERSONAL: Born January 20, 1975, in Seattle, WA; married October 8, 2005; wife's name Elizabeth. *Education:* Brown University, B.A., 1996; University of North Carolina at Chapel Hill, doctoral study.

ADDRESSES: Home—Santa Monica, CA. *Agent*—Dave Dunton, Harvey Klinger, Inc., 300 W. 55th St., Ste. 11V, New York, NY 10019. *E-mail*—info@ alexmcaulay.com.

CAREER: Writer. Also works as musician and recording artist, under the name Charles Douglas, including work with such groups as the Velvet Underground and the Pixies.

WRITINGS:

SUSPENSE NOVELS

Bad Girls, MTV Books (New York, NY), 2005.
Lost Summer, MTV Books (New York, NY), 2006.
Oblivion Road, MTV Books (New York, NY), 2007.

The novel *Bad Girls* has been published in several foreign countries, including the Czech Republic, Poland, and Spain.

SIDELIGHTS: Alex McAulay told *CA:* "I started writing because I had what I thought was a good idea for a book: an all-female version of *Lord of the Flies.* It came out of a conversation I had with my wife, Lisa. We wondered what the interactions between the characters would be like if they were all teenage girls, instead of young boys. That became the underlying concept behind my first novel, *Bad Girls.*

"My literary influences are pretty eclectic: J.G. Ballard, Paul Bowles, Jeanette Winterson, Stephen King, Angela Carter, John Fowles, and Alex Garland. My novels are also influenced by film directors, including David Lynch, Werner Herzog, Brian de Palma, Darren Aronofsky, and Jane Campion. My four favorite novels are *Lord of the Flies* by William Golding, *The Sheltering Sky* by Bowles, *High Rise* by Ballard, and *The Magus* by Fowles.

"I generally listen to music when I'm writing. Some of my favorite artists are David Bowie, Tegan & Sara, Nick Drake, Cat Power, Kate Bush, the Pixies, Liz Phair, Prince, the Velvet Underground, the Cure, the Long Winters, and New Order. I only write late at night. I usually begin writing around 11:00 p.m. and work until 3:00 or 4:00 a.m."

*　　*　　*

McDANIEL, Charles 1958-

PERSONAL: Born 1958. *Education:* Holds a B.A.; University of Missouri—Kansas City, M.A., 1995; Baylor University, Ph.D, 2002.

ADDRESSES: Home—Waco, TX. *Office*—Institute of Church-State Studies, Baylor University, 1 Bear Place, # 97308, Waco, TX 76798.

CAREER: Business entrepreneur and educator. Baylor University, Waco, TX, visiting professor, 2002—.

WRITINGS:

God and Money: The Moral Challenge of Capitalism, Rowman & Littlefield (Lanham, MD), 2007.

BIOGRAPHICAL AND CRITICAL SOURCES:

PERIODICALS

Library Journal, February 1, 2007, Charles Seymour, review of *God and Money: The Moral Challenge of Capitalism,* p. 76.

ONLINE

Baylor University: Faculty, http://www.baylor.edu/, (August 20, 2007), biography of Charles McDaniel.*

McDONALD, Sandra 1966-

PERSONAL: Born 1966. *Education:* Ithaca College, B.S.; University of Southern Maine, M.F.A.

ADDRESSES: Home—FL. *E-mail*—sandra@sandra mcdonald.com; sandra1012@attbi.com.

CAREER: Worked variously as a Hollywood assistant, software instructor, bureaucrat, and college professor. *Military service:* Served as a lieutenant with the U.S. Navy for eight years.

MEMBER: Science Fiction Writers of America, Florida Writers Association.

WRITINGS:

The Outback Stars (science fiction novel), Tor (New York, NY), 2007.

Contributor of stories to various periodicals, including *Realms of Fantasy, Strange Horizons, Talebones, Chizine,* and *Lone Star Stories.*

SIDELIGHTS: Sandra McDonald is a former U.S. Navy lieutenant who has transferred her experience to her first novel, *The Outback Stars,* described by *Science Fiction and Fantasy World* Web site reviewer Rob H. Bedford as "part space opera, part romantic military fantasy." One of the protagonists is Jodenny Scott, a female captain who has been injured in an accident in which many friends were lost. Space has been conquered through the use of Alcheringa, a transportation system that allows faster-than-light travel and which was designed by an ancient alien culture. Jodenny finds a place on a ship whose crew consists of many undesirable characters. Still suffering from guilt over the disaster, Jodenny is faced with mysterious happenings on the *Aral Sea,* one of the many huge freighters that travel in space between worlds, including missing officers and robots and a petty officer who has visions. The other protagonist, who eventually becomes romantically linked to Jodenny, is Terry Myell, who is also running from his past. Australian myth influences the plot.

Booklist reviewer Regina Schroeder concluded: "McDonald's characters are surprisingly interesting." A *Publishers Weekly* contributor wrote that McDonald "neatly ties the alien mystery with other plot threads at the end."

BIOGRAPHICAL AND CRITICAL SOURCES:

PERIODICALS

Booklist, March 15, 2007, Regina Schroeder, review of *The Outback Stars,* p. 33.
Library Journal, March 15, 2007, Jackie Cassada, review of *The Outback Stars,* p. 64.
Publishers Weekly, February 26, 2007, review of *The Outback Stars,* p. 65.

ONLINE

Ficlets, http://ficlets.com/ (October 1, 2007), Scalzi, "Author Interview: Sandra McDonald."
Outback Stars Web site, http://www.theoutbackstars. com (October 1, 2007).
Sandra McDonald Home Page, http://homepage.mac. com/samcdonald (October 1, 2007).
Science Fiction and Fantasy World, http://www. sffworld.com/ (July 30, 2007), Rob H. Bedford, review of *The Outback Stars.**

* * *

McDOWELL, Edwin 1935-2007
(Edwin S. McDowell, Edwin Stewart McDowell)

OBITUARY NOTICE— See index for *CA* sketch: Born May 13, 1935, in Somers Point, NJ; died of complications from Alzheimer's disease July 10, 2007, in Bronxville, NY. Journalist, biographer, and novelist. After twelve years with the *Arizona Republic* and six with the *Wall Street Journal,* McDowell filed stories for the *New York Times* from 1978 until his retirement in 2004. His specialties at the *Times* included the seemingly disparate topics of business travel, real estate, and book publishing. In Arizona McDowell had worked as a widely traveled foreign correspondent and editorial-page editor; while there he also wrote a biography, *Barry Goldwater: Portrait of an Arizonan* (1964). He penned at least three novels, including *Three Cheers and a Tiger* (1966), *To Keep Our Honor Clean* (1980), and *The Lost World* (1988).

OBITUARIES AND OTHER SOURCES:

PERIODICALS

New York Times, July 13, 2007, p. C10.

*   *   *

McDOWELL, Edwin S.
See McDOWELL, Edwin

*   *   *

McDOWELL, Edwin Stewart
See McDOWELL, Edwin

*   *   *

McFALL, Gardner 1952-

PERSONAL: Born July 10, 1952, in Jacksonville, FL; daughter of Albert Dodge (a U.S. naval officer) and Joan Livingston McFall; married Peter Forbes Olberg (an attorney), October 21, 1978; children: Amanda Wadsworth. *Education:* Wheaton College, B.A.; Johns Hopkins University, M.A., 1975; New York University, Ph.D., 1990.

ADDRESSES: Home—New York, NY. *E-mail*—gardner.mcfall@hunter.cuny.edu.

CAREER: Educator and author. Cooper Union for the Advancement of Science and Art, New York, NY, assistant professor of humanities, 1990-98; Purchase College, State University of New York, Purchase, lecturer in creative writing (poetry), 1993; Hunter College, City University of New York, New York, NY, adjunct assistant professor of children's literature, 2003—. Corporation of Yaddo, member, 1998—, and member of board of directors, beginning 2003. Residencies at MacDowell Colony and Yaddo; participant at writers' conferences.

AWARDS, HONORS: Discovery/*Nation* award for poetry, 1989; Thomas McAfee Prize for Poetry, *Missouri Review,* 1987.

WRITINGS:

Jonathan's Cloud (children's book), illustrated by Steven Guarnaccia, Harper & Row (New York, NY), 1986.
Naming the Animals, illustrated by Steven Guarnaccia, Viking (New York, NY), 1994.
The Pilot's Daughter (poetry), Time Being Books (St. Louis, MO), 1996.
(Editor) May Swenson, *Made with Words,* University of Michigan Press (Ann Arbor, MI), 1998.
(Author of introduction and notes) Kenneth Grahame, *The Wind in the Willows,* Barnes & Noble (New York, NY), 2005.

SIDELIGHTS: Gardner McFall told *CA:* "I began writing poems as a child, perhaps in response to the poems my maternal grandmother read to me by Robert Louis Stevenson. My mother encouraged me by asking me to memorize Edna St. Vincent Millay's poem 'God's World' in third grade and by giving me books of poems to read, notably those by Robert Frost and Robert Lowell. When we left the Naval Academy in 1960, where my father served as aide to the superintendent, the superintendent's wife gave me a copy of *The Golden Treasury of Poetry,* edited by Louis Untermeyer. I opened the book to Elizabeth Bishop's 'The Fish,' with a vivid drawing by Joan Walsh Anglund, and immediately felt poetry's power to transport and console. I knew that I wanted to become a writer after meeting Elizabeth Yates, author of *Amos Fortune: Free Man,* at my sixth-grade book fair at Friends' School in Virginia Beach.

"Because my father was a U.S. Naval officer, we traveled a lot, moving every two to three years until he was killed in 1966 in a sea operations accident. He had returned from a tour of duty in Vietnam where he flew over one hundred missions and was preparing for another tour there when he died. Writing became my anchor during the years when we traveled from place to place, and after my father's death it became a way of locating myself in grief.

"My children's book *Jonathan's Cloud* is about a cloud which floats into a boy's room and how the boy tries to keep it. When I gave a copy of this book to Elizabeth Yates, she said, 'Oh, this book is about death, about loss.' I think she was right, though I didn't realize it at the time I was working on it. All my work—whether poems, picture books, or the opera libretto I am currently writing—is about life's transience and the ways we try to handle it. Writing is one way, and the fact that language ultimately fails, is why I keep writing."

BIOGRAPHICAL AND CRITICAL SOURCES:

PERIODICALS

Publishers Weekly, December 6, 1993, review of *Naming the Animals,* p. 72.

School Library Journal, October, 1986, Anne E. Muherkar, review of *Jonathan's Cloud,* p. 163; April, 1994, Kathy Piehl, review of *Naming the Animals,* p. 108.

ONLINE

Hunter College Web site, http://www.hunter.cuny.edu/ (September 15, 2007), "Gardner McFall."

*   *   *

McKINNEY, Tina Brooks

PERSONAL: Born in Baltimore, MD; married; husband's name William; children: Shannan, Estrell.

ADDRESSES: Home—Covington, GA. *E-mail*—tybrooks2@gmail.com.

CAREER: Writer.

WRITINGS:

All That Drama (novel), Strebor Books International (Bowie, MD), 2004.
Lawd, Mo' Drama (novel; sequel to *All That Drama*), Strebor Books (Largo, MD), 2007.

Work represented in anthologies, including *Chocolate Seduction.*

SIDELIGHTS: In her debut novel *All That Drama,* Tina Brooks McKinney introduces Sammie Davis, a character loosely based on a friend. Sammie, a survivor of physical and mental abuse, has low self esteem, which she compensates for by sleeping with a number of partners, male and female. When she is seemingly out of control, her friend Marie, who has also suffered a similar past but who has more control, feels the need to distance herself from her self-destructive friend.

Sammie returns in *Lawd, Mo' Drama* with friend, Leah Simmons. Leah's husband walked out on her after the birth of their twins, one of whom is autistic. She has another small child, as well, is in fear of losing her home, and returns to work to support her children. She looks to her former husband's mother and to Sammie for support. Sammie, still involved with the wrong men, is in yet another abusive relationship.

Booklist reviewer Shelley Mosley noted that although this is a novel that features black women, "it's about challenges faced by all women."

In an interview with *Urban Review,* McKinney noted that autism now affects one in every one hundred fifty people. "These numbers are staggering," she said, "and I wanted people to see how it can change lives forever. Since the characters are based on real people and events, this novel was also personal to me."

BIOGRAPHICAL AND CRITICAL SOURCES:

PERIODICALS

Booklist, March 1, 2007, Shelley Mosley, review of *Lawd, Mo' Drama,* p. 64.

Publishers Weekly, February 5, 2007, review of *Lawd, Mo' Drama,* p. 41.

ONLINE

Rock Publications Web site, http://www.rock publications.com/ (October 1, 2007), "The Interview with Tina Brooks McKinney."

Tina McKinney Home Page, http://www.tinamckinney. com (October 1, 2007).

Urban Reviews, http://www.urban-reviews.com/ (October 1, 2007), interview.*

*   *   *

McWILLIE, Judith M. 1946-

PERSONAL: Born August 7, 1946, in Memphis, TN; daughter of James (a financial manager) and Elizabeth (a bank teller) McWillie. *Ethnicity:* "Caucasian." *Education:* University of Memphis, B.F.A., 1969; Ohio State University, M.F.A., 1971. *Religion:* Roman Catholic. *Hobbies and other interests:* Astronomy.

ADDRESSES: Home—Athens, GA. *Office*—Lamar Dodd School of Art, University of Georgia, Athens, GA 30602. *E-mail*—mcwillie@earthlink.net.

CAREER: University of Georgia, Athens, professor of drawing and painting, 1974—. INTAR Latin American Gallery, New York, NY, curator of exhibitions, 1989-92; consultant to Exhibitions International.

AWARDS, HONORS: James Mooney Award, Southern Anthropological Society, 2007, for *No Space Hidden: The Spirit of African American Yard Work.*

WRITINGS:

(With Grey Gundaker) *No Space Hidden: The Spirit of African American Yard Work,* University of Tennessee Press (Knoxville, TN), 2005.

Work represented in anthologies, including *Cultural Perspectives on the American South,* edited by Charles Regan Wilson, Gordon & Breach (New York, NY), 1991; *Dixie Debates,* edited by Richard H. King and Helen Taylor, Pluto Press (London, England), 1996; *Keep Your Head to the Sky: Interpreting African American Homeground,* edited by Grey Gundaker, University of Virginia Press (Charlottesville, VA), 1998; *The Art of William Edmondson,* edited by R. Freeman, University of Mississippi Press (Jackson, MS), 2000; and *Testimony: Vernacular Art from the African American South; The Ronald and June Shelp Collection,* edited by Anne Hoy, Harry N. Abrams (New York, NY), 2001. Contributor of articles and photographs to periodicals, including *Clarion, Visions Art Quarterly, Atlanta Art Papers, Artforum, Public Art Review,* and *Metropolis. Georgia Review,* member of board of directors, 1991-95.

SIDELIGHTS: Judith M. McWillie told *CA:* "I began writing as a result of my painting, which was rooted in abstract expressionism but specifically focused on religious themes in Roman Catholicism and African American ecstatic religion. In so doing I believed that I was proposing a new aesthetic for myself and challenging conventions in the region where I lived. I saw the South as linked, both demographically and aesthetically, to Africa, but this was not commonly acknowledged in the 1950s and early sixties. It seemed obvious at the time, however, that the musical traditions of blues and gospel, so globally successful, had visual counterparts. In the course of trying to establish this idea and explain the aesthetic origins of my paintings I began to photograph yards and sacred sites in the African American neighborhoods of Memphis.

"Later, when many of the people and sites I had photographed came to be described as 'folk' or 'outsider,' I believed that I had a responsibility to provide some context and empower the artists to speak for themselves, to describe their beliefs and motives.

"In 1984 I met Robert Farris Thompson after reading his profoundly important work, *Flash of the Spirit: African and African American Art and Philosophy.* Thompson discussed the Diaspora and its visual culture with a dignity lacking in the folk/outsider constituency. He encouraged me to publish my ideas and documentation. From that year until the publication of *No Space Hidden: The Spirit of African American Yard Work,* in 2005, I have been doing that while continuing to paint and teach studio art.

"I have several, sometimes contradictory, motives for writing. There is, of course, the documentary aspect, which focuses on the content of images and the words and ideas of practitioners, something that the art world is less concerned with today than in the past. At the same time, I want to make an aesthetic compendium of cultural forms that I consider to be beautiful in themselves. I am deeply moved by the aesthetics of African American vernacular art and yard displays, especially at their most raw and seemingly chaotic. This beauty is seeded with religious faith, but completely devoid of the sentimentality often associated with 'religious art.' So I want to share my gradual sensitization to this beauty and find it anew in locations beyond the American South. Recent travels in Cuba have proven to be especially generative in this regard.

"From a technical standpoint, the availability of computers made writing possible for me. Before word processors, I would not have been able to do it, because I think in nonlinear terms and must then rely heavily on cutting and pasting for coherence. I do an average of two writing projects a year, a schedule that is sometimes mitigated by my teaching duties. During projects I work late at night or in marathon weekend sessions—twelve hours a day or more.

"*No Space Hidden* is the culmination of thirty years of experience. Coauthor Grey Gundaker's scholarly methodology and integrity give it a special dimension that I, as a painter, could not have accomplished alone. However, I am especially fond of "Art, Healing, and Power in the Afro Atlantic South," a chapter in *Keep Your Head to the Sky: Interpreting African American Homeground,* in which I introduce tools for discussing vernacular art (practitioners' narratives, Robert Plant Armstrong's theories of 'the powers of presence,' Marcel Duchamp's fetishization of readymades) and suggest that studying vernacular art can generate theory that might also be applied to analyses and evaluations of contemporary art.

"First, I hope that [my books] honor the people in them and then I hope that they demonstrate a new way of discussing the effects of religion on both vernacular and contemporary art."

MELLY, Alan George Heywood
See MELLY, George

* * *

MELLY, George 1926-2007
(Good Time George, Alan George Heywood Melly, George Heywood Melly)

OBITUARY NOTICE— See index for *CA* sketch: Born August 17, 1926, in Liverpool, England; died July 5, 2007, in London, England. Jazz vocalist, critic, art collector, and author. Melly's flamboyant lifestyle and eccentric behavior entertained two generations of British jazz aficionados, and his knowledge of art and popular culture solidified his reputation as a critic and author. In the 1950s and 1960s Melly devoted himself to reviving and popularizing the classical or "trad" (traditional) jazz music of performers like Bessie Smith. His gravelly voice and risqué reenactment of bawdy lyrics made him a popular performer, especially at his frequent appearances at Ronnie Scott's jazz club in London, almost literally until the day he died. Melly attracted notice in the 1950s as a singer with Mike Mulligan's Magnolia Jazz Band. In the 1970s he reentered the jazz scene with John Chilton's Feetwarmers, where he was affectionately introduced as "Good Time George," (also the title of his theme song) and entertained a new generation of pub-goers, college students, and concert audiences. At the end of his career he performed with Digby Fairweather and His Half Dozen. In the 1950s, while performing with longtime friend Mulligan, Melly had also tested the waters of a writing career, and he spent most of the 1960s as a full-time critic and columnist for the London *Observer,* where he reviewed books, music, theater, and film, and commented on popular culture. He was particularly intrigued by surrealist art and was the owner of a significant private collection that he had begun to acquire as a young man. His writings on art include *A Tribe of One: Great Naive Painters of the British Isles* (1981) and *Paris and the Surrealists* (1991). Melly was not initially a fan of popular culture as it manifested itself in the music of performers like the Beatles, but he came to realize that an influential revolution was underway in England in the 1960s. He discussed this and related topics in his 1970 book *Revolt into Style: The Pop Arts in Britain.* His columns were collected in *Mellymobile, 1970-*

1981 (1982). Never one to shy away from the public eye, Melly also wrote several colorful and candid autobiographies, in which he related his decadent adventures with enthusiasm.

OBITUARIES AND OTHER SOURCES:

BOOKS

Melly, Diana, *Take a Girl like Me: Life with George,* Vintage (London, England), 2006.
Melly, George, *Owning Up,* Weidenfeld & Nicolson (London, England), 1965.
Melly, George, *Rum Bum and Concertina,* Weidenfeld & Nicolson (London, England), 1977.
Melly, George, *Scouse Mouse, or, I Never Got over It: An Autobiography,* Weidenfeld & Nicolson (London, England), 1984.
Melly, George, *Slowing Down,* Viking (London, England), 2005.

PERIODICALS

Chicago Tribune, July 6, 2007, sec.3, p. 10.
Los Angeles Times, July 6, 2007, p. B7.
New York Times, July 6, 2007, p. C9.
Times (London, England), July 6, 2007, p. 71.

*   *   *

MELLY, George Heywood
     See MELLY, George

*   *   *

MELMAN, Peter Charles 1971-

PERSONAL: Born 1971, in NY; married; wife's name Elena. *Education:* Tufts University, B.A., 1993; University of Louisiana-Lafayette, Ph.D.

ADDRESSES: Home—Brooklyn, NY. *Office*—Department of English and Theatre Arts, Hunter College High School, 71 E. 94th St., New York, NY 10128. *E-mail*—pmelman@hccs.hunter.cuny.edu.

CAREER: Writer. Podebrady, Czech Republic, English teacher, 1993-95; Zagat Restaurant Survey, New York, NY, restaurant critic and editorial assistant, 1995; Barnes & Noble, Lafayette, LA, clerk, 1996; Elliott Bay Book Company, Seattle, WA, clerk, 2001; BookCourt, Brooklyn, NY, clerk, 2002; Hunter College High School, New York, NY, teacher, 2002—.

WRITINGS:

Landsman: A Novel, Counterpoint Press (New York, NY), 2006.

SIDELIGHTS: Elias Abrams, the Jewish protagonist of Peter Charles Melman's *Landsman: A Novel,* is a petty criminal from New Orleans who enlists in the Confederate Army during the Civil War to evade a murder rap. War, he soon discovers, is even more brutal than the rough streets of his home town. Elias endures battles, capture, and torture, buoyed by his exchange of letters with Nora Bloom, a seventeen-year-old Southern girl whose initial letter comes to him at random when she acts on her rabbi's suggestion that she write to Confederate troops to boost their spirits. Elias, coarse and uneducated, comes to idealize Nora, and she inspires him to aim for a nobler life than that of a small-time gangster. Steven G. Kellman, writing in the *Jewish Ledger,* called *Landsman* a "wrenching coming-of-age drama set in an uncommonly dramatic age," and praised the novel's complexity and depth, noting that Elias's "harrowing" experiences of war earn him "a place in the human community." While *Jewish Literary Review* contributor Steve Pollak felt that *Landsman* sometimes suffered from "florid" prose and cliched dialogue, he nevertheless considered the book a "commendable" first novel. A *Publishers Weekly* reviewer expressed similar praise, describing the novel as a "solid debut" that provides a "colorful" portrait of Civil War-era New Orleans.

BIOGRAPHICAL AND CRITICAL SOURCES:

PERIODICALS

Library Journal, May 15, 2007, Molly Abramowitz, review of *Landsman: A Novel,* p. 81.

Publishers Weekly, January 22, 2007, Lauren Joyce, review of *Landsman,* p. 64; February 19, 2007, review of *Landsman,* p. 144.

ONLINE

Jewish Ledger, http://www.jewishledger.com/ (October 1, 2007), Steven G. Kellman, review of *Landsman.*

Jewish Literary Review, http://www.jewishliterary review.com/ (October 1, 2007), Steve Pollak, review of *Landsman.**

*   *   *

MENES, Orlando Ricardo 1958-

PERSONAL: Born May 12, 1958, in Lima, Peru; naturalized U.S. citizen; son of Orlando Francisco (in upholstery business) and Aída Francisca (a teacher's aide) Menes; married Ivis Teijeiro (a university instructor), June 26, 1994; children: Valerie, Adrian. *Ethnicity:* "Hispanic." *Education:* University of Florida, B.A., 1980, M.A., 1982; University of Illinois at Chicago Circle, Ph.D., 1998. *Religion:* Roman Catholic.

ADDRESSES: Home—South Bend, IN. *Office*—Department of English, University of Notre Dame, 4364 Foxfire Dr., Notre Dame, IN 46556. *E-mail*—orlando.menes.1@nd.edu.

CAREER: Computer Power, Inc., Jacksonville, FL, technical writer, 1987-88; University of Illinois at Chicago Circle, Chicago, lecturer, 1998-99; University of Dayton, Dayton, OH, assistant professor, 1999-2000; University of Notre Dame, Notre Dame, IN, assistant professor, 2000-07, associate professor, 2007—.

MEMBER: Modern Language Association of America, American Literary Translators Association, Associated Writing Programs.

WRITINGS:

POETRY

Borderlands with Angels, Bacchae Press (Bristolville, OH), 1994.

Rumba atop the Stones, Peepal Tree Press (Leeds, England), 2001.
(Editor and author of introduction) *Renaming Ecstasy: Latino Writings on the Sacred,* Bilingual Press (Tempe, AZ), 2004.
Furia, Milkweed Editions (Minneapolis, MN), 2005.

BIOGRAPHICAL AND CRITICAL SOURCES:

ONLINE

Orlando Menes Home Page, http://www.orlando menes.com (August 14, 2007).

*   *   *

MESSNER, Tammy Faye 1942-2007
(Tamara Faye Bakker, Tammy Bakker, Tammy Faye Bakker, Tamara Faye LaValley, Tammy Faye LaValley)

OBITUARY NOTICE— See index for *CA* sketch: Born March 7, 1942, in International Falls, MN; died of cancer, July 20, 2007, near Kansas City, MO. Television evangelist, singer, motivational speaker, and author. Messner has been called one of the most ridiculed women in America, yet she seemed to transcend the gossip columns and tabloids with a steadfast religious faith, calm courage in the face of scandal, and simple belief in the basic goodness of mankind. Her celebrity emerged from her first marriage to the notorious television evangelist Jim Bakker (pronounced like "baker"). Married to him when she was still a teenager, Messner followed him through the bad times into the good and back again, weighed down with her trademark eye makeup, praying for the sore of heart, and pleading for financial donations. The Bakkers traveled around the United States as itinerant revivalists, he preaching and she singing, praying, and performing puppet shows for children. In 1965 they were invited by television evangelist Pat Robertson to host *The 700 Club* on his Christian Broadcasting Network. When this partnership failed in 1972, the Bakkers established *The PTL Club* on the Trinity Broadcasting Network, and when that relationship soured, they became independent broadcasters. The money poured in, and they used some of it to build the Christian theme park Heritage USA. Much of the rest of the donations went to support the Bakkers' opulent lifestyle, which eventually aroused the suspicion of the Federal Communications Commission. In 1986 Jim Bakker was accused of a sexual dalliance with a former church secretary and a payoff to the woman to conceal the affair. Eventually he was defrocked by the Pentecostal Assemblies of God and indicted for fraud and conspiracy. Bakker was sent to jail, the television ministry was terminated, and the couple's personal empire fell into bankruptcy, but somehow Messner managed to remain above the debris field. She was never charged with a crime and, though she was mercilessly ridiculed, she was also pitied—eventually earning a certain amount of respect for her endurance if nothing else. By then Messner had divorced, remarried, and launched her own career as a motivational writer and speaker. She recorded gospel and country music, released a series of "You Can Make It" motivational tapes, and promoted her own line of cosmetics and wigs. Messner made guest appearances on numerous television programs. As one of the few Christian fundamentalists to include homosexuals among the children of God, she even co-hosted a television support program for gay men. Messner fought a long and highly televised battle against cancer, beginning in 1996, and finally passed way, almost literally on the air, in July of 2007. She was the author of the memoirs *I Gotta Be Me* (1987), *Tammy: Telling It My Way* (1996), and *I Will Survive . . . and You Will, Too!* (2003).

OBITUARIES AND OTHER SOURCES:

BOOKS

Messner, Tammy Faye, and Cliff Dudley, *I Gotta Be Me,* New Leaf Press (Green Forest, AZ), 1987.
Messner, Tammy Faye, *Tammy: Telling It My Way,* 1996.
Messner, Tammy Faye, *I Will Survive . . . and You Will, Too!,* 2003.
St. James Encyclopedia of Popular Culture, St. James Press (Detroit, MI), 2000.

PERIODICALS

Los Angeles Times, July 22, 2007, p. B11.
New York Times, July 23, 2007, p. A21.
Times (London, England), July 23, 2007, p. 49.

ONLINE

Tammy Faye Messner Home Page, http://www.tammyfaye.com (November 8, 2007).

OTHER

Bailey, Fenton, and Randy Barbato, *The Eyes of Tammy Faye* (documentary film), released by Lions Gate Films, 2000.
Bailey, Fenton, and Randy Barbaro, executive producers, *Tammy Faye: Death Defying* (television special), broadcast by Women's Entertainment Network, 2005.
Self, Jeffery, *Big Tent: The Tammy Faye Bakker Musical,* produced in a staged concert reading in New York, NY, at New World Stages, 2007.

*   *   *

MEYER, Donald
See MEYER, Donald J.

*   *   *

MEYER, Donald J. 1951-
(Donald Meyer, Donald Joseph Meyer)

PERSONAL: Born October 26, 1951, in Washington, DC. *Education:* Drake University, B.S., 1975; University of Washington, Seattle, M.Ed., 1978.

ADDRESSES: Office—Sibling Support Project, 6512 23rd Ave. N.W., Ste. 213, Seattle, WA 98117. *E-mail*—donmeyer@siblingsupport.org.

CAREER: Sibling Support Project, Seattle, WA, affiliate.

AWARDS, HONORS: Duncan Award, Children's Hospital and Regional Medical Center, Seattle, WA, 2007.

WRITINGS:

(With Patricia F. Vadasy and Rebecca R. Fewell) *Living with a Brother or Sister with Special Needs: A Book for Sibs,* drawings by R. Scott Vance, University of Washington Press (Seattle, WA), 1985, revised edition (as Donald Meyer), 1996.

(With Patricia F. Vadasy) *Sibshops: Workshops for Siblings of Children with Special Needs,* illustrated by Cary Pillo Lassen, P.H. Brookes Publishing (Baltimore, MD), 1994.

(Editor) *Uncommon Fathers: Reflections on Raising a Child with a Disability,* Woodbine House (Bethesda, MD), 1995.

(Editor) *Views from Our Shoes: Growing Up with a Brother or Sister with Special Needs,* illustrated by Cary Pillo, Woodbine House (Bethesda, MD), 1997.

(Editor; as Donald Meyer) *The Sibling Slam Book: What It's Really Like to Have a Brother or Sister with Special Needs,* Woodbine House (Bethesda, MD), 2005.

BIOGRAPHICAL AND CRITICAL SOURCES:

ONLINE

Sibling Support Project, http://www.siblingsupport.org (August 14, 2007).

*　　*　　*

MEYER, Donald Joseph
　　See MEYER, Donald J.

*　　*　　*

MEYERS, Harold Burton 1924-

PERSONAL: Born August 2, 1924, in AZ; married; wife's name Jean; children: four sons. *Education:* University of Colorado.

ADDRESSES: Home—Williamsburg, VA.

CAREER: Writer. Fort Lewis College, Hesperus, CO, English teacher, 1949-1950; University of Kansas-Lawrence, journalism teacher; *Grand Junction Sentinel,* executive editor; *Time* magazine, correspondent; *Fortune* magazine, New York, NY, senior editor.

AWARDS, HONORS: National Novella Award, Arts and Humanities Council of Tulsa and Council Oak Books, for *Geronimo's Ponies;* Best Book 2007, New Mexico Book Awards, for *The Death at Awahi.*

WRITINGS:

NOVELS

Geronimo's Ponies, Council Oak Books (Tulsa, OK), 1989.

Reservations, University Press of Colorado (Niwot, CO), 1999.

The Death at Awahi, Texas Tech University Press (Lubbock, TX), 2007.

SIDELIGHTS: In his three novels set on American Indian reservations in the early decades of the twentieth century, retired journalist Harold Burton Meyers draws on his childhood experience as the son of Indian Service teachers stationed on reservations in the southwest. *Geronimo's Ponies* is a coming-of-age story. David, the motherless son of an administrator on a Navajo reservation during the Great Depression, is drawn to his visiting Uncle Eph and decides to travel with him back to Texas. But David is disillusioned to see that Eph, who has obtained Indian ponies to sell along the way, cheats potential customers and lies about his family. David's journey provides him with the opportunity to learn about his mother's family and himself. The novel won the first National Novella Award given by the Arts and Humanities Council of Tulsa and Council Oak Books.

Reservations, also set on a Navajo reservation in the 1930s, focuses on activist teachers Will and Mary Parker, who oppose government assimilation policies for the Indians. They eventually win the respect of some of the Navajos, but remain outsiders, and their son Davey grows up during the Depression in social isolation. Vanessa Bush, writing in *Booklist,* noted the novel's "interesting view of reservation life from a white perspective."

Meyers deals with similar themes in *The Death at Awahi.* Quill Thompson has just arrived to take over as principal of the government school on the fictional Awahi pueblo in New Mexico in the 1920s; his wife has accompanied him reluctantly. Gradually they learn how to connect with the pueblo residents and to respect their customs. When, late in the book, an unpleasant missionary on the reservation is tortured and killed, the pueblo elders and the Thompsons must decide whether to destroy the evidence or alert the authorities. *Durango Herald* contributor Patricia Miller noted that the novel is filled with authentic period detail, and could serve as a "valuable resource for history teachers trying to show middle or high school students a slice of history they may not have encountered." Christine Wald-Hopkins, writing in the *Tucson Weekly,* described the book as a "graceful, culturally interesting medium for questioning the imposition of the United States culture on the native . . . and the subtle influence of the 'conquered' culture on its conquerors."

BIOGRAPHICAL AND CRITICAL SOURCES:

PERIODICALS

Booklist, May 15, 1999, Vanessa Bush, review of *Reservations,* p. 1670.
Durango Herald (Durango, CO), July 31, 2007, Patricia Miller, review of *The Death at Awahi,* p. 63.
Kirkus Reviews, December 15, 2006, review of *The Death at Awahi,* p. 1238.
New York Times Book Review, October 22, 1989, Burt Hockberg, review of *Geronimo's Ponies,* p. 22.
Publishers Weekly, April 19, 1999, review of *Reservations,* p. 63.
Tucson Weekly (Tucson, AZ), June 28, 2007, Christine Wald-Hopkins, "Native Tensions." p. 63.

* * *

MICHIE, Donald 1923-2007

OBITUARY NOTICE— See index for *CA* sketch: Born November 11, 1923, in Rangoon, Burma (now Yangon, Myanmar); died after an automobile accident, July 7, 2007, near London, England. Geneticist, industrial scientist, computer programmer, educator, administrator, and author. From his post at the University of Edinburgh in Scotland, where he taught for more than twenty-five years, Michie designed and programmed robotic devices that could "learn" from experience. As early as 1960 he designed the Menace (Matchbox Educable Noughts and Crosses Engine), a device that could play the game of tic-tac-toe. At the time, computers were in their infancy, so the first Menace was developed on paper and constructed of 300 matchboxes. Originally trained as a geneticist,

Michie (pronounced like "Mickey") taught surgical science. In 1965 the university created an Experimental Programming Unit, and in 1967 Michie was appointed a professor of machine intelligence. In the 1970s, Michie developed ExpertEase, a technique that would enable machines to identify rules based on collected data. He and his colleagues then built a robot called Freddy, which could actually learn by example to assemble an assortment of parts into a working object. Michie was named a professor emeritus in 1984, but soon afterward, as a founding member of the Turing Institute, he resumed his academic career at the University of Strathclyde in Glasgow. He also appeared as a guest lecturer at prominent universities in the United States and elsewhere around the world. Concurrently with his academic responsibilities, Michie directed the Intelligent Terminals company, a producer of the ExpertEase successor called SuperExpert. Michie was an early fellow of the British Computer Society. Over his long career, he was honored with other awards as well, including the Feigenbaum Medal of the World Congress on Expert Systems. Michie wrote or edited several books, including *On Machine Intelligence* (1974), *Intelligent Systems: The Unprecedented Opportunity* (1983), *The Creative Computer* (1984), and *Secrets of Colossus Revealed* (2001), a memoir of his World War II experiences as a code-breaker affiliated with the early and very secret computing machine called Colossus. Michie was the founder and longtime editor of the book series "Machine Intelligence," from which he resigned in 2000.

OBITUARIES AND OTHER SOURCES:

PERIODICALS

New York Times, July 23, 2007, p. A21.
Times (London, England), July 12, 2007, p. 51.
Washington Post, July 12, 2007, p. B7.

* * *

MIELE, Frank 1948(?)-

PERSONAL: Born c. 1948. *Education:* University of Georgia, A.B., 1970, M.S., 1972.

*ADDRESSES: Home—*Sunnyvale, CA. *Office—*Skeptic Magazine, P.O. Box 338, Altadena, CA 91001. *E-mail—*skepticmag@aol.com.

CAREER: Skeptic Magazine, Altadena, CA, columnist, advertising director, senior editor, 1994—.

AWARDS, HONORS: Spinoza Award, Skeptics Society, 1994, for "Giving the Devil His Due: Holocaust Revisionism as a Test Case for Free Speech and the Skeptical Ethic."

WRITINGS:

Intelligence, Race, and Genetics: Conversations with Arthur R. Jensen, Westview (Boulder, CO), 2002.
(With Walter Kistler) *Reflections on Life: Science, Religion, Truth, Ethics, Success, Society,* Foundations for the Future (Bellevue, WA), 2003.
(With Vincent Sarich) *Race: The Reality of Human Differences,* Westview Press (Boulder, CO), 2004.

Contributor to *Skeptic* magazine and other periodicals, including, *Mankind Quarterly, Perceptual and Motor Skills,* and *Intelligence.*

SIDELIGHTS: Frank Miele has worked as a senior editor and frequent columnist for *Skeptic Magazine,* where he has interviewed such scientists as evolutionist Richard Dawkins, psychologist Robert Sternberg, ecologist Garrett Hardin, and anthropologists Donald Johanson, Lionel Tiger, and Robin Fix. His extended e-mail conversations with research psychologist Arthur R. Jensen resulted in the 2002 title *Intelligence, Race, and Genetics: Conversations with Arthur R. Jensen.*

Miele, who grew up in New Jersey, first became interested in Jensen's theories of a possible genetic component to intelligence when he was an undergraduate at the University of Georgia in psychology, studying under R. Travis Osborne. At the time, he became a frequent contributor to the journal *Mankind Quarterly,* beginning his professional writing career with a review of the 1965 book *The Hittites,* by O.R. Gurney. Several other reviews followed, including one on M.F. Ashley Montagu's *The Concept of Race.* Shortly thereafter, Miele published an original article on the same theme, "The Race Concept." Working with his mentor, Osborne, Miele also authored "Heritability of Numerical Facility" for the journal *Perceptual and Motor Skills* in 1967. Two years later, Osborne and Miele wrote "Racial Differences in Environmental Influences on Numerical Ability as Determined by Heritability Estimates."

This was the same year that Jensen caused a stir in academia with an article published in the *Harvard Educational Review* maintaining that a person's IQ is mostly a result of heredity—including one's racial heritage—and that attempts to increase the IQ level are not very successful. The article, "How Much Can We Boost IQ and School Achievement?," was inflammatory because in it Jensen also argues that the fifteen-point difference in the average IQ range between whites and blacks is largely due to heredity rather than environment. This thesis was "construed as supportive of white racial superiority, and all hell broke loose," according to *Booklist* writer Ray Olson. Jensenism, as this hereditary theory of intelligence became known, was debated in the halls of universities and in the corridors of power in Washington.

Meanwhile, Miele, now doing postgraduate work at the University of Georgia, continued his research into the hereditary nature of certain types of intelligence. He also began to look into possible cultural biases in the WISC test, the primary tool for ascertaining IQ level. His "Cultural Bias in the WISC" was published in *Intelligence* in 1979. By 1994, Miele had begun to contribute articles to *Skeptic Magazine,* spurred on by a television interview of the magazine's founder dealing with Holocaust deniers. Miele's first article, "Giving the Devil His Due," explored the phenomenon of such deniers in the light of the rights of free speech and inquiry.

Soon Miele was a regular contributor to *Skeptic,* writing and interviewing on topics ranging from cloning to ecology to the controversial book *The Bell Curve,* another publication that stirred debate about race and intelligence. Miele ultimately became senior editor at *Skeptic,* but over the decades he had not lost his early interest Jensenism and the heritability of intelligence. Through a series of email interviews with Jensen, who became a University of California at Berkeley emeritus professor of psychology, Miele compiled his 2002 book, *Intelligence, Race, and Genetics.* A combination of "biography, autobiography, popular science, and polemical debate," according to Steve Sailer in *VDare,* "most of it in easy-to-digest Question and Answer style." A reviewer for *Publishers Weekly* commented that Miele "draws out this scientist with tough questions, engaging him in debate about the initial reaction to his theories, the *Bell Curve* wars, and the bias in IQ tests." A contributor to *Scientific American* online noted that "Miele hopes the exchange will enable the reader 'to decide for yourself whether Jensenism represents one man's search for provisional, not metaphysical, truth through the continuous and vigorous application of the methods of science.'" The same reviewer commented that the interview "read[s] like a conversation." On a similar note, Olson wrote: "This makes fascinating but often demanding reading and confirms that Jensen is no racist: exogamy, he says, facilitates higher intelligence." More praise for Miele's book came from *Intelligence* contributor A. Alexander Beaujean, who reported that "through his questions, Miele does an admirable job of presenting an overview of Jensen's colossal research, and he accomplishes this feat in an evenhanded and easy to understand fashion."

Miele collaborated with anthropologist Vincent Sarich to write *Race: The Reality of Human Differences*. The book focuses on the authors' view that the study of race is a valid scientific pursuit as opposed to the scientific view "that race is meaningless—a 'social construct,' divorced from physical reality and poisonous in its implications," as noted by *National Review* contributor Dan Seligman. In addition to pointing out the obvious physical differences between races, the authors turn to the modern study of DNA to present their case that races exhibit important differences in genetics that go beyond physical characteristics. In the process, they make their claim that the Human Genome Project, which has mapped the entire DNA makeup of human beings, has shown that there are correlations between intelligence and specific races. The authors also write about the potential public policy implications of their theories concerning race. Vernon Ford commented in *Booklist* that the book "challenges both the existence and the value of America's obsession with color blindness." Seligman added: "It exposes the race-doesn't-exist arguments as involved nonsense. It is a treasure trove of memorable evolutionary insights."

Some reviewers believed that the book would undoubtedly raise controversy. "It is not hard to predict the response to this book, not just the general response, but the scientific, technical one," wrote Paul R. Gross in the *New Criterion*. "For here, as in no other domain of contemporary science except, perhaps, in global climate research, political correctness reigns. There will be denunciations of Sarich and Miele; it has already begun." Nevertheless, Gross went on to write: "There is no bombast in *Race*. It is an effort to define for the general reader, in broadest terms, those features

of human genetics and anthropology testifying to a surprisingly recent origin of our lineage, but also to a long interval (before the present) of sufficient geographic separation of human subpopulations to have given rise to the currently recognizable races."

BIOGRAPHICAL AND CRITICAL SOURCES:

PERIODICALS

American Journal of Human Biology, November-December, 2004, George W. Gill, review of *Race: The Reality of Human Differences*, p. 721.

Booklist, October 15, 2002, Ray Olson, review of *Intelligence, Race, and Genetics: Conversations with Arthur R. Jensen*, p. 365; February 15, 2004, Vernon Ford, review of *Race*, p. 1031.

Intelligence, Volume 31, 2003, A. Alexander Beaujean, review of *Intelligence, Race, and Genetics*.

Library Journal, January 2004, David A. Timko, review of *Race*, p. 140.

National Review, April 19, 2004, Dan Seligman, "Facing Race," review of *Race*, p. 49.

New Criterion, April, 2004, Paul R. Gross, "Race: No Such Thing," p. 86.

Publishers Weekly, September 1, 2002, review of *Intelligence, Race, and Genetics;* January 12, 2004, review of *Race*, p. 50.

Quarterly Review of Biology, December, 2005, Leigh Van Valen, review of *Race*, p. 505.

Reference & Research Book News, May, 2004, review of *Race*, p. 72.

Skeptic, Volume 2, number 4, 1994, Frank Miele, "Giving the Devil His Due: Holocaust Revisionism as a Test for Free Speech and the Skeptical Ethic," pp. 58-70; Volume 3, number 2, 1995, Frank Miele, "An Interview with the Author of *The Bell Curve*," pp. 34-41; Volume 3, number 3, 1995, Frank Miele, "An Interview with Robert Sternberg on *The Bell Curve*," pp. 72-80; Volume 3, number 4, 1995, Frank Miele, "Darwin's Dangerous Disciple: An Interview with Richard Dawkins," pp. 80-85; Volume 4, number 1, 1996, Frank Miele, "The (Im)Moral Animal," pp. 42-49; Volume 4, number 2, Frank Miele, "Living within Limits and Limits on Living: Garrett Hardin on Ecology, Economy, and Ethics," pp. 42-46; Volume 5, number 1, 1997, Frank Miele, "Souled Out . . . or Sold Short?," pp. 46ff; Volume 7, number 2, 1999, Frank Miele, "How Close Are We to Cloning Time?," pp. 48ff; Volume 8, number 3, 2001, Frank Miele, "Quick and Dirty Guide to Chaos Theory and Complexity Theory," p. 5; spring, 2005, Michael Shermer, "The Great Race Debate," review of *Race,* p. 87.

Times Literary Supplement, February 25, 2005, Jerry A. Coyne, "Legends of Linnaeus: When 'Europeans Were Governed by Laws, Asians by Opinions and Africans by Caprice,'" p. 3.

ONLINE

Institute for the Study of Academic Racism (ISAR) Web site, http://www.ferris.edu/isar/ (May 6, 2003), "Bibliographies—Frank Miele."

Perseus Books Web site, http://www.perseusbooks group.com/ (September 24, 2007), brief profile of Frank Miele.

Scientific American Online, http://www.sciam.com/ books/ (May 6, 2003), review of *Intelligence, Race, and Genetics.*

VDare.com, http://www.vdare.com/ (December 1, 2002), Steve Sailer, "A King among Men: Arthur Jensen."*

* * *

MIGLIAZZO, Arlin C. 1951-

PERSONAL: Born September 20, 1951, in South Gate, CA; son of Charles J. (a school district administrator) and Dorothy (a homemaker) Migliazzo; married August 27, 1977; wife's name Judith C. (an elementary schoolteacher); children: Sara Marie, Nathan Charles. *Education:* Biola University, B.A., 1974; Northern Arizona University, M.A., 1975; further graduate study at University of California, Irvine, 1977-78; Washington State University, Ph.D., 1982; University of Michigan, postdoctoral study, 1987. *Politics:* Independent. *Religion:* Protestant.

ADDRESSES: Office—Department of History, Whitworth University, 300 W. Hawthorne Rd., Spokane, WA 99251; fax: 509-777-3711. *E-mail*—amigliazzo@ whitworth.edu.

CAREER: Biola University, La Mirada, CA, instructor in European and American history, 1977-78; Washington State University, Pullman, lecturer in

American history, 1979-81; Judson Baptist College, The Dalles, OR, assistant professor of history and political science, 1982-83; Whitworth University, Spokane, WA, began as assistant professor, became professor of history, 1983—, department chair, 1987-88, 1991-97, 1998-99, 2002-03, 2005-06, director of faculty development, 2000-03. Pacific Lutheran University, instructor, 1981; University of Pittsburgh, lecturer aboard the ship the S.S. *Universe,* 1986; Spokane Community College, adjunct professor, 1988; Keimyung University, Fulbright Professor of American History, 1990; Presbyterian Academy of Scholars and Teachers, member, 2001—; workshop director; conference presenter; judge of history competitions; public speaker; guest on media programs. Spokane City-County Historic Landmarks Commission, member, 2004—; consultant to Museum of Native American Cultures.

MEMBER: Conference on Faith and History, Southern Historical Association, South Carolina Historical Society, Eastern Washington State Historical Society, Phi Alpha Theta (chapter president, 1979-80).

AWARDS, HONORS: Grants from Washington Commission for the Humanities, 1986, National Endowment for the Humanities, 1987, and Pew Charitable Trust, 1991; Lilly Fellows grants, 1995, 1996; Fulbright scholar in Korea, 1990; fellow, Weyerhaeuser Center for Christian Faith and Learning, 1999; grant from William and Flora Hewlett Foundation, 2002.

WRITINGS:

(Associate editor) *Career Opportunities for Historians,* 2nd edition, Washington State University Press (Pullman, WA), 1981.

(Editor) *Land of True and Certain Bounty: The Geographical Theories and Colonization Strategies of Jean Pierre Purry,* Susquehanna University Press (Selinsgrove, PA), 2002.

(Editor) *Teaching as an Act of Faith: Theory and Practice in Church-Related Higher Education,* Fordham University Press (Bronx, NY), 2002.

To Make This Land Our Own: Community, Identity, and Cultural Adaptation in Purrysburg Township, South Carolina, 1732-1865, University of South Carolina Press (Columbia, SC), 2007.

Contributor to books, including *Indians, Superintendents, and Councils: Northwest Indian Policy, 1850-1855,* edited by Clifford E. Trafzer, University Press of America (Lanham, MD), 1986; *Models for Christian Higher Education: Strategies for Survival and Success in the Twenty-first Century,* edited by Richard T. Hughes and William B. Adrian, Eerdmans (Grand Rapids, MI), 1997; and *Called to Teach: The Vocation of the Presbyterian Educator,* edited by Duncan S. Ferguson and William J. Weston, Geneva Press, 2003. Contributor of articles, poetry, and reviews to periodicals, including *Korea Journal, South Carolina Historical,* and *Social Science Perspectives Journal.* Associate editor for integrative pedagogical strategies, *Fides et Historia,* 1993-94.

SIDELIGHTS: Arlin C. Migliazzo told *CA:* "I have realized for some time that we historians must be committed to a discipline that requires of its partisans a practiced schizophrenia. We recognize that our vocation proceeds from a commitment to render faithfully an accurate understanding of the past. At the same time we are fully aware of the fact that the past which we so much seek to know is gone forever, as is the vast majority of evidence verifying its existence.

"But while acknowledging the complexity of our task, historians cannot succumb to the cultural currents swirling through our own time that would have us believe that there is no 'true' history to uncover. To do so would not only compromise the integrity of our discipline; it would relegate our writing and teaching to impressive illusion—intriguing, and perhaps even entertaining—but ultimately offering only smoke and mirrors rather than our best take on the real thing. Sleight of hand might serve some well in other lines of work. It must remain anathema to historians.

"The distance between what actually occurred and why it did, on the one hand, and the fragmentary sources at our disposal to guide our attempts to recapture that which none of us directly witnessed, on the other, is where the historian must travel. Some may choose not to follow certain routes of inquiry, for the path is pot-holed, strewn with debris, and mucked up quite a little even where it is visible. But it does exist. And if we historians make only provisional journeys of reconnaissance along portions of its length, others will follow and edge closer to that far country of historical truth. We may never know the subjects of our inquiry as fully as we would desire, but just because we cannot know all of what really was does not mean we cannot know some of what was and is no more.

"As I reflect upon my years of teaching, research, and writing, I am most amazed that what always begins as an exploration into a place and time far removed from my own results in a deeper recognition of just how much we have in common with those who have gone before. I believe that what we learn of them and their life-ways connects us in space and time to the intrinsic humanness that binds us inextricably to them and to each other."

*   *   *

MILLS, Mark 1963-

PERSONAL: Born 1963.

ADDRESSES: Home—England.

CAREER: Novelist and screenwriter.

AWARDS, HONORS: John Creasey Memorial Dagger, BBC Audio Books, 2004, for *Amagansett.*

WRITINGS:

Amagansett (novel), Putnam (New York, NY), 2004.
The Savage Garden (novel), Putnam (New York, NY), 2007.

Also author of screenplays, including *The Reckoning.*

SIDELIGHTS: Mark Mills depicts life along the eastern tip of Long Island so successfully in his debut novel, *Amagansett,* that readers were surprised to learn that he didn't grow up there. In fact, he didn't even make his first visit to Amagansett until he was in his twenties, but the area so impressed him that he decided to make it the setting of his first novel. Hailed as a literate and thrilling murder mystery, *Amagansett* begins when a wealthy young woman whose family summers in the town is found dead. The action takes place in the late 1940s, as Amagansett's fishing community and Native American residents find themselves in a struggle to preserve their way of life against the onslaught of new wealth from the city. Two men team up to solve the crime: the Basque fisherman who found the body (and was having an affair with the victim), and a cynical police detective with a troubled past. A writer for *Kirkus Reviews* commended the novel for the "superb detail" of its setting, and noted that there is "not a cliche in sight." In *Booklist*, Bill Ott praised the skill with which Mills blends Long Island history into the story, concluding that "This is a novel to savor."

The Savage Garden, a mystery set in post-World War II Tuscany, drew similarly enthusiastic reviews. The novel focuses on art historian Adam Strickland, a Cambridge University undergraduate who is invited to the Villa Docci to study its Renaissance garden. He becomes intrigued by its owner, Signora Francesca Docci, and by the mystery surrounding the sudden death in 1577 of Flora, wife of the first owner. He is also increasingly puzzled by the circumstances under which Signora Docci's oldest son, Emilio, was shot by German troops. Pondering the secrets of Emilio's death, Adam discovers that the garden itself provides clues. *Library Journal* reviewer Susan Clifford Braun called the novel a "deftly plotted and suspenseful" story set in a "marvelously sensual locale." Barry Forshaw, writing in the London *Independent,* hailed *The Savage Garden* as a "mesmerising piece of writing" in which "iridescent" prose and a hauntingly mysterious plot are combined in a "striking tapestry." In the London *Guardian,* Laura Wilson wrote that *The Savage Garden* is "just as fascinating as [Mills's] magnificent first novel."

BIOGRAPHICAL AND CRITICAL SOURCES:

PERIODICALS

Booklist, August, 2004, Bill Ott, review of *Amagansett,* p. 1907; March 15, 2007, Bill Ott, review of *The Savage Garden,* p. 30.

Guardian (London, England), November 13, 2004, Colin Greenland, review of *Amagansett;* March 24, 2007, Laura Wilson, review of *The Savage Garden.*

Independent (London, England), March 7, 2007, Barry Forshaw, review of *The Savage Garden.*

Kirkus Reviews, July 15, 2004, review of *Amagansett,* p. 652; March 1, 2007, review of *The Savage Garden,* p. 198.

Library Journal, July 2004, Susan Clifford Braun, review of *Amagansett,* p. 72; March 1, 2007, Susan Clifford Braun, review of *The Savage Garden,* p. 75.

Publishers Weekly, July 12, 2004, review of *Amagansett,* p. 44; March 5, 2007, review of *The Savage Garden,* p. 37.

School Library Journal, January, 2005, Molly Connally, review of *Amagansett,* p. 159.

ONLINE

Bookreporter.com, http://www.bookreporter.com/ (October 8, 2007), Kate Ayers, review of *The Savage Garden.*

Crime Writers Association Web site, http://www.thecwa.co.uk/ (October 8, 2007), "The CWA's 2004 John Creasey Dagger Award."

HarperCollins Web site, http://www.harpercollins.co.uk/ (October 8, 2007), interview with Mark Mills.*

*   *   *

MIYAMOTO, Kenji 1908-2007

OBITUARY NOTICE— See index for *CA* sketch: Born October 17, 1908, in Yamaguchi, Japan; died July 18, 2007, in Tokyo, Japan. Communist party leader and author. As a longtime leader of the Communist party of Japan, Miyamoto rejected both Soviet and Chinese interpretations of Communist theory in favor of a less political and far more economic and social platform. He joined the Japanese Communist party in 1931 and guided it through more than sixty years of ups and downs. For twelve of the early years he led the party from a prison cell, after being convicted of conspiracy to murder (a crime to which he never confessed, and a conviction that was later annulled). After World War II, Miyamoto served as general secretary of the party's Central Committee from 1958 to 1997, except for twelve years from 1958 to 1970 that he spent as chair of the Presidium. Not only did Miyamoto reject the tenets of Soviet and Chinese Communism, including Marxist-Leninist theory; he also rejected the strategy of violent revolution. Miyamoto focused instead on the positive impact of Communism on social conditions such as education and housing. In the late 1950s, Miyamoto was prevented from actively serving his party by then-Supreme Commander of the Allied Powers General Douglas MacArthur, and the party leader never accepted Japan's alliance with the United States. Miyamoto wrote several books in the 1970s, including

The Road towards a New Japan (1970), Standpoint of the Communist Party in Japan (1972), Dialogues with Kenji Miyamoto (1972), Interviews with Kenji Miyamoto (1975), and Kenji Miyamoto on Our Time (1975).

OBITUARIES AND OTHER SOURCES:

PERIODICALS

Chicago Tribune, July 20, 2007, sec. 2, p. 13.

*   *   *

MOGHADDAM, Fathali M.

PERSONAL: Born in Iran. Education: University of Liverpool, B.A.; University of Surrey, M.Sc., Ph.D.

ADDRESSES: Office—Department of Psychology, Georgetown University, Box 571001, White-Gravenor Hall 306, Washington, DC 20057-1001; fax: 202-687-6050. E-mail—moghaddf@georgetown.edu.

CAREER: McGill University, Montreal, Quebec, Canada, former staff member; United Nations, former staff member; Georgetown University, Washington, DC, professor of psychology.

AWARDS, HONORS: Lifetime Achievement Award, Society for the Study of Peace, Conflict, and Violence, 2007.

WRITINGS:

(With Donald M. Taylor) Theories of Intergroup Relations: International Social Psychological Perspectives, Praeger (New York, NY), 1987, 2nd edition, 1994.
(With Donald M. Taylor and Stephen C. Wright) Social Psychology in Cross-Cultural Perspective, W.H. Freeman (New York, NY), 1993.
The Specialized Society: The Plight of the Individual in an Age of Individualism, Praeger (Westport, CT), 1997.

(With Charles Studer) Illusions of Control: Striving for Control in Our Personal and Professional Lives, Praeger (Westport, CT), 1998.
Social Psychology: Exploring Universals across Cultures, W.H. Freeman (New York, NY), 1998.
The Individual and Society: A Cultural Integration, Worth Publishers (New York, NY), 2002.
(Editor, with Rom Harré) The Self and Others: Positioning Individuals and Groups in Personal, Political, and Cultural Contexts, Praeger (Westport, CT), 2003.
(Editor, with Anthony J. Marsella) Understanding Terrorism: Psychosocial Roots, Consequences, and Interventions, American Psychological Association (Washington, DC), 2004.
(Editor, with Norman J. Finkel) The Psychology of Rights and Duties: Empirical Contributions and Normative Commentaries, American Psychological Association (Washington, DC), 2005.
Great Ideas in Psychology: A Cultural and Historical Introduction, Oneworld (Oxford, England), 2005.
From the Terrorists' Point of View: What They Experience and Why They Come to Destroy, Praeger (Westport, CT), 2006.
(With Rom Harré and Naomi Lee) Conflict Resolution through Positioning Analysis, Springer (New York, NY), 2007.
Multiculturalism and Intergroup Relations: Psychological Implications for Democracy in Global Context, American Psychological Association Press (Washington, DC), 2007.

SIDELIGHTS: Fathali M. Moghaddam is an Iranian-born, British-educated psychologist. He remained in Iran for five years after the Islamic Revolution before leaving to work with the United Nations and in Montreal at McGill University. Eventually he settled in Washington, DC, at Georgetown University as a professor of psychology. Throughout his career, Moghaddam has focused his research on the psychology of justice, inter-group relationship and conflict and, more recently, terrorism. In 2007 he was awarded the Lifetime Achievement Award from the Society for the Study of Peace, Conflict, and Violence.

In 2006 Moghaddam published From the Terrorists' Point of View: What They Experience and Why They Come to Destroy. Moghaddam takes a social psychological approach to the reasons why terrorists act as they do, primarily focusing on those from Muslim nations of the Middle East. He believes these individuals lack a proper channel to express their frustrations as they seek to find their identity in an ever-globalizing world, adding that the U.S. military approach does nothing to address the core issue. Elizabeth R. Hayford, writing in the *Library Journal,* called the text "useful" due to Moghaddam's personal and professional experience in the area. Hayford lamented, however, that "the combination of theoretical analysis and concrete examples sometimes makes for awkward and dense prose." A contributor to the *Midwest Book Review* found the book appropriate for a general readership, noting that "it'd be a shame not to recommend this outside the college-level collection."

BIOGRAPHICAL AND CRITICAL SOURCES:

PERIODICALS

Library Journal, November 15, 2006, Elizabeth R. Hayford, review of *From the Terrorists' Point of View: What They Experience and Why They Come to Destroy,* p. 81.
Midwest Book Review, October 1, 2006, review of *From the Terrorists' Point of View.*
Reference & Research Book News, November 1, 2006, review of *From the Terrorists' Point of View.*

ONLINE

Georgetown University Web site, http://www. georgetown.edu/ (March 10, 2002), author interview and profile.
Lund University Interdisciplinary Graduate Summer School and Forum Web site, http://www.icomm.lu. se/summerschool/ (August 22, 2007), author profile.

*   *   *

MONAGHAN, Nicola 1971-

PERSONAL: Born March 8, 1971, in Nottingham, England; daughter of an electrical fitter and a homemaker; married. *Education:* Graduated from the University of York, 1992; Nottingham Trent University, M.A., 2004.

ADDRESSES: Home—Nottingham, England. *Office—* School of English, University of Central England, Birmingham, Perry Barr, Birmingham B42 2SU, England. *Agent—*Luigi Bonomi Associates, 91 Great Russell St., London WC1B 3BS, England. *E-mail—* nicola.monaghan@uce.ac.uk; the.killingjar@yahoo.co. uk.

CAREER: National Academy of Writing, University of Central England, Birmingham, England, fellow; worked variously as a teacher, financial analyst, and software engineer.

AWARDS, HONORS: Betty Trask Award, Authors' Club Best First Novel Award, and Waverton Good Read, all for *The Killing Jar.*

WRITINGS:

The Killing Jar (novel), Chatto & Windus (London, England), 2006, Scribner (New York, NY), 2007.

Author of own Web log.

SIDELIGHTS: Nicola Monaghan's first novel, *The Killing Jar,* is set in the government housing projects of Nottingham, England. The story tells of Kerrie-Ann, a child forced to sell drugs at the age of ten by her addict mother's boyfriend. A few years later, her mother walks out on her and Kerrie-Ann is forced to survive on her own. She moves in with her boyfriend, Mark, and the two sell drugs by day and take them at night. Eventually Mark becomes abusive and Kerrie-Ann seeks to get out of her situation. In a London *Guardian* review, Joanna Hines called the novel "thought-provoking and compelling, right to the last page." *Booklist* contributor Joanne Wilkinson described the story as "utterly gripping." A contributor to *Publishers Weekly* concluded: "The stark material and unsentimental prose make for a wrenching look at devotion, crime, and violence."

Monaghan told *CA:* "The first time I realized I wanted to be a writer was when I was ten, and a teacher read out a story to the class and I got a reaction. Some people told me afterwards that they'd wanted my story to go on and on. This was my first-ever reader reaction, and I loved it and wanted more. It took me another twenty odd years, and several wrong turns, to finally be heading in this direction.

"I write most days and am one of those sickening people who don't really suffer from writers' block. I don't usually set myself any daily target but take it as it comes, and edit or do administration if the muse isn't on me. My characters are the people who lead me. They feel very real to me. Perhaps I'm a little mad. I love writing and can't imagine doing anything else. I also love teaching and find my students constantly stimulating and inspiring. Influences include Irvine Welsh, Chuck Palahnuik, Margaret Atwood, Al Kennedy, Alan Sillitoe. I have recently discovered Amy Hempel. Wow!"

BIOGRAPHICAL AND CRITICAL SOURCES:

PERIODICALS

Booklist, January 1, 2007, Joanne Wilkinson, review of *The Killing Jar,* p. 55.
Bookseller, December 16, 2005, review of *The Killing Jar,* p. 38.
City Paper (Philadelphia, PA), Stephen Peterson, review of *The Killing Jar.*
Financial Times, March 25, 2006, review of *The Killing Jar,* p. 49.
Guardian (London, England), March 31, 2007, Joanna Hines, review of *The Killing Jar.*
Publishers Weekly, November 13, 2006, review of *The Killing Jar,* p. 30.

ONLINE

National Association of Writers in Education Web site, http;//www.nawe.co.uk/ (January 9, 2004), author interview.
Nicola Monaghan Home Page, http://www.nicola monaghan.co.uk (August 16, 2007), author biography.
Nicola Monaghan MySpace Profile, http://www.my space.com/nicolamonaghan (August 16, 2007), author profile.
Nicola Monaghan Web log, http://www.nicola monaghan.blogspot.com (August 16, 2007), author profile.

Pulp.net, http://www.pulp.net/ (August 16, 2007), author profile.
Small Spiral Notebook, http://www.smallspiral notebook.com/ (June 19, 2007), Horam Kim, review of *The Killing Jar.*
University of Central England, Birmingham, School of English Web site, http://www.lhds.uce.ac.uk/ english/ (August 16, 2007), author profile.

*   *   *

MOREAU, Lynda

PERSONAL: Born in Winnfield, LA; daughter of Oran and Paula Moreau; married Mohammad Reza Saleh Ziabari (divorced); married Shannon Walgamotte; children: (first marriage) Daniel Jonathan; (second marriage) Genevieve Margaret. *Ethnicity:* "Southern American; French." *Politics:* "Jeffersonian Democrat." *Religion:* Roman Catholic. *Hobbies and other interests:* Genealogy, reading, antiques, travel.

ADDRESSES: Home—Metairie, LA. *E-mail*—dustbuny@ix.netcom.com.

CAREER: Cookbook editor.

MEMBER: Daughters of the American Revolution, Daughters of the Confederacy, Daughters of 1812, Colonial Dames XVII Century, Louisiana Colonials, Society of the Founders of the City of New Orleans, Junior League of New Orleans, Metairie Women's Club.

WRITINGS:

(Editor) *The Confederate Cookbook: Family Favorites from the Sons of Confederate Veterans,* Pelican Publishing (Gretna, LA), 2000.
(Editor) *Sweetly Southern: Delicious Desserts from the Sons of Confederate Veterans,* Pelican Publishing (Gretna, LA), 2004.

SIDELIGHTS: Lynda Moreau told *CA:* "My interest in Confederate history gave me the idea for the two cookbooks that were done with the cooperation of the Sons of Confederate Veterans. I thought it would be interesting to include photographs (when available) and anecdotal stories about the contributors' ancestors and the recipes they chose to include."

* * *

MORREY, Douglas 1974-
  (Douglas J. Morrey)

PERSONAL: Born December 18, 1974, in Falkirk, England. *Education:* University of Warwick, B.A., 1997, M.A., 1998, Ph.D., 2002.

ADDRESSES: Office—Department of French Studies, University of Warwick, Coventry, Warwick CV4 7AL, England. *E-mail*—d.j.morrey@warwick.ac.uk.

CAREER: University of Warwick, Coventry, Warwick, England, member of French studies faculty.

WRITINGS:

Jean-Luc Godard, Manchester University Press (Manchester, England), 2005.

* * *

MORREY, Douglas J.
  See MORREY, Douglas

* * *

MORRISON, Todd G. 1968-

PERSONAL: Born January 12, 1968, in Halifax, Nova Scotia, Canada; son of Donald and JoEllen Morrison. *Ethnicity:* "Caucasian." *Education:* University of Victoria, B.Sc. (with first-class honors), 1991; Memorial University of Newfoundland, M.Sc., 1995; Queen's University, Kingston, Ontario, Canada, Ph.D., 1998. *Politics:* New Democrat. *Hobbies and other interests:* Film, weight-lifting.

ADDRESSES: Home—Galway, Ireland. *Office*—Department of Psychology, National University of Ireland, University College, Galway, Upper New-Castle, Galway, County Galway, Ireland. *E-mail*—todd.morrison@nuigalway.ie.

CAREER: Red Deer College, Red Deer, Alberta, Canada, lecturer in psychology, 1991-94; National University of Ireland, University College, Galway, lecturer in psychology, 1994—.

MEMBER: Canadian Psychological Association, Association for Psychological Science.

WRITINGS:

(Editor) *Eclectic Views on Gay Male Pornography: Pornucopia,* Harrington Park Press (Binghamton, NY), 2004.
(Editor, with Bruce W. Whitehead) *Male Sex Work: A Business Doing Pleasure,* Harrington Park Press (Binghamton, NY), 2007.

Contributor of more than thirty articles to journals, including *Adolescence, Journal of Social Psychology, Sexuality and Culture, Journal of Psychology and Human Sexuality, Canadian Journal of Human Sexuality,* and *Psychology of Men and Masculinity.*

SIDELIGHTS: Todd G. Morrison told *CA:* "I believe that all research endeavors—in some capacity—are attempts at self-understanding. We gravitate toward things that perplex us, bother us, concern us, and we aim to find the answers that will lead to their resolution (for ourselves, at least). I study 'homonegativity,' for example, because it disturbs me deeply that gay men and lesbian women remain second-class citizens. I am enraged by the benefits that certain groups receive as a function of being interested in the 'right' genitalia.

"Conducting social scientific research on the topic of homonegativity provides a 'suitable' channel for this disturbance and, more importantly, may assist in the attainment of equality. One might say that my research and writing are grounded in a reality that is oft-times bleak, yet tempered—always—with the possibility that things can improve."

* * *

MULLANEY, James P.

PERSONAL: Born in Malverne, NY. *Education:* Attended Providence College.

ADDRESSES: *Home*—Long Beach, NY. *E-mail*—info@jamespmullaney.com.

CAREER: Novelist.

WRITINGS:

The Ministry of Culture (novel), Thomas Dunne Books/St. Martin's Press (New York, NY), 2007.

SIDELIGHTS: James P. Mullaney's debut novel, *The Ministry of Culture*, is set in Iraq in 1984 and tells the story of American journalist Michael Young, who is invited to Baghdad to report on the escalating war between Iraq and Iran. He befriends Ibrahim, an artist who works for Saddam Hussein's government but becomes politically radicalized after his fiancé is gang-raped by Iraqi soldiers and later commits suicide. Michael also develops a romantic attachment to fellow-journalist Daniella Burkett, a reporter for the London *Times*. When Michael's government minder is hospitalized after stepping on a landmine, Michael is drawn into the complexities of the partisan struggles that are threatening to tear the country apart; through this experience, according to a writer for *Publishers Weekly*, Michael "makes the rare acquaintance of his own better self."

A contributor to *Kirkus Reviews* felt that the novel's flat and unconvincing characterizations detracted from its appeal. *Library Journal* reviewer Victor Or, on the other hand, found the book "well-written and credible," though providing only a "perfunctory" treatment of serious themes. A writer in *Publishers Weekly*, however, praised *The Ministry of Culture* as a "harrowing" narrative about Saddam's Iraq and noted that the book is "that rare war narrative that doesn't depend on carnage for the lasting impressions it creates." Michael Leonard, writing on the *Curled Up with a Good Book* Web site, described the book as "at times both mesmerizing and dizzyingly repellent," and "a powerful evocation of a place on the edge, steadily being torn apart by violence and passion with a government that supervises and directs all its activity."

BIOGRAPHICAL AND CRITICAL SOURCES:

PERIODICALS

Kirkus Reviews, March 1, 2007, review of *The Ministry of Culture*, p. 190.

Library Journal, March 15, 2007, Victor Or, review of *The Ministry of Culture*, p. 62.
Publishers Weekly, February 12, 2007, review of *The Ministry of Culture*, p. 60.

ONLINE

Curled Up with a Good Book, http://www.curledup.com/ (October 9, 2007), Michael Leonard, review of *The Ministry of Culture*.*

*   *   *

MUNDY, Liza 1960-

PERSONAL: Born 1960; married; children: two. *Education:* Princeton University, A.B.; University of Virginia, M.A.

ADDRESSES: *Home*—Arlington, VA. *E-mail*—LM@LizaMundy.com.

CAREER: *Washington Post Magazine*, feature writer.

AWARDS, HONORS: Awards for essays, profiles, and science writing from Sunday Magazine Editors Association, Maryland-Delaware-D.C. Press Association, American Association of Sunday and Feature Editors, Missouri Lifestyle Journalism Awards, and Gay and Lesbian Alliance against Defamation; Kaiser Foundation Media fellow, 2003; Media Fellow, Marine Biological Laboratory, Woods Hole, MA, 2005.

WRITINGS:

Everything Conceivable: How Assisted Reproduction Is Changing Men, Women, and the World, Alfred A. Knopf (New York, NY), 2007.

Work included in *The Best American Science Writing 2003*, edited by Oliver Sacks. Contributor to periodicals, including *Slate*, *Lingua Franca*, *Redbook*, *Washington City Paper*, and *Washington Monthly*.

SIDELIGHTS: In *Everything Conceivable: How Assisted Reproduction Is Changing Men, Women, and the World*, Liza Mundy explains the science and the societal impact of in vitro fertilization (IVF) and other new technologies that are allowing people to overcome physical obstacles to parenthood. Before the late 1970s, infertile couples who wanted children had few options. The birth of the first "test-tube baby" in 1978, however, in the words of *New York Times Book Review* contributor Polly Morrice, "changed everything." New technologies have allowed many would-be parents—including gay and lesbian couples, men with low sperm counts, and women who either cannot find a partner or have delayed conception past the age of forty—to have children. While this is largely a positive development, Mundy writes, it also carries negative consequences that have been inadequately addressed, in particular the high incidence of multiple births—twins, triplets, or even more—among parents who undergo IVF. Multiples, who are often born prematurely, are at significantly greater risk than singles for adverse health conditions, many of which can be life-long. As Mundy explained in an interview with Lynn Harris on *Salon.com,* "In some ways, IVF science is driving evolution backward rather than forward. While assisted reproduction may someday lead to a master race of genetically designed humans . . . in the here and now what it's doing, often, is creating babies who are at a disadvantage, rather than unfairly enhanced."

Mundy covers her topic with admirable "breadth and thoroughness," according to a writer for *Publishers Weekly.* In addition to biological matters, she considers issues relating to income and social class (for example, the practice of buying donor eggs or surrogate motherhood from lower-income women); examines causes of infertility, including the possible role of pollution in lowering sperm counts; and discusses insurance, religion, and the need for government regulation. Critics welcomed *Everything Conceivable* as a meticulously researched, engaging, and compassionate book. Though Morrice, in the *New York Times Book Review,* felt that its focus on parents who want "biological ties" between themselves and their children could be "unsettling" to advocates of adoption, the critic nevertheless praised the book for its lucidity and depth. A writer for the *Economist* lauded the "insight and sensitivity" that Mundy brings to her subject, and the reviewer for *Publishers Weekly,* observing that Mundy's subject is one about which all readers should become informed, concluded that "there couldn't be a better starting point than this book."

BIOGRAPHICAL AND CRITICAL SOURCES:

PERIODICALS

Advocate, April 24, 2007, Charlotte Abbott, review of *Everything Conceivable: How Assisted Reproduction Is Changing Men, Women, and the World,* p. 59.

Booklist, March 1, 2007, Donna Chavez, review of *Everything Conceivable,* p. 46.

Economist, July 28, 2007, "Made, Not Begotten; Fertility Treatment," p. 86.

Library Journal, March 15, 2007, Elizabeth Williams, review of *Everything Conceivable,* p. 87.

New York Times Book Review, April 22, 2007, Polly Morrice, review of *Everything Conceivable.*

Publishers Weekly, February 19, 2007, review of *Everything Conceivable,* p. 161; March 5, 2007, "Of Test Tubes and Babies: PW Talks with Liza Mundy," p. 48.

SciTech Book News, September, 2007, review of *Everything Conceivable.*

ONLINE

Liza Mundy Home page, http://www.lizamundy.com (October 10, 2007).

Salon.com, http://www.salon.com/ (October 10, 2007), Lynn Harris, "Bionic Parents and Techno-Children."*

*   *   *

MUÑOZ, Manuel 1972-

PERSONAL: Born 1972, in Dinuba, CA. *Education:* Harvard University, B.A.; Cornell University, M.F.A.

ADDRESSES: Home—New York, NY. *Agent*—Stuart Bernstein, Representation for Artists, 63 Carmine St., 3D, New York, NY 10014.

CAREER: Writer.

AWARDS, HONORS: Constance Saltonstall Foundation Individual Artist's Grant in Fiction; National Endowmen for the Arts fellowship in fiction, 2006.

WRITINGS:

Zigzagger, Northwestern University Press (Evanston, IL), 2003.

The Faith Healer of Olive Avenue, Algonquin Books of Chapel Hill (Chapel Hill, NC), 2007.

Contributor to periodicals, including *New York Times.*

SIDELIGHTS: Hailed by *Fresno Famous* contributor Jefferson Beavers as a "promising voice in contemporary Latino literature, Manuel Muñoz has written two well-received collections of short fiction inspired by his childhood in California's San Joaquin Valley. The son of farmworkers, Muñoz spent his childhood summers working in the fields and, later, got a job in a school warehouse to earn money for school supplies and clothes. A bright student, he received encouragement at school and became the first person in his family to graduate from college. Attending Harvard was a culture shock; he had left home with only a hundred dollars to cover books and expenses, and did not fit in with the majority of students on campus, who came from privileged backgrounds. He coped, as he explains on his home page, by writing, which offered him "much-needed self-expression."

Zigzagger, Muñoz's first collection, focuses on gay Latinos who are on the cusp of adulthood. *Booklist* reviewer Hazel Rochman enjoyed the fact that Muñoz's treatment of this theme is "not the usual shame-about-coming-out stuff." The stories, according to *Los Angeles Times* contributor David Ebershoff, show the plight of Central Valley's loneliest characters: "gay boys who drive up and down the country roads to find one another; fathers broken by decades of field work, a bright young woman who has made it to twenty without getting pregnant, unlike every other girl she knows." Ebershoff noted the book's honesty and despair, emphasizing that Muñoz is "too truthful a writer to present false hope." *Zigzagger,* he added, "heralds the arrival of a gifted and sensitive writer."

Similar praise met publication of Muñoz's second collection, *The Faith Healer of Olive Avenue.* Set in Fresno, California, the book illuminates characters who long for escape, transcendence, or acceptance: a young gay man who defers his own life to care for his disabled mother; a grieving mother who discovers, when she cleans her dead son's room, that the man who died with him in a motorcycle accident was his lover; a father mourning his son's suicide. "Muñoz writes with restraint and without pretension," commented a *Publishers Weekly* contributor, "giving fearless voice to personal tragedies." Jeff Turrentine, writing in *New York Times Book Review,* called the book a "moving and tender" collection with a narrative energy that "derives from the friction between the characters' conflicting desires for love and acceptance, escape and permanence." Muñoz's stories, in Turrentine's view, transcend the categories of gay or Chicano fiction, and are universal. A writer for *Kirkus Reviews* expressed similar enthusiasm, describing *The Faith Healer of Olive Avenue* as "fine storytelling that achieves universality while remaining rooted in a particular time and place." Reviewing the book in the *Austin Chronicle,* Belinda Acosta wrote: "Each [story] lingers, staying with you like memories stirred from the scent in a lost loved one's shirt. In a word, [the book is] exquisite."

Muñoz told *CA:* "While at the Cornell M.F.A. program, I began a crucial mentorship with the Chicana writer Helena Maria Viramontes, who introduced me to key texts of Chicano/a literature and helped shape many of the early stories of *Zigzagger.* I cited her continued presence in my writing life in the acknowledgements to my second book, calling her 'a literary madrina . . . on every page here, and those still to come.'"

BIOGRAPHICAL AND CRITICAL SOURCES:

PERIODICALS

Austin Chronicle (Austin, TX), September 7, 2007, Belinda Acosta, review of *The Faith Healer of Olive Avenue.*

Booklist, November 15, 2003, Hazel Rochman, review of *Zigzagger,* p. 581; March 15, 2007, Keir Graff, review of *The Faith Healer of Olive Avenue,* p. 26.

Kirkus Reviews, February 1, 2007, review of *The Faith Healer of Olive Avenue,* p. 94.

Library Journal, January, 2004, Harold Augenbraum, review of *Zigzagger,* p. 162.

Los Angeles Times, February 1, 2004, David Ebershoff, review of *Zigzagger,* p. 9.

New York Times Book Review, August 5, 2007, Jeff Turrentine, review of *The Faith Healer of Olive Avenue.*

Publishers Weekly, February 5, 2007, review of *The Faith Healer of Olive Avenue,* p. 37.

School Library Journal, April, 2007, Teri Titus, review of *The Faith Healer of Olive Avenue,* p. 170.

ONLINE

LA36: Aloud, http://www.la36.org/ (November 30, 2007), interview with author.

Entertainment Weekly, http://www.ew.com/ (October 10, 2007), Vanessa Juarez, review of *The Faith Healer of Olive Avenue.*

88.7 KUHF, Houston Public Radio, http://www.kuhf.org/ (June 27, 2007), Chris Johnson, interivew with author.

Fresno Famous, http://www.fresnofamous.com/node/206/ (October 10, 2007), Jefferson Beavers, "His Version of Home."

La Bloga, http://labloga.blogspot.com/ (October 10, 2007), Daniel Olivas, interview with Manuel Muñoz.

Manuel Muñoz Home Page, http://www.manuel-munoz.com (October 10, 2007).

National Endowment for the Arts Web site, http://www.nea.gov/ (October 10, 2007), "Manuel Muñoz."

Nuestra Palabra, http://www.nuestrapalabra.org/ (October 10, 2007), "Harvard Graduate and Rising Star Manuel Muñoz in Houston."

PopMatters, http://popmatters.com/ (October 10, 2007), Rachel Smucker, review of *The Faith Healer of Olive Avenue.*

MURDOCK, Linda

PERSONAL: Born in Milwaukee, WI. *Education:* Western Illinois University, B.S.

ADDRESSES: Office—Bellwether Books, P.O. Box 9757, Denver, CO 80209. *E-mail*—murd@bellwetherbooks.com.

CAREER: Bond Gold Corp., Denver, CO, tax assistant, 1986-88; Accuracy First Printing, Denver, owner, 1988-2007. Bellwether Books, publisher and writer, 2001—; also affiliated with a planned management company.

WRITINGS:

A Busy Cook's Guide to Spices: How to Introduce New Flavors to Everyday Meals, Bellwether Books (Denver, CO), 2001.

Almost Native, How to Pass as a Coloradan, Bellwether Books (Denver, CO), 2004.

Mystery Lover's Puzzle Book, Crosswords with Clues from Your Favorite Mystery Series, Bellwether Books (Denver, CO), 2007.

BIOGRAPHICAL AND CRITICAL SOURCES:

ONLINE

Bellwether Books Web site, http://bellwetherbooks.com (August 15, 2007).

N-O

NATHAN, Leonard 1924-2007
(Leonard E. Nathan, Leonard Edward Nathan)

OBITUARY NOTICE— See index for *CA* sketch: Born November 8, 1924, in Los Angeles, CA; died of complications from Alzheimer's disease, June 10, 2007. Poet, literary critic, translator, educator, and author. Nathan once described himself to *CA* as "a poet in search of a saving grace." The search consumed him for decades and resulted in more than a dozen collections of his work. Nathan was nominated for a National Book Award in 1975 for *Returning Your Call.* His fellowship at the American Institute of Indian Studies in the 1960s inspired *The Likeness: Poems out of India* (1975). Nathan was a lifelong poet. For more than thirty years he was also a teacher of rhetoric at the University of California in Berkeley, retiring as a professor emeritus in 1991. He wrote a few works of literary criticism and through his translations introduced English-speaking readers to the poetry of Ramprasad Sen, Gunnar Ekelof, Anna Swit, and Aleksander Wat. As a translator he sometimes collaborated with poet Czeslaw Milosz, whose work he also introduced to a Western audience. Nathan's later poetry collections include *The Potato Eaters* (1999), *Tears of the Old Magician* (2003), and *Restarting the World* (2006).

OBITUARIES AND OTHER SOURCES:

PERIODICALS

Los Angeles Times, June 9, 2007, p. B11

NATHAN, Leonard E.
See NATHAN, Leonard

*   *   *

NATHAN, Leonard Edward
See NATHAN, Leonard

*   *   *

NAVIA, Luis E. 1940-

PERSONAL: Born 1940, in Colombia; moved to the United States at seventeen. *Education:* Queens College, City University of New York, B.A. (magna cum laude), 1963; New York University, M.A., 1966, Ph.D., 1972; Coast Navigational School, CA, certificate, 1975.

ADDRESSES: Home—Old Westbury, NY. *Office*— Department of Social Sciences, College of Arts and Sciences, New York Institute of Technology, Northern Blvd., Old Westbury, NY 11568-8000. *E-mail*— lnavia@nyit.edu.

CAREER: Worked at the United Nations and the *New York Daily News;* Hofstra University, New York, NY, instructor in foreign languages, 1965-67, adjunct professor of philosophy, 1987-92; Queens College, City University of New York, Queens, NY, lecturer in philosophy, 1965-70; New York Institute of Technology, Old Westbury, NY, professor of philosophy,

1968—; New York University, New York, NY, lecturer in philosophy, 1970; School of Visual Arts, New York, NY, adjunct professor of philosophy, 1978-92. Also served as consultant for Commission on Higher Education, Middle States Association, 1974-2005, New York Chiropractic College, 1986, St. Brigid/Our Lady of Hope Regional School, 1997, and Electronic Data Processing College of Puerto Rico, 2002-04. Program evaluator, philosophy department, University of Massachusetts at Dartmouth, 2002.

MEMBER: Council on Chiropractic Education (chairman of committee on ethics, 1983-86).

AWARDS, HONORS: Phi Beta Kappa Alumni Association Award, 1959; Outstanding Educators of America Award, 1975; National Endowment for the Humanities fellow, Princeton University, 1977; Presidential Service Award, New York Institute of Technology, 1985; award for service to the Long Island Philosophical Society, St. John's University, 2006.

WRITINGS:

(Editor, with Nicholas Capaldi) *Journeys through Philosophy: A Classical Introduction,* Prometheus Books (Buffalo, NY), 1977, new edition, with Nicholas Capaldi and Eugene Kelly, Prometheus Books (Buffalo, NY), 1982.

A Bridge to the Stars: Our Ancient Cosmic Legacy, Avery Publishing Group (Wayne, NJ), 1977.

(Editor, with Eugene Kelly) *Ethics and the Search for Values,* Prometheus Books (Buffalo, NY), 1980.

(With Nicholas Capaldi and Eugene Kelly) *An Invitation to Philosophy,* Prometheus Books (Buffalo, NY), 1981.

(Editor, with Eugene Kelly) *The Fundamental Questions: A Selection of Readings in Philosophy,* Kendall/Hunt Publishing (Dubuque, IA), 1985.

Socrates, the Man and His Philosophy, University Press of America (Lanham, MD), 1985.

Socratic Testimonies, University Press of America (Lanham, MD), 1987, University Press of America (Lanham, MD), 2002.

(With Ellen L. Katz) *Socrates: An Annotated Bibliography,* Garland (New York, NY), 1988.

Pythagoras: An Annotated Bibliography, Garland (New York, NY), 1990.

The Presocratic Philosophers: An Annotated Bibliography, Garland (New York, NY), 1993.

The Socratic Presence: A Study of the Sources, Garland (New York, NY), 1993.

The Philosophy of Cynicism: An Annotated Bibliography, Greenwood Press (Westport, CT), 1995.

Classical Cynicism: A Critical Study, Greenwood Press (Westport, CT), 1996.

Diogenes of Sinope: The Man in the Tub, Greenwood Press (Westport, CT), 1998.

The Adventure of Philosophy, Greenwood Press (Westport, CT), 1999.

Antisthenes of Athens: Setting the World Aright, Greenwood Press (Westport, CT), 2001.

Diogenes the Cynic: The War against the World, Humanity Books (Amherst, NY), 2005.

Socrates: A Life Examined, Prometheus Books (Amherst, NY), 2007.

Journal of Critical Analysis, editorial associate, 1973-82. Princeton University Press, referee, 1985; University of Notre Dame Press, reader-reviewer, 2003.

SIDELIGHTS: Colombian-born writer and educator Luis E. Navia received a Jesuit primary education in his native country before moving to the United States at the age of seventeen. Settling in New York, he went on to study philosophy at Queens College and later at New York University, eventually earning his doctorate. Navia worked various jobs before joining the faculty of the New York Institute of Technology in 1968, where he serves as a professor of philosophy. He has also written and/or edited a number of books, many of which delve into ancient Greek philosophical thought, focusing on such notable thinkers as Socrates and Diogenes. In *Diogenes the Cynic: The War against the World,* Navia examines the life and philosophy of Diogenes, who died in 323 BC and was survived by none of his writings. Navia looks at supporting materials and the accounts of others in order to create a framework of Diogenes' life. Dr. Tami Brady, writing for the *TCM Reviews* Web site, remarked: "This book is so complete, that the reader need not have prior knowledge of the subject matter." *Socrates: A Life Examined* also delves into the life of an ancient Greek philosopher about whom little is known, but Navia strives to piece together a picture of Socrates' life based on the writings of his contemporaries. *Booklist* reviewer Gilbert Taylor noted: "Navia shows where biographical agreement exists and where inference and speculation begin." *Classical Cynicism: A Critical Study* offers readers a broader look at the world of philosophical thought. Here Navia looks at trends rising from the counterculture in all parts of the world, and how they affect local philosophies. A reviewer for *Philosophy East and West* found the book to be "a rich and ready survey of the sources for and the traditions about the ancient Cynics."

BIOGRAPHICAL AND CRITICAL SOURCES:

PERIODICALS

Booklist, March 15, 2007, Gilbert Taylor, review of *Socrates: A Life Examined,* p. 6.

Internet Bookwatch, August, 2007, review of *Socrates.*

Philosophy East and West, January, 1998, review of *Classical Cynicism: A Critical Study,* p. 188.

Reference & Research Book News, May, 2006, review of *Diogenes the Cynic: The War against the World;* August, 2007, review of *Socrates.*

School Library Journal, April, 2007, Susanne Bardelson, review of *Socrates,* p. 173.

ONLINE

Legendary Times Web site, http://www.legendarytimes. com/ (October 9, 2007), "Prof. Dr. Luis E. Navia: Literature, Awards, Etc."

New York Institute of Technology Web site, http://iris. nyit.edu/ (October 9, 2007), King Cheek, faculty biography.

Publishers Weekly Online, http://www.publishers weekly.com/ (March 26, 2007), review of *Socrates.*

TCM Reviews, http://www.tcm-ca.com/ (October 9, 2007), Dr. Tami Brady, review of *Diogenes the Cynic.*

University of Delaware, American Philosophical Association Web site, http://apa.udel.edu/ (October 9, 2007), Haim Marantz, review of *The Fundamental Questions: A Selection of Readings in Philosophy.*

World Mysteries Forum, http://www.worldmysteries forum.ch/ (October 9, 2007), author biography.*

*   *   *

NUTTALL, Geoffrey F.
    See NUTTALL, Geoffrey Fillingham

NUTTALL, Geoffrey Fillingham 1911-2007
    (Geoffrey F. Nuttall)

OBITUARY NOTICE— See index for *CA* sketch: Born November 8, 1911, in Colwyn Bay, Denbighshire, Wales; died July 24, 2007, near Burcot, Worcestershire, England. Minister, church historian, educator, and author. Nuttall was ordained a Congregational minister in 1938, but his enthusiasm for church history knew few bounds. He was especially interested in the more liberal and charismatic, even radical, aspects of British Puritanism, an area rarely explored in depth by other scholars, and his focus was upon the seventeenth and eighteenth centuries. He thought of himself as a Separatist and dissenter, rather than a traditional Calvinist. Nuttall preached to Congregational (later United Reformed) congregations, but he spent much of his career as an academic. He taught church history and theology at the University of London, at New College, from 1945 to 1977, then at King's College, London, from 1977 to 1980. Nuttall was active in many church-historical organizations: a past president of the Congregational Historical Society, the Ecclesiastical Historical Society, and the United Reformed Church Historical Society. His historical interests reached beyond the Protestant denominations; he also studied such topics as the Chartres cathedral, Bernard of Clairvaux, Erasmus, and William Temple, Archbishop of Canterbury, often in Welsh, Latin, ancient Greek, and other languages in which he was fluent. Nuttall was a prolific writer, with no less than 600 titles to his credit, at least thirty of them full-length books. These include *The Holy Spirit in Puritan Faith and Experience* (1946), *Visible Saints: The Congregational Way, 1640-1660* (1957), *Christianity and Violence* (1972), *Studies in Christian Enthusiasm* (1983), and *Early Quakers and the Divine Presence* (2003).

OBITUARIES AND OTHER SOURCES:

BOOKS

Knox, R. Buick, editor, *Reformation, Conformity, and Dissent: Essays in Honour of Geoffrey Nuttall,* Epworth Press (London, England), 1977.

PERIODICALS

Times (London, England), August 29, 2007, p. 47.

O'CONNELL, Caitlin 1965-
(Caitlin O'Connell-Rodwell)

PERSONAL: Born 1965; married; husband's name Tim Rodwell. *Education:* Fairfield University, B.S.; University of Hawaii at Manoa, M.S.; University of California at Davis, Ph.D.

ADDRESSES: Home—San Diego, CA. *Office*—School of Medicine, Stanford University, 801 Welch Rd., Stanford, CA 94305. *E-mail*—ceoconnell@utopia scientific.org.

CAREER: Educator. Namibian Ministry of Environment and Tourism, Etosha National Park, Namibia, contract researcher for three years; Center for Conservation Biology, former research affiliate; Stanford University School of Medicine, Stanford, CA, postdoctoral fellow in Clark Center Bio-X Program, became assistant professor. Operates Triple Helix Productions (film company), with husband, Tim Rodwell. Cofounder and codirector, with husband, of Utopia Scientific (formerly Keystone Species International).

AWARDS, HONORS: Stanford University Department of Pediatrics and Hansen Experimental Physics Laboratory, postdoctoral fellowship; research grants from National Geographic Society, the U.S. Fish and Wildlife Service, the National Science Foundation, TRAFFIC International, and Stanford University; Rotary International Vocational Scholar.

WRITINGS:

The Elephant's Secret Sense: The Hidden Life of the Wild Herds of Africa, Free Press (New York, NY), 2007.

SIDELIGHTS: Caitlin O'Connell is an expert in evolution and conservation biology, with a particular interest in the elephant and its ability to sense seismic activity and other shifts in nature. She first became intrigued by the animals during the three years she spent in Namibia as a contract researcher working for the Namibian Ministry of Environment and Tourism, when she sought to alleviate the ongoing conflicts between local farmers and elephant herds. It was then that she first became aware of the elephant's ability to "hear" over large distances through their feet and trunks, based on the vibrations that travel through the ground. Further research resulted in O'Connell's book, *The Elephant's Secret Sense: The Hidden Life of the Wild Herds of Africa.* The book serves as combination memoir and scientific report, recounting O'Connell's experiences during her initial trip to Namibia as well as her continued research into elephant senses that she performed in California. She suggests that elephants are accustomed to communicating over distance through vibrations in the ground, and that this method of communication makes them extremely aware of their environment as well. A contributor to *Kirkus Reviews* dubbed the book "a remarkable account of elephant communication, though difficult in spots." A reviewer for *Publishers Weekly* found O'Connell's work to be "a successful combination of science and soulfulness, . . . studded with sympathetic insights and well-turned phrases."

BIOGRAPHICAL AND CRITICAL SOURCES:

BOOKS

O'Connell, Caitlin, *The Elephant's Secret Sense: The Hidden Life of the Wild Herds of Africa,* Free Press (New York, NY), 2007.

PERIODICALS

Australasian Business Intelligence, June 3, 2007, "Elephants down to Earth in Making Distance Calls to Neighbours."
Booklist, February 1, 2007, Nancy Bent, review of *The Elephant's Secret Sense,* p. 12.
Chronicle of Higher Education, November 10, 2006, Megan Lindow, "Eavesdropping on the Elephants."
Discover, July, 2001, Jocelyn Selim, "Reach Out and Stomp Someone," p. 13; March, 2007, Jennifer Barone, review of *The Elephant's Secret Sense,* p. 67.
Entertainment Weekly, March 30, 2007, Joan Keener, review of *The Elephant's Secret Sense,* p. 78.
Kirkus Reviews, February 1, 2007, review of *The Elephant's Secret Sense,* p. 115.
Library Journal, February 1, 2007, Ann Forister, review of *The Elephant's Secret Sense,* p. 94.

Natural History, April, 2002, Alan Burdick, "Four Ears to the Ground: For an Elephant, the Foot May Be a Powerful Listening Device," p. 86; May, 2006, "Ear to the Ground," p. 12.

Publishers Weekly, January 8, 2007, review of *The Elephant's Secret Sense,* p. 44.

Science News, April 28, 2007, review of *The Elephant's Secret Sense,* p. 271.

ONLINE

BookPage, http://www.bookpage.com/ (October 9, 2007), Carolyn Stalcup, "The Good Vibrations of an Elephant Herd."

Bookslut, http://www.bookslut.com/ (October 9, 2007), Barbara J. King, "Elephant Secrets, or, a Fever-Powered Trip from Virginia to Namibia."

Boston Globe Online, http://www.boston.com/ (June 28, 2007), Colin Nickerson, "Elephants' Toes Get the Message, Study Finds."

PBS Web site, http://www.pbs.org/ (October 9, 2007), author biography.

San Francisco Chronicle Online, http://sfgate.com/ (May 19, 2007), profile of Caitlin O'Connell.

Stanford University, Molecular Imaging Program Web site, http://mips.stanford.edu/ (October 9, 2007), faculty profile.

University of Hawaii, Malamalama Magazine, http://www.hawaii.edu/malamalma/ (October 9, 2007) Cheryl Ernst, "Understanding Elephants: UH Scholars Study Wild and Working Animals on Two Continents."

Utopia Scientific Web site, http://www.utopiascientific.org/ (October 9, 2007), founder profile.

* * *

O'CONNELL-RODWELL, Caitlin
See O'CONNELL, Caitlin

* * *

O'DELL, Carol D.

PERSONAL: Children: three daughters. *Education:* Jacksonville University, B.S.; Bethany Theological Seminary, studies in theology and church organization, 1983. *Hobbies and other interests:* Reading, writing, art, theology, philosophy, astronomy, cooking, traveling.

ADDRESSES: Home—Ponte Vedra Beach, FL. *E-mail*—writecarol@comcast.net.

CAREER: Writer. Has taught at writers' conferences and seminars. First Coast Writer's Festival, FL, committee member.

MEMBER: National Storyteller's Society, National League of American Pen Women, Authors Guild, Author's Writer's Programs, Zona Rosa Women Writers, Georgia Writers, Saint Louis Writer's Guild.

AWARDS, HONORS: Partial fellowships from Southeast Writers Conference, 2001, and Middle Georgia College, 2002, Summer Literary Series (St. Petersburg, Russia), 2005; John Woods Scholarship, Prague Summer Institute, 2006.

WRITINGS:

Mothering Mother: A Daughter's Humorous and Heartbreaking Memoir, Kunati (Largo, FL), 2007.

Also contributor to numerous magazines, periodicals, and journals, including, *HER: Home Education Resource, Jacksonville Magazine, Atlanta Magazine, America's Interracial, Margin, Pisgah Review, Andwerve Literary Journal, Flashquake.com,* and *Chicken Soup Celebrates Sister.*

SIDELIGHTS: Carol D. O'Dell is the author of fiction and creative nonfiction, including short stories, articles, and essays. In her first book, *Mothering Mother: A Daughter's Humorous and Heartbreaking Memoir,* O'Dell writes of caring for her mother as she slowly succumbs to both Alzheimer's disease and Parkinson's disease. The author details her hectic life as she deals with her mother, husband, and three children. In the process, she also recalls her mother as she once was—a six-foot-tall imposing figure and a firebrand minister. "When reading this haunting and substantive memoir, two other books came to mind: *A Year of Magical Thinking* by Joan Didion and *Tuesdays with Morrie* by Mitch Albom," wrote T.K. Kenyon on the *Suite 101* Web site. Kenyon went on to note that the O'Dell's "memoir . . . is a more realistic, gritty book than either one of those two." For example, O'Dell eventually must make a fateful, life-

or-death decision about whether or not her mother should be placed on a feeding tube. In another episode, she discovers her mother at night covered in feces. Several reviewers, including Kenyon, noted that, despite the difficult task of caring for her mother, the author includes humorous anecdotes. Mary Frances Wilkens, writing in *Booklist,* commented that O'Dell tells her story "with plenty of humor, a touch of martyrdom, and much love." Kenyon wrote: "Although this book is, in some places, emotionally difficult to read, it's a beautiful book about coming to terms with the death of a loved one."

BIOGRAPHICAL AND CRITICAL SOURCES:

BOOKS

O'Dell, Carol D., *Mothering Mother: A Daughter's Humorous and Heartbreaking Memoir,* Kunati (Largo, FL), 2007.

PERIODICALS

Booklist, February 15, 2007, Mary Frances Wilkens, review of *Mothering Mother,* p. 19.

ONLINE

Carol D. O'Dell Home Page, http://www.caroldodell.com (September 4, 2007).
Suite 101, http://recommended-non-fiction.suite101.com/ (April 8, 2007), T.K. Kenyon, review of *Mothering Mother.*
Writers Net, http://www.writers.net/writers/ (September 4, 2007), biography of Carol D. O'Dell.*

*   *   *

ODELL-SCOTT, David W. 1953-

PERSONAL: Born May 4, 1953, in Indianapolis, IN; son of Willis and JoAnn Scott; married August 16, 1975; wife's name Lauren (a minister and college professor); children: Megan, Paul. *Education:* Texas Christian University, B.A., 1975; Vanderbilt University, M.Div., 1980, Ph.D., 1989. *Politics:* Democrat. *Religion:* Christian Church (Disciples of Christ).

ADDRESSES: Home—Kent, OH. *Office*—Department of Philosophy, Kent State University, Kent, OH 44242-0001. *E-mail*—dodellsc@kent.edu.

CAREER: Vanderbilt University, Nashville, TN, adjunct instructor, 1984-90; Belmont University, Nashville, assistant professor of philosophy and religion, 1985-87; Fisk University, Nashville, assistant professor of philosophy and religion and department chair, 1987-90; Kent State University, Kent, OH, began as assistant professor, became associate professor, 1990-2003, professor of philosophy and department chair, 2003—, cofounder and codirector of Ohio Pluralism Project. Presenter of workshops on religion in America, 2000-06.

MEMBER: North American Paul Tillich Society, Society of Biblical Literature, American Academy of Religion, American Philosophical Association, Society for Phenomenology and Existential Philosophies.

AWARDS, HONORS: Selection among outstanding academic titles, *Choice,* 2006, for *Democracy and Religion: Free Exercise and Diverse Visions.*

WRITINGS:

A Post-Patriarchal Christology, Scholars Press (Atlanta, GA), 1991.
Paul's Critique of Theocracy: A/theocracy in Corinthians and Galatians, T & T Clark International (New York, NY), 2003.
(Editor) *Democracy and Religion: Free Exercise and Diverse Visions,* Kent State University Press (Kent, OH), 2004.
(Editor) *Reading Romans with Contemporary Philosophers and Theologians,* T & T Clark International (New York, NY), 2007.

Contributor to books, including *Gender, Tradition, and Romans: Shared Ground, Uncertain Borders,* edited by Cristina Grenholm and Daniel Patte, T & T Clark International, 2005. Contributor to journals, including *Encounter* and *Biblical Theology Bulletin.*

SIDELIGHTS: David W. Odell-Scott told *CA:* "I am concerned about the interactions between readers and texts, especially the issue of interpretive responsibility. Much of my interest has to do with the reading and interpretation of primary texts in the Christian corpus."

OLSON, Michael Keith

PERSONAL: Son of Robert "Pat" Olson.

ADDRESSES: Home—Santa Cruz, CA. *E-mail*—michael@tincan.us.

CAREER: Journalist, agriculturalist, freelance farm consultant. Worked variously as writer, photographer, and producer for the *San Francisco Chronicle,* the *Examiner,* NBC, ABC, the Australian Broadcast Commission, and KQED Public Television; *Food Chain* syndicated radio program, producer and host; MO MultiMedia Group, Santa Cruz, CA, president.

WRITINGS:

MetroFarm: The Guide to Growing for Big Profit on a Small Parcel of Land, TS Books (Santa Cruz, CA), 1994.
Tales from a Tin Can: The U.S.S. Dale from Pearl Harbor to Tokyo Bay, Zenith Press (St. Paul, MN), 2007.

SIDELIGHTS: Agriculturist and journalist Michael Keith Olson travels globally in his work as a consultant for farm projects. Over the course of his career, he has also served as a writer, producer, and photographer, his work appearing in such publications as the *San Francisco Chronicle* and the *Examiner,* and on network news programs for ABC, NBC, Australian television, and public television. Olson hosts and produces the syndicated radio program, "Food Chain," and is the president of MO MultiMedia Group in Santa Cruz, California. His first book, *MetroFarm: The Guide to Growing for Big Profit on a Small Parcel of Land,* stems from his interest in food production and farming, and is a guide to how to maintain a small farm within the confines of the city.

Olson's follow-up effort, *Tales from a Tin Can: The U.S.S. Dale from Pearl Harbor to Tokyo Bay,* is an homage to his father, Robert "Pat" Olson, who served on the U.S.S. *Dale* for three years following the attack on Pearl Harbor. In researching the project, Olson intertwined material gleaned from a series of oral histories produced by crew members with information from the ship's log and other data he considered likely to give readers an accurate historical perspective. A reviewer for *Publishers Weekly* called Olson's effort "an impressive accomplishment, bringing vividly to life the actions of a single warship that fought across half the world." *Booklist* contributor Roland Green considered the book "a sound addition to World War II naval literature."

When asked what first got him interested in writing, Olson told *CA:* "The desire to entertain and inform, which I saw, at a very early age, as a way of earning one's way in the world."

Olson cited authors Ernest Hemingway and Robert A. Heinlein, NBC, and "all things ancient China," as influences on his work.

He described his writing process as "The War of the Worlds: three a.m. to seven a.m."

When asked which of his books is his favorite, he answered: "Each of them, because they each represent a slice of my life."

Olson said he hopes that readers of his books "will get their money's worth."

BIOGRAPHICAL AND CRITICAL SOURCES:

PERIODICALS

Booklist, March 1, 2007, Roland Green, review of *Tales from a Tin Can: The U.S.S. Dale from Pearl Harbor to Tokyo Bay,* p. 58.
Publishers Weekly, December 11, 2006, review of *Tales from a Tin Can,* p. 60.

ONLINE

Destroyers.org, http://www.destroyers.org/ (October 9, 2007), James Healy, review of *Tales from a Tin Can.*
MetroFarm Web site, http://www.metrofarm.com (November 15, 2007).
Midwest Book Review, http://www.midwestbookreview.com/ (October 9, 2007), review of *Tales from a Tin Can.*
Tincan Web site, http://tincan.us (October 9, 2007).

OVERTVELDT, Johan Van 1955-

PERSONAL: Born August 24, 1955; married Hilde Jacobs, 1978; children: Matthias, David, Frederik, Laura. *Education:* University of Antwerp (UFSIA), license, 1977, Ph.D., 2001; Catholic University of Leuven, M.B.A., 1978. *Hobbies and other interests:* Read, bicycle, jog.

ADDRESSES: Home—Belgium. *Office*—Director, VKW Denktank, Sneeuwbeslaan 20, 2610 Wilrijk, Belgium.

CAREER: Trends magazine, Belgium, editor, 1978-82, head editor, 1992-99, chief economist, 1999-2004; Brussels Lambert Bank, staff member, 1982-87; Shoe-konfex (distribution chain of shoes and textiles), general director, 1987-91; BTR, automotive group advisor, 1991-92; VKW Metena, Belgium, director, 2004.

WRITINGS:

(With others) *Crash or Boom? De Wereldeconomie Op Het Einde Van Het Millennium,* Roularta Books (Roeselare, Belgium), 1999.

Fons Verplaetse, De Peetvader, Roularta Books (Roeselare, Belgium), 1999.

Marktzege(n): Zes Aanklachten Tegen Het Antiglobalisme, Pelckmans (Kapellen, Belgium), 2002.

De Euroscheppers: Macht En Manipulatie Achter De Euro, Pelckmans (Kapellen, Belgium), 2003.

The Chicago School: How the University of Chicago Assembled the Thinkers Who Revolutionized Economics and Business, Agate (Chicago, IL), 2007.

Contributor to periodicals, including *Knack, Trends, Time, Standard,* and the *Wall Street Journal.*

SIDELIGHTS: Johan Van Overtveldt is an expert in economics and serves as director of VKW Metena, a think tank located in Belgium that focuses primarily on issues related to the economy. In the past, he held a number of positions at *Trends,* a news magazine, including editor and chief economist. His writings have appeared in various news publications worldwide, including *Time,* the *Standard,* and the *Wall Street Journal.* He has also published several books, primarily in Belgium, and is best known on an international level for *The Chicago School: How the University of Chicago Assembled the Thinkers Who Revolutionized Economics and Business,* which was released in the United States in 2007. The book takes a look at the history of the study of business and economics at the University of Chicago, an institute of higher education whose graduates and professors have garnered an unusually high proportion of Nobel Prizes and other awards in the economics field. Overtveldt examines the theory behind the famed "Chicago School" of economics, which advocates a strongly free-market economy, and its proponents, as well as the history of disagreement both on campus and in the academic community on the whole. A reviewer for *ForeWord Magazine* online dubbed the book a "challenging and informative study." Writing in the *Economist,* a reviewer found: "This is an admirably detailed and thoroughly welcome history of a great centre of economic thought." A reviewer in *Publishers Weekly* concluded that the book's "exploration of the interaction between institution and idea is unique and fascinating."

BIOGRAPHICAL AND CRITICAL SOURCES:

PERIODICALS

Booklist, April 15, 2007, Mary Whaley, review of *The Chicago School: How the University of Chicago Assembled the Thinkers Who Revolutionized Economics and Business,* p. 10.

Economist, June 23, 2007, "Hyde Park Corner: Economics in Chicago," p. 96.

Internet Bookwatch, August, 2007, "The Chicago School."

Publishers Weekly, March 26, 2007, review of *The Chicago School,* p. 77.

Reference & Research Book News, May, 2007, review of *The Chicago School.*

ONLINE

American: A Magazine of Ideas, http://www.american.com/ (May 17, 2007), Alan D. Viard, "A Free-Market Outpost in the Midwest," review of *The Chicago School.*

ForeWord Magazine, http://www.forewordmagazine. com/ (October 9, 2007), review of *The Chicago School.*

Midwest Book Review, http://www.midwestbook review.com/ (October 9, 2007), review of *The Chicago School.*

Stockholm Network Web site, http://www.stockholm- network.org/ (October 25, 2005), "Lessons from US Social Security Reform."

VKW Metena Web site, http://www.vkwmetana.be/ (October 9, 2007), employee profile.*

P

PANNILL, Katherine
   See CENTER, Katherine

* * *

PASTOR, Ben 1950-
   (Verbena Pastor)

PERSONAL: Born 1950; birth name Verbena Pastor; married; husband's name Daniel; children: Alex (daughter).

ADDRESSES: Home—VT. *Office*—School of Graduate Studies, Norwich University, 158 Harmon Dr., Northfield, VT 05663.

CAREER: Norwich University, Northfield, VT, associate professor of graduate studies.

WRITINGS:

NOVELS

Lumen, Van Neste Books (Midlothian, VA), 1999.
Liar Moon, Van Neste Books (Richmond, VA), 2001.
The Water Thief, Thomas Dunne Books/St. Martin's Minotaur (New York, NY), 2007.

Contributor of academic articles and short fiction to periodicals, including *Alfred Hitchcock's Mystery Magazine, Strand, Ellen Queen's Mystery Magazine,* and *Yellow Silk.*

SIDELIGHTS: Ben Pastor writes mystery novels with historical settings, such as World War II-era Europe under Nazi occupation in *Lumen* and *Liar Moon,* and the time of the Roman Empire in *The Water Thief.* The latter book, taking place in the fourth century AD and featuring many real-life figures, finds former soldier and imperial historian Aelius Spartianus commanded by Emperor Diocletian to investigate the death, 200 years earlier, of Emperor Hadrian's male lover, Antinous. Aelius and Diocletian suspect that when Antinous drowned in the Nile River, it was neither accident nor suicide but murder. Over the course of his work, Aelius discovers evidence of a conspiracy against the empire, and some of his associates lose their lives while his own is threatened.

Several reviewers praised the novel's historical background as well as its mystery plot. Pastor's narrative touches on the empire's political and religious conflicts, the lives of its gay inhabitants, and the environment in its military outposts. Her vivid portrayal of Roman times makes *The Water Thief* "far richer than the traditional whodunit," observed Dennis Drabelle in the *Washington Post Book World.* A *Publishers Weekly* critic noted that Pastor spreads her story across "an elaborately detailed canvas." A *Kirkus Reviews* contributor, however, deemed the historical detail excessive, saying Pastor "buries her interesting story and well-drawn characters under an avalanche of research," while *Booklist* commentator Connie Fletcher found the Roman background riveting even though she thought that "the plot meanders." The *Publishers Weekly* reviewer had compliments for both plot and setting, summing up the novel as a "satisfyingly convoluted historical." In a similar vein, Drabelle concluded that Pastor "persuasively evokes an ancient world" and "works shrewd variations on the known facts."

BIOGRAPHICAL AND CRITICAL SOURCES:

PERIODICALS

Booklist, February 1, 2007, Connie Fletcher, review of The Water Thief, p. 36.

Kirkus Reviews, January 15, 2007, review of The Water Thief, p. 54.

Publishers Weekly, January 29, 2007, review of The Water Thief, p. 46.

Washington Post Book World, March 11, 2007, Dennis Drabelle, review of The Water Thief, p. 11.

ONLINE

Italian Mysteries.com, http://www.italian-mysteries. com (September 8, 2007), brief author biography and plot summary of Liar Moon.*

*   *   *

PASTOR, Verbena
    See PASTOR, Ben

*   *   *

PATON WALSH, Gillian
    See PATON WALSH, Jill

*   *   *

PATON WALSH, Jill 1937-
    (Gillian Paton Walsh, Gillian Paton Walsh)

PERSONAL: Born April 29, 1937, in London, England; daughter of John Llewellyn (an engineer) and Patricia Bliss; married Antony Edmund Paton Walsh (a chartered secretary), August 12, 1961 (marriage ended); married John Rowe Townsend (a writer), 2004; children: Edmund Alexander, Margaret Ann,

Jill Paton Walsh

Helen Clare. Education: St. Anne's College, Oxford, Dip.Ed., 1959, M.A. (with honors). Religion: "Skepticism." Hobbies and other interests: Photography, gardening, cooking, carpentry, reading.

ADDRESSES: Home—Cambridge, England. Agent—Bruce Hunter, David Higham Associates, 5-8 Lower John St., Golden Sq., London W1F 9HA, England.

CAREER: Enfield Girls Grammar School, Middlesex, English teacher, 1959-62; writer, 1962—. Whittall Lecturer, Library of Congress, Washington, DC, 1978. Visiting faculty member, Center for the Study of Children's Literature, Simmons College, Boston, 1978-86. Founder, with John Rowe Townsend, of Green Bay Publishers, 1986.

MEMBER: Society of Authors, Royal Society of Literature (fellow), Children's Writers Group.

AWARDS, HONORS: Book World Festival award, 1970, for Fireweed; Whitbread Prize (shared with Russell Hoban), 1974, for The Emperor's Winding

Sheet; *Boston Globe-Horn Book* Award, 1976, for *Unleaving;* Arts Council creative writing fellowship, 1976-77, and 1977-78; Universe Prize, 1984, for *A Parcel of Patterns;* Smarties Prize Grand Prix, 1984, for *Gaffer Samson's Luck;* named Commander of the British Empire, 1996; Phoenix Award, 1998, for *A Chance Child.*

WRITINGS:

FICTION FOR CHILDREN

Hengest's Tale, illustrated by Janet Margrie, St. Martin's Press (New York, NY), 1966.

The Dolphin Crossing, St. Martin's Press (New York, NY), 1967.

Fireweed, Macmillan (London, England), 1969, Farrar, Straus (New York, NY), 1970.

Goldengrove, Farrar, Straus (New York, NY), 1972.

Toolmaker, illustrated by Jeroo Roy, Heinemann (London, England), 1973, Seabury Press (New York, NY), 1974.

The Dawnstone, illustrated by Mary Dinsdale, Hamish Hamilton (London, England), 1973.

The Emperor's Winding Sheet, Farrar, Straus (New York, NY), 1974.

The Huffler, Farrar, Straus (New York, NY), 1975, published as *The Butty Boy,* illustrated by Juliette Palmer, Macmillan (London, England), 1975.

Unleaving, Farrar, Straus (New York, NY), 1976.

Crossing to Salamis (first novel in trilogy; also see below), illustrated by David Smee, Heinemann (London, England), 1977.

The Walls of Athens (second novel in trilogy; also see below), illustrated by David Smee, Heinemann (London, England), 1977.

Persian Gold (third novel in trilogy; also see below), illustrated by David Smee, Heinemann (London, England), 1978.

Children of the Fox (contains *Crossing to Salamis,* *The Walls of Athens,* and *Persian Gold*), Farrar, Straus (New York, NY), 1978.

A Chance Child, Farrar, Straus (New York, NY), 1978.

The Green Book, illustrated by Joanna Stubbs, Macmillan (London, England), 1981, illustrated by Lloyd Bloom, Farrar, Straus (New York, NY), 1982, published as *Shine,* Macdonald (London, England), 1988.

Babylon, illustrated by Jenny Northway, Deutsch (London, England), 1982.

A Parcel of Patterns, Farrar, Straus (New York, NY), 1983.

Lost and Found, illustrated by Mary Rayner, Deutsch (London, England), 1984.

Gaffer Samson's Luck, illustrated by Brock Cole, Farrar, Straus (New York, NY), 1984.

Torch, Viking (New York, NY), 1987.

Birdy and the Ghosties, illustrated by Alan Marks, Macdonald (London, England), 1989.

Can I Play Jenny Jones?, Bodley Head (London, England), 1990.

Can I Play Queenie?, Bodley Head (London, England), 1990.

Grace, Viking (New York, NY), 1991.

Can I Play Farmer, Farmer? Bodley Head (London, England), 1992.

Can I Play Wolf? Bodley Head (London, England), 1992.

When Grandma Came (picture book), illustrated by Sophie Williams, Viking (New York, NY), 1992.

Matthew and the Sea Singer, Farrar, Straus (New York, NY), 1993.

Pepi and the Secret Names, Lee & Shepard (New York, NY), 1995.

Connie Came to Play, Viking (New York, NY), 1995.

Thomas and the Tinners, Hodder Wayland (London, England), 1995.

When I Was Little Like You, Viking (New York, NY), 1997.

OTHER

(With Kevin Crossley Holland) *Wordhoard: Anglo-Saxon Stories,* Farrar, Straus (New York, NY), 1969.

Farewell, Great King (adult novel), Coward McCann, 1972.

(Editor) *Beowulf* (structural reader), Longman, 1975.

The Island Sunrise: Prehistoric Britain, Deutsch (London, England), 1975, published as *The Island Sunrise: Prehistoric Culture in the British Isles,* Seabury Press (New York, NY), 1976.

Five Tides (short stories), Green Bay, 1986.

Lapsing (adult novel), Weidenfeld & Nicolson (London, England), 1986, St. Martin's Press (New York, NY), 1987.

A School for Lovers (adult novel), Weidenfeld & Nicolson (London, England), 1989.

The Wyndham Case, St. Martin's Press (New York, NY), 1993.

Knowledge of Angels, Houghton Mifflin (Boston, MA), 1994.

A Piece of Justice: An Imogen Quy Mystery, St. Martin's Press (New York, NY), 1995.

A School for Lovers, Black Swan (London, England), 1996.

The Serpentine Cave, St. Martin's Press (New York, NY), 1997.

(With Dorothy Sayers, posthumously) Dorothy Sayers, *Thrones, Dominations: A Lord Peter Wimsey Mystery,* St. Martin's Press (New York, NY), 1998.

A Desert in Bohemia (adult novel), Doubleday (New York, NY), 2000.

(With Dorothy Sayers, posthumously) *A Presumption of Death: A New Lord Peter Wimsey/Harriet Vane Mystery,* St. Martin's Minotaur (New York, NY), 2002.

Debts of Dishonor: An Imogen Quy Mystery, St. Martin's Minotaur (New York, NY), 2006.

The Bad Quarto: An Imogen Quy Mystery, St. Martin's Minotaur (New York, NY), 2007.

Some of Paton Walsh's manuscripts and papers may be found in the Kerlan Collection, University of Minnesota, Minneapolis.

ADAPTATIONS: Gaffer Samson's Luck was adapted to audio in 1987; *Torch* was adapted as a television mini-series, 1992; *Knowledge of Angels* was adapted to audio in 1996 by Isis Audio; *A Parcel of Patterns* was adapted to audio in 1996 by Listening Library.

SIDELIGHTS: Jill Paton Walsh is noted for her works for young readers that deal realistically with life, death, and maturation. While her novels vary widely in terms of genre and style, as Judith Atkinson in *Twentieth-Century Children's Writers* noted, "the most immediately attractive features of these novels . . . are their absorbing plots and believable settings." "Of [the many] skilled and sensitive writers [for young people]," declared Sheila Egoff in *Thursday's Child: Trends and Patterns in Contemporary Children's Literature,* "[Paton] Walsh is the most formally literary. Her writing is studded with allusions to poetry, art and philosophy that give it an intellectual framework unmatched in children's literature." Paton Walsh's works examine eras and topics such as life, death, and honor in Anglo-Saxon England (*Hengest's Tale* and *Wordhoard*), Victorian child labor in England (*A Chance Child*), growing up in World War II England (*The Dolphin Crossing* and *Fireweed*), life in the Early Stone Age (*Toolmaker*), and loyalty in the midst of destruction in fifteenth-century Byzantium (*The Emperor's Winding Sheet*). She has also written several novels that center on the Cornish coast, where she spent part of her childhood.

Paton Walsh was born Gillian Bliss, a member of a loving family living in suburban London. Her father was an engineer, one of the earliest experimenters with television, and he and his wife actively stimulated their children to enjoy learning. "For the whole of our childhoods," Paton Walsh once wrote, "I, and my brothers and sister—I am the eldest of four—were surrounded by love and encouragement on a lavish scale. . . . And to an unusual degree everyone was without prejudices against, or limited ambitions for, girls. As much was expected of me as of my brothers."

Paton Walsh's early novels *Fireweed* and *The Dolphin Crossing* are based on her childhood experiences during World War II. The characters experience danger and insecurity along with new friendships. "For five crucial years of my childhood—from the year I was three to the year I was eight—the war dominated and shaped everything around me," Paton Walsh once explained "and then for many years, until well into my teens, postwar hardships remained. . . . I do not know if there was a plan of evacuation there when the war began, which my parents did not join in, or if Finchley did not seem a likely target," she continued. Finally her mother's stepfather, upset by a bombing raid, moved the family to his place in Cornwall, in the far west of England. Although Jill's mother soon returned with her younger children to her husband in London, Jill herself remained in Cornwall for the next five years, returning to her family only after her grandmother suffered a fatal heart attack.

The author used the familiar setting of Cornwall in *Goldengrove,* a book about the awkwardness that often accompanies growing up. The heroine is Madge, who, although almost fully grown, still eagerly anticipates her yearly visit to see her grandmother and cousin in Cornwall. When, one year, the visit proves disappointing, the grandmother understands that Madge's maturation is changing their relationship. Further, Madge must deal with two revelations that force her to question her faith in adults.

"I left St. Ives when I was just eight," Paton Walsh once recalled. "A part of me is still rooted on that rocky shore, and it appears again and again in what I write." She stepped out of the comfortable world she had known directly into wartime London. "That first night back," she remembered, "I lay awake listening to the clanging sounds, like dustbins rolling round the night sky, made by German rockets falling somewhere a little distance off.

"The children I talk to nowadays are very interested in the Second World War," Paton Walsh once remarked. "They think it must have been a time of excitement and danger, whereas it was actually dreadfully boring." Wartime restrictions and shortages meant that normal childhood activities—movies, radio, and even outdoor play—were severely limited. "I remember, in short, a time of discomfort and gloom, and, above all, upheaval." Part of the upheaval was caused by her mother's relatives, who had been wealthy colonists in Southeast Asia before the war, and who returned to England, newly impoverished, to live with her family. Because they had their own ideas of proper female behavior, Paton Walsh wrote, she never knew "whether it was good and clever to give voice to my opinions, or pushy and priggish; not knowing from one day to the next what sort of behavior would be expected of me. Yet in the long run I have benefited greatly from all this. I protected myself. I learned not to care what other people think. I would say what I liked, read what I was interested in, go on my own way, and ignore what the invading hoards of aunts and uncles thought, about me, or about anything else."

Paton Walsh attended a Catholic girl's school in North Finchley, whose environment was quite different from the liberality of her home life. When Paton Walsh left the school, it was to take a place at Oxford University. She once commented of this time: "I enjoyed myself vastly at Oxford, made friends, talked late into the night, and even worked sometimes, and work included lectures by both C.S. Lewis and J.R.R. Tolkien. The subject of the lectures and tutorials was always literature or philology—we wouldn't have dared ask those great men about their own work!—but the example they set by being both great and serious scholars, and writers of fantasy and books for children was not lost on me."

By the time Paton Walsh completed her degree, she was engaged to a man she had met at school. She obtained a teaching position, but soon discovered that she disliked being a teacher. "I didn't teach long," she once explained. "I got married in my second year as a teacher, and eighteen months later was expecting a child." The life of a housewife, however, did not suit her either: "I was bored frantic. I went nearly crazy, locked up alone with a howling baby all day and all night. . . . As plants need water and light, as the baby needed milk, I needed something intellectual, cheap, and quiet." So, she explained, "I began to write a book. It was a children's book. It never occurred to me to write any other kind."

The book she began to work on in those day, she said, "was, unfortunately, a dreadfully bad book. It had twelve chapters of equal length, with a different bit of historical background in each one." Eventually, Kevin Crossley-Holland, an editor with Macmillan, explained to Paton Walsh that to publish this particular book might be a bad idea. He then offered her an option on her next work. "I set to work joyfully on *Hengest's Tale*," she recalled, "a gory epic retold out of fragments of *Beowulf,* and I stopped work only for a fortnight—between chapter three and chapter four—when my second child, my daughter Margaret, was born. *Hengest's Tale* was my first published book. And I have never forgotten the difference it made to be able to say, to others, certainly, but above all, to myself, 'I am a writer.'"

Critics celebrate Paton Walsh's ability to evoke both character and setting, and through them to say something meaningful about growing up. She "has an astonishing ability to create appealing personalities," declared Elizabeth S. Coolidge in the *Washington Post Book World.* In reviewing *Unleaving,* in which Paton Walsh continues the story of Madge, the heroine of *Goldengrove,* Coolidge continued: "She has written a book about death, and what this means to a philosopher, a teenager, a grandmother and a very small child. Yet *Unleaving* is in no way a gloomy book, but one that leaves the reader with a warm and optimistic view of humankind." Alice Bach, writing in the *New York Times Book Review,* commented that "[Paton] Walsh doesn't tidy up the blight for which man was born."

For *Thrones, Dominations,* Paton Walsh took on the challenge of completing a manuscript of a Lord Peter Wimsey mystery found forty years after the death of its author, Dorothy L. Sayers. The book agent who turned in the manuscript had it since the 1930s, after Sayers had given it to him for safekeeping. In the coauthored book, Wimsey is recently married but soon finds himself on the case of an acquaintance's murder. Rex E. Klett, writing in the *Library Journal,* commented that the novel has all the "witty dialog, social satire, and red herrings of a classic Sayers." Noting Paton Walsh's contribution to the novel, *New Statesman* contributor Michael Leapman wrote: "The pace picks up when Walsh takes over. The dialogue gets crisper and there are twists on every other page."

Paton Walsh takes over the role of sole author for another Lord Peter Wimsey mystery, *A Presumption of Death,* this time featuring Harriet Vane, who has become Lady Wimsey. While Sir Wimsey is traveling abroad, Lady Wimsey takes up the case of a dead girl found during an air-raid drill in 1940 England. Klett, writing again in the *Library Journal,* called the mystery "a charmingly traditional British cozy." A *Publishers Weekly* contributor noted that Paton Walsh "does a far better job of honoring Sayers than she did in their first posthumous collaboration."

In a more recent mystery novel, *Debts of Dishonor: An Imogen Quy Mystery,* Imogen Quy—who previously appeared in *The Wyndham Case* and *A Piece of Justice: An Imogen Quy Mystery*—is a college nurse working at St. Agatha's, a fictional Cambridge college. When a benefactor to the school falls to his death, Imogen investigates. A *Kirkus Reviews* contributor observed that the novel is "geared toward the genteel reader." Writing on the *Monsters and Critics Books* Web site, Angela Youngman commented that "it keeps your attention throughout as you follow the twists and turns of the complex tale."

In addition to these mysteries, Paton Walsh has also written other novels for adults. Among these is *A Desert in Bohemia,* which focuses on the spread of communism following World War II. The novel follows numerous characters over several decades, including Russian exiles, idealistic communists, and an English family. A *Publishers Weekly* contributor noted that the "novel manages to be serious, important and philosophically provocative—and infused with narrative urgency, suspense, pathos and passion as well," adding that it also has "a cunningly orchestrated plot, a relentlessly chilling atmosphere and indelible character portraits." Patricia Gulian, writing in the *Library Journal,* called *A Desert in Bohemia* "beautifully written" and felt that "Walsh is at once complex and very simple."

AUTOBIOGRAPHICAL ESSAY: Jill Paton Walsh contributed the following autobiographical essay to *CA:*

I was born on the 29th of April, 1937, in North Finchley, a suburb of London. I made a bad job of it, and arrived damaged, with a condition known as Erb's palsy, which limits the movements of my right arm. This is in fact caused by stretching of the baby's arm during breech delivery; but it was not then very well understood, and my parents were told it was the result of brain damage of unknown extent.

I would have said for many years that my disability, so trifling in extent, as it turned out, had had no influence on my life; but I now think that it was in reality of great importance, not in any physical way, but psychologically. In the first place, all my life the people around me have supposed I would not be able to do things—like carrying trays, or standing on my hands—which I found, as soon I tried them, to be perfectly possible for me. And this has left me with a lifelong disposition to have a shot at things. Confronted with a difficult task, as constructing a built-in wardrobe, making a ballgown, or writing a publishable book, I am still inclined to tackle it, reflecting that if someone else can do it, I probably can. This is arrogant, of course, but it often proves true. It is arrogant, but then if I had been contented to do only what the doctors told my parents I would be able to do, I would have led a very narrow life! It is true, of course, that there are some things my arm prevents me from doing. Up to the present these are: lifting heavy objects from high shelves, being a bell-ringer, and putting curlers in my own hair.

Of course the worst fear that my unlucky parents had to deal with was the implied threat of mental handicap, and I made it worse by being very late to learn to talk. "You made up for it later!" my mother used to tell me. But when I had reached two-and-a-half with hardly any baby talk, they did begin to wonder. The day a neighbor leaned over my playpen and said, "And what do you do all day, little girl?" and I looked up and said, "Normally I play with bricks," the relief was very great.

Again, looking back, I am not surprised that I was wary of talking until I had got the grammar straight in my head, for my entire family made a nonstop game

Young Jill, her arm in a splint, with mother, father, and grandmother

out of what my grandfather called "Your language is foul, and mine is Fowler, or Knowing your Onions"—that is, of pedantically correcting each others' speech for the most minuscule errors of form or usage, accompanied by looking things up in *Modem English Usage,* by Fowler, or the *Shorter Oxford Dictionary,* edited by Onions.

When every utterance I delivered from cot or playpen was greeted with rapture by my parents and family, I was quickly convinced that I was good with words, and joined in the family game as rapidly and extensively as I could. Until the day she died, my mother, if I said something clever, or extravagantly articulate, would administer a subtle rebuke by looking at me thoughtfully and saying, "I *think* you're normal . . . "

For the whole of our childhoods I, and my brothers and sister—I am the eldest of four—were surrounded by love and encouragement on a lavish scale. On my father's side our family was of very modest origins indeed, but upwardly mobile—one reason perhaps for the delight in ultra-correct speech—there was no money behind us, but wealth of hopes. I might not be able to carry a tray, but I, or any of us, could win scholarships, get to university, become professors, politicians, inventors, captains of industry . . . anything we liked. And to an unusual degree everyone was without prejudices against, or limited ambitions for, girls. As much was expected of me as of my brothers. And therefore, of course, more, in a way. Perhaps my great-aunts, who had struggled out of real poverty to become primary school headmistresses, and self-taught intellectuals, were responsible for that.

But as well as all this affection and privilege, we did have hardships to contend with. We were fed and clothed, and housed, in a house which always had one warm room, but we were never well-off; there was never money for extras; and even if there had been, like everyone else in England we would have been in a land at war. For five crucial years of my childhood—from the year I was three to the year I was eight—the war dominated and shaped everything around me. And then for many years, until well into my teens, postwar hardships remained.

In the first place, my family lived in North Finchley. I do not know if there was a plan of evacuation there when the war began, which my parents did not join in, or if Finchley did not seem a likely target. What did happen is a family legend. My mother's mother had married again, just after my own parents' marriage, a moderately wealthy man who lived in Cornwall. He had business in London, and came to spend the night in our house. During the night we had to get up and get packed into the shelter in the garden three times, as the air-raid sirens went. However unlikely it was as a prime target, Finchley was getting bombed, as the enemy aircraft came in over London, turned right, and wheeled round to head home again, unloading any remaining bombs as they went. My Cornish grandfather was appalled. He said, over breakfast, "You can't live like this," and somehow all of us, and all our things were on the ten o'clock train, out of Paddington station, going to live with Gran in St. Ives.

St. Ives is an extremely beautiful place; a town of crooked, narrow sloping streets, a stone harbour on a wide bay, golden beaches, and a lighthouse on a distant island that can be seen from all over the town. A sweeping view of the town, beaches, and bay could be seen from every window of Gran's house, and a path to the beach led directly down from a gate at the foot of the garden. We seemed to have landed in heaven. We had certainly landed in a comfortable house—there were two full-time servants, and attics for us to sleep and play in. And, which impressed us more at the time, our Cornish stepgrandfather could afford to buy endless sweets on the black market, stuff his pockets with them when he went out, and give them away to any children he met in the town. I still remember his defence for this—"If *anyone* is having them, then anyone is having them!"

But if life in St. Ives was lovely for us, it was very hard on my mother, because it separated her from my

"Refugee" at St. Ives, about 1940

father. Of course the war separated many families from their fathers, but my father was not away fighting; he had not been allowed to join up. My father was a very brilliant engineer, whose job before the war had been first in radio, and then in television. He was the very first television cameraman in the world, but only because he was part of the tiny team of engineers who had launched public broadcast television before the war. Sometime after the war began he was sent to Malvern to help with research on radar. Travel on wartime trains between Malvern and St. Ives was very difficult. For this reason, and perhaps others I don't know about, my mother decided to go back to London.

But by the time she did, I had started at a little nursery school nearby, and my grandmother wanted to keep me, and argued that it would be better for me not to change schools. Both my brothers, and the youngest, my sister, were born by then, and my mother doubtless had her hands full, so I was left on my own in St. Ives.

And I don't remember missing the others at all. That's what my brothers and sister became to me, "the others," when they went home without me. Left with my grandmother I was spoiled, praised, and made much of in every way, and went on doing well at school. Wartime St. Ives was a small place, and I was known by name all over the town, and in every shop. One of the St. Ives fishermen lost a boat at Dunkirk, and my

grandfather had helped him replace it. The new boat was called *Little Jill.* Looking back, I will forgive myself for getting rather a good opinion of my own importance.

I left St. Ives when I was just eight, and I didn't go back there till I was thirty-six; but when I asked a stranger on the quays if he remembered a boat called *Little Jill* he looked at me hard, and said, "You had a brother younger'n you, didn't you?" and, in a minute or two more, "Grand ol' Liberal, your grandfer!" And it turned out that several people could remember me, and even remember having been in the same class in that little nursery school. A part of me is still rooted on that rocky shore, and it appears again and again in what I write.

But the safety, and the spoiling were not to last. Late in 1944 my grandmother died, very suddenly, of a heart attack. Lying in my bed, still awake, I heard her come up to bed unusually early, and run a bath. I slipped out of bed, and ran across the landing to hug her in her soft dressing gown, and tell her about something I had been reading. "Goodbye, Darling," she said. I laughed. "You mean Goodnight, Granny, not Goodbye," I said. "Yes," she told me. "Goodnight, don't read too long."

But I read long enough to hear a heavy thump; to hear people scrambling round the house, talking in agitated whispers. They were still doing it when I fell asleep.

Gran holding Jill, St. Ives

On the "golden beach" of St. Ives

And the next morning was like a nightmare. The other grown-ups in the house were my stepgrandfather's grown-up children, who had no children of their own, and, I think, didn't much like me. My poor grandfather kept to his room. They told me my grandmother was ill in bed, too ill to see anyone. But I had slipped in to her room the moment I woke, to wriggle down beside her for my morning cuddle, and a sugar lump dunked in tea that she would give me on a spoon from her tea-in-bed tray. I knew that she was not in bed, and the bed, smooth, flat, and cold had not been slept in. My head full of *Grimm's Fairy Tales* about wicked step-relations, and church talk about the wickedness of lying, I was horrified, and terrified. My terror lasted only as long as it takes a train from London to reach the end of England; just one day from waking up till early evening, but it has stayed with me vividly to the present day.

At dusk there was someone at the door. Someone told me, "Your mother is here," and I raced out in the darkness, and flung myself weeping, into the newcomer's arms. I was blurting out between tears that they were lying to me, that Granny had gone away and nobody would say. . . .

"My God," said my mother, "Has nobody told the child?" At which my grandfather, appearing at the top of the stairs, said in a choked voice, "Is that Patsy?" and put the lights on; and I saw that I was holding hard to someone whose face was wet with tears, clinging to my mother, and that I could not remember her at all.

I came home to London the following day. It was a strange sort of homecoming. There was thick snow on the ground; I had never seen snow, which seldom lies on the temperate, ocean-windswept ground of the far south-west of England. And in the London blackout I didn't exactly *see* it the night I came home; I just stumbled around it, and then when the door was opened, glimpsed it like a thick dirty quilt lying on the drive and steps. The house was strange to me; my parents had bought it while I was away. It was large and comfortable enough, an ordinary suburban semidetached house with a long garden, but in the war people couldn't paint, decorate, make themselves comfortable, or not easily, and the previous owners had painted it dark cream with brown doors and windows. There was a room for me, all my own and lushly furnished, but the worst surprise was that the house had strangers in it, quite settled strangers, treating it as their own home.

And that first night back I lay awake listening to the clanging sounds, like dustbins rolling round the night sky, made by German rockets falling somewhere, a little distance off. Everyone had given up trying to get into shelters. Instead we had a number chalked on the gatepost—the number of people sleeping in the house—and we each wore a brass disc about the size of a quarter, tied to our wrist, with a number on it. ZKDN/74/8 was mine.

The strangers in the house were my mother's adopted sister and her son, a shy and solemn boy the same age

With the "others": sister Liz, brothers Orvis and Geoff; Jill and mother behind

as me, and they were the first of my mother's relatives to get out of Burma, and home to England. Some of them—most of them, I think—had literally walked through the jungle to cross into India, bringing with them only what they could carry, and being glad to escape with their lives. Obviously, in bombed London they simply came to live with my mother; one set of them after another. Obviously, they were full of foreign and strange ideas, and it took them time to understand that they would have to work, that they would not have servants, that the world they were living in was not like the one they had been thrown out of by the Japanese.

Doris and her son Adrian, the first two, were, in fact—puzzled as I was at their presence—much the easiest to get on with. Doris was a sharp-tongued, intelligent woman, who always treated me as an equal, and is still, after many years of my adult life, a friend. And I think she was glad for Adrian to have some company his own age. He, I think, keenly felt himself to be an outsider, and played the prince with us, by showing us, and sharing with us, a large tin of sugar lumps which was in his mother's luggage, hidden in the attic. It is impossible to imagine, now, what wealth that tin seemed to contain! Of course, we did not gobble it up; reverently we received the lumps, one at a time, as gifts from Adrian. I think we had only the vaguest idea that they were not his to give us. It took many weeks before all the sugar was gone, and then we forgot about it, and began to use strips of aluminum foil with which the garden was showered like ticker tape every night, as presents or offerings between ourselves. The silver strips were to baffle enemy radar.

But the day came, in some crisis, when Doris offered my mother the sugar hidden in her luggage. Adrian, of course, could not escape blame; he was the only person apart from his mother who had known it was there. But nobody believed he could have eaten it all by himself, and he was pressed very hard to say who had eaten it with him, and share the punishment. With awesome nobility, Adrian claimed he had eaten every single lump himself.

"But Adrian, you don't even like sugar!" his mother pointed out, and we realised with dismay that it was true; Adrian had given the stuff to us, and never eaten his share. Still he stuck to his story, and took the punishment. He was confined to his room all day with nothing to eat. By stealth we fed him scraps, weeping

"The author as cover girl! (the magazine belonged to my stepgrandfather)"

with gratitude. Adrian's heroic action reappears, changed to suit the story, in *Goldengrove,* written a quarter of a century later. But it deserved to be remembered.

I for one, remembered him when he and his mother found somewhere to live, and moved out, to be followed by more of my mother's relatives, families of them, taking over the attics, and sharing meals with us, and somehow, always sitting in the fireside chair when my father got in from work, and not offering to move for him. Even after all this time I shall not name them. And I do, now, understand a lot more.

For it cannot have been easy for them. My mother's family had a background extremely different from my father's. She came of a family half Irish, and half aristocratic French. My French great-grandfather had run away from home—rumour had it because he was a third son, and third sons were destined for the Church—and made his fortune selling ice in the tropics; he founded the Rangoon Ice and Mineral Water Company. My relatives had led a wild colonial life, wealthy, waited on hand and foot by native servants, driving fast cars, throwing parties, doing amateur dramatics, and quarrelling picturesquely with each other.

I suppose someone must have run the ice factory, but none of the family seemed to my father to have done a day's work in their lives, and certainly they found life in wartime London, or come to that, any-time London, a severe shock, and if it took them time to come to terms with sudden poverty, and realise that they could not, because of my mother's loving heart, simply live indefinitely supported by my father, well, the adult I have now become would understand very well the terrible disorientation, and the nerves worn ragged by hardships of war which they were then suffering.

But at the time they caused terrible disruptions of our family life. There was the uproar over Mrs. Smith, for example. Mrs. Smith was my mother's charlady, and friend. She sat at table with us and shared the midday meal, and her children ran around the garden and playroom with us, simply because it had never entered my mother's head that they shouldn't. But one of my back-from-Burma relatives, horrified that she should be asked to sit down with a servant, made unforgivable remarks on the subject of ration books, as a result of which Mrs. Smith, though she went on working for my mother, and loving her dearly, never sat down again to share a meal with us.

But from my point of view still worse, the home-from-Burma brigade treated me with pointed dislike. Far from enjoying argument, and encouraging contributions, they thought it impudent for children to disagree with adults, and especially dislikeable in girls. Reading all the time was priggish, speaking up was pushy . . . they deliberately preferred my pretty younger sister, who smiled and flirted, and sat on her uncles' knees, as little girls often do, and set themselves to correct what they saw as unfairness in the way the two of us were treated. This seems to me now a kind of craziness. There are six years between my sister and me. When I was twelve, she was six. By the time she

was twelve, I was eighteen. How could it ever have been right to treat us the same? How could it ever have been reasonable for us to have the same bedtime? But, reasonable or not, that is how they felt, and I found myself slapped down sixty times a day for being what my father and grandfather encouraged me to be.

The only good result to emerge from all this was my better appreciation of my mother. My mother protected me as far as she could, while we all struggled along under the same roof. She told me to keep on reading and talking and take no notice. So that, seeing how unlike she was from her brothers and their wives, I began to see beneath her gentle and kind manner to her considerable strength of character. She was an intelligent woman, grossly undereducated. She had been sent to the sort of fashionable convent where girls learned French and manners and sewing, while her brothers were sent home to England to be properly educated. Nobody could say that the education of the boys had been very effective. My mother resented the unfairness of it, and all her life she was determined that her daughters should have the equal chances she had not had herself.

I look back now with great interest at this earliest part of my life. I can remember it in considerable detail, and as soon as I begin to think about those days I remember more and more, so that I could fill entire books with rambling memories. I would have much more difficulty remembering other, much more recent periods. The children I talk to nowadays are very interested in the Second World War. They think it must have been a time of excitement and danger, whereas it was actually dreadfully boring. There was nothing to do. The cinemas were closed, the swimming pool was closed, the blackout made it dangerous to go out after dark—it was months before as many people were killed by enemy action as were killed by cars with blacked-out headlights on roads with no street lights! Television was closed down, and we were before the age of pop music directed at young people on the radio. There was only reading; and how we read! Not of course, new children's books—paper was rationed, and there weren't any; just the rows and rows of classics on grandfather's shelves. It didn't matter whether we understood them; it was less boring to read them anyway than to stop reading!

I remember, in short, a time of discomfort and gloom, and, above all, upheaval. I'm sure you can imagine, from what I have written above, what a disturbed sort

"Amateur dramatics in Burma. My mother as a child, playing an angel!"

one day to the next what sort of behaviour would be expected of me.

Yet in the long run I have benefited greatly from all this. I protected myself. I learned not to care what other people think. I would say what I liked, read what I was interested in, go on my own way, and ignore what the invading hoards of aunts and uncles thought, about me, or about anything else. I knew that my parents and grandparents loved me. They loved us all, though we were all different. If my other relatives disliked me, well, I despised them. I thought them ignorant, overbearing, and silly. I realise that this doesn't make me seem very likeable, and I think I wasn't. But in the long run everyone has to march to their own tune, think, act, and choose for themselves. The adult attitude to other people's opinions which my childhood stamped on me is by and large a source of strength. Nowadays I like to listen to what other people think. I am interested in other people. But the least suggestion that one might alter one's own actions because of what other people think has me fighting mad in twenty seconds flat. I simply don't care. It is not what others expect of me, but what I expect of myself that governs me. I do try to be kind and polite. But I have never spent a moment's effort trying to be conventional or respectable! This kind of robust independence comes in handy if you are a woman, and you want to be a high-achiever, or an intellectual of any kind. I hope the world is easier nowadays for women, but certainly it was a far more difficult place when I was younger.

For at school, too, it was hard to work out what was expected of me. I was sent to a small Catholic convent, since my parents were nominally Catholic. It was supposed to be a "Grammar School," though nobody had ever gone from it to a university in its entire history—it was for girls only, of course. And Christ had never said "Blessed are the clever . . . " The nuns who taught me were suspicious of me. They liked girls who worked very hard, not those who found it easy. I daydreamed my time away, read under the desk, passed my exams, all to a continuous lecture about how I ought to try harder at sports, ought to pay attention, ought to read less, brush my hair more often . . . they were training us to be nuns or wives, they best liked people who came second or third in class, they thought it odd, and dangerous, to want a university degree. My year was a great shock to them. Six of us stayed on into the upper form; six of us did A-level

of time it was to grow up in. It was full of abrupt changes; the whole world was unreliable, all the way from the "aunt"—a friend of my grandmother's—who promised me a doll from Italy, and then got killed in an air raid before she produced it, to coming home from school never knowing who would be living in the house, or if my own bedroom would be just for me, or full of other people . . . above all never knowing whether it was good and clever to give voice to my opinions, or pushy and priggish; not knowing from exams. Three of us got university places. Mine was at Oxford, and caused the nuns to offer a mass for my soul!

Rather curiously, the nuns' attitude to boyfriends, lipstick, the Saturday night dances at the youth club, and the excitement caused by the few tennis matches or debate with the boys' Grammar School was eagerly benign. This didn't help me much, for I wasn't much good at having boyfriends. I liked to talk, not dance. My taste in clothes was truly awful. The others joked about me quite a bit. Nevertheless, I did get a boyfriend in the end. His name was Michael, and he was rather wild and Irish. He claimed to be a member of the IRA, which in those calmer times I had never heard of. And he too preferred talking to dancing. There was a pop song in the charts the year I met Michael called "Sweet Sixteen and Never Been Kissed." I was fifteen and three-quarters when a school debate threw us together. I set myself to keep him at bay till my birthday, and my school friends all had bets on whether or not I would make it. I did. It didn't strike any of us, I'm afraid, that this might be unkind. The nearest shave was on a moonlit walk home from a Saturday dance, when we stopped, and leaned over a gate together for sometime. He put an arm round me, and I thought I would lose the bet. "You know, Jill, you look almost beautiful in the dark!" he whispered. I collapsed in howls of laughter. He hadn't any sense of humour, however, and was mortally offended. By the time my birthday came he had recovered enough to send me a single yellow rose, in a florist's box. But he didn't last very long thereafter. When we had our parting quarrel I bought an ice-cream, I remember, to cheer myself up, and it worked! True love is harder to heal!

I suppose going to college marks the end of childhood. I enjoyed myself vastly at Oxford, made friends, talked late into the night, and even worked sometimes, and work included lectures by both C.S. Lewis and J.R.R. Tolkien. The subject of the lectures and tutorials was always literature or philology—we wouldn't have dared ask those great men about their own work!—but the example they set by being both great and serious scholars, and writers of fantasy and books for children was not lost on me. I was not, by Oxford standards, among the clever, and I had to stop dreaming and start to work! I met my husband while I was at Oxford, and was already engaged when I finished my degree, and got a teaching job in a school. I liked teaching; I hated

"Sweet sixteen and never been kissed!"

being a teacher. That is, I liked the company of young people, I liked discussing books with them, reading what they wrote for me, trying to get them through exams . . . I hated it when they all felt they had to duck out of sight of me on the bus home because they weren't wearing school hats, or when they were embarrassed at meeting me in the shops with their boyfriends. I didn't teach long; I got married in my second year as a teacher, and eighteen months later was expecting a child. Just before my son, Edmund, was born, I left teaching, with a washable baby's shawl as a goodbye present from my A-level class.

I was bored frantic. I went nearly crazy, locked up alone with a howling baby all day and all night. Edmund had a stomach problem that made him desperately slow to feed at the breast, and liable to vomit up the lot dramatically a few seconds later. Dramatically is no exaggeration—it used to hit the opposite wall! He and I and all the bedclothes in the house soon smelt of sick, mountains of washing piled up in the house, however hard I tried the baby was hungry all the time, and neither he nor I had any sleep for months. Doctors and clinic nurses alike warned me solemnly that only breast feeding would do, especially for a baby with stomach problems, so, naturally, nobody could help me, or get me even a few hours' rest. My husband, out at work all day, came home to study for professional exams. Nobody talked to me, for days on end. Finally a moment came when I realised that I would soon—before the day was out—crack up and be taken to a mental hospital. Would that help the baby? I

"Punting at Oxford"

wondered. Somebody else would be feeding him, anyway. A little spark of anger grew within me. I went out, leaving him, howling as usual, alone in the house, and bought at the chemist's on the corner, a baby's feeding bottle, a tin of dried milk, and a rubber teat. I went home, read the instructions, made up a feed, and sat down with the baby, ignoring my tight breasts, and gave him the bottle. He found the rubber teat easier; he gulped the lot down rapidly, and fell immediately contentedly asleep.

While he was asleep I *thought*. I thought about my own situation more intently than I ever remember doing, before or since. As plants need water and light, as the baby needed milk, I needed something intellectual, cheap, and quiet. I hauled out of the cupboard an old portable typewriter that my brother had given me, on leaving for America. I began to write a book.

It was a children's book. It never occurred to me to write any other kind.

Until the moment I began to write I did not know that I was a writer. I had vaguely wanted to be one, when at school, just because books were so important to me that I thought of writers as people think of doctors . . . but I had not tried to write, and I had not realised that I *was* a writer. But when I started on that battered typewriter, muffled as far as possible by being put on a folded blanket on the desk—I didn't want to wake the baby—I suddenly came clear to myself. This moment is a great one in your life; it will come to you, surely, sooner than it did to me—I am a late developer! When it comes, you will recognize it, or, rather you will suddenly recognize yourself.

I realised why the Burma mob had so disliked me, so tried to squash me . . . I had been watching them, weighing them up, deciding what I thought of them . . . writers watch all the time. You have to learn to do it tactfully. The best story about this aspect of being a writer I ever heard was told to me by an American friend, about a writer she knew who fell down the stairs of her apartment block, four floors of them, injuring herself badly, getting hospitalised for weeks. But as she went, bouncing, rolling, tipping head over heels, breaking this bone and that, she found herself watching herself go, and making a mental note what it felt like . . . "Ah!" she was saying to herself!

I realised why I had seemed too clever at school, too intellectual, and then not very bright at college, far too emotional. This particular combination, moderate brain power and strong feelings, is just what I needed now! Suddenly it all made sense. But why was it a children's book I was writing? That too makes sense to me now, though I took a year or two longer to work it out.

"The end of finals at Oxford"

With son Edmund, "when I was writing my first book"

If you go around asking people for the story of their lives, it is surprising how many of them begin by telling you about their teenage times; how they left college, or went to college against their parents' wishes, how they wouldn't take that job, or come in by midnight, or so on . . . . Most people's story of themselves begins with a conflict of some kind which taught them that they were different from others around them. If your first life-conflict hit you when you were fifteen, then you tend to think of childhood as very unimportant and boring. If you become a writer the hero of your book will be fifteen, or older. Most writers, now and in the past, have written about young adults, when you come to think of it. Charles Dickens is an exception; a lot of his heroes begin as children in the opening parts of his books. It is very well known that Dickens was sent to work in a blacking factory when he was only twelve; that he hated it, ran away, and was sent back. . . .

The epoch in life in which people first meet a crisis, in which they first begin to define themselves, their own needs, feelings, opinions, is the epoch which they will always feel the most important. The upheavals and changes and conflicts which the war brought to my life mean that for me childhood is the important and interesting stage of life. I like to write about children as characters, and I like to write for children as readers.

The book I was writing when all these grand thoughts occurred to me, was, unfortunately, a dreadfully bad book. It had twelve chapters of equal length, with a different bit of historical background in each one. It was about England in the reign of King Alfred. I finished it and sent it off to Oxford University Press. When, months later, I sent a letter of enquiry after it, it came back with a printed rejection slip. Bravely, weeping over the sticky label, I readdressed it and sent it off again, this time to Macmillan, where, by a stroke of enormous luck, there was a young man called Kevin Crossley-Holland newly installed as children's book editor. He, like me, had an Oxford English degree which had made him as nuts about the Anglo-Saxons as I was. He invited me out to lunch, and advised me not to publish my book, as it would damage my professional future. Instead he offered me fifty pounds for an option on my next book.

I was dazzled! To think that I had such a thing as a professional future! Fifty pounds! Enough for a better typewriter! I set to work joyfully on *Hengest's Tale,* a gory epic retold out of fragments of *Beowulf* and I stopped work only for a fortnight—between chapter three and chapter four—when my second child, my daughter Margaret, was born.

Hengest's Tale was my first published book.

And I have never forgotten the difference it made to be able to say, to others, certainly, but above all, to myself, "I am a writer."

Any writer will tell you how difficult second books are. But I was very lucky. I switched on the television set one gloomy afternoon, and saw a film of the evacuation of the British Army from Dunkirk. Newsreel footage, quite famous, of soldiers wading up to their armpits in the sea, holding their rifles above their heads, standing in line in the water to climb into little boats from England. Of course, I couldn't remember the newsreel; though I did remember the *Little Jill.* And right in the front of the picture one of the little boats was bobbing, while a soldier tried to haul himself on board. And at the tiller of the boat was a small boy—a strikingly young boy, maybe thirteen or so. I drew my breath, and looked closer, and as I did so the program moved on and the picture vanished from the screen. I knew we had been desperate to rescue our soldiers from France, and had used leaky old tubs and Thames steamers, and tiny private yachts and dinghies—but had we let children go right into battle to help? I was amazed, and duly went to look it up. And what a story I found! A boy of fourteen had been allowed to take a boat across the Channel four times in one day; they wouldn't let his mother take a turn, but they let the boy go back, in the evening, for that fourth trip. Incredible! The subject for my second book was unavoidable.

Of course memory wasn't much good, since I had been only three in 1940; I settled down to read every issue of the *Times* from the outbreak of war till Dunkirk, and of course to look at the illustrated magazines with drawings and photographs of which there were many before the times of television. And I talked to people who had adult memories of the time. My publishers were uncertain about the book; the Second World War was a new subject on the children's list. And Kevin had been replaced as children's editor by Marni Hodgkin, who was to be for many years my beloved first friend and supporter, and whose criticism taught me my trade, but whose first reaction on meeting me, and hearing me babble about Dunkirk was distinctly cagey. But *The Dolphin Crossing* has always been popular in England. It is still in print and still selling after all these years, and it boosted my confidence greatly.

In fact it seemed a shame to me to waste all the hard work that had gone into researching it; so I next thought that very little more reading newspapers would bring me through to the London Blitz, which I really could remember a bit about; and that is how *Fireweed* came to be written, from thrift over work! And work was becoming rather a problem, for by this time my third child, Clare, was born, and I was dealing with three children under four, and with no help of any kind. I have never had a lot of sympathy with people who tell me they would like to write a book if they had the time; I know that you always have the time for what you really want to do. I certainly was very busy with my three babies, but when I began writing *Fireweed* I was quickly swept away. I just couldn't stop writing it, and the whole project took only four months, from beginning to end; the most profitable

four months of my life. It was *Fireweed* that really made my name as a writer; it got marvellous reviews, in the United States as well as in England, and has never been out of print. Some time after I had finished writing it I was clearing out a bookcase, and I found a little paperback book which my father had given me, called *British War Artists*. It showed drawings by famous artists—Henry Moore was one of them—of the fantastic scenes of the London Blitz—the people sleeping on Underground stations, the ruins, and the fires, and suchlike. I flicked the pages; I had completely forgotten the book. And suddenly there was a picture from *Fireweed:* some air-raid wardens digging a body out of a pile of rubble. In the foreground, on the left-hand side, a young boy stands watching. I was amazed. I had caught my subconscious mind at work, for I certainly had not realised where the idea had come from; I really had thought only of the sensible idea of reusing all the research!

This whole question of where ideas for books come from is very intriguing. I suppose, "Where do you get your ideas?" is the question most often asked by the children I meet. I think they are hoping for useful guidance on how to get ideas for their English homework, and I am a bit ashamed to be so hopeless at helping. But I don't really know where I get ideas from; each one in turn seems like an accident. It's a question of being on the lookout for the kind of accident that makes the idea for a book.

There is always some work involved, of course; it doesn't just drop out of a tree and hit you like Newton's apple—and indeed an awful lot of apples must have dropped out of trees without making anybody think of the law of gravity! Newton was *ready* for that accident. It's a sort of long-distance daydreaming, the sort of thing which got me into trouble in school.

But I can say that a large part of it is giving loving attention to places; not necessarily beautiful places, just anywhere. Most of my books really have begun with thinking about the place they are set in. A good example is *A Chance Child*. We will jump a bit forward, and go to a time in my life when my children were in their early teens, and John Rowe Townsend's were in their later teens, and the two families shared a canal boat, a holiday cruiser, sixty-five-feet long, and six-feet-ten wide, with nine bunks, and a kitchen. Steering this thing along England's narrow waterways and getting it through seven-foot locks was everyone's

"As well as driving you mad they make you happy": Jill with daughter

favorite holiday activity; but the canals were built to bring coal and grain and bricks to city factories, and although for most of their length they go through open countryside, they also go right through the dirtiest parts of cities. One morning I was steering the boat—we called her *Wild Thyme*—through the middle of Birmingham. Everyone else was playing Monopoly in the cabin. I was gazing, horrified, at mile upon mile of derelict industry, stinking and blazing and hissing factories, dumps and wastelands . . . "How did it GET like this?" I wondered.

So when I got home I began to read up a bit about the Industrial Revolution. Very quickly my interest shifted from being about what it did to the landscape to what it did to the children of the time, who worked in factories and mines and workshops without any limit to hours of labour, or any thought for anyone's safety. I read voraciously for about a year before I actually began to write *A Chance Child,* and while I was reading the story of Creep was gradually taking shape in my mind.

The canals gave me two books; *The Huffler* also came from the experience of cruising on *Wild Thyme.*

As you would expect, having read this far, that lovely place, St. Ives in Cornwall, has also given me books, including those I think of with the most affection—

Goldengrove and *Unleaving.* These two books are very unlike the adventure war books with which I began. They are about a sensitive teenage girl, called Madge. I was thirty-five when I began to write *Goldengrove,* and I had not been back to St. Ives since the year I was eight, when my grandmother died.

I began to write from memory, and I assumed that my memory was a bit unreliable; somebody told me there weren't any trees on the cliff tops, where I remembered them, and my mother told me very emphatically that I was wrong to remember a cleft in the rocks called Godrevy, where the lighthouse stands. So I thought it would be better to work from memory, and pretend it was an imaginary place. And I couldn't do it. Imaginary people in real places is what I need. After a while I was stuck. The plot needed the children to buy a can of paint. And I couldn't remember any shops at all. My grandmother's house, and the cliffs and beaches were as clear as daylight in my mind, but no shops. So I bought a train ticket, and went back.

I went alone, out of season, and I bought a book to read on the train. I bought Quentin Bell's *Life of Virginia Woolf,* and from it I learned, as I went, that Virginia Woolf had spent her childhood holidays in St. Ives, and that *To the Lighthouse*—that book of hers that I loved so much, although it says it is happening on Skye, was really set in St. Ives. Her lighthouse and my lighthouse were the same one; and I remembered at once where "Talland House," the house her family rented for the summers, was—it was close to my grandmother's house, and shared the same view.

This gave me a very considerable emotional shock; *Goldengrove* was half-written, in a style somewhat like Virginia Woolf's; well, all in the present tense, anyway, because that was what had felt right to me. Now I knew why; I had caught my subconscious mind at it again, as when I found the book of war pictures. I was quite scared. If I had brought the manuscript with me, I might have torn it up.

I will always remember getting off the train late in the afternoon. A faint, late autumn sun was shining, and the sea was breaking briskly on the golden beaches just below the station. Behind me, all round my grandmother's house, and the other houses standing on the cliff crest, were trees; the trees I had remembered so clearly, and called the golden grove—and far across the bay was the lighthouse, standing on a rocky outcrop, and the rocks were cleft—I could see the white foam burst of breaking waves dividing the island. A great happiness engulfed me. Some of the happiness was a long-lasting aftermath of the married happiness of my grandmother and my stepgrandfather, who were, after all, newlyweds when they looked after me. Some of it was like finding treasure—the knowledge that my entranced memories of that magically beautiful place were hard and clear and truthful, and more accurate than the memories of other people who had thought to correct me.

The next morning, I walked in a patchwork town. I would be in a street where I could remember every detail, down to the cracks in the paving stones, and the shape of the shadows cast by houses across the lanes; and then I would turn the corner and find myself in a place which I had never seen before in my life. Within a few minutes I had met the man on the quay who remembered that I had a little brother . . . he took me out in his open boat, to go round Godrevy Island, past the rocks and crags and seals, but not to land. The light is remote controlled now, and the solitary keepers long since gone. I found the paint shop, easily. When I went home, three days later, to my manuscript I didn't have to change one word, not one, of what I had written from memory, and I defy anyone to guess how far I had actually written when I made the journey back! The old and the new memories fused perfectly, it seems to me.

Places. So important to me. I went to Greece to find the landscapes for a classical historical novel, written for adults, called *Farewell, Great King,* but when I got there I found Byzantine things, the marvellous mountaintop deserted city of Mistra above all, and the result of that was *The Emperor's Winding Sheet.* And there are more places singing to me; I haven't written anything yet for my love of New England. But the long-distance daydreaming about it has begun.

When I look back and wonder about where I get my ideas from, I can see another thing which I couldn't see while I was working. *A Parcel of Patterns,* for example, which is about the Plague in a village called Eyam, didn't start with a visit to Eyam. It started growing in my mind, and wanting to be written from the moment when John Rowe Townsend mentioned the historical story to me. All the villagers, voluntarily, had quarantined themselves to save the surrounding villages from the Plague. And that reminded me somehow, of air-raid shelters. Most of the people in the shelters behaved very bravely and well. Very ordinary people. The milkman was wonderful at making people share their blankets and sandwiches, and calming them down if they were frightened. A panic would have been dangerous. In the morning, when the all-clear sounded, Mike was just the milkman again. I am not interested in writing about great heroes, just ordinary people in difficult times. *Fireweed* and *The Emperor's Winding Sheet,* both about cities under siege, and *A Parcel of Patterns,* are probably all about Mike the milkman, really, if I can catch my subconscious at work!

But my most recent children's book starts with a place again. By and by the expense and trouble of that canal boat outweighed the fun, and we sold it, and bought instead, still shared between John and myself; a little cottage to work in, in peace. Somehow the older my children grew the harder it got to work at home! We didn't have enough money for a cottage in a beauty spot, so we landed in a fen village near Cambridge, on flat, flat land that floods in winter and attracts great flocks of Bewick's swans. At first I thought it dreadfully bleak and bare and depressing . . . then gradually I saw how strange and beautiful it is. Our cottage is a row house, and two doors down was an old man who was gruff and kind and friendly . . . it didn't take long for me to wonder what a child would feel who had to move house, and who landed just where we had done; and the result was *Gaffer Samson's Luck.*

I don't know where I'll go next. That's part of the endless fun.

For being a writer *is* fun. It is a very pleasant and rewarding kind of life, but it is not easy to write about! The actual *writing* is basically very dull. A writer spends long hours alone, sitting at a typewriter, and if you think of words rattling onto paper very fast you have the wrong picture; little short bursts, with very long silences for thought is far more like it. The best possible output for me is a thousand words a day. If you could watch me working, most of the time I wouldn't even be typing, just mooching. Of course, there is some interest. These days I have a word-processor to work on, and a very nice photocopier, with which I can put pictures on my letters. Like most writers I love stationery; these days a stationer's affects me as a sweet shop used to do just after the war

St. Ives: "The view from Grandmother's house"

when we were all starved of chocolate. I treat myself to pretty folders, coloured banks of paper, shiny pink pencils, envelopes with windows for the word-processed address to show through, rubber stamps, rainbow boxes of paper-clips, and so on endlessly. They don't help me to write, but I like them so much! And they do help with the nightmare about white paper; I sometimes wake up with this nightmare, that I'm typing very fast and frantically, and the paper is coming up blank. . . .

I don't earn a great deal of money, but I have a very privileged life. In the first place, all the time my children have been growing up I have been able to look after them, to be there when they come in from school, to cook for them, and cherish them, and at the same time to work at my chosen career. That is a huge benefit. Then there is the general niceness of being in charge of oneself, and so being able to go out when the sun shines, and continue thinking under the cherry tree, whenever it feels right. And then there is, after all, some excitement. When you need to visit far-off places in order to write about them, for instance. I have, after all, been twice to Greece, and twice to Turkey in order to be able to describe the settings for *Children of the Fox* and *The Emperor's Winding Sheet.*

Whatever I'm interested in at the time, I am able to pursue. When I was writing *A Chance Child,* which has a scene down a coal mine, I realised that it would be a help if I had ever been down a coal mine myself. Or, come to that, if I had ever seen a working cotton mill. And one or two letters got me the invitations I needed. The mine was very surprising; not a bit like what I had expected. I thought it might have been claustrophobic, but it wasn't really, because it moved all the time—the roof cracking and falling in as they shifted the jacks along the coalface. I must be one of very few women who has ever crawled on hands and knees, with a lamp in her hat, along 800 yards of "scufflings." It was the safety precautions which made the mine feel dangerous; they made us wear little brass identity discs, with a number; our names were against the numbers in the book at the head of the lift shaft;—I knew just what those were for!

The people in the cotton mill had long memories. Everything was fine now, they told me, "but when I were a lad. . . . " and they gave me many of the details I needed to know.

The most rewarding thing of all has been the way my books have opened up America to me. In 1976 a book called *Unleaving* won the *Boston Globe-Horn Book* Prize. My friend Ethel Heins, who was then the editor of the *Horn Book,* rang me up, and told me the good news. She asked me to write an acceptance speech, and send it to her to read aloud at the prize-giving dinner.

I was blowed if I would! Instead I splashed out the prize money on an airline ticket, and gave my speech myself. So I landed in America for just one week at a week's notice.

"Grandmother's house, indicated by arrow"

Jill Paton Walsh, 1986

something I had written; and as time has gone by I have won the friendship of many other writers and readers and book-lovers. I feel lucky in this, beyond my deserts. A special pleasure of being a children's writer is in getting letters from readers all over the world; I bet children's writers get more, and more interesting letters than writers for adults!

A writer is what I shall be as long as there is a daydream in my head, and I have strength to sit up and type.

Jill Paton Walsh contributed the following autobiographical essay to *CA* in 2007:

The year 1986, in which my autobiography for Gale was published, turned out to be a crucial year for me. In that year my youngest child, my daughter Clare, left home for university, and I too left home, to live with

"Visiting America—on the old North Bridge, Concord, Massachusetts": from left, Clare and Edmund Paton Walsh, Penny Townsend (daughter of author John Rowe Townsend), and Margaret Paton Walsh

Britishers either love or loathe the United States; I love it, or, at least, I love as much of it as I have seen, which is mostly New England. I was something of a new girl at first; I remember that I asked a New York taxi driver what that building was as we drove past Grand Central Station, and he said, "Lady, where you bin all your life?" But I have now visited the States often enough to feel very much at home, and I have nearly stopped asking silly questions. I have been invited back repeatedly, always, after that first time, with my friend John Rowe Townsend, and I have become, "Permanent Visiting Fellow" of the Center for the Study of Children's Literature at Simmons College in Boston.

In both England and America the best thing about being a writer is the friends it enables you to make. John Rowe Townsend, with whom I share my life as far as possible, got in touch with me originally because of

John Rowe Townsend, in a village on the outskirts of Cambridge. We asked the Estate Agent to find us something within twenty minutes of the Cambridge University Library, and so it was. This great change in my private life was matched by a shift in my professional life, for it was the year in which *Lapsing,* my first novel for adults, was published.

When I finished the Gale autobiography I still wrote of myself, and thought of myself, as a children's author, although I always maintained, and I still believe, that any book good enough to offer to children must be good enough for an adult reader. *Lapsing* was an autobiographical subject—it's about a young woman at Oxford, getting into a complex love triangle, and leaving the Catholic Church as a result. It felt very personal, and in many ways it kept me from writing adult novels for the first twenty years of my working life. Somehow I always knew it would be my first subject as an adult writer, and I needed, it turned out, a quarter of a century to distance myself enough to see the story in it, and to write it without tears. Once *Lapsing* was published I began to write alternately for adults and for children. I wrote short books for younger readers—picking up from *Gaffer Samson's Luck.*

An unplanned and unexpected change, perhaps as a result of the arrival by and by of a sequence of John's grandchildren, to whom I was a loved, and I hope loving wicked stepmother, was that I became able to write picture books. Of course I don't mean (worse luck!) that I was suddenly able to draw and paint, but I had a sequence of good ideas for stories that could be told in pictures. I can remember exactly when the first of these ideas arrived in my head. It was during a Children's Literature New England conference taking place in Cambridge, which John and I had helped to organize. It was going beautifully, with wonderful speeches, and wonderful weather, and I came home very excited and extremely exhausted, and sat in an armchair doing nothing. This is something I very seldom do. While I sat slumped and idle, I thought about John's little granddaughter Madeleine, whom I had been cuddling and playing with very recently. I thought how miraculously beautiful she was, and how full of love and joy she made the adults around her feel—she was a new wonder of the world! I should say that she is not alone in that; all babies are beautiful and full of hope. But it was Madeleine who caused the thought to occur to me then.

The thought begins: *I have been to Mount Desert Island, far away, and seen the shape of a great whale, rolling in the deep, but I have never, no never, seen anything as tremendous as you!* And with some nice elaboration that is the line of *When Grandma Came.* The illustrator was Sophie Williams.

I very greatly enjoyed writing picture books, because they are collaborations, very unlike the lonely work of writing a novel. My contribution was to make a story that would break nicely at each turn of the page, not stopping as a sentence does with a stop, but pausing as a sentence does with . . . and fitting exactly onto a thirty-two page dummy book, made of folded A4. Each page should have a sentence on it needing a different picture from the page before. Then the illustrator gets to work. When the pictures are ready I can pare down the text to nearly nothing, removing anything that was told in the picture. You don't need adjectives in a picture book! As well as myself and an illustrator, there would be an editor and a book designer. When the team works well the process is very satisfying.

Until 1997 I continued to write short chapter books and picture books for children alongside adult writing, but the landscape of my inner world was slowly changing, and the ability to write for children gradually left me. I am very sorry about this, and would gladly welcome another idea for a children's book if one came to me. I have often asked myself why I lost it, and there are several possible reasons. The most obvious one is that I was no longer much in company with children. My own children were grown up. John has seven grandchildren and I now have three, but none of his live very near us, and mine are in Australia. Love can cross worlds and oceans, but the everyday rub-along contact with children, which means that you know what they are like without having to think about it, doesn't. But perhaps the real reason has more to do with the growing distance between my own childhood and my present self. The world I was a child in is now very far away, and a lot of things that shape childhoods have changed beyond recognition. I feel that the world of a child now is partly a foreign country to me. I don't expect the inner world of children has changed as much as their outer world. Hope and fear and boredom and puzzlement at adults is probably pretty much what it always was, but that inner world of childhood is now distant to me for two reasons. One is simply that it is a long time ago. I was twenty-six when I started to

Jill with her new grandson Anthony

write, and I am nearly seventy now. It makes a difference! But the other reason is that I have written now so much. I have quarried my memories of childhood for over thirty books for children, and I have used up most of the gold. Since 1997, when my last picture book was published, *When I was Little Like You,* illustrated by Stephen Lambert, I have written only for adults.

Next after *Lapsing* I wrote a novel based on Mozart's opera *Cosi fan Tutti,* which has always annoyed me by condemning the women for infidelity, while excusing the men. I had a lot of fun with it, and it got very good reviews, but it didn't sell particularly well, so it laid the foundation for the big crisis which met my next book, *Knowledge of Angels.* I have always thought that *Knowledge of Angels* was the book I was born to write.

It is about a child found above the snowline in the mountains having apparently been reared by wolves. The churchmen into whose hands she falls have her taught to speak in isolation, so that they can find out by asking her the answer to a question which interests them—is knowledge of God inborn, or must it be taught? Incredibly, this really did happen in eighteenth-century France to a child called "The Maid of Challons." I should tell you at once that *Knowledge of Angels* is not in any way a children's book. Nor is it a young adult book, being very bleak and full of intellectual argument. But ironically a lot of young adults have read it, as I will explain in a minute. *Knowledge of Angels* was published in the United States by Houghton Mifflin, but in England it failed to find a publisher. In the end, when the U.S. edition was about

to be printed Peter Davison, the U.S. editor, offered to print a few extra copies, otherwise my English friends would never read it.

John said "**** them all, we'll do it ourselves," and we rang Peter back and said "Can you make that a thousand?" and, amazingly, he did. His thousand copies had a new title page stripped in, with a publisher's name: Green Bay Publications, which John and I had made up for our tiny publishing enterprises, because in the Bible the wicked "grow and flourish like the green bay tree." After we had made this decision our friends Linda and Robert Yeatman, who at that time had a tiny imprint doing country-life nonfiction books came to our aid, asked to join in the enterprise, sharing costs risks and profits (we didn't think there would be any!) and insisted that we needed a PR firm.

The fact that we were doing it ourselves made a good story, and the publicity firm did very well for us. The book began flying out of the shops, and soon we needed to reprint. We sold paperback rights and foreign rights, and the book reached the shortlist for the Booker Prize that year. Three years later it was set for the English school exams called A-levels that sixteen- and seventeen-year-olds sit. It has sold a lot of copies, and briefly made me very famous.

During the time when he was trying in vain to place it with British publishers, my agent began to worry, I think, in case I starved. He wondered if I would like to do what many others have done in a tight corner—take to crime. He meant writing it, of course, not perpetrating it! "There are still readers for old-fashioned detective stories," he said. "You might find it fun." There flashed through my mind a sequence of half-remembered detective stories. Joking with myself I proposed a dead body found in a locked library. I considered a gallery of amateur detectives—I don't know anything about police procedures—and discovered that I really disliked the gun-toting, good-as-a-tough-man female detectives I had read, and also the brutal forensic approach. I settled on a gentle, observant woman who works as a college nurse. She has time for people, they confide in her, and that's how she comes to know the crucial details that solve the mystery. She is Imogen Quy—her initials are IQ!—and I am very fond of her.

There are now four Imogen Quy detective novels, and there will be more, by and by.

Jill with her friends in the Lake District

What with the fuss about *Knowledge of Angels,* and the fact that I was now writing detection, I was approached by the trustees of the estate of Dorothy L. Sayers, and asked if I could finish a "Lord Peter Wimsey" novel that she left unfinished at her death. This was *Thrones, Dominations.* The manuscript was with other Sayers papers in a collection at Wheaton College, Illinois. That meant a trip to the United States, which of course I welcomed as a chance to see old friends and visit John's daughter who was then living in Chicago. It was a daunting task to finish in 1995 a work which had been abandoned in 1936, without the join showing. But I like a challenge, and it was successful at least in covering the join—not one reader or reviewer has correctly spotted it. I am often asked where it is, but I am not telling!

I have now written a second "Wimsey" novel, *A Presumption of Death,* as well as two more literary novels, *The Serpentine Cave* and *A Desert in Bohe-*

mia. The Serpentine Cave is set in St. Ives, Cornwall, the scene of my childhood, and two of my best children's books, *Goldengrove,* and *Unleaving* (since reissued in one volume as an adult title). I no longer depend on memory to write about St. Ives, because John and I have a flat there, with a view down to the town and across the bay, nearly identical to the view from my Grandmother's house, which is just a few steps further up the hill. We spend several months of the year there, very happily.

As well as all the changes in my writing life, there has been change in my private life. Antony Paton Walsh, my first husband, fell ill and died in 2003. Being after all these years free to marry without hurting anyone's feelings, John and I were married in 2004. We still share a study, and work side by side in Cambridge. We still travel a lot—I think I have crossed the Atlantic about sixty times, to work with Children's Literature New England, of which John and I are adjunct board

Jill's wedding to John, pictured with his granddaughters Rosie and Maddie as bridesmaids

members, or to visit friends or family. My elder daughter has become an American citizen, and lives in Alaska. And now that I have grandchildren growing up in Australia we make that long journey too. I am still writing, though more slowly than before, and instead of alternating between a children's book and an adult book, as I did for some years, I now alternate between a literary novel and a detective story.

I have had, and am still having an interesting and happy life, and I count myself lucky beyond my deserts

BIOGRAPHICAL AND CRITICAL SOURCES:

BOOKS

Children's Literature Review, Volume 2, Thomson Gale (Detroit, MI), 1976.

Contemporary Literary Criticism, Volume 35, Thomson Gale (Detroit, MI), 1985.

Egoff, Sheila A., *Thursday's Child: Trends and Patterns in Contemporary Children's Literature*, American Library Association (Chicago, IL), 1981.

Something about the Author Autobiography Series, Volume 3, Thomson Gale (Detroit, MI), 1987.

Twentieth-Century Young Adult Writers, St. James Press (Detroit, MI), 1994.

PERIODICALS

Booklist, December 15, 2000, Margaret Flanagan, review of *A Desert in Bohemia*, p. 788.

Christian Century, June 3, 1998, Gwenette Orr Robertson, review of *Thrones, Dominations: A Lord Peter Wimsey Mystery*, p. 585.

Commonweal, May 8, 1998, Elizabeth Bartelme, review of *Thrones, Dominations*, p. 26.

Entertainment Weekly, January 12, 2001, Mark Harris, review of *A Desert in Bohemia*, p. 76.

First Things, August, 2001, review of *A Desert in Bohemia*, p. 76.

Horn Book, November, 2000, Gregory Maguire, review of *The Green Book*, p. 682.

Kirkus Reviews, February 1, 2003, review of *A Presumption of Death: A New Lord Peter Wimsey/ Harriet Vane Mystery*, p. 192; March 15, 2006, review of *Debts of Dishonor: An Imogen Quy Mystery*, p. 265.

Library Journal, January, 1998, Rex E. Klett, review of *Thrones, Dominations*, p. 147; November 1, 2000, Patricia Gulian, review of *A Desert in Bohemia*, p. 138; February 1, 2003, Rex E. Klett, review of *A Presumption of Death*, p. 120.

New Statesman, October 31, 1986, review of *Lapsing*, p. 31; February 20, 1998, Michael Leapman, review of *Thrones, Dominations*, p. 47.

New Yorker, November 27, 1989, Faith McNulty, review of *Birdy and the Ghosties*, p. 142.

New York Times Book Review, August 8, 1976, Alice Bach, review of *Unleaving*, p. 18; June 16, 1985, Phyllis Theroux, review of *Gaffer Samson's Luck*, p. 30; June 14, 1992, Roger Sutton, review of *Grace*, p. 31; March 15, 1998, Joyce Carol Oates, review of *Thrones, Dominations*, p. 16.

Publishers Weekly, January 5, 1998, review of *Thrones, Dominations*, p. 62; October 9, 2000, review of *A Desert in Bohemia*, p. 71; November 27, 2000, Yvonne Nolan, "Jill Paton Walsh Novel Ideas along the Cam," p. 48; January 20, 2003, review of *A Presumption of Death,* p. 59, and Leonard Picker, "Lord Peter Wimsey and Harriet Vane Redux," p. 60; February 20, 2006, review of *Debts of Dishonor,* p. 139.

School Library Journal, June, 2001, Penny Stevens, review of *A Desert in Bohemia,* p. 184.

Times Literary Supplement, March 29, 1985, review of *Goldengrove,* p. 349; November 29, 1985, review of *Gaffer Samson's Luck,* p. 1358; November 28, 1986, review of *The Butty Boy,* p. 1347; November 22, 1991, P.J. Kleeb, review of *Grace,* p. 24.

Washington Post Book World, May 2, 1976, Elizabeth S. Coolidge, review of *Unleaving,* p. L13.

ONLINE

Bookreporter.com, http://www.bookreporter.com/ (September 6, 2006), Barbara Lipkien Gershenbaum, review of *A Presumption of Death.*

Jill Paton Walsh Home Page, http://www.greenbay. co.uk (June 9, 2007).

Monsters and Critics Books, http://books.monstersand critics.com/ (April 6, 2006), Angela Youngman, review of *Debts of Dishonor.*

Shots Magazine, http://www.shotsmag.co.uk/ (June 9, 2007), Mike Stotter, "Wimsey, Sayers and Me," interview with Jill Paton Walsh.

*   *   *

PEACOCK, Molly 1947-

PERSONAL: Born June 30, 1947, in Buffalo, NY; immigrated to Canada, 1992, naturalized citizen (dual citizenship), 2006; daughter of Edward Frank and Pauline Peacock; married Jeremy Benton, 1970 (divorced, 1976); married Michael Groden, August 19, 1992. *Education:* State University of New York at Binghamton, B.A. (magna cum laude), 1969; Johns Hopkins University, M.A. (with honors), 1977.

ADDRESSES: Home—Toronto, Ontario, Canada. *Agent*—Kathleen Anderson, Anderson Literary Management, 12 W. 19 St., 2nd Fl., New York, NY 10011; Hilary McMahon and Bruce Westwood, Westwood Creative Artists, 94 Harbord St., Toronto, Ontario M5S 1G6, Canada. *E-mail*—molly@molly peacock.org.

Molly Peacock Hauser

CAREER: State University of New York at Binghamton, director of academic advising, 1970-73, coordinator of innovational projects in office of the dean, 1973-76; Johns Hopkins University, Baltimore, MD, honorary fellow, 1977-78; Delaware State Arts Council, Wilmington, poet-in-residence, 1978-81; Friends Seminary, New York, NY, learning specialist, 1981-92; One-to-One poetry consulting, 1990—; Bucknell University, Lewisburg, PA, poet-in-residence, 1993-94. Visiting lecturer at YMCA, New York, 1986—, Hofstra University, Hempstead, NY, 1986, 1988, Columbia University, 1987, Barnard College, 1989-90, New York University, 1989, and Sarah Lawrence College; writer-in-residence, University of Western Ontario, 1995-96; Spalding University, graduate faculty member; actor in her one-woman play of poems, *The Shimmering Verge.*

MEMBER: Poetry Society of America (president, 1989-94), Writers' Union of Canada.

AWARDS, HONORS: Resident at MacDowell Colony, 1975-76, 1979, 1982, 1985, 1989, and Yaddo Colony, 1980, 1982; awards from Creative Artists Public Service, 1977; award from Ingram Merrill Foundation, 1981; New York Foundation for the Arts award, 1985, 1990; National Endowment for the Arts Fellowship, 1990; Lila Wallace Fellowship, 1994; Woodrow Wilson Fellowship, 1995.

WRITINGS:

POETRY

And Live Apart, University of Missouri Press (Columbia, MO), 1980.

Raw Heaven, Random House (New York, NY), 1984.

Take Heart, Random House, 1989.

Original Love, W.W. Norton (New York, NY), 1995.

Understory, Northeastern University Press (Boston, MA), 1996.

(Editor, with others) *Poetry in Motion: 100 Poems from the Subways and Buses,* Norton (New York, NY), 1996.

Cornucopia: New and Selected Poems, 1975-2002, W.W. Norton (New York, NY), 2002.

(With Georgianna Orsini and Robert Phillips) *An Imperfect Lover,* Cavankerry Press, 2002.

The Second Blush, W.W. Norton (New York, NY), 2008.

OTHER

Paradise, Piece by Piece (memoir), Putnam (New York, NY), 1998.

How to Read a Poem—And Start a Poetry Circle, Riverhead Books (New York, NY), 1999.

(Editor) *The Private I: Privacy in a Public World,* Graywolf Press (St. Paul, MN), 2001.

Contributing editor, *House and Garden* magazine, 1996. Also contributor to journals, including *Shenandoah, Mississippi Review, New Letters, Southern Review, Massachusetts Review, Ohio Review, Paris Review, New Yorker, Nation,* and *New Republic.*

SIDELIGHTS: American poet Molly Peacock uses strong rhyme schemes, skillful alliteration, and biting humor to explore such themes as fate, family, sexuality, pain, and the many facets of love. Writing in the *Washington Post Book World,* David Lehman observed that "Peacock has a luxuriantly sensual imagination—and an equally sensual feel for the language. In mood her poems range from high-spirited whimsy . . . to bemused reflection. . . . Whatever the subject, rich music follows the tap of her baton." Annette Allen, in the *Dictionary of Literary Biography,* commented on Peacock's poetic structures, stating that "Peacock's

skillful wielding of form ensures a continual dialectic between the inner world of memory and feeling and the external world. She accomplishes this dynamic, the balance between inner and outer worlds, by employing sound patterns that keep the poem close to unconscious rhythms and by using images or metaphors from the civilized and the natural worlds."

Peacock's first collection, *And Live Apart,* introduces her preoccupation with the past. Instead of employing a bitter or hostile approach, Peacock views her personal history from the enlightened perspective of one who has reconciled herself to its shortcomings. Robert Phillips noted in *Hudson Review* that Peacock's "concerns are big ones: the separations we make between one another, the reversals of love, the inescapability of fate, inevitabilities of inheritance, a concern for the language of emotion in conversation." He went on to say that *And Live Apart* "is notable for plumbing the past without sentimentality, and for finding new solutions to old dilemmas."

Raw Heaven, which received wider critical attention, stresses the manipulative aspects of desire and the ineffable quality of sex and sensuality. In the poem "Desire," for example, Peacock compares sexual yearning to a pet's constant demands for affection. Several critics expressed admiration for her vivid, illuminating imagery, elegant rhymes, and bold consideration of such taboo topics as menstruation, childbirth, and masturbation. *Boston Review* critic Matthew Gilbert observed: "What makes this book a 'drive for what is real,' even more than her forceful longings, is Peacock's devotion to the strength of vision. She reveres the power of uninhibited perception, imagining herself as one daring to witness the world." Some reviewers, however, criticized what they considered Peacock's overabundant use of wordplay, rhyme, and the sonnet form. J.D. McClatchy noted in *New York Times Book Review* that Peacock's "wordplay, so high-spirited, is often aimless," while Christopher Benfey observed in *Parnassus* that "her rhymes—and these sonnets are relentlessly rhyming—are rarely part of the sense of the poem, nor are they particularly adept."

In *Take Heart,* Peacock continues to address inviolable topics, including the horrors and repercussions of physical and mental child abuse. Many of the volume's opening poems deal with the death of Peacock's father and her childhood memories of his alcoholism. Several critics praised her ability to illuminate universal concerns through intimate memories. In "Say You Love Me," for instance, her drunken father's aggressive demand for her unconditional love evolves into a study of humanity's need for acceptance and reassurance. Similarly, "Buffalo"—in which Peacock harshly recollects waiting in bars while her father drank—becomes a condolence for the bartenders who "shrink / from any conversation to endure / the serving, serving, serving of disease." *Los Angeles Times Book Review* critic Ian Gregson noted: "Peacock is conspicuously courageous in the subjects she is willing to tackle. The [reason] she's mostly successful in doing so in *Take Heart . . .* is because she's discovered a technique that meticulously follows the labyrinthine twists and turns of these emotional tangles."

Peacock begins to move away from more formally structured verse in *Original Love*. In this work, as Frank Allen stated in *Library Journal,* she addresses "the boundaries between men and women, mother and daughter, and one's mind, body, and senses." A reviewer in *Publishers Weekly* also noted that Peacock uses "explicit eroticism" to explore "three loves—for lover, mother, self." Like her other works, *Original Love* directly and unrelentlessly examines such subjects as sexuality, desire, death, and human fallibility. Regarding Peacock's work as a whole, Allen observed: "The intelligence and music of her work, the belief in exploring consciousness with honesty, the sheer beauty of the language—all contribute to the 'pleasure of the text.' Because all the pain and joy of living are in [Peacock's] poetry, people will continue to turn to her poems."

Peacock published her memoir, *Paradise, Piece by Piece* in 1998. In it she outlines her difficult childhood and the way her father's alcoholism tore at the family base. She also shows how by escaping that unpleasant place in her life, she was able to develop as a poet. She also discusses her decision to not have children. *Booklist* contributor Donna Seaman noted that "Peacock's lucid prose is as honest and precise as her poems." Mary Paumier Jones, writing in *Library Journal,* remarked that "she speaks with candor, humor, and insight on her topic."

In 1999 Peacock published *How to Read a Poem—And Start a Poetry Circle.* This book seeks to assist those interested in reading poetry to use a structured approach in order to better understand it. Reviews for the instructional book were mostly positive. A contributor to *Publishers Weekly* commented that "Peacock sets a wonderfully idiosyncratic example for responding to poetry." In *Booklist,* Seaman concluded that "her lucid interpretations provide a welcoming introduction to the art of reading poetry, and her suggestions for forming a poetry circle are meant to encourage poem-struck readers to articulate and share their passion."

The Private I: Privacy in a Public World, published in 2001, is a collection of essays on the values placed on privacy in the age of reality TV and daily celebrity exposés. The collection includes contributions from Jonathan Franzen, Dorothy Allison, and Kathleen Norris, Barbara Feldon, and Evans D. Hopkins. Reviews, however, were mixed. Mark Bay, writing in *Library Journal,* complimented the writing style, but commented that the essays "offer little real sociological substance and consequently are of little research value." Writing in *Lip,* Suzanne Cody concluded, "This excellent overall collection reminds us that personal boundaries are important, that there is a difference between desiring privacy and harboring secrets."

Cornucopia: New and Selected Poems, 1975-2002 brings together many of Peacock's best poems from earlier collections with a few new poems added in. As the poems included are among her most celebrated, reviews for the collection were positive. Seaman, again writing in *Booklist,* remarked that "there's a delicious tang to Peacock's vital poems." James Beschta, writing in *Kliatt,* stated: "At her best, her wide-reaching domestic subject matter dominates the poems to the point that poetic convention becomes transparent or invisible."

AUTOBIOGRAPHICAL ESSAY: Molly Peacock contributed the following autobiographical essay to *CA:*

Two girls, fourteen and eleven, eat the dinner the older one has cooked as the July shadows lengthen on all the suburban lawns. School is long over and won't begin again for equally as long. They are deep into the green barbarity of a childhood summer. They listen to the swish of each car as it slows down so that the children playing baseball in the street have time to disperse, and each slowing down causes them a prick of anxiety because it might be their father's car. The later it becomes the more certain it is that he will he

Molly Peacock, 1994

parakeet squawks in its cage. The sun hangs lower in the sky. This time when the sounds of the baseball players disperse, the car wheels into her own driveway. She drops the plate back into the dishwater, grabs the towel, and immediately wipes the knives. She pushes them into the drawer, shuts the drawer, and turns around. "Hi, Dad. Dinner's on the stove. Want to eat?"

She says this before she looks at his face. It is rough-red as a piece of ham. "No, I don't want nothin' to eat," the face says. The arm of her father picks up the saucepan full of creamed corn drying out on the burner from being set continually on "Low." The arm of her father flings the pan of corn at the wall. The dull creamed corn drips down the pink kitchen wall.

"You don't have to have corn, Dad. I made you some pork chops."

"Don't want no pork chops!" The workshirted arm of her father picks up the iron frying pan from the big burner on "Low."

"Dad! Don't throw it!"

He doesn't throw it.

Remember what you said just now, Molly thinks to herself, and remember how you said it. The timing. Remember how you got him not to throw the pan. Maybe you can do it again. Get him not to throw the pan when his arm grabs it like that. While she is organizing these thoughts in her mind, he has gone to the corner cabinet.

In the corner cabinet is a lazy Susan filled not with food or dishes but with files of receipts for the quarterly taxes of Peacock's Superette. Pink and yellow receipts, hundreds of them, clipped together, rubber banded, stuck in between other receipts, notebooks, little pads with columns of figures, and rolls of adding machine paper with columns of figures.

As the arm of her father opens the corner cabinet and whirls the lazy Susan faster and faster, the receipts come flying out. But they don't fly fast enough. The arm of her father, both arms of her father start grabbing the receipts and hauling them down onto the

drunk, but what he will do is not certain. They have the dinner heating on the stove, drying out in the pans. They eat with a mix of summer doldrums and a kind of haste to finish before he comes. Then they won't have to eat with him. The day is long; it's still light out. The littler one puts her dishes in the sink and goes out to play baseball. The older one does the dishes, washing the knives first, just as her mother told her, then continuing on with the rest. "Dry those knives and put them in the drawer before your father gets home. Never leave a knife out, Molly."

Molly is obedient. Molly is good. She never leaves a knife out. Molly is not obedient or good because of her fierce moral fiber, but because she is frightened her father might kill her. Her mother has said that her father might do this. That's why she has to put the knives away. Wash them first. She slops through the suds, the scatter rug below the sink is drenched. The counter, then onto the floor. The kitchen is awash in receipts. Some stick to the creamed corn on the pink walls, some fall into the frying pan with the chops on the stove.

The frying pan, she thinks. I should have let him throw the pan. Next time, remember to let him throw the pan. Remember. Don't say anything. Let him throw it.

Because this is worse.

The side doorbell rings.

Molly ignores it. Her father is swearing, "Fuck the store! Don't want no dinner!" And mumbling, "Fuckin' shit, fuckin' bitch." He wades through the receipts toward the kitchen table. All this time his daughter has been moving around the kitchen, keeping at a safe distance. She makes no move to clean anything up. If she began to clean it up she'd have to turn her back. And if she turned her back, he might kill her. She watches in fascination at the destruction. Her father's legs lumber him toward her. She backs up. He turns toward the kitchen table. The doorbell rings again. Her father is still swearing. He plants his legs as two columns. His arms grab the tabletop and tip it over. Salt, pepper, napkins, and her father's place setting fly off the table. She's glad she cleaned up the other dishes. And put away the knives.

Now her father is down on his knees, bracing them against the upside down table, and using his powerful arms to wrench off the table legs one by one. It is a solid hardwood table. She has learned about adrenaline from the pediatrician who has treated her numerous allergies. Suddenly she thinks, what amount of adrenaline is coursing through him now? The doorbell rings again. He continues swearing, "Cunt, cunt," and methodically braces himself to break the last table leg. She backs into the foyer and closes the kitchen door just before her father takes a table leg and beats it like a club against the tabletop on the floor.

It is a neighbor girl at the side door. "Wanna come out and hang around, go to the drugstore?" It is the girl with cigarette burns on her legs she says are mosquito bites she scratched and made worse. Molly looks down. She still has a dishtowel in her hand. Behind the door her father grunts as he methodically beats the

table. His workbooted feet make a swishing sound as he moves through the flimsy carpet of receipts. How much can she hear? What would she make of it?

"I can't. Go with you. I . . . " Molly trails off. "I . . . ," think of something normal she tells herself, think of a regular excuse, what regular parents do to normal kids. "I'm grounded," she says almost enthusiastically as she finds her normal lie. "I've got to stay in and do the dishes. He's making me." Imagine, doing something dumb and wrong and normal, and then getting punished, and then having it be over, she thinks.

Behind the kitchen door it's over temporarily. No grunts, no swearing. Then, "Molly," he growls, "get in here and clean up this goddamn mess."

"You see? Lookit, I've gotta go."

"Yeah. Well, see ya."

Inside Molly looks at her father with every ounce of censure she can muster. "Oh Dad, what's Mommy going to say?"

"Don't worry about your mother. I'll worry about your mother. Get into your room. I'll clean this up." Now he is pale and repentant. She knows he won't do anything more, like follow her into her room and start breaking things there. He is ashamed and cleans it up by himself.

After he leaves for Peacock's Superette, Molly creeps out to the kitchen. She thinks of calling the neighborhood girl, but stays in the kitchen instead, then goes into the living room to watch TV. The kitchen floor and walls are clean, the receipts somehow piled back into the corner cabinet. Of course the knives were put away earlier. She had seen to that. And he hadn't broken the chairs. Four hard maple chairs are lined up against the wall, waiting, a bit like a police lineup.

It is far too dark to play baseball now. The kids outside are playing a flashlight game. Then parents begin to call them in, so her sister comes home. The kitchen lights are ablaze, but Molly sits in the dark in the living room with only the light of the TV. "Hey, Mol, what happened to the table?" Gail asks. "I saw Dad dragging the pieces out to the garbage."

"He broke it. He broke up the table. He threw his dinner at the wall and broke the table."

"Jesus. Lookit those chairs lined up—they look like Goldilocks and the three bears," her sister says in awe.

Later their mother arrives. "What the hell happened to the kitchen table?"

"Dad broke it."

"No wonder he was such a lamb at the store," her mother says.

Even though I have told this episode countless times to friends, in therapy, and used parts of it in my poetry, I could not write it here in the first person. The only way I could tell it was to make myself and Gail and my father characters in a story.

"What happened here?" my mother asked the next morning when she opened the door to the cabinet where all the receipts were shoved in disorder.

"Dad. He did it when he broke the table."

My mother didn't ask me to tell her more about it, nor did I volunteer. She simply took in the information, groaned, and started reorganizing the receipts. "This will take me a week," she muttered. She did not say he was wrong, she did not say it was his disease, she did not say she was sorry I had to be there during it all, but neither did she wholly deny it happened. She treated it like a horrible fact of life, a hurricane you had to clean up after. I had no sense at all that change in my family was possible.

Sometimes the difference between how I see my life and how others see it is the matter of my skin. Of course, others see it as the border of my body, as anybody else's skin is the boundary between them and the world. But I have often seen my skin as permeable. And sometimes I have felt that I do not have a

"My parents, Edward Frank (Ted) and Pauline (Polly) Peacock," 1945

skin at all. At these times anybody in the world has access to me. I do not feel separate from them. This means that during those times I have found myself in a state of continuous empathy with other people. This empathic state puts me in danger of losing my self because I am attending so closely to the needs of someone else. Well into my thirties I struggled to have an identity, to have a form or shape to my life which seemed constantly to be bleeding into—or being bled by—others.

Many people, especially many women, have felt this sensation, but I felt it all the time as a teenager and as a young woman. The identity crisis that adolescents usually undergo, the questions of *Who am I?* and *What constitutes me?* were kept alive in my life. I carried far too many responsibilities to say I was in an extended state of adolescence, but there was a certain adolescent pain, the psychic growing pain, present all the time.

Years later, having to support myself as a poet, I entered a profession which requires one of the highest levels of sustained human nurturance outside of actual nursing: I became a learning disabilities specialist. The permeable skin I had allowed me to identify with the children I tried to help. These students had trouble processing language. The permeable skin also became part of my identity as a poet. It gave me an understanding of the world from the inside out.

I knew quite early I was engaged in a survival struggle, but I felt I would be alone in it, as alone as each person in my family was. It was not until I was twenty-seven, nearly twenty years ago, that I realized I could ask for help. It was my good fortune to ask for this help from Joan Stein, a psychotherapist so attuned to me that I have been able, over the years, to integrate the many aspects of me that were born and developing along, much like a healthy family of various dimensions inside me. The process of psychotherapy, what the British analyst Adam Phillips calls a "theory of censorship" (and means by this, I think, the development of ways to lift the pressure of the many internal censors our family life and growing personalities attempt to impose on us), has allowed the births and rebirths of these aspects of me, and has allowed me to see their shape, my boundaries.

For ten years (1947–1957) we lived in the duplex in Buffalo, New York, with my grandparents, then, when they retired, sold the duplex and moved to a small pink-and-white suburban house in Tonawanda, north of Buffalo. But the mortgage payments were crippling, not to mention finding the money for the cases of beer and cartons of cigarettes necessary to keep our new nuclear family afloat. My dad, Ted (Edward Frank Peacock), began to work two jobs, his regular job at the electric company, driving the truck with a huge yellow lift to repair downed wires, and a night job pumping gas in a service station a few blocks away. Anticipating my father's breaking point, my mother found a way of taking care of all of us financially, eliminating the gas station job, and getting the beer and cigarettes at cost.

What my mother, Pauline (Pauline Ruth Peacock, née Wright), found to do was to emulate her own father. My grandfather Gilbert Wright's general store and Esso station (which stood at a crossroads in the orchard country of rural upstate New York called LaGrange)—with its secret peephole to spy for gypsies and the miracles of its wooden shelves of fudge bars, soda pop, clothespins, flour, oil, auto parts—fascinated all its customers, including the regulars, my grandfa-

"I'm in the foreground, with my mother and Gail behind me," about 1952.

ther's cronies, a group of pipe-smoking farmers in bib overalls. Pauline convinced Ted to borrow money from his credit union to start a business: PEACOCK'S SUPERETTE. The Superette, a low cement building next to a liquor store on a main road between Buffalo and Niagara Falls, had none of the slow conviviality of LaGrange Garage. The Superette sported metal shelves, not brightly painted wooden ones, and cement floors with rows of coolers stocked with brown pint bottles and green quart bottles and flimsy aluminum cans of beer and ale.

The new arrangement Pauline constructed was that Ted would come home from his job at four, I would make him dinner, iron his shirt, and send him off to the store. There he would relieve her, so that she could come home and eat dinner. Gail and I were to come home alone from school and do our homework until the dinner I made was ready. I was to supervise my sister's homework. This was to be the clockwork, weekday routine. On weekends Pauline and Ted were to alternate shifts at the store.

Pauline would cook on Sundays. Now this is an extreme schedule for any family. The burden on my mother from her two jobs of house and store, on my father from his two jobs, on me from the two jobs of school and house, and on my sister from the job of

"Again in the foreground, with my father and Gail, picking up marbles," about 1954

school as a learning disabled child and home with a smartypants older sister who hated her mothering role all weigh so heavily in the mere description that it is exhausting for me to imagine it. Now add alcoholism.

Twelve- and thirteen-year-old humans are some of the frailest animals alive. I spent ten years of my life watching them, first as a teacher, then as a learning disabilities specialist. It is a truism among teachers that the age you teach is the age of your greatest personal crisis. Having worked with hundreds of girls and boys of the age at which I began my life as a false wife and false mother, I can say with verified sadness that no matter how adult such adolescents appear, they are not adults, but in a tunnel of travel into adult consciousness. However successful I am as a poet, or as a teacher, or even simply as an adult, there is an ever-decreasing but still apparent part of me frozen in that tunnel, for I was not allowed to traverse it in my own time or in my own skin.

Three years of high school without change in fear, or vigilance. Sometimes the fear abates, but it never completely leaves. Sometimes I turn my attention elsewhere, but a part of me never removes my attention from the possible source of danger, which isn't only my father, but Ted and Gail and Pauline and myself in four strands of color that wind and wind. Of

course the changes of growth and degeneration occur, but these aren't clear to me. My father's alcoholism degenerates. His daughters' sexuality accelerates. His wife's depression deepens. Everybody gains weight, except Gail. Either food or drink fills us up, but danger fills her up.

"I'm going out with this great guy tonight," Gail whispers over the minute steaks I've burned. "Don't tell Mom, Molly, you're always such a tattletale." I was a tattletale; she was right. "He's coming over at seven and we're going to go to the Falls." Niagara Falls was not within walking distance.

"How old is this guy? Does he drive a car?" I say incredulously.

"Sure he drives. He's nineteen. He goes to night school, isn't that cool?"

"Cool," I say, nonplussed.

"He was at the JV basketball game. He likes basketball."

"Likes basketball?"

"Yeah, but Molly, don't tell Mom, what he really likes is cars. He likes to drive 'em."

"Cars?"

My sister was a JV cheerleader. I had coached her for hours before the tryouts. I hadn't been chosen as a cheerleader, but like a teenage stage mother I'd decided that my Gail should rectify my inabilities and mistakes. And so I'd hounded and nagged her until she learned a great routine and was honored with a position on the squad. She was too hip, though. She smoked; she never did her homework. I felt I was a shitty mother and worse as a sister. I just couldn't keep an eye on her. When, when, I asked myself, did she become like this?

"Look, I better call Mom," I began, but she mocked me.

"Better call Mo-om," breaking the syllable in two like a saltine.

"The guy's nineteen! He's two years older than I am!" I squawked.

"So who says you have to be the oldest thing around here? This guy is cool. Wait'll you meet him. He knows Mom, too. He hangs out at the store sometimes." The only guys who hung out at the store were dropouts. My mother collected them.

"Keep an eye on your sister," my grandparents often said.

Be vigilant. You can never tell what will happen.

She looked to me as the mother I hated to be. She told the truth to me, more or less. And whatever truth she told increasingly horrified me. She was blonde and sexual and loved danger. Personally, danger left me cold. I'd been in enough of it. I was endangered every night waiting for Ted to come home.

"That's him!" my sister squealed as she heard a muffled noise at the door.

"How could it be him? I didn't hear a car drive up."

I still listened for my father's car in the driveway every night. I listened for how he drove, whether the turn was reckless and the brake was jammed on at the last minute, or whether it was a smooth, pantherlike crawl, the turquoise Chrysler oiled with only a couple of beers. Late, later, after countless shots of whisky with beer chasers, meant either rage at full force, or maybe only a dead sleep, or maybe a few slurred questions tucked around an insult and then the blackout. A couple of beers maybe meant OK, he'd get changed and go to relieve my mother at the store, but it also meant fuller consciousness, questions, where was my sister going, what was I doing, and possible anger. This meant anything could happen.

My sister was unlocking the door and speaking to a figure in the dark she didn't ask into the light of the hallway. She left him standing outside in the cold while she ran for her coat and grabbed the keys to my mother's ancient pink Plymouth that was mysteriously harbored in the rivulet of our driveway. How had my mother gotten to work, anyway?

"You're taking Mom's car?" I was incredulous.

"I told you, Molly, he likes cars. He loves to drive. He's a really great driver, too. We'll he back before they know it's missing."

"Put those car keys on the hook!" I hissed as she swung out the door. She knew I wouldn't tackle her on the front steps. She knew I'd be slightly afraid of the nineteen-year-old boy. She knew I was confused and couldn't decide whether I was her mother or her sister, and she knew I wouldn't tell our mother because I was supposed to he her mother and I failed. And she also knew, somehow, that my mother's car would be there for the taking. The Plymouth wheeled out of the driveway with the wild teenage daughter I couldn't control.

My father came home drunk but obedient to some unknown-to-me command from my mother that he pick her up at the store and bring her home. I said my sister was at her girlfriend's house. Just after he left, my sister came home with my mother's car, and there the two of us sat, watching "Adventures in Paradise," when my parents drove up at 10:30 p.m. I never understood how my mother had gotten to work without a car, how my sister knew this, or how my father understood the arrangement; nor did my parents— unless my mother knew some version of this from my sister—know whom my sister was with and in what vehicle. My family arrangements were often like this. I felt I had all the responsibility, and none of the control. Nothing I kept an eye on stayed still; it vaporized. Yet I had to keep my eye on my sister, and especially on my father. If I took my eyes off him, he might kill me.

Continually my mother reminded me to do the dishes immediately after eating and to put away the knives. "You don't want to give anybody an opportunity," my mother said. "Anybody" meant my father. It took me almost a decade of exposure to other people's lives before what a therapist said to me made sense: "She expected you to be hurt, Molly." And I expected this too.

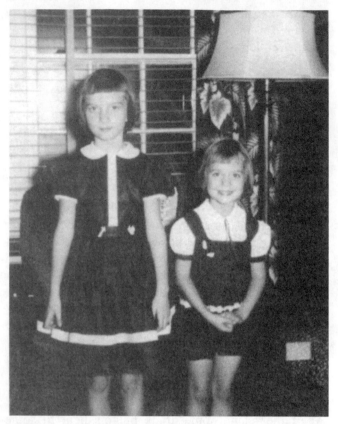

Molly and Gail at Christmas, 1955

A spring night in my senior year of high school. My sister out with her friends. I lie on my bed looking at the curtains I've designed and sewn and looking at the two orange heads of Nefertiti I've wedged as bookends for the books of poetry I've begun collecting. I have only a few friends, and they are school friends. If my mother is out when my father is home, I feel I have to stay home as well. It takes me decades to understand I am a substitute, a sacrifice. Then I only thought, if I'm not here, who knows what could happen? I have to stay home, because if I am home I will be able to . . . prevent . . . what?

Well, one thing I can prevent is his coming into my room. My bedroom has no door. It is an extension built onto the house through my sister's bedroom. Her room does have a door, but I do not want to lead him to burst through it; therefore I meet him on common ground: the kitchen and the living room. The key is to remain ever watchful. You can never tell when he will come home or what he will do when he gets there. The best tactic is to stay alert and stay away from the things of yours he could destroy.

Every evening is a defensive military maneuver, and I use the tactics of the powerless everywhere: fore-thought and watchfulness. I also use the good girl tactic, since it is at my disposal. I am the good girl, the obedient one. If I obey perfectly all the instructions, I can trot out obedience in my defense. I can ward off evil with my structure of goodness, of servitude. Oh yes, I am a servant. I serve my family's needs, not out of that desire for connection, not out of that love that makes us long to fulfill the needs of those whom we love, but out of self-defense, a brittle, two-faced cunning that knows the armor of the Good. And it is armor I need, for I have no skin. At best I am "thin-skinned" and sensitive, sensitive because the borders that define me are so frail.

But I have my lessons to do, and I have the phone to talk on to my occasional friends, not about socializing, but about homework and the appalling number of school activities I join. I'm in every club and on every committee. Of course there's nothing to come home for after school, so I don't. There's another reason I join everything. I want to be visible in school. I've never been rushed to a sorority. (How can I have people to my house? Who knows what will happen?) And out of a desire to reaffirm that I can be something other than a nobody, I manage to get myself elected to things, chosen for things. I do the publicity for this and this, make the posters, make the phone calls. I work on the newspaper, on the yearbook. Finally I am chosen editor of the yearbook. Everything looks normal; I am succeeding.

And I am succeeding as the substitute abused wife of my father: I am alive. A spring night here in my room admiring the overstuffed chair I acquired and the cover for the chair my grandmother helped me make and the bedspread she helped me dye to match it, and I listen. I listen for the car in the driveway. Every night for all the years between twelve and eighteen I listen for the car, and often I hope he is dead. I hope he gets into a car accident and dies. I think my father must be the luckiest man in Buffalo. He is the embodiment of the luck of the Irish. How can he be alive when he drives like that? It is about a year since my last try at getting him into Alcoholics Anonymous. I have ended a campaign which begged my mother every morning to leave him and begged him every sober early weekend morning to go to AA. I read him the ten questions from the *Buffalo Evening News* that if you answer yes to any five you are an alcoholic.

My mother surprised me. She said, "You're hurting your father." Is she crazy? I thought. He's hurting us.

Maternal grandparents, Ruth and Gilbert Wright, about 1967

Me. Nothing seemed to change, except the years passing at school. I was going to go to college. I was going to get out of there, to escape a burden that was both very big and very inappropriate. The secrecy surrounding my father's alcoholism hooded every perspective. My mother had found a way of supporting us, but it was also a way of abdicating responsibility as a wife and a mother. I can still touch the anger at her strange abandonment, the lack of love and care that resulted, and that held me in a kind of perpetual pause of growth throughout my teenage years. When I was required during literature classes or during my silly home economics classes to imagine a family, or to imagine what my own future family might be like, I could only picture my present painful one. This picture I looked away from again and again as I tried to make a life as an ordinary human being, though I was not so ordinary. I had a gift for language and a burning desire to use it to understand my life. Therefore, though I tried to turn away from it, in poem after poem I focused on that internalized picture.

No one who knew my mother well actually used her formal name, Pauline. Everyone called her Polly. Polly, as a child, had felt lovingly bonded to her grandmother,

Molly. Her mother (my grandmother, Ruth) had named my newborn mother Ruth Isabelle, after herself. Family legend has it that my grandfather simply started calling my mother Polly, and her name was formally changed to Pauline Ruth, dropping the wretched Isabelle. As a girl my mother lived for weeks at a time on the glorious farm with her grandparents, preferring it to the house and general store down the road where her mother was. Her brother was preferred in her parents' household, and Polly was relished by her grandparents, especially Molly, after whom I am named. When she married my father, she became Polly Peacock, a goofy name she feistily defended.

I know the history of these names is confusing—I myself was confused by it as a little girl—but I explain it here because the confusion is so emblematic of the confused identity of the child who shares too intimately a mother's thoughts. There was only one consonant difference between my mother and me, yet I was also her obstacle. I continually felt that if I didn't exist, she somehow would have a better life. How could I, as her child, bear being her obstacle? I could become her mirror. I could reflect to her the assurances she needed to be who she was.

It was a staggering job to return this mirroring, more so because the mirroring my mother did for me was often obscured. Common wisdom says that mothers are supposed to be the mirrors of their children, for in their eyes will be reflected their children's growth and identities. But very often my mother was depressed, so depressed that the mirrors of her eyes were dull, and nearly impossible to see myself in. At these times, my mother read. I sat at her side playing—often reading myself, or writing and drawing—and admonishing myself not to interrupt her, though she tolerated what probably were a stream of interruptions from me. My mother read to escape. And I have often thought that I became a writer in order to have my mother read me. Although it is difficult to develop a positive picture of a family to internalize if the picture your mother draws for you is negative—or at least my own experience has taught me that—my mother's escape, reading, did allow me to develop other ideas of families, because as soon as I could read I loved to read about them.

Polly was an avid reader of westerns and romances. Gail and I teased her about her favorite author, Louis L'Amour, as soon as we found out what *amour* was. Before she turned to buying paperbacks to read behind

LaGrange crossroads in rural upstate New York, the site of Grandfather Gilbert Wright's general store and Esso station

the counter at the Superette, the three of us went weekly to the library. I did everything Pauline did, so I became a reader, too. My learning-disabled sister, hyperactive, unable to focus, did not. My mother and I, swept into fantasy worlds at the drop of a paragraph, had one more reason to see Gail as a foreigner. This was in 1955, thirty years before schools began diagnosing learning disabilities. Pauline's escapist reading began in her own family when she herself was four and learned to read at a one-room schoolhouse, taken there every day on the back of a blind farm horse who knew the way. When her grandparents hooked up their team to their wagon and went to town for weekly supplies, Pauline stayed at the farm to ride her pony but instructed them to bring her back a book.

If I had had grandparents who hitched up a wagon and went to town, I too would have wanted to stay home and be brought a book. To wander bareback on a pony to a riverbank pretending to be this or that, and then to lie, deliciously prone on that riverbank, and get lost in a book: I cannot think of a childhood afternoon more

ideal. Very luckily I was invited to spend summers with my mother's parents at the hamlet of LaGrange. A few weeks of each of my own childhood summers were as golden as those my mother described, though my mother's summers grew into apple-picking falls, and I left my grandparents' house to return to Buffalo to resume my roles as a poorly prepared substitute wife and mother. As Polly aged, she often lapsed into stories about her youth and prefaced each story with how wonderful her girlhood was. For her, childhood contained the best moments of life before adulthood went awry. For me, whose life has been so much the opposite, but who had that little taste of what she described and re-described, those stories are clouded in my anger. I heard "Oh, I had a wonderful childhood!" with sharpening rage over the years.

It sounds hyperbolic, but the legacy of childhood reading probably saved my life. My experience of horror—my parents' fights, the terror I felt when the drinking was out of hand and into violence, at the least my parents' voices raised, at the worst my father pushing my mother down the cellar stairs, my sister and I running to push her back up into safety—led me to separate my experience into what happened "outside" my head and what happened "inside." Inside were fantasies of health and power and control. I was Lola the spy who controlled all (I played Lola privately well into my sophomore year of high school) or I was Mary of *The Secret Garden* or Jo of *Little Women*. I developed these fantasies from reading. The voices of authors, the comfort and wisdom and emotion expressed, allowed me to grow internally, secretly, to nurture a hidden self all on my own, the self I would save, the self I would become, unbeknownst to my family, almost unbeknownst to my conscious, practical, adult facade, the outer self I built to bear the burdens of my father's alcoholism and my mother's depression. The voices of those authors parented me. The books I read were my escape, the authors' voices mirrors of my feelings, nurturers of my imagination. All my inner world was yearnings, yearnings for solitude and freedom.

Of course I fantasized I was an orphan, that these parents were really not my own. Perhaps my real parents would come and get me. My fantasy life was composted from the emotional peelings and scraps of my parents' lives put out to rot in the backyard of literature, the weather of literature beating on them, turning them into loam. Although my parents' arguments must have had words, I do not recall them but only remember the achingly wordless non-explanations of their behavior, the silence to my questions, the silencing of my questions, the requirement that I turn inside in order to stay sane, although many children turn inside, split off entirely, and become insane. My imagination, fueled by literature, kept alive an anchored, growing, interior life, one I could articulate to myself because of literary models, models who would save me. The books gave me this gift. But unbeknownst to me I was gifted already. I was imaginative and verbal and, best of all, I was to learn that I could write.

Polly always closed her book and put it carefully away when Ted came home. His entry into the house always threatened disruption. The threat that I felt to my life, even though my father in fact never spanked, hit, or touched me (and in fact rarely hugged or was physically affectionate toward me) had its taproot in my father's threat to my mother's life. Ted was a hysterical nipper of a fighter, biting, darting, then sweating,

bashing, and thrashing as my mother's recalcitrance fanned his hysteria into blinder rage. Polly was a growler, growling this or that comment, refusing to up her pitch, keeping a steady negative monotone that refused to react to his emotionalism, fanning it. The ways they expressed themselves completely frustrated their understanding of one another, Polly constantly protecting herself from Ted's emotional fireworks, Ted's need for an ear met instead by her protective resistance. Neither of them ever could change his or her mode.

Bright morning in the Buffalo duplex house. Gail is three and I am six. Daddy comes home after working the graveyard shift. Breakfast. French toast. Sharp rectangular delineations of sunlight on the floor. Playing, eating, unaware of the escalating voices until our mother's usual growl of stubborn annoyance hikes itself into a surprising soprano pitch, and our father's yapping descends to a deep, lung-rattling bass. The hefty Scotty dog I think he's like and the big unflappable setter I think she's like have reversed and become monstrous. They are not like dogs anymore, but like canine horrorsaurs. He is pushing her toward the open cellar door and she is screaming, "Ted, Ted don't do it!" and he is panting, "I'll kill you, you bitch," and as his broad workshirted back blocks the doorway, she is already backing down the cellar stairs. He prods her collarbone with his pointer finger. Then he pushes her again. "Ted, not in front of the kids!" is her signal to us and we run, Gail tiny enough to push between his legs to get to her, me sliding past them on the stairs. Now Gail and I are below them, pushing up against our mother's legs as he pushes down on her. It is a tangle of legs and stairs, his workpants and boots pushing down against her bare calves and slippers, while Gail and I push up against her, trying to hold her up and save her, and in saving her rescue our lives, because he is a monster now, a dragon, faced puffed and red. Her face as she twists toward us is drained an almost painted white. She looks like a geisha girl beneath her black hair. "Ted, watch out! The kids!" she screams, diverting his attention. She is the cunning girl and he is the blustering dragon, brought for a moment to his senses, outwitted because we have diverted him. He backs up the stairs, she follows, we follow her, we are saved, all of us, because of the kids, watch out for them.

The stereotypical Asian images of terrifying maleness in the shape of a red dragon and terrified femininity painted chalk white, ashen in fear, leapt into relief in my mind and seem permanently installed there. I cannot think of him in rage except to recall the dragon, or her except to recall the courtesan, highly stylized images for this Navy boy come home from World War II to work at the electric company and this farm girl come to the city. Even if he seemed like a little terrier and she like a large, long-haired lazy setter, they were a strong man and a weaker woman. He could overpower her. He could kill her. Kill us. Me. Usually the fights were verbal. Physical violence was only hinted at, but because this perennial threat wasn't quite empty, it was always powerful. Only after I escaped to college did I hear, long distance from my dorm room, the stories of increased physical violence, the police, my mother's and sister's fear escalating until they ran away. My parents divorced, and Peacock's Superette was sold, and my father briefly remarried, worked, retired early from countless alcohol-related health problems, and died; my mother finished her working life as a secretary in a hospital, never remarried, then retired and lived a life of glorious solitude until the illness of her last year, carefully budgeting her money to eat an inexpensive lunch out every day with a paperback romance or western in front of her, happy with her book, with the food which she did not have to make, brought to her by a series of solicitous waitresses with waiting coffee pots, and happy with the voice of the author speaking to her, soothing, exciting, engaging, surprising. Now I am an author.

The serious split between an internal safety I struggled to create and preserve and an external atmosphere of verbal suggestions of violence, sharpened my ideas of inner life and public life to a glittering edge. What I truly was I felt could not be revealed at the cost of its death. As a result, no one could really know me. The loneliness this causes is almost unspeakably profound. Anyone who is driven this far inward risks the "not coming back" of serious mental illness, the splitting off of internal and external experience that can become at its worst multiple personalities. But I did not suffer a splitting off from the world so severe. When I think of the circumstances that allowed my escape from extreme illness, of the many individual adults both inside and outside my family who helped me, and of the sheer luck of my physical stamina and intelligence, the circumstance with the most profoundly rescuing shape is art. Since the first time my mother gave me a pencil and scrap paper to occupy myself, I have consistently felt the joy of processing my experiences into pictures and words. As a girl I drew and painted, and as I learned more about language I wrote, and then

read. My inner life had a way out. I did not have to hold my spirit prisoner. Many times throughout my young life I imagined myself in prison, without pencil or paper. I practiced for this deprivation by imagining writing in my head and memorizing it. I was determined for my gift to save me, even if I became deprived of its instruments.

Gail next door at Grandma's, Daddy far away at work, Mommy reads her library book settled deep in a red upholstered chair with doilies on the arms to cover the cigarette burns. Mommy wears Daddy's dark green T-shirt without a bra and a pair of baggy jeans. Her shiny black hair with its exciting streak of gray to the left of her widow's peak is pushed back from her cream-white forehead. The wall behind her is green, dark as the forest green of the T-shirt. It is 1952. I am five. She is thirty-three. No woman on Gunnell Avenue in Buffalo, New York, goes braless, wears jeans, buys red chairs and puts them in deep green rooms, then sits down to read a library book, popping an occasional chocolate-covered cherry into her mouth after she's finished her cigarette. She's whizzed through her housework, the dinner fixings are on the counter. She is alone, alone and happy to be in her own world.

Little mouse at her side, I try to read a letter her mother, my grandmother Ruth in the country, has sent me, but I don't attend school yet and do not know how. I have my pencil and my drawing pad. I am using my inner resources. Mommy doesn't like people who can't sit and be quiet and use their inner resources. But I can't read! In exasperation I poke through the carefully constructed boundary of Mommy's world. "Read it to me, Mom."

"Read it to me, Mom, OK?"

Her hazel eyes are trained on her book.

"Read me Gram's letter, OK?"

After a few verbal tries, I place the letter on top of the open book, and Mommy turns and reads it aloud. I have never gotten a letter before, and this is an interesting thing to have, though I wonder what to do with it now.

"Well, when you get a letter, you write back," Mommy explains.

"OK," I say, picking up my pencil, making stray letter-like lines on the page. But my lines are disappointing. They don't really look like writing.

"Why don't you draw Gram a picture?" Mommy lazily says.

I *always* draw pictures. *Babies* draw pictures. "No! I want to write a letter back!"

"Oh, all right, here's the alphabet, Molly." Mommy scrawls the alphabet across the top of the paper. "Now, write DEAR GRAM." She underlines the individual letters. Of course I can't remember the order of "Dear Gram" out of ADEGMR, and I am aware that Mommy has reached her limit, so I do not ask again, but try to figure out for myself how to write them, and after a fashion, I have covered the page in something akin to a personal cuneiform. It is the hardest thing I've ever done. I couldn't be more pleased. And Mommy couldn't be more pleased. I make her smile. I draw a smile from those straight, slightly purplish lips whose carmine lipstick has disappeared to find a better home on the filter tips of cigarette butts in a square glass ashtray, an ashtray so heavy that when my father let it fly against the wall in an argument it didn't even break. Nothing can break the pleasure of this solitude of this afternoon. Like two sides of an open locket, the side that read and the side that wrote to reach the reader, my mother and I lay inside the red and green jewelbox of the afternoon.

The mutual possession of our selves, without the diverting presence of my sister or the inflaming presence of my father, gave me the sense, reinforced by my mother over and over again, that *this* was how one ought to live. "Everybody should have their own room," my mother would say. "The only way for a family to survive is for each person to have their own room." My mother had never heard of Virginia Woolf. She didn't have a room of her own as an adult until she was nearly fifty years old, divorced, and with her children grown. None of us had rooms to ourselves, and even when my sister and I did, later in a different house, the rooms *had no doors.* Invasion was always both physically and emotionally possible. My mother's quest for a room became invested in me, and the magnitude of my need for it irrevocably shaped my life—and the lives of the people I've loved, especially the men I've lived (or tried to live) with.

Part of that driven need for a room of my own was to have room for my gift as an artist. I both drew and wrote until I reached high school. I knew I wanted to be "something special" but I didn't know what that special thing was until I got to college and decided, in a very tentative way, to try to become a poet. I know people who have denied their gifts, and I have watched their personalities wizen and shrivel, almost before my eyes, from that denial. My gift was too large, too pleasurable, too life-affirming to deny. It gave me life by ensuring my life. Without it, I would not have survived. I did not know this consciously, but since I first was able to express myself I have guarded that gift with a fierceness I have long heard described as the characteristic protective fierceness of motherhood. I take pleasure in the gift, and, animal-like, claw the mental air at any interference with the tenderness of its growing being.

Sex and babies. Five tiny neighborhood girls all jumping up and down on two of their children's twin beds, squealing and tickling one another in the silky, rabbit warren mess of sheets that smell of childbody sleep thick between the crumpled ridges. Burrow into Gail's bed with the shock of Gailsmell while the others use my bed as a trampoline before Grandma, alarmed at the squawk of the springs, hauls us all downstairs: I stick my finger up my underpants and find the hole, fingersized, see a color in my mind, black/red, bring my finger out and smell it. Ah! The smell of me.

"All right now, all of you girls have to go home after you finish your oatmeal cookies. Come on now, little Diane, let's get a move on." My grandmother Mildred, my father's mother who lives next door to us, has the quality of a businesslike Shetland sheepdog nosing at the heels of the three lambs she ushers out the door. She is glad to sit down. Five girls, ages four to seven, are a handful. But she leans toward me from her chair and puts her arms loosely around me. "Oh you naughty girls! I'll have to make those beds all over again."

"Hey Gram, look what I found," I say, suddenly daring. She has said "naughty" with benign acceptance. I know she thinks we weren't really naughty. I stick my finger up my underpants into my vagina and bring my finger out and thrust it under her nose. "Smell this!"

"Eeewwwhhh!" she exclaims in delight, "what a cupcake smell!" Her eyes glisten with a kind of excitement, surprise, curiosity, and wonder. I search her face

Paternal grandparents, Mildred and Howard Peacock, about 1950

for whether this is all right. I have found the secret place she also knows about, inside the place I pee from. I'm not clear at all about why this is a secret, but it is all right. "Let's go remake the beds," she says, corralling me and Gail up the stairs. I know not to startle my mother in the way that I startled Gram, just the way I know not to use the beds as trampolines, although I think it's fine to use the beds as trampolines *quietly* not making a disturbance.

Quietly. For all my railing at my mother's abandonment and sometimes downright neglect—one time I was forced to come home from school with a note asking my mother to please get me to brush my teeth—the policy of Quietly, and the unloosed aspect of neglect that was benign, allowed me to be uncivilized, sensuous, a barbarian. This is not the kind of thing that prepares you well for your college interviews, but it created a privacy in which my sexuality was allowed to take its own course. After I learned how to masturbate, I wasn't to be interrupted at it, disturbed in the midst, often questioned, admonished . . . my sexuality went on burgeoning without direct notice. The neglect that left me in terror, that left me holding the bag of family responsibility, left me in peace and

quiet about sex. Along with writing, sex became another healthy, undisturbed part of my life.

When I worked with middle schoolers in English classes, we all enjoyed writing poems about tumbling down birth canals and the voyage from the womb to the outside. The children astonished me with their memories and images of being born: blood, and egg yolks, and pulsations galore, the imagery freshly present for them in a way it was only embedded for me. Being born is a highly contemporary subject for children's poetry. No one would have asked us to write about being born in 1955. One of my oldest friends, Katie Kinsky, a painter, swears she thought women had babies from their armpits because the deodorant commercials of the fifties showed a mysterious statue of the Venus de Milo, camera aimed at the pit of her cut-off arm and the voiceover murmuring about "that place." The language was so veiled she thought that armpits had to be the most secret part of the body.

Because my mother had a cesarean section for my sister, I thought all babies were born that way. It was only when Polly overheard me majestically explaining to Gail how babies were delivered that she corrected me. I was probably eight or nine. I simply couldn't imagine a baby coming out of my vagina, and I was horrified. It would hurt! "Oh, you expand," my mother said. Expand???

I was an angry little girl who almost never directly expressed that anger. My experience of anger was one of blowing up—not exploding, but my whole body blowing up until I was the size of an imaginary sumo wrestler. I could not name this feeling. Only as an adult did I recognize it as anger. At the time when Polly said, "Oh, you expand," I generally experienced my anger as confusion and distortion and being filled like a human balloon. This filling up felt painful and exhausting. It was a perverse pregnancy, a holding in of anger until it grew, and grew. Always having contained my anger, I never had a chance to see it being born, or expressed, and to feel a normal human cycle of being full and being empty.

Sex and babies. To have a baby "out of wedlock" was so terrible there was no worse crime. Manslaughter charges got dropped, prison sentences ended, but having a baby out of wedlock ruined your life forever. I had trouble connecting pregnancy and sex until I was in junior high. I knew you had to have a father in order to have a baby. But somehow I thought "married" conferred "future father" status on a man. However, I learned that there was a terrible danger of being "in trouble," of getting pregnant out of wedlock. I never connected my delight in myself to the sex that led to "in trouble" because I avoided knowing how children came to be and because I never asked questions. (My parents did not like to have to answer them. A child's questions shed an unwittingly bright light on their unhappiness. I grew to be a hyper-involved listener, gleaning the answers to my questions from fragments of phrases and innuendos. But sex was not a fully discussed subject, and I couldn't pick up enough information. Because, as a teenager, I was leery about bringing friends home, I didn't have the intimate conversations with them that might have led to other information.)

One day Gram drove me to see Beryl. I was eight or nine, and she was on a mission of no mercy to Beryl. I was the excuse not to stay long, just enough time to eye the mess Beryl was in and report back to other interested parties. She had had a baby out of wedlock and lived on welfare. To be on welfare was almost as bad as to be in trouble. Beryl was ironing. There probably are people alive now or in the past who don't mind ironing, or who even love it, but I have never met one. (Ironing may be distinguished from many men and women's love of washing and drying laundry, which the lovers of laundry see as a redemptive act. I know no lovers of fresh sheets flapping on the line or shirts resurrected from their final spin who also have this deep affection for ironing.) Beryl was particularly affecting because she had a withered arm which hung at her side when she ironed.

The baby slept rather politely in a wicker laundry basket I myself wouldn't have minded curling up in. I was tired from being dragged from store to store by my tireless, domineering fireball of a grandmother. Beryl lived in welfare housing. This meant that she lived in a kind of barracks where nothing was planted to obscure the cement foundation, the grass was cut down to a yellow stubble, and the screening in the screen door sagged in convexity. This was what happened when you got in trouble. What was worse was that people like my grandmother would come and throw old baby clothes on your ripped davenport and humiliate you with a lot of judgmental questions. My grandmother *was* someone I could ask questions of and

I did a substantial amount of quizzing on the fascinating, horrifying Beryl who was so skinny that her apron—obviously meant for someone who in those days would have been called more "ample"—wrapped around her one and a half times. Her eyes were red, and her hair was thin and frizzy from a home permanent that had gone wrong. "It'll grow out," my grandmother said drily. I would not be Beryl, I decided, although the image of Beryl came to me many times as I stood at the ironing board in our half-finished suburban basement, surrounded by baskets of Ted's, Polly's, Gail's and my rumpled clothes, never taken from the dryer on time. The sheer servitude of that General Electric steam iron that linked me to every housewife, housekeeper, and laundress became so fraught for me that I still can't iron more than three pieces of clothing without feeling pinned by the wings.

"I'm going to marry a collie," I announced to Gram on the way home. Some girls choose horses, some cats, some ballet shoes, and some dogs as emblems of their growing selves. Having chosen dogs for their ability to read emotions, to protect, to adore—all the qualities, alas, that Polly and Ted may have had but could not give to me—and having an encyclopedic bent, I took all the dog books out of the library and tried to memorize all the breeds. (Later, with my country grandmother Ruth in charge, I traipsed the landscape identifying flowers in the same impulse to anchor down the world.) Polly introduced me to *Lad, a Dog*. I was a goner. From sidewalk booksales to the tiny libraries at the backs of English classrooms I fetched all the Albert Payson Terhune dog novels and ate them, then ate them again. God bless him for having written so many, especially what I remember as the incomparable *Unseen*, which gives us both romance *and* dogs.

As I watched the "Lassie" family on TV, despising that horrible sap of a boy Lassie rescued week after week but loving the farm life and the gentle goddess-like understanding of June Lockhart, the boy's mother, I reached the point of tears. (Oh, little girl who wouldn't let herself cry over the loss of what she wondered whether she deserved anyway. . . .) I did not cry at the program, knowing I would fail my mother's standard of appropriate toughness, though I would have liked to have cried, and if Gail had punched me then or if I had been injured in fake play, I would have used the opportunity to cry. The program, as the novels did, gave me a way to envision a safe life. Many people rail at the perfected, inhumanly bland vision of

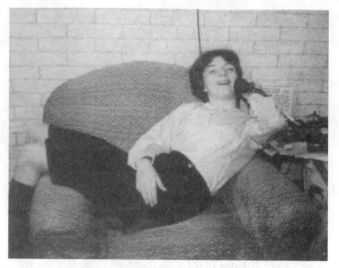

On the telephone with Michael Groden, 1964

the fifties' television family, but it was a comfort to me. I knew it was not real. Real was home. But the kindness the "Lassie" parents showed for their son and the dog, as well as the gravely fierce kindness the dog showed toward the boy, showed *me* kindness by displaying behavior I didn't often get to see.

Animals for girls, and certainly for women poets from Emily Dickinson to Elizabeth Bishop, become a form of natural identity, identity in its unhampered state, greedy, unsocialized, an essential nature accepted simply, not transformed into the posture of continuous giving-unto-others that girls and women often must assume. I wished I could be a dog. I wished I could have a dog to recognize the essential me with its knowing eyes, just as Blake looks into the Tyger's eyes. The combination of the kindness of the family and the protection, adoration, and recognition of the dog caused such a longing for another life to well up in me that I nearly cried. I was seven years old. Would I get what I wanted? Now I had a new answer to those awful, awful questions adults always asked me, "Who are you going to marry when you grow up? And how many children will you have?"

"Lassie," I would say, "I'm going to marry Lassie." (But how would I ever meet such a celebrity as Lassie? Did such animals come to Buffalo? Also, Lassie would be dead by the time I needed to get married. I had heard there were *replacement* Lassies, a ghastly fact I could barely assimilate. . . .) Becoming more realistic, I would simply reply, "A collie, I am going to marry a collie." There on the windswept moor I

would stand with my husband, a big, big collie with its foreleg casually, protectively, but not remotely possessively, around my shoulder. "So what kind of children are you going to have with a *dog*?" the adults asked, then answered their own question with, "*Puppies!*"

"Maybe we'll have puppies," I'd announce, then say more primly, "or we won't have anything. You can't have children with a dog." In this wish for my doghusband was a wish for cherished protection as well as a fair certainty that no progeny would come from the union. But I never got as far as imagining doing it with a dog. What was doing it, anyway? Oh, if only my parents could be dogs. Oh, to be a feral child, brought up by wolves!

"Maybe we should get a dog," I recently said to my husband who has two cats who have come to include me in their sphere of interest. "What kind of dog?" Mike says. "Oh, I don't know," I say cagily. "Do you have a favorite kind?" "A small one," Mike says. Not a collie. Oh, well, I'm years and years beyond collies. Forty years. "What kind of a small one?" "A miniature collie. I like those dogs."

I did not marry this man by accident. I married him by design, although the design took thirty years and two countries, and became so vast and intricate it shaped our lives in ways only experience and greater forces could be responsible for. I am only responsible for the first move, a move I made in high school, long after I abandoned the fantasy of a collie for a husband, but not very long at all after I surrendered a fantasy about my father that I knew was entirely untrue but wanted so hard to believe I spoke it as true.

The little girl who said the cigarette burns on her legs were infected mosquito bites, the one who came to the door while my father was tearing off the hardwood maple table legs, grew up to become a creep in high school who had not been rushed to a sorority. I too had not been rushed, but I resolved to escape creephood, and did this by being yearbook editor, the keeper of the records of what everybody was, and by organizing activities, and by, as Polly put it as she sipped her instant Maxwell House and ate a peanut donut, "not being a sheep." Really, I would have adored being a sheep if I could have just got on sheep's clothing, but I could not, and so with the Creepette I walked home.

Graduation day, June 1965: Molly (in cap and gown), with sister, Gail, and Mike

I had nothing but contempt for her, who looked up to me and believed every word I said, just like a little sister except she was my own age. But by the time I reached my sophomore year, I didn't have a single real friend. All the phone calls and checking in to see if we had gotten our periods yet that charged my group of girlfriends in junior high were gone. The years of friends squealing on the couches of our living rooms were long, long over. I was not in a sorority as my former friends were, and I had no group but those artificial clubs institutionalized by the school. I could not invite anyone home, even the Creepette. By my junior year I especially could not ask her, to whom I had lied, lied horribly and unconsciously.

"I hate my father," Creepette said as we trudged through the ice of an unshoveled sidewalk, thrown shoulder to shoulder. "He drinks too much beer. He's mean to my mother. He's not like *your* father. I know how much you like your father. I know how nice he is to you, Molly. You probably don't even understand how I could hate my father so much."

Absolutely stunned, I stammered, "Well my father isn't *that* nice."

"I know he like brings you presents and stuff, like when he comes back from business trips and everything."

BUSINESS TRIPS! Oh God, how much had I lied? My lies were being presented to me as truth! When had I uttered them? When had I articulated my fantasy?

My mother dies. My sister is sent away. My father stops drinking, becomes an executive, and buys a penthouse apartment where I keep house for him, waiting in glorious solitude above downtown Buffalo, the traffic spinning below me, reading on our charcoal gray sectional couch surrounded by our shell pink walls for him to come home.

How much had I actually told her? Carefully, I question her. I refer to my mother and the store. She nods. OK, I didn't tell my mother was dead. I mention my sister. She talks about her sister. OK, sister here, not sent away. I say I'm going home. To Pilgrim Road.

"Where the hell do you live but on Pilgrim Road?" the Creepette snorts. She is tired of this ridiculous conversation. She only thinks my father is kind and doesn't drink. Well, that was the main part of the fantasy anyway. Like urine spreading through the seat of my pants, the realization, fast, warm, embarrassing and untellable, spread through my consciousness: I had fantasized, and I had *told*. I couldn't distinguish reality from fantasy. I was crazy. I had lied. My father drank. He was mean to my mother. He was just like her father. I was just like her. I was a creep, too. And I was crazy. At least the Creepette told the truth. I was lying. There was no shell pink room.

Except the one inside me. Was I crazy?

Was I? Was I? OK, I hadn't lied all that much.

Only to one person. *God, don't see her anymore, avoid her. At all costs don't walk home from school with her again.* She will show you to yourself in a way you will not be able to stand. *Stay longer after school,* I told myself, *work on the yearbook, hide in the stairwell, do anything.* I never walked home with her again. Now I had no friends at all, not even a creep to be contemptuous of.

The room inside me was empty. There was just that faint glow of pink in the air around the trees that in the north means eventually, after two more months of mud and cold and disbelief it will ever come, there will be spring. Oh no. I was a junior in high school, pretty old for fantasies about kind, rich fathers. And smart, too. My poor alcohol brain-damaged father had become smart in my fantasy, smarter than I was. I felt really stupid now. *Don't be stupid!* With spring came a deadline. (My self-imposed deadline.) I was going to be asked to the Junior Prom. I was going to get dressed up in something those sorority girls never thought of and I was going to go. And not alone, either. I was going to get someone to ask me. This was reality. I was going to face reality. No more fantasies, Molly. Forget the penthouse. Get going. It is February 19. The Junior Prom is in June. You have three months to get a boyfriend and keep him until the Junior Prom. So go get one. Now.

Sex, attainable. Michael Groden was the smartest boy in my class. He had the kind of mind that snaps back like a brand new window shade. He had gotten perfect scores on both his math and his verbal PSATs. Not only was he the smartest boy in my class, he was smarter than many classes of kids—no one in the history of the school had gotten perfect scores. He had done the impossible. Michael Groden was a kind boy who had friends among smart, not too nerdy boys. And he was Jewish. Polly had conveyed to me the stereotype that Jewish men were nice and always took out the garbage for their wives, bought them diamond rings, and *did not drink*. I wasn't going to go after a fraternity boy. That was a lost cause. But not just anybody was taking me to the Prom. I didn't think I was very pretty, certainly not pretty and waiflike as my sister was, off in the wilds of junior high. I was going to go after Mike Groden. I was going to go after him and I was going to get him. I was going to focus on him as I focused on my fantasy, but he was real. And I was going to get him, because he was achingly lonely. His loneliness was palpable, a force field around him. His hands jerked and shook when he answered questions in his nervously fierce intelligently shaking voice. I was going to set my hair, and put on makeup, and reach out to him. And he was going to fall.

Sex. Oh, how glad I am you are fallen. We have fallen in the backseat, we have fallen on the high school lawn. We have fallen on the plastic seats of the couch in your basement. We have fallen on my living room floor. I have reached you. And I have brought you home. Polly is always at work now. Gail is always out. Ted stays later and later at the bars. It is . . . a little bit safe . . . I am calculating. I am loved, so together we calculate . . . what we will do if my parents appear. I do not tell him all the really terrible stuff. What am I, crazy? I cannot even tell myself that terrible stuff. But in all the calculating I have not counted on falling myself. I have, but I do not admit it often. How can I let go? Not to be vigilant, not to be aware, aware, aware . . . how can I? I might get killed.

But, Mike Groden, your shirts smell so good. When we dance my nose fits under your shoulderbone and I drink in the smell of Tide soap and skin underneath. Skin. I have one. He has one. We have borders to our bodies. Oh honey, I wear a black dress to the Prom and carry a rose instead of a corsage and you cooperate. We are smart. I am not wearing pink carnations and a pink pouffy dress. I am an artiste. (An artiste of *what* it doesn't occur to me to determine. An intellectuelle.) Mike Groden works after school. He is steady. He has bought a car. A car is my equivalent of Polly's diamond ring. He delivers me to my stream of dentist appointments. This is my equivalent of taking out the garbage. He has condoms in his wallet, but don't worry, we don't take them out for another two years. We are slow. We do everything in our own rhythm.

Yes, yes, we're going to mess this up, of course, because neither of us has any model for keeping it going, and besides, we go off to college and have many neurotic adventures and mess up our lives and have our successes and thirty years later we get married, and it is a love story: happiness like this at our ages is a palpable, recognizable fact, not the wafting of a feeling. And throughout our three decades of odysseys we have much in common, so much so that when we get back together we quickly pick up the old, first threads.

Gail off with the cheerleading squad. Ted at his bar. Polly at the store. Late spring. Mike Groden at the screen door on which I have posted a note: *Come in. Lock the screen door behind you. Then go to the kitchen table and find another note.* I hear him come in from where I am ensconced: in a bubble bath with nearly three times the recommended dose of bubble juice to achieve the right effect—covered in stiff whipped foam as in a *Playboy* photograph. Mike Groden in the kitchen reading the next note to proceed to my room and take off all his clothes.

"Molly, are you here?"

"Yes, yes," I whisper, "I'm here in the bathroom, but don't come in here!" (He wouldn't have *dreamed* of coming in.)

"Where's your parents? Are we alone?"

"Yes, we're alone. They won't be home for hours. Do what the notes say!"

When you've removed all your clothes but your underpants, come to the bathroom.

And so he does. And so his eyes pop out of his sockets because there I am. We've done everything but. It is the spring of our senior year. We won't actually make love until the fall when Mike is away at Dartmouth and I take a fifteen-hour bus ride from my state university to Hanover, New Hampshire, but this spring evening in the bath is what we remember together with delight as we think of our earliest sexuality with one another, and marvel that our instincts were so right that our first choice turned out to be our best, lasting choice.

"What if your parents come home?"

"Well, I don't think they will, but we'll have to listen for them and then run to my room."

"I'd better go get our clothes to have them ready just in case, Molly."

I knew he was right. What on earth had I been thinking of to trust fate so? I had been thinking of my body. I had been looking in the full-length mirror on my closet door at my almost eighteen-year-old body trying on my swimsuit for the coming summer and thinking of D.H. Lawrence and Henry Miller, whom I could never get through except to find the dirty parts, and Kenneth Rexroth's *100 Poems from the Chinese* with the first woman's sexual voice I had ever heard, the Empress Li Ching Chao who lay in her orchid boat, and then thinking of my own body: *How ripe it is,* I thought, *how ripe I am.* Ripe for what I wasn't exactly sure.

Molly Peacock and Michael Groden during their marriage ceremony, August 19, 1992, Port Angeles, Washington

"Let's just wash each other first. All over. Then we'll get out together."

"OK," he said as I gave him the washcloth and the soap.

He was real. He was as real as my father, and as different from my father as he could be. He could have been the father to my children, as I could have been the mother to his. Our first choice was our best choice, we know that now that we are forty-seven and in our elaborately designed commuter marriage between my apartment in New York City, which we have made ours, and Mike's house in London, Ontario, Canada, which we have made ours.

When he touched my shoulders with the soapy cloth and proceeded down my breastbone and around each breast, I remembered Marie, the mother of the boys next door. Twelve or thirteen years before, Marie gave me a bath one night. How extraordinarily lightly she swiped the cloth over my arms and legs. "My boys are always covered in scrapes and bruises and scabs from the rough way they play," she said, "so I wash them very lightly, so they don't hurt and so all their bruises can heal." I was astonished.

"Do they get *clean*?" I asked her. "They get clean enough." I thought you got clean only if you really scrubbed, and held Marie suspect from the point of view of Polly's cleanly values, but loved the sensuous treat of such elaborate care, and loved the safety of the big towel she wrapped around me before she led me off to pajamas, bed, and thoroughly undisturbed sleep.

What special instinct for self-preservation, what luck, led Mike and I to one another then was not only lifesaving, but enhancing. We allowed one another to grow. Our sexual companionship and literary friendship, probably the two most important, self-defining aspects of our lives then, are probably the most important now. We seemed then, and now, to free one another and to support one another simply as curious and sympathetic witnesses to the other's behavior, and ways of thinking, and needs. After we reached our freshman year in colleges many miles away from one another our fabric of support began to fray. It was not only distance, it was a creeping contempt I always felt for him that eroded my other feelings. My fear of my father, my repulsion of him, my lonely unexpressed desire for his affection, my sadness that I did not have his love all manifested themselves in my contempt not only for him, but for Mike, especially when he did something nice for me. I simply couldn't believe a man was doing something nice for me. I thought there had to be something wrong with him; certainly there was something wrong with me. I was so deeply ashamed of my family, and so deeply ashamed of myself. Finally we broke up, and between the ages of nineteen and thirty-eight we completely lost touch with one another.

"Mike Groden!" I said to the nervously thin young woman who had joined the happy, lazy dinner trio of my former seventeenth-century literature professor, his novelist buddy, and myself, their guest of honor. My second book had come out, and I'd been invited to give a reading at State University of New York at Binghamton, where I had gone to college. The three of us had eaten nearly everything on the small menu, and here we were joined by our very late fourth for dinner, a perfectly decent woman I hated on sight because she was very very thin—we had been gobbling our chocolate cakes—and because she ordered only one thing to eat: a bowl of consommé. "I believe I know someone you used to know," she said, looking up from the brown watercolor in the bowl, "Mike Groden."

"Mike Groden! I remember the smell of his shirts! When we used to slow dance, my nose would rest right under his shoulderbone, and when I think of him I can't help but think of the smell of Tide, or All, or Wisk, or whatever it was then. . . . " I trailed off, having seen the discomfort on her face, and realized I had stepped in it; she must have been his girlfriend, his lover.

"He's been ill, you know," she said. "He's been very sick. He's a cancer survivor."

A cancer survivor? So, he had survived something terrible and was alive, even as I had survived something terrible to be alive. He had written a respected book, she said, and he had been the editor of the colossal many-volumed facsimile of James Joyce manuscripts. He did not have children; he had ambition, the ambition of the survivor of something terrible. This I recognized very well. I don't know what I said to her. I remember I pressed my address on her and asked if she would give it to him, but she said she was on her way to Paris and would be unlikely to see him for a long time. What could that mean? I thought. Only that she would prevent my message to him. But meanwhile she told me the name of the university where he taught, and I knew I could reach him there, if I wanted.

Unknown to me, that weekend Mike Groden would read a review of my second book, *Raw Heaven,* in the *New York Times Book Review.* He would find my address from my publisher and write to me. We would begin a long, slow, luxuriously platonic adult friendship that would last for another eight years. And one day we would finally talk about that bath.

Molly Peacock contributed the following update to *CA* in 2007:

The biography I wrote for the *Contemporary Authors* autobiography series, Volume 21, published in 1995, was composed of early drafts from my memoir, *Para-*

dise, Piece by Piece, later published in 1998 by River-head. As a poet just becoming interested in prose, I dove into the emotional states I recollected from childhood and into the history of my marriage to Michael Groden, which began in high school and was interrupted by almost two decades before it resumed again. Those emotional states were so potent that they destroyed chronology, and I thought I would use this update to make a brief statement which includes that chronology, and which looks at the years between 1995 and 2007.

UPDATED CHRONOLOGY:

1947–1977

I was born in Buffalo, New York, on June 30, 1947, at 10:30 a.m., and I spent my first decade with my parents, Pauline and Edward (Ted) Peacock, my sister Gail, my grandparents, Mildred and Howard Peacock, my uncle Howard, my aunt Dorothy (his first wife, who died in childbirth) and my aunt Joan (his second wife) and their two very young children, Howard and Guy. My parents, sister and I lived in one half of a duplex at 15 Gunnell Avenue in North Buffalo, and my grandparents, uncle and his family lived in the other side. We were an extended working-class family, and my father worked for Niagara Mohawk Power Company, reading meters and driving a truck. My grandfather was also a local truck driver. My mother did not work at this time.

In the summer of 1957, when I was ten, our family moved to 147 Pilgrim Road, in the Buffalo, New York suburb of Tonawanda. I attended Benjamin Franklin Junior High School, where I was taught English by the remarkable Mrs. Bernice Baeumler, and where I began to write seriously, almost daily, at her suggestion. At this time my mother opened Peacock's Superette, spending long hours at the store. This happened at the same time as my father's increasingly violent alcoholism, and it marked the disintegration of our family. I wrote about the impact of this in *Contemporary Authors* 1995. During the summers from the ages of ten to fourteen, I visited my mother's parents, Gilbert and Ruth Wright, in LaGrange, New York, a rural hamlet about ninety minutes from Buffalo, and attended Vacation Bible School at LaGrange Baptist Church. Because of the irreligious examples my mother and my grandfather Wright set, I never felt compelled to

believe any of the fundamentalist Christian rules and regulations. The summers, for me, were golden moments in which I read and wrote my first poems, and grew to my full height, five feet six.

I went on to Kenmore East Senior High, graduating in 1965, along with my steady boyfriend, Michael Groden. I loved English, French, history, and art, but I spent every summer re-taking my math course. We lived on Pilgrim Road until 1967, when I was a sophomore in college, and my parents finally divorced, ending a long siege of a marriage plagued by my father's alcoholism.

I attended Harpur College, later State University of New York at Binghamton, now Binghamton University, from 1965 to 1969, graduating magna cum laude after studying poetry with Milton Kessler. It was an electric time at the university, where the brilliance of classmates like Camille Paglia, Art Spiegelman, and Deborah Tannen, and the charisma of Milton Kessler sparked my commitment to poetry, and to becoming an artist.

I struggled with becoming a poet, since I wanted, after the draining experiences of my childhood and adolescence, to live a quiet, so-called normal life with my first husband, Jeremy Benton. I even stopped writing for a few years, but found myself unable to repress the images, thoughts, and music inside me, and I began to write again. This marriage, very nurturing to both of us, lasted from 1970 to 1976. After publishing a few poems in the early 1970s, I went to the MacDowell Colony for artists, and then on to The Writing Seminars at The Johns Hopkins University, where I had the luck to fall in with a remarkable group of writers, including lifelong friends Phillis Levin, Rachel Hadas, Lisa Zeidner, and Tom Sleigh, and to receive a remarkable education from Richard Howard and Michael Fried. I received an M.A. in Creative Writing with honors from Johns Hopkins in 1977, and a postgraduate fellowship for another year.

1977–1995

I became Poet-in-Residence for the schools in the State of Delaware from 1978 to 1981. After my first book, *And Live Apart,* was published by University of Missouri Press in the spring of 1981, I left Delaware for New York City, where I made a safe landing at Friends Seminary School. Here I taught seventh-grade English and worked with learning-disabled children there from 1981 to 1992. During this time I had the great luck to meet the young poetry editor of the *Paris Review,* Jonathan Galassi, who published my poems and who, when he moved to Random House, published my second book, *Raw Heaven,* in 1984, the year my father died. This book of sonnets, sensuous in nature, was reviewed in the *New York Times Book Review* by J.D. McClatchy, and my reputation as a poet began to flourish.

When Galassi moved on to Farrar, Straus and Giroux, I stayed at Random House, where Miranda Sherwin, a young editor, published my third book of poems, *Take Heart,* in 1989. This is a book heavily influenced by my return to psychotherapy with the same therapist I had seen earlier in Binghamton, New York. Now she practiced in New York City. During these years I lived in a tiny studio apartment at 321 East 71st Street. My friend from graduate school, Phillis Levin, lived in Greenwich Village. Our literary friendship grew. We exchanged every single poem we wrote, and we still do. During this time I had a long relationship with composer Marc-Antonio Consoli, and we regularly went to the artists colonies Yaddo and MacDowell as guests in the summers.

Even though I was writing sonnets, I had not particularly thought of myself as a New Formalist, but I was adopted as one by Dana Gioia, whom Phillis Levin and I met one fall night in 1983 at the Madison Avenue Pub after a reading at Books and Company, a bookstore near the Whitney Museum. During this time I also volunteered on the Board of the Poetry Society of America, and became president in 1988, succeeding William Mathews. With Elise Paschen, then director of the PSA, we began the program Poetry in Motion on the subways and buses of New York City. We had no idea that the program would become as successful as it turned out to be. The program has become a tourist attraction on the subways, and it has been instituted in other cities across North America. We worked hard to open the PSA to all the diverse aesthetics in poetry at the time, New Formalists, free verse writers, and L=A=N=G=U=A=G=E poets. In 1989 I moved downtown, to 505 East 14th Street, in Stuyvesant Town, to be near both Friends Seminary and the Poetry Society on Gramercy Park. In 1991 I began commuting to

Molly and her husband, Michael Marc Royce

London, Ontario, Canada to visit Michael Groden, my high school boyfriend, with whom I recently reconnected, now a professor of English at the University of Western Ontario.

1995–2007

I married Michael Groden on August 19, 1992. For me, making a longed-for connection with another human being at the age of forty-five meant a leap from a guarded state into an unguarded one, and this required a balance and flexibility I had to learn. I found that I could actually write a poem while I was in the same room as my husband. He never tried to step into my mind. I had never been with such a person before. Oh, yes, I had. I had chosen him in high school as my boyfriend, and twenty-nine years later, when we finally married, I understood why my initial instincts were right.

Though I kept my apartment and still worked in New York after we were married, I returned to his house in London, Ontario, where he provided the space and time out from my city life. There my New York obligations withered and something like a table of time opened before me, a dining room table, all cleared, just waiting for a person to begin a project. I began a memoir, building it around a choice I made and felt was quite right for me but didn't truly understand and didn't quite have words for. The choice was not to have children. (I confirmed this again with my husband before our marriage.) I began to learn a whole new art, creative nonfiction, and it was my agent, Kathleen Anderson, who taught me. She patiently line-edited draft after draft of a memoir that was both easy and painful to write. I just sat in front of the computer—yes, I was using a computer now, not an IBM Selectric typewriter—and it poured out. During this time I also held various honorary positions at universities: Stadler Poet-in-Residence at Bucknell University in 1993, poet-in-residence at the University of Western Ontario in 1995, Visiting University Professor at University of California, Riverside in 1998. *Paradise, Piece by Piece* was published by Riverhead Books in the U.S. and McClelland and Stewart in Canada in 1998.

It was the height of the publishing boom, and I was whisked across North America on a book tour that seemed glamorous from the outside (stunning hotels and readings stacked like the food on plates in glamorous restaurants) but in fact, pressed me to a level of public performance that I never expected. It amazes me that I got anything written, but I also wrote another book, *How to Read a Poem—And Start a Poetry Circle.* These essays about reading thirteen of my talisman poems led to an invitation to collaborate with Wisconsin Public Radio host Jean Feraca. Since 1998, I have conducted quarterly poetry reading circles with callers on Feraca's show, "Here on Earth."

Although this looks like a frenzy of activity (and it was very, very active), my marriage, which is a cozy, talking sort of marriage, full of humor and shared points of view about the outside world, and full of a gentle play of ideas in the air, grew in its strength and stability. My psychotherapist and I also established a telephone relationship. I no longer considered myself "in" therapy, in series of biweekly appointments, but "in contact" with my therapist, checking in every few months for the refocusing perspective it offers on my over-focused attempts to deal with life. My friendships altered with my marriage and my bi-national life. Though I made new friends in Canada, I invested a great deal of energy in maintaining my friendships in New York, and, as my New York friends scattered around the world, in many other places. Telephones, cell phones, e-mails, all create part of that softened, personal, alternate life that for me underpins the public commitments of readings and lectures.

During the writing of the memoir, from 1992 to 1997, I did not forget my poetry, and I published *Original Love* in 1995 with W.W. Norton and Company. *Original Love* contains the poems from that tumultuous time. (My mother died of lung cancer in 1992, four months after we were married; and my sister, with whom I had reconnected because of our mother's illness and because of the memoir, died of throat cancer in 1996.) Adding to the peculiar mix of turmoil and respite of these years was the shift in my way of earning a living. I left the safe haven of Friends Seminary School, where I taught from 1981 to 1992, and I slowly began to invent a freelance life as a teacher and editor of poetry in one-to-one appointments with serious writers of poetry.

Over the past twenty-five years I have helped many emerging poets edit and publish books. Using private music instruction as a model, I developed a way to work, at first in person, and then by telephone, with poets in an ongoing investigation of their creative processes. I've become a student of people's creative impulses as a result. I've noticed that at certain crisis stages, those moments of now-or-never that people seem to have as they climb on hospital gurneys, face certain birthdays, etc. they become determined to re-dedicate part of themselves to a lost art. I never thought that would happen to me because I dedicated myself to poetry at a fairly young age.

But human growth, I've learned, is more like plant growth than I previously thought. (I became a gardener almost at the instant I became a permanent resident of Canada in 1993. Since 2006 I have been a dual citizen of both the United States and Canada.) My grandmother, Ruth Wright, used to send a chill up my spine when she viciously (to my adolescent mind) lopped off the tops of her windowsill geraniums: "For side growth," she said. Of course I was too busy growing in one direction upwards to understand this. But for mature plants, the stimulation of the side nodes of growth along the stem of a plant promotes health and the restoration of all the leaves that have been shed near the roots. Crisis lops off top growth and sends out side growth. That's both how I happened to learn the new art of nonfiction, and, to my surprise, after menopause (another life event that sends students to me) how I began acting.

In 2002, as W.W. Norton was publishing *Cornucopia: New and Selected Poems,* I began to develop *The Shimmering Verge,* a one-woman show in poems which I wrote and performed, inspired by the process of col-

Molly in **Verge** Sue Bradnam

lecting the poems from my first four books, by the stories and explanations about the poems that I have developed for readings, and by the essays I wrote for *How to Read a Poem—And Start a Poetry Circle*. Part of the inspiration for the show was a venue offered by the Cathedral of St. John the Divine in New York City, where I was poet-in-residence at the American Poets' Corner from 1999 to 2004. At the Cathedral I became involved in organizing marathon Maundy Thursday readings of Dante's *Divine Comedy*. This whiff of producing and directing in a spiritual space, coupled with meeting Canadian producer-director Louise Fagan, led to the mounting of *The Shimmering Verge*, which toured from 2003 to 2006 and included a limited Off Broadway engagement in March, 2005, at Urban Stages Theatre in New York City.

During the learning of the acting techniques and the physical training, as well as doing part of the producing, I knew that engaging in a performing art, while part of that side growth, was also part of my effort to remain visible as a productive, mature woman in a culture, yes, even in a poetry culture, that prefers its women either young or old and gray and where a productive, active woman in her forties and fifties seems to pass behind a veil of invisibility. *The Shimmering Verge* allowed me to use that veil, literally playing with the idea of a shimmering verge. But a performing art is not a literary art, and I have the private personality of a poet, not the personality of an actor. I understood this instinctively but can only articulate it now that the show is on hiatus. All through the show's development, I wrote another book of poems. I knew I would only have the briefest time to write them, so I gave myself an assignment: fourteen lines, single image. I started the book in Ireland, where

my husband, a scholar who writes about James Joyce, spends a good deal of time, and so, as a result, do I. Of course, the poems haven't turned out to obey those rules, but they helped guide me toward my latest book, *The Second Blush,* which will be published by W.W. Norton in 2008.

During the tour, my husband gave me the gift only a scholar could give to a poet for her birthday. I had been keeping drafts of poems all my life, tossing them into what had grown to sixty boxes of idiosyncratically labeled, vaguely dated paper. He sorted them. When Binghamton University acquired the papers, they were ready for textual study, each poem I've ever written in a separate file.

BIOGRAPHICAL AND CRITICAL SOURCES:

BOOKS

Contemporary Authors Autobiography Series, Volume 27, Thomson Gale (Detroit, MI), 1995.
Contemporary Literary Criticism, Volume 60, Thomson Gale (Detroit, MI), 1990.
Contemporary Poets, 6th edition, St. James Press (Detroit, MI), 1996.
Dictionary of Literary Biography, Volume 120: *American Poets since World War II, Third Series,* Thomson Gale (Detroit, MI), 1992.
Peacock, Molly, *Paradise, Piece by Piece,* Putnam (New York, NY), 1998.

PERIODICALS

American Book Review, May, 1999, review of *Paradise, Piece by Piece,* p. 25; November, 2001, review of *The Private I: Privacy in a Public World,* p. 14.
Booklist, November 1, 1984, review of *Raw Heaven,* p. 30; April 15, 1989, review of *Take Heart,* p. 1425; March 15, 1995, Elizabeth Gunderson, review of *Original Love,* p. 1302; April 15, 1998, Donna Seaman, review of *Paradise, Piece by Piece,* p. 1414; March 15, 1999, Donna Seaman, review of *How to Read a Poem—And Start a Poetry Circle,* p. 1273; May 15, 2001, Donna Seaman, review of *The Private I,* p. 1713; August 2002, Donna Seaman, review of *Cornucopia: New and Selected Poems, 1975-2002,* p. 1913.

Boston Review, December, 1984, Matthew Gilbert, review of *Raw Heaven,* pp. 30-31.

Canadian Book Review, 1998, review of *Paradise, Piece by Piece,* p. 77.

Georgia Review, fall, 1984, review of *Raw Heaven,* p. 628; fall, 1989, review of *Take Heart,* p. 589.

Globe and Mail (Toronto, Ontario, Canada), November 2, 2002, review of *Cornucopia,* p. D22.

Hudson Review, autumn, 1981, Robert Phillips, review of *And Live Apart,* p. 427.

Kenyon Review, summer, 1991, Steve Kronen, review of *Take Heart,* p. 161.

Kliatt, May, 2004, James Beschta, review of *Cornucopia,* p. 32.

Library Journal, January, 1985, Robert Hudzik, review of *Raw Heaven,* p. 88; April 1, 1989, Barbara Hoffert, review of *Take Heart,* p. 92; February 15, 1995, Frank Allen, review of *Original Love,* p. 159; May 15, 1998, Mary Paumier Jones, review of *Paradise, Piece by Piece,* p. 86; May 1, 1999, Ellen Sullivan, review of *How to Read a Poem—And Start a Poetry Circle,* p. 77; June 1, 2001, Mark Bay, review of *The Private I,* p. 163.

Lip, May 7, 2001, Suzanne Cody, review of *The Private I.*

Los Angeles Times Book Review, August 20, 1989, Ian Gregson, review of *Take Heart,* p. 3; June 1, 2003, review of *Cornucopia,* p. R14.

Michigan Quarterly Review, fall, 1996, Bruce Bonds, review of *Original Love,* p. 734.

Midwest Book Review, April, 2005, review of *An Imperfect Lover.*

Ms., May, 1998, review of *Paradise, Piece by Piece,* p. 88.

New England Review, winter, 1986, review of *Raw Heaven,* p. 230.

New Republic, July 17, 1989, Christopher Benfey, review of *Take Heart,* pp. 31-34.

New York Times Book Review, December 2, 1984, J.D. McClatchy, review of *Raw Heaven,* pp. 54-55; October 22, 1989, Jay Parini, review of *Take Heart,* p. 16.

North American Review, December, 1989, review of *Take Heart,* p. 58.

O, the Oprah Magazine, February, 2006, "This Is Your Life!," p. 53.

Parnassus, spring, 1985, Christopher Benfey, review of *Raw Heaven,* pp. 500-512.

Poetry, November, 1985, Grace Schulman, review of *Raw Heaven,* p. 107; April, 1990, Henri Cole, review of *Take Heart,* p. 38.

Publishers Weekly, July 13, 1984, review of *Raw Heaven,* p. 42; February 24, 1989, Genevieve Stuttaford, review of *Take Heart,* p. 227; February 27, 1995, review of *Original Love,* p. 98; May 4, 1998, review of *Paradise, Piece by Piece,* p. 194; March 29, 1999, review of *How to Read a Poem—And Start a Poetry Circle,* p. 100; May 7, 2001, review of *The Private I,* p. 238; July 22, 2002, review of *Cornucopia,* p. 171.

Quill & Quire, April, 1998, review of *Paradise, Piece by Piece,* p. 27; June 1999, review of *How to Read a Poem—And Start a Poetry Circle,* p. 56.

Saturday Review, July, 1985, review of *Raw Heaven,* p. 67.

Southern Humanities Review, winter, 1986, review of *Raw Heaven,* p. 91; fall, 1990, Diann Blakely Shoaf, review of *Take Heart,* p. 397.

Times Literary Supplement, December 24, 2004, Carrie Etter, review of *Cornucopia,* p. 32.

Tribune Books (Chicago, IL), August 6, 1989, review of *Take Heart,* p. 5.

Virginia Quarterly Review, spring, 1985, review of *Raw Heaven,* p. 54; autumn, 1989, review of *Take Heart,* p. 137.

Washington Post Book World, September 2, 1984, David Lehman, review of *Raw Heaven,* p. 6.

ONLINE

Bookslut, http://www.bookslut.com/ (August 25, 2007), author interview.

Molly Peacock Home Page, http://www.mollypeacock.org (August 25, 2007).

Poets.org, http://www.poets.org/ (August 25, 2007), author profile.

Writers' Union of Canada, http://www.writersunion.ca/ (August 25, 2007), author profile.*

*   *   *

PERLMAN, Rhea 1948-

PERSONAL: Born March 31, 1948, in Brooklyn, NY; daughter of Philip (a doll and toy- part salesman and actor) and Adele Perlman; married Danny DeVito (an actor), 1981; children: Lucy Chet, Gracie Fan, Jake Daniel Sebastian. *Education:* Hunter College, City University of New York, degree. *Politics:* Democrat.

ADDRESSES: Agent—International Creative Management, 8942 Wilshire Blvd., Beverly Hills, CA 90211.

CAREER: Actor and author. Formerly worked as a waitress, telephone salesperson, and as a secretary. Stage appearances include (as Lorna) *What! And Leave Bloomingdale's?,* New York, NY, 1973; (as Columbine) *A Phantasmagoria Historia of D. Johann Fausten Magister, PHD, MD, DD, DL, Etc.,* New York, NY, 1973; (as Marjorie; Broadway debut) *The Tale of the Allergist's Wife,* New York, NY, 2002; and (as Bertha) *Boeing Boeing,* London, England, 2006.

Feature film credits include: (as Woman on ferry) *Hot Dogs for Gauguin,* 1972; (as Mother), *Swap Meet,* 1979; (as June Burns) *Love Child,* Warner Bros., 1982; (as voice of Reeka) *My Little Pony: The Movie* (animated), De Laurentiis Entertainment Group, 1986; (as Mavis) *Over Her Dead Body,* Vestron Video, 1990; (as Grace) *Ted and Venus,* Double Helix Films, 1991; (as Miss Joanne Simpson) *Class Act,* Warner Bros., 1992; (as Lois) "The Wedding Ring," *Amazing Stories: Book One,* 1992; (as voice of 9-Eye) *From Time to Time,* 1992; (as Lydia Nunn) *There Goes the Neighborhood,* Paramount, 1992; (as Voice of Mother Bird) *We're Back! A Dinosaur's Story* (animated), Universal, 1993; (as Deputy Honey) *Canadian Bacon,* Gramercy, 1995; (as Zinnia Wormwood) *Matilda,* TriStar, 1996; (as Phyllis Saroka) *Sunset Park,* TriStar, 1996; (as Martha the meter maid) *Carpool,* Warner Bros., 1996; and *Final Analysis; Love in Venice; Radio Flyer;* and short films *Minestrone* and *The Sound Sleeper.*

Television film credits include: (as Rae Finer) *I Want to Keep My Baby!,* CBS, 1976; (as Jean) *Stalk the Wild Child,* NBC, 1976; (as Cheryl) *Having Babies II,* ABC, 1977; (as Judy) *Mary Jane Harper Cried Last Night,* CBS, 1977; *Intimate Strangers,* ABC, 1977; (as Jan) *Like Normal People,* ABC, 1979; (as Tawney Shapiro) *Drop-Out Father,* CBS, 1982; (as Francine Kester) *The Ratings Game,* The Movie Channel, 1984; (as Claudia) *Dangerous Affection,* NBC, 1987; (as Shirley) *To Grandmother's House We Go,* ABC, 1992; (as Jerri Blair) *A Place to Be Loved,* CBS, 1993; (as Emma) *Spoils of War,* ABC, 1994; (as Esther) *Houdini,* TNT, 1998; (as Phyllis Markowitz) *In the Doghouse,* Showtime, 1998; (as Ms. Beezlebug) *H-E Double Hockey Sticks,* ABC, 1999; (as Thelma) *A Tail of Two Bunnies,* ABC, 2000; (as Dr. Parella) *Secret Cutting,* USA Network, 2000; (as Jackie Kennedy) *How to Marry a*

Billionaire: A Christmas Tale, Fox, 2000; (as Mrs. Wabash) *Other People's Business,* 2003; (as Penny) *Stroller Wars,* 2006; and (as Reisel) *Love Comes Lately,* 2007. Television series credits include *Likely Stories, Volume II,* 1983; *Cheers,* NBC, 1982-1993; *Pearl,* CBS, 1996; and *Kate Brasher,* CBS, 2001; as well as appearances on *Taxi,* 1979-82, *Saturday Night Live,* 1983, 1987, *Amazing Stories,* 1987, *Matlock,* 1987, *The Simpsons,* 1994, *Mad about You,* 1999, *Ally McBeal,* 2001, *Frazier,* 2002, *Karen Sisco,* 2003; and *Keven Hill,* 2004.

Presenter in numerous network television specials and awards presentations, beginning 1985. Executive producer of television series *Pearl,* 1996, and film *Bye Bye Benjamin,* 2006.

AWARDS, HONORS: Emmy Award nominations for Best Supporting Actress in a Comedy Series, 1982, 1983, 1987, 1988, 1990, 1991, 1993, and awards, 1984, 1985, 1986, 1989, American Comedy Award for Funniest Supporting Female Performer in a Television Series, 1989, Golden Globe nomination for Best Supporting Actress in a Television Series, 1985, 1987, 1988, 1989, 1990, 1992, and TV Land Legend Award (with others), 2006, all for *Cheers.* Volunteer for literacy advocacy groups.

WRITINGS:

"OTTO UNDERCOVER" SERIES

Born to Drive, illustrated by Dan Santat, Katherine Tegen Books (New York, NY), 2006.
Canyon Catastrophe, illustrated by Dan Santat, Katherine Tegen Books (New York, NY), 2006.
Water Balloon Doom, illustrated by Dan Santat, Katherine Tegen Books (New York, NY), 2006.
Toxic Taffy Takeover, illustrated by Dan Santat, Katherine Tegen Books (New York, NY), 2006.
The Brink of Ex-Stink-Tion, illustrated by Dan Santat, Katherine Tegen Books (New York, NY), 2006.
Brain Freeze, illustrated by Dan Santat, Katherine Tegen Books (New York, NY), 2007.

SIDELIGHTS: Many adults know Rhea Perlman as the Emmy Award-winning actress who starred as Carla Tortelli on the long-running television series *Cheers,* which aired on CBS from 1982 until 1993. To young readers, however, Perlman's name recognition comes as the author of the "Otto Undercover" series, which features a mix of humor and fast action in titles such as *Born to Drive, Canyon Catastrophe, Water Balloon Doom, Toxic Taffy Takeover, Brink of Ex-stink-tion,* and *Brain Freeze.* Each book in the series is noted for its wordplay, and includes anagrams, palindromes, and words spelled backwards for comic effect.

In series opener *Born to Drive,* readers meet Otto Pillip, a precocious preteen inventor and race-car driver who has built the fastest car on Earth. Living with his aunts FiFi and FooFoo since his parents set off on an expedition to discover a missing continent, Otto must rescue racecar (note the palindrome) from two elementary-school dropouts who hope to use it to win the million-dollar prize at the upcoming Yazoo 200 auto race. *Canyon Catastrophe* finds Otto Pillip working as an undercover agent, this time hoping to stop a villain bent on bombing the Grand Canyon, and in *Water Balloon Doom* his nemesis is the evil Prune Man, a ne'er-do-well hoping to take over the planet's ocean water. A hypnotist able to exert mind-control through a potent candy recipe is the focus of *Toxic Taffy Takeover,* while a particularly smelly evildoer terrorizes Africa in *The Brink of Ex-Stink-tion,* until Otto and Racecar come to the continent's aid. I-Skreem, a villain who is somehow involved in the disappearance of Otto's parents, is the focus of *Brain Freeze,* the concluding volume in Perlman's series. Perlman "breaks the novel into tiny, easy-to-digest bits," in order to make the books "a fun read, especially for hard-to-motivate readers," explained Walter Minkel in his *School Library Journal* review of *Canyon Catastrophe.* While a *Publishers Weekly* contributor found the story in *Born to Drive* somewhat "slim," the critic noted that illustrator Dan Santat's "brash cartoons" inject energy to the upbeat story, and commented that readers would enjoy decoding the story's wordplay (help is hidden in the margin of each page).

BIOGRAPHICAL AND CRITICAL SOURCES:

PERIODICALS

Entertainment Weekly, October 4, 1999.
Publishers Weekly, December 19, 2005, review of *Born to Drive,* p. 65.

School Library Journal, July, 2006, Walter Minkel, review of *Born to Drive,* p. 109; January, 2007, H.H. Henderson, review of *Water Balloon Doom,* p. 100.

ONLINE

Otto Undercover Web site, http://www.ottoundercover. com (October 27, 2007).*

*   *   *

PFEIFER, Carl J. 1929-2007

OBITUARY NOTICE— See index for *CA* sketch: Some sources cite middle name as Jacob, others as James; born June 22, 1929, in St. Louis, MO; died of complications from Alzheimer's disease, July 12, 2007, in Dubuque, IA. Priest, educator, columnist, and author. Pfeifer was ordained a Jesuit priest in 1961 and remained one for many years, until he realized he was about to fall in love with his colleague and coauthor, a Franciscan nun named Janaan Manternach. They resigned from their religious orders, married in 1976, and continued their partnership as man and wife. They saw themselves as Catholic educators whose mission would reform the traditional, rather stilted "Baltimore catechism" by breathing life and anecdote into the twenty-nine-volume series they called *Life, Love, Joy* (1968), which was also published as *This Is Our Faith.* Pfeifer was a lecturer at the Catholic University of America in Washington, DC, when he met Manternach and began the academic collaboration that would change his life. He had also taught high school and lectured at St. Louis University. Pfeifer was a panelist for the *Bauman Bible Telecasts* from 1967 to 1992 and wrote several columns, including "Know Your Faith" and "Photomeditations," syndicated by the National Catholic News Service in the 1970s. From 1998 to 2002 he wrote "Core Beliefs" and "Did You Know?" for the magazine *FaithWorks.* "Photomeditations" enabled him to combine his own photographs with his spiritual musings. Pfeifer wrote several books, often with Manternach. These include *The Living Faith in a World of Change* (1973), *Creative Catechists: A Comprehensive, Illustrated Guide for Training Religion Teachers* (1983), *People to Remember: Thirty Stories and Activities about Saints and Heroes for Youth Today* (1987), and *How Creative Catechists Use Stories* (2000).

OBITUARIES AND OTHER SOURCES:

PERIODICALS

Los Angeles Times, August 11, 2007, p. B8.
Washington Post, August 4, 2007, p. B6.

*   *   *

PHARES, Walid 1957-

PERSONAL: Born 1957, in Lebanon; immigrated to the United States, 1990. Education: Earned degrees from Saint Joseph University and the Lebanese University in Beirut; Université de Lyons, master's degree; University of Miami, Ph.D.

ADDRESSES: E-mail—phares@walidphares.com.

CAREER: Fox News Channel, Middle East correspondent; Foundation for the Defense of Democracies, Washington, DC, senior fellow; European Foundation for Democracy, Brussels, Belgium, senior fellow; National Defense University School for National Security Executive Education (SNSEE), Washington, DC, visiting professor, 2007. Previously worked as a lawyer in Beirut, Lebanon; as the publisher of several multilingual periodicals, 1982-87; for MSNBC, terrorism analyst; Florida International University, Miami, lecturer; University of Miami, Miami, lecturer; Florida Atlantic University, Boca Raton, professor of Middle East Studies, 1993-2006.

WRITINGS:

Lebanese Christian Nationalism: The Rise and Fall of an Ethnic Resistance, L. Rienner (Boulder, CO), 1995.
Future Jihad: Terrorist Strategies against America, Palgrave Macmillan (New York, NY), 2005.
The War of Ideas: Jihadism against Democracy, Palgrave Macmillan (New York, NY), 2007.

Contributor to periodicals, including Global Affairs, Middle East Quarterly, International Journal of Security Studies, Journal of South Asian and Middle Eastern Studies, Philadelphia Inquirer, National Review, and the Chicago Sun-Times.

SIDELIGHTS: Walid Phares was born and raised in Lebanon, and received his education there as well as in Lyons, France, and Miami, Florida, eventually earning a Ph.D. in international relations and strategic studies. An expert on the Middle East, Phares has worked as a foreign correspondent in that region for the Fox News Channel. He has also served as a professor and a fellow for several defense organizations in Washington, DC. Phares is the author of several books on the Middle East and the dynamic tension between that part of the world and the United States. Lebanese Christian Nationalism: The Rise and Fall of an Ethnic Resistance addresses the roots of Christianity in Lebanese history.

Phares's next book, Future Jihad: Terrorist Strategies against America, published several years following the terrorist attacks of September 11th, has a somewhat broader scope, and offers readers a brief history of the concept of the jihad, from its roots in Islamic beliefs to its more current use in the global political arena. Phares explains how the jihad is being applied today, and why Western economic and political ideology make Western nations a target for such religious-minded types of terrorist acts. Dave Martin, reviewing on the Bookbag, remarked of Phares's effort: "As a learning experience, this is an invaluable resource for someone . . . who knows little about the religious or political motivations of Al-Qaeda and their followers."

In The War of Ideas: Jihadism against Democracy, Phares continues his explanation of the motivations driving Muslim terrorists who believe in the call for a war against those who do not share their religious beliefs. A contributor for Kirkus Reviews called the book "provocative reading."

BIOGRAPHICAL AND CRITICAL SOURCES:

PERIODICALS

Choice, March, 1996, A.R. Norton, review of Lebanese Christian Nationalism: The Rise and Fall of an Ethnic Resistance, p. 1215.
International Wire, May 26, 2004, "Analysis with Walid Phares"; June 22, 2004, "Interview with Florida Atlantic University's Walid Phares"; January 30, 2005, "Interview with Mideast Politics Professor Walid Phares."

Kirkus Reviews, December 15, 2006, review of *The War of Ideas: Jihadism against Democracy,* p. 1260.

Officer, February, 2007, Will Holahan, "The Even Longer War," p. 43.

U.S. Newswire, June 24, 2003, "Walid Phares, Lebanese Professor of Middle East Studies, Ethnic and Religious Conflict, to Discuss 'Jihad against America,'" p. 1008175.

ONLINE

Benador Associates Web site, http://www.benador associates.com/ (October 9, 2007), biography of Walid Phares.

Bookbag, http://www.thebookbag.co.uk/ (October 9, 2007), Dave Martin, review of *Future Jihad: Terrorist Strategies against America.*

Cedar Key News Online, http://cedarkeynews.com/ (October 9, 2007), Linda Dale, review of *Future Jihad.*

Foundation for Defense of Democracies Web site, http://www.defenddemocracy.org/ (October 9, 2007), biography of Walid Phares.

Fox News Web site, http://www.foxnews.com/ (October 9, 2007), contributor profile.

Front Page Online, http://www.frontpagemag.com/ (March 20, 2007), Jamie Glazov, review of *Future Jihad.*

National Review Online, http://article.nationalreview.com/ (August 2, 2006), "Tehran & Damascus Move to Lebanon: Walid Phares on the Mideast."

Walid Phares Home Page, http://www.walidphares.com (October 9, 2007).*

*   *   *

PHELAN, Joseph 1963-

PERSONAL: Born 1963. *Education:* King's College, Cambridge, M.A., King's College, London, Ph.D.

ADDRESSES: Office—Faculty of Humanities, Clephan Building, De Montfort University, Leicester LE1 9BH, England. *E-mail*—jphelan@dmu.ac.uk.

CAREER: Educator, editor, writer, and reviewer. De Monfort University, Leicester, England, senior lecturer in English.

WRITINGS:

(Editor) *Clough: Selected Poems,* Longman (New York, NY), 1995.

The Nineteenth-Century Sonnet, Palgrave Macmillan (New York, NY), 2006.

(Editor, with John Woolford and Daniel Karlin) *The Poems of Browning,* Volume 3, Palgrave Macmillan (New York, NY), 2007.

Contributor to books, including *Utopia Matters: Politics and Theory,* edited by Fatima Vieira, University of Porto Press, 2005. Contributor to professional journals, including *Revue de Littérature Comparée, Higher Education Review, New Dictionary of National Biography, Biography: An Interdisciplinary Quarterly, Journal of Victorian Culture, Review of English Studies,* and the *Journal of Anglo Studies.*

SIDELIGHTS: Joseph Phelan teaches English literature and is the editor of *Clough: Selected Poems,* which presents a selection of poetry by nineteenth-century writer Arthur Hugh Clough. *Notes and Queries* contributor Bernard Richards remarked of the work: "Phelan is an extremely sympathetic and expert reader of Clough, and the introduction is a most elegant and informative essay." Phelan also includes extensive footnotes and letters by Clough. Richards noted that Phelan takes extra care in presenting the particulars of the language that Clough uses, including slang and biblical language. Richards also wrote: "There is a fine section on Clough and the legacy of Romanticism. The approach is to place the poet as much as possible in the context of his time."

In *The Nineteenth-Century Sonnet,* the author provides a critical look at the history and development of the sonnet throughout the nineteenth century. In the process, Phelan explores such issues as why the fourteen-line sonnet returned to popularity in the nineteenth century after being largely ignored in the eighteenth century. Among the topics discussed are the "Wordsworthian" sonnet revival, sonnet and autobiography, the political sonnet, the devotional sonnet, and the amatory sonnet sequence. Phelan also discusses why the sonnet has remained an enduring popular form of poetry. Among the poets he examines are Wordsworth, Keats, Elizabeth Barrett Browning, and George Meredith. In the introduction to her book, *Little Songs:*

Women, Silence, and the Nineteenth-Century Sonnet, Amy Christine Billone points out that Phelan "[gives] space to female as well as male sonneteers."

BIOGRAPHICAL AND CRITICAL SOURCES:

BOOKS

Billone, Amy Christine, *Little Songs: Women, Silence, and the Nineteenth-Century Sonnet,* Ohio State University Press (Columbus, OH), 2007.

PERIODICALS

Notes and Queries, December, 1998, Bernard Richards, review of *Clough: Selected Poems,* p. 506.

ONLINE

De Montfort University Web site, http://www.dmu.ac.uk/ (September 6, 2007), faculty profile of author.*

* * *

PIERCE, Nora
(Nora Elena Pierce)

PERSONAL: Married; children: one. *Ethnicity:* Native American, Lebanese. *Education:* Attended Stanford University.

ADDRESSES: Home—CA. *Office*—Department of English, Stanford University, Bldg. 460, Margaret Jacks Hall, Stanford, CA 94305. *Agent*—J. Adams, Levine Greenberg Literary Agency, Inc., 307 7th Ave., Ste. 2407, New York, NY 10001. *E-mail*—nepierce@stanford.edu.

CAREER: Writer. Stanford University, Stanford, CA, lecturer in creative writing; previously worked as a bartender.

AWARDS, HONORS: Wallace Stegner fellowship, Stanford University; PEN Emerging Voices fellowship.

WRITINGS:

The Insufficiency of Maps: A Novel, Atria Books (New York, NY), 2007.

SIDELIGHTS: Nora Pierce studied creative writing at Stanford University, where she was the recipient of a prestigious Wallace Stegner fellowship. She went on to lecture within the program. Her first published book, *The Insufficiency of Maps: A Novel,* was published in 2007 to critical praise. A coming-of-age story, the novel follows the protagonist, a young girl called Alice, as she gradually progresses from what appears to be a normal, everyday type of life, to something that is actually quite off the beaten path. The daughter of an alcoholic schizophrenic mother, Alice finds herself in foster care and eventually runs away. Alice's love for her mother warps her perceptions of her parent's mental illness and colors the way she reacts to her frequently erratic behavior. Like Pierce, Alice is half Native American, and that sense of culture and displacement is very much apparent in Alice's experiences as well. Lindsay Maples, in a review for the *Aniston Star Online,* commented: "An innocence and subtlety pervade Pierce's storytelling, with sensory details that evoke award-winning novelist Michael Ondaatje's descriptions of childhood in the Sri Lankan jungle in his memoir. Every character Alice comes into contact with is real; the reader can see, smell, touch the world around her." A reviewer for *Publishers Weekly* dubbed the book a "forceful debut." Susan Rife, reviewing in the *Herald Tribune Online,* found the book to be difficult going, but ultimately concluded that it was "filled with graceful images and a heart-rending story."

BIOGRAPHICAL AND CRITICAL SOURCES:

PERIODICALS

Library Journal, March 1, 2007, Debbie Bogenschutz, review of *The Insufficiency of Maps: A Novel,* p. 77.
Publishers Weekly, February 12, 2007, review of *The Insufficiency of Maps,* p. 64.

ONLINE

Aniston Star Online (Aniston, AL), http://www.dailyhome.com/ (May 20, 2007), Lindsay Maples, "Vivid Imagery More Than Sufficient."

Herald Tribune Online (Sarasota, FL), http://www.heraldtribune.com/ (April 26, 2007), Susan Rife, "Mapping an Inner World."

Nora Pierce Home Page, http://www.norapierce.com (October 9, 2007).

San Francisco Chronicle Online, http://sfgate.com/ (July 12, 2007), Reyhan Harmanci, "Crazy Love," review of *The Insufficiency of Maps.*

Small Spiral Notebook, http://www.smallspiralnotebook.com/ (October 9, 2007), Adam Goldwyn, review of *The Insufficiency of Maps.**

*   *   *

PIERCE, Nora Elena
See PIERCE, Nora

*   *   *

PIRNIE, Amy
See DAVIES, Freda

*   *   *

PITE, Ralph

PERSONAL: Male.

ADDRESSES: Home—Wales. *Office*—Cardiff School of English, Communication and Philosophy, Cardiff University, Humanities Bldg., Colum Dr., Cardiff CF10 3EU, Wales.

CAREER: Writer. University of Cardiff, Cardiff, Wales, professor of English literature; previously taught at the University of Cambridge and the University of Liverpool.

WRITINGS:

Dante's Influence on Coleridge and Keats: The Circle of Our Vision, Cambridge University Press (Cambridge, England), 1989, published as *The Circle of Our Vision: Dante's Presence in English Romantic Poetry,* Clarendon Press (Oxford, England), 1994.

Hardy's Geography: Wessex and the Regional Novel, Palgrave (New York, NY), 2002.

Paths and Ladders (poems), Brodie Press (Bristol, England), 2003.

(Editor, with Hester Jones) *W.S. Graham: Speaking towards You,* Liverpool University Press (Liverpool, England), 2004.

Thomas Hardy: The Guarded Life, Picador (London, England), 2006, Yale University Press (New Haven, CT), 2007.

(Series editor) *Lives of Victorian Literary Figures, V: Mary Elizabeth Braddon, Wilkie Collins, and William Thackeray,* Pickering & Chatto (Brookfield, VT), 2007.

SIDELIGHTS: Ralph Pite is a writer, educator, and academic, and has served as a professor of English at the University of Cambridge, University of Liverpool, and University of Cardiff. His primary areas of interest include Dante, English Romanticism, Thomas Hardy, and poet W.S. Graham, and he is the author of books on the lives of the writers of the Romantic and Victorian periods, as well as a volume of his own poetry, *Paths and Ladders.*

The Circle of Our Vision: Dante's Presence in English Romantic Poetry addresses the influence of Dante's writings on the poets of the English Romantic period, with careful attention paid to the works of Shelley, Keats, Byron, and Coleridge. In particular, he focuses on the religious references of the poets, noting the relationship to Dante's *The Divine Comedy.* But Pite does not limit himself by claiming Dante was the sole influence on these writers, merely noting that he was an important one. Michael O'Neill, in a contribution to the *Review of English Studies,* had a mixed opinion of Pite's results, noting that the book "combines impressively the scholarly and the nuanced. Yet the pursuit of nuance can lead to tortuousness." However, Tim Fulford, in a review in the *Modern Language Quarterly,* remarked: "Pite is able to depict with great clarity why Dante mattered to them and why he might matter to us as readers of their work."

In *Thomas Hardy: The Guarded Life,* Pite strives to offer readers a look inside the mind of the famous writer, attempting to link elements of his life to the themes of his work. The task is more difficult than it might have been, given Hardy's private nature and the destruction of many of his personal records and papers following his death. However, Pite makes ample use of what resources were available to him, attempting to divine the writer from his creative output, and to see through any false information left behind as part of Hardy's estate in an attempt to discourage future biographers. Brenda Wineapple, writing in *Biography,* was unimpressed with Pite's book, calling it "a rather airless psychological study." Richard King, in a review in the *Sydney Morning Herald Online,* remarked: "To make connections between art and life is the literary biographer's raison d'etre, but truly great art outsoars its beginnings: its greatness depends on its universality. This is something to bear in mind when reading this absorbing book." Sophie Ratcliffe, reviewing the book in the *New Statesman,* observed: "Pite admits that Hardy's life is a stubborn mystery, and his biography embraces the writer's seemingly self-conscious inconsistency. An impressive, and impressively human, book, it will be particularly useful for those researching Hardy." Sally Cunneen, in a review in *America,* praised Pite's approach to his material, stating: "Pite mines the writer's novels and poetry with great sensitivity, using them to illuminate Hardy's life at every stage."

BIOGRAPHICAL AND CRITICAL SOURCES:

PERIODICALS

America, April 30, 2007, Sally Cunneen, "Behind the 'Serene Public Image,'" p. 32.

Biography, summer, 2007, Brenda Wineapple, review of *Thomas Hardy: The Guarded Life.*

Booklist, March 1, 2007, Bryce Christensen, review of *Thomas Hardy,* p. 53.

Modern Language Quarterly, March, 1996, Tim Fulford, review of *The Circle of Our Vision: Dante's Presence in English Romantic Poetry,* p. 112.

New Statesman, July 3, 2006, Sophie Ratcliffe, "A Man with Many Sides," p. 62.

New York Times Book Review, March 18, 2007, Brenda Wineapple, "Wessex Man," p. 20.

Review of English Studies, November, 1996, Michael O'Neill, review of *The Circle of Our Vision,* p. 598.

Weekly Standard, May 21, 2007, Barton Swaim, "Thomas of the Hardys: The Poet-Novelist of Old England."

ONLINE

Guardian Online, http://books.guardian.co.uk/ (June 3, 2006), Jem Poster, "Secrets and Lives" review of *Thomas Hardy.*

Metroactive.com, http://www.metroactive.com/ (June 27, 2007), Michael S. Gant, review of *Thomas Hardy.*

New York Sun Online, http://www.nysun.com/ (March 7, 2007), Brooke Allen, "The Very Rich Hours of Thomas Hardy."

Spectator Online, http://www.spectator.co.uk/ (June 17, 2006), Lloyd Evans, review of *Thomas Hardy.*

Sydney Morning Herald (Sydney, Australia), http://www.smh.com.au/ (September 6, 2006), Richard King, review of *Thomas Hardy.*

Times Literary Supplement Online, http://tls.timesonline.co.uk/ (December 6, 2006), review of *Thomas Hardy.*

University of Liverpool, Centre of Poetry and Science Web site, http://poetryandscience.co.uk/ (October 9, 2007), biography of Ralph Pite.*

*   *   *

PITOL, Sergio 1933-

PERSONAL: Born 1933, in Puebla, Mexico. *Education:* Studied in Mexico City, Mexico. *Politics:* Democratic socialist. *Religion:* Agnostic.

ADDRESSES: Home—Xalapa, Mexico.

CAREER: Writer, translator, educator. Served as university professor in Xalapa, Mexico, and Bristol, England; diplomat for Mexico, including cultural attaché to Warsaw, Paris, Moscow, and Budapest, and Mexican ambassador to Czechoslovakia, 1960-88.

AWARDS, HONORS: Cervantes Prize, 2005.

WRITINGS:

Infierno de todos (cuentos), Universidad Veracruzana (Xalapa, Mexico), 1964, Editorial Seix Barral (Barcelona, Spain), 1971, Universidad Veracruzana (Xalapa, Mexico), 1997.

Sergio Pitol: voz del autor (sound recording), Universidad Nacional Autónoma de México (Mexico City, Mexico), 1968.

Del encuentro nupcial, Tusquets Editores (Barcelona, Spain), 1970.

Los climas, Editorial Seix Barral (Barcelona, Spain), 1972.

El tanido de una flauta (novella), Ediciones Era (Mexico City, Mexico), 1972, Grijalbo (Mexico City, Mexico), 1987.

De Jane Austen a Virginia Woolf: seis novelistas en sus textos, Secretaría de Educación Pública (Mexico City, Mexico), 1975.

Asimetría: antología personal, Universidad Nacional Autónoma de México (University City, Mexico), 1980.

Nocturno de bujara, Siglo Veintiuno Editores (Mexico City, Mexico), 1981.

Juegos florales, Siglo Veintiuno Editores (Mexico City, Mexico), 1982.

Cementerio de tordos, Ediciones Océano (Mexico City, Mexico), 1982.

Olga Costa, Gobierno del Estado de Guanajuato (Guanajuato, Mexico), 1983.

El desfile del amor, Editorial Anagrama (Barcelona, Spain), 1984.

Vals de Mefisto, Editorial Anagrama (Barcelona, Spain), 1984.

Domar a la divina Garza, Anagrama (Barcelona, Spain), 1988.

La vida conyugal, Ediciones Era (Mexico City, Mexico), 1991.

El relato Veneciano de Billie Upward, Monte Avila Editores (Caracas, Venezuela), 1992.

Juan Soriano: el perpetuo rebelde, Consejo Nacional para la Cultura y las Artes: Ediciones Era (Mexico City, Mexico), 1993.

Luis García Guerrero, Gobierno del Estado de Guanajuato (Guanajuato, Mexico), 1993.

El arte de la fuga, Ediciones Era (Mexico City, Mexico), 1996.

Rocío Maldonado, Grupo Financiero Serfin (Mexico City, Mexico), 1996.

Miradas a la obra de Sergio Galindo, Instituto de Investigaciones Linguistico-Literarias (Xalapa, Mexico), 1996.

Sonar la realidad: una antología personal, Plaza & Janés (Barcelona, Spain), 1998.

Pasión por la trama, Ediciones Era (Mexico City, Mexico), 1998.

Un largo viaje, Universidad Nacional Autónoma de México (Mexico City, Mexico), 1999.

El viaje, Ediciones Era (Mexico City, Mexico), 2000.

Diario Argentino, A. Hidalgo (Buenos Aires, Argentina), 2001.

Hasta Manana y Buenos Días, Gobierno del Estado de Aguascalientes (Aguascalientes, Mexico), 2001.

El Oscuro Hermano Gemelo, Gobierno del Estado de Veracruz (Veracruz Llave, Mexico), 2001.

De la realidad a la literatura, Tecnológico de Monterrey (Monterrey, Mexico), 2002.

Obras Reunidas, Fondo de Cultura Económica (Mexico City, Mexico), 2003.

Los Mejores Cuentos, Editorial Anagrama (Barcelona, Spain), 2005.

El Mago de Viena, Pre-Textos (Valencia, Spain), 2005.

El Viaje de una vida: Sergio Pitol, Premio Cervantes 2005: Exposicion y Catálogo, Servicio de Publicaciones de la Universidad de Alcalá (Alcala, Mexico), 2006.

SIDELIGHTS: Writer and diplomat Sergio Pitol was born in Puebla, Mexico. He studied law and literature in Mexico City, and went on to join the Mexican diplomatic corps, serving first as a cultural attaché for Mexico to various foreign cities, including Warsaw, Paris, Budapest, and Moscow, and eventually becoming the Mexican ambassador to Czechoslovakia. In addition to his diplomatic career, Pitol worked as a translator, taught at the university level, and has written numerous books. His translations have brought the classic works of several foreign writers into prominence in Mexico, including Jane Austen, Anton Chekhov, Henry James, and Joseph Conrad. In addition, his own writings have brought him considerable respect, both in Latin America and abroad. In 2005, he was awarded the prestigious Cervantes Prize. Pitol credits reading with making difficult phases of his life bearable, such as the loss of his parents and an extended illness. He maintains that these hardships in his life have also been responsible for shaping his own style as a writer, using humor and ridicule in the face of misery. In *El Mago de Viena,* as with much of his work, Pitol offers readers a combination of various methodologies, including memoir, essay, fiction, and literature. While the book is in first person and often recounts events in Pitol's life, it is by no means a true autobiography. In a sense, Pitol's work reflects real life in the sense that it is all-encompassing and leaves no aspect of the world behind. Will H. Corral, writing for *World Literature Today,* commented: "Pitol's world relies exclusively on the examined literary life, without Socratic obfuscations."

BIOGRAPHICAL AND CRITICAL SOURCES:

PERIODICALS

EFE World News Service, December 1, 2005, "Mexican Wins Big Spanish Literary Award"; December 7, 2005, "Mexican Writer Hails Cervantes and 'Don Quixote';" April 21, 2006, "Sergio Pitol Praises the Yearning for Freedom in Cervantes' Works."

M2 Best Books, December 5, 2005, "Winner of the 2005 Cervantes Prize Announced."

World Literature Today, spring, 1998, George R. McMurray, review of *El arte de la fuga;* July 1, 2006, Will H. Corral, review of *El Mago de Viena,* p. 79.

Xinhua News Agency, December 1, 2005, "Mexican Writer Pitol Wins Spain's Cervantes Prize"; April 21, 2006, "Mexican Novelist Wins Spain's Cervantes Prize."

ONLINE

America Reads Spanish Web site, http://www.americareadsspanish.org/ (October 10, 2007), author biography.

CBC/Radio Canada Web site, http://www.cbc.ca/ (April 21, 2006), Cervantes Prize announcement.

International Literature Festival Berlin Web site, http://www.literaturfestival.com/ (October 10, 2007), author biography.*

*   *   *

PORIZKOVA, Paulina 1965-

PERSONAL: Born April 9 1965, in Prostejov, Czechoslovakia; became a U.S. citizen; married Rick Ocasek (a musician and record producer), August 23, 1989; children: Jonathan Raven, Oliver Orion; Eron, Christopher, Derek (stepchildren). *Hobbies and other interests:* Classical piano and art.

ADDRESSES: Home—New York, NY.

CAREER: Writer, model, and actress. Former supermodel whose work included a six-million-dollar-a-year contract with Estée Lauder. Has appeared in films and on television. Films include *Portfolio,* 1983, *Covergirl,* 1984, *Anna,* 1987, *Her Alibi,* 1989, *Arizona Dream,* 1993, *Female Perversions,* 1996, *Wedding Bell Blues,* 1996, *Long Time Since,* 1997, *Thursday,* 1998, *After the Rain,* 2000, *The Intern,* 2000, *Partners in Crime,* 2000, *Roommates,* 2001, *Dark Asylum,* 2001, *Au plus près du paradis,* 2002, *People I Know,*

2002, *Second Best,* 2004, and *Knots,* 2004. Television work includes appearances on *Saturday Night Live* and *Ned and Stacey.*

WRITINGS:

(With Joanne Russell) *The Adventures of Ralphie the Roach,* illustrated by Adam Otcasek, Doubleday (New York, NY), 1992.

(And director) *Roommates* (screenplay), 2001.

A Model Summer (novel), Hyperion (New York, NY), 2007.

Contributor to *Travelers' Tales Prague and the Czech Republic: True Stories.*

SIDELIGHTS: Onetime supermodel Paulina Porizkova has expanded her career to include acting and writing. Her first writing effort was the children's book *The Adventures of Ralphie the Roach,* which Porizkova wrote with her friend and fellow model Joanne Russell. The story focuses on Ralphie and his family, who live in a place called Roachtown behind a shelf in an empty house. However, someone is moving into the house, and Ralphie and the other residents of Roachtown face extermination.

It would be more than a decade before Poirzkova's next book was published, this time an adult novel titled *A Model Summer.* While the novel's protagonist, Jirina, bears many resemblances to the author, Porizkova told Carla Hay in an interview posted on the Lifetime Television Web site that the events are not necessarily all true, noting: "Kind of everything and kind of nothing [is based on real events]. I lent [the Jirina character] some of my experiences, but it's not me and it's not my life. When I first went to Paris, I had a slightly different personality from my protagonist. I was much tougher than the girl I created, and I have a much better sense of humor. So I was much better prepared for that world than she is. The book is not a memoir; it's a memory."

The novel features a Swedish-Czechoslovakian teenager name Jirina who, despite being tall and skinny and no classical beauty, attracts the attention of a Parisian owner of a modeling agency. As the young girl enters the world of modeling, she goes from being very naive to a seasoned veteran who understands all too well the ups and downs of the high-fashion and modeling industries. As time goes on, Jirina comes to realize that being a model is not her ideal career. She comes to find it degrading and boring. Nevertheless, she meets a host of interesting people, including a gentleman who rescues her from a bad situation and an Australian photographer who captures her heart. Commenting on the protagonist, a *Publishers Weekly* contributor noted that her "drive is palpable and her voice believable." A reviewer writing on *BellaOnline* commented: "Porizkova gives us front row seats to witness the ugly side of beauty." Several other reviewers also noted the insights into the modeling world provided by the author. "For anyone looking for a unique read that offers an insider's look into the world of modeling, *A Model Summer* is a fantastic read," wrote Tracy Farnsworth in a review posted on *Roundtable Reviews. Front Street Reviews* contributor Sarra Borne noted: "Paulina Porizkova clearly expresses her creativity in her debut novel. It is a fascinating subject that she describes vividly and quite expertly."

BIOGRAPHICAL AND CRITICAL SOURCES:

PERIODICALS

Booklist, March 1, 2007, Carolyn Kubisz, review of *A Model Summer,* p. 64.

Entertainment Weekly, August 18, 1995, Laura C. Smith, "My Husband the Car," profile of author and husband, p. 68; April 6, 2007, Tina Jordan, "8 Things You Don't Know about Paulina Porizkova," p. 19.

Marie Claire, May, 2007, review of *A Model Summer,* p. 126.

Newsweek, November 23, 1992, review of *The Adventures of Ralphie the Roach,* p. 72.

New York Times, April 1, 2007, Winter Miller, "Pampering Two Left Feet," p. 4.

New York Times Book Review, April 8, 2007, Alex Kuczynski, "In Her Fashion," review of *A Model Summer,* p. 9.

People, July 1, 1985, "Don't Be Catty: At 20, Is Paulina Porizkova the World's Most Beautiful Model or Isn't She?," p. 95; February 6, 1989, Peter Travers, "Her Alibi," p. 15.

Publishers Weekly, October 19, 1992, review of *The Adventures of Ralphie the Roach,* p. 78; January 29, 2007, review of *A Model Summer,* p. 41.

Redbook, October, 1992, Stephanie Mansfield, "Paulina Porizkova: Starting Over at 27," p. 104.

School Library Journal, February, 1993, JoAnn Rees, review of *The Adventures of Ralphie the Roach,* p. 77.

Sports Illustrated, February, 1989, Douglas S. Looney, "1984, 1985: The Pearls of Paulina," p. 191.

Vogue, April, 2007, Eve MacSweeney, "Long Tall Stories; Eighties Supermodel Paulina Porizkova Has Lived Several Lives Already," p. 352.

ONLINE

AskMen, http://www.askmen.com/ (October 10, 2007), profile of author.

BellaOnline, http://www.bellaonline.com/ (October 10, 2007), review of *A Model Summer.*

Front Street Reviews, http://www.frontstreetreviews.com/ (October 10, 2007), Sarra Borne, review of *A Model Summer.*

Internet Movie Database, http://www.imdb.com/ (October 10, 2007), biography of author and information on author's film work.

Lifetime Television Web site, http://www.lifetimetv.com/ (August 24, 2007), Carla Hay, "Paulina Porizkova: From Supermodel to Budding Novelist."

Roundtable Reviews, http://www.roundtablereviews.com/ (October 10, 2007), Tracy Farnsworth, review of *A Model Summer.*

World Hum, http://www.worldhum.com/ (October 10, 2007), David Farley, "Paulina Porizkova: A Model Traveler," interview with author.*

*   *   *

POTTER, Franz J. 1969-

PERSONAL: Born 1969. *Education:* University of East Anglia, Ph.D.

ADDRESSES: Home—Thousand Oaks, CA. *Office*—Academic and Administrative Headquarters, National University, 11355 N. Torrey Pines Rd., LaJolla, CA 92037. *E-mail*—fpotter@nu.edu.

CAREER: Educator and writer. National University, LaJolla, CA, assistant professor.

WRITINGS:

(Editor) *The Monster Made by Man: A Compendium of Gothic Adaptations,* Zittaw Press (Concord, NH), 2004.

The History of Gothic Publishing, 1800-1835: Exhuming the Trade, Palgrave Macmillan (New York, NY), 2005.

(Editor and author of introduction) *Romances and Gothic Tales,* Zittaw Press (Concord, NH), 2006.

SIDELIGHTS: As the editor of *The Monster Made by Man: A Compendium of Gothic Adaptations,* Franz J. Potter focuses on gothic short stories, or what were once derivatively referred to as the "trade Gothic." These gothic stories were usually not viewed favorably by the critics, especially in comparison with the famous gothic novels of the late eighteenth and early nineteenth century, such as Horace Walpole's *The Castle of Otranto* and Mary Shelley's *Frankenstein.* Nevertheless, Potter makes a case for their value in his introduction and gathers together nine tales from serial magazines and omnibuses published primarily between 1825 and 1830. All the authors published their works anonymously, and the stories show both the derivative and creative nature of gothic short stories. Many of them focus on similar themes, such as intervention by supernatural forces, including the dead directing the living to seek revenge. For example, the title story borrows its theme from *Frankenstein,* while another adapts the wandering Jew myth. Noting the collection's "extremely interesting and learned Introduction, historical notes and a rich bibliography," *Agony Column* Web site contributor Mario Guslandi wrote of *The Monster Made by Man*: "Naïve and shallow as their themes can appear, those tales maintain their ability to fascinate and entertain." Guslandi also pointed out that Potter's contribution to the collection should be recognized. The reviewer commented: "If you're neither an academic nor a literary scholar, you may just enjoy the tales without bothering to browse the editor's annotations. However, I strongly advise you to do so because they are enlightening and definitely worth reading."

BIOGRAPHICAL AND CRITICAL SOURCES:

ONLINE

Agony Column, http://trashotron.com/agony/ (October 5, 2007), Mario Guslandi, review of *The Monster Made by Man: A Compendium of Gothic Adaptations.*

National University Web site, http://www.nu.edu/ (September 6, 2007), biography of Franz J. Potter.*

PRAP, Lila 1955-
(Lilijana Praprotnik-Zupančič)

PERSONAL: Born September 28, 1955, in Celje, Yugoslavia (now Slovenia); daughter of Albert (a civil engineer) and Vida (a bookkeeper) Praprotnik; married Bori Zupančič (an art therapist), January 30, 1982; children: Izidor. *Education:* University of Ljubljana, diploma in architectural engineering.

ADDRESSES: Home—Škofia Vas, Slovenia. *E-mail*—lilijana.praprotnik@guest.arnes.si.

CAREER: Architect in Wiesbaden, West Germany (now Germany), 1980-81; teacher at a high school for civil engineering in Celje, Yugoslavia (now Slovenia), 1981-84; industrial designer in Gorenje Velenje, Yugoslavia, 1986-89; freelance artist, 1989—.

AWARDS, HONORS: Included in honor list, International Board on Books for Young People, 2002; Slovenian awards include Levstik Award, 2001, and honors for best children's book, 2002, 2005.

WRITINGS:

CHILDREN'S BOOKS

Živalske Uspavanke, Mladinska Knijiga (Ljubljana, Slovenia), 2000, translation published as *Animal Lullabies,* NorthSouth Books (New York, NY), 2006.

Why? (originally published in Slovenian, 2002), Kane/Miller Book Publishers (La Jolla, CA), 2005.

(Illustrator) Barbara Jean Hicks, *I Like Colors,* Random House (New York, NY), 2005.

1001 Stories, Kane/Miller Book Publishers (La Jolla, CA), 2006.

(Illustrator) Barbara Jean Hicks, *I Like Black and White,* Tiger Tales (Wilton, CT), 2006.

Daddies, NorthSouth Books (New York, NY), 2007.

Also illustrator or author and illustrator of books published solely in Slovenian, most often by the publisher Mladinska Knijiga.

SIDELIGHTS: Lila Prap told *CA:* "I began to think about making books for children when my son was small and I wanted to amuse him with the word games and nonsense answers that I had invented with my dad in my own childhood. We had great fun, and a lot of things can be learned this way. With my books I'd like to stimulate parents and their children to have fun reading together and to make their own word games.

"All things that come into my life influence my work: reading books, watching films, especially about animals, going for walks, traveling, everyday problems . . . but mostly unexpected discoveries that appear when I simply play with materials, words, or colors.

"I make picture books mostly, so sometimes I begin with an idea of the text or sometimes with the illustrations. My texts are very short poems or prose, understandable to very small children, so the main things in my books are the ideas. A good idea for a picture book is not so easy to get; sometimes it takes almost a year before I think out something useful. The best ideas come when I'm working with something else.

"I'm inspired by the magic world of childhood. Everything is new, everything has to be discovered, each day is a new adventure, and there is no limit between dreams and reality. I want to make an example, to answer a child's 1,001 questions, to motivate the child to explore language and different types of writing, or to look at the tiniest living creatures as examples of the different ways of life that surround us. I want to motivate daddies to play with children, or children to play with daddies, to show how to lull a child to sleep, to tell a story in a thousand different ways. Mostly I use animal figures to tell something. I found them to be a good mediator. Animals can represent fear, power, weakness, curiosity, or other unexplainable things that children encounter in the earliest periods of their lives.

"One of my greatest inspirations for making more books after the first one has been the positive reaction of children and their parents to my books."

*   *   *

PRAPROTNIK-ZUPANČIČ, Lilijana
    See PRAP, Lila

PRASAD, Chandra 1975-

PERSONAL: Born 1975, in New Haven, CT; married Basil Petrov. *Education:* Graduate of Yale University, 1997.

ADDRESSES: Home—CT.

CAREER: Freelance writer, 1997—.

WRITINGS:

Outwitting the Job Market: Everything You Need to Locate and Land a Great Position, Lyons Press (Guilford, CT), 2004.
Death of a Circus (novel), Red Hen Press (Granada Hills, CA), 2006.
(Editor and contributor) *Mixed: An Anthology of Short Fiction on the Multiracial Experience,* introduction by Rebecca Walker, W.W. Norton (New York, NY), 2006.
On Borrowed Wings: A Novel, Atria Books (New York, NY), 2007.

Contributor of articles to periodicals and Web sites, including the *Wall Street Journal, India Abroad, India New England, Monster.com,* and *Vault.* Contributor of short stories to periodicals, including *Faultline.*

SIDELIGHTS: In a *New York Times* profile of Chandra Prasad, Kathryn Shattuck commented on the author's novels and wrote: "Chandra Prasad's writing reverberates with the familiar, from images of the south-central Connecticut towns where she grew up and still lives to the storied campus of Yale University, where she was educated. But her perspective is that of an outsider, nose pressed to the glass, peering in." Chandra began her freelance writing career by focusing on workplace issues. Her first book was *Outwitting the Job Market: Everything You Need to Locate and Land a Great Position.* Writing in a review posted on *Quintessential Careers,* Randall S. Hansen noted: "I was struck at how well Prasad covers all aspects of job-hunting in a very easy-to-read style, with numerous tips and examples to guide the wary job-seeker."

In her first novel, *Death of a Circus,* the author writes of Lor Cole, a young black man living in Connecticut in the early twentieth century. Bored with his life, Lor dreams of running away with the circus and eventually lands a job as a high-wire walker. Although he becomes a circus star, Lor must still contend with the diverse community that makes up a circus. Allison Block, writing in *Booklist,* called *Death of a Circus* a "richly textured first novel packed with glamour and grit."

Prasad next served as editor of and contributor to *Mixed: An Anthology of Short Fiction on the Multiracial Experience.* The anthology, for which Prasad wrote the foreword, features a diverse range of multiracial writers. "*Mixed* reveals . . . commonalities and the unique ways they manifest themselves in particular times, places and people," wrote Cheryl Harris Sharman in the *San Francisco Chronicle.* Prasad also contributes a short story to the anthology. Titled "Wayward," the tale features a teenage girl—the daughter of an Indian mother and Russian father—who is exposed to discrimination by a young child she is babysitting. Vanessa Bush, writing in *Booklist,* called the anthology "an absorbing and thought-provoking collection of stories." *New Statesman* contributor Mary Fitzgerald noted: "There is some exquisite writing here."

Prasad's *On Borrowed Wings: A Novel* is also set in Connecticut and tells the story of a young woman, Adele Pietra, who pretends to be her deceased brother so she can attend Yale University. Commenting that the novel is no "standard crossdress-to-impress tale," *New Haven Advocate* contributor Christopher Arnott also called the novel "accessible, a good bedtime read," adding that "it isn't a cloying romance novel in literary clothes or a heavy-handed metaphor." A subplot of the novel revolves around Adele taking a work-study job with a professor who is conducting research to prove that the upper classes are superior. A *Publishers Weekly* contributor noted that the author "renders believable a girl who becomes herself in a most unlikely way."

BIOGRAPHICAL AND CRITICAL SOURCES:

PERIODICALS

Booklist, July 1, 2006, Vanessa Bush, review of *Mixed: An Anthology of Short Fiction on the Multiracial Experience,* p. 31; November 15, 2006, Allison Block, review of *Death of a Circus,* p. 30.

Hamden Journal (Shelton, CT), June 14, 2007, "Author Delves into Identity."

Library Journal, June 15, 2006, Rebecca Stuhr, review of *Mixed,* p. 63.

New Haven Advocate, June 21, 2007, Christopher Arnott, review of *On Borrowed Wings: A Novel.*

New Statesman, October 16, 2006, Mary Fitzgerald, "Spelling out Diversity," review of *Mixed,* p. 60.

New York Times, February 18, 2007, Kathryn Shattuck, "Writing; A High-Wire Act Balancing Race, Gender and a Lonely Determination," profile of author.

Publishers Weekly, March 12, 2007, review of *On Borrowed Wings,* p. 32.

San Francisco Chronicle, August 27, 2006, Cheryl Harris Sharman, review of *Mixed.*

ONLINE

BookLoons, http://www.bookloons.com/ (October 10, 2007), Hilary Williamson, review of *Outwitting the Job Market: Everything You Need to Locate and Land a Great Position.*

Chandra Prasad Home Page, http://www.chandra prasad.com (October 10, 2007).

CT Central, http://www.ctcentral.com/ (October 10, 2007), Patricia D'Ascoli, "Chandra Prasad's Debut Novel Reflects Fascination with the '30s Yale, Gender Issues."

CT Festival of Words, http://www.ctfestivalofwords. com/ (October 10, 2007), brief profile of author.

Quintessential Careers, http://www.quintcareers.com/ (October 10, 2007), Randall S. Hansen, review of *Outwitting the Job Market.*

South Asian Women's Network, http://www.sawnet. org/books (October 10, 2007), "Chandra Prasad," profile of author.

True Careers Inc. Web site, http://www.truecareers. com/ (October 10, 2007), "Outwitting Discrimination: New Job Market Tactics for Women and Minorities," interview with author.*

*   *   *

PRESLEY, Michael

PERSONAL: Born in Grenada, West Indies; immigrated to United States, 1978. *Education:* Stony Brook University, B.A.

ADDRESSES: Home—Brooklyn, NY.

CAREER: Writer.

WRITINGS:

Tears on a Sunday Afternoon, Strebor Books (Largo, MD), 2007.

"BLACKFUNK" NOVEL SERIES

Blackfunk, 2nd revised edition, Blackfunk Publishing (Brooklyn, NY), 2001.
Blackfunk II: No Regrets, Blackfunk Publishing (Brooklyn, NY), 2002.
Whatever It Takes (Blackfunk III), Blackfunk Publishing (Brooklyn, NY), 2004.

SIDELIGHTS: Michael Presley is a short-story writer and novelist whose first three novels are part of a series titled "Blackfunk." The series takes place in an urban world where love is difficult, if not impossible, to find and has been replaced by sexual manipulation. The "Blackfunk" books follow characters who seek authentic relationships and love in their life. "I wanted to show us [black Americans] as professionals: doctors, engineers, lawyers—successful people with issues," the author told Victoria Christopher Murray in an interview in the *Black Issues Book Review.* In his fourth novel, *Tears on a Sunday Afternoon,* the author presents a sexually graphic story about a man named Donald who finds himself in a bizarre situation, that is, living with his wife and her lesbian lover. Although Donald is no paragon of virtue, he loves his son and wants to get him out of a situation he sees as abusive, largely because of his father-in-law, Mr. Malcolm, who hates Donald. However, Donald's wife has all the money, and Donald has gotten used to living in a mansion and driving fast cars. The protagonist also faces the fact that his father-in-law has underworld connections that could prove dangerous. Donald soon finds his chance to get out when a beautiful woman presents an indecent and possibly illegal proposition that would make Donald enough money to get away with his son. Calling the novel of sexual betrayal and intrigue "hugely entertaining," David Pitt, writing in *Booklist,* went on to note that some readers may not like the swearing and graphic sex contained in the novel but that "all others will be thrilled."

BIOGRAPHICAL AND CRITICAL SOURCES:

PERIODICALS

Black Issues Book Review, September, 2001, review of *Blackfunk,* p. 73; March-April, 2005, Victoria Christopher Murray, "On the Way Up: Two Emerging Authors Succeed in the Fast-Paced World of Literary Entrepreneurship," p. 70.
Booklist, February 1, 2007, David Pitt, review of *Tears on a Sunday Afternoon,* p. 33.

ONLINE

Blackfunk Web site, http://www.blackfunk-book.com (October 5, 2007).*

*   *   *

PRYCE, Lois 1973-

PERSONAL: Born 1973; married.

ADDRESSES: *Home*—London, England. *Agent*—Faye Bender Literary Agency, 337 W. 76th St., #E1, New York, NY 10023. *E-mail*—lois@loisontheloose.com.

CAREER: Writer. Worked for Virgin Megastore as specialist music buyer for London's Oxford Street store; for record labels and production companies; and as a product manager at the British Broadcasting Corporation (BBC).

WRITINGS:

Lois on the Loose: One Woman, One Motorcycle, 20,000 Miles across the Americas (memoir), Thomas Dunne Books/St. Martin's Press (New York, NY), 2007.

SIDELIGHTS: Lois Pryce had an office job with the British Broadcasting Corporation when, finding herself bored, decided to take an epic motorcycle trip. "I thought, 'I can't work at the BBC for ever," the author told Benedicte Page in an interview in the *Bookseller.* "I fancy an adventure, I've always had itchy feet, and when I was 22 I bought a boat to live on, so I do like silly adventures." The result is her adventure memoir *Lois on the Loose: One Woman, One Motorcycle, 20,000 Miles across the Americas.* Called "part memoir, part travelogue, part motorcycle-babe grandstanding" by Ina Hughs in a review in the

Knoxville News Sentinel, the memoir follows Pryce as she buys a dirt bike, debates and finally settles on a touring route, and then sets off on her trip from Anchorage, Alaska, to Ushuaia, Argentina. The author describes the various landscapes and adventures she encounters as well as the people she meets along the way, especially those who help her when she finds herself in difficult predicaments. Black-and-white photographs are included. In the review in the *Knoxville News Sentinel,* Hughs noted "the colorful language, the funny and poignant stories, and the feisty spirit that shines on every page." A *Publishers Weekly* contributor wrote: "Armchair travelers will delight in this funny, vivid account and—almost—wish they'd done it themselves."

Pryce told *CA:* "I have read books all my life, and always enjoyed writing stories when I was at school. It never occurred to me until recently that I could do it as my job!

"Although I am an avid reader, there is no writer that has particularly influenced me, except maybe Spike Milligan—his World War II diaries are hilarious and touching and showed me that you can apply humor to every situation.

"I used to write at the end of the day. Now I do it first thing in the morning. It usually starts off with a lot of staring at a blank screen, then scribbling down some notes, making far too many cups of tea before actually getting on with it. It seems I have to wade through mud for an hour and then it starts to flow."

When asked the most surprising thing she has learned as a writer, Pryce said: "That when it's flowing I get an almost drug-like high!

"I hope [my books] will encourage adventure."

BIOGRAPHICAL AND CRITICAL SOURCES:

BOOKS

Pryce, Lois, *Lois on the Loose: One Woman, One Motorcycle, 20,000 Miles across the Americas,* Thomas Dunne Books/St. Martin's Press (New York, NY), 2007.

PERIODICALS

Booklist, February 1, 2007, Sarah Watstein, review of *Lois on the Loose,* p. 18.
Bookseller, April 29, 2005, "Biker Babe Sells Travel Memoir to Arrow," p. 11; November 3, 2006, Benedicte Page, "Time for Adventure: Lois Pryce Got Bored of the Office—So She Took Off across South America on a Motorbike Instead," interview with author, p. 23.
Knoxville News Sentinel, April 15, 2007, Ina Hughs, "This Read Takes You on a Ride."
Publishers Weekly, December 11, 2006, review of *Lois on the Loose,* p. 55.

ONLINE

Gadling, http://www.gadling.com/ (March 8, 2007), Justin Glow, "Talking Travel with Lois Pryce," interview with author.
Lois Pryce Home Page, http://www.loisontheloose. com (August 27, 2007).

Q-R

QUINN, Paula

PERSONAL: Married; children: three.

ADDRESSES: Home—New York, NY. *E-mail*—paula@paulaquinn.com.

CAREER: Writer. Historical romance novelist.

WRITINGS:

Lord of Desire, Warner Books (New York, NY), 2005.
Lord of Temptation, Warner Forever (New York, NY), 2005.
Lord of Seduction, Warner Forever (New York, NY), 2006.
Laird of the Mist, Warner Forever (New York, NY), 2007.

SIDELIGHTS: Paula Quinn, an author of historical romances, told *Romance Review Today* Web site contributor Ann Cooke: "I—love medieval history, when men fought with swords and sometimes died for what they believed in. My favorite times to research and write about are the Conqueror era, when Duke William of Normandy became king of England." Cooke's first historical romance, *Lord of Desire,* was called "an exquisitely written and sensuous historical" by a contributor to *Love Romances & More.* The novel features Lord Brand "the Passioniate" Risande and Lady Brynnafar, whose father was defeated by Brand and must relinquish his castle to him. The novel

follows Brynnafar as she decides that she will marry Brand to save the family castle but is surprised to find that she is falling in love with him. However, after his former lover cheated on him, Brand has vowed never to marry. John Charles, writing in *Booklist,* commented that the author provides "enough historical details to give a vivid sense of time and place." Nancy Davis noted in a review posted on *Romance Reader at Heart:* "Paula Quinn can pat herself on the back for coming out with such a marvelous debut romance. Rich in detail, filled with wonderful characters and a good plot, *Lord of Desire* is a delectable medieval treat."

Lord of Temptation contains "sharp repartee and [a] dramatic finale," according to a *Publishers Weekly* contributor. The story takes place after the Norman conquest of England and features wealthy warrior Lord Dante Risande who, though many women pursue him, cannot win the love of the only woman he wants, Gianelle, who has worked for cruel masters. When a previous master dies, Gianelle is suspected of murder and Risande sees his chance to protect her and win her love. "Attention to detail, story pacing and perfect rhythmic writing style make this a great second book for a new author," wrote a contributor to *Fresh Fiction.* Writing in *Booklist,* John Charles commented that the author's "second engaging historical romance . . . is an excellent choice for readers who like powerful, passion-rich medieval romances."

Gareth ap Owain wins a tournament and the right to ask for Lady Tanon Risande's hand in marriage in Quinn's third romance, *Lord of Seduction.* Lady Tanon, who had hoped to marry for love, is resigned to the marriage but soon has her hopes rekindled that love and marriage will coexist in her life. "Passion, peril, and plenty of medieval political intrigue are the primary ingredients" in *Lord of Seduction,* wrote John Charles in *Booklist.* Kim Atchue-Cusella, writing on *BookLoons,* commented that the author "crafts a story in which the details . . . make you feel as if you are there with her characters. I sighed over the gentleness of the hero and the charm of the heroine."

Quinn told *CA:* "Anything romantic influences my work. Whether it's a song, a painting, a movie, a couple I see on the street. . . . I'm a sappy romantic of the worst sort. History also has a strong place in my heart. I love it. When I first read about William of Normandy a dozen stories popped into my head almost immediately.

"Usually I do a complete character analysis before I begin a story. The characters have been living in my head for some time before I even begin their story, so doing the character analysis is easy. Still, I want to really get inside their heads and know what makes them tick. Sometimes I write the first draft of the story by hand. (Because of my crazy love for pens!) Most of the time I have the beginning, middle, and ending already established so I know where the story is going. Or where I'd like it to go. The characters change things along the way, though, so I'm always prepared for that.

"The most surprising thing I have learned as a writer is that people love my books as much as I do. An author's stories are like their children. I know they aren't perfect, but I like to believe they are. Each word, each sentence is wrought with a birth pang, and when a reader enjoys those words and sentences it's worth all the blood, sweat, and tears it sometimes took to write them.

"All my books hold a special place in my heart for different reasons. Some have characters I like a little more than others. Some were easier to write, while others have a storyline that I can relate to more. If I had to choose one that had a more profound effect on me while I was writing it, it would be *Laird of the Mist.* My favorite place in the world is Scotland, and who doesn't love a story about Highlanders? But it was very important for me to tell a little bit of the history of the MacGregor clan. To touch upon the sorrows of their time and the only thing that can truly mend a vengeful heart. Love.

"When I began writing professionally I remember wanting my stories to reach just one woman who was unhappy in a bad relationship. I wanted to somehow give her hope that there are knights in shining armor still out there. Sure, they're not easy to find, but they are out there and the search is worth it. Don't settle for less. Men of honor are not a fantasy. Happily ever afters do happen."

BIOGRAPHICAL AND CRITICAL SOURCES:

PERIODICALS

Booklist, August, 2005, John Charles, review of *Lord of Desire,* p. 2006; December 15, 2005, John Charles, review of *Lord of Temptation,* p. 30; December 1, 2006, John Charles, review of *Lord of Seduction,* p. 32.
Publishers Weekly, December 12, 2005, review of *Lord of Temptation,* p. 44.

ONLINE

BookLoons, http://www.bookloons.com/ (October 10, 2007), Marie Hashima Lofton, review of *Lord of Desire;* Kim Atchue-Cusella, review of *Lord of Seduction.*
Fresh Fiction, http://freshfiction.com/ (July 4, 2005), Angela Johnson, review of *Lord of Desire;* (January 9, 2006), Margaret Ohmes, review of *Lord of Temptation;* (November 17, 2006), Margaret Ohmes, review of *Lord of Seduction.*
Hachette Book Group USA Web site, http://www.hachettebookgroupusa.com/ (October 10, 2007), profile of author.
Historical Romance Writers, http://historicalromance writers.com/ (June 9, 2005), review of *Lord of Desire;* (August 24, 2005), review of *Lord of Desire.*
Love Romances, http://www.loveromances.com/ (October 10, 2007), interview with author.
Love Romances & More, http://www.loveromancesand more.com/ (October 10, 2007), reviews of *Lord of Desire, Lord of Temptation,* and *Lord of Seduction.*
Mystic Castle, http://www.themysticcastle.com/ (October 10, 2007), review of *Lord of Seduction.*
Once upon a Romance, http://www.onceupona romance.net/ (October 10, 2007), Lori Graham, review of *Lord of Seduction.*

Paula Quinn Home Page, http://paulaquinn.com (October 10, 2007).

Paula Quinn MySpace Profile, http://www.myspace.com/paulaquinn (October 10, 2007).

Road to Romance, http://www.roadtoromance.ca/ (October 10, 2007), Julie Brown, review of *Lord of Desire.*

Romance Reader at Heart, http://romancereaderatheart.com/ (October 10, 2007), Nancy Davis, reviews of *Lord of Desire* and *Lord of Temptation;* Deana Monteleone, review of *Lord of Seduction.*

Romance Readers Connection, http://www.theromancereadersconnection.com/ (October 10, 2007), Deborah Hern, review of *Lord of Desire.*

Romance Review, http://www.aromancereview.com/ (October 10, 2007), reviews of *Lord of Desire, Lord of Temptation,* and *Lord of Seduction.*

Romance Review Today, http://www.romrevtoday.com/ (October 10, 2007), Ann Cooke, "Interview with Paula Quinn."

Roundtable Reviews, http://www.roundtablereviews.com/ (October 10, 2007), Tracy Farnsworth, review of *Lord of Desire.*

*   *   *

RALLISON, Janette 1966-
(Sierra St. James)

PERSONAL: Born 1966; married; children: five children.

ADDRESSES: Home—Chandler, AZ. *E-mail*—jrallisonfans@yahoo.com.

CAREER: Novelist.

WRITINGS:

YOUNG-ADULT NOVELS

Deep Blue Eyes and Other Lies, Deseret (Salt Lake City, UT), 1996.

Dakota's Revenge, Deseret (Salt Lake City, UT), 1998.

Playing the Field, Walker (New York, NY), 2002.

All's Fair in Love, War, and High School, Walker (New York, NY), 2003.

Life, Love, and the Pursuit of Free Throws, Walker (New York, NY), 2004.

Fame, Glory, and Other Things on My To-Do List, Walker (New York, NY), 2005.

It's a Mall World after All, Walker (New York, NY), 2006.

How to Take the Ex out of Ex-Boyfriend, Walker (New York, NY), 2007.

Revenge of the Cheerleaders, Walker (New York, NY), 2007.

UNDER NAME SIERRA ST. JAMES

Trial of the Heart, Deseret (Salt Lake City, UT), 1999.

Masquerade, Bookcraft (Salt Lake City, UT), 2001.

Time Riders, Bonneville Books (Springville, UT), 2004.

What the Doctor Ordered, Deseret (Salt Lake City, UT), 2004.

ADAPTATIONS: Several of Rallison's novels have been adapted as audiobooks.

SIDELIGHTS: Janette Rallison began writing at age six, and many of her books draw on her memories of growing up in a small town in eastern Washington. Specifically, Rallison focuses on the concerns shared by most teen girls—dating, dating, and dating—and her entertaining novels, such as *All's Fair in Love, War, and High School, Fame, Glory, and Other Things on My To-Do List,* and *How to Take the Ex out of Ex-Boyfriend,* feature heroines attempting to discover, rekindle, jump-start, or repair a love relationship with the boy of their dreams. When mining her own memories dors not yield the perfect character or plot element, Rallison has been known to adapt events from her teenage daughter's life. Living with a teenager "is sort of like living in your own reality show, but with fewer commercials," the author explained on her home page. "I borrow from [my daughter's] . . . life a lot. In fact while I was writing *It's a Mall World After All* I once lifted dialogue for a scene right off the text message log in my daughter's cell phone."

Rallison began her publishing career with the teen romance *Deep Blue Eyes and Other Lies,* which was released in 1996. Another of her early novels, *Playing the Field,* finds thirteen-year-old McKay trying to keep his head above water in algebra class, because a bad grade will mean the end of his spot on the school baseball team. When his friend Tony suggests that he wrangle free tutoring from a brainy math student by pretending that he has a crush on her, McKay buys into the scheme. Ultimately, Serena discovers the plot, Tony proves to be a less-than-loyal buddy, and soon McKay realizes that he has to approach his life, and his relationships, with a little more integrity. McKay is a likeable and well-grounded hero, noted *Booklist* contributor John Peters, the critic adding that Rallison delivers her message "without lectures" and by presenting "a set of situations that readers will have little trouble relating to." Noting Rallison's use of "humor and realistic characters," Linda Bindner concluded in her *School Library Journal* review of *Playing the Field* that the novel will "be a hit with anybody interested in . . . baseball, friends, and that mysterious . . . first crush."

Described by a *Kirkus Reviews* writer as a "witty, often hilarious romp," *All's Fair in Love, War, and High School* finds popular head cheerleader Samantha Taylor frustrated by her inability to pull decent scores on the SAT exam. To balance out her college applications with some positive credentials, the teen decides to run for student body president. Unfortunately, Samantha's dry, sarcastic humor will not serve her well on the campaign trail, so she enlists the help of ex-boyfriend Logan to plan her election strategy. This strategy has an unsettling effect on her personal life, however; not only does Samantha lose her current beau (and thus have no date for the Junior Prom), but the bet she has made with Logan that she can hold back her sarcasm for an entire week seems as doomed as her future college career. In *Publishers Weekly,* a critic wrote that Rallison's use of "appealing characters and snappy dialogue give this light fare a satisfying bite."

Fame, Glory, and Other Things on My To-Do List finds New Mexican high-school junior Jessica dreaming of a Hollywood film career. When her role in the school play—an "unintentionally hilarious politically correct rewrite of *West Side Story,*" according to a *Kirkus Reviews* writer—is threatened, so is her future, so she decides to court Jordan, a new student at school, when she finds out that his divorced father is a famous actor. Although Jordan wants his dad's identity to remain a secret so that he can be judged on his own merits, Jessica disagrees and cuts their relationship short. When

she realizes that fame is less important than lasting friendship, the teen decides to set matters right and this time puts more sincere energy into winning Jordan back. In her review in *Booklist,* Hazel Rochman praised Jessica's "cool, hilarious first-person" narration and noted the novel's themes of "rivalry, the embarrassment, and the romance between friends and lovers."

Incorporating a nod to Jane Austen, in the opinion of one reviewer, *It's a Mall World after All* introduces two teens who, despite their continual verbal sparring, are destined for one another. In addition to her part-time job as a perfume spritzer at a local shopping mall, her work helping an underprivileged boy, and her effort to keep up her honor-student status, compassionate Charlotte still has time to fret about friend Brianna's errant boyfriend, Bryant. When her efforts to catch Bryant in an indiscretion are continually foiled by Bryant's friend, the rich, preppy Colton, Charlotte gradually finds her frustration with Colton shifting to attraction despite their many differences. Although Rallison's heroine has a quirky personality that sometimes gets her into trouble, she is nonetheless an "appealing" character, according to a *Kirkus Reviews* writer. *It's a Mall World after All* offers teens the best of all worlds, in the opinion of *Booklist* reviewer Debbie Carton. In Carton's view, the novel is "a fun romp of a read that's . . . [also] light and breezy," and the *Kirkus Reviews* writer concluded that Rallison's story offers up "plenty of laughs and some insights too."

A common dating quandary—how to deal with a boyfriend's annoying friends—factors into the plot of Rallison's 2007 novel *How to Take the Ex out of Ex-Boyfriend.* When sixteen-year-old Giovanna's boyfriend Jesse chooses to support the campaign of a snobby friend rather than aid her twin brother in his run for student council president, she rashly ends the relationship. Too late, she realizes that she made a mistake, and now her job is to make Jesse jealous enough of her new dates to take time out of his campaign-manager duties and woo her back. Although a *Publishers Weekly* reviewer noted that Jesse's appeal to Giovanna is "somewhat of a mystery," *How to Take the Ex out of Ex-Boyfriend* benefits from a "spunky protagonist" and a "satisfying" end to the teen-friendly story. In *School Library Journal,* Stephanie L. Petruso recommended the novel to fans of authors Meg Cabot and Cathy Hopkins, calling it a "breezy look at high school life," and a *Kirkus Reviews* writer dubbed the book characteristic Rallison: "fast-paced and funny."

BIOGRAPHICAL AND CRITICAL SOURCES:

PERIODICALS

Booklist, May 15, 2002, John Peters, review of *Playing the Field,* p. 1597; November 1, 2004, Debbie Carton, review of *Life, Love, and the Pursuit of Free Throws,* p. 486; October 15, 2005, Hazel Rochman, review of *Fame, Glory, and Other Things on My To-Do List,* p. 43; January 1, 2007, Debbie Carton, review of *It's a Mall World after All,* p. 83.

Bulletin of the Center for Children's Books, July, 2002, review of *Playing the Field,* p. 416.

Kirkus Reviews, October 15, 2003, review of *All's Fair in Love, War, and High School,* p. 1275; August 1, 2004, review of *Life, Love, and the Pursuit of Free Throws,* p. 748; August 15, 2005, review of *Fame, Glory, and Other Things on My To-Do List,* p. 921; October 1, 2006, review of *It's a Mall World after All,* p. 1023; May 15, 2007, review of *How to Take the Ex out of Ex-Boyfriend.*

Publishers Weekly, November 24, 2003, review of *All's Fair in Love, War, and High School,* p. 65; June 25, 2007, review of *How to Take the Ex out of Ex-Boyfriend,* p. 61.

School Library Journal, April, 2002, Linda Bindner, review of *Playing the Field,* p. 156; September, 2003, Lynn Evarts, review of *All's Fair in Love, War, and High School,* p. 219; November, 2004, Sharon Morrison, review of *Life, Love, and the Pursuit of Free Throws,* p. 153; November, 2005, Amy Patrick, review of *Fame, Glory, and Other Things on My To-Do List,* p. 146; December, 2006, Heather M. Campbell, review of *It's a Mall World after All,* p. 152; July, 2007, Stephanie L. Petruso, review of *How to Take the Ex out of Ex-Boyfriend,* p. 108.

Voice of Youth Advocates, June, 2002, review of *Playing the Field,* p. 122; June, 2004, Eileen Kuhl, review of *All's Fair in Love, War, and High School,* p. 135; February, 2005, Amanda Zalud, review of *Life, Love, and the Pursuit of Free Throws,* p. 84; October, 2005, review of *Fame, Glory, and Other Things on My To-Do List,* p. 312; April, 2007, review of *It's a Mall World after All,* p. 55.

ONLINE

Janette Rallison Home Page, http://www.janette rallison.com (October 27, 2007).*

RAMADAN, Tariq 1962-

PERSONAL: Born 1962, in Switzerland; son of Said Ramadan; married. *Education:* University of Geneva, M.A., Ph.D.; attended Al-Azhar University in Cairo, Egypt.

ADDRESSES: Office—Office-39 rue de la boulangerie 93200 Saint-Denis, Paris, France; European Studies Centre, St. Antony's College, University of Oxford, 70 Woodstock Rd., Oxford OX2 6JF, England. *E-mail*—office@tariqramadan.com.

CAREER: Professor and writer. University of Oxford, St. Antony's College, Oxford, England, and Lokahi Foundation, London, England, visiting fellow, 2005-06, senior research fellow, 2006—. Visiting professor at Erasmus University, Holland.

WRITINGS:

Les Musulmans dans la laïcité: responsabilités et droits des musulmans dans les sociétés occidentales, Tawhid (Lyon, France), 1994, 3rd edition 2000.

Islam, le face á face des civilisations, Quel projet pour quelle modernité?, Les Deux Rives (Lyon, France), 1995, 4th edition 2001.

Aux sources du renouveau musulman, un siècle de réformisme islamique, Bayard Editions/Centurion (Paris, France), 1998, Tawhid (Lyon, France) 2001.

Muslims in France, Islamic Foundation (Leicester, England), 1999.

To Be a European Muslim, Islamic Foundation (Leicester, England), 1999.

Entre l'homme et son coeur, Tawhid (Lyon, France), 2000.

Islam, The West and the Challenges of Modernity, Islamic Foundation (Leicester, England), 2000, 2nd edition 2004.

(With Alain Gresh) *L'Islam en questions,* Actes Sud (Paris, France), 2000, Actes Sud (Babel, France), 2002.

Dar ash-shahada, l'Occident, espace du témoignage, Tawhid (Lyon, France), 2002.

De l'Islam, Tawhid (Lyon, France), 2002.

Jihad, violence guerre et paix en islam, Tawhid (Lyon, France), 2002.

La foi, la voie, la résistance, Tawhid (Lyon, France), 2002.

Musulmans d'Occident, construire et contribuer, Tawhid (Lyon, France), 2002.

Globalisation, Muslim Resistances, Tawid (Paris, France), 2003.

Les Musulmans d'Occident et l'avenir de l'Islam, Actes Sud (Paris, France), 2003, translation published as *Western Muslims and the Future of Islam,* Oxford University Press (New York, NY), 2004.

Muhammad: vie du prophète: les enseignements spirituels et contemporains, Presses du Chatelet (Paris, France), 2006, translation published as *In the Footsteps of the Prophet: Lessons from the Life of Muhammad,* Oxford University Press (New York, NY), 2007, also published as *The Messenger: The Meaning of the Life of Muhammad,* Penguin (London, England), 2007.

Contributor to books, including *Péril islamiste?,* by Alain Gresh, Complexe (Brussels, Belgium), 1995; *La tolérance ou la liberté? Les leçons de Voltaire et de Condorcet,* by Claude-Jean Lenoir, Complexe (Brussels, Belgium), 1997; *Islam, Modernism and the West,* edited by Gema Martin Munoz, I.B. Tauris (London, England), 1999; *La spiritualité, un défi pour notre socieété,* with Michel Bertrand, Michel Morneau, Luc Pareydt, Tawhid and Réveils (Lyon, France), 2000; *La Méditerranée, Frontières et passages,* by Thierry Fabre, Actes Sud (Babel, France), 1999; *L'irrationnel, menace ou nécessité?,* Le Monde, Le Seuil (Paris, France), 1999; *ILa non-violence? Des images idéales à l'épreuve du réel,* Féd. Nationales des enseignants de yoga, Dervy (Paris, France), 2000.

SIDELIGHTS: Tariq Ramadan is an academic who has contributed to the worldwide debate concerning Muslims in the West and the Islamic revival in the Muslim world. In addition to social justice and dialogue, Ramadan—predicted by the editors at *Time* magazine to be one of the twenty-first century's most influential people—proposes a reconciliation between European Muslims and European lifestyles. "We need to separate Islamic principles from their cultures of origin and anchor them in the cultural reality of Western Europe," the author told Nicholas Le Quesne in an interview for *Time Online.* The author went on to note: "I can incorporate everything that's not opposed to my religion into my identity, and that's a revolution." Ramadan is viewed as a controversial figure by some observers, who also accuse him of anti-Semitism. Ramadan's visa to the U.S. was revoked in 2004, preventing him from accepting a professorship at the University of Notre Dame.

The author has written several books focusing on Islam, Muslims, and the West. For example, in his 2004 book, *Western Muslims and the Future of Islam,* Ramadan, according to a contributor to the *Economist,* provides a "mix of orthodox and radical ideas, mingling social activism, religious tolerance and feminism with close adherence to Muslim tradition."

In *In the Footsteps of the Prophet: Lessons from the Life of Muhammad,* the author focuses on the teachings of the prophet of Islam. "The purpose of the book was not to correct or to come with new revelations about his life," the author told Steve Paulson in an interview for *Salon.com.* "It's really a rereading of his life, stressing two dimensions. The first one is spiritual. We can extract from his life the spiritual lessons for now and forever. And the second dimension is about contemporary lessons as to our relationships with our neighbor, with nature, with people from other religions. So it's really to come back to the teachings, the lessons and the meditations."

"For the non-Muslim reader the book offers a window onto a classic Islamic theme, while at the same time wrestling with urgent contemporary issues," wrote Richard McGregor in the *Christian Century.* "The book will also be welcomed among thoughtful Muslims, both in the West and the Islamic world, as an articulate progressive reading of a very traditional story." A *Publishers Weekly* contributor referred to *In the Footsteps of the Prophet* as an "excellent, engaging book" and also noted that the author "ably demonstrates why Muhammad is a spiritual paragon to the followers of Islam." Writing in the *Library Journal,* Sandra Collins commented: "Thoughtful and accessible, this book offers much of interest to those looking for a relatively uncritical spiritual discussion."

BIOGRAPHICAL AND CRITICAL SOURCES:

BOOKS

Favrot, Lionel, *Tariq Ramadan devoile,* Lyon Mag' Hors Serie (Lyon, France), 2004.

PERIODICALS

Biography, summer, 2007, Stephanie Giry, review of *In the Footsteps of the Prophet: Lessons from the Life of Muhammad,*

Christian Century, May 29, 2007, Richard McGregor, review of *In the Footsteps of the Prophet,* p. 37; August 21, 2007, "European Muslim: The Multiple Identity of Tariq Ramadan," p. 30.

Commentary, June, 2007, David Warren, "A Kinder, Gentler Islam?," p. 72.

Economist, March 6, 2004, "The Provoker; a Muslim Philosopher in Europe," p. 46.

Foreign Policy, November-December, 2004, "Who's Afraid of Tariq Ramadan?," p. 20.

Library Journal, March 15, 2007, Sandra Collins, review of *In the Footsteps of the Prophet,* p. 77.

Middle East Quarterly, summer, 2005, Isabelle Tahar Miller, "Tariq Ramadan Devoile."

National Catholic Reporter, January 7, 2005, "Tariq Ramadan," p. 4.

New Statesman, June 21, 2004, Andrew Hussey, "Tariq Ramadan: Some Call Him 'the Most Dangerous Man in Europe,rsquo; Others 'the Martin Luther of Islam.rsquo; Just How Sinister Is He?," p. 32; September 12, 2005, "Not a Fanatic after All? The Sun Thinks He's Dangerous and the US Won't Let Him In, but He Is Welcome at Oxford and the Home Office Wants Him as an Adviser. Andrew Hussey Interviews the Muslim Thinker Tariq Ramadan," p. 16.

New York Times, February 4, 2007, Ian Buruma, "Tariq Ramadan Has an Identity Issue."

Publishers Weekly, November 27, 2006, review of *In the Footsteps of the Prophet,* p. 47.

Tikkun, July-August, 2007, "Is Tariq Ramadan Too Beautiful to Be True?," p. 23.

Time, April 26, 2004, Bruce Crumley, "Tariq Ramadan: Modernist or Extremist?," p. 116.

Time International, September 6, 2004, Elaine Shannon and Vivienne Walt, "Sins of the Grandfather," p. 15.

ONLINE

American Civil Liberties Union, http://www.aclu.org/ (October 10, 2007), brief profile of author.

New Republic, http://www.tnr.com/ (October 10, 2007), profile of author.

Prospect Magazine, http://www.sant.ox.ac.uk/ (October 10, 2007), Ehsan Masood, "Tariq Ramadan-,rdquo; interview with author.

St. Antony's College, Oxford University Web site, http://www.sant.ox.ac.uk/ (October 10, 2007), faculty profile of author.

Salon.com, http://www.salon.com/ (February 20, 2007), Steve Paulson, "The Modern Muslim," interview with author.

Tariq Ramadan Home Page, http://www.tariqramadan.com (October 10, 2007).

Time Online, http://www.time.com/ (October 10, 2007), Nicholas Le Quesne, "Trying to Bridge a Great Divide," profile of author.

What Is Enlightenment?, http://www.wie.org/ (October 10, 2007), brief profile of author.

*   *   *

RANNEY, Joseph A. 1952-

PERSONAL: Born May 19, 1952, in Urbana, IL. *Education:* University of Chicago, B.A., 1972; Yale Law School, J.D., 1978.

ADDRESSES: Office—Marquette University Law School, Sensenbrenner Hall, 1103 W. Wisconsin Ave., P.O. Box 1881, Milwaukee, WI 53201; DeWitt, Ross, & Stevens, Capitol Sq. Office, 2 E. Mifflin St., Madison, WI 53703. *E-mail*—jar@dewittross.net.

CAREER: Lawyer, historian, educator, and writer. DeWitt, Ross, & Stevens, Madison, WI, lawyer and shareholder; Marquette University, Milwaukee, WI, adjunct professor of law. Legal Services of Northeastern Wisconsin, board of directors, 1982-1988, treasurer, 1985-1987, and president, 1987-1988. Also serves on the board of the Exchange Center for Child Abuse Prevention; former member of the Dane County Bar Association board of directors and former president and board member of Legal Services of Northeastern Wisconsin. *Military service:* U.S. Army, 1972-1975.

MEMBER: American Bar Association, Dane County Bar Association, State Bar of Wisconsin, Phi Beta Kappa.

AWARDS, HONORS: Charles Dunn Award for Legal Writing, State Bar of Wisconsin, 1993; President's Award for Meritorious Achievement, State Bar of Wisconsin, 2003.

WRITINGS:

Wisconsin's Legal History: An Article Series, Wisconsin Supreme Court (Madison, WI), 1998.

Trusting Nothing to Providence: A History of Wisconsin's Legal System, University of Wisconsin Law School (Madison, WI), 1999.

In the Wake of Slavery: Civil War, Civil Rights, and the Reconstruction of Southern Law, Praeger Publishers (Westport, CT), 2006.

Author of articles on legal history.

SIDELIGHTS: Joseph A. Ranney is a lawyer and legal historian who has written several books focusing on historical aspects of the law. In *Trusting Nothing to Providence: A History of Wisconsin's Legal System,* for example, the author provides what may be the first comprehensive history of one state's legal system. *Library Journal* contributor Margaret M. Jobe called the book "a thorough examination of . . . Wisconsin's legal history." Ranney focuses on the legal aspects of Reconstruction following the Civil War in his book *In the Wake of Slavery: Civil War, Civil Rights, and the Reconstruction of Southern Law.* The author writes of how Southern states, facing social turmoil, reconstructed their legal systems as they sought to regain social, economic, and political equilibrium. According to the author, the states reformed their laws with little interference from the Federal government. In addition to exploring various laws, such as the Jim Crow Laws, the author profiles many of the central legal and political figures of the South in the late 1860s. A *Reference & Research Book News* contributor called the book "a fascinating account" of how the legal system changed in the South. Elliot Mandel, writing in *Booklist,* referred to *In the Wake of Slavery* as a "careful and well-organized study."

BIOGRAPHICAL AND CRITICAL SOURCES:

PERIODICALS

Booklist, February 1, 2007, Elliot Mandel, review of *In the Wake of Slavery: Civil War, Civil Rights, and the Reconstruction of Southern Law,* p. 27.

Library Journal, May 15, 2001, Margaret M. Jobe, review of *Trusting Nothing to Providence: A History of Wisconsin's Legal System,* p. 65.

Reference & Research Book News, February, 2007, review of *In the Wake of Slavery.*

ONLINE

DeWitt, Ross, & Stevens Web site, http://www.dewittross.com/ (August 27, 2007), biographical information on author.

Lawyers.com, http://www.lawyers.com/ (August 27, 2007), career information on author.

Marquette University Law School Web site, http://law.marquette.edu/ (August 27, 2007), faculty profile of author.

* * *

RANSOM, Roberto 1960-

PERSONAL: Born May 8, 1960, in Mexico City, Mexico; married; children: three. *Ethnicity:* Irish, Irish American. *Education:* Universidad Nacional Autónoma de Mexico, B.A.; University of Virginia, M.A., Ph.D.

ADDRESSES: Home—Chihuahua, Mexico.

CAREER: Writer, educator.

AWARDS, HONORS: National Prize for Children's Literature, Mexico, 2003.

WRITINGS:

En esa otra tierra, Alianza Editorial (Mexico City, Mexico), 1991.

Historia de dos leones, Ediciones El Aduanero (Naucalpan, Mexico), 1994, translation by Jasper Reid published as *A Tale of Two Lions: A Novel,* Norton (New York, NY), 2007.

Desaparecidos, animales y artistas, Consejo Nacional para la Cultura y las Artes (Mexico City, Mexico), 1999.

La línea del agua, Joaquín Mortiz (Mexico City, Mexico), 1999.

Te guardaré la espalda, Joaquín Mortiz (Mexico City, Mexico), 2002.

SIDELIGHTS: Mexican-born writer Roberto Ransom is the author of several books in his native Spanish, but *A Tale of Two Lions: A Novel* is the first of his works to be published in English translation. The book is actually a series of three linked stories, whose common thread is two cats: Cattino, a pet cat that might in actuality be a lion, and Pasha, a stuffed lion that might actually be real. In the first tale, a count is jealous of the attention his wife lavishes on her pet cat, Cattino, even as they await the arrival of their guests for a dinner party. The second story follows the adventures of Pasha, a stuffed and mounted lion who is supposedly under the watchful eye of Jeremiah Jones, a tourism official who is paid to dress as a big-game hunter for the tourists. When Pasha vanishes, Jones is accused of stealing the creature. In the final story, Pasha and Cattino meet. Tiffany Lee-Youngren, in a review for the *San Diego Union-Tribune Online,* found the book failed to live up to its critical acclaim, stating: "There's a difference between simple and lacking, and Ransom's stories leave far too much up to the imagination, and far too little for extrapolation." However, Barbara Fisher, reviewing for the *Boston Globe Online,* found the stories to be charming, and the two cats "delightfully unreliable narrators well suited to the enigmatic stories they have to tell." Alexander McCall Smith, reviewing in the *New York Times Book Review,* commented that "while Ransom's book is charming, it is perhaps a bit too brief to explore its theme of lions lost and found."

BIOGRAPHICAL AND CRITICAL SOURCES:

PERIODICALS

Kirkus Reviews, November 15, 2006, review of *A Tale of Two Lions: A Novel,* p. 1151.

New York Times Book Review, January 28, 2007, Alexander McCall Smith, "Big Cats," p. 21.

Publishers Weekly, November 20, 2006, review of *A Tale of Two Lions,* p. 37.

ONLINE

Boston Globe Online, http://www.boston.com/ (January 7, 2007), Barbara Fisher, "Short Takes," review of *A Tale of Two Lions.*

Coordinacion Nacional de Literatura, http://www. literaturainba.com/ (October 10, 2007), Spanish author biography.

San Diego Union-Tribune Online, http://www.signon sandiego.com/ (May 6, 2007), Tiffany Lee-Youngren, "A Child Might Be the Best Guide When Trapped 'In the Country of Men.'"*

*   *   *

RATCLIFF, R.A. 1963-
   (Rebecca Ann Ratcliff)

PERSONAL: Born 1963.

ADDRESSES: *Home*—CA.

CAREER: Writer, consultant, educator. Previously taught history at the University of San Francisco and the University of California at Berkeley; lectured on cryptologic history at the National Security Agency intelligence school.

WRITINGS:

Delusions of Intelligence: Enigma, Ultra, and the End of Secure Ciphers, Cambridge University Press (New York, NY), 2006.

Contributor to journals, including *Intelligence, National Security,* and *Cryptologia.*

SIDELIGHTS: R.A. Ratcliff is an expert on cryptologic history, and has lectured on the subject at the National Security Agency intelligence school. She has also taught history on the university level, at both the University of San Francisco and the University of California at Berkeley. She works as a consultant in Silicon Valley and is a contributor to various periodicals, including *Intelligence, National Security,* and *Cryptologia.* Her first book, *Delusions of Intelligence: Enigma, Ultra, and the End of Secure Ciphers,* was published in 2006. The book addresses intelligence communications during World War II from the point of view of the Germans, including an analysis of the supposedly fool-proof encryption machine, Enigma, that the Germans utilized during the war. Ratcliff goes on to highlight the ways in which the Allied Forces took advantage of opportunities for advancement in technology and accessing intelligence whenever the Germans made errors in judgment or their encryptions failed. A reviewer for *Publishers Weekly* called the book "provocative," and Graeme S. Mount, reviewing in the *Canadian Journal of History,* pointed out that "Ratcliff provides balance. This is not simply a story of Allied successes and German mistakes." Mount went on to note that, "without an understanding of Ultra, one cannot understand the military campaign against the Axis belligerents."

BIOGRAPHICAL AND CRITICAL SOURCES:

PERIODICALS

Canadian Journal of History, winter, 2006, Graeme S. Mount, review of *Delusions of Intelligence: Enigma, Ultra, and the End of Secure Ciphers,* p. 579.
Foreign Affairs, January 1, 2007, Lawrence D. Freedman, "Military, Scientific, and Technological— Delusions of Intelligence: Enigma, Ultra, and the End of Secure Ciphers," p. 161.
Publishers Weekly, June 12, 2006, review of *Delusions of Intelligence,* p. 43.*

* * *

RATCLIFF, Rebecca Ann
    See RATCLIFF, R.A.

* * *

REDDI, Rishi

PERSONAL: Born in Hyderabad, Andhra Pradesh, India; immigrated to the United States, naturalized citizen; married; children: a daughter. *Education:* Swarthmore College, graduated, 1988; Northeastern University School of Law, J.D., 1992.

ADDRESSES: *Home*—Brookline, MA. *Agent*— Lippincott Massie McQuilkin, 80 5th Ave., Ste. 1101, New York, NY 10011.

CAREER: Writer and lawyer. Has worked as an enforcement attorney for state and federal environmental protection agencies, and as a lawyer for the Massachusetts Secretary of Environment. Also serves on the board of directors of South Asian American Leaders of Tomorrow.

AWARDS, HONORS: Pushcart Prize honorable mention, 2004; fellow, Bread Loaf Writers' Conference, 2007; Individual Artist's Grant, Massachusetts Cultural Council.

WRITINGS:

Karma and Other Stories, Ecco (New York, NY), 2007.

Short story appeared in *Best American Short Stories 2005;* contributor of short stories to periodicals, including the *Harvard Review, Louisville Review* and *Prairie Schooner.* English translations of Telugu short fiction has appeared in *Partisan Review.*

ADAPTATIONS: One of Reddi's stories was recorded for National Public Radio's *Selected Shorts* program.

SIDELIGHTS: A practicing lawyer, Rishi Reddi is also an accomplished short-story writer whose first collection of stories, *Karma and Other Stories,* was called a "startlingly mature collection" by a contributor to the *New Yorker.* Many of the seven stories take place in a fictionalized Boston community populated by Telugu Indian immigrants. (Telugu is a language spoken primarily in southern India.) "I wrote about what I'm familiar with and what's important to me: the stories around Indian immigration to this country, what we sacrifice and what we gain as immigrants," Reddi told Jeanne Fredriksen in an interview on the *India Currents* Web site. The author added: "Why do some people choose to give up everything that is familiar to them—family, home, and community—to travel to another country and culture and start from scratch?" The author's stories often focus on conflict within families, such as the differences between a successful doctor in America and his newly arrived mother from India in the story "Bangles." Others explore the differences between Indian and American or Western culture, such as the story "The Validity of

Love," in which two young, hip American women of Indian descent disagree about arranged marriages. "This excellent debut collection is deceptively easy to read," wrote Marta Segal Block in *Booklist*. A *Kirkus Reviews* contributor commented: "Reddi's voice is gentle and her eye watchful, and the dilemmas of her often-isolated characters are by no means solely those of the immigrant community."

BIOGRAPHICAL AND CRITICAL SOURCES:

PERIODICALS

Booklist, January 1, 2007, Marta Segal Block, review of *Karma and Other Stories*, p. 57.

Kirkus Reviews, December 1, 2006, review of *Karma and Other Stories*, p. 1195.

New Yorker, April 9, 2007, review of *Karma and Other Stories*, p. 85.

Prairie Schooner, fall, 2002, Rishi P. Reddi, "Karma," short story by author.

Publishers Weekly, December 4, 2006, review of *Karma and Other Stories*, p. 33.

ONLINE

India Currents, http://www.indiacurrents.com/ (April 5, 2007), Jeanne Fredriksen, "Instant Karma," review of *Karma and Other Stories*.

Lippincott Massie McQuilkin Literary Agents Web site, http://www.lmqlit.com/ (August 28, 2007), brief profile of author.

Rishi Reddi Home Page, http://www.rishireddi.net (August 28, 2007).

Small Spiral Notebook, http://www.smallspiral notebook.com/ (August 28, 2007), Cara Setichek, "Cara Seitchek interviews Rishi Reddi, author of *Karma and Other Stories*."

*   *   *

REGAN, Linda 1959-

PERSONAL: Born November 5, 1959, in London, England; married Brian Murphy (an actor), March 14, 1993.

ADDRESSES: Agent—Andrew Manson Personal Management, 288 Munster Rd., London SW6 6BQ, England. *E-mail*—lindareganonline.co.uk.

CAREER: Actress and writer. Has acted on stage, television, and film. Movies include *Carry On England*, 1977, and *The Last Horror Movie*, 2003. Television credits include British series *Hi-De-HI!*, 1984-1988; *Birds of a Feather*, 1991; *Framed*, 1993; *The Knock*, 1995; *Harry and Cosh*, 2002-04; *Doctors*, 2004; *Holby City*, 2007. Appeared in numerous stage plays in Great Britain, including *You're Only Young Twice*, national tour; *Alan Aykbourn's Norman Conquests*, tour; *Stepping Out*, The Mill at Sonning; *The Rivals* and *Norman Conquests*, both at Hever Castle Open Air Theatre; *MacBeth*, Cannizaro Open Air Theatre; *Day in the Death of Joe Egg*, Chelmsford Civic Theatre; *Filthy Firar*, Orange Tree Theatre; *Dirty Linen*, West End; *The Legend*, in the role of Marylin Monroe; *Once in a Lifetime*, directed by Trevor Nunn, in the role of Florabelle. Has also acted with the Royal Shakespeare Company, performed book readings, and worked as a resident actress on BBC Radio 4 plays.

WRITINGS:

"DI BANHAM AND SERGEANT ALISON GRAINGER" CRIME SERIES

Behind You!, Creme de la Crime (Chesterfield, England), 2006.

Passion Killers, Creme de la Crime (Chesterfield, England), 2007.

SIDELIGHTS: A working actress in Great Britain since she was a child, Linda Regan uses her background working on the stage for her "DI Banham and Sergeant Alison Grainger" crime series. "My head is full of crime fiction," Regan noted in an interview on the *Shots* Web site. "I've always wanted to write it down—and now I've got the chance." The first book in the series, *Behind You!*, introduces readers to Detective Inspector Banham, who is still trying to recover emotionally from the murder of his wife and baby daughter ten years earlier. The novel finds the inspector investigating the death of an actress killed by a stage weight falling on her during a performance on the British pantomime circuit. Before long, with the help of Sergeant Grainger, whom the inspector secretly loves, the inspector knows the death was no accident. Another murder soon occurs, and Banham and Grainger also face a hostage crisis. *Booklist* contributor Emily Melton noted "the combination of offbeat characters and forceful prose." Several reviewers praised the author's evocation of the British theatre life. "The book certainly brings the unique ambience of small-town pantomime to vivid life," commented a contributor to the *Shots* Web site. Sharon Wheeler, writing on *ReviewingTheEvidence. com,* noted that the author is "good on the world she knows best—the theatre."

BIOGRAPHICAL AND CRITICAL SOURCES:

PERIODICALS

Booklist, February 1, 2007, Emily Melton, review of *Behind You!,* p. 36.

ONLINE

Internet Movie Database, http://www.imdb.com/ (August 28, 2007), information on author's film work.
Linda Regan Home Page, http://www.lindaregan online.co.uk (August 28, 2007).
ReviewingTheEvidence.com, http://www.reviewingthe evidence.com/ (August 28, 2007), Sharon Wheeler, review of *Behind You!*
Shots, http://www.shotsmag.co.uk/ (August 28, 2007), interview with author.

*   *   *

RICH, Simon 1984-

PERSONAL: Born 1984; son of Frank (a newspaper columnist) and Gail (a book editor) Rich. *Education:* Harvard University, B.A., 2007. *Hobbies and other interests:* Run, cook, and play music with friends.

ADDRESSES: Home—New York, NY. *Agent*—Levine Greenberg Literary Agency, 307 7th Ave., Ste. 2407, New York, NY 10001.

CAREER: Writer.

WRITINGS:

Ant Farm: And Other Desperate Situations, Random House Trade Paperbacks (New York, NY), 2007.

Contributor to periodicals, including the *New Yorker* and *Mad* magazine.

SIDELIGHTS: Simon Rich graduated from Harvard University in 2007, where he served a stint as president of the satirical *Harvard Lampoon.* He also sold his first book prior to graduation, *Ant Farm: And Other Desperate Situations,* a collection of comedic short sketches that focuses on the tragic end of childhood and what that means for each person setting out as a newly minted adult. Three of the pieces appeared in the *New Yorker* prior to the book's release. Nick A. Zaino III, in a review for *Paste,* noted that Rich's position on the *Lampoon* staff and as the son of *New York Times* columnist Frank Rich might easily have garnered him his book deal, but went on to state that the quality of his writing stood on its own. Zaino concluded: "*Ant Farm* is simple, smart and easily digestible, and that's a potent combination these days." Rich himself addressed obvious comparisons to his father in an interview with James Sullivan for the *Boston Globe Online,* noting the differences in their approaches: "My dad writes about the fate of the free world, and I write about dogs, video games, and bears." *Forbes Online* reviewer Marisa Rindone noted: "It is clear that Simon Rich has potential . . . and he has a definite talent for boiling situations down to their desperate, at times touching, cores." *Booklist* reviewer Allison Block opined that Rich "displays a knack for extracting humor from scenarios of discomfort and despair."

BIOGRAPHICAL AND CRITICAL SOURCES:

PERIODICALS

Booklist, March 1, 2007, Allison Block, review of *Ant Farm: And Other Desperate Situations,* p. 53.
Library Journal, April 15, 2007, Joyce Sparrow, review of *Ant Farm,* p. 89.

Publishers Weekly, February 5, 2007, review of *Ant Farm,* p. 50.

ONLINE

Boston Globe Online, http://www.boston.com/ (April 1, 2007), James Sullivan, "Scared Silly," review of *Ant Farm.*
Forbes Online, http://www.forbes.com/ (September 4, 2007), Marisa Rindone, "Ant Farm and Other Daydreams."
Gothamist Web site, http://gothamist.com/ (June 22, 2007), "Simon Rich, Author, Ant Farm."
Harvard Crimson Online, http://www.thecrimson.com/ (April 6, 2007), Zachary M. Seward, "Rich '06-'07 Scores a Home Run in Debut."
Levine Greenberg Literary Agency Web site, http://www.levinegreenberg.com/ (October 10, 2007), author profile.
Paste, http://www.pastemagazine.com/ (April 19, 2007), Nick A. Zaino III, review of *Ant Farm.*
Simon Rich MySpace Page, http://www.myspace.com/simonrich (October 10, 2007).*

* * *

RICHARDSON, Brian W. 1966-
(Brian William Richardson)

PERSONAL: Born 1966. *Education:* University of Victoria, B.A. (political science) and B.A. (philosophy), both (with first-class honors), 1989, M.A. (political science), 1992; University of Hawaii, M.A. (philosophy), 1996, Ph.D. (political science), 2001, M.LIS., 2002, Ph.D. (philosophy), 2005.

ADDRESSES: Home—Honolulu, HI. *Office*—Library, Windward Community College, 45-720 Keaahala Rd., Kaneohe, HI 96744. *E-mail*—richards@hawaii.edu.

CAREER: Bolen Books, Victoria, British Columbia, Canada, bookstore clerk, 1980-91; Windward Community College, Kaneohe, HI, instructor. Conference presenter; guest on radio programs; public speaker.

MEMBER: Hawaii Library Association (member of executive board, 2006—), Beta Phi Mu.

AWARDS, HONORS: Grants from Hawaii Council for Humanities, 2005, 2006.

WRITINGS:

Longitude and Empire: How Captain Cook's Voyages Changed the World, University of British Columbia Press (Vancouver, British Columbia, Canada), 2006.

Contributor to *Canadian Review of Comparative Literature;* also reviewer for other periodicals.

SIDELIGHTS: When asked who or what influences his work, Brian W. Richardson told *CA:* "The struggle with understanding and writing about the works of some key philosophers, including Thomas Hobbes, G.W.F. Hegel, and Ludwig Wittgenstein.

"[My writing process] is really a rewriting process: printing out a draft, marking it up, entering the corrections, and then printing out another draft."

Richardson identified *A Confederacy of Dunces* by John Kennedy Toole and *Animal Farm* by George Orwell as two of his favorite books, "because they show how foolish people (or animals) can be.

"I hope *Longitude and Empire: How Captain Cook's Voyages Changed the World,* replaces the reverence that is paid to Captain Cook with a greater understanding of how the voyages connect to the intellectual history of Europe and the world."

* * *

RICHARDSON, Brian William
See RICHARDSON, Brian W.

* * *

RIFFLE, Ernest
See BERGMAN, Ingmar

RINGWALD, Christopher D.

PERSONAL: Married Amy Biancolli (a writer and critic); children: three. *Education:* Georgetown University, B.S.; Columbia University, M.S.; St. Bernard's Institute, M.A.

ADDRESSES: Office—Sage Colleges, 140 New Scotland Ave., Albany, NY 12208. *E-mail*—ringwc@sage.edu; ringwald@capital.net.

CAREER: Journalist, writer, and educator. Advocates for Human Potential, Inc., senior writer; Sage Colleges, Albany, NY, visiting scholar and director of the Faith & Society Project. Former reporter for the *Times Union,* Albany.

AWARDS, HONORS: General Excellence Award, Hearst Newspapers, 1990; 2002 Albany Author of the Year; first-place award from the Catholic Press Association, 2003, 2006.

WRITINGS:

Faith in Words: Ten Writers Reflect on the Spirituality of Their Profession, ACTA Publications (Chicago, IL), 1997.
Jewish Farming Communities of Northeastern New York, Rathbone Gallery: Sage Colleges (Albany, NY), 1998.
The Soul of Recovery: Uncovering the Spiritual Dimension in the Treatment of Addictions, Oxford University Press (New York, NY), 2002.
A Day Apart: How Jews, Christians, and Muslims Find Faith, Freedom, and Joy on the Sabbath, Oxford University Press (New York, NY), 2007.

Contributor to periodicals, including the *Wall Street Journal, Washington Post, Commonweal, Governing,* and *Christian Science Monitor.*

SIDELIGHTS: Christopher D. Ringwald has written on mental health, religion, books, law, social policy, and conflict and reconciliation in Iraq and Uganda. His books have primarily focused on various aspects of religion. For example, his 2002 book, *The Soul of*

Recovery: Uncovering the Spiritual Dimension in the Treatment of Addictions, explores the role that spirituality plays in different addiction treatment programs. The author discusses specific aspects of various programs' spiritual components, such as meditation and prayer, and also explores controversial issues associated with faith-based treatments. Much of the book is based on the author's numerous interviews with doctors, scientists, counselors, and addicts' family members. "This is an important book," wrote William A. Barry in a review in *America.* Commenting on the author's profiles of recovery addicts, Barry noted: "Many of these are moving tributes to the power of some kind of belief, even if it is only belief in the treatment group." Other reviewers also had praise for *The Soul of Recovery.* For example, *Insight on the News* contributor John Elvin called it "a very solid, thoroughly documented . . . book."

A Day Apart: How Jews, Christians, and Muslims Find Faith, Freedom, and Joy on the Sabbath is an examination of how the Jewish, Christian, and Muslim faiths share the idea that a day should be set aside for rest and contemplation. The author explores each religion's view of the Sabbath and its importance and describes the specific customs associated with each religion's observance, as well as modern controversies surrounding these customs. The author also follows his own family's observance of the Sabbath and the observances of two other families. "For Ringwald . . . [and the other families] setting a day apart, helps them pace themselves in a world where we claim we can't find time for anything," wrote a contributor to the Albany *Times Union. A Day Apart* received widespread praise from critics. Anthony J. Elia, writing in the *Library Journal,* commented that this "splendid book is a welcome addition to the contemporary discussions of interreligious conversations." *Booklist* contributor Bryce Christensen noted the author's "careful scholarship."

Ringwald told *CA:* "When I was a student at Our Lady of Mercy grammar school, a teacher assigned me to write up a newspaper on school activities. The issue was cancelled. 'Too negative,' she said. She then had me report on Christmas activities in all the grades. That was cancelled as well. Again, too negative. And about Christmas! But thanks to that teacher, I fell in love with the exercise of going somewhere, talking to the people there, and reporting on them and their lives. I resumed journalism in college, notably with a series of columns examining Georgetown University's Catholic identity and fidelity thereto. Ever since, I have tended to ask people about their beliefs, why they hold these, and how these shape their lives. This combines with an interest in journalism that matters, that touches on the important issues of life. (I also enjoy writing on other topics, such as books and art, and lighter topics, such as quirky social trends and habits and idiosyncratic characters.) My interest in writing sharpened when I worked on an international human rights law project in Washington, DC. Though our targeted lobbying and educational work saved lives, I saw that journalists who informed the world about oppression could have a larger impact.

"I seek to make a difference and, like all good reporters, to inform, educate and entertain. At the same time, I took to heart Henry James' advice: 'Try to be one of those people on whom nothing is lost.' Nothing is too small or insignificant to bear some importance, perhaps unseen or yet unrealized. A great influence and potential dwells in many an overlooked aspect of people and life. One needs only to pay attention, think it through, and get it down on paper. I am particularly interested in publicizing the fate of oppressed people and exploring the role of faith in social reconciliation after war or conflict and in personal recovery from addictions, madness, and other troubles.

"I write to figure out what I think. I write as soon as possible in the process to begin making sense of the material I've collected and to see what's missing. While reporting, I take notes in shorthand using reporter pads. I also record thoughts and events in pocket notebooks, journals, and legal pads. More and more, I draft on paper with pen or pencil. My thoughts are more fluid and sensible than when drafting on the computer. Subsequent drafts are online. I print, edit endlessly, and have others read and suggest revisions.

"The biggest surprise is how much fun it can be to work incredibly hard in researching and writing anything, from an essay to a book. My last book, *A Day Apart,* offered many an hour of bliss. The production and promotion was less blissful. But I always remember that it is an honor to write a book and have it published, and then to have people read it and engage with the fruit of my long days and years of work and discovery. I am thankful that my wife, Amy Biancolli, a movie critic and musical biographer, supports these endeavors, and for the friends, colleagues, editors and agents who make the work possible.

"I have great affection for my first book, *Faith in Words: Ten Writers Reflect on the Spirituality of Their Profession,* since it was my first. The next one, *The Soul of Recovery,* was exhausting but continues to reverberate. The most recent was a joy. In each case, I wrote a book I would have wanted to read on the topic. I trust that each delights and helps some people. With all three, I hope people will better know and understand how and why belief or faith shapes and saves lives. I hope also to show the many ways that men and women find God or the many ways that God finds us."

BIOGRAPHICAL AND CRITICAL SOURCES:

PERIODICALS

Alcoholism & Drug Abuse Weekly, September 16, 2002, "Book Examines Spirituality in Addiction Treatment," p. 6.

America, October 7, 2002, William A. Barry, "Keep the Faith," p. 23.

Christian Century, August 7, 2002, James C. Howell, review of *A Day Apart: How Jews, Christians, and Muslims Find Faith, Freedom, and Joy on the Sabbath,* pp. 34-36.

Insight on the News, June 17, 2002, John Elvin, "Found: Faith-Based Cures for Drug Abusers," p. 35.

Library Journal, February 1, 2007, Anthony J. Elia, review of *A Day Apart,* p. 77.

Times Union (Albany, NY), February 18, 2007, "New Book Explores How Jews, Christians, Muslims Gain More from Taking a Day of Rest."

ONLINE

Sage Colleges Web site, http://www.sage.edu/ (August 28, 2007), faculty profile of author.

University at Albany Web site, http://www.albany.edu/ (October 12, 2007), faculty profile of author.

ROSEN, Steven 1955-
  (Satyaraja Dasa)

PERSONAL: Born 1955. *Religion:* Hindu.

ADDRESSES: Home—NY.

CAREER: Writer. *Journal of Vaishnava Studies,* editor in chief.

WRITINGS:

NONFICTION

Food for the Spirit: Vegetarianism and the World Religions, Bala Books (New York, NY), 1987.

India's Spiritual Renaissance: The Life and Times of Lord Chaitanya, Folk Books (Brooklyn, NY), 1988.

Archeology and the Vaishnava Tradition: The Pre-Christian Roots of Krishna Worship, Firma KLM (Calcutta, India), 1989.

(Editor) *Vaisnavism: Contemporary Scholars Discuss the Gaudiya Tradition,* Folk Books (New York, NY), 1992.

Passage from India: The Life and Times of His Divine Grace A.C. Bhaktivedanta Swami Prabhupada: A Summary Study of Satsvarupa Dasa Goswami's Srila Prabhupada Lilamrta, Munshiram Manoharlal Publishers (New Delhi, India), 1992.

(Editor) *Vaisnavī: Women and the Worship of Krishna,* Motilal Banarsidass Publishers (Delhi, India), 1996.

Diet for Transcendence: Vegetarianism and the World Religions, Torchlight (Badger, CA), 1997.

The Reincarnation Controversy: Uncovering the Truth in the World Religions, Torchlight (Badger, CA), 1997.

Gita on the Green: The Mystical Tradition behind Bagger Vance, Continuum (New York, NY), 2000.

(Editor) *Holy War: Violence and the Bhagavad Gita,* Deepak Heritage Books (Hampton, VA), 2002.

The Hidden Glory of India, Bhaktivedanta Book Trust (Los Angeles, CA), 2002.

From Nothingness to Personhood: A Collection of Essays on Buddhism from a Vaishnava-Hindu Perspective, Rasbihari Lal (Vrindavan, India), 2003.

Holy Cow: The Hare Krishna Contribution to Vegetarianism and Animal Rights, Lantern Books (New York, NY), 2004.

Essential Hinduism, Praeger (Westport, CT), 2006.

Krishna's Song: A New Look at the Bhagavad Gita, Praeger (Westport, CT), 2007.

SIDELIGHTS: Steven Rosen, who took the name Satyaraja Dasa as a Hindu disciple, has written extensively on Hinduism and is editor of an academic journal on the religion's most widespread form, Vaishnavism. He is a disciple of A.C. Bhaktivedanta Swami Prabhupāda, a spiritual leader who was also the subject of one of Rosen's books. Rosen's writings include both works on Hinduism in general and others on specific aspects of the faith.

One of the more general books is *Essential Hinduism,* which covers the religion's history, beliefs, and rituals. *Library Journal* contributor C. Brian Smith called Rosen "the ideal author" to explain Hinduism and particularly Vaishnavism. Rosen's text, Smith added, "is of a high caliber," making the work of interest to scholars yet accessible to lay readers.

A look at a particular aspect of the Hindu religion— and others—is *The Reincarnation Controversy: Uncovering the Truth in the World Religions.* Rosen discusses the positions of Buddhism, Christianity, Judaism, and Islam in addition to Hinduism. He provides a "succinct survey" of what these faiths say about reincarnation, related Patricia Monaghan in *Booklist.* She found his exploration of Hindu and Buddhist beliefs particularly good but praised the rest of the work as well, deeming it "an excellent review" despite its "unnecessarily sensational title."

BIOGRAPHICAL AND CRITICAL SOURCES:

PERIODICALS

Booklist, October 1, 1997, Patricia Monaghan, review of *The Reincarnation Controversy: Uncovering the Truth in the World Religions,* p. 290.

Library Journal, February 1, 2007, C. Brian Smith, review of *Essential Hinduism,* p. 77.

Reference & Research Book News, February, 2007, review of *Essential Hinduism.**

*　　*　　*

ROSS, Ann B.

PERSONAL: Children: two daughters, one son. *Education:* Attended Armstrong College and Blue Ridge Technical College; University of North Carolina at Asheville, B.A.; University of North Carolina at Chapel Hill, M.A., Ph.D. *Hobbies and other interests:* Reading, needlepoint, horseback riding, spending time with family.

ADDRESSES: Home—Hendersonville, NC. *E-mail*—aross@missjulia.com.

CAREER: Novelist. Former professor of literature and humanities at University of North Carolina at Asheville. Also worked as an operating room nurse for five years.

WRITINGS:

The Murder Cure, Avon Books (New York, NY), 1978.
The Murder Stroke, 1981.
The Pilgrimage, Macmillan (New York, NY), 1987.

"MISS JULIA" SERIES

Miss Julia Speaks Her Mind, William Morrow (New York, NY), 1999.
Miss Julia Takes Over, Viking (New York, NY), 2001.
Miss Julia Throws a Wedding, Viking (New York, NY), 2002.
Miss Julia Hits the Road, Viking (New York, NY), 2003.
Miss Julia Meets Her Match, Viking (New York, NY), 2004.
Miss Julia's School of Beauty, Viking (New York, NY), 2005.
Miss Julia Stands Her Ground, Viking (New York, NY), 2006.
Miss Julia Strikes Back, Viking (New York, NY), 2007.
Miss Julia Paints the Town, Viking (New York, NY), 2008.

SIDELIGHTS: Novelist Ann B. Ross is the author of *Miss Julia Takes Over* and other works in her best-selling "Miss Julia" series, which features a proper but feisty septuagenarian from North Carolina. "I identify with Miss Julia to the extent that we've both been raised as Southern gentlewomen—to be gracious, agreeable, and socially correct in all that we do, regardless of how we actually feel," Ross commented in an interview on her home page. Asked if she based Miss Julia on someone from her own life, the author remarked, "I suppose I can say that she is a combination or blend of a lot of strong-minded, straight-talking women I've known. It is fascinating to me, though, that many readers tell me that they know 'a Miss Julia,' and they wonder if I've met their aunt or grandmother or neighbor."

Ross, who taught literature and the humanities at the University of North Carolina at Asheville, introduced her popular character in *Miss Julia Speaks Her Mind,* a 1999 title. After the sudden death of her husband, Wesley Lloyd Springer, a prudent banker and a mainstay of their small community, Julia DeWitt Springer receives yet another shock when Wesley's mistress, Hazel Marie Puckett, and their illegitimate nine-year-old son, Little Lloyd, arrive penniless at her doorstep. Despite criticism from her neighbors, Miss Julia reluctantly agrees to house the pair while fending off a greedy pastor who has designs on her inheritance. A critic in *Publishers Weekly* called the work "fast-paced and funny," and *Library Journal* reviewer Christopher Koranowsky similarly noted that Ross's "dialog produces laugh-out-loud responses."

In *Miss Julia Takes Over,* the strong-willed widow grows concerned when Hazel Marie doesn't return from her date with Wilson T. Hodge, a scheming church fundraiser. With the police of little assistance, Julia hires private investigator J.D. Pickens to locate the pair, though she insists on accompanying him as he pursues the case across the state. According to *Booklist* reviewer Mary Ellen Quinn, Ross permits "the reader to laugh gently at . . . Miss Julia while thoroughly enjoying the view through her eyes."

When Sheriff Coleman Bates and lawyer Binkie Enloe announce their engagement, Miss Julia offers to let them use her home for the ceremony in *Miss Julia Throws a Wedding.* All of her plans seem for naught, however, when Binkie develops cold feet and wants to back out, among other calamities. "Ross gets a bit carried away with wedding details, but her cheeky style works flawlessly once Miss Julia digs into the romantic intrigue," a *Publishers Weekly* critic stated. In *Miss Julia Hits the Road,* the determined Southerner comes to the rescue of her longtime housekeeper, Lillian, whose home is threatened by a rapacious developer. Miss Julia teams with her love interest, lawyer Sam Murdoch, to organize a marathon fundraising event that finds her donning leather chaps and hopping on the back of a Harley Davidson. "Along with the opinionated and indomitable heroine, the series charms readers with its gentle humor and small-town southern setting," noted Quinn.

In *Miss Julia Meets Her Match,* the fifth work in Ross's series, Miss Julia confronts the owners of a dubious religious theme park and downplays rumors that another of her late husband's paramours has come to Abbotsville. In *Miss Julia's School of Beauty,* the spunky protagonist reluctantly agrees to help Hazel Marie with a beauty contest for Miss Abbot County Sheriff's Department, only to find the pageant contestants are sorely in need of assistance. Miss Julia's personal life is in shambles, too, as her quickie marriage to Sam may not be completely legal. "Fun for series fans, although a few of Ross' characters teeter dangerously close to being stereotypes," observed Quinn.

When Brother Vernon Puckett, Hazel Marie's troublesome uncle, disputes the parentage of Little Lloyd, Miss Julia and Sam attempt to retrieve some of her late husband's DNA in *Miss Julia Stands Her Ground.* While Sam is away, Miss Julia's home is broken into and her engagement ring is stolen in *Miss Julia Strikes Back.* With the help of Little Lloyd, Etta Mae Wiggins, and private eye Frank Tuttle, Miss Julia heads to Florida to recover the missing goods. Quinn described the novel as "a wacky and mildly suspenseful escapade."

BIOGRAPHICAL AND CRITICAL SOURCES:

PERIODICALS

Booklist, June 1, 1999, Nancy Pearl, review of *Miss Julia Speaks Her Mind,* p. 1795; July, 2001, Mary

Ellen Quinn, review of *Miss Julia Takes Over,* p. 1983; May 15, 2002, Mary Ellen Quinn, review of *Miss Julia Throws a Wedding,* p. 1577; April 15, 2003, Mary Ellen Quinn, review of *Miss Julia Hits the Road,* p. 1451; April 15, 2004, Mary Ellen Quinn, "Ann B. Ross' Miss Julia," p. 1426; March 15, 2005, Mary Ellen Quinn, review of *Miss Julia's School of Beauty,* p. 1267; March 1, 2007, Mary Ellen Quinn, review of *Miss Julia Strikes Back,* p. 69.

Library Journal, June 15, 1999, Shannon Haddock, review of *Miss Julia Speaks Her Mind,* p. 110; January, 2000, Christopher Koranowsky, review of *Miss Julia Speaks Her Mind,* p. 200.

Publishers Weekly, May 24, 1999, review of *Miss Julia Speaks Her Mind,* p. 62; July 16, 2001, review of *Miss Julia Takes Over,* p. 160; April 8, 2002, review of *Miss Julia Throws a Wedding,* p. 205; March 31, 2003, review of *Miss Julia Hits the Road,* p. 45.

ONLINE

Ann B. Ross Home Page, http://www.missjulia.com (October 11, 2007).

Armchair Interviews, http://www.armchairinterviews. com/ (October 11, 2007), Julie Failla Earhart, review of *Miss Julia Stands Her Ground.*

Penguin Group Web site, http://us.penguingroup.com/ (October 11, 2007), "Ann B. Ross."*

*   *   *

ROTH, Louise Marie 1970-

PERSONAL: Born 1970; married; children: two sons. *Education:* McGill University, B.A., 1992; New York University, M.A., 1998; New York University, Ph.D., 2000.

ADDRESSES: Home—AZ. *E-mail*—lroth@email. arizona.edu.

CAREER: University of Arizona, Tucson, associate professor of sociology.

AWARDS, HONORS: Research grants from the National Science Foundation, University of Arizona, and Rogers Program on Law in Society.

WRITINGS:

Selling Women Short: Gender Inequality on Wall Street, Princeton University Press (Princeton, NJ), 2006.

Also author of blog on *Huffington Post.* Contributor to *Workplace/Women's Place: An Anthology,* 2nd edition, Roxbury Publishing (Los Angeles, CA), 2002. Contributor to periodicals, including *American Sociological Review, Sociological Forum, Sociological Inquiry, Sociological Quarterly,* and *Sociological Perspectives.*

SIDELIGHTS: Louise Marie Roth is a professor of sociology who specializes in gender issues. One of her particular areas of expertise is sex discrimination in employment. That topic is the basis of her book, *Selling Women Short: Gender Inequality on Wall Street.* In this volume, Roth explores the issue of inequities in the world of high finance. The book is based on her doctoral thesis, for which she compared the career and salary tracks of seventy-six men and women, with similar qualifications, who began Wall Street careers during the 1990s. Her findings indicate that despite regulations against gender discrimination, the best-paid members of that work force were consistently white, aggressive, heterosexual men. Though women and men may have started out on equal footing, various factors come together to direct female workers into sectors where pay is less, or to clients whose businesses have less funding than those of the more successful brokers—a situation that results in smaller bonuses. Despite official regulations, there is great importance attached to personal relationships between clients and brokers, and sealing these relationships sometimes hinges on activities such as hunting trips and visits to strip clubs—expeditions on which women might well feel uncomfortable and out-of-place. Roth's research indicated that having children also tended to damage a woman's career, even if she continued to work long hours, because she was perceived as less serious and less committed to her job. Reviewing Roth's book for *American: A Magazine of Ideas,* Laura Vanderkam commented: "The results of her survey are disconcerting for those of us who generally trust the free market to end discrimination." A reviewer for *Here Is the City* called *Selling Women Short* "a powerful new indictment of how the very systems put into place to address discrimination have allowed more subtle, but no less insidious, forms of discrimination."

BIOGRAPHICAL AND CRITICAL SOURCES:

PERIODICALS

Booklist, November 1, 2006, Mary Whaley, review of *Selling Women Short: Gender Inequality on Wall Street,* p. 11.

Library Journal, December 1, 2006, Wendy Wendt, review of *Selling Women Short,* p. 137.

USA Today, March 1, 2004, "Wall Street Still Favors Men," p. 8.

ONLINE

American: A Magazine of Ideas, http://www.american.com/ (November 21, 2006), Laura Vanderkam, "What Are Women Worth?"

Deal Breaker, http://www.dealbreaker.com/ (August 27, 2007), review of *Selling Women Short.*

Ethical Corporation Web site, http://www.ethicalcorp.com/ (August 27, 2007), "Special Reports: Extracting the Male from a Malefaction."

Here Is the City, http://news.hereisthecity.com/ (February 11, 2006), review of *Selling Women Short.*

Huffington Post, http://www.huffingtonpost.com/ (August 27, 2007), biographical information on Louise Marie Roth.

Louise Roth's Home Page, http://fp.arizona.edu/soc/lroth.htm (August 27, 2007).

University of Arizona News, http://uanews.org/ (September 14, 2006), Jeff Harrison, review of *Selling Women Short.*

*   *   *

RUDY, Susan 1961-
(Susan Rudy Dorscht, Susan Arlene Rudy Dorscht)

PERSONAL: Born May 7, 1961, in London, Ontario, Canada; daughter of Elvin (a high school principal) and Dorene (a human resources executive) Rudy; married Brian Dorscht, December 30, 1983 (divorced, October, 2007); companion of Frances Bowen (a university professor of business); children: Erin Frances, Julian Kathryn. *Ethnicity:* "Mennonite." *Education:* Wilfrid Laurier University, B.A. (hons.), 1984; University of New Brunswick, M.A., 1985; York University, Ph.D., 1988. *Politics:* New Democrat.

ADDRESSES: Home—Calgary, Alberta, Canada. *Office*—Department of English, University of Calgary, 2500 University Dr. N.W., Calgary, Alberta T2N 1N4, Canada. *E-mail*—susan.rudy@ucalgary.ca.

CAREER: University of Calgary, Calgary, Alberta, Canada, assistant professor, 1988-93, associate professor, 1993-99, professor of English, 1999—, department chair, 2003—. McGill University, visiting scholar at Centre for Research and Teaching on Women, 2002.

MEMBER: Modern Language Association, Canadian Association of Chairs of English (chair, 2007-08), Association of Canadian and Quebec Literatures (president, 1994-96), Association of Canadian College and University Teachers of English.

AWARDS, HONORS: Killam Foundation resident fellow, 1999; grants from Social Sciences and Humanities Research Council of Canada, 2001, and Canadian Federation for the Humanities, 2004.

WRITINGS:

(Under name Susan Rudy Dorscht) *Women, Reading, Kroetsch: Telling the Difference,* Wilfrid Laurier University (Waterloo, Ontario, Canada), 1991.

(Editor, with Nicole Brossard, and author of introduction) *Fluid Arguments* (essays), Mercury Press (Toronto, Ontario, Canada), 2005.

(With Pauline Butling) *Poets' Talk: Interviews with Marie Annharte Baker, Dionne Brand, Jeff Derksen, Daphne Marlatt, Robert Kroetsch, Erin Moure, and Fred Wah,* University of Alberta Press (Edmonton, Alberta, Canada), 2005.

(With Pauline Butling) *Writing in Our Time: Canada's Radical Poetries in English (1957-2003),* Wilfrid Laurier University Press (Waterloo, Ontario, Canada), 2005.

Contributor to books, including *The Politics of Art: Eli Mandel's Poetry and Criticism,* edited by E. Jewinski and A. Stubbs, Rodopi Press, 1993; *Precarious Present/Promising Future? Ethnicity and Identities in Canadian Literature,* edited by Janice Kulyk Keefer, Danielle Schaub, and Richard Sherwin, Magnes Press (Jerusalem, Israel), 1996; and *Assembling Alternatives: Reading Postmodern Poetries Transnationally,* edited by Romana Huk, Wesleyan University Press (Middletown, CT), 2003. Contributor to scholarly journals, including *Essays on Canadian Writing, International Journal of Canadian Studies, Canadian Fiction, Signature: Journal of Theory and Canadian Literature, Room of One's Own: Canadian Feminist Quarterly of Literature and Commentary,* and *Canadian Literature.* Editor of special issues, *Open Letter: Canadian Journal of Writing and Theory,* 2000, *English Studies in Canada,* 2001, 2003.

*   *   *

RUDY DORSCHT, Susan
     See RUDY, Susan

*   *   *

RUDY DORSCHT, Susan Arlene
     See RUDY, Susan

*   *   *

RUSSELL, Letty M. 1929-2007
   (Letty Mandeville Russell)

OBITUARY NOTICE— See index for *CA* sketch: Born September 20, 1929, in Westfield, NJ; died of cancer, July 12, 2007, in Guilford, CT. Minister, theologian, educator, and author. Russell was ordained a minister of the United Presbyterian Church in 1958, when women were less welcome at the pulpit than they are today. She was educated in the ministry at Harvard University and Union Theological Seminary in New York City, where she earned a doctorate in 1969. Russell was also one of the first women invited to teach at the Yale University Divinity School in the early 1970s, and she remained there for the rest of her academic career, teaching part-time after her formal retirement in 2001. Russell was described as an early champion of feminist theology, even before the notion of feminism took hold of the national conscience in the 1970s. As a minister in Harlem throughout most of the 1950s and 1960s she taught Bible classes that focused on oppressed people everywhere and women in particular. Her interpretation of the scriptures at that time, however, stressed the biblical theme of freedom rather than what some others perceived as a message of sexist oppression. She also promoted a round-table approach to participation in the church, rather than a discourse directed by a formal authority figure. In the 1980s Russell was a founding member of the Women's Theological Center in Boston, where she promoted the pursuit of feminist scholarship in a seminary setting. Her own scholarship is reflected in more than a dozen books, including Human Liberation in a Feminist Perspective: A Theology (1974), *Household of Freedom: Authority in Feminist Theology* (1987), and *Church in the Round: Feminist Interpretation of the Church* (1993). Russell's edited collections include *Feminist Interpretation of the Bible* (1985) and *Hagar, Sarah, and Their Children: Jewish, Christian, and Muslim Perspectives* (2006).

OBITUARIES AND OTHER SOURCES:

BOOKS

Farley, Margaret A., and Serene Jones, editors, *Liberating Eschatology: Essays in Honor of Letty M. Russell,* Westminster John Knox Press (Louisville, KY), 1999.

* * *

RUSSELL, Letty Mandeville
See RUSSELL, Letty M.

S

SAENZ, Gil 1941-
(Gilbert Saenz)

PERSONAL: Born October 17, 1941, in Detroit, MI; son of Valentine and Lena M. Saenz. *Ethnicity:* "Mexican-American." *Education:* Wayne State University, B.A., 1968. *Politics:* Democrat. *Religion:* Roman Catholic. *Hobbies and other interests:* Music.

ADDRESSES: Home—Melvindale, MI. *E-mail*—gilbertsaenz@comcast.net.

CAREER: Poet. Worked as a government employee in the field of information technology until retirement in 2004. *Military service:* U.S. Air Force, 1960-63.

MEMBER: Academy of American Poets, U.S. Diplomatic Courier Association, Poetry Society of Michigan.

WRITINGS:

POETRY

Moments in Time, illustrated by George Perazza, privately printed (Detroit, MI), 1995.
Dreaming of Love, Pentland Press (Raleigh, NC), 1999.
Poems of Life (bilingual in English and Spanish), Laredo Publishing (Beverly Hills, CA), 2001.
Spaces in Between: A Collection of Poems, 1st Books Library (Bloomington, IN), 2002.

(Editor) *The Other Side of Darkness: MDDA Anthology,* MDDA of Metro Detroit (Detroit, MI), 2003.

Also author of the short work "Colorful Impressions," with illustrations by George Perazza, privately printed, 1993. Contributor to *Downriver Reflections: Downriver Poets & Playwrights Member Anthology,* Volume 2, edited by Bob Rankin, 2007.

SIDELIGHTS: Gil Saenz told *CA:* "Writing, especially the writing of poetry, has been one of my main interests for many years now. It has been a source of great friendships and acquaintances. Even though I worked for the government until 2004, I managed to fit in some type of writing activity. I would write entries in my daily log book to describe the individual calls that I received while I was working on the customer service desk; sometimes this would amount to a small paragraph of narrative comments. I wanted to be able one day to write prose or poetry that could be enjoyed and admired by my readers.

"I don't have a systematic way of writing poems. I keep my notebook handy and write down my thoughts from time to time. I can always refer back to them to see if I have some good ideas or inspirations

"My poems usually are the result of certain ideas or feelings that are very striking to me. Poetry writing is the same as other types of writing. The more you practice, the closer you get to capturing your real insights on a particular subject. In this sense I feel that I am always changing, growing, and evolving."

SAENZ, Gilbert
   See **SAENZ, Gil**

*   *   *

SANTOGROSSI, Stephen

PERSONAL: Married to a psychologist; children: one daughter.

ADDRESSES: Home—Pomona, CA.

CAREER: Writer and business manager. Has also worked as an electronics technician, an insurance claims adjuster, and a disk jockey in Palm Springs, CA.

AWARDS, HONORS: St. Martin's Press/Malice Domestic Contest winner for best first traditional mystery, for *A Stranger Lies There.*

WRITINGS:

A Stranger Lies There (novel), St. Martin's Minotaur (New York, NY), 2007.

SIDELIGHTS: Stephen Santogrossi is the author of *A Stranger Lies There,* the winner of the St. Martin's Press/Malice Domestic Contest for best first traditional mystery. The novel centers on Tim Ryder, an unassuming carpenter who awakens one morning to find a corpse on the front lawn of his Palm Springs, California, home. A former student radical in the 1970s, Ryder wonders if the murder is connected to his role in a bungled bank robbery intended to fund the campaign of an antiwar presidential candidate; Ryder provided testimony against his group's ringleader, Glenn Turret, who just finished serving a thirty-year term in prison. The police investigating the case, however, consider Ryder a chief suspect, and they even cast suspicion on his wife, Deirdre, a former drug addict who works as a substance abuse counselor. When Ryder suffers an unexpected loss and discovers a clue the police have missed, he determines to solve the crime himself. According to a critic in *Publishers Weekly,* Santogrossi's "well-drawn characters, unexpected resolution and sharp casual insights make for an energizing read." Harriet Klausner, writing on the *I Love a Mystery* Web site, similarly noted: "The characters are fully developed, especially the reluctant hero Tim," and a contributor in *Kirkus Reviews* described *A Stranger Lies There,* as "a beautifully understated portrait of a hero who's a lot better at grieving than detecting."

BIOGRAPHICAL AND CRITICAL SOURCES:

PERIODICALS

Kirkus Reviews, April 1, 2007, review of *A Stranger Lies There.*
Publishers Weekly, March 19, 2007, review of *A Stranger Lies There,* p. 47.

ONLINE

Armchair Interviews, http://www.armchairinterviews. com/ (October 11, 2007), Diane Kasperski, review of *A Stranger Lies There.*
I Love a Mystery, http://www.iloveamysterynewsletter. com/ (October 29, 2007), Harriet Klausner, review of *A Stranger Lies There.*
New Mystery Reader, http://www.newmysteryreader. com/ (October 11, 2007), Susan Illis, review of *A Stranger Lies There.**

*   *   *

SAPPHIRE 1950-
   (Ramona Lofton)

PERSONAL: Born Ramona Lofton, 1950, in Fort Ord, CA; children: two. *Education:* Attended San Francisco City College in the 1970s; City College of New York, Brooklyn, NY, B.A. (with honors), 1983; Brooklyn College, M.F.A., c. 1993.

ADDRESSES: Home—New York, NY. *Office*—New School University, 55 W. 13th St., New York, NY 10011. *Agent*—Charlotte Sheedy Literary Agency, 65 Bleecker St., New York, NY 10012.

CAREER: Performance artist, educator, and author. Children's Aid Society, New York, NY, parent-child mediator, c. 1980s; reading instructor in Harlem and the Bronx, NY, c. 1980s-90s; New School University, New York, NY, faculty member; previously taught literature, fiction and poetry workshops at the State University of New York at Purchase, Trinity College, and the Writer's Voice in New York, NY; taught graduate writing workshops in M.F.A. programs at Fairleigh Dickinson University and Brooklyn College. Has also worked as a go-go dancer and house cleaner.

AWARDS, HONORS: Year of the Poet III Award, *Downtown* magazine, 1994; MacArthur Foundation Scholarship for poetry, 1994; First Novelist Award, Black Caucus of the American Library Association, and Stephen Crane Award for First Fiction, Book-of-the Month Club, both 1997, for *Push;* Outstanding Achievement in Teaching Award, City of New York, for work with literacy students in Harlem and the Bronx.

WRITINGS:

Meditations on the Rainbow: Poetry, Crystal Bananas Press (New York, NY), 1987.
American Dreams (poems and prose), Serpent's Tail/High Risk (New York, NY), 1994
Push (novel), Knopf (New York, NY), 1996.
Black Wings & Blind Angels: Poems, Knopf (New York, NY), 1999.

Contributor of prose and poetry to anthologies, including *Women on Women: An Anthology of American Lesbian Short Fiction,* edited by Joan Nestle and Naomi Holoch, Plume (New York, NY), 1990; *Critical Condition: Women on the Edge of Violence,* edited by Amy Scholder, City Lights Books (San Francisco, CA), 1993; and *High Risk 2: Writings on Sex, Death, and Subversion,* edited by Amy Scholder and Ira Silverberg, Plume (New York, NY), 1994. Also contributor to *Portable Lower East Side,* and to other periodicals.

SIDELIGHTS: A traumatic upbringing and later work with traumatized students in Harlem inform the work of African American poet and novelist Sapphire. The daughter of an abusive father and an alcoholic mother, who abandoned the family when Sapphire was barely a teenager, this controversial writer frequently addresses themes of incest, rape, and child abuse, as well as racism.

Born Ramona Lofton, Sapphire grew up in a middle-class family in California. Both of her parents were in the military, and the family moved frequently within the United States and Europe during Sapphire's early childhood. When Sapphire was thirteen, they settled in Los Angeles, and Sapphire's mother left the family. After leaving high school and connecting with the black power movement and later with drugs, Sapphire adopted her new name. She told D.T. Max of *Harper's Bazaar:* "It was a New Age thing. I had read somewhere that the rays emitted by sapphires can change the molecular structure of other gemstones—and that was exactly what I wanted to do with my life." She studied chemistry, and then dance, at San Francisco City College before moving to New York in 1977.

Sapphire worked at a variety of odd jobs while starting to experiment with poetry and performance art in Greenwich Village in the early 1980s. But the decade was a difficult one for the writer. She reconnected with her mother in the late 1970s, but her mother died in June of 1986. That same year, Sapphire's brother, who was then homeless and suffered from schizophrenia, was murdered in a Los Angeles park. She also began to have memories of incest. She confronted her father with her suspicions that he had sexually abused her, but he denied it. Sapphire's sister, however, confirmed the events Sapphire remembered. Other friends died during the next three years, marking an intensely dark period in her life, but she later recalled that coming through that time was actually freeing. In *Harper's Bazaar* the author noted: "A shade opened up, and suddenly my life was rescued for me."

In 1989 Sapphire wrote a poem called "Wild Thing," which was inspired in part by the "wilding" of a jogger in Central Park that had made national news. Her poem was written in the voice of one of the young men accused of the rape, and her empathy for the young man, whom she imagined as abused and oppressed himself, stirred the anger of both liberal feminists and conservatives of the Religious Right. (The convictions of the five men accused of the crime were challenged in 2002, after DNA evidence and the confession of another man called the verdict into question). Reverend Donald Wildmon discovered the poem and was outraged by one of its images, which presents Jesus in a sexual situation with an altar boy. Taking the lines out of context (Sapphire intended the image to represent the abuse of children by members of the clergy), Wildmon and Senator Jesse Helmes used the poem to attack the National Endowment for the Arts (NEA), which funded the journal in which the poem first appeared. John Frohnmayer, then head of the NEA, defended the poem and was eventually forced to resign. In his memoir, *Leaving Town Alive,* Frohnmayer continued to support Sapphire's work, writing: "[The poem is] not meant to make us feel good. It's not meant as an apology for a violent act. And it's certainly not meant to be sacrilegious, unless pedophilia is part of religious dogma. The poem is meant to make us think and reflect on an incredibly brutal act in an allegedly civilized society."

Sapphire was also thrust into the spotlight as her poem became a symbol of government-funded filth for some and an icon of free speech for others. The event made her feel exploited, and yet she realized that her fame could also bring further opportunity. "My dreams were not enhanced by someone holding my work up in Congress and calling me a pervert," she said in *Harper's Bazaar,* "On the other hand, there I was, suddenly a public figure." Sapphire was committed to the idea of literature as a tool for change. In an interview with Fran Gordon in *Poets & Writers,* she said: "I know literature helps." The author added: "My life was not the same after I read *The Prison Letters of George Jackson.* My perception of American culture changed."

Sapphire's first major book, a collection of prose and poems, is called *American Dreams.* The writing is confrontational and the images the author presents are graphic. The work's opening poems chronicle a black middle-class family headed by an abusive father and passive mother, and continues with poems for Sapphire's deceased brother and that explore the ugly stereotypes of blacks and Africans in popular culture. Jeannine DeLombard, describing the book in the *New York Times Book Review,* wrote: "At its best, Sapphire's poetry takes the stuff American's illusory dreams are made of—Top 40 songs, brand names, nursery rhymes, pop icons—and turns it inside out." Reviewers found the work powerful. In *American Book Review,* Margaret Randall called Sapphire's writing "unrelenting." Though Randall suggested that "disembodied penises, wilding, battery, rape, betrayal, S & M, sickness and death far outweigh connection, creativity, the retrieval of memory or the power of righteousness" in *American Dreams,* she nonetheless called Sapphire a writer of "considerable craft" and "haunting power."

With her debut novel, *Push,* Sapphire gained a wider readership. The novel tells the story of Claireece "Precious" Jones, a Harlem teenager pregnant by her father for the second time. Precious is also abused by her mother; she loses her first child when authorities determine the baby has Down syndrome. Worse, after delivering her second child and being ousted from her home, she discovers she has HIV. The story is told in graphic detail through the voice of Precious; Sapphire uses vernacular to convey the illiteracy that creates one more obstacle for her protagonist. The extreme horror that fills Precious's life comes across as nearly unreal. As Paula L. Woods wrote in the *Los Angeles Times Book Review,* however, Sapphire's characterization of the girl brings her to life: "Although right-wingers might dismiss the real-life Preciouses of this world as the Willie Hortons of welfare, Sapphire gives the fictional Precious something that surveys and case studies do not—a mind, a heart and a ferocious rage to survive that ignite the book and make it strangely compelling for all of the horror Precious relives in the telling." Sapphire herself felt that Precious was a special character, as she explained to Gordon in *Poets & Writers:* "I knew that with *Push* I had created a beautiful character that people loved in spite of themselves. People who love to hate people like her loved her."

After the success of *Push,* Sapphire felt compelled to continue taking risks. Though her next book, *Black Wings & Blind Angels: Poems,* returned to the format of mixed prose and poetry, it was with a greater sense of distance from the rage that marked her earlier work. Speaking about the poem "Breaking Karma #8" in *Poets & Writers,* Sapphire commented that "in the rehashing, in the ruminating, in the obsessing, the incident is now, as tragic as it is, placed in perspective—and in the scheme of humanity, is a small incident." Characterizing the evolving style of Sapphire's work, a contributor to *Publishers Weekly* wrote: "This second volume of verse finds her less aggressive, mixing her hostilities and anxieties with a newly bemused nostalgia."

In her prose, Sapphire draws on her own childhood experiences as well as her time living and working with children in Harlem throughout the 1980s and 1990s. Talking to Mark Marvel in *Interview,* Sapphire said: "I saw a complete generation grow up while I was living in Harlem. I moved into a building in '83 and moved out in '93." Sapphire continued: "I saw girls who had their first babies at fourteen. I listened to someone I had gone over a little primer with talking about their friend who got shot." The author added: "I saw the way things get repeated." Discussing social themes implicit in *Push,* Sapphire told Gordon that while "there was an . . . agenda-ridden part of me that wanted to talk about the welfare system," her primary aim was "to tell a really pure, unadulterated story about a girl." "I didn't want to preach," she continued, "but I did want to show what was happening." Sapphire added: "I don't think there's anything wrong with that—that's history."

BIOGRAPHICAL AND CRITICAL SOURCES:

BOOKS

Contemporary Black Biography, Volume 14, Thomson Gale (Detroit, MI), 1997.

Frohnmayer, John, *Leaving Town Alive,* Houghton Mifflin (New York, NY), 1993.

Newsmakers 1996, Issue 4, Thomson Gale (Detroit, MI), 1996.

PERIODICALS

Advocate, September 28, 1999, Richard Tayson, "Ready, Aim, Sapphire," p. 96.

American Book Review, March-May, 1995, Margaret Randall, "Dreams Deferred," p. 26.

Black Issues Book Review, March, 2000, review of *Black Wings & Blind Angels: Poems,* p. 44.

Booklist, January 15, 1994, Whitney Scott, review of *American Dreams,* pp. 894-895; May 1, 1996, Lillian Lewis, review of *Push,* p. 1470; October 1, 1998, review of *Push,* p. 317.

Book World, March 12, 2000, review of *Black Wings & Blind Angels,* p. 6.

Entertainment Weekly, April 8, 1994, Suzanne Ruta, review of *American Dreams,* p. 52.

Harper's Bazaar, November, 1995, Katie Roiphe, "Making the Incest Scene," pp. 65, 68-71; July, 1996, D.T. Max, "Pushing the Envelope," pp. 108-112.

Harvard Gay & Lesbian Review, fall, 1996, review of *Push,* p. 37, and *American Dreams,* p. 43.

Interview, June, 1996, Mark Marvel, "Sapphire's Big Push," pp. 28-30.

Kenyon Review, spring, 1995, Terese Svoboda, "Try Bondage," pp. 157-159.

Lambda Book Report, May-June, 1995, Jewelle Gomez, "Cutting Words," pp. 6-8; September, 1996, Jacquie Bishop, review of *Push,* pp. 12-14.

Library Journal, November 1, 1999, review of *Black Wings & Blind Angels,* p. 107.

London Review of Books, February 6, 1997, review of *Push,* p. 25.

Los Angeles Times Book Review, July 7, 1996, Paula L. Woods, "Pushed to Survival," review of *Push,* pp. 1, 9.

Ms., March-April, 1994, June Jordan, review of *American Dreams,* p. 70; July-August, 1996, Jewelle Gomez, review of *Push,* p. 82.

Newsweek, June 3, 1996, Jeff Giles, "Beginners' Pluck," review of *Push,* pp. 72-75.

New York Times, June 14, 1996, Michiko Kakutani, "A Cruel World, Endless until a Teacher Steps In," review of *Push,* p. B8.

New York Times Book Review, February 27, 1994, Jeannine DeLombard, review of *American Dreams,* p. 26; July 7, 1996, Rosemary Mahoney, "Don't Nobody Want Me. Don't Nobody Need Me," p. 9.

Observer (London, England), December 8, 1996, review of *Push,* p. 17.

Perspectives in Psychiatric Care, April-June, 1997, Suzanne Lego, review of *Push,* pp. 29-31.

Poets & Writers, January, 2000, Fran Gordon, "Breaking Karma: A Conversation with Sapphire," pp. 24-31.

Publishers Weekly, January 10, 1994, review of *American Dreams,* p. 58; April 22, 1996, review of *Push,* p. 61; September 27, 1999, review of *Black Wings & Blind Angels,* p. 99.

Reviewer's Bookwatch, May, 2005, Akua Sarr, review of *Push.*

Review of Contemporary Fiction, spring, 1997, Susann Cokal, review of *Push,* pp. 186-187.

Times Literary Supplement, October 11, 1996, Alex Clark, review of *Push,* p. 24.

Tribune Books (Chicago, IL), July 21, 1996, Achy Obejas, "Living Hell," p. 3.

Village Voice Literary Supplement, April, 1994, review of *American Dreams,* p. 28; December 8, 1996, review of *Push,* p. 17.

Voice of Youth Advocates, August, 2002, review of *Push,* p. 175.

Women's Review of Books, November, 1996, Gayle Pemberton, review of *Push,* p. 1.

Atlantic Center for the Arts Web site, http://www. atlanticcenterforthearts.org/ (September 25, 2007), profile of Ramona Lofton.

Comet, http://cometmagazine.com/ (April 26, 2007), "Seeking Hope Sharing Insight with Author Sapphire."*

*　　*　　*

SARILA, Narendra Singh 1927-

PERSONAL: Born January 2, 1927, in India; married Rani Rohini Devi, 1945 (divorced); married Countess Rita von Oberndorff, 1955 (divorced, 1958); married Kumari Shefali Kunwar, 1972; children: (second marriage) Rajkumari, (third marriage) Samar. *Education:* Educated at Mayo College, Ajmer, Allahabad University, and Magdalene College.

CAREER: Diplomat and civil servant. Heir to the princely state of Sarila in central India; aide-de-camp to Lord Louis Mountbatten, the last Viceroy of British India, 1948; served in the Indian Foreign Service, 1948-85; deputy permanent representative of the Indian Delegation to the United Nations, New York, NY, 1963-65; officer on special duty, Kashmir Affairs, 1967-68; joint secretary dealing with Pakistan and then United Nation affairs in the External Affairs Ministry, 1968-72; special delegate to the Indian Delegation to the United Nations during the Bangladesh crisis and war, 1971; ambassador to Spain 1972-74; ambassador to Brazil, 1974-77; ambassador to Libya (with concurrent accreditation to Malta), 1977-81; ambassador to Switzerland (with concurrent accreditation to the Vatican), 1981-82, ambassador to France, 1982-85; Nestle India, New Dehli, chairman of the board, 1994-2000, chairman emeritus, 2000—.

WRITINGS:

The Shadow of the Great Game: The Untold Story of India's Partition, HarperCollins Publishers India (New Delhi, India), 2005.

Contributor to periodicals, including *International Herald Tribune* and *Times of India.*

SIDELIGHTS: Narendra Singh Sarila, formerly a prince of the Indian state of Sarila and the aide-de-camp to Lord Louis Mountbatten, the last Viceroy of British India, is the author of *The Shadow of the Great Game: The Untold Story of India's Partition.* The book is "a useful look at a tumultuous series of events," observed Jay Freeman in a review for *Booklist.* The 1947 partition of British India into the independent nations of Pakistan and India resulted in extreme violence and the displacement of millions of people. In his work, Sarila asserts that, contrary to conventional wisdom, "the British favoured partition and worked successfully to achieve it because they did not trust a Congress government to provide a bulwark against Russian incursions into the area," noted Philip Ziegler in the *Spectator.* Further, he stated: "Only a strong, independent Pakistan could be relied on to protect the Himalayan frontiers and the rich oil fields of the Middle East."

The Shadow of the Great Game received decidedly mixed reviews. "Sarila has undoubtedly added to, and sometimes significantly altered, our understanding of what went on during the lead-up to Partition, but his book rambles," remarked *Telegraph* contributor Peter Parker. Ziegler, calling *The Shadow of the Great Game* a "thoughtful, interesting, if essentially wrong-headed book," also wrote that "even if the reader does not accept Narendra Singh Sarila's thesis, it still deserves attention." The author "shines a light on the diplomatic world of hints, pressures and concealed motives on the route to partition that he has uncovered through painstaking research," noted Jad Adams in the *Telegraph.*

BIOGRAPHICAL AND CRITICAL SOURCES:

PERIODICALS

Booklist, February 1, 2007, Jay Freeman, review of *The Shadow of the Great Game: The Untold Story of India's Partition,* p. 20.

Organiser, November 27, 2005, M.V. Kamath, "Muslim Pak Suited British Interests," review of *The Shadow of the Great Game.*

Spectator, September 23, 2006, Philip Ziegler, "Not So Duplicitous as Painted," review of *The Shadow of the Great Game.*

Times of India, June 22, 2005, K. Subrahmanyam, "Pakistan a British Creation."

ONLINE

Indian Express, http://www.indianexpress.com/ (September 23, 2005), Saeed Naqvi, "Wide Angle: Book Release That Speak Volumes," review of *The Shadow of the Great Game.*

Telegraph Online, http://www.telegraph.co.uk/ (September 20, 2006), Peter Parker, "At Once Medieval and Modern," review of *The Shadow of the Great Game;* (September 28, 2006), Jad Adams, "The Ill-Fated Battle for Indian Independence," review of *The Shadow of the Great Game.*

Tribune Online (Chandigarh, India), http://www.tribuneindia.com/ (October 16, 2005), M. Rajivlochan, "What Led to Freedom," review of *The Shadow of the Great Game.*

Watandost, http://watandost.blogspot.com/ (May 27, 2007), Rabab Naqvi, "Documenting Partition," review of *The Shadow of the Great Game.**

*   *   *

SAVREN, Shelley 1949-

PERSONAL: Born June 7, 1949, in Cleveland, OH; daughter of Albert and Helen Savren; married Elijah Imlay (a social worker), July 27, 2006; children: Talia Savren. *Education:* Ohio State University, B.A., 1973; Central Michigan University, M.A., 1974; Antioch University, Los Angeles, M.F.A., 2006. *Religion:* Jewish.

ADDRESSES: Home—Ventura, CA. *Office*—Oxnard College, 4000 S. Rose Ave., Oxnard, CA 93033. *E-mail*—poets@jetlink.net.

CAREER: Poet. Gavilan College, Gilroy, CA, part-time teacher, 1975; San Diego Community College District, San Diego, CA, part-time teacher, 1976; Southwestern College, Chula Vista, CA, part-time teacher, 1989-92; Oxnard College, Oxnard, CA, member of English faculty, 1992—. University of California, San Diego, extension teacher, 1976. Participant in California Poets in the Schools. Has taught poetry writing workshops in a prison, juvenile justice systems, civic centers, and public, private, and special schools. Gives readings from her works, including tours of U.S. cities; conference presenter and poetry workshop facilitator.

MEMBER: PEN USA, Association of Writers and Writing Programs, Poets and Writers, American Academy of Poets, Teachers and Writers Collaborative.

AWARDS, HONORS: Grants from Community Arts of San Diego, 1977-78, California Arts Council, 1979-93, and National Endowment for the Arts, 1986-89; Adjunct Faculty Award, Southwestern College, 1992; John David Johnson Memorial Poetry Award, *Poet,* 1994; Mark Dever Full-Time Faculty Award, Oxnard College, 1995; fellow of SouthCoast Writing Project, 1994.

WRITINGS:

POETRY

Gathering My Belongings, Greater Golden Hill Poetry Express (San Diego, CA), 1984.
Photo Album, Greater Golden Hill Poetry Express (San Diego, CA), 1987.
The Common Fire, Red Hen Press (Granada Hills, CA), 2004.

Contributor of poetry to many literary magazines, including *Hawaii Pacific Review, Poet, Rockhurst Review, Solo, Rattle, Bridges, ArtLife, Askew, Chickasaw Plum, Eclypse,* and *Prairie Schooner.*

*   *   *

SCHOENHALS, Michael

PERSONAL: Education: Earned degree from Stockholm University, 1987.

ADDRESSES: Office—Centre for Languages and Literature, Lund University, Box 201, SE-221 00 Lund, Sweden. *E-mail*—mschoenhals@silkroadstudies.org; michael.schoenhals@ostas.lu.se.

CAREER: Lund University Centre for Languages and Literature, Lund, Sweden, professor of modern Chinese society; Institute for Security and Development Policy, senior research fellow. Visiting professor at Institute of Asian Research, University of British

Columbia, 2004-05; visiting scholar at Contemporary China Research Institute, Chinese Academy of Social Sciences, 2005-06.

AWARDS, HONORS: Researcher of Excellence Award, Swedish Research Council, 2003.

WRITINGS:

Saltationist Socialism: Mao Zedong and the Great Leap Forward 1958, Foereningen foer Orientaliska Studier (Stockholm, Sweden) 1987.

Doing Things with Words in Chinese Politics: Five Studies, Institute of East Asian Studies, University of California (Berkeley, CA), 1992.

(Editor) *China's Cultural Revolution, 1966-1969: Not a Dinner Party,* M.E. Sharpe (Armonk, NY), 1996.

(With Roderick MacFarquhar) *Mao's Last Revolution,* Belknap Press of Harvard University Press (Cambridge, MA), 2006.

Contributor to books, including *Contemporary China and Its Outside World,* edited by Zhu Jiamu, Dangdai Zhongguo Chubanshe (Beijing, China), 2006. Member of the editorial board of *Pacific Affairs, China Quarterly, Totalitarian Movements and Political Religions, Copenhagen Journal of Asian Studies, European Journal of East Asian Studies,* and *Contemporary Chinese Thought.*

SIDELIGHTS: Michael Schoenhals, a Swedish writer and educator, is the coauthor of *Mao's Last Revolution,* an "exhaustively researched" account of China's Great Proletarian Cultural Revolution, observed *Washington Post Book World* contributor Orville Schell. In the work, Schoenhals and Roderick MacFarquhar examine Mao Zedong's repressive ten-year social experiment and political campaign, extending from 1966 to 1976, that resulted in the persecution, imprisonment, and death of millions. According to *New York Times Book Review* critic Judith Shapiro, "*Mao's Last Revolution* provides a detailed account of the salvos, currents, countercurrents, conspiracies, waves, cleansings and purges for which the era is known." "Using sources that range from official party and government documents to letters, diaries and interviews with surviving participants and victims," noted a contributor in the *Economist,* "the authors

document the orders that went out, the mayhem that resulted and the fear it all struck in the hearts of people across the country." "A feast for the student of China," remarked Ross Terrill in the *Weekly Standard,* the volume "is a challenge for the general reader. Authoritative and tightly documented, it is rather dense with political maneuver and Communist gobbledygook. But it is fluently written, and it tells the known truth about the Cultural Revolution at a time when the Beijing regime cannot bring itself to do so." In Schell's opinion, Schoenhals and MacFarquhar "have provided the most definitive roadmap to date of China's odyssey through those tumultuous times."

BIOGRAPHICAL AND CRITICAL SOURCES:

PERIODICALS

Economist, September 2, 2006, "Big Bad Wolf; China," review of *Mao's Last Revolution,* p. 77.
Foreign Affairs, November-December, 2006, Lucian W. Pye, "Asia and Pacific," review of *Mao's Last Revolution.*
New York Review of Books, September 21, 2006, Jonathan D. Spence, "China's Great Terror," review of *Mao's Last Revolution.*
New York Times Book Review, October 8, 2006, Judith Shapiro, "Red Guards," review of *Mao's Last Revolution.*
Washington Post Book World, October 29, 2006, Orville Schell, "Great Disorder under Heaven," review of *Mao's Last Revolution.*
Weekly Standard, March 19, 2007, Ross Terrill, "Mao's Madness," review of *Mao's Last Revolution.*

ONLINE

Institute for Security and Development Policy, http://www.isdp.eu/ (October 11, 2007), "Michael Schoenhals."

*   *   *

SCHONE, Robin

PERSONAL: Married Don Schone. *Education:* Graduated from Rockford College.

ADDRESSES: Home—Roselle, IL. *E-mail*—robin@ robinschone.com.

CAREER: Novelist. Also worked as a marketing research analyst.

AWARDS, HONORS: RITA Award nominee for best sensual historical romance, 2001, for *Gabriel's Woman.*

WRITINGS:

Awaken, My Love, Avon Books (New York, NY), 1995, revised edition, Kensington Brava (New York, NY), 2001.
The Lady's Tutor, Kensington Brava (New York, NY), 1999.
(With Beatrice Small, Susan Johnson, and Thea Devine) *Captivated* (anthology), Kensington Brava (New York, NY), 1999.
(With Bertrice Small, Susan Johnson, and Thea Devine) *Fascinated* (anthology), Kensington Brava (New York, NY), 2000.
The Lover, Kensington Brava (New York, NY), 2000.
Gabriel's Woman, Kensington Brava (New York, NY), 2001.
Scandalous Lovers, Kensington Brava (New York, NY), 2007.

SIDELIGHTS: Robin Schone is the author of *Scandalous Lovers* and other erotic romance novels. "I can't imagine writing a romance book that isn't erotic, because in my mind it is the sexual chemistry that makes the relationship between a man and a woman so very special," Schone told *Romantic Bookcorner* interviewer Angela Weiss. "Likewise, I can't imagine writing erotica without romance, because to me, the sexual love between a man and a woman is the most powerful force in the universe."

A woman travels back in time to the nineteenth century in *Awaken, My Love,* Schone's debut work. Inspired by the *Kama Sutra,* the novel concerns Elaine Metcliffe, a middle-aged computer analyst who finds herself inhabiting the body of Morrigan, the wife of English baron Lord Charles Mortimer. "This well-written erotic romance will arouse the passion of sub-genre fans," commented Harriet Klausner on her Web site, *Harriet Klausner's Book Review.*

The Lady's Tutor concerns a woman's attempts to rekindle a passionless marriage by learning the art of seduction. Though Elizabeth Petre, the Victorian heroine, requests the assistance of Ramiel Devington, the bastard son of an English countess and an Arab sheikh, she insists that he instruct her without touching her. The author "combines a highly charged sexual romance with a strong storyline," noted *Romantic Times* online critic Kathe Robin. In *The Lover,* a wealthy spinster hires a physically scarred lothario to help her lose her virginity, little realizing his true motivation for accepting the offer. Schone "deals with betrayal, loss of innocence and sexual hunger, all in an astute, adult, intricate manner," remarked Linda Mowery in the *Romance Reader.*

Gabriel's Woman centers on Victoria Chambers, who trades her virginity for safety after she is stalked by a mysterious stranger. She finds a protector in Gabriel, a cautious stranger with a haunted past. A *Romantic Times* online reviewer described *Gabriel's Woman* as an "erotic and emotionally powerful work." In *Scandalous Lovers,* widow Frances Hart and widower James Whitcox begin a torrid affair after meeting at London's Men and Women's Club, where sex is discussed openly. On her Web site, Schone remarked, "*Scandalous Lovers,* is not only my favorite book, but Frances and James are my two favorite characters. He's a sophisticated barrister, and she's an unsophisticated grandmother, yet together they find the courage to be what they need to be instead of what society tells them they should be." According to *Booklist* reviewer John Charles, Schone "gives readers some surprisingly nuanced characterization and an expertly evoked Victorian setting."

"I love stepping into the shoes of my characters," Schone told Karen Scott on the *Karen Knows Best Blog.* "I love experiencing history as they would have experienced it. My goal is to write in such a manner that my readers may also step into the shoes of my characters, so that they, too, can experience the history and the wonder and the despair and the laughter and the tears and the love. And hope."

BIOGRAPHICAL AND CRITICAL SOURCES:

PERIODICALS

Booklist, February 1, 2007, John Charles, review of *Scandalous Lovers,* p. 38.

ONLINE

Clean Sheets, http://www.cleansheets.com/ (March 15, 2000), Bill Noble, "Yes, Dorothy, That Is Your Clitoris! An Interview with Bestselling Author Robin Schone."

Harriet Klausner's Book Reviews, http://harriet klausner.wwwi.com/ (August 15, 2007), Harriet Klausner, reviews of *Awaken, My Love* and *Scandalous Lovers.*

Karen Knows Best Blog, http://karenknowsbest. blogspot.com/ (November 22, 2005), Karen Scott, "Tuesday Special Author Interview: Robin Schone."

RBL Romantica, http://www.geocities.com/Paris/ Opera/7895/schoneinterview.html (August 15, 2007), "RBL Presents Robin Schone."

Robin Schone Home Page, http://www.robinschone. com (August 15, 2007).

Romance Reader, http://theromancereader.com/ (August 15, 2007), Meredith McGuire, review of *Awaken, My Love;* (August 15, 2007), Linda Mowery, reviews of *Captivated, The Lady's Tutor,* and *The Lover.*

Romantic Bookcorner, http://www.die-buecherecke.de/ (February, 2000), Angela Weiss, "Interview with Robin Schone"; (June, 2000), Angela Weiss, "Interview with Robin Schone about Her New Book *The Lover.*"

Romantic Times, http://www.romantictimes.com/ (August 15, 2007), Maria C. Ferrer, review of *Awaken, My Love;* (August 15, 2007), Kathe Robin, reviews of *Captivated, The Lady's Tutor, The Lover, Gabriel's Woman,* and *Scandalous Lover.*

Writing Playground, http://writingplayground.com/ bleacherarchive.html (May-June, 2006), Marilyn Puett, "Q&A with Robin Schone."*

*   *   *

SCOTCH, Allison Winn

PERSONAL: Married; children: one son, one daughter. *Education:* University of Pennsylvania, B.A., 1995.

ADDRESSES: Home—New York, NY. *Agent*—Elisabeth Weed, Weed Literary, 55 E. 65th St., Ste. 4E, New York, NY 10065. *E-mail*—Allison@allison winn.com.

CAREER: Freelance writer. Also worked in public relations and marketing.

MEMBER: American Society of Journalists and Authors.

WRITINGS:

The Department of Lost & Found (novel), William Morrow (New York, NY), 2007.

Author of *Allison Winn Scotch* Web log. Contributor to Web sites, including ivillage.com, msn.com, and women.com. Contributor to periodicals, including *American Baby, American Way, Cooking Light, Family Circle, Fitness, Glamour, Men's Health, Parents, Prevention, Redbook, Self, Shape, Woman's Day,* and *Women's Health.*

SIDELIGHTS: Freelance writer Allison Winn Scotch, a frequent contributor to magazines such as *American Baby* and *Parents,* is the author of *The Department of Lost & Found,* a novel about an ambitious political assistant whose life comes unglued after she is diagnosed with breast cancer. "The idea for *The Department of Lost & Found* came to me instantly and easily," Scotch remarked to Therese Walsh in a *Writer Unboxed* interview. "I was caught up in the grief of mourning one of my best friends to breast cancer, and I just sat down one day, imbued with the voice of this character, who was fighting the disease herself. The novel has no relation to my friend's life at all, but the germ of the idea did spring from my experience in helping her with her battle . . . and, of course, provided a good deal of catharsis in coping with her death."

The Department of Lost & Found centers on Natalie Miller, a thirty-year-old senior aide to a New York senator. As Natalie struggles with the devastating effects of chemotherapy, she begins to reassess her life's goals and tracks down her former boyfriends in an effort to explore her approach to relationships. Scotch's debut novel received generally positive reviews. A contributor in *Marie Claire* described the work as "smart and well-written," and *Booklist* critic Elizabeth Dickie noted that the author "handles the topic of cancer with humor and hope, never dipping into the maudlin."

BIOGRAPHICAL AND CRITICAL SOURCES:

PERIODICALS

Booklist, March 1, 2007, Elizabeth Dickie, review of *The Department of Lost & Found,* p. 64.
Marie Claire, May, 2007, review of *The Department of Lost & Found,* p. 127.
Publishers Weekly, February 12, 2007, review of *The Department of Lost & Found,* p. 60.

ONLINE

Allison Winn Scotch Home Page, http://www.allisonwinn.com (October 11, 2007).
Allison Winn Scotch Web Log, http://allisonwinnscotch.blogspot.com (October 11, 2007).
Trashonista Web Site, http://www.trashionista.com/ (June, 2007), review of *The Department of Lost & Found.*
Writer Unboxed, http://writerunboxed.com/ (May 4, 2007), Therese Walsh, "Interview: Allison Winn Scotch."*

*   *   *

SHAFER, Audrey

PERSONAL: Born December 7, in Philadelphia, PA; father a playwright, mother a costume designer; children: Thomas, Rebecca. *Education:* Harvard University, A.B., 1978; Stanford University, M.D., 1983. *Hobbies and other interests:* Poetry.

ADDRESSES: Home—Mountain View, CA. *E-mail*—ashafer@stanford.edu.

CAREER: Anesthesiologist, educator, and author. University of Pennsylvania, Philadelphia, resident in anesthesia, 1984-86; Veterans Affairs Palo Alto Health Care System, Palo Alto, CA, staff anesthesiologist, 1989—; Stanford University School of Medicine, Stanford, CA, fellowship in clinical pharmacology, 1986-87; associate professor of anesthesia, 1997—, and member of faculty of Stanford Center for Biomedical Ethics, beginning 2003.

MEMBER: American Society of Anesthesiologists.

WRITINGS:

Sleep Talker: Poems by a Doctor/Mother, Xlibris (Philadelphia, PA), 2001.
The Mailbox (young adult novel), Delacorte Press (New York, NY), 2006.

Contributor to books, including *Cultural Sutures: Medicine and Media,* edited by Lester D. Friedman, Duke University Press, 2004. Contributor to academic journals, including *Anesthesiology, Journal of Medical Humanities, Academic Medicine,* and *Family Medicine.* Contributor of poems to periodicals and anthologies.

SIDELIGHTS: Audrey Shafer is an anesthesiologist at the Veterans Affairs Palo Alto Health Care System and an associate professor at Stanford University, where she directs the Arts, Humanities and Medicine Program. "I think the arts can help mitigate suffering," Shafer told Steven Winn of the *San Francisco Chronicle.* In addition to her work in the medical field, Shafer is also the author of the young-adult novel *The Mailbox,* "an evocative picture of the weblike nature of human existence and the interconnectedness of seemingly disparate experiences," according to *School Library Journal* contributor Faith Brautigan.

Raised by parents involved in theatre, Shafer developed an early interest in literature and the arts. "I grew up backstage, because my mother was a costume designer," she told *Gas Pipeline* online interviewer Patricia Rohrs. "Hence my childhood was influenced by playwrights, particularly Shakespeare, Molière and [Samuel] Beckett. My father, a playwright, was heavily involved with the Philadelphia literati of the time, who were mostly poets. I remember a poetry reading by Gerald Stern whose poem included the image of a Fanta orange soda bottle—my first clue that poetry could contain ordinary details." Shafer, who began writing poetry as a teenager, credits Denise Levertov with stimulating her interest in the written word; before she became a faculty member at Stanford, Shafer attended a poetry workshop conducted by Levertov. "She taught me that writing is a way to see the world," Shafer commented to Rohrs. Since then, Shafer has published a number of poems in magazines and anthologies, and she released *Sleep Talker: Poems by a Doctor/Mother* in 2001.

Shafer published her debut work of fiction, *The Mailbox*, in 2006. Geared for teen readers, the story concerns an orphaned boy's relationship with his uncle, a reclusive Vietnam veteran. The idea for the novel came to Shafer a few years earlier, during the buildup to the Iraq War, as she noticed that her patients at the veteran's hospital felt the need to talk to her before they entered the operating room. As she told Rohrs, "Many described their own wartime experiences; others commented on the youth and innocence of those being deployed—the veterans were deeply concerned about young people being put 'in harm's way.' I was moved by this witnessing and by hearing their deep-felt empathy."

The Mailbox centers on twelve-year-old Gabe, a foster child who had been shuttled from one home to another until he was sent to live with his Uncle Vernon in Virginia. After returning from his first day of school, the sixth-grader finds his uncle dead on the floor; grief-stricken and worried about having to reenter the foster care system, the youngster decides not to report the death. When Gabe comes home the next day, however, Vernon's body has disappeared, and an anonymous note left in the mailbox states, "I have a secret. Do not be afraid." As the days pass, the mysterious correspondent helps Gabe to survive, and through a series of messages the youngster develops a better understanding of his uncle's past. Shafer "builds a story finely balanced between mystery—who is Gabe's benefactor?—and meditation," observed *Washington Post Book World* contributor Elizabeth Ward, and a critic in *Kirkus Reviews* remarked that the narrative "conveys the power of memory to help heal wounds." According to *BookPage* online reviewer Dee Ann Grand, Shafer "weaves a remarkable story clearly influenced by her deep understanding of the characters involved."

BIOGRAPHICAL AND CRITICAL SOURCES:

PERIODICALS

Bulletin of the Center for Children's Books, December, 2006, Deborah Stevenson, review of *The Mailbox,* p. 191.

Kirkus Reviews, October 1, 2006, review of *The Mailbox,* p. 1024.

San Francisco Chronicle, July 23, 2003, Steven Winn, "Scientists Are Coming Around to the Idea That Art Can Heal."

School Library Journal, November, 2006, Faith Brautigan, review of *The Mailbox,* p. 152.

Washington Post Book World, November 26, 2006, Elizabeth Ward, review of *The Mailbox,* p. 191.

ONLINE

Audrey Shafer Home Page, http://www.ashafer.com (October 17, 2007).

BookPage, http://www.bookpage.com/ (November, 2006), Dee Ann Grand, "Enveloped in Secrets," review of *The Mailbox.*

Gas Pipeline Online, http://med.stanford.edu/anesthesia/newsletter/ (November, 2006), Patricia Rohrs, "Audrey Shafer, MD, Author of *The Mailbox.*"*

KidsReads.com, http://www.kidsreads.com/ (October 17, 2006), Terry Miller Shannon, review of *The Mailbox.*

Stanford Center for Biomedical Ethics Web site, http://bioethics.stanford.edu/ (October 27, 2007), "Audrey Shafer."

Stanford University Web site, http://www.stanford.edu/ (October 17, 2007), "Audrey Shafer."

*   *   *

SHEFCHIK, Rick

PERSONAL: Born in Duluth, MN; married, wife's name Barbara; children: Claire, David. *Education:* Graduated from Dartmouth College, 1974. *Hobbies and other interests:* Golf, playing guitar.

ADDRESSES: Home—Stillwater, MN. *E-mail*—rshefchik@comcast.net.

CAREER: Journalist. *Duluth News-Tribune,* Duluth, MN, reporter, for three years; *St. Paul Pioneer Press,* St. Paul, MN, reporter and columnist, 1980-2006.

AWARDS, HONORS: Best first novel nomination, Mystery Writers of America, for *Amen Corner.*

WRITINGS:

Amen Corner, Poisoned Pen Press (Scottsdale, AZ), 2007.

SIDELIGHTS: Rick Shefchik, a journalist who spent more than two decades at the *St. Paul Pioneer Press,* is the author of *Amen Corner,* his debut work of fiction. In the novel, Shefchik introduces Sam Skarda, a Minneapolis police detective on medical leave after being wounded in a shooting incident. A former collegiate golfer, Skarda receives an invitation to play at the prestigious Masters golf tournament after he wins the U.S. Publinx tournament. When Skarda arrives at Augusta National Golf Club, he learns that the body of the Rules Committee chairman has been found in the pond in front of the celebrated twelfth green. Though members of a feminist group protesting the tournament are initially suspected of the murder, the culprit is actually Lee Doggett, an ex-convict who has vowed revenge on media director Ralph Stanwick and flies into a rage when he realizes he has killed the wrong man. When a reporter is later found dead, Skarda is asked to investigate the crimes.

Though Shefchik reveals the killer's identity early in the book, "this in no way lessens the appeal of the mystery as the author is able, for the most part, to successfully maintain a high level of suspense throughout," noted a contributor to *Mysterious Reviews.* "The straight-ahead crime plot works best as a MacGuffin for a fact-packed roman à clef about a singular American institution," a critic in *Kirkus Reviews* stated, and Bill Ott, writing in *Booklist,* observed that Shefchik "combines a surprisingly grisly plot and a convincing villain with plenty of more or less realistic golf action."

BIOGRAPHICAL AND CRITICAL SOURCES:

PERIODICALS

Booklist, February 1, 2007, Bill Ott, review of *Amen Corner,* p. 36.
Kirkus Reviews, February 1, 2007, review of *Amen Corner,* p. 105.
Publishers Weekly, January 1, 2007, review of *Amen Corner,* p. 35.

ONLINE

Harriet Klausner's Book Review, http://harrietklausner. wwwi.com/ (August 15, 2007) review of *Amen Corner.*

Mysterious Reviews, http://www.mysteriousreviews. com/ (August 15, 2007) review of *Amen Corner.*
Rick Shefchick Home Page, http://www.rickshefchik. com (August 15, 2007).*

*   *   *

SHEN, James 1909-2007
(James C.H. Shen)

OBITUARY NOTICE— See index for *CA* sketch: Born June 15, 1909, in Shanghai, China; died July 12, 2007, in Taipei, Taiwan, China. Journalist, information officer, interpreter, diplomat, and author. Shen worked as a journalist in China in the 1930s and an officer of the government information ministry in the 1940s. Educated at the University of Missouri in Columbia, Shen was assigned as director of the ministry's San Francisco bureau from 1943 to 1947. When China fell into the hands of Communist revolutionary Mao Tse-tung in 1949, Shen cast his lot with the opposing Nationalist forces of Chiang Kai-shek in exile on the island of Taiwan. He was an English interpreter for the exiled leader in the 1950s, then joined the foreign affairs ministry in the de-facto capital city Taipei, where he directed the Government Information Office in the early 1960s. At that time much of the western world treated Taiwan as the official center of Chinese government, and Shen was appointed ambassador to Australia in 1966; he became vice minister of foreign affairs in 1968. He was the Taiwanese ambassador to the United States from 1971 to 1979, when President Richard M. Nixon reestablished diplomatic relations with mainland China, formally recognized the Communist government, and rendered Shen's job obsolete. The diplomat returned to Taiwan, where he spent the rest of his life. Shen's bitterness toward the United States is reflected in the title of his 1983 book, *The U.S. & Free China: How the U.S. Sold Out Its Ally.* His other writings, from happier times, include a collaboration with former U.S. Ambassador to Japan Edwin O. Reischauer and former U.S. Secretary of State Dean Rusk, *China's Open Wall* (1972).

OBITUARIES AND OTHER SOURCES:

PERIODICALS

Los Angeles Times, July 17, 2007, p. B11.

SHEN, James C.H.
   See SHEN, James

*   *   *

SHEPARD, Alicia C. 1953-

PERSONAL: Born 1953; daughter of Whiting Newton (a sales executive) and Florence (a store manager) Shepard; married Paul Robert Hodierne, 1984; children: Cutter (son). *Education:* George Washington University, B.A., 1978; University of Maryland, M.A., 2002.

ADDRESSES: Home—Arlington, VA. *E-mail*—alicia@ woodwardandbernstein.net; shepard@american.edu.

CAREER: Journalist and educator. *San Jose Mercury News,* San Jose, CA, reporter, 1982-87; sailed around the world and taught English in Japan, 1987-89; *American Journalism Review,* senior writer, for ten years; American University, Washington, DC, adjunct professor of journalism. Visiting professor at University of Texas at Austin, 2005-06.

AWARDS, HONORS: Three National Press Club awards for media criticism; Foster Distinguished Writer award, Penn State University, 2003.

WRITINGS:

(With Cathy Trost) *Running toward Danger: Stories behind the Breaking News of 9/11,* with foreword by Tom Brokaw, Rowman & Littlefield Publishers (Lanham, MD), 2002.
Woodward and Bernstein: Life in the Shadow of Watergate, John Wiley (Hoboken, NJ), 2007.

Contributor to periodicals, including *Los Angeles Times,Washingtonian, People,New York Times, Washington Post,* and *Chicago Tribune.*

SIDELIGHTS: Journalism professor Alicia C. Shepard is the author of *Woodward and Bernstein: Life in the Shadow of Watergate,* a dual biography of Bob Woodward and Carl Bernstein, the *Washington Post* report-

ers who uncovered the Watergate scandal that later brought down the administration of U.S. President Richard M. Nixon. Their account of the investigation was detailed in the best-selling book *All the President's Men,* which was adapted into an Academy Award-winning film starring Robert Redford and Dustin Hoffman. "After Watergate—possibly the most important event for journalism, politics, and the presidency in the last one hundred years—Woodward and Bernstein became living legends," Shepard noted on her Web site. "They left an indelible high-water mark that every American journalist has had to confront since." According to Greg Wyshynski in the *Connection Newspapers,* Shepard's "is the first book to follow the duo through their Watergate work, the multimedia mania and cult of celebrity that surrounded them in its *All the President's Men* aftermath, and their professional triumphs and tragedies over the next three decades."

Woodward and Bernstein had its roots in an oral history Shepard wrote for *Washingtonian* magazine in 2003. While researching the article, Shepard conducted extensive interviews with both men; for her book, she combined that information with archival material from the University of Texas, historian and author David Halberstam, and film director Alan J. Pakula, as well as some 200 additional interviews. "What floored me in my research in Texas were the scores and scores of fan letters people wrote Woodward and Bernstein," Shepard told *News Hounds* interviewer Marie Therese. "They were only Metro reporters and still only about 30, and yet, so many Americans felt that they were like Batman and Robin (not saying which is which!). People had a lot of faith in them." "It's amazing to remember how young and unempowered they were (each earning less than 20,000 dollars a year as metro reporters with Bernstein on the verge of losing his job) when fame and fortune hit them like a tidal wave," noted Marjorie Kehe in the *Christian Science Monitor.* "Both almost immediately made second marriages that didn't last (and then shared a divorce lawyer) and were forced—in their different ways—to learn to navigate the strange new landscape of life as a famous person."

In addition to recounting Woodward and Bernstein's work on the Watergate story, Shepard "does an even more admirable job of digging into their personalities, exposing their foibles and tracing the paths their lives have taken in the more than thirty years since Watergate entered the nation's vocabulary," wrote Lee Coppola in the *Buffalo News.* Though the men remain close friends, their careers have diverged greatly; Woodward, an assistant managing editor at the *Washington Post,* has written a number of best-selling books about national politics, while the less prolific Bernstein made an ill-fated move to network news. "Mr. Woodward has been so much more productive than Mr. Bernstein that it seems inevitable that his work should dominate a dual biography," wrote Carl Rollyson in the *New York Sun.* "It is to Ms. Shepard's credit, however, that interest in Mr. Bernstein never flags. She treats his marital and professional failures sympathetically without excusing his bad behavior or injudicious career moves." "It's probably inevitable that someone should write a biography of these two American folk heroes," commented *Market Watch* contributor Jon Friedman. "A biographer's work is even more complicated when the subjects are still alive and evolving—and frequently making headlines. Woodward and Bernstein are lucky that an observer as sensitive and careful as Shepard accepted the challenge."

BIOGRAPHICAL AND CRITICAL SOURCES:

PERIODICALS

Boston Globe, December 17, 2006, Jan Gardner, "Whence WoodStein," review of *Woodward and Bernstein: Life in the Shadow of Watergate.*

Buffalo News, December 10, 2006, Lee Coppola, "The Personal Side of Watergate Authors," review of *Woodward and Bernstein.*

Christian Science Monitor, November 7, 2006, Marjorie Kehe, "Two Lives Ever Defined by Watergate," review of *Woodward and Bernstein,* p. 14.

Editor & Publisher, August 2, 2006, Joe Strupp, "Upcoming Book Takes Sharp Look at Woodward and Bernstein"; October 18, 2006, Joe Strupp and Greg Mitchell, "New Bio of Woodward and Bernstein Is 'No Love Letter.'"

Library Journal, October 1, 2002, Audrey Snowden, review of *Running toward Danger: Stories behind the Breaking News of 9/11,* p. 109.

New Yorker, December 4, 2006, review of *Woodward and Bernstein.*

New York Sun, October 25, 2006, Carl Rollyson, "The Outsiders with the Ultimate Inside Scoop," review of *Woodward and Bernstein.*

Oregonian, November 26, 2006, Steve Weinberg, "After Watergate—Fame, Wealth and Bitterness," review of *Woodward and Bernstein.*

Waco Tribune-Herald, February 3, 2006, Carl Hoover, "Pop Culture Made Woodward, Bernstein into Superheroes."

ONLINE

Alicia C. Shepard Home Page, http://www.woodward andbernstein.net (August 20, 2007).

Blog Critics, http://blogcritics.org/ (November 11, 2006), Nancy Gail, review of *Woodward and Bernstein.*

Connection Newspapers, http://www.connection newspapers.com/ (November 30, 2006), Greg Wyshynski, "Notes on a Scandal," review of *Woodward and Bernstein.*

Creative Ink, http://creativeink.blogspot.com/ (October 18, 2006), Wendy Hoke, "What Watergate Did for Journalism."

Market Watch, http://www.marketwatch.com (November 29, 2006), Jon Friedman, "Lifting the Veil on Woodward and Bernstein," review of *Woodward and Bernstein.*

News Hounds, http://www.newshounds.us/ (November 13, 2006), Marie Therese, review of *Woodward and Bernstein* and interview with Alicia C. Shepard.

Poynter Online, http://www.poynter.org/ (October 3, 2003), Bill Mitchell, "Mainline Those Quotes: A Story Form That Works," interview with Alicia C. Shepard.

Washington Post, http://www.washingtonpost.com/wp-srv/politics/special/watergate/index.html (October 27, 2006), "Q&A: Author Alicia Shepard."*

*   *   *

SHINNIE, Peter
See SHINNIE, P.L.

*   *   *

SHINNIE, Peter L.
See SHINNIE, P.L.

*   *   *

SHINNIE, Peter Lewis
See SHINNIE, P.L.

SHINNIE, P.L. 1915-2007

(Peter Shinnie, Peter L. Shinnie, Peter Lewis Shinnie)

OBITUARY NOTICE— See index for *CA* sketch: Born January 18, 1915; died July 9, 2007. Archaeologist, Africanist, historian, linguist, educator, and author. Shinnie went to Africa with the training and intention to be an Egyptologist, but his fate lay farther afield. After World War II he went to the Sudan to work as a field archaeologist and became a government commissioner there. He spent many years studying the ancient Meroe people of the Kush, located in the Nubian region of northern Sudan, approaching their civilization with the spade of an archaeologist and the heart of a historian. After Sudan's independence from Egyptian and English oversight in the 1950s, Shinnie's job went to a native Sudanese, and the scholar made his way southward toward Uganda, where he worked briefly as the director of antiquities, then westward to Ghana. He became a specialist in the strip of Africa south of the Sahara Desert where these countries lay. Perhaps because of his several career moves, Shinnie's perspective was that of an Africanist not rooted in any particular region, nor was he focused on a specific time period. He was interested in cultural changes over time as they were manifested in a people's history, language, oral traditions, and artifacts. The closest he came to his original career goal of Egyptology was the time he spent just south of Egypt studying the culture of ancient Nubia. Shinnie taught archaeology at the University of Ghana for eight years, then returned to the Sudan to teach at the University of Khartoum until 1970, when he left Africa for Canada. He was a professor at the University of Calgary until 1980, when retirement enabled him to return to Africa for occasional research expeditions, though by then the land of the Meroe was mostly in the flood plain of the new Aswan Dam. Shinnie's dedication to Meroe culture was recognized near the end of his life when he was awarded the Sudanese Order of the Two Niles. Shinnie's books, more than a dozen in number, reflect his interests: *Meroe: A Civilization of the Sudan* (1967), *The African Iron Age* (1971), and *Ancient Nubia* (1996). He was also the founder and editor of newsletters and journals intended to keep scholars around the world in touch with ongoing research. These include *Kush* and *Nyame Akuma,* the latter of which was available at no cost to people living and working in Africa.

OBITUARIES AND OTHER SOURCES:

PERIODICALS

Times (London, England), October 11, 2007, p. 68.

*   *   *

SHORT, Kenneth Richard M.
See SHORT, K.R.M.

*   *   *

SHORT, Kenneth Richard MacDonald
See SHORT, K.R.M.

*   *   *

SHORT, K.R.M. 1936-2007

(Kenneth Richard M. Short, Kenneth Richard MacDonald Short)

OBITUARY NOTICE— See index for *CA* sketch: Born February 16, 1936, in Woodbury, NJ; died July 30, 2007. Historian, educator, minister, editor, and author. Short went to England as a Fulbright scholar and ended up living and teaching there for nearly twenty years. When he became aware of the value of audiovisual materials and mass communications for the teaching of history, his proximity to primary European sources enabled him to study these topics in their own right. He was the founding editor of the *Historical Journal of Film, Radio, and Television* in 1979 and a general editor of the Cambridge University Press book series "Cambridge Studies in the History of Mass Communications." Short taught British history at British secondary schools from 1968 to 1988 before returning to the United States to teach communications history at the University of Houston from 1988 to 2003. He was also a director of the International Telecommunications Research Institute and, before that, an affiliate of the International Association for Audio-Visual Media in Historical Research and Education, the British Universities Film and Video Council, the Inter University History Film Commission, and the British Film Institute. Short was convinced that newsreels and other documentary audiovisual materials were absolutely necessary to an understanding of the history of the twentieth century. Aside from his scholarly pursuits, Short was also an ordained priest of the Church of England and served Episcopal congregations in Texas and Colorado. Short edited several collections related to the history of mass communications, including *Feature Films as History* (1981), *Film and Radio Propaganda in World War II* (1983), and *Western Broadcasting over the Iron Curtain* (1986). He also wrote the book *Universal Newsreels and the Fall of Nazi Germany* (1990).

OBITUARIES AND OTHER SOURCES:

PERIODICALS

Times (London, England), October 9, 2007, p. 65.

*   *   *

SIEGBAHN, Kai 1918-2007
(Kai M. Siegbahn, Kai Manne Börje Siegbahn, Kai Manne Boerje Siegbahn)

OBITUARY NOTICE— See index for *CA* sketch: Born April 20, 1918, in Lund, Sweden; died of heart failure, July 20, 2007, in Angelholm, Sweden. Physicist, educator, and author. Siegbahn shared the Nobel Prize in physics in 1981 for his development of high-resolution electron spectroscopy for chemical analysis (or ESCA). It was his own father who had won the same prize more than fifty years earlier for his work on X-ray spectroscopy, but it was the son's technique that proved to be sensitive enough for widespread use as an industrial application. The ESCA technique uses electrons, rather than X-rays or lasers, to test the chemical composition of materials, but it also enables scientists to determine the purity, contamination, or corrosion level of the materials and to identify new chemical elements undetectable by other means. It can be used to analyze a wide range of materials: solid, liquid, gas; organic or inorganic; pure or alloyed; the only excluded elements are helium and hydrogen. ESCA can be applied to identify chemical elements even at the molecular and atomic levels. Siegbahn also made improvements to the spectrometer and other measuring devices to take full advantage of the

benefits offered by the ESCA process. Siegbahn had been working on his projects for nearly thirty years. His research began to yield solid results as early as 1954 in his work with sodium chloride, and the first commercially viable electronic spectrometer was produced in 1969. Siegbahn was a researcher at the Nobel Institute of Physics from 1942 to 1951. He was a member of the faculty at the Swedish Royal Institute of Technology when he recorded his initial discoveries. He moved to the University of Uppsala in 1954, where he was a professor of physics and a department head until 1984. Siegbahn was active in many scientific organizations, among them the International Union of Pure and Applied Physics, which he headed in the early 1980s. He was a recipient of many scientific awards in lifetime in addition to the Nobel Prize. Siegbahn's writings include the books *ESCA: Atomic, Molecular, and Solid State Structure Studied by Means of Electron Spectroscopy* (1967) and *ESCA Applied to Free Molecules* (1969).

OBITUARIES AND OTHER SOURCES:

PERIODICALS

Chicago Tribune, August 8, 2007, p. 11.
Los Angeles Times, August 8, 2007, p. B8.
New York Times, August 7, 2007, p. C11.
Times (London, England), August 9, 2007, p. 64.
Washington Post, August 6, 2007, p. B5.

*   *   *

SIEGBAHN, Kai M.
See SIEGBAHN, Kai

*   *   *

SIEGBAHN, Kai Manne Boerje
See SIEGBAHN, Kai

*   *   *

SIEGBAHN, Kai Manne Börje
See SIEGBAHN, Kai

SIEGEL, Robert Anthony

PERSONAL: Born in New York, NY; son of a criminal defense lawyer; married to Karen E. Bender (a writer); children: Jonah, Maia. *Education:* Harvard University, B.A., 1992; University of Iowa, M.F.A., 1992; also attended the University of Tokyo. *Religion:* Jewish.

ADDRESSES: Home—Wilmington, NC. *Agent*—Geri Thoma, Elaine Markson Literary Agency, 44 Greenwich Ave., New York, NY 10011. *E-mail*—robert@robertanthonysiegel.com; siegelr@uncw.edu.

CAREER: Writer and educator. University of North Carolina Wilmington, assistant professor of creative writing.

AWARDS, HONORS: Mombusho fellowship, Japanese Ministry of Education, 1983-85; Michener-Engle fellowship, University of Iowa, 1992; writing fellowship, Fine Arts Work Center at Provincetown, 1992-93.

WRITINGS:

All the Money in the World (novel), Random House (New York, NY), 1997.
All Will Be Revealed (novel), MacAdam Cage (San Francisco, CA), 2007.

Contributor of short stories to periodicals, including *Portland Review, Post Road Magazine* and *Cimarron Review.*

SIDELIGHTS: Robert Anthony Siegel, a professor at the University of North Carolina Wilmington, is the author of the novels *All the Money in the World* and *All Will Be Revealed.* "In my view, good fiction is always driven by emotion," Siegel noted on his faculty page at the university's Web site.

All the Money in the World concerns the relationship between wealthy defense attorney Louis Glasser and his son, Jason, a student at Harvard. When Brian Brianson, one of Louis's shady clients, is arrested in a sting operation, he attempts to gain favor with the authorities by falsely accusing Louis of a crime. As his life falls apart, Louis turns to Jason for support. "Although this first novel is well written, there are questions left unanswered," observed *Library Journal* contributor Shirley Gibson. A critic in *Publishers Weekly* offered a more positive assessment, noting that the author "succeeds in making the lives and actions of all his characters . . . real and heartfelt." *All the Money in the World* "doesn't end with a grand pronouncement," Siegel told interviewer Luke Ford on *Luke Ford.net.* He added, "I was trying to hold within the bounds of normal human experience rather than trying to create a neat dramatic arc. It's true to life. People go through terrible things and sometimes the one reward is having survived."

Set in late-nineteenth-century New York City, *All Will Be Revealed* centers on Augustus Auerbach, a disabled recluse who has made a fortune in pornography. When one of his models convinces Auerbach to attend a séance at the home of Verena Swann, a spiritual medium, he becomes convinced that she has channeled the soul of his late mother. Auerbach and Swann begin an unlikely love affair that is later threatened by Swann's greedy brother-in-law. According to Miriam Parker, a contributor in *BustedHalo.com,* "The plot of the novel moves deftly from Auerbach's point of view to Verena Swann's and back again, showing the worlds that they each inhabit and the insecurities that are inherent in their lives of deception." A critic in *Publishers Weekly* called *All Will Be Revealed* "a richly detailed and seedily seductive narrative."

BIOGRAPHICAL AND CRITICAL SOURCES:

PERIODICALS

Library Journal, April 1, 1997, Shirley Gibson, review of *All the Money in the World,* p. 131; March 1, 2007, Susan O. Moritz, review of *All Will Be Revealed,* p. 78.
Publishers Weekly, March 31, 1997, review of *All the Money in the World,* p. 64; December 18, 2006, review of *All Will Be Revealed,* p. 40.

ONLINE

BustedHalo.com, http://www.bustedhalo.com (August 15, 2007), Miriam Parker, "Pulling the Curtains Back," review of *All Will Be Revealed* and "Busted: Robert Anthony Siegel's Literary Novel."

Maureen Sawa, *The Library Book: From Camels to Computers,* Tundra Books (Plattsburgh, NY), 2006.

Evan Solomon, *The Sabre-Toothed Tiger,* Puffin Canada (Toronto, Ontario, Canada), 2007.

Cynthia Pratt Nicolson and Paulette Bourgeois, *The Jumbo Book of Space,* Kids Can Press (Toronto, Ontario, Canada), 2007.

SIDELIGHTS: Bill Slavin told *CA:* "I have been drawing since I can remember and have wanted to illustrate books for just about as long. My first commercial success was an antismoking-in-bed poster I did in grade three, which won first prize and earned me twenty-five dollars. Grade three was an important year because it was also the year I produced my first illustrated book, called *Zok the Caveman.*

"After high school I attended Sheridan College, where I studies cartooning and graphic story illustration. I have worked in and around the publishing industry since 1979, working for many years as an artist director, illustrator, and layout artist for a small publishing house in the Ottawa Valley. After moving back to Toronto, I became involved with doing illustrations for educational computer software programs, while continuing to try to get a job doing what I have really always wanted to do—illustrating kids' books. I eventually contracted with Kids Can Press to illustrate Paulette Bourgeois's book *Too Many Chickens!* Since then I have illustrated a number of children's books, and that is now my primary sources of income. It is work that I love, and I consider myself a most fortunate person to be working in this industry.

"Today I am living in paradise in an old farmhouse on the edge of the village of Millbrook. I live with my wife, Esperança Melo, who is also an artist and is an integral part of all I do, and our cat, Merlin. We have formed a company called Kinder Box, and from 1995 to 2002 we were both members of the Millbrook Gallery, a gallery collective of nineteen local artists. I primarily work in acrylics or watercolor and inks.

"I tend to work quickly and impetuously at my art, but I am learning to slow down and smell the resins.

"In regard to my fiction work, until recently I have had very little contact with the authors whose books I am illustrating, and I feel that in most cases this allows the written and visual narrative to reach its full potential. Generally the author is quite willing to give the illustrator free rein; needless to say, this is a great act of trust on the part of the writer. More recently I have been working in closer collaboration with the author on some projects right from the outset, and I am finding this sort of collaboration an exciting and interesting development in my work. I occasionally put my own hand to writing, something I enjoy doing, although my primary focus is illustration. In 1996 I wrote my own story, *The Stone Lion,* and in 2005 I cowrote and illustrated *Transformed: How Everyday Things Are Made.*

"Although my first love is and always will be the storybook, nonfiction illustration makes up a significant part of my work and poses its own challenges. My real lack of interest in things scientific seems to have made me uniquely qualified to illustrate this genre. I believe it is the desire to make my work interesting to *me* that defines how I embrace these subjects, and the result is an approach to the illustrations that is not overly ponderous or didactic. Having said this, I have a real love for history and am thrilled by books or the parts thereof that have a historical slant. Coming full circle, I believe my love for the narrative found in picture-book illustration is reflected in my nonfiction illustration."

*   *   *

SMITH, Gary Scott 1950-

PERSONAL: Born 1950. *Education:* Grove City College, B.A., 1972; Gordon-Conwell Theological Seminary, M.Div., 1977; Johns Hopkins University, M.A., 1979, Ph.D., 1981. *Hobbies and other interests:* Tennis, basketball, weight lifting, travel, hiking.

ADDRESSES: Office—Department of History, Grove City College, 100 Campus Dr., Grove City, PA 16127. *E-mail*—gssmith@gcc.edu.

CAREER: Historian and educator. Grove City College, Grove City, PA, 1978—, professor of history, department chair, and coordinator of humanities core.

AWARDS, HONORS: Named Professor of the Year, Grove City College, 2000; Pennsylvania Professor of the Year, Carnegie Foundation for the Advancement of Teaching, 2001; fellowship research grants, Earhart Foundation, 2001-02 and 2004-05.

WRITINGS:

The Seeds of Secularization: Calvinism, Culture, and Pluralism in America, 1870-1915, Christian University Press (Grand Rapids, MI), 1985.

(Editor, with W. Andrew Hoffecker) *Building a Christian World View,* Presbyterian and Reformed Publishing (Phillipsburg, NJ), Volume 1: *God, Man, and Knowledge,* 1986, Volume 2: *The Universe, Society, and Ethics,* 1988.

(Editor) *God and Politics: Four Views on the Reformation of Civil Government: Theonomy, Principled Pluralism, Christian America, National Confessionalism,* Presbyterian and Reformed Publishing (Phillipsburg, NJ), 1989.

The Search for Social Salvation: Social Christianity and America, 1880-1925, Lexington Books (Lanham, MD), 2000.

Faith and the Presidency: From George Washington to George W. Bush, Oxford University Press (New York, NY), 2006.

Contributor of scholarly articles to periodicals and of chapters to books.

SIDELIGHTS: Gary Scott Smith, a professor of history at Grove City College, is the author of *Faith and the Presidency: From George Washington to George W. Bush.* Smith "draws on extensive archival research to describe how faith helped shape presidential character, political philosophy and the interplay between beliefs and policies," remarked Thomas O'Boyle in the *Pittsburgh Post-Gazette.* The author examines the religious practices of eleven U.S. Presidents, including Thomas Jefferson, Abraham Lincoln, Dwight D. Eisenhower, and Ronald Reagan. He writes that Jefferson, branded as an atheist by his political opponents, was actually a student of the Bible, that Woodrow Wilson believed dancing to be sinful, and that Franklin Roosevelt often interrupted meetings in the Oval Office to contact his home church. Smith pays particular attention to what he calls "civil religion," which promotes social justice and character building, noting that Lincoln, Roosevelt, and Reagan "above others, understood how to invoke religion to reinforce cherished ideals and strengthen America's commitment to core values, delivering speeches that were essentially sermons, and providing moral leadership," O'Boyle observed. Steve Young, reviewing *Faith and the Presidency* in the *Library Journal,* praised the author's scholarship, noting "the wealth of source material and historical detail he has amassed on a fascinating and important topic."

Smith told *CA:* "I became interested in writing because of the fascinating books I read, the desire to express creativity, and the hope of providing people with greater knowledge and better understanding of people and historical events. Moreover, writing books about historical topics involves a great deal of detective work, which I enjoy.

"Because of my heavy teaching schedule, I do most of my writing during the summer and other breaks in the academic schedule. When working on a project, I typically write eight to twelve hours per day. I usually try to research a chapter of a book or an article in substantial detail before I begin to write. I craft a first draft of the article or chapter and then try to determine what information I still need to finish it. I normally do four or more drafts of each piece and ask colleagues to critique the next to the last version.

"My favorite book is *Faith and the Presidency* because it involved a lot of research in the archives of numerous presidential libraries, deals with a topic in which there is significant interest, and has afforded me numerous opportunities to speak to varied groups about its content.

"I hope my books will help people better understand and appreciate history and inspire readers to think about the larger issues they discuss."

BIOGRAPHICAL AND CRITICAL SOURCES:

PERIODICALS

Library Journal, December 1, 2006, Steve Young, review of *Faith and the Presidency: From George Washington to George W. Bush,* p. 132.

Pittsburgh Post-Gazette, December 31, 2006, Thomas O'Boyle, review of *Faith & the Presidency.*

ONLINE

Grove City College, http://www.gcc.edu/ (August 15, 2007), "Gary Scott Smith."

SMOLINSKI, Jill

PERSONAL: Divorced; children: Danny. *Education:* Central Michigan University, B.A., 1983.

ADDRESSES: Home—Los Angeles, CA.

CAREER: Writer. Former staff member, *Teen* magazine; has worked for nonprofit agency promoting ridesharing since 1990.

WRITINGS:

Supermodels!: Everything You Want to Know about Cindy Crawford, Claudia Schiffer, Niki Taylor, and Many Others!, Lowell House Juvenile (Los Angeles, CA), 1993.

(With Carol J. Amato and Eric Ladizinsky) *Fifty Nifty Super Science Fair Projects,* Lowell House (Los Angeles, CA), illustrated by Kerry Manwaring, 1995.

Holiday Origami, illustrated by Mary Ann Fraser, Lowell House Juvenile (Los Angeles, CA), 1995, new edition (with Andrea Urton), illustrated by Dianne O'Quinn Burke and Mary Ann Fraser, Lowell House Juvenile (Los Angeles, CA), 1999.

Scary Origami, illustrated by Anita McLaughlin, Lowell House Juvenile (Los Angeles, CA), 1995.

Sixty Super Simple Travel Games, illustrated by Leo Abbett, Lowell House Juvenile (Los Angeles, CA), 1997.

Fifty Nifty Super Animal Origami Crafts, illustrated by Charlene Olexiewicz, Lowell House Juvenile (Los Angeles, CA), 1998.

Sixty Super Simple More Travel Games, illustrated by Leo Abbett, Lowell House Juvenile (Los Angeles, CA), 1998.

Girls Wanna Have Fun: Friendship Origami, illustrated by Charlene Olexiewicz, Lowell House Juvenile (Los Angeles, CA), 1999.

The First-Timer's Guide to Origami, illustrated by Neal Yamamoto, Lowell House Juvenile (Los Angeles, CA), 2000.

Contributor to *American Girls about Town,* 2004. Contributor of articles to women's magazines. Author of *My Life List* Web log.

NOVELS

Flip-Flopped, Thomas Dunne Books/St. Martin's Press (New York, NY), 2002.

The Next Thing on My List: A Novel, Shaye Areheart Books (New York, NY), 2007.

ADAPTATIONS: The Next Thing on My List has been optioned for film by New Line Cinema.

SIDELIGHTS: Jill Smolinski realized her dream of writing fiction in 2002 when she published her debut novel, *Flip-Flopped.* The work centers on Keely Baker-Kekuhi, a scientist who leaves her Midwestern home to live in Hawaii, where she is assigned to study an extinct volcano. Keely's husband leaves her for a hula dancer and then demands custody of their young son. Keely's life takes an unexpected turn for the better when she meets Ian Gardiner, a British art dealer who is friendly with Davy Jones, the lead singer of The Monkees and Keely's childhood crush. "The best thing about *Flip-Flopped* is its offbeat sense of humor, which is fueled by Smolinski's creativity," observed *Romance Reader* critic Susan Scribner. Beth Warrell, writing in *Booklist,* praised the author's "honest and funny look at the loss of love and the process of grieving."

The Next Thing on My List: A Novel, Smolinski's second book, concerns June Parker, an aimless thirty-four-year-old who undergoes a life-changing experience after her young acquaintance, Marissa Jones, is killed in a car accident. June takes possession of Marissa's list of "20 Things to Do by My 25th Birthday," which includes riding in a helicopter and kissing a stranger, and determines to finish the tasks in her friend's honor. "I think women in particular have a habit of putting things off for 'later'—when the kids are grown, when we lose weight, when the house is in perfect order," Smolinski told *Reader Views* contributor Juanita Watson. "Unfortunately, this idyllic later doesn't always come—and in the meantime, we're left with a day-to-day life that feels hollow, and we can't figure out why. June sets out to complete a list, and she doesn't have the luxury of procrastinating because she's doing it on behalf of someone else. In the process, she learns the value of taking charge of her own dreams." *Reader Views* critic Cherie Fisher called *The Next Thing on My List* "a wonderfully written heartwarming story about a woman's self-discovery," and *Library Journal* reviewer Lisa Craig-Davis stated, "June's odyssey is funny, charming, and moving."

BIOGRAPHICAL AND CRITICAL SOURCES:

PERIODICALS

Booklist, June 1, 2002, Beth Warrell, review of *Flip-Flopped,* p. 1688.
Library Journal, April 15, 2007, Lisa Davis-Craig, review of *The Next Thing on My List: A Novel,* p. 76.
Publishers Weekly, January 1, 2007, review of *The Next Thing on My List,* p. 30.

ONLINE

Jill Smolinski Home Page, http://www.jillsmolinski.com (August 15, 2007).
My Life List, http://todayslifelist.blogspot.com (August 15, 2007), author's Web log.
MySpace.com, http://www.myspace.com (August 15, 2007), "Jill Smolinski."
Reader Views, http://www.readerviews.com/ (March, 2007), Cherie Fisher, review of *The Next Thing on My List;* (August 15, 2007), Juanita Watson, "Interview with Jill Smolinski."
Romance Reader, http://www.theromancereader.com/ (August 15, 2007), Susan Scribner, review of *Flip-Flopped.*
Trashionista, http://www.trashionista.com/ (July 5, 2007), Diane Shipley, "Author Interview: Jill Smolinski."*

*   *   *

SNYDER, Tom 1936-2007

OBITUARY NOTICE— See index for *CA* sketch: Born May 12, 1936, in Milwaukee, WI; died of complications from leukemia, July 29, 2007, in San Francisco, CA. Broadcast journalist. Snyder was a pioneer of late-late-night light news. It was his job to keep viewers' eyes glued to the television set long after the entertainment- and talk-show hosts had signed off for the night. The late-late-night format afforded him

more latitude in subject matter and interviewing technique than more-conventional newscasts that were broadcast earlier in the day, and Snyder took full advantage of it. He recognized that viewers would not postpone their bedtime unless he could capture and hold their interest. After a modest start at television stations around the country, Snyder made his mark as the host of *The Tomorrow Show,* which followed Johnny Carson's popular talk show on NBC-TV for nearly ten years, from 1973 to 1982. Snyder was willing to talk about almost anything with anyone. His topics ranged from social issues such as open marriage, suicide, and prostitution, to politics, law, and the entertainment world. He interviewed a wide range of guests as well, from the Dalai Lama to convicted killer Charles Manson to labor leader Jimmy Hoffa and disgraced former vice president Spiro Agnew. Snyder's style was hard-hitting and sometimes antagonistic; it generated almost as much criticism as praise, but it kept his audience awake. After the demise of *The Tomorrow Show,* Snyder moved from Los Angeles to New York City to anchor *Eyewitness News* for ABC-TV, but the transition was not successful. Deprived of the freedom of a late-night time slot, the show's ratings fell as critics and viewers began to see a blander version of the television personality profile that had made him famous. He moved from one program and network to another and enjoyed a modest success with *The Late Late Show with Tom Snyder* on CBS-TV from 1995 to 1999.

OBITUARIES AND OTHER SOURCES:

PERIODICALS

Chicago Tribune, July 31, 2007, pp. 1, 6.
Los Angeles Times, July 31, 2007, p. B8.
New York Times, July 31, 2007, p. A21.

*   *   *

SOODALTER, Ron

PERSONAL: Married; wife's name Jane; children: Jesse, Melora. *Education:* Earned a bachelor's degree and two master's degrees. *Hobbies and other interests:* Folk music, collecting Western memorabilia.

ADDRESSES: *Home*—Chappaqua, NY. *E-mail*—Ron@RonSoodalter.com.

CAREER: Writer and educator. Has taught at Riker's Island Prison, New York, NY, at a bilingual school in Harlem, NY, and at a high school in upstate NY; worked as curator of history museum in CO; professional flamenco guitar player; scrimshaw artist.

WRITINGS:

Hanging Captain Gordon: The Life and Trial of an American Slave Trader, Atria Books (New York, NY), 2006.

Contributor to *Smithsonian* and *True West.*

SIDELIGHTS: Ron Soodalter is the author of *Hanging Captain Gordon: The Life and Trial of an American Slave Trader.* Soodalter first became interested in the tale of Nathaniel Gordon as a college student in the 1960s. "Diving into the primary sources had all the aspects of a treasure hunt," the author remarked in an interview on his Web site. "At the outset, all I really knew was that President [Abraham] Lincoln had resisted considerable political pressure, and allowed a young sea captain to hang for slave trading." It would take Soodalter almost four decades to complete his history, during which he worked as a museum curator, taught at Riker's Island Prison, and collected traditional folk ballads. "When I finally sat down to write the Gordon story, it was with the accumulated information—and perspective—gleaned and gathered through these various pursuits," the author wrote on his Web site.

In *Hanging Captain Gordon,* Soodalter details the trial of Gordon, a thirty-four-year-old sea captain whose ship, carrying a cargo of African slaves, was seized by federal authorities in 1860, beginning a complex legal process that ended in Gordon's execution two years later. The author's "fascinating and disturbing account of this obscure episode in our history is a story replete with political intrigue," observed *Booklist* reviewer Jay Freeman. *Boston Globe* critic Chuck Leddy remarked: "Soodalter does a fine job explaining just how unusual Gordon's prosecution was. The captain was in the wrong place at the wrong time when he got caught, but nobody involved thought he would be convicted or executed. Soodalter details forty years of lax enforcement, outright bribery, and judicial nullification of the 1820 slave-trade law." Though Soodalter

remarked that he initially sympathized with Gordon, "a loving husband and father," he reversed his attitude toward Gordon with time and perspective. "The true tragedy lies in our government's unforgivably lax approach to enforcing the slave trade laws, in its refusal to cooperate with Great Britain when cooperation would have meant ending the slave traffic decades earlier, and in letting men like Gordon evade punishment as a matter of policy," he stated.

BIOGRAPHICAL AND CRITICAL SOURCES:

PERIODICALS

Booklist, February 1, 2006, Jay Freeman, review of *Hanging Captain Gordon: The Life and Trial of an American Slave Trader,* p. 22.
Boston Globe, August 1, 2006, Chuck Leddy, "Execution Case Puts Slave Trade under the Microscope," review of *Hanging Captain Gordon.*
History: Review of New Books, summer, 2006, Julie Allison Mujic, review of *Hanging Captain Gordon.*

ONLINE

Ron Soodalter Home Page, http://www.ronsoodalter. com (August 15, 2007).

*   *   *

SPRIGGE, Timothy
   See SPRIGGE, Timothy L.S.

*   *   *

SPRIGGE, Timothy Lauro Squire
   See SPRIGGE, Timothy L.S.

*   *   *

SPRIGGE, Timothy L.S. 1932-2007
   (Timothy Sprigge, Timothy Lauro Squire Sprigge)

OBITUARY NOTICE— See index for *CA* sketch: Born January 14, 1932, in London, England; died of heart failure, July 11, 2007. Philosopher, educator, and author. Sprigge once told *CA* that his work as a philosopher was devoted to "the nature of reality" rather than the study of abstract concepts and semantics. He taught at the University of London in the early 1960s, then at the University of Sussex from 1963 to 1979. He moved to the University of Edinburgh in 1979, where he was named a professor emeritus of logic and metaphysics in 1990. Sprigge's writings include *Santayana: An Examination of His Philosophy* (1983), *The Vindication of Absolute Idealism* (1983), *Theories of Existence* (1984), *The Rational Foundations of Ethics* (1988), and *James and Bradley: American Truth and British Reality* (1993).

OBITUARIES AND OTHER SOURCES:

PERIODICALS

Times (London, England), September 6, 2007, p. 74.

*   *   *

STANGROOM, Jeremy

PERSONAL: Education: London School of Economics, Ph.D. *Hobbies and other interests:* Computers, travel, running, playing squash.

ADDRESSES: Office—Butterflies and Wheels, 98 Mulgrave Rd., Sutton, Surrey SM2 6LZ, England. *E-mail*—jerry@philosophersnet.com;   jerry@philosophers.co.uk; jerry@jeremystangroom.com.

CAREER: Writer, Web site designer, and computer programmer.

AWARDS, HONORS: Prospect magazine book of the year, 2006, for *Why Truth Matters.*

WRITINGS:

NONFICTION

(Editor, with Julian Baggini) *New British Philosophy,* Routledge (New York, NY), 2002.

(Editor, with Julian Baggini) *What Philosophers Think,* Continuum (New York, NY), 2003.

(Editor, with Julian Baggini) *Great Thinkers A-Z,* Continuum (New York, NY), 2004.

(With Ophelia Benson) *The Dictionary of Fashionable Nonsense: A Guide for Edgy People,* Souvenir (London, England), 2004.

(Editor) *What Scientists Think,* Routledge (New York, NY), 2005.

The Great Philosophers, Arcturus (London, England), 2005.

(With Ophelia Benson) *Why Truth Matters,* Continuum (New York, NY), 2006.

(Editor, with Julian Baggini) *What More Philosophers Think,* Continuum (New York, NY), 2007.

(With Julian Baggini) *Do You Think What You Think You Think? The Ultimate Philosophical Handbook,* Plume (New York, NY), 2007.

Little Book of Big Ideas: Philosophy, Chicago Review Press (Chicago, IL), 2007.

Identity Crisis: Against Multiculturalism, Continuum (New York, NY), 2008.

Founder, with Julian Baggini, and new media editor of *Philosophers' Magazine,* 1997—. Editor, with Ophelia Benson, of Web site *Butterflies and Wheels.* Editor, with James Garvey, of"Contemporary Social Issues" series for Continuum. Contributor to periodicals.

SIDELIGHTS: Jeremy Stangroom's books include profiles of important thinkers in philosophy and science and attempts at debunking what he considers nonsensical thought. His work often aims to make seemingly arcane concepts accessible to general readers. Of *What Scientists Think,* for instance, he told *Scientist* magazine contributor Stephen Pincock: "The book should be comprehensible even to people who have no background in science."

What Scientists Think collects Stangroom's interviews with twelve leading scientists of the late twentieth and early twenty-first centuries. Some of the interviewees address contentious topics, with Steve Jones discussing Charles Darwin's theories, which remain unaccepted by adherents of some religions, and Colin Blakemore explaining scientific testing on animals. Others in the book include Steven Pinker on evolutionary psychology and Susan Greenfield on consciousness.

Stangroom, being an expert on philosophy, "takes a rather philosophical approach" in the book, Pincock reported, concentrating "on science that relates to the

ADDRESSES: Home—New York, NY; and Charlotte, NC. *Office*—New York Times, 229 W. 43rd St., New York, NY 10036-3959. *E-mail*—ronstodghill@aol. com.

CAREER: New York Times, New York, NY, staff writer. Former editor-in-chief, *Savoy*.

WRITINGS:

NONFICTION

(With Kweisi Mfume) *No Free Ride: From the Mean Streets to the Mainstream*, One World (New York, NY), 1996.

Redbone: Money, Malice, and Murder in Atlanta, Amistad (New York, NY), 2007.

Contributor to periodicals, including *Time, Essence,* and *Business Week.*

SIDELIGHTS: Ron Stodghill tells a sensational true-crime story in his book *Redbone: Money, Malice, and Murder in Atlanta*. It concerns the 1996 murder of Lance Herndon, a wealthy young African-American businessman who was brutally slain in his Atlanta home while that city was hosting the Olympic Games. A native of New York, Herndon had headed south to become one Atlanta's most successful young entrepreneurs. A millionaire with a taste for the high life, Herndon was known for his extravagant spending and his highly promiscuous sex life. He was particularly attracted to light-skinned, petite African-American women, whom he called "redbones." Dionne Baugh was one of his sexual partners, and after becoming enraged with Herndon over a legal matter, she bludgeoned him to death as he slept in his bedroom, in one of Atlanta's most exclusive neighborhoods. An *Essence* reviewer advised that the book, is so filled with sensational details that it seems "as if you're reading a novel." A *Kirkus Reviews* contributor found that Stodghill does "a creditable job of setting up the crime," but felt that the character of the victim, while intriguing, "never does come into focus." A *Publishers Weekly* writer stated that in addition to creating "an absorbing yarn," Stodghill presents a "cogent" analysis of society, money, and power in Atlanta.

BIOGRAPHICAL AND CRITICAL SOURCES:

PERIODICALS

Essence, March, 2007, review of *Redbone: Money, Malice, and Murder in Atlanta*, p. 80.
Kirkus Reviews, December 15, 2006, review of *Redbone*, p. 1261.
Nieman Reports, spring, 2003, "Ron Stodghill, a Senior Writer and Former Midwest Bureau Chief at Time, Has Been Named the New Editor."
Publishers Weekly, December 4, 2006, review of *Redbone*, p. 43.*

* * *

STONE, Judith 1950-

PERSONAL: Born 1950.

CAREER: Writer and editor.

WRITINGS:

In the Jaws of Death, illustrated by Beth Hutchins, Raintree Publishers (Milwaukee, WI), 1980.
Minutes to Live, illustrated by Rob Sauber, Raintree Publishers (Milwaukee, WI), 1980.
Light Elements: Essays in Science from Gravity to Levity (nonfiction), Ballantine Books (New York, NY), 1991.
(With Nicole Gregory) *Heeling Your Inner Dog: A Self-Whelp Book* (nonfiction), Times Books (New York, NY), 1993.
When She Was White: The True Story of a Family Divided by Race (biography), Miramax (New York, NY), 2007.

Contributor to periodicals, including *New York Times, Elle, Vogue,* and *Newsday.* Contributing editor, *O, the Oprah Magazine.* Humor columnist, *Discover.*

SIDELIGHTS: Judith Stone displays her sense of humor while at the same time exploring interesting scientific quirks in her book *Light Elements: Essays in Science from Gravity to Levity.* Her subjects range from the humanity shown by an ape who uses sign language, to the reasons why the sound of fingernails scratching a chalkboard is so unpleasant to hear, to the ways that the belches of cows contribute to global warming. Other essays introduce little-known scientists such as Calvin Schwabe, who recommends eating broth made from earthworms, and discuss the manipulation of workplace environments with mood-altering scents. Reviewing the book for *Publishers Weekly,* Penny Kaganoff commented that the author's humor "makes science not only intelligible but entertaining as well."

Stone takes on a serious topic in the biography *When She Was White: The True Story of a Family Divided by Race.* The book covers the life of Sandra Laing, who was born in South Africa during the 1950s. Her parents were white, and supporters of apartheid, yet Sandra was born with African features and dark skin. Neighbors persecuted Sandra's mother, believing that the child was the product of an adulterous affair, but both parents vowed that Sandra was theirs, and speculated that her appearance was from some inter-racial union in their ancestry. Sandra was expelled from her all-white school for her appearance, and of-ficially classified as "Coloured." Her parents won a legal battle to regain her "White" status. A few years later, Laing eloped with a black man and went to live in a poor black township, which ultimately led to her being disowned by her family. The story is "riveting" in its portrayal of the harm brought about by the apartheid system, according to Hazel Rochman in *Booklist.* Deborah Way, a reviewer for *O, the Oprah Magazine,* also felt the book was outstanding for its exposé of the cruelty inherent in apartheid; she further praised Stone as a writer who produced "beautifully restrained prose, with a keen eye for detail and a strong sense of place."

BIOGRAPHICAL AND CRITICAL SOURCES:

PERIODICALS

Booklist, March 1, 2007, Hazel Rochman, review of *When She Was White: The True Story of a Family Divided by Race,* p. 47.
Good Housekeeping, May, 2007, review of *When She Was White,* p. 212.
Internet Bookwatch, August, 2007, review of *When She Was White.*

Kirkus Reviews, March 1, 2007, review of *When She Was White,* p. 213; March 1, 2007, review of *When She Was White,* p. S8.
O, the Oprah Magazine, April, 2007, Deborah Way, review of *When She Was White,* p. 58; May, 2007, "Correction," p. 42.
Publishers Weekly, April 5, 1991, Penny Kaganoff, review of *Light Elements: Essays in Science from Gravity to Levity,* p. 142; February 26, 2007, review of *When She Was White,* p. 76.
Vogue, April, 2007, Genevieve Bahrenburg, review of *When She Was White,* p. 286.

ONLINE

Boston Globe Online, http://www.boston.com/ (April 21, 2007), review of *When She Was White.**

*   *   *

STONE, R.W.

PERSONAL: Born in Chicago, IL; married; children: two. *Hobbies and other interests:* Korean martial arts, horseback riding, firearms collecting.

ADDRESSES: Home—FL. *Office*—Veterinary Trauma Center, 244 W. Orange St., Groveland, FL 34736; fax: (352) 429-7715.

CAREER: Veterinary Trauma Center, Groveland, FL, veterinarian.

WRITINGS:

Trail Hand: A Western Story (novel), Five Star (Water-ville, ME), 2006.

Also author of the e-book *A Very Shiny Nose.* Contribu-tor of more than seventy scientific articles to veterinary journals.

SIDELIGHTS: R.W. Stone had worked as a veterinar-ian for nearly thirty years before publishing his first novel. That book, *Trail Hand: A Western Story,* was inspired by the classic Western adventures of Max

Brand, Zane Grey, Louis L'Amour, and Luke Short. In the story, Owen Burke is a lone American cowhand who finds himself in the company of a group of Mexican vaqueros, as they move a valuable herd of horses from Mexico to California. There is tension between Burke and a vaquero named Chavez, who is jealous of the American's attention to the daughter of Enrique Allende, a wealthy ranch owner. Later, while scouting ahead of the herd, Owen is ambushed, assaulted, and left to die. Meanwhile, the horse herd is stolen by rustlers. Burke survives, but is framed by Chavez for setting up his own beating and being in league with the rustlers. Reviewing *Trail Hand* for *Booklist,* Wes Lukowsky stated that Stone "bursts onto the western scene with a suspenseful yarn replete with action." Lukowsky also described Owen Burke as "a very likable narrator," and welcomed Stone and Burke as "fresh" additions to the Western genre.

BIOGRAPHICAL AND CRITICAL SOURCES:

PERIODICALS

Booklist, December 1, 2006, Wes Lukowsky, review of *Trail Hand: A Western Story,* p. 35.

ONLINE

AuthorsDen, http://www.authorsden.com/ (September 28, 2007), biographical information about R.W. Stone.

* * *

SULLIVAN, Sherry E. 1961-

PERSONAL: Born 1961. *Education:* Ohio State University, Ph.D.

ADDRESSES: Office—Department of Management, College of Business Administration, Bowling Green State University, 3008A Business Admin Addition, Bowling Green, OH 43403. *E-mail*—ssulliv@cba.bgsu.edu.

CAREER: Educator, writer, and consultant. Memphis State University, Memphis, TN, associate professor; Bowling Green State University, Bowling Green, OH, associate professor and director of the Small Business Institute; consultant for not-for-profit businesses and executive career coach.

MEMBER: Southern Management Association (Southern Regional Network director for the careers division, 1991-93; board member, 1993-96, 1999-2002; networking event cochair, 1994, 2002; women in management division executive committee member, 1994-97; networking event chair 1996; careers division program chair, 1996; careers division chair, 1998; Sage Award Committee, 1996-98, 2000-2001; Gender and Diversity in Organizations board member; fellow), Midwest Academy of Management (track chair, 1997; treasurer, 1997-99), United States Association for Small Business and Entreprencurship, International Division (secretary, 2003; chair-elect, 2005), Southwest Academy (division secretary and track chair).

AWARDS, HONORS: Patton Scholar, Bowling Green State University, 1995; Janet Chusmir Outstanding Service Award for mentoring and service, National Academy of Management, 2002; University Author-Scholar, Bowling Green State University, 2003; Outstanding Educator, Reed Center, 2003; grants from the U.S. Department of Education and the Society for Human Resource Management; scholarships from Reader's Digest Corp., 21st Century Leaders, and the Ohio State University.

WRITINGS:

The Opt-Out Revolt: Why People Are Leaving Companies to Create Kaleidoscope Careers, Davies-Black Publishing (Mountain View, CA), 2006.

(Editor, with Yehuda Baruch and Hazlon Schepmyer) *Winning Reviews: A Guide for Evaluating Scholarly Writing,* Palgrave Macmillan (New York), NY 2006.

Contributor to periodicals, including *Journal of Management, Journal of Applied Psychology, Academy of Management Executive, Human Resource Management Review, Career Development Quarterly, Organizational Dynamics, Business Horizons,* and *Journal of Vocational Behavior, Group and Organization.* Associate editor of SMA careers division newsletter, 1989-

93, editor, 1993-95; associate editor of *International Journal of Small Business and Entrepreneurship*, 2003—. Member of editorial boards of journals, including *Cross-Cultural Management: An International Journal*, 1994-97, *Group and Organizational Management*, 1997—, *Journal of Managerial Psychology*, 2001—, *International Journal of Small Business and Entrepreneurship*, 2002—.

SIDELIGHTS: Sherry E. Sullivan is an associate professor of management at Memphis State University and author, with Lisa A. Mainiero, of *The Opt-Out Revolt: Why People Are Leaving Companies to Create Kaleidoscope Careers*. The book examines why both men and women are choosing to go it alone rather than climb the corporate ladder. Using quantitative and qualitative research from a five-year period, the authors reason that for cultural, biological, and psychological reasons, more people are choosing to restructure their careers, with the ultimate goal of spending more time outside of the company walls. Heidi Senior in the *Library Journal* noted that "job seekers, career changers, and researchers will find this book useful." In *Armchair Interviews*, Celia Renteria Szelwach recommended the book, commenting that "human resources professionals, academics, and executive/career transition coaches will gain value from reading this book." She concluded: "It's a keeper!"

BIOGRAPHICAL AND CRITICAL SOURCES:

PERIODICALS

California Bookwatch, December 1, 2006, "The Opt-Out Revolution."

Library Journal, September 1, 2006, Heidi Senior, review of *The Opt-Out Revolt: Why People Are Leaving Companies to Create Kaleidoscope Careers*, p. 158.

Publishers Weekly, June 12, 2006, review of *The Opt-Out Revolt*, p. 42.

Stamford Advocate, August 25, 2006, "Book Gets to the Core of Career Change."

ONLINE

Armchair Interviews, http://www.armchairinterviews.com/ (August 10, 2007), Celia Renteria Szelwach, review of *The Opt-Out Revolt*.

Bowling Green State University College of Business Administration Web Site, http://www.cba.bgsu.edu/ (September 10, 2007), biography of Sherry Sullivan.

Opt-Out Revolt, http://www.theoptoutrevolt.com (September 10, 2007).*

T

TABORI, George 1914-2007

OBITUARY NOTICE— See index for *CA* sketch: Original name, Gyorgy Tabori; born May 24, 1914, in Budapest, Austria-Hungary (now Hungary); died July 23, 2007, in Berlin, Germany. Playwright, scriptwriter, novelist, translator, journalist, broadcaster, director, and actor. Tabori is known internationally as a playwright of the Holocaust whose work examined some of the most brutal and frightening elements of life under Nazi rule. The author himself escaped the Nazi occupation of Eastern Europe as an emigré living in London, but his father was killed at Auschwitz and his mother barely talked her way out of the same fate. Tabori was born into a Jewish family and raised in relative comfort, ostensibly as a Roman Catholic. He had left Eastern Europe before Hitler's rise to power and was living in England as a naturalized British citizen when World War II began. Tabori spent the war years working as a journalist, translator, and foreign correspondent. After the war he moved to the United States, working in Hollywood as a screenwriter and occasional novelist, then in New York City as a playwright and translator-adaptor of dramatic works by his friend and colleague Bertolt Brecht. The screenplays include the Alfred Hitchcock movie *I Confess* (1953); the novels include *Beneath the Stone* (1945), the suspenseful story of a British parachutist's meal with a Prussian officer behind enemy lines. But it is Tabori's stage plays that critics remember most vividly. He was widely praised for using irony and humor (albeit dark humor) to explore the horrors of the Holocaust, the relations between Germans and Jews, and the ramifications of anti-Semitism with audiences who would not be receptive to his grim message in any other form. Some critics have described his subjects as characters wholly beyond redemption, but Tabori himself once said, rather enigmatically, that the theme of his work was actually the act of love. *The Emperor's Clothes,* produced on Broadway in 1953, is about a young man who falls into the hands of the Hungarian secret police. Facing interrogation and torture, the prisoner, instead of sacrificing his beliefs to save himself, finally reinforces them by a courageous demonstration of integrity. *The Cannibals* (1967) is the story of inmates of a concentration camp who are forced to choose between cannibalism of their own and the gas chamber. *Mein Kampf* (1989) has been described as a farce, but the play is the story of a young Adolf Hitler and his relationship with the Viennese Jew who becomes his mentor and helps to shape the future leader's world view. Tabori returned to Europe in the 1970s, where he settled in Germany as an actor, director, and playwright, notably with the Berliner Ensemble. In 1992 Tabori was awarded the George Büchner Prize of the Deutsche Akademie für Sprache und Dichtung for what the awarding body called "courage in using irony and humour to explain to Germans the grim history of relations between Germans and Jews."

OBITUARIES AND OTHER SOURCES:

BOOKS

Contemporary Dramatists, 6th edition, St. James Press (Detroit, MI), 1999.

Dictionary of Literary Biography, Volume 245: *British and Irish Dramatists since World War II, Third Series,* Thomson Gale (Detroit, MI), 2001.

Reference Guide to Holocaust Literature, St. James Press (Detroit, MI), 2002.

PERIODICALS

Los Angeles Times, July 25, 2007, p. B9.
New York Times, July 27, 2007, p. C11.
Times (London, England), October 2, 2007, p. 56.
Washington Post, July 26, 2007, p. 86.

*   *   *

TAYLOR, Patrick 1941-

PERSONAL: Born 1941, in Bangor, County Down, Northern Ireland; immigrated to Canada, 1970; married; wife's name Kate; children: Sarah. *Education:* Attended Campbell College, Belfast; graduated in medicine from Queen's University of Belfast, 1964. *Hobbies and other interests:* Sailing and navigation; building ship models.

ADDRESSES: Home—Bowen Island, British Columbia, Canada. *E-mail*—editere@shaw.ca; editere@yahoo.com.

CAREER: Medical doctor, specializing in obstetrics and gynecology. Practiced in Ulster, Northern Ireland; teacher and researcher in the field of human infertility, in Canada; University of British Columbia, Vancouver, emeritus professor of medicine, and St. Paul's Hospital, head of obstetrics and gynecology, retired, 2001.

AWARDS, HONORS: Campbellian Prize for Literature, 1958, for "On Shootinge: An Essay in the Style of Francis Bacon"; three lifetime achievement awards in medicine, including the Lifetime Award of Excellence, Canadian Fertility and Andrology Society.

WRITINGS:

Only Wounded: Ulster Stories, Key Porter Books (Toronto, Ontario, Canada), 1997.

(With T.F. Baskett)*The Complete Anthology of "En Passant," 1989-1999* (humor collection), Rogers Media (Toronto, Ontario, Canada), 1999.

NOVELS

Pray for Us Sinners, Insomniac Press (Toronto, Ontario, Canada), 2000.
The Apprenticeship of Doctor Laverty, Insomniac Press (Toronto, Ontario, Canada), 2004, published as *An Irish Country Doctor* (Volume 1 in "Irish Country Books" series), Forge (New York, NY), 2007.
Now and in the Hour of Our Death, Insomniac Press (Toronto, Ontario, Canada), 2005.
An Irish Country Village (Volume 2 in "Irish Country Books" series), Forge (New York, NY), 2008.

TEXTBOOKS

(With V. Gomel, A.A. Yzpe, and J.E. Rioux, *Laparoscopy and Hysteroscopy in Gynecologic Practice*, Year Book Medical Publishers (Chicago, IL), 1986.
(Translator) J.E. Hamou, *Hysteroscopy and Microhysteroscopy: Text and Atlas*, Appleton & Lange (Norwalk, CT), 1991.
(With J.A. Collins) *Unexplained Infertility*, Oxford University Press (Oxford, England), 1992.
(With A.G. Gordon) *Practical Laparoscopy*, Blackwell Scientific Publications (London, England), 1993.
(With A.G. Gordon) *Practical Hysteroscopy*, Blackwell Scientific Publications (London, England), 1993.
(With V. Gomel) *Diagnostic and Operative Gynecologic Laparoscopy*, Mosby (St. Louis, MO), 1995.

Contributor to professional journals and periodicals, including *Pacific Yachting, West Coast Yachting*, and *48 Degrees North*. Author of monthly medical humor columns "En Passant," 1989-1999, "Medicine Chest," 1990-94, and "Taylor's Twist," 1993-2002. Book reviewer for *Stitches: The Journal of Medical Humour.* Editor-in-chief, *Snakes Alive: The Journal of the Belfast Medical School*, 1962-63, and *Canadian Obstetrics and Gynaecology*, 1991-2001. Senior editor, *The Society of Obstetricians and Gynaecologists of Canada: The First Fifty Years*, Pantheon (New York,

NY), 1994. Associate editor of several professional journals, including *Journal of Reproductive Medicine, International Journal of Fertility, Human Reproduction,* and *Canadian Journal of Surgery.*

ADAPTATIONS: Film rights to *Pray for Us Sinners* have been purchased by Captive Entertainment.

SIDELIGHTS: Patrick Taylor practiced medicine in an Northern Irish village with many similarities to Ballybucklebo, the fictional setting of his novel *An Irish Country Doctor,* which was originally published in Canada as *The Apprenticeship of Doctor Laverty.* The novel is, in fact, based on journals Taylor kept during his early years of medical practice. While carrying on a distinguished career as a doctor, Taylor also proved himself as a writer, publishing several textbooks, humor columns in professional journals, and even a book of short stories and a novel prior to *An Irish Country Doctor,* the first book in a projected four-volume series.

The book's main character, Barry Laverty, is a naive young graduate of medical school, who takes a job as a physician's assistant in Ballybucklebo, a small town in Northern Ireland. Unlike most of his classmates, Laverty did not seek conventional success, but was attracted instead to the beauty and seeming tranquility of the backwater town. Laverty's recent medical studies and modern practices are a world away from medicine as it is practiced by his employer, Dr. Fingal Flahertie O'Reilly. As the book progresses, Laverty does realize that he has much to learn from the older doctor, as well as some things to teach. A subplot follows Laverty's romance with Patricia, an engineering student. A *Kirkus Reviews* writer found the plot "a bit thin," but described the book as one "with likable characters and atmospheric dialogue." A reviewer for *Publishers Weekly* warned of an "occasional whimsy overload," but added that despite that, "Taylor's novel makes for escapist, delightful fun."

BIOGRAPHICAL AND CRITICAL SOURCES:

PERIODICALS

Kirkus Reviews, December 15, 2006, review of *An Irish Country Doctor,* p. 1242.

Publishers Weekly, December 4, 2006, review of *An Irish Country Doctor,* p. 35.

ONLINE

MyShelf.com, http://www.myshelf.com/ (October 5, 2007), review of *An Irish Country Doctor.*
Patrick Taylor Home Page, http://www.patrick taylor.ca (October 5, 2007).*

* * *

TAYLOR, Sarah McFarland 1968-

PERSONAL: Born 1968; daughter of Arthur R. (a former television executive and college president) and Marion McFarland (manager of marketing publications at a securities brokerage company) Taylor; married Kevin Charles Looper, May 11, 1997. *Education:* Brown University, B.A.; Dartmouth University, M.A.; University of California at Santa Barbara, Ph.D.

ADDRESSES: Office—Department of Religion, Northwestern University, Crowe Hall, 1860 Campus Dr., Evanston, IL 60208-0850. *E-mail*—sarah@ northwestern.edu; SMcFT@aol.com.

CAREER: Northwestern University, Evanston, IL, assistant professor of religion, 2000—.

MEMBER: American Academy of Religions (cochair, Religion and Ecology group).

AWARDS, HONORS: Rockefeller Foundation Humanities Fellowship, 2001-2002; Louisville Institute dissertation fellowship; Woodrow Wilson Foundation Career Enhancement Fellowship; Andrew Mellon Postdoctoral Fellowship; Joseph H. Fichter Award for study of women and religion; Albert C. Clark Prize for work on African American religions.

WRITINGS:

Green Sisters: A Spiritual Ecology (nonfiction), Harvard University Press (Cambridge, MA), 2007.

Contributor to *This Sacred Earth: Religion, Nature, Environment,* 2nd edition, Routledge (New York, NY), 2004, and to monograph *The Struggle for Life: A Companion Volume to William James's The Varieties of Religions Experience,* Society for the Scientific Study of Religion, 1995. North American religions editor, *Encyclopedia of Religion and Nature,* Continuum Press (New York, NY), 2002. Contributor to periodicals, including *Journal of Theta Kappa* and *Epochê.*

SIDELIGHTS: Sarah McFarland Taylor's book *Green Sisters: A Spiritual Ecology* had its genesis in her doctoral dissertation, which involved a four-year study of the greening of Catholicism in America, focusing on a group of activist nuns who ran a community-supported farm. Taylor has also made presentations on similar topics, including the work of activist nuns to halt the spread of "Frankenfoods," or foods produced through biotechnology methods.

Green Sisters explores the ways that nuns around the United States have extended the traditional Catholic concern with social justice to include a mission to heal planet Earth and protect its resources. This movement takes many forms, from the use of alternative energy and housing, to the creation of community-supported, organic farms and gardens, to the development of "green" religious ceremonies. At times, the work of these nuns has been misunderstood or interpreted as being contrary to their church, even though they do not see it as such themselves.

"*Green Sisters* is an academic work of wide-ranging research and mysticism, social justice, feminism, Catholicism, or monasticism," stated Margaret Bullitt-Jonas on the *Sojourners* Web site. "*Green Sisters* makes an important contribution both to contemporary American religious history and to women's religious history."

BIOGRAPHICAL AND CRITICAL SOURCES:

PERIODICALS

Booklist, March 15, 2007, June Sawyers, review of *Green Sisters: A Spiritual Ecology,* p. 6.
Catholic New Times, July 3, 2005, Cristina Vanin, review of *Green Sisters,* p. 20.

New York Times, May 11, 1997, biographical information about Sarah McFarland Taylor.

ONLINE

American Academy of Religion, http://www.aarweb.org/ (October 2, 2007), biographical information about Sarah McFarland Taylor.
Gainesville.com, http://www.gainesville.com/ (October 2, 2007), Nathan Crabbe, "Ecological Endings: Green Burials Are Catching On."
Northwestern University Department of Religion, http://www.religion.northwestern.edu/ (October 3, 2007), biographical information about Sarah McFarland Taylor.
Science Musings Blog, http://www.sciencemusings.com/ (April 13, 2007), review of *Green Sisters.*
Sojourners, http://www.sojo.net/ (October 2, 2007), Margaret Bullitt-Jonas, review of *Green Sisters.**

*   *   *

TELLKAMP, Uwe 1968-

PERSONAL: Born 1968.

ADDRESSES: E-mail—info@rowohlt.de.

CAREER: Writer.

AWARDS, HONORS: Dresden Poetry Prize, 2004; Ingeborg Bachmann Prize, 2004, for work in progress.

WRITINGS:

NOVELS

Der Hecht, Die Träume Und Das Portugiesische Cafe, Faber & Faber (Leipzig, Germany), 2000.
Der Eisvogel (title means "The Icebird"), Rowohlt Berlin (Berlin, Germany), 2005.

SIDELIGHTS: Uwe Tellkamp was the winner of the prestigious Dresden Poetry Prize in 2004, in a competition open to German and Czech-speaking authors. That same year, he was awarded the Ingeborg Bachmann Prize in an annual competition that involves writers reading unpublished manuscripts and then taking criticism from a panel of judges, with the proceedings being broadcast on national television. Tellkamp's winning work used the framework of a trolley ride around Dresden to support his thematic and linguistic flights.

Tellkamp's novel, *Der Eisvogel,* is, in the words of *World Literature Today* reviewer Gregory H. Wolf, "an intriguing, complexly written novel with a number of interwoven themes such as social criticism, a father-son conflict, and, most notably, terrorism." The reviewer compared Tellkamp's novel to a "mosaic," as it is made up of shifting viewpoints and perspectives, moving back and forth in time after it begins at the protagonist's trial for a shooting. The man, named Wiggo, is thirty years old. Despite being the son of a successful banker and having earned his Ph.D., he is unemployed and adrift in life. Injured in a terrorist attack, Wiggo begins to tell his life story, with many interruptions from other narrators. Wolf felt that *Der Eisvogel* is "an engaging read," and that the references to terrorism and contemporary social and political issues, along with the author's "elevated linguistic register and narrative style, invite readers to contemplate and reflect on violent extremism, the use of power and terrorism, and the future of legitimate political representation."

BIOGRAPHICAL AND CRITICAL SOURCES:

PERIODICALS

World Literature Today, July 1, 2006, Gregory H. Wolf, review of *Der Eisvogel,* p. 71.

ONLINE

Dresdner Literaturbüro, http://www.dresdner-literaturbuero.de/ (October 2, 2007), biographical information about Uwe Tellkamp.
Literary Saloon, http://www.complete-review.com/ (October 2, 2007), "Ingeborg-Bachmann-Preis."
Sign and Sight, http://www.signandsight.com/ (October 2, 2007), Clemens-Peter Haase, "Highlights of German Contemporary Literature."*

TEMPLE, Peter 1946-

PERSONAL: Born 1946, in South Africa; immigrated to Australia, 1980. *Hobbies and other interests:* Cabinetmaking, horse racing.

ADDRESSES: Home—Ballarat, Victoria, Australia.

CAREER: Worked as a journalist and editor for newspapers and magazines, including *Australian Society;* taught journalism, editing, and media studies at a number of universities; self-employed writer/editor, 1995—.

AWARDS, HONORS: Four Ned Kelly awards, for *Bad Debts,* 1996, *Shooting Star,* 1999, *Dead Point,* 2000, and *White Dog,* 2003; Colin Roderick Award, Federation for Australian Literary Studies, 2005; Duncan Laurie Dagger award, 2007, for *The Broken Shore.*

WRITINGS:

"JACK IRISH" SERIES; NOVELS

Bad Debts, HarperCollins (Pymble, New South Wales, Australia), 1996, MacAdam/Cage (San Francisco, CA), 2005.
Black Tide, Bantam (Sydney, New South Wales, Australia), 1999, MacAdam/Cage (San Francisco, CA), 2005.
Dead Point, Bantam (Sydney, New South Wales, Australia), 2000.
White Dog, Text (Melbourne, Victoria, Australia), 2003.

OTHER NOVELS

An Iron Rose, HarperCollins (Pymble, New South Wales, Australia), 1998.
Shooting Star, Bantam (Milsons Point, New South Wales, Australia), 1999.
Dead Point, Bantam (Sydney, New South Wales, Australia), 2002.
Identity Theory, MacAdam/Cage (San Francisco, CA), 2004, published as *In the Evil Day,* Quercus (London, England), 2006.

The Broken Shore, Text (Melbourne, Victoria, Australia), 2005, Farrar, Straus (New York, NY), 2007.

SIDELIGHTS: Peter Temple is an Australian crime writer who has garnered awards for his best-selling books, many of which have been reprinted in Britain and the United States. A former journalist and educator, in 1995 Temple turned his entire attention to writing, and the following year his first book, *Bad Debts,* was published. It is the first in a series featuring Jack Irish, a criminal attorney whose hobby is cabinetmaking and who enjoys betting on horses. Jack is not actually Irish, but of German-Jewish extraction. In this first book former client Danny McKillop has been released from prison and leaves him a desperate message asking for help. Before Jack returns the call, Danny is killed. Jack hunts for his murderer, finds romance, and becomes involved in a horse-racing plot. A *Publishers Weekly* contributor wrote: "The engaging Jack and his friends are absolutely original and unfailingly amusing." Temple has received several Ned Kelly awards, which are the Australian equivalent of the Edgar Award in the United States, including three for books in this series.

Temple moved to Australia in 1980, and his novels reflect the atmosphere, culture, and rugged terrain of that country. *Mostly Fiction* Web site contributor Sudheer Apte wrote that "permeating the entire narrative is the ever-present coastline of southern Australia, of cold, jagged cliffs and violent seas. It may be a cliche to say that the place is itself a character in the novel, but it applies to *The Broken Shore.*

The protagonist is Victoria police detective Joe Cashin, who has returned to his childhood home with his two dogs to restore the old family dwelling and attempt to heal from both physical and emotional trauma. In the relative peace of the rural setting, local millionaire businessman Charles Bourgoyne is murdered, and Joe heads the investigation. When three Aboriginal teens are caught trying to sell the dead man's watch, the police move in on them and kill two. The third boy drowns himself offshore. The case is closed, but Joe, who has Aboriginal family members, is not satisfied with its conclusion. In this novel Temple treats a number of themes, including the poor treatment of Australian Aborigines and the ecology of the wilderness.

Booklist reviewer Keir Graff concluded his review by writing that "this deeply intelligent thriller starts slowly, builds inexorably, and ends unforgettably." A *Publishers Weekly* contributor called *The Broken Shore* "an unforgettable read."

In a *Bookreporter.com* interview, Temple was asked if, since he was born in South Africa, he would use that country as a setting. Temple replied: "I left South Africa out of profound distaste for the white regime and for a long time I had no wish to be reminded of the place. It has changed, however, and so have I. I set a chapter of *Identity Theory* in South Africa and one of the lead characters is South African. Given time, there are certainly plenty of themes I would like to explore in the country's recent history."

In *Identity Theory,* published in England as *In the Evil Day,* the action takes place across the globe—in South Africa, England, the United States, and Wales. Con Niemand is a former South African mercenary who now works in security, protecting wealthy South Africans from lingering violence. He comes into possession of a videotape that implicates American soldiers in the murders of the residents of a small South African village, and this raises alarms worldwide and leads to orders to kill him. A London newspaperwoman tries to buy the tape but is thwarted by people she thought she could trust. John Anselm is a journalist who was kidnapped in Lebanon and brain damaged due to a beating in which his head was bashed with a rifle butt. Anselm works in surveillance and is given the job of tracking Niemand, which soon leads them to a confrontation.

In reviewing the novel for the *Curled Up with a Good Book* Web site, Luan Gaines described *Identity Theory* as "an excellent, well-written thriller that evokes malevolent shadows of intrigue and special ops, all the unnamable things we confine to spy movies." *Library Journal* reviewer Lawrence Rungren called the novel "a violent page-turner." *January Magazine* Web site contributor David Honeybone, who reviewed the British edition, wrote: "Anselm and Niemand battle with their own demons throughout this book, and as a result they make for wholly credible protagonists."

BIOGRAPHICAL AND CRITICAL SOURCES:

PERIODICALS

Booklist, October 15, 2004, Frank Sennett, review of *Identity Theory,* p. 393; March 15, 2007, Keir Graff, review of *The Broken Shore,* p. 30.

Entertainment Weekly, June 1, 2007, Jennifer Reese, review of *The Broken Shore,* p. 70.

Library Journal, October 1, 2004, Lawrence Rungren, review of *Identity Theory,* p. 74; May 15, 2007, Wilda Williams, review of *The Broken Shore,* p. 85.

Publishers Weekly, October 10, 2005, review of *Bad Debts,* p. 36; April 2, 2007, review of *The Broken Shore,* p. 38.

ONLINE

Age Online, http://www.theage.com.au/ (August 31, 2006), Jason Steger, "Crime Writer Judged a Serial Winner."

Bookreporter.com, http://www.bookreporter.com/ (September 26, 2007), author interview.

Brisbane Writers Festival Web site, http://www. brisbanewritersfestival.com.au/ (September 26, 2007), author biography.

Curled Up with a Good Book, http://www.curledup. com/ (September 26, 2007), Luan Gaines, review of *Identity Theory.*

Epinions, http://www.epinions.com/ (September 26, 2007), reviews of *Bed Debts, Black Tide,* and *Dead Point.*

January Magazine, http://www.januarymagazine.com/ (September 26, 2007), David Honeybone, "Peter Temple: Lies, Lies and Videotape."

Mostly Fiction, http://www.mostlyfiction.com/ (January 29, 2006), Jana L. Perskie, review of *Bad Debts;* (May 29, 2007), Sudheer Apte, review of *The Broken Shore.**

*   *   *

THEROUX, Louis 1970-
(Louis Sebastian Theroux)

PERSONAL: Born May 20, 1970, in Singapore; son of Paul (a writer) and Ann Theroux; married Susanna Kleeman (divorced). *Education:* Attended Oxford University, England.

ADDRESSES: Home—London, England; New York, NY. *Agent*—Capel & Land Ltd., 29 Wardour St., London W1D 6PS, England.

CAREER: Writer, journalist, television host, television producer, and screenwriter. Host of television series *Weird Weekends,* British Broadcasting Corporation (BBC) network and Bravo. Has appeared on numerous other television shows, including *TV Nation.* Also worked as a journalist in California and as a writer for *Spy* magazine.

AWARDS, HONORS: BAFTA (British Academy of Film and Television Arts) award for best factual presenter, 2001 and 2002.

WRITINGS:

The Call of the Weird: Travels in American Subcultures, Da Capo Press (Cambridge, MA), 2007.

Writer for television and documentaries, including *TV Nation,* 1994; *Weird Christmas,* 1998; *Weird Weekends,* 1999; *Louis and the Brothel,* 2003; *Louis, Martin & Michael,* 2003; and *Louis and the Nazis,* 2003.

SIDELIGHTS: Louis Theroux became famous in England with the British Broadcasting Corporation (BBC) television series *Weird Weekends.* The show featured Theroux as he chronicled America's subcultures, from the porn industry and "gangsta" rappers to religious zealots and White Power activists. In his first book, titled *The Call of the Weird: Travels in American Subcultures,* the author revisits ten of the characters he met while filming for his television series. "His prose is conversational yet concise," wrote Michael Upchurch in the *Seattle Times,* adding: "His psychological reading of his interviewees is probing, even if he does run into some brick walls of mutual incomprehension." Lucy Hughes-Hallett, writing in the *Spectator,* noted: "One of the saving graces of his relationship with his interviewees, and therefore of this book, is that he tends to become rather fond of them."

Among the people Theroux revisits for *The Call of the Weird* are a retired porn star who is bored in his computer job, a man named Thor Templar who claims to have killed space aliens, and a former member of the Aryan Nations named Jerry Gruidl. As for his own feelings about the strange people he profiles, the author told Sathnam Sanghera on Sanghera's Web site: "There is something deeply romantic about these strange bearded renegades who carry guns and are willing to lay down their lives for their vision of correct living, even if it comes to nothing. There is something about their ambition that fulfills my slightly pessimistic view of human perfectibility."

Reviewers generally praised Theroux's first book. "The book is a charming travelogue of unusual people encountering a more bland world," noted a contributor to the *Weirdwriter* Web site. "It doesn't offer profound insights, but it does offer a good time." A *Kirkus Reviews* contributor referred to the book as "a mixed bag of peculiar encounters with bizarre citizens, alternately fascinating and sad."

BIOGRAPHICAL AND CRITICAL SOURCES:

PERIODICALS

AdWeek, September 27, 1999, Kathleen Sampey, "Fringe Benefits," p. 5.

Bookseller, October 12, 2001, "Weidenfeld Signs Louis Theroux," p. 35; March 12, 2004, "Louis Theroux Is About to Research His First Book, Which Pan Macmillan Will Publish Next Autumn. May Contain Traces of Nuts. Sees Him Return to the US, without Camera Crew, to Meet Again Some of His Offbeat Subjects," p. 33; July 15, 2005, review of *The Call of the Weird: Travels in American Subcultures,* p. 36.

Financial Times, June 13, 2005, Karl French, "Television—Karl French Critics' Choice," p. 16; October 8, 2005, Sathnam Sanghera, "Much Smarter Than He Looks an Act? Well Not Entirely, but There's Nothing Naive or Befuddled about TV's Master of Weird in Person or Prose, writes Sathnam Sanghera," p. 3; November 19, 2005, Claudia Webb, "In Brief—The Call of the Weird: Travels in American Subcultures," p. 39; November 29, 2005, "One Life Critics Choice—Television," p. 16.

Guardian Unlimited (London, England), March 4, 2002, Simon Hattenstone, "This Is a Setup," interview with author; January 27, 2007, "Is This It?," interview with author; March 31, 2007, Louis Theroux, "God's Squad."

Independent (London, England), October 4, 2005, Deborah Ross, "Louis Theroux: 'Even if You Find What Someone Does Hideous, You Can Still Enjoy Their Company and Find Them Interesting,'" interview with author; August 21, 2006, Sophie Morris, "Louis Theroux: My Week in Media," interview with author.

Kirkus Reviews, November 15, 2006, review of *The Call of the Weird,* p. 1168.

Library Journal, January 1, 2007, Melissa Stearns, review of *The Call of the Weird,* p. 132.

Marketing, February 27, 2003, "Marketing Mix: Hush Descends on Hamiltons," p. 52.

Miami Herald, March 14, 2007, Lisa Arthur, review of *The Call of the Weird.*

Multichannel News, September 20, 1999, Linda Haugsted, "Theroux Makes the Most of His Bravo 'Weekends,'" p. 40.

New Statesman, March 25, 2002, Ann Widdecombe, "When Ann Met Louis: Critics Felt That the Ingenu Theroux Had Gone Too Far, nut, Says His Recent Victim Ann Widdecombe, All's Fair in Fly-on-the-Wall," p. 38; February 12, 2007, Andrew Billen, "Nothing Ventured, Nothing Gained: Two Documentaries Show It's Important to Choose Your Subject Carefully," p. 46.

New York Times, February 7, 2007, William Grimes, "Back on the Road, Tracking the Red, White and Odd," p. E8.

PR Week, April 5, 2002, "Diary: The Clifford Mic Incident: We Shall Never Know," p. 24.

Publishers Weekly, November 20, 2006, review of *The Call of the Weird,* p. 50.

Seattle Times, March 7, 2007, Michael Upchurch, review of *The Call of the Weird.*

Spectator, October 22, 2005, Lucy Hughes-Hallett, "A Bemused and Amused Bystander," p. 46.

Sun (London, England), June 27, 2007, Melissa Kent, "Louis Theroux Gets the Chop."

ONLINE

BBC, http://www.bbc.co.uk/ (August 13, 2001), "The Weird World of Louis Theroux"; (June 26, 2007), "Louis Theroux: Under the Knife"; (January 26, 2007), "Weird, or Just Wanting?," profile of author.

Call of the Weird Official Website, http://www.thecalloftheweird.com (October 15, 2007).

Capel & Land Agency Web site, http://www.capelland.com/ (October 15, 2007), profile of author.

Guardian Unlimited—The Blog TV & Radio, http://blogs.guardian.co.uk/tv/ (February 2, 2007), Sarah Phillips, "Louis Theroux, I Love You."

International Movie Database, http://www.imdb.com/ (October 15, 2007), information on author's film work.

Internet Trash, http://internettrash.com/ (October 15, 2007), profile of author.

Irish KC, http://irishkc.com/ (March 30, 2007), "Kansas' Phelps in BBC Documentary."

My Manifesto, http://www.aphrodigitaliac.com/ (November 29, 1999), "Louis Theroux's Weird Weekends."

Quick Stop Entertainment, http://www.quickstop entertainment.com/ (October 15, 2007), Ken Plume, "Interview with Louis Theroux."

Rupert's Blog, http://rupertward.wordpress.com/ (October 15, 2007), "The Most Hated Family in America."

Salon.com, http://www.salon.com/ (October 22, 1999), Cynthia Joyce, "Beyond the Fringe," profile of author.

Sathnam Sanghera Web site, http://www.sathnam.com/ (October 15, 2007), Sathnam Sanghera, "Louis Theroux Interview."

Slush Pile.net, http://www.slushpile.nct/ (June 20, 2007), interview with author.

Time.com, http://www.time.com/ (October 29, 1999), "Thank God It's Friday: Weird Weekend's Louis Theroux," interview with author.

TV.com, http://www.tv.com/ (October 15, 2007), information on author's television work.

UKTV, http://uktv.co.uk/ (October 15, 2007), profile of author.

Weirdwriter: Exploring the Fields of the Weird, http://browriter.blogspot.com/ (March 27, 2007), review of *The Call of the Weird.**

*   *   *

THEROUX, Louis Sebastian
    See THEROUX, Louis

*   *   *

THOMPSON, Kate 1956-

PERSONAL: Born 1956, in Halifax, Yorkshire, England; partner of Conor Minogue; children: Cliodhna and Dearbhla (daughters). *Education:* Studied law.

ADDRESSES: Home—Ireland. *Agent*—Sophie Hicks, Ed Victor Ltd., 6 Bayley St., Bedford Sq., London WC1B 3HE, England. *E-mail*—kate@katethompson. info.

CAREER: Writer.

AWARDS, HONORS: Bisto prize, 2002, for *The Beguilers,* 2003, for *The Alchemist's Apprentice,* 2004, for *Annan Water,* and 2006, for *The New Policeman;* Children's fiction prize, London *Guardian,* Whitbread Children's Book award, and the Dublin Airport Authority Children's Book of the Year Award, all 2005, all for *The New Policeman.*

WRITINGS:

There Is Something (poetry), Signpost Press (Bellingham, WA), 1992.

Down among the Gods, Virago (London, England), 1997.

Thin Air, Sceptre (London, England), 1999.

An Act of Worship, Sceptre (London, England), 2000.

The Alchemist's Apprentice, Bodley Head (London, England), 2001.

The Beguilers, Dutton Children's Books (New York, NY), 2001.

Annan Water, Bodley Head (London, England), 2004.

The New Policeman, Bodley Head (London, England), 2005, Greenwillow Books (New York, NY), 2007.

The Fourth Horseman, Bodley Head (London, England), 2006.

The Last of the High Kings, Bodley Head (London, England), 2007.

"SWITCHERS" SERIES

Switchers, Bodley Head (London, England), 1997, Hyperion Books for Children (New York, NY), 1998.

Midnight's Choice, Bodley Head (London, England), 1998, Hyperion Books for Children (New York, NY), 1999.

Wild Blood, Bodley Head (London, England), 1999, Hyperion Books for Children (New York, NY), 2000.

The Switchers Trilogy, Red Fox (London, England), 2004.

"MISSING LINK" SERIES

The Missing Link, Bodley Head (London, England), 2000, also published as *Fourth World,* Bloomsbury (New York, NY), 2005.

Only Human, Bodley Head (London, England), 2001, Bloomsbury (New York, NY), 2006.

Origins, Bodley Head (London, England), 2003, Bloomsbury (New York, NY), 2007.

SIDELIGHTS: Kate Thompson was born in England to activist parents and spent the majority of her time growing up riding and racing horses. Thompson traveled the world, including going to the United States and India, before settling in Ireland in 1981 and seriously writing poetry and novels. Many of Thompson's novels are science fiction and oftentimes deal with lore or locales of Ireland. Writing primarily for younger audiences, she is one of the few authors who writes fantasy novels for children.

The first novel Thompson published was *Switchers,* which later developed into a trilogy. The story follows teenaged Tess and Kevin in their mission to prevent the jelly-fish-like krool from sending the planet into another ice age. The krool devour anything in their path, but the pair are gifted with the ability to change into any animal, real or imaginary, that they want. Reviews for Thompson's debut novel were mixed. A contributor to *Publishers Weekly,* noting the occasional poetic language, praised Thompson for her ability to join "elements from mythology and science fiction with insights into animal nature." John Peters, writing in *Booklist,* found parts of the story that suggested Thompson "hasn't thought through every detail." Writing on the *Rambles* Web site, Donna Scanlon claimed that "Thompson's plot is completely engrossing, and the characters of Tess and Kevin are very well drawn and sympathetic."

Thompson rounded out the series with *Midnight's Choice* and *Wild Blood* before moving to her next trilogy, the "Missing Link" series. The first book in the series, *Fourth World,* continues a key concept from the previous series in playing on the link between humans and animals. Christie accompanies his mentally impaired foster brother, Danny, when he sets out to meet his birth mother, Maggie. Christie is suspicious, however, when Maggie sends a talking bird and dog to travel with them. Christie later finds out that Maggie is a neo-Dr. Moreau, splicing human DNA with that of animals creating a range of hybrids, Danny included. In a *Horn Book Magazine* review, Vicky Smith found holes in the genetic arguments Thompson makes. Smith commented, however, that even "if the exact nature of the genetic work is rather sketchily developed, the characters are not." Susan L. Rogers, writing in *School Library Journal,* thought that "Christie's narrative voice seems far too sophisticated for his age." Rogers conceded, however, that it brings the story "more heft than the average plot-driven series opener." A contributor to *Kirkus Reviews* concluded that Thompson "weaves some stimulating ideas into this suspenseful tale and leaves plenty of unanswered questions for future installments." Thompson continued the series, publishing *Only Human* one year later, and following up with *Origins.*

Published in 2005, *The New Policeman* won the 2006 Bisto prize, 2005 Whitbread Children's Book award and the London *Guardian* Children's fiction prize, and was named the 2005 Dublin Airport Authorities children's book of the year. Fifteen-year-old Irish musician J.J. Liddy discovers a link between his world and that of eternal youth in an attempt to literally give his mother more time in the day to play music. While in this fantasy land, he faces dark rumors about his family and attempts to fix a leak in time between the two worlds. Reviews for the independent novel were positive. Judith A. Hayn, writing in the *Journal of Adolescent & Adult Literacy,* commented that "Thompson takes the reader into a dreamland, coupled with the reality of Ireland as part of the European Union of 2005, and captivates her readers until the charming tale ends in surprise." Gillian Engberg noted in a *Booklist* review that readers would "overlook any creaky plot connections and fall eagerly into the rich, comic language and the captivating characters and scenes." Writing in *School Library Journal,* Heather M. Campbell added that "those who follow this story through to the end will not be disappointed."

BIOGRAPHICAL AND CRITICAL SOURCES:

PERIODICALS

Booklist, March 15, 1998, John Peters, review of *Switchers,* p. 1245; April 15, 2000, Sally Estes, review of *Wild Blood,* p. 1543; May 15, 2005, Jennifer Mattson, review of *Fourth World,* p. 1660; May 15, 2006, Jennifer Mattson, review of *Only Human,* p. 61; February 1, 2007, Gillian Engberg, review of *The New Policeman,* p. 47.

Bookseller, February 18, 2005, review of *The New Policeman,* p. 40; February 17, 2006, review of *The Fourth Horseman,* p. 32.

Children's Bookwatch, July, 2005, review of *Fourth World.*

Horn Book Magazine, January-February, 2002, Anita L. Burkam, review of *The Beguilers,* p. 85; May-June, 2005, Vicky Smith, review of *Fourth World,* p. 333; May-June, 2006, Vicky Smith, review of *Only Human,* p. 332; March-April, 2007, Betsy Hearne, review of *The New Policeman,* p. 206.

Journal of Adolescent & Adult Literacy, May, 2007, Judith A. Hayn, review of *The New Policeman,* p. 690.

Kirkus Reviews, April 1, 2005, review of *Fourth World,* p. 427; May 1, 2006, review of *Only Human,* p. 468; December 15, 2006, review of *The New Policeman,* p. 1273.

Kliatt, January, 2007, Paula Rohrlick, review of *The New Policeman,* p. 19.

M2 Best Books, September 30, 2005, "Kate Thompson Awarded Guardian Children's Fiction Prize."

Publishers Weekly, June 8, 1998, review of *Switchers,* p. 61; October 29, 2001, review of *The Beguilers,* p. 65.

School Library Journal, July, 2000, Patricia A. Dollisch, review of *Wild Blood,* p. 111; October, 2001, Steven Engelfried, review of *The Beguilers,* p. 173; October, 2005, Susan L. Rogers, review of *Fourth World,* p. 175; March, 2007, Heather M. Campbell, review of *The New Policeman,* p. 220; April, 2007, review of *The New Policeman,* p. 73.

ONLINE

Contemporary Writers in the UK, http://www.contemporarywriters.com/ (October 8, 2007), author profile.

Rambles, http://www.rambles.net/ (October 8, 2007), Donna Scanlon, review of *Switchers.*

SLA, http://www.sla.org.uk/ (January 5, 2006), "Kate Thompson Wins Whitbread Children's Book Award."*

*   *   *

THOMPSON, Ronda 1955-2007

PERSONAL: Born October 14, 1955, in Ponca City, OK; daughter of Sam and Yvonne Widener; died of ovarian and pancreatic cancer, July 12 (one source says July 11), 2007; married Mike Thompson, 1984; children: Marley, Matthew; Chrystal (stepchild).

CAREER: Author. Worked as a mortgage loan processor, bank teller, dog groomer, construction worker, and grocery store clerk.

MEMBER: Romance Writers of America.

AWARDS, HONORS: Hughie Award, Romance Book Lovers, for *Love at First Bite;* winner of other writing awards.

WRITINGS:

ROMANCE FICTION

Welcome to Paradise, Zebra (New York, NY), 1998.

Isn't It Romantic?, Lionhearted Publishing, 1998.

Prickly Pear, Leisure Books (New York, NY), 1999.

Cougar's Woman, Leisure Books (New York, NY), 1999.

In Trouble's Arms, Leisure Books (New York, NY), 2000.

Scandalous, Leisure Books (New York, NY), 2000.

(With Amanda Ashley and Christine Feehan) *After Twilight,* Love Spell (New York, NY), 2001.

Desert Bloom, Leisure Books (New York, NY), 2001.

Call of the Moon, Love Spell (New York, NY), 2002.

Violets Are Blue, Leisure Books (New York, NY), 2002.

Walk into the Flame, Leisure Books (New York, NY), 2003.

(With Maggie Shayne, Amanda Ashley, and Sherrilyn Kenyon) *Midnight Pleasures,* St. Martin's Paperbacks (New York, NY), 2003.

Love at First Bite, St. Martin's Paperbacks (New York, NY), 2006.

Confessions of a Werewolf Supermodel, St. Martin's Paperbacks (New York, NY), 2007.

"WILD WULFS OF LONDON" SERIES; PARANORMAL ROMANCE NOVELS

The Dark One, St. Martin's Paperbacks (New York, NY), 2005.

The Untamed One, St. Martin's Paperbacks (New York, NY), 2006.

The Cursed One, St. Martin's Paperbacks (New York, NY), 2006.

SIDELIGHTS: After enjoying a successful career as a romance writer, beginning with the publication in 1998 of her first novel, *Welcome to Paradise,* Ronda Thompson died unexpectedly of pancreatic and ovarian cancer in 2007. She left behind over a dozen romances, including contemporaries, historicals, and paranormal tales. Before her writing career began, the author raised three children and held a variety of jobs ranging from mortgage processor to construction worker. She had loved romance novels since her teenage years, however, and was a great fan of the prolific Barbara Cartland. With her children grown, Thompson had some time to write. "I took some creative classes, got involved with writers groups and in 1996 I sold my first novel," she recalled on her Web site.

Her first novels were contemporary romances, including *Isn't It Romantic?,* in which two people on a blind date discover that one is an author and the other the critic who trashed her book. *Romantic Times* online reviewer Chandra Y. Sparks promised that readers would "laugh out loud" at the story. Humor laces many of Thompson's other books as well, though she also has a serious side to her romances.

Moving on to historical fiction, Thompson, who grew up in Texas, loved to ride horses, and even participated in rodeos, naturally favored a Wild West setting. This is the case in such books as *Prickly Pear, Cougar's Woman, Desert Bloom,* and *Walk into the Flame.* The author pleased critics in many cases with the tension—sexual and otherwise—between her heroes and heroines. In *Prickly Pear,* for instance, the characters are a former gunslinger who is trying to make good, and a recalcitrant woman trying to impress her father. "High-tension desire and quick tempers between Wade and Cam make for an exciting, delicious read," according to Anne Black in the *Romantic Times. Desert Bloom* is about a young woman seeking revenge on the father who sold her into prostitution. She runs away from the family that saved her from prostitution, and the love interest is found in Gregory, the man sent to find her again. Harriet Klausner, lauding the novel in *Best Reviews,* commented that the author proves she "can make silk out of a cow's ear as she recreates a whore and a rat into lead protagonists with redeeming qualities."

Conflicts between white settlers and Native American tribes set the stage for a number of Thompson's Wild West books. In *Cougar's Woman,* for example, a high society woman is kidnapped by Apaches and promised to Clay Black, a white man who has been raised by the tribe. *Walk into the Flame* also features Apache characters, as well as the white woman they adopted as part of the tribe when she was abandoned as a child. *Romantic Times* critic Gerry Benninger appreciated the way Thompson strove to make the often violent conflict between whites and American Indians realistic, but feared that the "well-written" tale becomes a "bit too harsh," concluding that this "makes the requisite happy ending unbelievable." Harriet Klausner, writing in *Blether: The Book Review Site,* similarly suggested that the novel "reads more like a deep historical fiction than a love story."

Many of the last books Thompson wrote are paranormal tales featuring werewolves. These works include *Call of the Moon, Confessions of a Werewolf Supermodel,* and the "Wild Wulfs of London" series. A kind of segue between her westerns and paranormals, *Call of the Moon,* features Tala Soaringbird, a Native American who is a "chosen one" and supposed to protect her people from werewolves. However, she notices that one werewolf seems kinder than the others she has fought and she begins to fall in love with him. *Romantic Times* contributor Jill M. Smith appreciated that the author "put a clever and intriguing new spin on werewolf mythology. Rich with ancient myths and modern-day passion, *Call of the Moon* is very satisfying reading." *Confessions of a Werewolf Supermodel,* on the other hand, is a contemporary werewolf story with flashes of humor. The premise of a woman who is a supermodel with an uncomfortable secret makes for an "amusing chick lit werewolf tale," according to Klausner in *Genre Go Round Reviews.*

The "Wild Wulfs of London" series, which includes *The Dark One, The Untamed One,* and *The Cursed One,* has different members of the Wulf clan starring in each tale. The Wulfs have the unfortunate fate of suffering from a family curse that makes them all werewolves. Wulfs in each installment run into women with whom they naturally fall in love. The relationships are, of course, complicated, affording Thompson plenty of opportunity to blend romance, the supernatural, and humor into her tales. Terri Clark, reviewing the first book in *Romantic Times,* commented that the author "created a deliciously dark world and blended it with speckles of humor, great passion and exceptional characters." *Booklist* contributor Nina C. Davis, however, felt that the second book is "predictable," although an "interesting development" toward the end made her anticipate the next installment. Of the last book, Kathe Robin asserted in her *Romantic Times* review that "Thompson cleverly blends paranormal elements into a fine-tuned historical romance with well-crafted characters and a tender, blossoming romance."

BIOGRAPHICAL AND CRITICAL SOURCES:

PERIODICALS

Booklist, November 15, 2002, John Charles, review of *Call of the Moon,* p. 583; October 15, 2005, Nina C. Davis, review of *The Dark One,* p. 36; December 1, 2006, Nina C. Davis, review of *The Cursed One,* p. 32.

ONLINE

Best Reviews, http://thebestreviews.com/ (July 1, 2002), Harriet Klausner, review of *Desert Bloom.*

Blether: The Book Review Site, http://reviews.blether. com/ (September 25, 2007), Harriet Klausner, reviews of *Walk into the Flame* and *Midnight Pleasures.*

Fantastic Fiction, http://www.fantasticfiction.co.uk/ (September 25, 2007), brief biography of Ronda Thompson.

Genre Go Round Reviews, http://genregoroundreviews. blogspot.com/ (September 5, 2007), Harriet Klausner, review of *Confessions of a Werewolf Supermodel.*

Romance Reader at Heart, http://romancereader atheart.com/ (September 25, 2007), Shannon Johnson, reviews of *The Untamed One* and *The Cursed One.*

Romantic Times, http://www.romantictimes.com/ (September 25, 2007), Kathe Robin, reviews of *Desert Bloom, The Untamed One,* and *The Cursed One;* Jill M. Smith, reviews of *Call of the Moon, Midnight Pleasures, After Twilight,* and *Love at First Bite;* Terri Clark, review of *The Dark One;* Gerry Benninger, reviews of *Walk into the Flame, In Trouble's Arms,* and *Violets Are Blue;* Joan Hammond, review of *Scandalous;* Anne Black, reviews of *Prickly Pear* and *Cougar's Woman;* and Chandra Y. Sparks, review of *Isn't It Romantic?*

Ronda Thompson Official Website, http://www. rondathompson.com (September 25, 2007).

OBITUARIES

ONLINE

Dear Author, http://dearauthor.com/ (July 11, 2007).
NovelSpot, http://novelspot.net/ (July 13, 2007), "Cancer Awareness."
Romance at Heart Magazine Online, http://romanceat heart.com/ (September 25, 2007).*

* * *

THOMSON, Jennifer A. 1947-
(Jennifer Ann Thomson)

PERSONAL: Born 1947. *Education:* University of Cape Town, B.Sc.; Cambridge University, M.A.; Rhodes University, Ph.D.; postdoctoral study, Harvard Medical School. *Hobbies and other interests:* Hiking.

ADDRESSES: Office—Department of Molecular and Cell Biology, University of Cape Town, Private Bag Rondebosch 7701, Cape Town, South Africa. *E-mail*—jat@science.uct.ac.za.

CAREER: University of Witwatersrand, Witwatersrand, South Africa, began as lecturer, became associate professor of genetics; Council for Scientific and Industrial Research, founder and director of Laboratory for Molecular and Cell Biology; University of Cape Town, Cape Town, South Africa, professor of microbiology. Lecturer on genetically modified organisms. Member of board, International Service for the Acquisition of Agribiotech Applications, BIO-EARN, and European Action Group on Life Sciences (EAGLES).

MEMBER: South African Academy of Science, South African Women in Science and Engineering (cofounder and chair).

AWARDS, HONORS: Fellow, Royal Society of South Africa; UNESCO/L'Oreal Woman in Science for Africa award, 2004.

WRITINGS:

NONFICTION

Recombinant DNA and Bacterial Fermentation, CRC Press (Boca Raton, FL), 1988.

Genes for Africa: Genetically Modified Crops in the Developing World, UCT Press (Lansdowne, South Africa), 2002.

GM Crops: The Impact and the Potential, CSIRO Publishing (Collingwood, Victoria, Australia), 2006, published as *Seeds for the Future: The Impact of Genetically Modified Crops on the Environment,* Comstock Publishing (Ithaca, NY), 2007.

Contributor to books, including *Innovative Approaches to Plant Disease Control,* edited by I. Chet, John Wiley (New York, NY), 1987; *Biotechnological Prospects for Plant Pathogen Control,* edited by I. Chet, Wiley-Liss (New York, NY), 1993; and *Biotechnology and Sustainable Development: Voices of the South and North,* edited by I. Serageldin and G.J. Persley, CABI Publishing, 2003. Contributor of numerous articles to professional journals, including *South African Medical Journal, Applied Microbiology, Gene,* and *Applied Bacteriology.*

SIDELIGHTS: Jennifer A. Thomson is a South African professor of microbiology and an expert in the field of genetically engineered organisms (GMOs). Some groups, particularly in Europe, argue that GMOs are potentially dangerous to humans and the environment, and advocate strict control or even abolition of them. Thomson and others are strongly in support of their use. She believes that plants that have been modified to resist drought and disease can be greatly beneficial and even help in alleviating human suffering. Thomson has been the leader of a team of biologists seeking to create a maize plant that can resist the maize streak virus, which is widespread in Africa and stunts the growth of plants. Thomson stated in a piece written for the *Africa News Service:* "African farmers already suffer from drought, disease, internal trade barriers, corruption and lack of property rights; refusing them the benefits of genetically modified food is a cruel and nasty trick."

Reviewing Thomson's book *Seeds for the Future: The Impact of Genetically Modified Crops on the Environment* for *Library Journal,* Irwin Weintraub pointed out that while it is aimed primarily at a specialized audience, "it should be read by all who want to get beyond the debate to a lucid understanding of GM crops and their place in modern biotechnology." *Seeds for the Future* was also highly recommended by Carol Haggas in *Booklist,* where she called it "critical reading for members of the scientific community and concerned consumers."

BIOGRAPHICAL AND CRITICAL SOURCES:

PERIODICALS

Africa News Service, April 1, 2004, "UCT Professor Savours Taste of Scientific Success"; February 7, 2006, "Cruel to Deny Africa a Hand Up."

Australasian Business Intelligence, August 6, 2006, "Scientist Set for GM Push into Africa."

Australian Doctor, June 1, 2007, Reynard, "Letter Writer Not Limelighter."

Booklist, March 1, 2007, Carol Haggas, review of *Seeds for the Future: The Impact of Genetically Modified Crops on the Environment,* p. 47.

Ecos, December, 2006, review of *GM Crops: The Impact and the Potential,* p. 32.

Library Journal, March 1, 2007, Irwin Weintraub, review of *Seeds for the Future,* p. 103.

M2 Presswire, November 7, 2002, "We Cannot Be Indifferent to Genetically Modified Crops, Secretary-General Says in Introducing Lecture Speakers."

SciTech Book News, September, 2007, review of *Seeds for the Future.*

ONLINE

African Agricultural Technology Foundation, http://www.aatf-africa.org/ (October 5, 2007), biographical information about Jennifer A. Thomson.

International Food Policy Research Institute, http://www.ifpri.org/ (October 5, 2007), biographical information about Jennifer A. Thomson.

University of Cape Town Department of Molecular and Cell Biology Web site, http://www.mcb.uct.ac.za/ (October 5, 2007), biographical information about Jennifer A. Thomson.*

*   *   *

THOMSON, Jennifer Ann
See THOMSON, Jennifer A.

TIRMAN, John

PERSONAL: Born in IN; married Nike Zachmanoglou; children: Coco (daughter). *Education:* Indiana University, B.A., 1972; Boston University, Ph.D., 1981.

ADDRESSES: Home—MA. *E-mail*—tirman@mit.edu; john@johntirman.com.

CAREER: Winston Foundation for World Peace, Washington, DC, executive director, 1986-99; Social Science Research Council, Washington, DC, program director; Massachusetts Institute of Technology, Cambridge, executive director of Center for International Studies, 2004—. Trustee and U.S. chair, Institute for War and Peace Reporting, International Alert, and the Foundation for National Progress. Worked at *Time* magazine, New York, NY. Creator of educational Web site *Cyprus Conflict.*

AWARDS, HONORS: Fulbright scholar in Cyprus; Human Rights Award, United Nations Association.

WRITINGS:

NONFICTION

(Editor) *The Fallacy of Star Wars,* Vintage Books (New York, NY), 1984.
(Editor) *The Militarization of High Technology,* Ballinger (Cambridge, MA), 1984.
(Editor) *Empty Promise: The Growing Case against Star Wars,* Beacon Press (Boston, MA), 1986.
Sovereign Acts: American Unilateralism and Global Security, Harper & Row (New York, NY), 1989.
Spoils of War: The Human Cost of America's Arms Trade, Free Press (New York, NY), 1997.
Making the Money Sing: Private Wealth and Public Power in the Search for Peace, Rowman & Littlefield Publishers (Lanham, MD), 2000.
(Editor) *The Maze of Fear: Security and Migration after 9/11,* New Press (New York, NY), 2004.
(Editor, with Ramesh Thakur and Edward Newman) *Multilateralism under Challenge? Power, International Order, and Structural Change,* United Nations University Press (New York, NY), 2006.

100 Ways America Is Screwing Up the World, Harper Perennial (New York, NY), 2006.
(Editor, with Marianne Heiberg and Brendan O'Leary) *Terror, Insurgencies, and States: Breaking the Cycles of Protracted Violence,* University of Pennsylvania Press (Philadelphia, PA), 2007.

Contributor to periodicals, including *Nation, International Herald Tribune, Los Angeles Times, Boston Globe, Washington Post, Wall Street Journal,* and *New York Times.*

SIDELIGHTS: John Tirman is a political scientist who has published numerous books on international affairs. His 1984 book *The Fallacy of Star Wars* was an early and important critique of the Strategic Defense Initiative (SDI), a controversial ballistic missile defense system first proposed by Ronald Reagan. Tirman wrote another volume critical of U.S. policy in 1997, *Spoils of War: The Human Cost of America's Arms Trade.* In this book, he faults the arms industry and arms traders for supplying weapons to some of the world's most oppressive governments. He illustrates the way in which conflicts of interest can lead to massive violations of human rights. For example, he states that concerns about Arab fundamentalism, extreme nationalism in Turkey, and local concern in the state of Connecticut about the loss of jobs linked with the Sikorsky military helicopter led to large-scale, systematic destruction of lives and villages across Kurdistan. Tirman argues that arms trading is morally unjustifiable, and reports that not only conservatives, but many politicians who identify themselves as liberal Democrats support arms trading. Nader Entessar, reviewing the book in *Library Journal,* described it as an "engaging and challenging look" at the disturbing repercussions of U.S. arms sales overseas. Harvey Wasserman, writing in the *Progressive,* stated that Tirman "proves a savvy commentator on both belt-way politics and the need to convert the national economy to peacetime production."

Tirman's experience as the founder of the Winston Foundation for World Peace provided him with abundant background material for *Making the Money Sing: Private Wealth and Public Power in the Search for Peace.* In this book, Tirman points out the ways in which money can act as agent of social and political improvement—in concert with hard work, courage, and intelligence. Unfortunately, the opposite is often true. Walter C. Uhler, reviewing *Making the Money Sing* in the *Bulletin of the Atomic Scientists,* called this book a "riveting indictment of an immoral and counterproductive arms-for-protection policy in the Middle East. His book should become a primer on the politics the United States should avoid."

Tirman criticized U.S. policy around the world once more in *100 Ways America Is Screwing Up the World.* The tone of this book is somewhat light, and yet, the author insists that the content is not a joke. Among the "100 Ways" listed that U.S. actions have gone wrong—or have gone as planned, but with unfortunate results for the rest of the world—he includes racial bigotry, a culture that glorifies violence, the Vietnam War, pollution, obsession with celebrities, and the spread of the culture of Walt Disney. The author also lists ten positive things he feels the United States has brought to the world, including generosity, the rule of law, and a welcoming attitude toward immigrants. A *Publishers Weekly* reviewer wrote that Tirman possesses "a sly style and makes his often predictable points with unexpected panache." Speaking with Jessica Bennett for *Newsweek Online,* Tirman explained his purpose in writing *100 Ways America Is Screwing Up the World.* "We have a very, very powerful impact throughout the world, and I don't think most Americans realize that. And that's part of what I'm trying to convey here. Let's think about what we're doing, because it really has tremendous consequences."

BIOGRAPHICAL AND CRITICAL SOURCES:

BOOKS

Tirman, John, *Making the Money Sing: Private Wealth and Public Power in the Search for Peace,* Rowman & Littlefield Publishers (Lanham, MD), 2000.

PERIODICALS

Booklist, October 1, 1997, Mary Carroll, review of *Spoils of War: The Human Cost of America's Arms Trade,* p. 293.
Bulletin of the Atomic Scientists, March 1, 1998, Walter C. Uhler, review of *Spoils of War,* p. 64.

Chronicle of Philanthropy, November 30, 2000, Gwen A. Williamson, "Philanthropy Can Shape Society, Politics for the Better, Author Claims."
Library Journal, October 15, 1997, Nader Entessar, review of *Spoils of War,* p. 77.
M2 Best Books, February 9, 2006, "Not Guilty Plea Entered by Turkish Publisher."
National Catholic Reporter, February 4, 2005, Lena Khan, "Abolishing Mistrust," p. 25.
Progressive, July, 1998, Harvey Wasserman, review of *Spoils of War,* p. 42.
Publishers Weekly, September 1, 1997, review of *Spoils of War,* p. 89; June 12, 2006, review of *100 Ways America Is Screwing Up the World,* p. 42.
Reference & Research Book News, May, 2007, review of *100 Ways America Is Screwing Up the World.*

ONLINE

BlogCritics, http://blogcritics.org/ (October 31, 2007), Larry Sakin, interview with John Tirman.
John Tirman Home Page, http://www.johntirman.com (October 5, 2007).
Massachusetts Institute of Technology Center for International Studies Web site, http://web.mit.edu/ (October 5, 2007).
Newsweek Online, http://www.msnbc.msn.com/ (July 27, 2006), Jessica Bennett, interview with John Tirman.
University of Colorado at Boulder, http://www.colorado.edu/ (October 5, 2007), biographical information on John Tirman.*

*   *   *

TONSETIC, Robert
    See TONSETIC, Robert L.

*   *   *

TONSETIC, Robert L.
    (Robert Tonsetic)

PERSONAL: Male.

CAREER: Writer. *Military service:* U.S. Army, served in Vietnam as infantry commander in the 4th Battalion, 12th Infantry Regiment.

WRITINGS:

NONFICTION

Warriors: An Infantryman's Memoir of Vietnam, Ballantine (New York, NY), 2004.

Days of Valor: An Inside Account of the Bloodiest Six Months of the Vietnam War, Casemate (Philadelphia, PA), 2007.

SIDELIGHTS: Robert L. Tonsetic's experiences as an American infantry commander in the Vietnam War are the source of both of his books, *Warriors: An Infantryman's Memoir of Vietnam* and *Days of Valor: An Inside Account of the Bloodiest Six Months of the Vietnam War. Days of Valor* is a detailed, chronological accounting of the actions of the 199th Light Infantry Brigade, beginning in December, 1967, and continuing to May, 1968—the time of the infamous Tet offensive. Using reports from eyewitnesses, diaries and letters from those involved, staff reports, and photographs, the book gives a full picture of the many battles engaged in by the 199th during those months. "The treatment of this period is superb," stated Edward Fennell in a review of the book for the *Empire Page* Web site. "It does not attempt to politicize either the war or demonize the enemy. It is simply one man's attempt to put a magnifying glass to a war and the professional soldiers who fought it." Throughout the book, Tonsetic refers to himself in the third person, but he "relies heavily on evocative first-person testimony from his fellow infantrymen to paint a picture of almost nonstop combat," remarked a reviewer for *Publishers Weekly.*

BIOGRAPHICAL AND CRITICAL SOURCES:

BOOKS

Tonsetic, Robert, *Warriors: An Infantryman's Memoir of Vietnam,* Ballantine (New York, NY), 2004.

Tonsetic, Robert, *Days of Valor: An Inside Account of the Bloodiest Six Months of the Vietnam War,* Casemate (Philadelphia, PA), 2007.

PERIODICALS

Library Journal, February 15, 2007, Edwin B. Burgess, review of *Days of Valor,* p. 134.

Publishers Weekly, January 22, 2007, review of *Days of Valor,* p. 180.

ONLINE

Empire Page, http://www.empirepage.com/ (October 1, 2007), Edward Fennell, review of *Days of Valor.**

* * *

TOOZE, Adam
See TOOZE, J. Adam

* * *

TOOZE, J. Adam
(Adam Tooze)

ADDRESSES: Office—Jesus College, University of Cambridge, Cambridge CB5 8BL, England. *E-mail*—jat27@cam.ac.uk.

CAREER: University of Cambridge, Jesus College, Cambridge, England, senior lecturer in modern European economic history, Gurnee Hart Fellow in history and Director of Studies.

AWARDS, HONORS: Philip Leverhulme Prize for modern history, 2002; H-Soz-Kult Historisches Buch Prize, 2002, for *Statistics and the German State 1900-1945: The Making of Modern Economic Knowledge.*

WRITINGS:

NONFICTION

Statistics and the German State, 1900-1945: The Making of Modern Economic Knowledge, Cambridge University Press (New York, NY), 2001.

The Wages of Destruction: The Making and Breaking of the Nazi Economy, Allan Lane (London, England), 2006, Viking (New York, NY), 2007.

Contributor to books, including *Imagining Nations,* 1998. Contributor to periodicals, including *Economic History Review.*

SIDELIGHTS: J. Adam Tooze is a historian who specializes in modern economics, particularly in the economics of the Third Reich in Germany. The era that saw the Nazi regime seize power in Europe has been researched, analyzed, and reported in painstaking detail, and yet, Tooze's book *The Wages of Destruction: The Making and Breaking of the Nazi Economy* manages to make a significant new contribution to the field of Nazi history. According to Bertrand Benoit, a reviewer for the *Financial Times,* Tooze's book is an "astonishingly erudite study" that "not only uncovers new explanatory strands for the events that led to and ended the war, but smashes a gallery of preconceptions on the way."

One of those preconceptions is the notion that Germany went to war in 1939 as a powerful industrial nation. In fact, Tooze shows in *The Wages of Destruction* that at that time, Germany's agricultural output was poor, its resources were few, and the standard of living for most of its people was far below that in the United States or the United Kingdom. Germany's economy was really on the brink of collapse, and the country's poor financial health may have been the greatest reason for its eventual defeat by the allies, according to Tooze's book. The author explains the specific ways that Germany's economic situation affected the course of the war. For example, a desperate need for resources was behind Germany's ruthless looting of the territories it occupied. Countries to the east were used as sources of food, workers, and raw materials for the benefit of Germany. British and American bombing campaigns further crippled German industry and the country's economy. Tooze also offers insight into Hitler's economic aspirations, explaining how the dictator not only regarded the United States as an enemy, but also as a role model. The huge size of the United States and its expansion west, at the expense of the Native American tribes, was something Hitler hoped to mirror with an eastward expansion and genocide of the inhabitants of the countries he occupied. Reviewing the book for the *Live Journal* Web site, Randy McDonald commented: "Tooze's economic history is gripping, not only because it's an economic history that presents compelling arguments but because of its insights into Nazism."

The Wages of Destruction was recommended in *Kirkus Reviews* as "a strong contribution to the historical literature surrounding WWII and the Nazi era; indeed, one of the most significant to arrive in recent years." *History Today* reviewer Nicholas Stargardt stated that Tooze's book stands as "the definitive account of the Nazi economy," but went on to add that the author "has done much more than that. He has also rewritten the history of the Second World War. By thinking afresh about what Hitler's war aims really were and how the Nazi leadership attempted first to win and then prolong a war for which they knew they never possessed sufficient resources, Tooze has produced the most striking history of German strategy in the Second World War that we possess. This is an extraordinary achievement."

BIOGRAPHICAL AND CRITICAL SOURCES:

PERIODICALS

Booklist, March 15, 2007, Brendan Driscoll, review of *The Wages of Destruction: The Making and Breaking of the Nazi Economy,* p. 8.

Financial Times, August 5, 2006, Bertrand Benoit, review of *The Wages of Destruction,* p. 29.

History Today, December, 2006, Nicholas Stargardt, review of *The Wages of Destruction,* p. 64.

Kirkus Reviews, February 1, 2007, review of *The Wages of Destruction,* p. 117.

Library Journal, February 15, 2007, Antonio Thompson, review of *The Wages of Destruction,* p. 134.

Spectator, June 24, 2006, Noble Frankland, review of *The Wages of Destruction.*

ONLINE

Live Journal, http://rfmcdpei.livejournal.com/ (September 14, 2007), Randy McDonald, review of *The Wages of Destruction.**

*   *   *

TORDAY, Paul 1946-

PERSONAL: Born 1946; married second wife; children: (first marriage) two sons; (second marriage) two stepsons. *Education:* Attended Pembroke College, Oxford University.

ADDRESSES: Home—Northumberland, England.

CAREER: Worked in engineering and industry for thirty years.

AWARDS, HONORS: Bollinger Everyman Wodehouse Prize for Comic Writing, 2007, for *Salmon Fishing in the Yemen.*

WRITINGS:

Salmon Fishing in the Yemen (novel), Harcourt (Orlando, FL), 2007.

SIDELIGHTS: Paul Torday worked in industry and engineering for some three decades. After his retirement, he turned his attention to writing a book, one that takes in his love of fishing and his knowledge of the Middle East, gleaned from many business trips to that region over the years. The result was *Salmon Fishing in the Yemen,* a satirical novel that follows the actions of Dr. Alfred Jones, a scientist who is assigned the task of bringing salmon fishing to the Middle Eastern desert, in part to deflect criticism of the war there.

In an interview with Danuta Kean, published on the Orion Publishing Group Web site, Torday discussed the changes he saw occurring in the Arab culture over a ten-year period, due to the pressures of Western influences, tourism, and financial concerns. He observed that Western cultures failed to appreciate the richness of Arab culture, wrongly regarding it as primitive and crude. "It is a very sophisticated and ancient world and it is really super-patronising to think that we can bring ideas to them that they haven't already thought of and tried and found wanting," he noted. One of the central themes in his book is that of faith versus reason, and as the author said to Kean: "The contrast between people who pray five times a day and people who shop five times a day is marked."

In the story, the character of Alfred clings to his scientific, rational worldview as he proceeds with his seemingly impossible project. Eventually, though, he must admit to himself that passion and hope are also vital to life. Alfred's story is told though the use of conventional narrative, diary entries, newspaper clippings and the like. Reviewing the novel for the *Scotland on Sunday* Web site, Daneet Steffens remarked:

"It is light, but succeeds in an ambitious project: making a book about fishing readable, even touching. Fish may not be your bag, but it is the capacity for commitment and belief that makes for good reading." Matt Thorne, reviewing for the London *Telegraph Online,* described it as "feel good comedy with surprising bite." Some reviewers were particularly impressed with the author's skill in creating his characters. For example, Janelle Martin commented on the *Gather* Web site: "Through deft handling and shifting viewpoints, Torday's characters are well-rounded and almost leap off the page. . . . His attention to detail ensures that, with time, even characters who initially appear wooden exhibit unexpected depths and demand the reader's empathy."

BIOGRAPHICAL AND CRITICAL SOURCES:

PERIODICALS

Booklist, March 1, 2007, Thomas Gaughan, review of *Salmon Fishing in the Yemen,* p. 64.

Bookseller, January 26, 2007, review of *Salmon Fishing in the Yemen,* p. 13.

Economist, March 3, 2007, review of *Salmon Fishing in the Yemen,* p. 89.

Library Journal, March 1, 2007, David A. Berona, review of *Salmon Fishing in the Yemen,* p. 78.

M2 Best Books, May 8, 2007, "Paul Torday Wins Bollinger Prize for Comic Fiction."

New Statesman, January 22, 2007, Nadia Saint, review of *Salmon Fishing in the Yemen,* p. 60.

Publishers Weekly, February 19, 2007, review of *Salmon Fishing in the Yemen,* p. 149.

ONLINE

Curled Up with a Good Book, http://www.curledup.com/ (October 10, 2007), Janelle Martin, review of *Salmon Fishing in the Yemen.*

Gather, http://www.gather.com/ (October 2, 2007), review of *Salmon Fishing in the Yemen.*

Guardian Online, http://books.guardian.co.uk/ (February 24, 2007), Tim Mackintosh-Smith, review of *Salmon Fishing in the Yemen.*

Orion Publishing Group Web site, http://www.orionbooks.co.uk/ (October 1, 2007), Danuta Kean, interview with Paul Torday.

Scotland on Sunday, http://scotlandonsunday.scotsman. com/ (October 2, 2007), Daneet Steffens, review of *Salmon Fishing in the Yemen.*
Telegraph Online, http://www.telegraph.co.uk/ (October 2, 2007), Amanda Craig, review of *Salmon Fishing in the Yemen.**

*   *   *

TREMLETT, Giles

PERSONAL: Education: Graduated from Oxford University.

ADDRESSES: Home—Spain. *Agent*—Capel & Land, Ltd., 29 Wardour St., London W1D 6PS, England. *E-mail*—giles.tremlett@guardian.co.uk.

CAREER: Journalist. *Guardian,* London, England, correspondent in Spain.

WRITINGS:

Ghosts of Spain. Travels through a Country's Hidden Past (nonfiction), Faber & Faber (London, England), 2006.
Catherine of Aragon (biography), Faber & Faber (London, England), 2008.

SIDELIGHTS: Giles Tremlett is an Englishman who has lived and worked as a journalist in Spain for many years. His first book, *Ghosts of Spain: Travels through a Country's Hidden Past,* gives a sense of the country's history and its many paradoxes, as experienced by Tremlett. He comments on the vast differences between Spanish and British traditions of childrearing —stating that Spanish children are treated as treasures, while British children have often been largely ignored by their parents—and notes that atypically, Spanish teenagers report being extremely happy with their families. Overall, the country seems to have a forward-looking attitude and to be prospering. Yet Tremlett's book also explore's Spain's dark side. During the 1930s, civil war tore at the nation; there were atrocities and massacres committed on both sides, and in the end, a dictatorship was established, with its own long list of cruel and unjust acts. Yet, once the dictatorship of Francisco Franco was abolished in the 1970s, the Spanish population as a whole seemed largely determined to forget about the past and move ahead. As more years passed and evidence of past crimes came to light—including the discovery of mass graves full of war victims—old divisions inevitably began to resurface. Tremlett offers his opinion that Spain still suffers because of her collective denial of the past several decades. He examines the philosophies and stances of various ethnic groups within Spain (such as the Basques, Catalans, and Galacians), and explores the repercussions of past war crimes and how they affect current generations. He paints a picture of the Spanish national character, including their surprising tendency to hypochondriac behavior, and their meekness in the face of medical practitioners. He also takes in recent historical events, such as the 2004 train bombing in Madrid.

"There is more sunshine than ghostliness in this vivid and sensitive book, which will interpret Spain to present-day visitors as Gerald Brenan and V.S. Pritchett did for former generations," commented Christopher Howse in the *Spectator.* William Grimes, writing for the *New York Times,* also recommended the book as "a highly informative, well-written introduction to post-Franco Spain." *Library Journal* contributor Linda M. Kaufmann summarized *Ghosts of Spain* as "a provocative and vividly written book that is part history, part political and social commentary, and part love letter."

BIOGRAPHICAL AND CRITICAL SOURCES:

BOOKS

Tremlett, Giles, *Ghosts of Spain: Travels through a Country's Hidden Past,* Faber & Faber (London, England), 2006.

PERIODICALS

Library Journal, February 15, 2007, Linda M. Kaufmann, review of *Ghosts of Spain,* p. 140.
Morning Edition, July 17, 2002, "Interview: Giles Tremlett Talks about the Arrest in Spain of Three Suspected Al-Qaeda Operatives."

New York Times, February 21, 2007, William Grimes, review of *Ghosts of Spain,* p. 10.

New York Times Book Review, April 1, 2007, Sarah Wildman, review of *Ghosts of Spain,* p. 9.

Spectator, March 18, 2006, Christopher Howse, "Coming to Terms with the Past," p. 50.

ONLINE

Guardian Unlimited, http://books.guardian.co.uk/ (March 19, 2006), Jason Webster, review of *Ghosts of Spain.*

Life of Zhisou, http://mrzhisou.wordpress.com/ (September 1, 2006), review of *Ghosts of Spain.*

Rambles.net, http://www.rambles.net/ (October 2, 2007), David Cox, review of *Ghosts of Spain.* *

*   *   *

TRINCHIERI, Camilla
    See CRESPI, Camilla T.

*   *   *

TURNER, Nikki

PERSONAL: Children: two. *Education:* Attended North Carolina Central University.

ADDRESSES: Home—Richmond, VA.

CAREER: Writer.

WRITINGS:

FICTION

A Hustler's Wife (novel), Triple Crown Publications (Columbus, OH), 2003.

A Project Chick, Triple Crown Publications (Columbus, OH), 2003.

(With others) *Girls from Da Hood,* Urban Books (Dix Hills, NY), 2004.

(With others) *Girls from Da Hood 2,* Urban Books (Dix Hills, NY), 2005.

The Glamorous Life (novel), One World (New York, NY), 2005.

Nikki Turner Presents Street Chronicles: Tales from Da Hood 3, One World (New York, NY), 2006.

Riding Dirty on I-95 (novel), Ballantine Books (New York, NY), 2006.

Nikki Turner Presents Street Chronicles: Christmas in the Hood, One World Books (New York, NY), 2007.

Nikki Turner Presents Street Chronicles: Girls in the Game, One World Books (New York, NY), 2007.

(With 50 Cent) *Death before Dishonor: A 50 Cent and Nikki Turner Original,* G-Unit Books (New York, NY), 2007.

Forever a Hustler's Wife (novel), One World/ Ballantine Books (New York, NY), 2007.

The Black Widow, One World/Ballantine (New York, NY), 2008.

ADAPTATIONS: Film rights to *A Hustler's Wife* and *Death before Dishonor* have been sold.

SIDELIGHTS: Nikki Taylor's first novel, *A Hustler's Wife,* was a tremendously popular, contemporary love story set in the ghetto culture. The story concerns Des Taylor, who leads a criminal life, and his love, Yarni. The book stayed on the *Essence* best-seller chart for more than two years after its publication. Taylor followed up with a sequel, *Forever a Hustler's Wife.* In the sequel, Yarni, a lawyer, fights for Des's freedom. Having been imprisoned for ten years for a crime he did not commit, Des Taylor is finally pardoned and released. He and Yarni now have a child, but nevertheless, Des returns to his old ways. After two years of freedom, he is again framed for murder. The couple must also contend with other crimes, including another murder, a kidnapping, and an attempted rape. Rollie Welch, reviewing the book in *Library Journal,* found the characters somewhat "typecast" but stated that the book stands out from others in the "street-lit" genre, thanks to its "veiled editorials about the legal system and religious hypocrisy."

Turner's success with *A Hustler's Wife* enabled her to start her imprint, One World/Ballantine Books, with the series "Nikki Turner Presents." Her objective, she stated, was to find "great stories and original voices . . . stories that don't march to the same beat as other street lit," she was quoted as saying in the *Black Issues Book Review.* Turner, and other writers in the genre, have been criticized for presenting criminal lifestyles in a glamorous way. Taylor responded to those concerns in an interview with Imani Powell for *Essence,* saying: "Urban lit touches on many ugly issues that we as a society don't like to discuss. It's easier to condemn it than to recognize that this lifestyle does exist. These are all issues that go on in our day-to-day lives. No matter where you live or what background you come from, these subjects exist and no one is immune. I don't glorify 'the game,' but I do tell an honest story."

Turner told a "gritty, fast-paced street tale with heart" in her 2006 offering, *Riding Dirty on I-95,* according to a *Publishers Weekly* reviewer. The protagonist is Mercy Jiles, a spirited young woman whose father was killed for a gambling debt when she was only seven years old. Since then, Mercy has struggled to survive despite her mother's neglect and the abuse she has suffered in various foster homes. She becomes romantically involved with C-Note, a drug dealer and murderer, who soon has Mercy transporting drugs for him. Eventually she breaks away from the relationship, but years later, after she has become a successful screenwriter, Mercy meets C-Note again. *Riding Dirty on I-95* "offers a vivid, nonjudgmental glimpse into a world of broken ambitions, backstabbers and self-loathers," stated a *Publishers Weekly* reviewer.

BIOGRAPHICAL AND CRITICAL SOURCES:

PERIODICALS

Black Issues Book Review, March 1, 2004, "Nikki Turner," p. 8; September 1, 2006, "Urban Lit Goes Legit: Authors Headline New Ventures to Bring Street Cred into the World of Corporate Publishing," p. 20.

Booklist, April 15, 2005, Lilian Lewis, review of *The Glamorous Life,* p. 1434; March 1, 2006, Lillian Lewis, review of *Riding Dirty on I-95,* p. 70.

Bookseller, November 18, 2005, "50 Cent to Pen Street Fiction from S&S," p. 7.

Ebony, April, 2007, Lynette R. Holloway, "5 Questions for Nikki Turner," p. 38.

Essence, May, 2007, Imani Powell, "Hustle & Flow: Nikki Turner, the Self-Proclaimed Queen of Hip-Hop Fiction, Addresses Her Detractors and Talks about Her New Novel," p. 92.

Library Journal, March 1, 2007, Rollie Welch, review of *Forever a Hustler's Wife,* p. 78.

Publishers Weekly, February 20, 2006, review of *Riding Dirty on I-95,* p. 133; February 5, 2007, review of *Forever a Hustler's Wife,* p. 42.

ONLINE

Fountain Bookstore, http://www.fountainbookstore.com/ (October 8, 2007), biographical information on Nikki Turner.

Nikki Turner Home Page, http://www.nikkiturner.com (October 8, 2007).

Publishers Weekly Online, http://www.publishersweekly.com/ (April 27, 2006), "One World Launches Nikki Turner Book Line."

Tayari Jones's Blog, http://www.tayarijones.com/ (May 11, 2006), "Nikki Turner Presents . . . "*

U-V

UNGER, Roberto Mangabeira 1947-

PERSONAL: Born 1947, in Rio de Janeiro, Brazil; mother a journalist and poet; married; children: four. *Education:* Attended college in Brazil; Harvard University, law degree. *Hobbies and other interests:* Playing the cello.

ADDRESSES: E-mail—robertomangabeira@gmail. com; unger@law.harvard.edu.

CAREER: Harvard University, Cambridge, MA, from assistant professor to Roscoe Pound Professor of Law, c. 1969—. Directed a foundation for needy children in Brazil, c. 1980s; unsuccessfully ran for Chamber of Deputies seat, Brazil, 1990. Visiting scholar, Yale University, 1999.

WRITINGS:

Knowledge & Politics, Free Press (New York, NY), 1975.

Law in Modern Society: Toward a Criticism of Social Theory, Free Press (New York, NY), 1976.

Participação, salário e voto: um projeto de democracia para o Brasil, Paz e Terra (Rio de Janeiro, Brazil), 1978.

Passion: An Essay on Personality, Free Press (New York, NY), 1984.

The Critical Legal Studies Movement, Harvard University Press (Cambridge, MA), 1986.

False Necessity—Anti-necessitarian Social Theory in the Service of Radical Democracy (Volume 1 in *Politics: A Work in Constructive Social Theory*), Cambridge University Press (New York, NY), 1987, new edition, Verso Books (New York, NY), 2004.

Plasticity into Power: Comparative-Historical Studies of the Institutional Conditions of Economic and Military Success (Volume 3 in *Politics: A Work in Constructive Social Theory*), Cambridge University Press (New York, NY), 1987, new edition, Verso Books (New York, NY), 2004.

Politics: A Work in Constructive Social Theory, Cambridge University Press (New York, NY), 1987.

Social Theory, Its Situation and Its Task (Volume 2 in *Politics: A Work in Constructive Social Theory*), Cambridge University Press (New York, NY), 1987, new edition, Verso Books (New York, NY), 2004.

A alternativa transformadora: como democratizar o Brasil, Editora Guanabara Koogan (Rio de Janeiro, Brazil), 1990.

(With Ciro Gomes) *O próximo passo: uma alternativa prática ao neoliberalismo,* Topbooks (Rio de Janeiro, Brazil), 1996.

What Should Legal Analysis Become?, Verso (New York, NY), 1996.

Politics the Central Texts: Theory against Fate, edited and introduced by Zhiyuan Cui, Verso (New York, NY), 1997.

Democracy Realized: The Progressive Alternative, Verso (New York, NY), 1998.

(With Cornel West) *The Future of American Progressivism: An Initiative for Political and Economic Reform,* Beacon Press (Boston, MA), 1998.

Respuestas al neoliberalismo, IIPS (La Paz, Bolivia), 1999.

A segunda via: presente e futuro do Brasil, Boitempo Editorial (São Paulo, Brazil), 2001.

Politics, Verso (New York, NY), 2004.

What Should the Left Propose?, Verso (New York, NY), 2005.

Free Trade Reimagined: The World Division of Labor and the Method of Economics, Princeton University Press (Princeton, NJ), 2007.

The Self Awakened: Pragmatism Unbound, Harvard University Press (Cambridge, MA), 2007.

Contributor to books, including *Law and New Governance in the EU and the US,* edited by Grainne de Burca and Joanne Scott, 2006; contributor to periodicals.

SIDELIGHTS: In some ways, Roberto Mangabeira Unger's life is a reflection of his maternal grandfather, a man he much admired. Octavio Mangabeira was a former astronomer turned Brazilian politician when his oratory skills were discovered. Unger himself has gone from an academic to becoming a fresh political voice. As a young man, Unger left Brazil for Harvard University to study law. In 1970, however, there was a military crackdown in Brazil, and Unger decided not to go back home. He became, instead, one of Harvard's youngest-ever law professors. By the 1980s he was considered the leader of the Critical Legal Studies (CLS) movement at Harvard. The central idea of CLS is that people presume incorrectly that the principles forming the basis of the legal system are inherent and not the product of values set up to define power relationships within society. In other words, laws in the United States favor principles that help retain the status quo of power and have no true basis in neutral, universal principles. "The overall goal of C.L.S. is to remove the constraints and hindrances imposed on individuals by unjust social hierarchy and class," explained Calvin Woodard in a *New York Times* review of Unger's *The Critical Legal Studies Movement.*

Unger and his like-minded colleagues felt that the legal system could legitimately be challenged and allowed to evolve to create a more just society. Unger first set down some of his basic ideas in his debut book, *Knowledge & Politics,* which created a huge stir in the academic and legal community. The book "mounted a sharp attack on liberal political philosophy, which he accused of reducing life to a series of false antinomies—rules versus values, reason versus desire," according to Eyal Press in *Lingua Franca.* Left-leaning in his beliefs, Unger feels that liberalism and other similar political schools are stagnating because of their unwillingness to change and adapt. One key point

where Unger differs from many on the Left is his idea that society should not be based so much on equality as on individual capability.

As with his insistence that society and the law should evolve, Unger himself is perfectly willing to allow his theories to change, as is evident in his written work. Reviewing *Politics: A Work in Constructive Social Theory,* William Connolly wrote in the *New York Times:* "Freedom as rising to highest human fulfillment now gives way to freedom as mastery over the contexts that form us: 'We are our fundamental practices. But we are also the permanent possibility of revising them,' he says. Productivity, innovation, empowerment, reconstruction, experimentation, context-breaking and self-assertion become key terms in the Unger lexicon." Pointing out the flaws in such schools as Marxism and Naturalism because they make certain inflexible assumptions, Unger says the "general idea [should be] . . . to enhance the flexibility of governing institutions so that they become effective instruments of individual and collective agency." Many of Unger's critics have seen his views as too utopian, for he "refuses to believe human beings are inherently brutish in the Hobbesian sense," related Woodard. Though Woodard believed that Unger "and his followers weaken their cause by adopting the style of Continental philosophy," the critic also stated that "one cannot fail to be impressed by his high idealism and intelligence."

In some of his works, Unger proposes radical ideas. For instance, *Democracy Realized: The Progressive Alternative* "proposes not so much a blueprint but a profoundly new direction that includes high levels of government investment and taxes, required voting and forced savings to buffer states from the influence of international investors," according to *New York Times* contributor Jeff Madrick. In the more recent *The Self Awakened: Pragmatism Unbound,* Unger goes so far as to assert that there should be "a world revolution that is spiritual as well as political," according to reviewer Leon H. Brody in *Library Journal.* Brody remarked that Unger's is a difficult work drawing on a broad spectrum of disciplines, such as politics, religion, and philosophy. Moreover, he added, this "highly informed, insightful, and demanding" book argues for political and legal reform as a necessity for humanity's spiritual growth.

In a review of Unger's *What Should the Left Propose?* in the *Guardian Unlimited,* John Sutherland commented that Unger has evolved into a less utopian-minded and more pragmatic social philosopher. Unger increasingly tries to apply his theories to practical, real-world problems, such as the globalization of economies. Sutherland quoted Unger as asserting: "In a world of democracies, . . . the different states of the world should represent a form of moral specialisation. . . . Humanity can develop its powers and possibilities only by developing them in different directions. But if this pluralism is to be compatible with the deepening of human freedom, it must have as one of its premises that a person born into one of these human worlds, but antipathetic to its special character, should be able to escape it. So for all these reasons, one should look to a world in which the freedom of movement is continuously but cautiously expanded."

Unger has also tried to apply his academic work to the real world. Since the 1990s, he has become increasingly active in his native Brazil's politics. He ran unsuccessfully for office in 1990 and then supported finance minister Ciro Gomes in the 1998 and 2002 elections for president. Unger himself has had a number of radical ideas for improving life in Brazil, focusing on one of its largest cities, São Paolo, in particular. Here he proposed a new tax on cars to be used for public transportation systems, government regulation of shantytowns, and a rezoning plan for the city to create multiple pseudocenters, which resemble minicities within the city. While many of Unger's proposals may never be realized as he has conceived them, his highly original theories on society and the law have stimulated political debate worldwide.

BIOGRAPHICAL AND CRITICAL SOURCES:

PERIODICALS

Booklist, October 15, 1998, Mary Carroll, review of *The Future of American Progressivism: An Initiative for Political and Economic Reform,* p. 395.

Ethics & International Affairs, October, 2002, Samuel Moyn, review of *False Necessity—Antinecessitarian Social Theory in the Service of Radical Democracy,* p. 135.

Institutional Investor, May 1997, Lucy Conger, "Tilting at Neoliberalism," p. 91.

Library Journal, March 1, 2007, Leon H. Brody, review of *The Self Awakened: Pragmatism Unbound,* p. 87.

Lingua Franca, March, 1999, Eyal Press, "The Passion of Roberto Unger: A Harvard Law Professor Jettisons His Past and Sets Out to Destabilize Latin America."

New York Times, July 8, 1984, Jerome Neu, "Looking Around for Our Real Selves," review of *Passion: An Essay on Personality,* section 7, p. 24.

Tikkun, July-August, 2007, review of *The Self Awakened,* p. 81.

Times Higher Education Supplement, February 24, 2006, Huw Richards, "Ideas Man Decides It's Time to Act: An Interview with Roberto Unger."

Utopian Studies, winter, 2001, Vincent Geoghegan, review of *Democracy Realized: The Progressive Alternative,* p. 266.

ONLINE

Guardian Unlimited, http://www.guardian.co.uk/ (February 28, 2006), John Sutherland, "He Wants to Be President of Brazil, and He Believes in the Human Right to Live Anywhere."

Harvard University Law School Web site, http://www.law.harvard.edu/ (October 22, 2007), faculty profile of Roberto Managabeira Unger.

New York Times Online, http://www.nytimes.com/ (November 23, 1986), Calvin Woodard, "Toward a 'Super Liberal State,'" review of *The Critical Legal Studies Movement;* (February 7, 1988), William Connolly, "Making the Friendly World Behave"; (July 6, 1998), Tina Rosenberg, "The Latin Left Searches for a Practical Agenda"; (August 24, 1999), Celia W. Dugger, "Sri Lanka Peacemaker's High-Risk Life, and Death"; (October 7, 1999), Simon Romero, "A Brazilian Politician Stirs Fear and Debate on Debt"; (June 11, 2000), Sam Dillon, "Presidential Challenger in Mexico Pitches Tent in Two Camps"; (July 2, 2000), Paul Berman, "Mexico's Third Way"; (July 9, 2000), Ginger Thompson, "Mexico's Voters Spoke"; (August 2, 2001), Jeff Madrick, "The Mainstream Can't or Won't Recognize Some Basic Facts about World Poverty."

Play Ethic, http://theplayethic.typepad.com/ (December 8, 2005), "The Self Unbound," review of *The Self Awakened.*

Roberto Unger Home Page, http://www.robertounger.com (October 22, 2007).*

VACHON, Dana 1979-

PERSONAL: Born 1979, in Greenwich, CT. *Education:* Duke University, B.A., 2002.

ADDRESSES: Home—New York, NY.

CAREER: JPMorgan (private bank), New York, NY, analyst for three years; currently a freelance writer.

WRITINGS:

Mergers & Acquisitions (novel), Riverhead Books (New York, NY), 2007.

Author of Web log *DNasty.* Contributor to periodicals, including *Salon.com, Men's Vogue, New York Times,* and the *International Herald Tribune.*

ADAPTATIONS: Movie rights to *Mergers & Acquisitions* have been sold.

SIDELIGHTS: Frequently compared to Jay McInerney's novel *Bright Lights, Big City, Mergers & Acquisitions* is Dana Vachon's debut work about young professionals living a rich but morally bereft life in New York City. Vachon's novel concerns twenty-somethings who get their investment-banking jobs mostly through family connections rather than talent; the author's admission that the story is largely based on real life is a big reason many readers find it fascinating. After graduating from Duke University, Vachon found work at JPMorgan as an analyst, a job he was not really qualified to do, just like his protagonist Tommy Quinn, who works in J.S. Spenser's mergers and acquisitions department. Vachon's roman à clef is blatantly aimed at satirizing the incompetence, outright greed, and ethically bankrupt environment of large financial corporations. He also spoofs the shallow lives of the young men and women who pursue money, sex, and drugs unashamedly. The epitome of this behavior is Tommy's friend, Roger Thorne, "a blue-blood would-be Master of the Universe so completely up front about his debauched lack of interest in anything beyond booze, babes, drugs and money that he is impossible to hate," according to Ben White in a *Financial Times* article; White called Roger the book's "finest creation." Va-

chon has said most of the other characters in his story are based on friends and relatives, with the exception of Tommy's love interest, Frances, a sexy but mentally disturbed art student. *Recorder* critic Kellie Schmitt commented that Frances is actually the least intriguing of the novel's characters, making her "wonder whether Vachon truly has a good imagination—or just happened upon some rich material."

Vachon was not at JPMorgan very long before it was purchased by Chase Manhattan, after which time he felt the corporate culture soon went into decline. Realizing that he was not really competent at his job and yearning for something more, he began writing about the financial world in his spare time. He would sneak off to a coffee shop, where he penned articles and began writing a Web log called *DNasty,* where he offered revealing, anonymous commentaries about his experiences. A well-known Internet Web logger, Elizabeth Spiers, took note and created a link from her Web log to Vachon's. Literary agent David Kuhn then contacted Vachon and suggested he write a book. *Mergers & Acquisitions* was the result, and Vachon earned a 650,000-dollar advance on the title.

Critics have variously labeled the book flawed, promising, and entertainingly humorous. While a *Kirkus Reviews* writer asserted that "the novel never succeeds in establishing a coherent fictional world, let alone delivering a roman a clef," White called it "wickedly funny and smartly written." Yet the critic admitted the work is not perfect: "Vachon's novel is flawed in serious ways. But it is also at times enormously entertaining and revelatory. And . . . it holds the promise of much greater things to come." Schmitt decided that "it'd be nice to have a little more substance" to the story, concluding that "it's a compelling read, if only in that guilty-pleasure kind of way." "Vachon has penned a convincing depiction of young turks on Wall Street and the thin, pretty, blonde women who bed them," reported a contributor to *Curled Up with a Good Book,* describing it as "annoyingly immature—consider the requisite fart and spew jokes—and yet as fascinating as watching a train wreck in slow motion."

BIOGRAPHICAL AND CRITICAL SOURCES:

PERIODICALS

Financial Times, March 31, 2007, Ben White, "Fiction—Greed Is God. An Impressive First

Novel about the High Life and Low Motives of a Junior Investment Banker," p. 31.

Investment Dealers' Digest, July 16, 2007, Aleksandrs Rozens, "Wall Street's Other Book Value."

Kirkus Reviews, February 1, 2007, review of *Mergers & Acquisitions,* p. 97.

Library Journal, March 1, 2007, Sheila Riley, review of *Mergers & Acquisitions,* p. 79.

Marie Claire, April 2007, Colleen Oakley, "Author Q&A: Dana Vachon on His Novel, *Mergers & Acquisitions,*" p. 122.

New York, April 2, 2007, Carl Swanson, "DNasty Boy: Dana Vachon, the Investment Banker Turned Blogger Turned Novelist, Is One Very Sincere Satirist," p. 74.

New York Times Book Review, April 22, 2007, D.T. Max, "Money Talks," p. 15.

New York Times, March 25, 2007, Melena Ryzik, "Made in Manhattan," p. 4.

Publishers Weekly, May 9, 2005, Sara Nelson, "Too Much of a Good Thing?," p. 5; January 8, 2007, review of *Mergers & Acquisitions,* p. 29.

Recorder, May 11, 2007, Kellie Schmitt, "M&A Misadventures: A Tale of Wall Street's Young, Rich and Oh-So-Bad Boys."

Variety, April 30, 2007, John Clarke Jr., "Lit Hipsters Vie for H'wood's Eye," p. 3.

ONLINE

Curled Up with a Good Book, http://www.curledup.com/ (October 22, 2007), review of *Mergers & Acquisitions.*

Gawker, http://gawker.com/ (March 28, 2007), "Dana Vachon Backlash Begins in Gritty, Blue-Collar Paper."

Radar, http://www.radaronline.com/ (April 11, 2007), Neel Shah, "On the Scene: Dana Vachon Makes His Mama Proud."

Reading Matters, http://kimbofo.typepad.com/readingmatters/ (April 7, 2007), Rex Allen, review of *Mergers & Acquisitions.**

* * *

VALDES, David Luis
See VALDES GREENWOOD, David

VALDES GREENWOOD, David 1967-
(David Luis Valdes)

PERSONAL: Born 1967; son of Jolene B. Valdes (a home health aide); married Jason John Greenwood (a speech therapist), December 31, 2004; children: Lily Ruth. *Education:* Atlantic Union College, B.A.; Emerson College, M.F.A., 1994.

ADDRESSES: Home—MA. *Office*—English Department, Tufts University, 210 East Hall, Medford, MA 02155.

CAREER: Author. Tufts University, Medford, MA, lecturer in English.

AWARDS, HONORS: Humana Festival award; Edward Albee PlayLab award; Midwest Theatre Network award; Massachusetts Cultural Council award; Clauder Competition award; two commissions from EST/Sloan Project.

WRITINGS:

Homo Domesticus: Notes from a Same-Sex Marriage, Da Capo Press Lifelong Books (Cambridge, MA), 2007.

A Little Fruitcake: A Boyhood in Holidays, Da Capo Press (Cambridge, MA), 2007.

Columnist and arts writer, *Bay Windows,* 1994-2000; contributing writer, *Boston Phoenix,* 1996-2004; columnist, *Boston Globe,* 2005-06.

PLAYS

Brave Navigator (acting edition), Baker's Plays (Quincy, MA), 2000.

Day Eight: Snow Globe, Baker's Plays (Quincy, MA), 2003.

Dream of Jeannie-by-the-Door, Broadway Play Publishing (New York, NY), 2007.

SIDELIGHTS: David Valdes Greenwood is the author of two memoirs focusing on distinct chapters of his childhood and adult life. In *A Little Fruitcake: A Boy-*

hood in Holidays, Valdes Greenwood recalls both the cherished and wacky moments spent with his eccentric family at Christmas. The book is organized into twelve essays, one for each of the holiday's twelve days. Conversely, *Homo Domesticus: Notes from a Same-Sex Marriage* is the story of the life that Valdes Greenwood and his husband, James, have forged together. It begins with their auspicious meeting at a college campus event, follows their commitment ceremony in 1995 and legal Massachusetts wedding in 2005, and includes the adoption of their infant daughter. Valdes Greenwood sets out to prove that same-sex marriages struggle through their fair share of the usual conflicts—financial difficulties, poor communication, disruptive in-laws—and are more similar than many think to heterosexual relationships. Holly Dolezalek described *Homo Domesticus* in a review for *Gay Marriage World* as "a hilarious treatise on serious subjects, like the right of gays to marry and adopt—and how to do both without murdering each other." *Gay and Lesbian Review Worldwide* contributor Terri Schlichenmeyer wrote: "Reading this book is rather like having a latte with your best friend who just got married and can't wait to tell you everything. Fortunately, given this degree of intimacy, [Valdes] Greenwood is a born storyteller, and the story he tells is one you'll be delighted to hear."

BIOGRAPHICAL AND CRITICAL SOURCES:

PERIODICALS

Booklist, February 15, 2007, Whitney Scott, review of *Homo Domesticus: Notes from a Same-Sex Marriage,* p. 19.
Gay and Lesbian Review Worldwide, May-June, 2007, Terri Schlichenmeyer, "Scenes from a Marriage," review of *Homo Domesticus,* p. 46.
New York Times, January 2, 2005, "David Valdes, Jason Greenwood," wedding announcement, p. 11.
Publishers Weekly, February 26, 2007, "Wendy Holt at Da Capo Bought World Rights to 'A Little Fruitcake: A [Boyhood] in Holidays,'" p. 23.

ONLINE

Gay Marriage World, http://www.gaymarriageworld.com (August 21, 2007), review of *Homo Domesticus.*

VASSALLO, Russell A. 1934-

PERSONAL: Born April 24, 1934, in Newark, NJ; son of Anthony D. and Philomena Vassallo; married October 5, 1987; wife's name Virginia G.; children: Carolyn Vassallo Ward, Russell A. III, Christopher D., Marianne Vassallo Mosca. *Ethnicity:* "Italian-American." *Education:* Seton Hall University, B.A., 1958, J.D., 1961. *Politics:* Independent. *Religion:* Christian. *Hobbies and other interests:* Animal rescue, horseback riding and training, target shooting, farming, marketing, travel.

ADDRESSES: Home—Liberty, KY. *Office*—Krazy Duck Productions, P.O. Box 105, Danville, KY 40423. *E-mail*—russ@krazyduck.com.

CAREER: Trial attorney in Bloomfield, NJ, 1971-99; Krazy Duck Productions, Danville, KY, publisher and writer, 2003—. Also worked as insurance adjuster and private investigator.

MEMBER: Publishers Marketing Association, National Rifle Association, Kentucky Mountain Saddle Horse Association, New Jersey State Bar Association.

AWARDS, HONORS: Winner of inspirational short story contest, *Reader Views,* for "A Heart Betrayed."

WRITINGS:

Tears and Tales: Stories of Human and Animal Rescue (nonfiction), Krazy Duck Productions (Danville, KY), 2005.
The Horse with the Golden Mane: Stories of Adventure, Mystery, and Romance (short stories), Krazy Duck Productions (Danville, KY), 2007.

Work represented in anthologies, including *Horse Tales for the Soul.* Also author of articles and short stories.

SIDELIGHTS: Russell A. Vassallo told *CA:* "My writing is therapeutic, giving me an opportunity to express myself while obtaining the approval of those who read my writings. It also gives me the chance to record the events of my life: personal experiences, people I have encountered who I believe others should know about. In a sense I write to immortalize those who have formed a part of my life, so that someone will know they existed. I write to let others know that I was here. Often I write to quell a mood or give vent to some emotion. Most of all, I write because I know it is 'in me' to write.

"My writing is influenced by many people and other factors. My wife is my single-most important audience. If I please her, I am content to let others read what I write. I write for my children and grandchildren that they may know a little more about me. My writing is also influenced by my peers and my editor. All my work is professionally edited, for there is no good writer without a good editor (despite what I tell her). The greatest influences on my life have been the great literary masters. From Kipling I derive plot and adventure; from Kenneth Roberts the value of history; from Steinbeck a study of people and social times; from Cervantes the myth of imagination; from Maugham character development. I am influenced by people and events and a desire to touch others with vivid emotion.

"My writing process is difficult. I start with the raw seed of a story with no idea of beginning or ending, just a thread of what I want to write about. It goes underground for a time, as if forgotten. Sometimes I do not write for weeks, although I feel I am writing internally. Then, when I am least able, as for example when I am driving to a faraway location or standing in a rainstorm in the middle of a field, the first line or the last line strikes me like a bolt. I know how to start my story. From that, all else flows right to a smash conclusion.

"Then begins the true writing process. The beginning and end usually do not change, but I begin to dab in more description, more character, a twist here or there. I rewrite again. And then again. I wake up in the middle of the night and add more, wondering why I am punishing myself. The second or third or fourth draft is then finished. I think it's wonderful. Best I have ever done. I leave it for two or three weeks. Go back and read it again. It's awful! How could something I thought so good be so rotten? I burn the manuscript but leave the original on my computer. Perhaps it, too, will go away in the morning.

"Somewhere from all this emerges a story full of adventure, emotion, sincerity, love, sentiment; but I am drained. I swear I will never again subject myself to such torture. I publish a book. People tell me it's great. The sales mount up. Ten copies sold. Twenty. I run out of friends and family, and the friends I have are threatening to leave if I write another book. Even my dogs begin to look at me as if I am mad. Perhaps I am mad. Poe suffered hallucinations. Perhaps mine is that I can write or sell stories. No! I will never again do this to myself.

"And then I am standing in that field again. It's raining. I huddle under a tree, and the raindrops are slithering like icy snakes down the back of my neck. That opening sentence is right there in front of me. I take out my penknife and chisel out the first sentence in the bark of a tree. And then I look to the sky and pray, 'Oh God, not again. Please hit me with a lightning bolt or something.' And the answer rolls like thunder from the sky. 'Who told you to be a writer? Didn't I tell you to be a lawyer and make a decent living?' All I can do is nod my head in shame. 'You're right, Mom. I should have listened.'

"I am inspired to write by the experiences of my lifetime and the manner in which events transpired in my life. I came out of a very rough section of Newark, New Jersey, attended college and law school, worked as an insurance adjuster, worked as a private investigator, then as an attorney. I met many people from many cultures. I traveled a good deal. All of this now fins its way into my stories. Most of my stories are based on some true event, some real person in my life. It's easy to write about the things one knows. Giving it life is the difficult part.

"Making people feel my characters, enjoy my stories, that's the challenge. Because my experience is so widespread and vast, I can write in many areas. I can write about animals, people, and traverse the fields of fiction and nonfiction. One of the books on my computer is about the field of divorce and my experience as an attorney. Another reveals the lives of the animals that reside with me and how they came to be here. Another covers some of the mobsters and common people I grew up with in Newark.

"I hope I never become so stilted that I can only write on one topic."

BIOGRAPHICAL AND CRITICAL SOURCES:

ONLINE

Krazy Duck Productions, http://www.krazyduck.com (August 16, 2007).

VELICKOVIC, Nenad 1962-

PERSONAL: Born 1962, in Sarajevo, Yugoslavia (now Bosnia and Herzegovina).

ADDRESSES: E-mail—omnibus@bih.net.ba.

CAREER: Institute for Literature, Sarajevo, Bosnia and Herzegovina, secretary, early 1990s; University of Sarajevo, Sarajevo, literature faculty; author. *Military service:* Served in Bosnia and Herzegovina (BiH) Army for four years.

WRITINGS:

Konačari (novel), Durieux (Zagreb, Croatia), 1997, translated by Celia Hawkesworth as *Lodgers,* Northwestern University Press (Evanston, IL), 2005.

Sexicon-Sexpressionism (essays), 1998.

Duvo u Sarajevu (short stories; title means "Devil in Sarajevo"), Feral Tribune (Split, Croatia), 1998.

Sahib: Impresije iz depresije (novel; title means "Sahib; or, Impressions from a Depression"), Kultura & Rasvjeta (Split, Croatia), 2002.

Izdržite jos malo, nećete još dugo, Omnibus (Sarajevo, Bosnia and Herzegovina), 2003.

Otac moje kćeri (novel; title means "My Daughter's Father"), Stubovi kulture (Belgrade, Serbia), 2003.

(Editor) *Inso(mno)lent P(r)ose,* translated by Celia Hawkesworth, Knjizevna radionica (Sarajevo, Bosnia and Herzegovina), 2003.

Pedalo (play), first produced in London, England, at the Blue Elephant, 2005.

Also author of television and radio scripts, short stories, and essays.

SIDELIGHTS: Born in Sarajevo, Nenad Velickovic refused to flee his homeland when war in Yugoslavia began to break up the nation. Instead, as Tatjana Jukic related in a *Style* article, he "stayed and survived the siege. As a consequence, his texts, written mainly during the siege of the city, are ruled primarily by the rapidly and radically shifting cultural and political dominant." His first novel, *Konačari,* was published in 1997 and later translated into English as *Lodgers.* Set in the worn-torn Sarajevo of 1992, the story is about a Muslim family that finds shelter in the museum where the father is a curator. He tries to protect the museum's collection from looters; meanwhile, his teenage daughter, Maja, narrates the tale. Maja tries to make the best of things while there with her odd grandmother, vegetarian mother, her pessimistic stepbrother, and his wife. Despite the grim surroundings where even fresh water is hard to come by, Velickovic puts a great deal of humor into his story using Maja's witty perspective. Ales Debeljak, writing in *World Literature Today,* described the narrative tone as "gallows humor," adding: *Lodgers* supplies one of the best examples of 'war literature' wherein the aesthetic qualities are not suffocating in the straitjacket of patriotic imperative." Using Maja's perspective helps the author view the tragedy of war from the interesting perspective of a young teen who does not fully comprehend what is happening and remains somewhat self-absorbed. The result is "a first-rate work that shows the action but does not raise a moral-pedagogical finger," according to Debeljak. "Velickovic reveals an artistry that defeats the forces of brutality with wit, indirection, and boundless good humor," concluded Michael Pinker in the *Review of Contemporary Fiction.*

One of the themes in Velickovic's writings is the clash between Eastern and Western cultures. His *Sahib: Impresije iz depresije,* for example, is about an Englishman who comes to Bosnia on a diplomatic mission. On the pretext of trying to establish Western ideals of government, he portrays the motives of his country as closer to colonization than democratization. The author uses text from e-mails for much of the narrative, revealing at the end of the book that the e-mails are actually real correspondences with the authors' names changed. "The meeting of the Orient with the Occident serves as a good source for all sorts of humorous situations, misunderstandings, and witticisms, with which Velickovic's book abounds," commented Ana Lucic in the *Review of Contemporary Fiction,* adding that *Sahib,* is occasionally "a Swiftian satire, having as its main target the colonizing policies behind the rhetoric of liberating and democratizing nations."

BIOGRAPHICAL AND CRITICAL SOURCES:

PERIODICALS

Review of Contemporary Fiction, summer, 2003, Ana Lucic, review of *Sahib: Impresije iz depresije,* p. 136; spring, 2006, Michael Pinker, review of *Lodgers,* p. 148.

Style, fall, 1996, Tatjana Jukic, "Souls and Apples, All in One: Bosnia as the Cultural Nexus in Nenad Velickovic's 'Konacari.'"

World Literature Today, July-August, 2006, Ales Debeljak, review of *Lodgers,* p. 72.

ONLINE

Nenad Velickovic Home Page, http://www.velickovic.ba (October 27, 2007).*

*   *   *

VERON, J. Michael

PERSONAL: Born in Lake Charles, LA; son of Earl (an attorney and judge) and Verdy Veron; married; wife's name Melinda; children: five. *Education:* Tulane University, B.A., J.D.; Harvard University, graduate law degree. *Hobbies and other interests:* Golf.

ADDRESSES: Home—Lake Charles, LA.

CAREER: Attorney, 1976—; Scofield, Gerard, Veron, Singletary & Pohorelsky (law firm), Lake Charles, LA, currently a partner; Louisiana State University, member of law faculty. Committee member, U.S. Golf Association.

MEMBER: Lake Charles Country Club (president).

AWARDS, HONORS: Inducted into the Law Center Hall of Fame, Louisiana State University.

WRITINGS:

The Greatest Player Who Never Lived: A Golf Story (novel), Sleeping Bear Press (Chelsea, MI), 2000.

The Greatest Course That Never Was: The Secret of Augusta National's Lost Course (novel), Sleeping Bear Press (Chelsea, MI), 2001.

The Caddie (novel), Thomas Dunne Books/St. Martin's Press (New York, NY), 2004.

Shell Game: One Family's Long Battle against Big Oil (nonfiction), Lyons (Guilford, CT), 2007.

Also author of *Litigation Handbook: A Method of Trial Practice.* Contributor to law journals; also author of articles on golf.

SIDELIGHTS: J. Michael Veron is a respected attorney and law firm partner with a passion for the game of golf. He combined his professional and avocational interests to create a fiction trilogy that includes the novels *The Greatest Player Who Never Lived: A Golf Story, The Greatest Course That Never Was: The Secret of Augusta National's Lost Course,* and *The Caddie.* Honoring the game with a blend of love for its history and an air of mysticism reminiscent of *The Legend of Bagger Vance* by Steven Pressfield, the books find a common thread in Bobby Jones. Jones was a real-life golf legend who won thirteen national championships during the 1920s and 1930s and later designed the course for the Augusta National. He, like Veron, was also an attorney.

In *The Greatest Player Who Never Lived,* Jones helps the fictional Beau Steadman achieve greatness on the course, until Beau has to go into hiding when he is accused of murder. But Beau occasionally comes out of hiding to play golf anyway. The remarkable story is discovered by a law student named Charley Hunter, who finds the correspondence between Beau and Bobby among Jones's legal files. In the sequel, *The Greatest Course That Never Was,* Hunter is a practicing lawyer when he comes across another mystery. This one is about a course that Jones designed that is even more remarkable than the one at Augusta. However, nobody seems to know about it except the rare golfer who is allowed the chance to play there. The last book in the trilogy, *The Caddie,* features yet another troubled but talented golfer. Bobby Reeves is bailed out of jail by Jones, who sees potential in the young man if only he can get his mind more on the game. "This is Veron's third mystical-toned golf novel and should have no trouble attracting duffing fans," predicted Gilbert Taylor in *Booklist.*

Abandoning fiction for nonfiction, Veron drew on his own family history to write *Shell Game: One Family's Long Battle against Big Oil.* From the 1960s until 1981, Veron's family leased land to Shell Oil for drilling. Part of the contract included the condition that Shell clean up its mess after the end of the lease. When the company abandoned the land, leaving machinery and pollution behind, Veron pursued the company for a year, trying to get them to clean the site. After repeated failures, he finally took them to court. Facing a hostile judge and corporate attorneys backed by a wealthy company, Veron managed to win the case using his skills, excellent witnesses, and the fact that truth was on his side. Comparing Veron's account to the novel *A Civil Action,* by Jonathan Harr, a *Publishers Weekly* contributor considered *Shell Game* to be more "biased" against big business, but added that "this simpler good-versus-evil tale is a cracking good read." *Library Journal* contributor Ilse Heidmann concluded that the "engaging plot, colorful characters, well-written narration, and an ultimately happy ending make this a satisfying work."

BIOGRAPHICAL AND CRITICAL SOURCES:

PERIODICALS

Booklist, April 1, 2004, Gilbert Taylor, review of *The Caddie,* p. 1350.
Library Journal, March 1, 2007, Ilse Heidmann, review of *Shell Game: One Family's Long Battle against Big Oil,* p. 103.
Publishers Weekly, January 29, 2007, review of *Shell Game,* p. 54.

ONLINE

Bookreporter.com, http://www.bookreporter.com/ (October 27, 2007), Stuart Shiffman, review of *The Caddie.*
J. Michael Veron Home Page, http://www.jmichael veron.com (October 27, 2007).*

*   *   *

VER STEEG, Clarence L. 1922-2007
(Clarence Lester Ver Steeg)

OBITUARY NOTICE— See index for *CA* sketch: Born December 28, 1922, in Orange City, IA; died of cancer, July 2, 2007, in Evanston, IL. Historian, educator, and author. Ver Steeg spent nearly his entire career at Northwestern University, where he taught U.S. history from 1950 until 1992. Deeply attached to the university and its campus, he was an instrumental member of the planning committee responsible for reclaiming adjacent land from Lake Michigan in the 1960s to expand the campus. He also dedicated himself to elevating the status of Northwestern from a regional college to a nationally respected research university. Ver Steeg wrote many articles and several books, including *Robert Morris, Revolutionary Financier,* for which he received the Albert J. Beveridge Award of the American Historical Association in 1952. Other writings include *Southern Colonies in the Eighteenth Century, 1689-1783* (1975) and *American Spirit: A History of the United States* (1982). With historian Richard Hofstadter, Ver Steeg edited *Great Issues in American History: From Settlement to Revolution, 1584-1776* (1969).

OBITUARIES AND OTHER SOURCES:

PERIODICALS

Chicago Tribune, July 9, 2007, p. 6.

*   *   *

VER STEEG, Clarence Lester
See VER STEEG, Clarence L.

*   *   *

VIGORITO, Tony

PERSONAL: Born in PA.

ADDRESSES: Home—Northern CA. *E-mail*—tony@ justacoupleofdays.com.

CAREER: Former professor of social theory; has taught at Antioch College, Ohio University, and Ohio State University.

WRITINGS:

Just a Couple of Days (novel), privately printed, 2001, Harcourt (Orlando, FL), 2007.

SIDELIGHTS: Tony Vigorito has written several novels but did not find a publisher until his *Just a Couple of Days* was released by Harcourt in 2007. Originally self-published, the satirical book is a parody of government, the military, and other institutions that seek to control people. The tale is set at the fictional Tynee University, where geneticist Flake Fountain works. He is friends with Blip Korterly, an unemployed sociology professor, who is married to another professor on the Tynee faculty. Flake is approached by representatives of the military, which has developed a virus that affects people's ability to communicate. The intention is to use the virus as a weapon, but to protect American troops Flake is asked to develop a vaccine. In performing secret experiments on prison inmates, complications arise when Blip is briefly arrested for a minor crime and is given the virus. Released, Blip spreads the disease to others at a party with unexpected results that address Vigorito's theme of the futility of trying to control people. "The final apocalyptic vision is a twist not seen since Kurt Vonnegut's *Cat's Cradle,*" reported Joshua Cohen in a *Library Journal* review. A *Kirkus Reviews* contributor, however, felt that "suspense takes a backseat to philosophizing and linguistic fireworks" and that Vigorito's attempts at satire are "not quite enough to sustain a full-length novel." Similarly, a *Publishers Weekly* writer decided that the author's "inability to go big with humor or vision leaves this feeling like [Thomas] Pynchon ultra-lite." Nevertheless, Royce Carlson asserted on the *Zenzibar* Web site that *Just a Couple of Days* "provokes thought and laughter and shows that freedom is, indeed, a bigger game than power."

BIOGRAPHICAL AND CRITICAL SOURCES:

PERIODICALS

Kirkus Reviews, January 15, 2007, review of *Just a Couple of Days,* p. 50.

Library Journal, February 15, 2007, Joshua Cohen, review of *Just a Couple of Days,* p. 115.

Publishers Weekly, January 8, 2007, review of *Just a Couple of Days,* p. 31.

ONLINE

Just a Couple of Days Web site, http://www.justa coupleofdays.com (October 27, 2007).

Listen and Be Heard, http://listenandbeheard.net/ (October 27, 2006), Kara Hartz, "A Couple Days Read."

Redbrick, http://www.redbrick.dcu.ie/ (October 27, 2007), Cian Synnott, review of *Just a Couple of Days.*

Tony Vigorito MySpace Page, http://www.myspace. com/tonyvigorito (October 27, 2007).

Zenzibar, http://www.zenzibar.com/ (October 27, 2002), Royce Carlson, review of *Just a Couple of Days.*

* * *

VLAUTIN, Willy 1968(?)-

PERSONAL: Born c. 1968, in Reno, NV.

ADDRESSES: Home—Portland, OR.

CAREER: Cofounder of band Richmond Fontaine; songwriter and musician; also worked for ten years for a trucking company.

WRITINGS:

The Motel Life (novel), Harper Perennial (New York, NY), 2006.

Author of lyrics for his band, Richmond Fontaine, including the release of several compact discs. Contributor to periodicals, including *Cold Drill, Chiron Review, Sun Dog Southeast Review,* and *Zembla.*

ADAPTATIONS: Movie rights to *The Motel Life* were sold to Guillermo Arriaga.

SIDELIGHTS: The front man and founder of the alternative country band Richmond Fontaine, Willy Vlautin has known many struggles in his life. His distinctly nonmainstream musical group has never gained a large following in the United States, though they have found better success in Europe and the United Kingdom and have released a number of compact discs. Vlautin writes lyrics and sings for the band, and his music is known for being distinctly dark and "about the sort of blue collar folk that corporate US treats with contempt," according to Brian Denny in a *Morning Star Online* article. Now gaining some financial stability, Vlautin yearns for a more stable life than can be offered by a band constantly on the road. "The camaraderie of being in a band is my favourite thing. Other than that, I was a shy guy, I just wanted to go home," he admitted to Peter Murphy on the *Laura Hird* Web site. Taking his writing to a new level, he penned his first novel, *The Motel Life.*

As unrelievedly depressing as many of his songs, *The Motel Life* is about two brothers who never seem to get a break. Their mother died when they were young, and their father abandoned them. Sticking together, they lead a vagabond life, escaping their miserable existence with the help of drugs and alcohol. One day, their world goes from bad to worse when they hit and kill a teen with their car. Ditching the body, the brothers flee from the authorities, trying to escape from the inevitable. Calling the novel a "gritty debut" with spare prose reminiscent of the work of S.E. Hinton, a *Publishers Weekly* contributor wrote that Vlautin "transmits a quiet sense of resilience and hopefulness" despite the subject matter. Christine Perkins, writing in *Library Journal,* held a contrary opinion. Describing the prose as "meandering" and "choppy," Perkins felt that this is an "inconsistent effort." Other critics were more positive, with Murphy asserting that *The Motel Life* is "the work of a careful and conscientious writer."

Vlautin plans to continue his new career as novelist with a book about a woman who tries to escape an abusive relationship.

BIOGRAPHICAL AND CRITICAL SOURCES:

PERIODICALS

Bookseller, November 17, 2006, "Vlautin Signs Up for Two More Books with Faber," p. 13.

Entertainment Weekly, June 1, 2007, Clark Collis, "Richmond Fontaine," p. 68.
Library Journal, May 15, 2007, Christine Perkins, review of *The Motel Life,* p. 85.
New York Times Book Review, June 24, 2007, John Wray, "Let's Get Lost," review of *The Motel Life,* p. 22.
Publishers Weekly, February 26, 2007, review of *The Motel Life,* p. 53.

ONLINE

Americana, http://www.americana-uk.com/ (October 27, 2007), "Willy Vlautin (Richmond Fontaine)."
Austinist, http://austinist.com/ (September 19, 2007), interview with Willy Vlautin.
Comes with a Smile, http://cwas.hinah.com/ (October 27, 2007), Stav Sherez, "Richmond Fontaine," interview with Willy Vlautin.
KQED Web site, http://www.kqed.org/ (May 1, 2007), review of *The Motel Life.*
Laura Hird Web site, http://www.laurahird.com/ (October 27, 2007), Peter Murphy, interview with Willy Vlautin.
Morning Star Online, http://www.morningstaronline.co.uk/ (November 10, 2004), Brian Denny, "Star Interview: Willy Vlautin."
Oregonian Online, http://www.oregonlive.com/ (April 22, 2007), Jeff Baker, "His Sad Stories Didn't Sell, Nor Did His Music. Willy Vlautin Perservered."
Richmond Fontaine MySpace Page, http://www.myspace.com/richmondfontaine (October 27, 2007).
SF Weekly, http://www.sfweekly.com/ (June 27, 2007), Jennifer Maerz, "Manifesting Dead-End Destinies Willy Vlautin Attempts the Great Escape."
Uncut, http://www.uncut.co.uk/ (October 27, 2007), Allan Jones, interview with Will Vlautin.
Willy Vlautin Home Page, http://www.willyvlautin.com (October 27, 2007).*

W-Z

WAGNER, Andreas 1967-

PERSONAL: Born January 26, 1967.

ADDRESSES: Office—Biochemistry Institute, University of Zurich, Winterthurestrasse 190, CH-8057 Zurich, Switzerland. *E-mail*—aw@bioc.uzh.ch.

CAREER: University of Zurich, Zurich, Switzerland, member of chemistry faculty.

WRITINGS:

Robustness and Evolvability in Living Systems, Princeton University Press (Princeton, NJ), 2005.

*   *   *

WAGNER, Jan Costin 1972-

PERSONAL: Born 1972, in Germany; married. *Education:* Attended Frankfurt University.

CAREER: Journalist and freelance author.

WRITINGS:

Nachtfahrt (novel), Eichborn (Berlin, Germany), 2001.

Ice Moon (mystery novel; originally published in Germany as *Eismond*), translated by John Brownjohn, Harvill Secker (London, England), 2006.

Das Schweigen (novel), Eichborn Berlin (Frankfurt on Main, Germany), 2007.

SIDELIGHTS: A journalist and freelance writer in his native Germany, Jan Costin Wagner is also an author of murder mysteries. His first to be translated into English, *Ice Moon,* is about a young police detective working on a disturbing case after the recent death of his wife from cancer. The serial killer, who likes to murder his victims in the least violent and quietest way possible, also narrates much of the book. Detective Kimmo Joentaa feels himself drawn into the case, sensing a kind of connection between himself and the killer. Reviewers of this psychological crime novel noted occasional flaws in it, but overall found it intriguing and gripping. A *Publishers Weekly* writer, for example, felt the author "sometimes shifts awkwardly" to the point of view of the murderer, but added that the "characters are well drawn" in this "absorbing" novel. Writing in *Booklist,* Thomas Gaughan was disappointed that the setting in Finland does not come through in the book, yet he described the thriller as a "superior crime novel." And while *Curled Up with a Good Book* contributor Luan Gaines complained that "the lack of passion that permeates the book alienated me to some degree, and I failed to make a connection with the protagonist," Maxine Clarke asserted in *Euro Crime* that "the main strength of this excellent book is the character study of Kimmo Joentaa."

BIOGRAPHICAL AND CRITICAL SOURCES:

PERIODICALS

Booklist, March 1, 2007, Thomas Gaughan, review of *Ice Moon,* p. 66.
Publishers Weekly, February 12, 2007, review of *Ice Moon,* p. 65.

ONLINE

Curled Up with a Good Book, http://www.curledup.com/ (October 27, 2007), Luan Gaines, review of *Ice Moon.*
Euro Crime, http://www.eurocrime.co.uk/ (April 1, 2007), Maxine Clark, review of *Ice Moon.*
Reading Matters, http://kimbofo.typepad.com/readingmatters/ (March 25, 2007), review of *Ice Moon.**

* * *

WALSH, Gillian Paton
See PATON WALSH, Jill

* * *

WALTZER, Jim 1950-

PERSONAL: Born 1950.

ADDRESSES: E-mail—jmwaltzer@verizon.net.

CAREER: Author.

WRITINGS:

Tales of South Jersey: Profiles and Personalities, Rutgers University Press (New Brunswick, NJ), 2001.
(With Rod Kennedy) *Monopoly: The Story behind the World's Best-Selling Game,* Gibbs Smith (Salt Lake City, UT), 2004.
Sound of Mind (thriller novel), Five Star (Waterville, ME), 2007.

SIDELIGHTS: Jim Waltzer published the nonfiction *Tales of South Jersey: Profiles and Personalities* and *Monopoly: The Story behind the World's Best-Selling Game* before releasing his first novel, *Sound of Mind.* The premise of the book is that the main character, Richard Keene, has a remarkably keen sense of hearing. It is so good that at one point it drove him nearly insane and put him in a mental hospital. After recovering and being released, Keene gets a job working as an audiometric technician. One day in his apartment building, he accidentally overhears what he believes to be a murder. When he reports what he heard to law enforcement authorities, however, they do not believe him. The problem is that the apartment where Keene thought he heard the crime in progress is occupied by a renowned doctor; moreover, the police cannot find a body or any evidence of murder. Convinced that his hearing did not lead him astray, Keene sets out to find the killer on his own in a tale that Harriet Klausner described as a "fascinating thriller" on her Web site. *Booklist* critic David Pitt commented that the story reminded him of the movie *The Conversation,* in which the sound of a murder's being committed is caught on tape, but the reviewer felt that Waltzer's take is original, "sharply plotted and engagingly written."

BIOGRAPHICAL AND CRITICAL SOURCES:

PERIODICALS

Booklist, March 1, 2007, David Pitt, review of *Sound of Mind,* p. 70.

ONLINE

Harriet Klausner Web site, http://harrietklausner.wwwi.com/ (October 27, 2007), Harriet Klausner, review of *Sound of Mind.*

* * *

WASLEY, Ric

PERSONAL: Married; children: two sons, one daughter. *Education:* University of Kentucky, B.A., 1968. *Hobbies and other interests:* Cross-country and downhill skiing, motorcycling, waterskiing, brewing beer, golf.

ADDRESSES: Home—Boston, MA.

CAREER: Professional folk singer and author; has worked in media and advertising, beginning c. 1975.

AWARDS, HONORS: Short story award, *Boulevard Magazine.*

WRITINGS:

Acid Test (murder mystery; "McCarthy Family" series), self-published through iUniverse, 2004.
Shadow of Innocence (murder mystery; "McCarthy Family" series), Kunati (Largo, FL), 2007.

Contributor to periodicals.

SIDELIGHTS: Ric Wasley has a steady career working in advertising for a media company and is a married man with three children. He still looks back fondly to the 1960s, though, when he was a folk singer and was able to meet such famous musicians as Joan Baez and Bob Dylan. He kept a detailed journal of this time in his life, "traveling around on my motorcycle, playing as a single folk act, and later in a VW Mini-bus touring with my rock band," as he recalled in an interview reproduced on the *Authors Den* Web site. This background information would later serve as setting material for his murder mysteries. His main characters in the stories, Mick McCarthy and his girlfriend, Bridget, help Mick's father, who runs a detective agency. They "often go 'under-cover' when working on a case, and travel around as folk-singing duo," the author explained in the interview.

Shadow of Innocence is set during the 1968 Newport Rock Festival, where a friend of Mick's is accused of murder. Mick naturally answers his friend's call to try to clear his name, getting caught up in the clash between the sex, drugs, and rock 'n' roll crowd versus the rich, staid community where the festival is being held. While David Pitt, writing in *Booklist,* felt the plot is "a little dumsy" and the writing "a tad clunky," he still concluded that the book is, overall, "colorful and exciting."

BIOGRAPHICAL AND CRITICAL SOURCES:

PERIODICALS

Booklist, March 1, 2007, David Pitt, review of *Shadow of Innocence,* p. 70.

ONLINE

Authors Den, http://www.authorsden.com/ (October 27, 2007), interview with Ric Wasley.
McCarthy Family Mysteries Web site, http://www.mccarthyfamilymysteries.com (October 27, 2007).
Ric Wasley MySpace Page, http://www.myspace.com/ricwasley (October 27, 2007).*

*　　*　　*

WERSHLER-HENRY, Darren 1966-
  (Darren Sean Wershler-Henry)

PERSONAL: Born 1966, in Winnipeg, Manitoba, Canada; son of a Royal Canadian Mounted Police officer. *Education:* University of Manitoba, B.A. (first-class honors), 1988; University of Alberta, M.A., 1989; York University, Ph.D., 2005.

ADDRESSES:　　　　*E-mail*—darren@alienated.net; dwershlerhenry@wlu.ca.

CAREER: Worked as a technical writer, c. 1996-97; Coach House Books, Toronto, Ontario, Canada, senior editor, 1998-2002; Wilfrid Laurier University, Waterloo, Ontario, assistant professor of communications, 2002—.

WRITINGS:

Nicholodeon: A Book of Lowerglyphs (poetry), Coach House Books (Toronto, Ontario, Canada), 1997.
(With Scott Mitchell) *Internet Directory 2000,* Prentice Hall Canada (Toronto, Ontario, Canada), 1999.
(With Mark Surman) *Commonspace: Beyond Virtual Community,* Financial Times (Toronto, Ontario, Canada), 2000.
The Tapeworm Foundry andor the Dangerous Prevalence of Imagination (poetry), House of Anansi Press (Toronto, Ontario, Canada), 2000.
(With Hal Niedzviecki) *The Original Canadian City Dweller's Almanac: Facts, Rants, Anecdotes and Unsupported Assertions for Urban Residents,* illustrated by Marc Ngui, Viking Canada (Toronto, Ontario, Canada), 2002.

Free as in Speech and Beer: Open Source, Peer-to-Peer and the Economics of the Online Revolution, Prentice Hall (New York, NY), 2002.

(Editor, with Mark Higgins and Stephen Pender) *The Common Sky: Canadian Writers against the War,* Three Squares Press (Toronto, Ontario, Canada), 2003.

(With Bill Kennedy) *Apostrophe* (includes links to hypertext poetry site), ECW Press (Toronto, Ontario, Canada), 2006.

The Iron Whim: A Fragmented History of Typewriting, Cornell University Press (Ithaca, NY), 2007.

Contributor of essays, articles, and poetry to periodicals, including *Sulfur, Prairie Fire, Quill & Quire, Grain, Boston Review, Brick, Boundary 2, Open Letter, Matrix, Postmodern Apocalypse, Semiotext(e) Canada(s), West Coast Line, Gone to Croatan: Origins of American Dropout Culture,* and *Rampike.*

SIDELIGHTS: A writer, educator, and former editor, Darren Wershler-Henry has explored cutting-edge poetry in such experimental forms as concrete poems and hypertext. Since his college days, he has been fascinated by how technology—from the typewriter to the computer—has influenced our writing and even our culture, as ideas blend with technology to create new forms of expression. While still a graduate student, for instance, he and another poet named Christian Bök wrote the "Virus 23 Meme," which they then had published on a mailing list in 1993. The "meme" was a raw idea they implanted in the list and that then was spread to recipients of the magazine *Future,* spreading the idea to others like a virus.

The former editor of the innovative Canadian publishing house Coach House Books, as a poet Wershler-Henry is particularly known for his experiments in concrete poetry, or verses for which the visual component of the written word is important to grasp their meaning. For example, in one poem he repeats the word "sun" over and over and then has the word "moon" also repeat. On the page, the two words come closer and closer together, and eventually the word "moon" eclipses the "sun." The author explained in an interview reprinted on the *Rock Critics* Web site that "what concrete poetry does when it works, is it reveals the everyday aspect of language." He added: "I think what concrete poetry does is it says . . . language is a material thing, as material as the table we're sitting at or the pen that you write with. And words are tools, they're things—you can do things with them."

Long interested in computer technology and the Internet, Wershler-Henry worked with poet Bill Kennedy to produce the innovative work *Apostrophe.* The printed version actually includes some of the results from 2002 of an Internet experiment posted at http://www.apostropheengine.ca. The Web site includes a long poem written by Kennedy, and when a reader comes across a line that interests him or her, or that he or she feels is relevant to his or her life, the reader then clicks that line. Wershler-Henry created the novel links that then use search engines to find relevant text associated with the line from the poem; then the program actually "writes" a new poem for the reader. In essence, the Internet itself is a coauthor of the poem. "Net effect? A weird sense of déjà vu, reflected through cyberspace," remarked Rachel Pulfer on the *Taddle Creek* Web site. She added: "Hyperlinking the lines of a poem to a search engine, and enabling readers to generate their own poems riffing off one of those lines, takes a pretty creative brain." Calling the concept "ingenious," *Pop Matters* writer Jason B. Jones felt there was value to the printed version of *Apostrophe* as well. For one thing, it archives the results of previous visitors' reactions to the Web site; secondly, "the uncanny coherence of the poems anthropomorphizes the author, that is, the web itself."

It is not just new technology that influences writing, though, as Wershler-Henry's *The Iron Whim: A Fragmented History of Typewriting* explains. Originally written as his doctoral dissertation, the book, with a number of revisions, was not published until 2007. Here, Wershler-Henry describes the complex history of the typewriter's evolution, but he also goes into the many influences it has had on society. For example, in the early twentieth century typing pools were mostly comprised of women, and this helped bring them into the workforce, thus eventually lending impetus to the feminist movement. Wershler-Henry also discusses how the mechanical writing device, replacing the pen and pencil, influenced the way writers ranging from Mark Twain to Jack Kerouac and Truman Capote composed their works. A central theme in the book is "the notion that typewriters made writers feel they were being dictated to," according to Joan Acocella in a *New Yorker* review. Acocella also related Wershler-Henry's thesis that "there was a mythology that what was typewritten was true, that the machine somehow caused writers to bare their souls." Acocella further commented, "Both these ideas are surprising—furthermore, they seem to contradict each other—but Wershler-Henry never really tries to prove them or reconcile them." In the *New York Times Book Review* Joshua Glenn reported that Wershler-Henry concludes that the replacement of the typewriter with the computer is a positive development: "Unlike typewriting, a discourse whose rules are determined 'by mechanical devices and hierarchies,' he writes reassuringly, 'computing is a discourse whose rules are determined by the functioning of software and networks.'"

BIOGRAPHICAL AND CRITICAL SOURCES:

PERIODICALS

Danforth Review, January 1, 2006, Derek Beaulieu, "Type Cast: Darren Wershler-Henry," interview and review of *The Iron Whim: A Fragmented History of Typewriting.*

New Yorker, April 9, 2007, Joan Acocella, "The Typing Life," review of *The Iron Whim.*

New York Times Book Review, May 6, 2007, Joshua Glenn, "Prison Made of Type," p. 26.

ONLINE

Darren Wershler-Henry Home Page, http://alienated.net/dwh (October 28, 2007).

Electronic Poetry Center Web site, http://epc.buffalo.edu/ (October 28, 2007), brief biography of Darren Wershler-Henry.

Pop Matters, http://www.popmatters.com/ (November 13, 2006), Jason B. Jones, review of *Apostrophe.*

Rock Critics, http://rockcriticsarchives.com/ (October 28, 2007), Scott Woods, "Concrete Jungle: Interview with Darren Wershler-Henry."

Taddle Creek, http://www.taddlecreekmag.com/ (October 28, 2007), Rachel Pulfer, "Collaboration Is the Medium of Darren Wershler-Henry's Message."

This Magazine, http://www.thismagazine.ca/ (November-December, 2005), Suzanne Alyssa Andrew, review of *The Iron Whim.**

*   *   *

WERSHLER-HENRY, Darren Sean
See WERSHLER-HENRY, Darren

WHITAKER, Zai
(Zahida Futehali)

PERSONAL: Born in Mumbai, India; daughter of Zafar and Laeeq Futehali; married Rom Whitaker (a naturalist), 1974; children: two sons.

ADDRESSES: Home—India.

CAREER: Educator, naturalist, and writer. Chennai Snake Park and Crocodile Bank, Chennai, India, founder with husband, Romulus Whitaker; teacher at Abacus Montessori School, Chennai, and Kodai International School; Outreach School, Bangalore, India, principal. Consultant on wildlife preservation issues.

WRITINGS:

Up the Ghat (novel), Affiliated East-West Press (New Delhi, India), 1992.

Andamans Boy, illustrated by Ashok Rajagopalian, Tulika (Chennai, India), 1998.

(With husband, Rom Whitaker) *Crocodile Fever: Wildlife Adventures in Guinea,* photographs by Rom Whitaker, Orient Longman (Hyderabad, India), 1998.

Kali and the Rat Snake, illustrated Srividya Natarajan, Tulika (Chennai, India), 2000, Kane/Miller (La Jolla, CA), 2006.

Salim Ali for Schools, Permanent Black (India), 2003.

Cobra in My Kitchen: Stories, Poems, and Prose Pieces, illustrated by Saddhasattwa Basu, Rupa (India), 2005.

The Boastful Centipede and Other Creatures in Verse, illustrated by Ajanta Guhathakurta, Penguin USA (New York, NY), 2007.

Also author of *Snakeman,* a biography of her husband published in India. Contributor to periodicals, including *International Wildlife.*

SIDELIGHTS: A native of Mumbai, India, and the wife of noted conservationist Rom Whitaker, Zai Whitaker is principal of the Outreach School in Bangalore, where she dedicates her efforts to providing an education to the children growing up in rural areas. In her books for children, which include *Cobra in My*

Kitchen: Stories, Poems, and Prose Pieces, Andamans Boy, and *Kali and the Rat Snake,* Whitaker draws on her lifelong interest in nature as well as her work as a naturalist and with the women of the Irula tribe of hunter-gatherers and snake catchers. In *Cobra in My Kitchen,* she collects the articles, poems, and stories she has written to share her love of nature with young children, while *Andamans Boy* and *Kali and the Rat Snake* are inspired by the knowledge Whitaker gained through her work as cofounder of the Chennai Snake Park and Crocodile Bank.

In *Andamans Boy,* Whitaker takes readers to the islands of the Andaman sea, home to the Jarawa tribe, where they meet ten-year-old Arif. An orphan since his parents died in an accident, Arif lives with his unloving aunt and uncle until he runs away to Chennai, and encounters a series of adventures while attempting the trip from there to the Andamans. In *Kali and the Rat Snake* a boy has trouble making friends at school due to the stigma attached to his father's job: the man is a snake-catcher for the Iruli tribe. However, when a large rat snake appears in Kali's classroom, the boy uses what he has learned from his father and becomes a hero to his classmates. Noting that Whitaker's story "moves at a good pace," Mary Hazelton added in her *School Library Journal* review that *Kali and the Rat Snake* "has much to offer children learning about other cultures."

Based on the life of Whitaker's great uncle, *Salim Ali for Schools* profiles a noted Indian ornithologist. In her book, Whitaker recounts how Salim Ali, a pioneer in the study of India's birdlife, "went all over India's princely states, surveying the bird life in them, travelling mostly on foot, and only much later in a Willys station wagon, which he drove 'like a battle tank'," according to *Hindu* contributor Ranjit Lal. In addition to writing about Ali, Whitaker is also the author of *Snakeman,* a biography of her husband.

BIOGRAPHICAL AND CRITICAL SOURCES:

PERIODICALS

Hindi, June 7, 2003, Ranjit Lal, review of *Salim Ali for Schools.*

Kirkus Reviews, September 1, 2006, review of *Kali and the Rat Snake,* p. 914.

School Library Journal, October, 2006, Mary Hazelton, review of *Kali and the Rat Snake,* p. 130.

Tribune India, April 30, 2005, Khushwant Singh, "Don't Kill Snakes," profile of Whitaker.

ONLINE

Penguin Books India Web site, http://www.penguin booksindia.com/ (October 27, 2007), "Zai Whitaker."*

*   *   *

WHITING, Charles 1926-2007
(Richard Douglas, Duncan Harding, Ian Harding, John Kerrigan, Leo Kessler, Klaus Konrad, K.N. Kostov, L. Kostov, Charles Henry Whiting)

OBITUARY NOTICE— See index for *CA* sketch: Born December 18, 1926, in York, England; died of renal failure, July 24, 2007, in York, England. Educator, historian, and author. Whiting was the author of no less than 350 books in his lifetime, almost all of them about World War II. He served in the British Army toward the end of the war and afterward, then used his experience to write from the perspective of the ordinary, often unsung, soldier. His work was divided into historical studies, including titles under the pseudonym Leo Kessler, and action-adventure novels, under a variety of pen names. Whiting worked as a history teacher until his success as an author enabled him to retire from that pursuit, and many of his early writings were historical accounts of military operations and the men who participated in them. His books were sometimes critical of the motives of military leaders, especially when their decisions led to excessive casualties that Whiting considered unnecessary. One example is *The Battle of Hurtgen Forest: The Untold Story of a Disastrous Campaign* (1989). Another topic of interest to the author was what he saw as the deteriorating relationship between British and American forces as the war progressed; he described one such event in *The Field Marshal's Revenge: The Breakdown of a Special Relationship* (2004). Whiting did not neglect the other side of the conflict. He wrote often of German leaders and military activities, such as *Siegfried: The Nazis' Last Stand* (1982). Whiting was also a prolific novelist of the military-adventure genre. His novels of soldiers at war have been described as action-packed and violent thrillers, and, while they did not earn the author any major literary awards, they were enormously popular among his readers. Even his earliest efforts, such as *The Frat War* (1954), were well received. Whiting's most widely recognized pseudonym was the Kessler *nom de plume,* which he used for more than thirty years.

OBITUARIES AND OTHER SOURCES:

PERIODICALS

Times (London, England), September 18, 2007, p. 65.

*   *   *

WHITING, Charles Henry
See WHITING, Charles

*   *   *

WIESE, Anne Pierson

PERSONAL: Born in Minneapolis, MN. *Education:* Received degrees from Amherst College and New York University Graduate Writing Workshop.

ADDRESSES: Home—New York, NY.

CAREER: Poet.

AWARDS, HONORS: First-Place Poetry Prize, Writers@Work fellowship competition, 2002; "Discovery"/*The Nation* Poetry Contest winner, 2004; second prize, Arvon International Poetry Competition, Arvon Foundation, 2004; New York Foundation for the Arts fellow in poetry, 2005; Walt Whitman Award, 2006, for *Floating City: Poems.*

WRITINGS:

Floating City: Poems, Louisiana State University Press (Baton Rouge, LA), 2007.

Contributor to anthologies, including *Broken Land: Poems of Brooklyn,* New York University Press (New York, NY), 2006. Contributor of poetry to journals, including *Nation, Prairie Schooner, Raritan, Atlanta Review, Southwest Review, Alaska Quarterly Review, Quarterly West, Rattapallax, Carolina Quarterly, South Carolina Review, West Branch,* and *Hawai'i Pacific Review.*

SIDELIGHTS: Anne Pierson Wiese received the 2006 Walt Whitman Award for her first collection of poetry, *Floating City: Poems.* "She lives in Brooklyn," explained Lisa Chamberlain in a review for *Polis,* "and her poetry so absolutely captures the essence of life in the city—the small moments of beauty and tragedy, how the natural and the built environments can combine to create magic." "Weise," Patricia Monaghan wrote in her *Booklist* review of the collection, "leaps across conventional divides and shows us urban life's complexity."

Wiese's work evokes comparisons with the opus of the English Romantic writers of the late eighteenth and early nineteenth centuries. "It's easy to discern," stated Douglas Basford in *Unsplendid: An Online Journal of Poetry in Received and Nonce Forms,* "that Wordsworth is the governing ghost (confirmed in a later sonnet, 'Composed upon Brooklyn Bridge, July 6, 2003'), primarily in that Wiese always endeavors to 'look steadily upon [her] subject.'" "She delights as much in Chinese restaurant employees washing down tables with tea between lunch and dinner," Basford continued, ". . . as she does in New York's green spaces, being more than a mere denizen but an aficionado of the parks. She's profoundly aware of Nature as an impenetrable, indestructible element, capable of overwhelming the imagination, much in the way that Wordsworth was." Wiese, Basford concluded, is a "promising [voice] asserting the viability of received forms."

BIOGRAPHICAL AND CRITICAL SOURCES:

PERIODICALS

Booklist, March 1, 2007, Patricia Monaghan, review of *Floating City: Poems,* p. 55.

ONLINE

Louisiana State University Press, http://www.lsu.edu/ (October 9, 2007).

Nation, http://www.thenation.com/ (October 9, 2007), "Happy 30th Anniversary Discovery/*The Nation.*"

Polis, http://polisnyc.wordpress.com/ (October 9, 2007), Lisa Chamberlain, review of *Floating City.*

Unsplendid: An Online Journal of Poetry in Received and Nonce Forms, http://www.unsplendid.com/ (October 9, 2007), Douglas Basford, "'Taking the Ears at Their Peak': McHenry and Wiese's Debut Books."*

*   *   *

WILLIAMS, Prescott H. 1924-
(Prescott Harrison Williams, Jr.)

PERSONAL: Born June 20, 1924, in Detroit, MI; son of Prescott Harrison (a sales representative) and M. Louise (a homemaker and hat maker) Williams; married Jane Tweed McMillan (a director of a child development center and antiques dealer), September 9, 1950; children: Prescott Harrison III, Andrew James, Margaret Louise Williams Tufts, Todd Radford (deceased). *Ethnicity:* "Irish, English, German, and Cree." *Education:* Wheaton College, Wheaton, IL, B.A., 1947; Princeton Theological Seminary, B.D., 1950. *Politics:* "Independent, active voter." *Religion:* Christian.

ADDRESSES: Home—Austin, TX.

CAREER: Presbyterian minister and teacher until retirement in 1990. Teacher of classes for senior citizens.

WRITINGS:

(Editor, with Theodore Hiebert) *Realia Dei: Essays in Archaeology and Biblical Interpretation in Honor of Edward F. Campbell, Jr. at His Retirement,* Duke University Press (Durham, NC), 1999.

SIDELIGHTS: Prescott H. Williams told *CA:* "My primary motivation for writing was my students' needs for guidance and orientation to important resources in the study of the Hebrew Old Testament, the Qumran (Dead Sea Scrolls), ancient Middle Eastern history, languages, and archaeology—and related subjects. I produced a key to the Latin textual notes in the Hebrew Old Testament, which was published in Stuttgart and distributed with the Hebrew book. The serious questions of students during courses of study led to unpublished outlines, essays, and guides, which I distributed free. My inspiration was my own enjoyment of learning, my students' curiosity, and their greater understanding of Bible-related issues."

*   *   *

WILLIAMS, Prescott Harrison, Jr.
See WILLIAMS, Prescott H.

*   *   *

WILSON, Antoine 1971-
(Antoine Leonide Thomas Wilson)

PERSONAL: Born 1971, in Montreal, Quebec, Canada; married. *Education:* Received degrees from University of California, Los Angeles, and University of Iowa Writers' Workshop.

ADDRESSES: Home—Los Angeles, CA. *Agent*—Zoe Pagnamenta, PFD New York, 373 Park Ave. S., 5th Fl., New York, NY 10016. *E-mail*—info@antoinewilson.com.

CAREER: Writer. University of California, Los Angeles, Extension Writing Program, teacher of writing.

AWARDS, HONORS: Wisconsin Institute for Creative Writing, fellow.

WRITINGS:

The Young Zillionaire's Guide to Distributing Goods and Services (young adult), Rosen Publishing Group (New York, NY), 2000.

You and a Death in Your Family (young adult), Rosen Central (New York, NY), 2001.

The Assassination of William McKinley (young adult), Rosen Publishing Group (New York, NY), 2002.

S.E. Hinton (young adult), Rosen Central (New York, NY), 2003.

The Interloper: A Novel, Handsel Books (New York, NY), 2007.

Contributing editor, *A Public Space.* Contributor to *Paris Review* and the *Best New American Voices* anthology.

SIDELIGHTS: Antoine Wilson's first work of fiction, *The Interloper: A Novel,* is a story of revenge gone awry. Owen Patterson wants two things out of life: healing for his wife Patty, in mourning for the meaningless killing of her little brother C.J., and vengeance on C.J.'s murderer, Henry Joseph Raven. Although Raven has been caught, tried, and sentenced to a twenty-year prison term, Owen wants a more personal accounting. "He plans to entrap Raven emotionally through letters supposedly written by a lonely, available female," explained a *Kirkus Reviews* contributor; "once Raven is hooked, the woman will end the relationship, Raven will be crushed and Patty will find closure." The plan quickly goes awry, in part because Owen draws on his own tortured past for inspiration—in particular, his feelings for his now-dead lover and cousin Eileen. "What was mildly comedic," stated a contributor to the *Five Branch Tree* blog, "soon succumbs entirely to the dark side of the human psyche, then feeding off itself until there's nothing left but the inevitable tragedy."

"One question being negotiated in *The Interloper,*" Wilson told Lisa Kunik in an interview in the *Small Spiral Notebook,* "is whether it is, as Owen puts it, 'the noblest mistake to see humanity in everyone.' There's an ethical collision. Of course we want to see humanity in everyone; we want to believe that everyone is capable of feeling, for instance. But what about someone like Raven? Is he indeed unfeeling?" "I don't know the answers to these questions," Wilson concluded, "but in this novel I tried to open a space in which they could be negotiated, albeit in an oblique way."

Wilson said that he was able to write a book that deals with loss in a comedic sense in part because his own half-brother was murdered. "After the book made its way into the world," he declared in an interview for *LAist,* "it occurred to me that someone who never had a murder in their family might never write this kind of book. It's dark, but the darkness that unfolds was something I had to live with and cope with using the full spectrum of emotions. I didn't feel there was a clash with the funny stuff—I just kept thinking it was darkly comic. But if someone set out to write this book . . . the schism might be a little more obvious and it might not work."

BIOGRAPHICAL AND CRITICAL SOURCES:

PERIODICALS

Kirkus Reviews, February 1, 2007, review of *The Interloper: A Novel,* p. 98.

Ploughshares, fall, 2007, James Alan McPherson, "James Alan McPherson Recommends *The Interloper.*"

Publishers Weekly, March 19, 2007, review of *The Interloper,* p. 39.

School Library Journal, February, 2001, Mary Mueller, review of *The Young Zillionaire's Guide to Distributing Goods and Services,* p. 139; August, 2001, Martha Gordon, review of *You and a Death in Your Family,* p. 207; August, 2003, Nicole M. Marcuccilli, review of *S.E. Hinton,* p. 186.

ONLINE

Antoine Wilson Home Page, http://www.antoine wilson.com (October 9, 2007), author biography and blog.

Antoine Wilson MySpace Page, http://www.myspace. com (October 9, 2007), author biography.

Big Mouth Indeed Strikes Again, http://bigmouth indeedstrikesagain.blogspot.com/ (August 17, 2007), Amy Guth, interview with Antoine Wilson.

Five Branch Tree, http://fivebranchtree.blogspot.com/ (October 9, 2007), "*The Interloper;* Antoine Wilson, 2007."

LAist, http://www.laist.com/ (May 22, 2007), "LAist Interview: Antoine Wilson."

Small Spiral Notebook, http://www.smallspiral notebook.com/ (October 9, 2007), Lisa Kunik, "Lisa Kunik Interviews Antoine Wilson, Author of *The Interloper.*"

* * *

WILSON, Antoine Leonide Thomas
See WILSON, Antoine

WINDSOR, Charles Philip Arthur George
See CHARLES, PRINCE OF WALES

*   *   *

WINE, Sherwin T. 1928-2007
(Sherwin Theodore Wine)

OBITUARY NOTICE— See index for *CA* sketch: Born January 25, 1928, in Detroit, MI; died after an automobile accident, July 21, 2007, in Essaouira, Morocco. Rabbi and author. Wine was known to many as the rabbi who didn't believe in God or, as he put it himself, who suspended belief in a supreme being for lack of empirical evidence. Wine was a legitimate, ordained Reform rabbi who led Jewish congregations in Detroit and its sister city, Windsor, Ontario, Canada, between 1956 and 1964. At some point, while ministering to a congregation in the Detroit suburb of Birmingham, he came to doubt the existence of God, but he continued to observe the ethical and cultural practices of Judaism. Wine began to call himself a secular humanist, or secular Jew. He attracted national attention, including the censure of other, more traditional rabbis, but Wine also gathered a following of like-minded souls throughout the United States and Canada. Wine and his fellow humanists practiced the tenets of Judaism but replaced the worship of God with a celebration of man. Wine founded the Society for Humanistic Judaism in 1969 and the Center for New Thinking in 1977. He was active in the International Institute for Secular Humanistic Judaism, the International Association of Humanist Educators, Counselors, and Leaders, the International Federation of Secular Humanistic Jews, the North American Committee for Humanism, and the Conference on Liberal Religion. Wine promoted his views in several books, including *A Philosophy of Humanistic Judaism* (1965), *High Holidays for Humanists* (1979), *Judaism beyond God: A Radical New Way to Be Jewish* (1985), *Celebration: A Ceremonial and Philosophic Guide for Humanists and Humanistic Jews* (1988), and *Staying Sane in a Crazy World* (1995).

OBITUARIES AND OTHER SOURCES:

PERIODICALS

Chicago Tribune, July 23, 2007, p. 4.
Los Angeles Times, July 26, 2007, p. B8.

New York Times, July 25, 2007, p. A16.
Washington Post, July 24, 2007, p. B7.

*   *   *

WINE, Sherwin Theodore
See WINE, Sherwin T.

*   *   *

WIRZBA, Norman 1964-

PERSONAL: Born 1964; married; wife's name Gretchen; children: Emily, Anna, Benjamin, Luke. *Education:* University of Lethbridge, Alberta, B.A. (with distinction), 1986; Yale University Divinity School, M.A. (religion), 1988; Loyola University, Chicago, M.A. (philosophy), 1991, Ph.D., 1994. *Hobbies and other interests:* Gardening, hiking, playing sports, and making things out of wood.

ADDRESSES: Home—Georgetown, KY. *Office*—Department of Philosophy, Georgetown College, 309 Pawling Hall, Georgetown, KY 40324. *E-mail*—Norman_Wirzba@georgetowncollege.edu.

CAREER: Northern Illinois University, Dekalb, and Loyola University, Chicago, IL, lecturer in philosophy, 1992-93; University of Saskatchewan, St. Thomas More College, Saskatoon, Saskatchewan, Canada, assistant professor of philosophy, 1993-95; Georgetown College, Georgetown, KY, associate professor, 1995-2006, professor of philosophy, 2006—, department chair, 1995—.

WRITINGS:

(Editor and author of introduction) Wendell Berry, *The Art of the Commonplace: Agrarian Essays of Wendell Berry,* Counterpoint (Washington, DC), 2002.
(Editor) *The Essential Agrarian Reader: The Future of Culture, Community, and the Land,* University Press of Kentucky (Lexington, KY), 2003.
The Paradise of God: Renewing Religion in an Ecological Age, Oxford University Press (New York, NY), 2003.

(Editor, with Bruce Ellis Benson) *The Phenomenology of Prayer,* Fordham University Press (New York, NY), 2005.

Living the Sabbath: Discovering the Rhythms of Rest and Delight, Brazos Press (Grand Rapids, MI), 2006.

(Editor, with Bruce Ellis Benson) *Transforming Philosophy and Religion: Love's Wisdom,* Indiana University Press (Bloomington, IN), 2008.

Contributor to books, including *Postmodern Philosophy and Christian Thought,* Indiana University Press, 1999. Contributor to periodicals, including *Christian Century, Christian Reflection, Orion, Christianity and Literature,* and *Living Pulpit.*

SIDELIGHTS: Norman Wirzba, a writer and educator, serves as a professor and chair of the philosophy department at Georgetown College in Georgetown, Kentucky. Wirzba's primary areas of interest include the history of philosophy, agrarianism, environmental philosophy and ethics, and Christian theology. He is the author and/or editor of several volumes on modern philosophy and religion, particularly agrarianism. Agrarianism is concerned with a return to agrarian values, the creation of local communities, and personal self-reliance. Wirzba is the editor of Wendell Berry's *The Art of the Commonplace: Agrarian Essays of Wendell Berry* and of the related volume *The Essential Agrarian Reader: The Future of Culture, Community, and the Land,* a "collection of eminently quotable and passionately argued essays," as Ilse Heidmann called it in the *Library Journal.* In *The Paradise of God: Renewing Religion in an Ecological Age,* Wirzba offers an argument against those religious followers who claim that God, having given man dominion over the Earth, wants humanity to do whatever they wish to the planet, including use up its resources. Wirzba's argument states that the Bible actually stands in favor of environmentalism, and proceeds to illustrate how he came to his conclusion. Diane Bergant, in a review in *Theological Studies,* found that Wirzba's effort "rightly credits the new insights into the balance of nature with both a recognition of the harm done by the extreme form of anthropocentrism holding sway in the Western world, and a realization of the need to develop a new way of understanding the unique place of humankind within the broader ecological scheme."

Living the Sabbath: Discovering the Rhythms of Rest and Delight looks at the commonly held theories regarding what it means to keep the Sabbath, traditionally referred to as the day of rest. Wirzba suggests that, rather than resting, one should take the day as an opportunity to reflect and to separate one's mind from the chaos and turmoil of the typical week. A reviewer for *Publishers Weekly* opined: "This book will humble, fascinate, but most of all challenge spiritual seekers to pursue the fullness of Sabbath."

BIOGRAPHICAL AND CRITICAL SOURCES:

PERIODICALS

America, September 30, 2002, Stephen Bede Scharper, "Rooted in Place," p. 27.
Christian Century, December 27, 2003, Bill McKibben, "Food Fight: Local Farming vs. Agribusiness," p. 20; February 6, 2007, Arthur Paul Boers, review of *Living the Sabbath: Discovering the Rhythms of Rest and Delight,* p. 42.
Dallas Morning News, April 18, 2007, "Review of Religious Books and a Web Site."
Library Journal, May 1, 2002, Ilse Heidmann, review of *The Art of the Commonplace: Agrarian Essays of Wendell Berry,* p. 125; August, 2003, Ilse Heidmann, review of *The Essential Agrarian Reader: The Future of Culture, Community, and the Land,* p. 118.
Modern Age, summer, 2003, Jeremy Beer, "An Alternative Conservative."
Nation, July 1, 2002, Eric Zencey, "A Whole Earth Catalogue," p. 35.
Publishers Weekly, September 8, 2003, review of *The Art of the Commonplace,* p. 13; June 12, 2006, review of *Living the Sabbath,* p. 46.
Sojourners Magazine, April, 2007, "Real Re-creation," p. 52.
Theological Studies, September, 2005, Dianne Bergant, review of *The Paradise of God: Renewing Religion in an Ecological Age,* p. 702.
Tikkun, September 1, 2004, Roger S. Gottlieb, "Religion and Ecology," p. 77.

ONLINE

Baptist Seminary of Kentucky Web site, http://www.bsky.org/ (October 10, 2007), author profile.

Camping Is Not Optional Web site, http://www.campingisnotoptional.com/ (October 10, 2007), author profile.

* * *

WOIK, Julie 1963-

PERSONAL: Born April 15, 1963, in Hartford, WI; daughter of Robert and Ellen Woik; married Guy Finnemore (an antique furniture restorer), September 1, 1995. *Ethnicity:* "Caucasian." *Education:* High school graduate; also attended a technical school.

ADDRESSES: Home—Sarasota, FL. *E-mail*—finnwoik@verizon.net.

CAREER: Sarasota Memorial Hospital, Sarasota, FL, psychiatric technician, 1984-90; private duty nurse, 1990-94; officer manager for various companies, 1994—.

WRITINGS:

The Garden Gathering (children's book; "The Life and Times of Lilly the Lash" series), Advocate House (Sarasota, FL), 2007.

SIDELIGHTS: Julie Woik told *CA:* "Writing for me has been a gift. The poems or stories I have written have come to me without my asking for them. I get an idea, and I must write it down or I won't be able to stop thinking about it. My inspiration comes from everything and everyone. I'm observant and enjoy the whole life process. Sometimes thing turn out differently than I had planned, but it is always the right path for my personal journey.

"I wrote a few poems when I was young, and that carried into my adult life.

"People, the environment, what's happening in the world [influence my work]. I have to admit, I'm a tad bit frightened by what is going on in this world. Sometimes I become quite anxious about it all. Writing something positive is simply the right thing for me to do. What I have discovered in my forty-four years of life is that although there are people in our society making choices that are less than desirable, there are *many* more wonderful people trying to make this world a better place. They spend each and every day of their lives trying to make a difference. That is what influences me . . . LOVE.

"At first, [writing] just came to me without asking. I would write down the words that came to me in the night, spend time putting them together, and that was it, a poem was born. Then, after being encouraged to think more seriously about my writing, I decided to sit down and see if I could do it 'upon demand.' Now, in a quiet room, I sit down to my laptop, hop into whatever I am writing about, and words just flow onto the page."

When asked the most surprising thing she has learned as a writer, Woik said: "That a good book is very important to people. There are millions of books to choose from, but when a person finds a good one, they will tell you, and everyone else, about it! I have been overwhelmed by the comments people have gone out of their way to relay to me. I am grateful and blessed.

"I'm hoping to turn the world on its head! Since the series focuses on strong self-esteem and learning life lessons, I'm thinking that the books might turn out a whole generation of secure, loving, accepting, responsible, and respectful adults. Just that one tiny little thing, that's all I'm asking for."

* * *

WOODIWISS, Kathleen
See WOODIWISS, Kathleen E.

* * *

WOODIWISS, Kathleen E. 1939-2007
(Kathleen Erin Hogg, Kathleen Woodiwiss, Kathleen Erin Woodiwiss)

OBITUARY NOTICE— See index for *CA* sketch: Born June 3, 1939, in Alexandria, LA; died of cancer, July 6, 2007, near Princeton, MN. Romance novelist.

Woodiwiss was a homemaker and "stay-at-home mom" in the 1960s and 1970s. She had no training to become a novelist, but she knew what she wanted to read and couldn't find what she wanted at the local bookstore, so she wrote it herself. Her first novel did not fit the profile of a typical romance novel, and Woodiwiss had a hard time finding a publisher. When *The Flame and the Flower* finally saw the light of day in 1972, it flew off the shelves onto the best-seller lists, and its author never looked back. Woodiwiss crafted her fiction with all the ingredients of typical romance fare, but she "super-sized" it in every way. For that achievement she has been called the reinventor of the modern romance novel. Unlike most romance novels of the early 1970s, Woodiwiss's novels are long, usually 500 to 600 pages in length. Like other romance writers, she set her tales in exotic places or against historical backgrounds, in which her heroines had to face difficulties of gothic proportions: lost fortunes, lost babies, lost chastity, forced marriage, heartless encounters. These are typical dilemmas, but in Woodiwiss's hands, all were a backdrop to the central drama, which, for the first time in the genre, was the romance itself. Her heroines were characteristically beautiful, soft, and helpless, at least at the beginning; her heroes were larger than life: handsome, strong and strong-willed, charismatic, and ultimately irresistible. The love story never remained in the background for long—it *was* the story, rendered in such descriptive detail that some critics dubbed the author a master of erotic historical fiction, a distinction that Woodiwiss herself always countered with an indignant denial. In truth, however, Woodiwiss's heroines rarely retained their chastity for long, and their undoing was often against their will. For this and other reasons, champions of women's causes have not routinely embraced her work. Serious critics of literature have, for the most part, either ignored Woodiwiss or denounced her, but some of her harshest detractors have also acknowledged that they enjoyed her stories nonetheless. All of her books achieved best-seller status, sold in the millions, and remained in print or were reprinted long after their original debuts. Woodiwiss received a lifetime achievement award from the Romance Writers of America in 1988. She wrote more than a dozen novels, several of which were also recorded as audio books. The titles include *Shanna* (1977), *Forever in Your Embrace* (1992), *A Season beyond a Kiss* (2000), and *Everlasting,* published posthumously in 2007.

OBITUARIES AND OTHER SOURCES:

PERIODICALS

Chicago Tribune, July 13, 2007, sec. 2, p. 12.
Los Angeles Times, July 13, 2007, p. B9.
New York Times, July 12, 2007, p. C13.
Washington Post, July 14, 2007, p. B6.

* * *

WOODIWISS, Kathleen Erin
    See WOODIWISS, Kathleen E.

* * *

WYSE, Lois 1926-2007
    (Lois Helene Wyse)

OBITUARY NOTICE— See index for *CA* sketch: Born October 30, 1926, in Cleveland, OH; died of stomach cancer, July 6, 2007, in New York, NY. Advertising executive and author. Wyse achieved her greatest career success as an advertising executive. She also wrote more than sixty books, which, with the exception of a novel or two, were rarely about the world of advertising and business. Wyse and her then-husband created Wyse Advertising in Cleveland, Ohio, in 1951, adding an office in New York City in 1966. Wyse served as the president and creative director for many years. Her most recognizable successes were the long-running slogan "With a name like Smucker's, it has to be good" and her renaming of a small chain of home-goods stores from "Bed and Bath" to "Bed, Bath & Beyond." During her business career Wyse was a founding member of the Committee of 200, a gathering of women executives, and Catalyst, a research organization that focused on topics of interest to women. Over the years Wyse's work spread well beyond the boardroom. She created a magazine column, "The Way We Are," that appeared in *Good Housekeeping* for thirteen years, ending in 1998. Wyse also produced dozens of books. At least eighteen of them could be classified as uplifting or motivational booklets of verse intended for the greeting-card market. Some others, like *The Rosemary Touch* (1974) and *Kiss, Inc.* (1977), are novels drawn on her own expertise regarding the advertising industry. At least a half-dozen are children's books, and several others, like *Funny, You Don't Look Like a Grandmother* (1989) and *Family Ties: The Legacy of Love* (2001), are anecdotal collections about family life and topics related to living (and aging) as a woman in contemporary society. One of the handful of nonfiction books directly related to Wyse's years in the business world is called *Company Manners: How to Behave in the Workplace in the '90s.*

OBITUARIES AND OTHER SOURCES:

PERIODICALS

Chicago Tribune, July 8, 2007, sec. 4, p. 6.
Los Angeles Times, July 7, 2007, p. B11.
New York Times, July 7, 2007, p. B10.

*   *   *

WYSE, Lois Helene
    See WYSE, Lois

*   *   *

ZELMAN, Leon 1928-2007

OBITUARY NOTICE— See index for *CA* sketch: Born June 12, 1928, in Szczekociny, Poland; died July 11, 2007. Information officer, newspaper editor, executive, and author. In 1945 Zelman was liberated from a Nazi detention camp as an emaciated, tubercular teenager who had lost both parents and his brother to the Holocaust. Somehow he recovered his health, earned a doctorate at the University of Vienna, and spent the rest of his life working on behalf of other displaced Jews and Holocaust survivors. Zelman cofounded the newspaper *Das Judische Echo* in 1951, while he was still a university student; he later became the editor in chief. In 1963 he joined the Austrian National Travel Agency in Vienna, where his assignment was to promote immigration to Austria from the State of Israel and to encourage travel between the two countries. He then established the Jewish Welcome Service in 1978 to help Israeli immigrants settle into the city of Vienna by providing financial assistance as needed and by hosting tours and lectures about daily living in Austria. He was particularly concerned, according to some reports, about allaying the reluctance and fears of those Austrian Jews who were returning to a place that they had once left in a state of terror and panic. Zelman wrote a book about his own Holocaust experience in 1995 with the assistance of coauthor Armin Thurnher. The English translation appeared as *After Survival: One Man's Mission in the Cause of Memory,* in 1998.

OBITUARIES AND OTHER SOURCES:

BOOKS

Zelman, Leon, and Armin Thurnher, *After Survival: One Man's Mission in the Cause of Memory,* Holmes & Meier (New York, NY), 1998.

PERIODICALS

Times (London, England), July 30, 2007, p. 46.

✓